HISTORY
of the WORLD *in*
1,000 OBJECTS

DK SMITHSONIAN ✺

HISTORY
of the WORLD *in*
1,000 OBJECTS

LONDON, NEW YORK, MELBOURNE, MUNICH, AND DELHI

DK LONDON

Senior Art Editors Anna Hall, Ina Stradins

Senior Editors Peter Frances, Janet Mohun

Project Art Editors Alison Gardner, Clare Joyce, Simon Murrell, Duncan Turner, Francis Wong

Project Editors Gill Pitts, Louise Tucker

Editors Lili Bryant, Manisha Majithia, Steve Setford, Kaiya Shang, Debra Wolter

US Editors Jill Hamilton, Margaret Parrish, Jane Perlmutter

Editorial Assistant Henry Fry

Indexer Hilary Bird

Picture Researcher Liz Moore

New Photography Angela Coppola, Dave King, Richard Leeney, Gary Ombler

Jacket Designer Laura Brim

Jacket Editor Maud Whatley

Jacket Design Development Manager Sophia MTT

Senior Preproduction Producer Luca Frassinetti

Producer Mary Slater

Managing Art Editor Michelle Baxter

Managing Editor Angeles Gavira Guerrero

Art Director Philip Ormerod

Publisher Sarah Larter

Associate Publishing Director Liz Wheeler

Publishing Director Jonathan Metcalf

DK INDIA

Managing Art Editors Sudakshina Basu, Govind Mittal

Managing Editors Kingshuk Ghoshal, Rohan Sinha

Project Art Editor Amit Malhotra

Art Editors Sanjay Chauhan, Vikas Chauhan, Heena Sharma, Upasana Sharma, Shreya Anand Virmani

Assistant Art Editors Anjali Sachar, Riti Sodhi

Senior Editors Neha Gupta, Vineetha Mokkil

Project Editors Neha Pande, Priyaneet Singh

Editor Suefa Lee

Jacket Designer Suhita Dharamjit

Managing Jacket Editor Saloni Singh

Assistant Editors Sneha Sunder Benjamin, Deeksha Saikia

Production Manager Pankaj Sharma

DTP Manager Balwant Singh

DTP designers Rajesh Singh, Mohammad Usman, Dheeraj Singh

SMITHSONIAN ENTERPRISES

President Christopher A. Liedel

Senior Vice President Carol LeBlanc

Vice President Brigid Ferraro

Licensing Manager Ellen Nanney

Key Accounts Manager Cheryl Stepanek

Product Development Manager Kealy Wilson

First published in the United States in 2014
by DK Publishing

4th floor, 345 Hudson Street, New York, New York 10014

14 15 16 17 18   10 9 8 7 6 5 4 3 2 1

001—192895—Oct/2014

Published in Great Britain by Dorling Kindersley Limited.

A catalog record for this book is available
from the Library of Congress.

ISBN 978-1-4654-2289-7

DK books are available at special discounts when purchased in bulk for sales promotions, premiums, fund-raising, or educational use. For details, contact: DK publishing Special Markets, 345 Hudson Street, New York, New York 10014 or SpecialSales@dk.com.

Printed and bound in Hong Kong

Discover more at
www.dk.com

CONTRIBUTORS

EARLY SOCIETIES
Jane McIntosh
Senior Researcher for Civilizations in Contact, a Public Engagement Project in the Faculty of Asian and Middle Eastern Studies, University of Cambridge, UK.

ANCIENT CIVILIZATIONS
Peter Chrisp
Author of more than 70 history books, including DK's Atlas of *Ancient Worlds*, *Ancient Greece (E Explore)*, *Ancient Rome (E Explore)*, and the *Shakespeare Eyewitness Guide*.

TRADE AND EMPIRE
Philip Parker
Historian and writer whose books include DK's Eyewitness Companion Guide: *World History*, *History Year by Year*, *Science Year by Year*, *History of Britain and Ireland*, and *Engineers*.

ENLIGHTENMENT AND IMPERIALISM
Dr. Carrie Gibson
Writer who has contributed to *The Guardian* and *Observer* newspapers and author of *Empire's Crossroads: A History of the Caribbean from Columbus to the Present Day*; gained a doctorate in 18th- and 19th-century history from the University of Cambridge, UK.

INDUSTRY AND INDEPENDENCE
R. G. Grant
History writer who has published more than 40 books, including *Battle*, *Soldier*, *Flight*, and *Battle at Sea*, and *World War I* for DK.

A SHRINKING WORLD
Sally Regan
Contributor to several books for DK, including *History*, *World War II*, *History Year by Year*, and *Science*; award-winning documentary maker whose films include *Shell Shock* and *Bomber Command* for Channel 4 in the UK.

Additional writing by R. G. Grant and Jack Challoner

CONSULTANTS

Lauren Barnes
Access Officer, Durham University Oriental Museum, UK

Dr. Roger Collins
Honorary Fellow, School of History, Classics and Archaeology, University of Edinburgh, UK

Professor Richard Overy
Professor of History, University of Exeter, UK

Len Pole
Former curator of Saffron Waldon Museum, UK

SMITHSONIAN CONSULTANTS

NATIONAL MUSEUM OF NATURAL HISTORY
J. Daniel Rogers Curator of Archaeology, Department of Anthropology • **Salima Ikram** Egyptology Unit Head, Department of Anthropology • **Noel Broadbent** Archaeologist, Department of Anthropology **William Fitzhugh** Curator of Archaeology and Director of Arctic Studies Center, Department of Anthropology **James Harle** Map curator volunteer • **Bruce Smith** Senior Archaeologist, Department of Anthropology **Adrienne Kaeppler** Anthropologist, Curator of Oceanic Ethnology, Department of Anthropolgy • **Joshua Bell** Anthropologist, Department of Anthropology **Candace Greene** Program Analyst, Collections and Archival Programs • **Jeffrey Post** Geologist, National Gem and Mineral Collection • **Alexander Nagel** Research Associate, Department of Anthropology

FREER GALLERY OF ART AND ARTHUR M. SACKLER GALLERY
J. Keith Wilson Curator of Ancient Chinese Art **James T. Ulak** Senior Curator of Japanese Art **Debra Diamond** Associate Curator of South and Southeast Asian Art • **Massumeh Farhad** Chief Curator and Curator of Islamic Art • **Louise Cort** Curator of Ceramics **Stephen Allee** Associate Curator for Chinese Painting and Calligraphy

NATIONAL MUSEUM OF AMERICAN HISTORY
Kenneth Slowik Curator, Division of Culture and the Arts **Stacey Kluck** Supervisory Curator, Division of Culture and the Arts • **David Miller** Curator, Division of Armed Forces History • **Joan Boudreau** Curator, Division of Culture and the Arts • **Steve Velasquez** Curator, Division of Home and Community Life • **Jennifer Locke Jones** Chair and Curator, Division of Armed Forces History • **Harold Wallace** Curator, Division of Work and Industry

NATIONAL AIR AND SPACE MUSEUM
Alex Spencer Curator, Division of Aeronautics **F. Robert Van der Linden** Chairman, Division of Aeronautics • **Andrew Johnston** Research Specialist, Center for Earth and Planetary Studies • **Hunter Hollins** Program Specialist, Department of Space History

NATIONAL PORTRAIT GALLERY
Nik Apostolides Associate Director
James Barber Historian

COOPER-HEWITT NATIONAL DESIGN MUSEUM
Sarah Coffin Curator • **Cindy Trope** Museum Specialist **Susan Brown** Museum Specialist

NATIONAL MUSEUM OF THE AMERICAN INDIAN
Ramiro Matos Associate Curator, Office of Latin America

EXTERNAL CONSULTANTS
Colleen Batey Senior Lecturer, Archaeology, University of Glasgow • **Wirt Wills** Professor of Archaeology, University of New Mexico • **Walter Turner** Historian, North Carolina Transportation Museum

CONTENTS

ENLIGHTENMENT AND IMPERIALISM

1450–1750

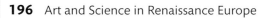

INDUSTRY AND INDEPENDENCE

1750–1900

A SHRINKING WORLD

1900 TO PRESENT

TIMELINES OF WORLD HISTORY

FOREWORD

There is something magical about the survival of human-made objects from the past. A piece of jewelry, a cup, a sword, or a sandal that has, often arbitrarily, survived the general tide of oblivion seems in some degree to bridge the gulf of years that separates us from the world of our ancestors—whether inhabitants of ancient Egypt or the Roman Empire, the Aztecs of Mexico or Japanese samurai. A collection of such artifacts can vividly represent a long-lost civilization, its daily life, its art and culture, its ways of making war and conducting trade, its rituals and its beliefs.

Many objects have come to us from ancient times through the rituals surrounding death. Our knowledge of the ancient Egyptians, for example, would be much poorer but for their habit of burying personal possessions with the dead. The exquisite decoration and furnishing of palaces and places of worship has been another rich source of surviving artifacts. We are also beholden to the desire of people to record the great events of their own time, which has given us Trajan's column in Rome and the Norman Bayeux Tapestry. Some objects were created to celebrate heroes or gods, like the statues of ancient Greece and Rome. Some are exquisite craft work, such as Japanese Samurai armor and the gold figurines of the West African Asante. Others are famous puzzles, such as the Rosetta Stone, which eventually allowed scholars to decipher Egyptian hieroglyphs.

Objects are particularly important when evoking human societies that have left no written records, such as that of the hunters and farmers of the Neolithic era. But objects are also a rich source of information about the more recent past. Historical documents such as England's Magna Carta and the United States Constitution have remained alive as a basis for current political practice, as well as existing as physical objects preserved for posterity. The Watt steam engine shows the mix of practical good sense, skill, and basic science that was to advance the Industrial Revolution, while the Ford Model T transports us back to the early days of modern motorized society.

Collected together in this book, objects from all periods generate a striking impression of the overarching shape of human history and its development from stone tools to spaceflight. They also take us on a breathtaking journey through the ever-varying stages of the human adventure.

R. G. GRANT

Persian life
This Persian illuminated manuscript is from a book of poems completed in 1548. Brightly colored pigments were used to produce works that show aspects of daily life including style of dress and architecture.

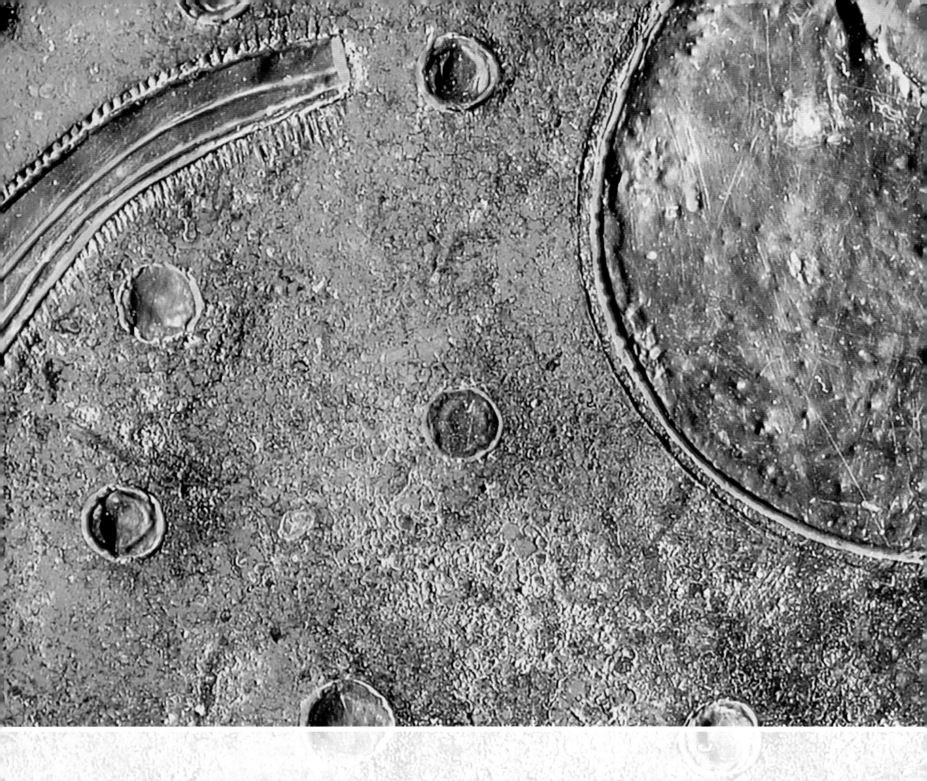

After 12,500 BCE, as temperatures rose, vegetation changed and ice sheets melted, and people adopted new ways of living, including agriculture in some areas. As farming and settled life spread, populations increased, and new technologies such as metalworking and monumental construction began. Between 3000 and 1000 BCE, the first civilizations, with cities and writing, emerged in Mesopotamia, Egypt, the Indus Valley, China, Mesoamerica, and Andean South America.

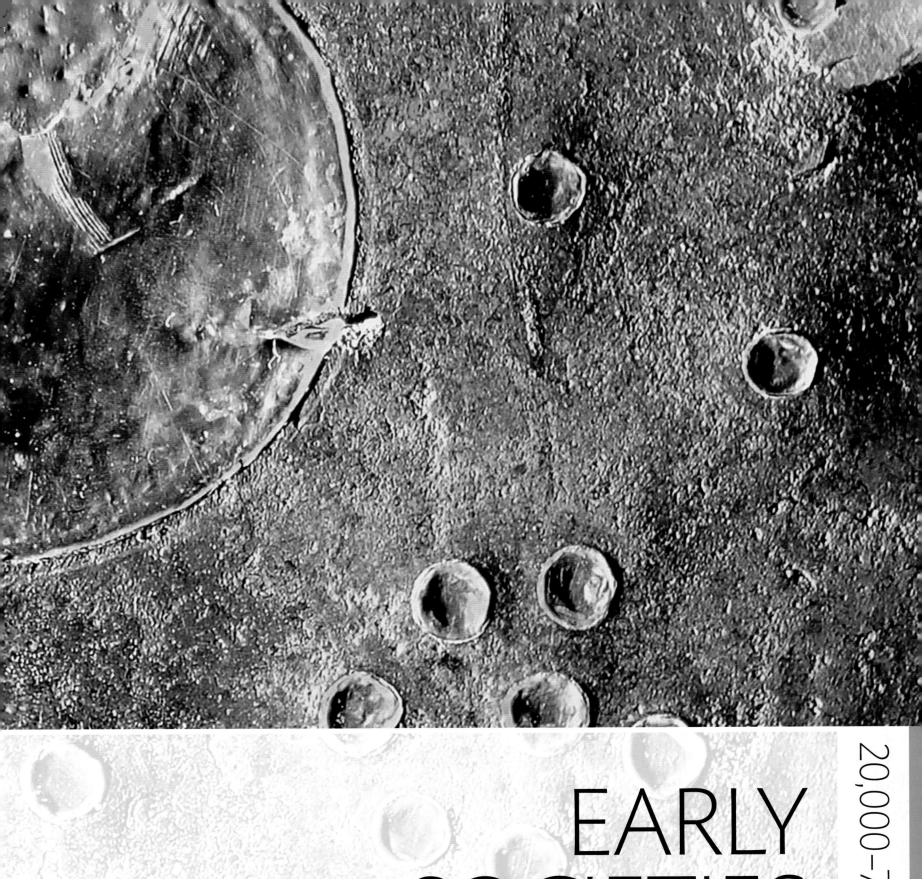

EARLY
SOCIETIES

EARLY HUMANS SHAPING THE WORLD

Humanity's extraordinary success is due to our ingenuity in devising cultural means to overcome our physical limitations. Early stone tools seem crude, but they were the first step on the road to computers, the Moon, and beyond. Along the way we developed language, allowing the sharing of knowledge, skills, and ideas.

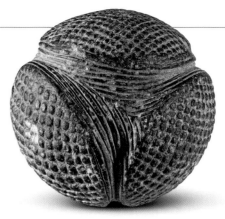

Mysterious serpentine ball
We don't know why balls were carved from stone in northeast Scotland, but the skill required suggests they were highly valued.

Settling down ▽
The huge Neolithic village of Catalhöyük in Turkey had closely packed houses entered through the roof via a ladder. The main room had a hearth, cabinets, benches, and platforms for sitting and sleeping. The walls often had paintings of bulls.

Our early ancestors evolved in Africa and spread into Asia and Europe. Around 2.5 million years ago, they developed stone tools, initially to cut through tough hides to access meat. This began a period called the Stone Age, divided into the Paleolithic, Mesolithic, and Neolithic. Paleolithic people tamed fire for protection, warmth, and cooking. Several human species continued to evolve. One, the Neanderthals, began burying their dead and caring for their disabled. Around 200,000 BCE, *Homo sapiens* (modern humans) emerged in Africa.

Outcompeting other human species, by 11,500 BCE they had spread across Asia, Europe, and the Americas and crossed open ocean to Australia. They had created art, sewn clothing, made shelters, and domesticated dogs.

THE FIRST FARMERS

Late Paleolithic people inhabited an ice age world. By around 9600 BCE, however, the world's climate was similar to today's. Communities began exploiting newly available resources, and in some areas settled permanently instead of traveling to

obtain seasonally available resources. For different reasons in different areas, some communities began cultivating plants, and in some parts of the world herding animals. As agriculture and a settled way of life brought population growth, Neolithic farmers expanded into new areas.

To obtain useful materials from other places, sedentary communities developed exchange networks. They also sought luxuries with which they could demonstrate their superiority over others. These included fine stone and eventually, in some areas, metals.

TECHNOLOGY AND INNOVATION

The earliest known tools were of stone. Using their cutting edges, wood and other materials could also be made into tools. Over hundreds of thousands of years, tools became more specialized, designed for particular tasks, and the range of materials expanded to include clay, leather, fibers, shell, and, later, metals.

■ THE FIRST TOOLS

point for digging and boring

sharp edge for cutting

comfortable grip for holding in hand

Handax
The first stone tools, made around 2.5 million years ago, had one simple cutting edge. Handaxes, from around 1.65 million years ago, were carefully shaped digging, cutting, and general-purpose tools.

BLADE CORE

UNMODIFIED BLADE

SNAPPED BLADE

Obsidian core and blades
Modern humans invented blades, which they used as cutting tools or reshaped for other purposes. Many small blades could be struck from a single core.

■ HUNTING

fluted base for attaching to haft

Clovis point
Elegant points were made by the North American Clovis culture as tips for spears, which were used as projectiles to hunt bison and mammoths. This example was found in a mammoth skeleton.

barb

barb

Barbed harpoon
Fishing, begun by early modern humans, became increasingly important after the last ice age. Fishing gear included wood, bone, and antler fishhooks and harpoons, nets, and elaborate fishtraps.

tang for attaching to arrow shaft

Flint arrowheads
Bows and arrows, to kill prey at a safe distance, were invented in the late Paleolithic. Later times saw many improvements in their efficiency, such as these arrowheads with barbs to embed them more securely in prey.

■ AGRICULTURE

decorative deer's head

Early sickle
As grains became important in the diet, sickles were developed to harvest them, as well as to cut reeds used in matting, basketry, and construction.

twig wedge to prevent movement

ancient perforated pebble weight

modern replica stick

row of inset flint bladelets

bone haft

Digging stick
Digging sticks were used to dig up tubers and to make holes to plant seeds and bulbs. A stone weight on the stick increased its power of penetration.

■ EARLY SAW

edge chipped to form series of teeth

Egyptian saw
Although some multipurpose tools continued to be made, over time tools for specific purposes proliferated. This cast of an early Egyptian saw, made around 3000 BCE, is one such specialized tool.

■ AXES

horizontally mounted blade

strong cutting edge

polished surface

hole for attaching to haft

replica handle

leather thong binding

Neolithic diorite ax
In the later Stone Age after 10,000 BCE, people developed new techniques, grinding and polishing hard stone to make axes for felling trees and other purposes.

Stone shaft-hole ax
As metal objects spread in 3rd-millennium BCE Europe, communities that did not use metal made fine stone imitations of them, not as tools but as prestige fashion items.

Mesolithic stone tool
Heavy stone tools served various purposes, such as adzes to plane and trim wood, and picks perhaps to dig up plants or knock limpets off rocks.

ART AND CULTURE

In many parts of the world, the late Paleolithic saw the flowering of art, including painting, engraving, and sculpture. Fired clay came into use at this time, providing a medium with huge scope for later artistic expression, as did textiles woven from plant fibers. Stone monuments, often with a ritual purpose, were created from at least 9500 BCE (see, for example, Stonehenge, p.40).

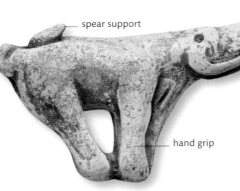

spear support

hand grip

Mammoth spearthrower
This fine bone carving from France combined practical utility as a spearthrower with artistic sensitivity to the natural world.

CAVE ART

The most impressive Paleolithic artworks are the cave paintings found in France. Their purpose is unknown, although some cave art may have played a part in initiation or religious rites. It is unlikely animals were drawn to bring success in a hunt—the people who painted this horse and mammoth at Lascaux hunted reindeer almost exclusively.

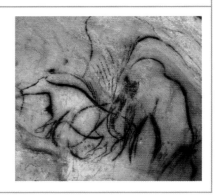

HOME LIFE

People with a mobile lifestyle could only afford to carry a few small objects. Sedentary communities, however, could accumulate possessions, including fragile pottery and heavy querns (grindstones). After 11,500 BCE, such communities included some hunter-gatherers and most farmers. With the spread of farming across much of the world, objects proliferated.

WOODEN WEAVING COMB

CLAY LOOM WEIGHT

Weaving equipment
Weaving on simple looms began in Neolithic times, using cotton in India and South America, and flax and other plant fibers in western Asia and Europe. More complex looms, and silk and alpaca and sheep's wool, came into use later.

decorated handle

SPATULA **SPOON** **FORK**

Bone cutlery from Catalhöyük
The shift to sedentary life and agriculture in many regions brought dietary changes and the associated development of new cooking and eating utensils.

hard stone quern

sandstone rubber

Grinding tools
Cereal grains (also seeds and nuts) were ground into flour, to cook as bread, porridge, or gruel. Grinding with a quern and rubber became an arduous daily task for many women.

◼ POTTERY

typical scalloped rim

applied decoration

Later Jomon pot
Pottery was independently invented many times, in different parts of the world. The earliest pots, including Jomon wares, come from late Paleolithic East Asia.

incised designs and impressions made by cord

typical zoned decoration

bell-like beaker shape

Bell Beaker culture pot
The Bell Beaker culture made a distinctive style of pottery beaker with an upside-down bell shape, in parts of Europe after 2900 BCE.

incised decoration

Wagon-shaped pot
Invented in the 4th millennium BCE, wheeled transportation, using draft animals, revolutionized work by making it easier to transport heavy or bulky goods. This pot was found in Eastern Europe.

fixed axle

solid wheel

BELIEFS AND RITUALS

The religious beliefs of people who lived before writing was invented are unknown to us: we can only identify the results of their behavior, with more or less certainty, and speculate on their meaning. Past peoples' richly varied ways of treating their dead, artistic representations, and places with offerings (and sometimes sacrifices) provide some clues.

beaten sheet gold appliqué

hole for attaching to clothing

raised decoration

Rich grave goods
As communities expanded, social differences developed within them. The treatment of the dead often reflected their status in life, with rich grave goods denoting important people.

Burial art
Some European late Neolithic megalithic tombs included stones bearing geometric designs. These designs may have held some religious significance. They sometimes also appear on the associated grave goods, such as plaques, made from a hard stone called schist, found in southern Spain and Portugal.

burial design visible only to dead person inside the tomb

SCHIST PLAQUE

CIST (STONE BOX) COVER

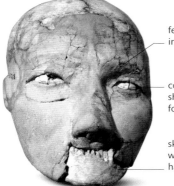

features modeled in painted plaster

cowrie shells for eyes

skull visible where plaster has fallen off

Jericho plastered head
In some parts of early Neolithic West Asia, bodies were buried beneath house floors, but skulls were removed and modeled with lifelike features, probably for use in ancestor rituals.

clay mask

plant packing inside

Chinchorro mummy
Some cultures preserved their dead by mummification; the earliest were the South American Chinchorro, from 5000 BCE. They removed the flesh, reassembled the bones, and replaced the skin.

■ HUMAN FIGURINES

Late Neolithic figurine
Stone figurines were made by cultures across the world. Some were for use in rituals; others were decorative, or made social statements, or were toys.

schematic arms

slot for mounting figurine

Venus figurines
These female figures, from late Paleolithic Europe, are known as Venus figurines. Made from mammoth ivory, stone, and baked clay, they have strongly emphasized hips and breasts, and are generally faceless. They may have played some part in rituals.

featureless head

FIRED CLAY

small arm

damaged area

pronounced buttocks

hair, a feature rarely shown

tiny arms resting on breasts

small, tapering legs

LIMESTONE

MAMMOTH IVORY

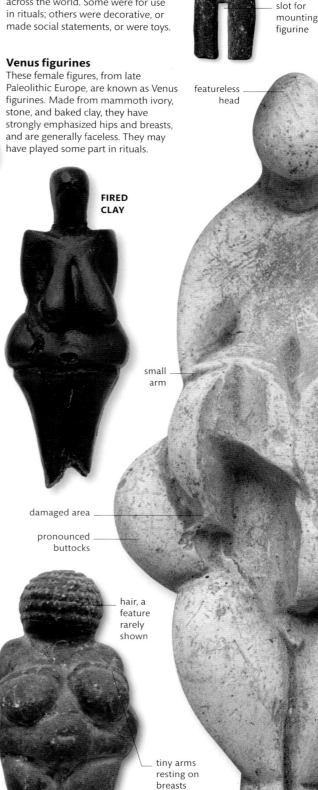

THE ENIGMA OF THE INDUS CIVILIZATION

Around 2500 BCE, the world's first planned towns and cities appeared throughout the Indus region (part of present-day India and Pakistan). Indus society was highly organized and produced many fine artifacts, but some details of the culture remain obscure because their script has not yet been deciphered.

Lands of the unicorn
A unicorn is the most common design found on Indus seals, often with a ritual brazier, as seen in this partial impression.

Public buildings ▽
Mohenjo-daro, in present-day south Pakistan, was the largest Indus city, covering more than 620 acres (250 hectares) and with a population of perhaps 100,000 people. Many of its structures, which included more than 700 wells, were built of baked bricks of standardized size.

Most Indus towns and cities had a massive raised sector, the citadel, with monumental public buildings. These included the Great Bath at Mohenjo-daro, which was probably a place of ritual purification. Indus political organization remains a mystery, partly because the writing invented by the Indus people defies decipherment. However, society was organized and controlled, with a good standard of living and highly developed craft specialization. A warehouse and workshops at Lothal in southern Gujarat, as well as Harappa in the Punjab, exemplify the role of towns and cities in manufacturing, storing, and distributing goods for external trade and circulation within the Indus realm. Rivers provided transport networks, and goods were carried by herders moving between seasonal pastures. Hunter-gatherers brought in ivory and other materials from beyond the settled lands.

GULF TRADERS

The valleys, mountains, and coasts of the Indus state provided agricultural and pastoral abundance and many raw materials. The Indus people also obtained metal ores and lapis lazuli from Afghanistan. They shipped lapis lazuli to Mesopotamia, along with carnelian and other gemstones, ivory, timber, gold, copper, and other materials, probably in exchange for silver and woolen textiles.

After 1800 BCE, unknown changes brought about the disintegration of the Indus realm. Towns and cities were abandoned, and writing ceased. However, farming communities continued to flourish in many parts of the region.

BELIEFS AND RITUALS

The symbols used on Indus objects (including some seals, see opposite) suggest that the Indus religion had some similarities to later Hinduism. These included deities resembling Shiva and Parvati, and reverence for aspects of the natural world, particularly powerful animals such as the bull and the tiger. Some copper tablets depicting a hairy man with horns suggest that a form of shamanism was part of Indus folk religion.

pannier headdress

neck choker

pendant necklace

beaded belt

Votive offering
Stains on figurines with large pannier headdresses suggest they may have been used as ritual lamps.

pipal leaf

unicorn head

Indus script

Sacred tree
The pipal tree was venerated by the Indus people, as it would be by Hindus, and the unicorn had an important role in Indus iconography.

trident headdress

yogic position

"Proto-Shiva"
This three-faced deity is surrounded by a bull, rhino, tiger, and an elephant. It has been suggested that he is a precursor of the god Shiva.

Mythological scene
Some seals depict a deity wrestling two tigers, as here, while others feature a half-tiger, half-goddess composite figure.

ADORNMENT

The Indus people set great store by personal adornment, wearing necklaces, pendants, hair and ear ornaments, rings, anklets, and bead belts, made from materials such as metal, ivory, faience (glazed ceramic), terracotta, shell, and stone. Bangles were particularly important. Indus beadmakers were extremely skilled in working gemstones such as agate, carnelian, serpentine, and steatite.

gold rod bent to form circular bangle

Gold bangle
Indus women generally wore bangles. Their materials give clues to social status: pottery or shell for the majority, silver or gold for the elite.

Ear ornament
This ornament has lost its inlay, perhaps of carnelian. The edge decoration is of gold wire, soldered onto the domed disk.

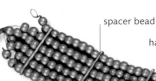

spacer bead

half-moon end cap

Neck ornament
The design of this gold neck choker, which has been broken in two, reveals a high level of skill on the part of the goldsmith who made it.

ART AND CULTURE

The uniformity of Indus culture suggests it was part of a well-organized, controlled society. Skilled artisans manufactured high-quality goods from materials such as fine flint quarried in Sindh, gemstones mined in Gujarat, and seashells. Indus art included a few bronze and stone sculptures, miniature images of animals carved on seals (see above), and vibrant terracotta figurines.

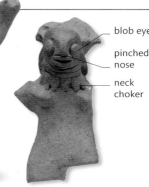

Terracotta bull
Indus figurines portrayed domestic and wild creatures, including pet dogs, rhinos, birds, and squirrels. Bulls were the most popular subject.

blob eyes

pinched nose

neck choker

Naked lady
Female figurines usually wear nothing apart from jewelry. Only rarely are they portrayed clothed and undertaking domestic tasks.

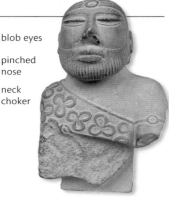

"Priest-king"
This tiny stone sculpture, only 7 in (17.5 cm) high, is often said to represent an Indus ruler, but there is no evidence to support this.

TECHNOLOGY AND INNOVATION

Indus towns and cities were all set out in a well-defined grid pattern, and the residents enjoyed a highly sophisticated water supply and drainage system. Specialized Indus craft products included fine flint and copper tools, and a wide range of pottery. Fine cotton textiles—dyed various colors including yellow, blue, and red—were made at home.

Cubic stone weights
Indus officials used standardized weights, ranging from a base unit of 0.03 oz (0.9 g) up to 23.9 lb (10.9 kg) or 12,800 units.

modern wooden replica yoke-pole

Bullock cart
This model shows that the Indus people had passenger carts as well as traditional bullock carts used to transport food and goods.

solid disk wheel

THE CRADLE OF CIVILIZATION

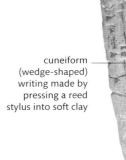

cuneiform (wedge-shaped) writing made by pressing a reed stylus into soft clay

The world's first civilization emerged in southern Mesopotamia, the birthplace of writing, around 3300 BCE. Early city-states were united around 2350 BCE, and Babylon became the capital of later empires in this region. In northern Mesopotamia (Assyria), linked culturally with the south, empires emerged from around 1800 BCE. Later, the Assyrians expanded to control all of western Asia.

Making a mark
Inscribed clay nails set into the walls of major public buildings, such as temples, bear texts describing the kings' close involvement in their construction.

Strength and beauty ▷
Babylon grew into a magnificent city. It boasted massive city walls, the ziggurat of Marduk (the "Tower of Babel"), and the Ishtar Gate and Processional Way, clad in glazed brick friezes of bulls and dragons. Similar tiles in the palace throne room depicted fearsome lions.

Southern Mesopotamia created many innovations of world significance during the 4th millennium BCE. Farming on the lower Tigris and Euphrates rivers depended on irrigation. The invention of the seeder plough made preparation of the soil easier and maximized productivity. Crops included barley, dates, and vegetables. Cattle kept for ploughing also gave milk and dung fertilizer. Sheep were now bred for wool, woven into textiles. Pastured locally or grazed farther afield by shepherds, sheep and goats also provided milk, meat, and leather.

The temple dominated society at this time. Grain from temple lands was used to pay people working for the temple as farmers, laborers, artisans, or traders. Such public service or employment, paid in grain rations and cloth, continued later, when power passed to secular rulers.

The first cities appeared around 3300 BCE in Sumer, centered on temples. The first known is Uruk, which yielded clay tablets inscribed with the earliest writing, invented to aid the temple authorities in their administrative tasks. By the mid-3rd millennium BCE, texts also included literature, such as epic tales of the early Uruk king Gilgamesh. Secular authority, vested in kings, who were originally war leaders, grew in importance as city-states came into conflict over land and water for irrigation.

THE FIRST EMPIRES

Around 2350 BCE, Sargon of Akkad created the Akkadian Empire, uniting the south. He standardized many aspects of the administration, including weights and measures. The later Ur III Empire imposed stiflingly detailed bureaucratic control. Following Ur III's fall in 2004 BCE, smaller city-states rose to power, but these were conquered in the 18th century BCE by Hammurabi of Babylon (famous for his "law code" inscribed on a stone stela).

Agriculturally rich, Babylonia was poor in raw materials. It traded copper from Oman and later Cyprus; lapis lazuli and tin from Afghanistan; and lumber, gold, ivory, and gemstones from the Indus. In exchange, it offered manufactured goods, especially fine textiles produced on an industrial scale in workshops staffed by women and children.

NORTH AND SOUTH

Diplomatic correspondence reveals shifting patterns of alliance and hostility between the major later 2nd millennium BCE powers: Egypt (see p.26), the Hittites (see p.43), Mitanni in northern Mesopotamia, and the Kassites in Babylonia. The small northwestern state of Assyria expanded as Mitanni declined. Its fortunes fluctuated, but for long periods it dominated western Asia. Palace relief sculptures bring Assyrian campaigns vividly to life (see p.21). One depicts King Sennacherib's beautiful terraced garden at Nineveh, perhaps the original of the Hanging Gardens attributed to Babylon.

Babylonia conquered Assyria in 612 BCE, but then fell to the Persians in 539 BCE. However, Mesopotamia's cultural legacy included inventions such as glass, the potter's wheel, and improved knowledge of medicine, astronomy, and complex mathematics including geometry.

> " I have **no equal** among even the most distant rulers... **Everything is achievable** by me."
>
> Shulgi, king of the Ur III Empire (2094–2047 BCE), *A praise poem of Shulgi*

POLITICS AND POWER

In city-states, the king and people had a shared sense of identity, and citizen assemblies had some decision-making power. Larger states were administered through officials from the ruler's own family, city, or tribe, but shared cultural values ensured the king remained answerable to the gods for his subjects' prosperity.

symbols of Babylonian deities

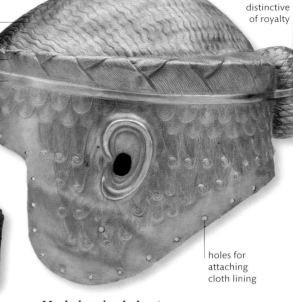

carefully combed lines of hair

bun, distinctive of royalty

braided hair

gold rendition of gold ribbon

curling locks

holes for attaching cloth lining

Babylonian temple text
Kings often founded temples and restored and embellished earlier ones. They recorded these pious deeds on clay texts placed in the foundations or in inscriptions.

Boundary stone
Kassite kudurrus (boundary stones) were documents recording royal grants of land to those who had served their rulers well. They were publicly displayed in temples.

Accounting tablet
Writing was invented around 3300 BCE to manage the administration of temple receipts, outgoings, and labor. Most surviving later texts are also administrative.

Meskalamdug helmet
This beautiful helmet of beaten gold is from a grave at the Ur cemetery, possibly that of King Meskalamdug. It would have been parade armor, not worn in battle.

lapis lazuli background

king clad in fleece kilt, his status shown by larger size

shell inlays and mosaic pieces

noble seated on wooden stool with decorative animal legs

red limestone

lyre player

VICTORY FEAST

war captive carrying captured booty

pair of asses from a chariot team

fisherman carrying fish

sheep, goats, and cattle for victory feast

Standard of Ur

This unusual object from the Ur royal graves may have been a royal standard (or flag) or the sound box of a musical instrument. One side is decorated with scenes of warfare. The panel of the other side depicts the preparations for and celebration of the victory shown on the war side.

WAR SIDE

BATTLE AND CONFLICT

Warfare between rival city-states and with enemies from the hills and desert is recorded at length in Mesopotamian literature and art. Armies originally had infantry and chariots; cavalry was added in the 1st millennium BCE. The highly efficient Assyrian military were greatly feared. Subject peoples paid tribute and were defended against their enemies, but rebellions were mercilessly suppressed.

Assyrian siege
Siege warfare inspired frequent improvements in ways of defending and attacking cities, such as fortifications and wooden siege towers and ladders.

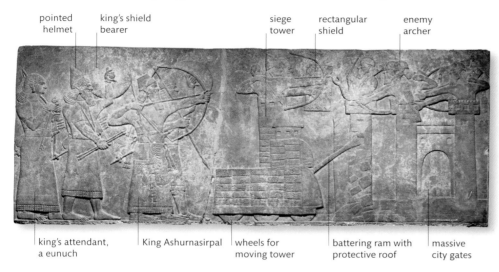

pointed helmet | king's shield bearer | siege tower | rectangular shield | enemy archer

king's attendant, a eunuch | King Ashurnasirpal | wheels for moving tower | battering ram with protective roof | massive city gates

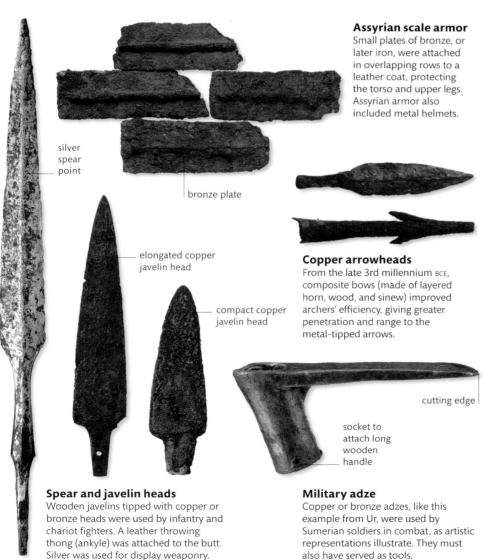

Assyrian scale armor
Small plates of bronze, or later iron, were attached in overlapping rows to a leather coat, protecting the torso and upper legs. Assyrian armor also included metal helmets.

silver spear point

bronze plate

elongated copper javelin head

compact copper javelin head

Copper arrowheads
From the late 3rd millennium BCE, composite bows (made of layered horn, wood, and sinew) improved archers' efficiency, giving greater penetration and range to the metal-tipped arrows.

cutting edge

socket to attach long wooden handle

Spear and javelin heads
Wooden javelins tipped with copper or bronze heads were used by infantry and chariot fighters. A leather throwing thong (ankyle) was attached to the butt. Silver was used for display weaponry.

Military adze
Copper or bronze adzes, like this example from Ur, were used by Sumerian soldiers in combat, as artistic representations illustrate. They must also have served as tools.

BELIEFS AND RITUALS

The temple enjoyed great political and social power throughout Mesopotamian history. Sumerian cities each had their own gods but acknowledged the supremacy of the storm god, Enlil. Babylon's city god Marduk later became the principal deity, mirroring the political rise of Babylon itself. Although the Assyrians worshipped their city god, Ashur, they also venerated the Babylonian pantheon.

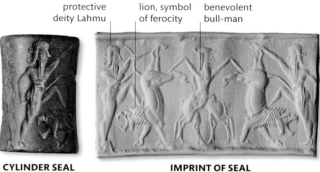

protective deity Lahmu | lion, symbol of ferocity | benevolent bull-man

CYLINDER SEAL   **IMPRINT OF SEAL**

Mythical combat scene
Cylinder seals often bore motifs with religious significance. This traditional theme of gods or heroes wrestling bulls or lions was particularly popular in Akkadian times.

traditional fleece kilt

Sumerian priest
Priests officiated at religious ceremonies, offered prayers, interpreted omens to discover the gods' views of proposed actions, and oversaw temple business matters.

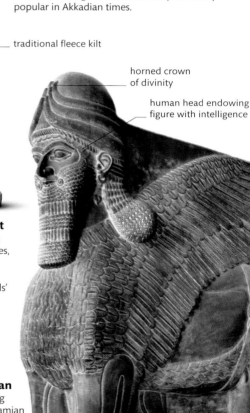

horned crown of divinity

human head endowing figure with intelligence

Nimrud guardian
Many awe-inspiring figures in Mesopotamian art had a benign role. Gigantic winged human-headed lions and bulls representing protective spirits guarded the gateways of Assyrian temples and palaces.

five legs in total to allow viewing from front or side

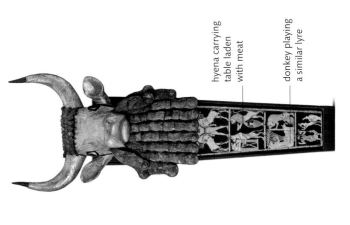

hyena carrying table laden with meat

donkey playing a similar lyre

RAM CAUGHT IN A THICKET

In the 1920s, the British archaeologist Sir Leonard Woolley discovered some remarkable burials at Ur (in modern Iraq), dating from around 2550–2400 BCE. Most graves in the huge cemetery were simple pits, but 16 were barrel-vaulted chambers, often with large associated grave pits approached by a shaft. They contained lavishly rich grave goods, and Woolley identified them as royal graves. One pit grave also contained rich furnishings, including a beautiful gold helmet and two gold bowls inscribed "Meskalamdug," an early king of Ur. One royal grave yielded a seal inscribed "Puabi the queen."

The objects from these graves represented enormous wealth and extraordinary artistic creativity. They were made from imported exotic materials, such as gold, silver, lapis lazuli, Indus carnelian, and fine stone. They included not only vessels and jewelry but also animal-headed lyres, a gaming board with mosaic decoration, a sled drawn by asses, and gilded furniture. While some objects were the deceased's personal possessions, buried for their continued enjoyment, others were meant as gifts to placate the grim underworld deities in the hope of receiving favorable treatment in the joyless afterlife.

In addition to the principal, royal person, the 16 graves contained the bodies of others who may have been sacrificed: at least 26 in Puabi's grave and 74 in what Woolley called the Great Death Pit. Their positions and associated finds showed them to be guards, grooms, musicians, and personal attendants, most of them women. Woolley argued these were willing victims, who chose to die with their royal master or mistress. Recent investigations show that some, at least, died from blows to the head, but whether all were sacrificed is still uncertain. No other Mesopotamian cemetery contains such sacrifices.

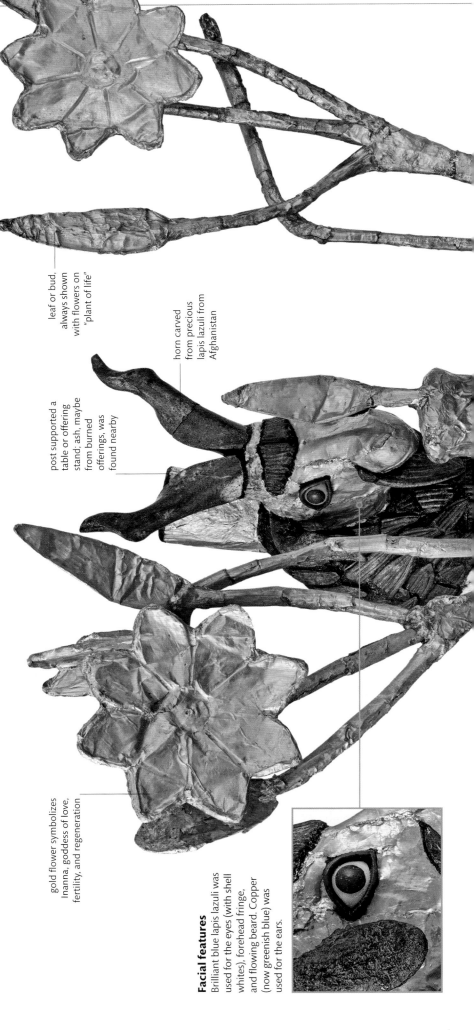

Bull-head lyre
Wooden lyres were found with many of the female attendants. Their sound boxes ended in an animal head, usually that of a bull or cow, decorated with lapis lazuli, shell, and gold.

leaf or bud, always shown with flowers on "plant of life"

horn carved from precious lapis lazuli from Afghanistan

post supported a table or offering stand; ash, maybe from burned offerings, was found nearby

gold flower symbolizes Inanna, goddess of love, fertility, and regeneration

Facial features
Brilliant blue lapis lazuli was used for the eyes (with shell whites), forehead fringe, and flowing beard. Copper (now greenish blue) was used for the ears.

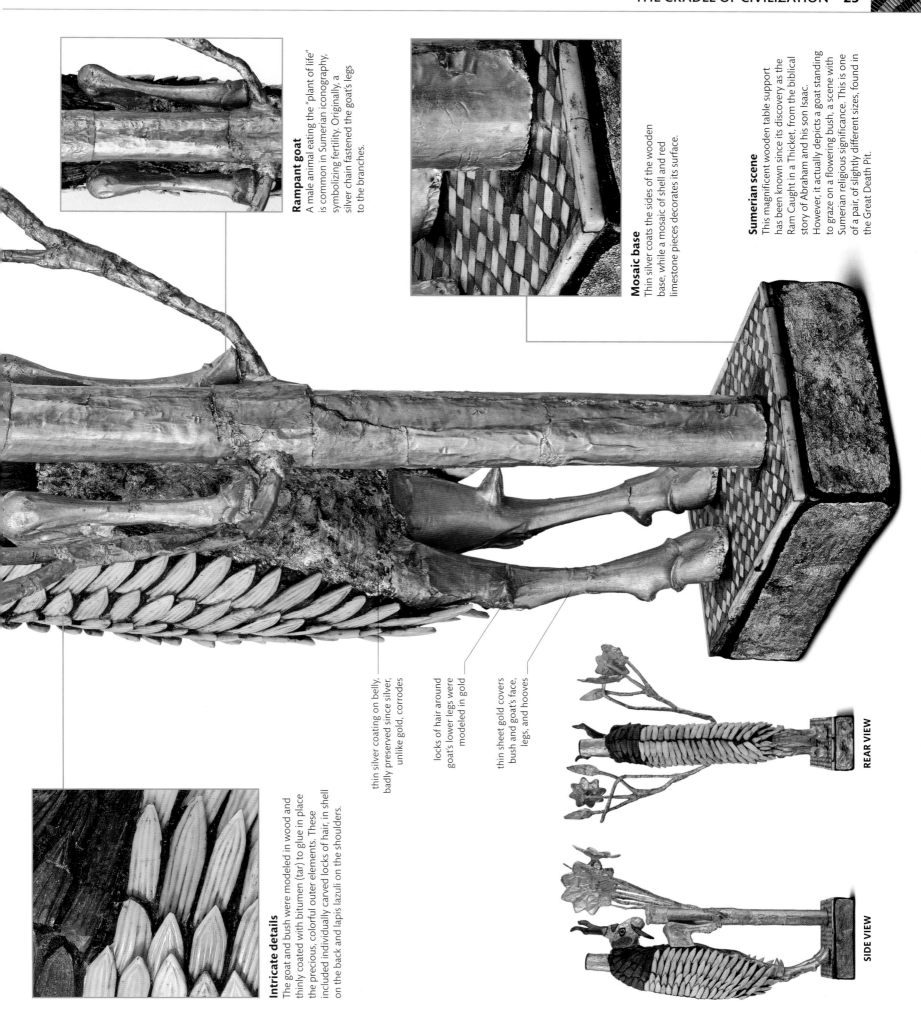

Rampant goat
A male animal eating the "plant of life" is common in Sumerian iconography, symbolizing fertility. Originally, a silver chain fastened the goat's legs to the branches.

Mosaic base
Thin silver coats the sides of the wooden base, while a mosaic of shell and red limestone pieces decorates its surface.

Sumerian scene
This magnificent wooden table support has been known since its discovery as the Ram Caught in a Thicket, from the biblical story of Abraham and his son Isaac. However, it actually depicts a goat standing to graze on a flowering bush, a scene with Sumerian religious significance. This is one of a pair, of slightly different sizes, found in the Great Death Pit.

Intricate details
The goat and bush were modeled in wood and thinly coated with bitumen (tar) to glue in place the precious, colorful outer elements. These included individually carved locks of hair, in shell on the back and lapis lazuli on the shoulders.

thin silver coating on belly, badly preserved since silver, unlike gold, corrodes

locks of hair around goat's lower legs were modeled in gold

thin sheet gold covers bush and goat's face, legs, and hooves

REAR VIEW

SIDE VIEW

HOME LIFE

Cups, bowls, dishes, goblets, and jars for cooking and serving food at home were usually made of pottery. Well-off households also acquired metal and stone vessels, often made of exotic imported materials. Many of these vessels were buried at Ur in both royal graves and those of lesser people.

Decorated bowl
Distinctive soapstone bowls were manufactured at Tepe Yahya and Jiroft, in modern Iran, and Tarut, in Saudi Arabia, in the 3rd millennium BCE. They were widely traded.

scorpion design | typical hatched infill

Boat-shaped bowl
Silver was imported from Anatolia to make luxury tableware and decorative objects. Weighed silver was used as a form of currency.

beer vat | reed tube

CYLINDER SEAL | **FEAST SCENE IMPRESSION**

Beer drinkers
Sumerian barley beer was unfiltered so it was drunk through a long tube. Three tubes, of gold, silver, and copper encased in lapis lazuli, were found in Queen Puabi's grave.

Soapstone tumbler
Many tumblers of gold, silver, and stone were found at Ur. Soapstone, being soft and therefore easy to carve, was frequently used for stone vessels and seals.

Alabaster vase
Stone was used in early Mesopotamia to make luxury vessels. Most was imported, from Iran and farther afield, but alabaster was locally available.

CLOTHING AND ADORNMENT

Intact rich graves are rarely found, so most information on Mesopotamian clothing and adornment comes from texts or art. These reveal that Sumerian men, for example, wore fleece kilts and the women wore woolen wrap-around robes. The largest collection of surviving jewelry is from the royal cemetery at Ur (see p.22).

Finger rings
These rings were made from very finely twisted gold wire, soldered to plain gold bands. Ordinary people wore rings made of copper.

Garment cuff
Beaded cuffs were found with many of the women in the Great Death Pit. Surviving threads show that these were sewn onto short-sleeved red garments.

lapis lazuli bead

gold bead

carnelian disk bead

poplar leaves of engraved beaten gold

Wreaths, pendants, and necklaces
Elaborate hairstyles were held in place by a gold or silver ribbon wound around several times. Over this were arranged wreaths of gold poplar and willow leaves. The double spiral of the gold pendant was a common symbolic element in Mesopotamian decoration.

biconical carnelian bead | carved lapis lazuli bead

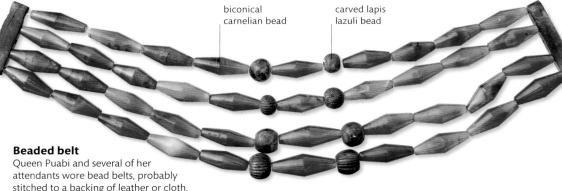

Beaded belt
Queen Puabi and several of her attendants wore bead belts, probably stitched to a backing of leather or cloth, sometimes with pendant rings of gold or shell.

Unusual choker
A number of the female attendants in the royal graves wore unusual chokers made of triangular beads. The gold beads were made of sheet metal doubled over.

carved lapis lazuli bead | gold tube for suspension cords

lapis lazuli fly

fluted gold bead

lapis lazuli bead

gold fly

Indus
carnelian
bead

twisted
gold wire
pendant

hair comb topped
by 7 gold flowers

carnelian-tipped
gold willow leaves

gold sheet
ribbons

hammered
sheet gold

Loop earrings
Many of the women found
in the Ur cemetery wore
earrings. These large gold
crescent-shaped earrings
were probably worn hanging
down, with the thin wire over
the top of the ear.

multiple strands of
gold, lapis lazuli,
silver, agate, and
carnelian beads

silver support for
petal, now missing

gold leaf petal

gold and lapis
lazuli head

banded agate bead

gold ring
to attach
cylinder
seal

gold pendant rings
hanging from belt

frit (vitreous
paste) petal

silver
hair support

Hair comb
Queen Puabi and several
attendants in the royal
graves wore "Spanish
combs," which supported
an elaborate raised hair
arrangement. The flowers
would appear to be
growing out of the hair.

Dress pins
Pins fastened a cloak
draped over one
shoulder and passed
under the other arm.
Often the wearer's
cylinder seal was
attached by a chain to a
ring near the pin's head.

Queen Puabi's finery
With great skill, Woolley used the
position of surviving elements to
reconstruct original forms. These
included the queen's elaborate hair
arrangement, outlined by her gold
ribbons and headdress, and her
magnificent cape, made of long
pendant strands of beads.

EGYPTIAN LIFE AND AFTERLIFE

From its inception, ancient Egypt was defined by its religious beliefs. Worship of all-powerful deities was part of daily life, and ancient Egyptians believed that when they died they would enjoy an afterlife. Its pharaohs, kings who were regarded as gods, controlled the vast resources of the kingdom, using them to build architecture on a grand scale and tombs filled with beautiful objects.

Behind the mask
After bandaging, a mummy's face was often covered by an idealized portrait mask, made of gilded and painted cartonnage (linen and glue stiffened with plaster).

Scenes from real life ▷
The tomb of the astronomer and scribe Nakht, who lived around 1400 BCE, is decorated with magnificent paintings depicting scenes from life at that time. Here he hunts birds in a papyrus thicket, watched by his wife and three children.

Egypt is often called "the gift of the Nile," and ancient Egypt owed much to the river. Its annual floods brought water and fertile silt to sustain agriculture and, by the late 4th millennium BCE, supported a few towns, with growing regional control. The regions of Upper and Lower Egypt were eventually united in 3100 BCE by the legendary King Menes, who made his capital centrally at Memphis. A pattern of alternating regional division and centralized control was repeated throughout subsequent Egyptian history. During times of prosperity and under strong rulers, the land was united; when troubles arose, weakened rulers lost overall control and the kingdom disintegrated into smaller political realms enjoying varying degrees of independence.

OLD KINGDOM

Comparatively little is known of Egypt's first two dynasties (the Early Dynastic period). The Old Kingdom began with the 3rd dynasty in 2686 BCE. Its pharaohs built the first pyramids (see p.28). They obtained gold from Nubia and traded with the city of Byblos (see p.47) for lumber. The Sun god Re became Egypt's supreme deity. However, poor floods and subsequent famine brought political disintegration from 2181 BCE (the First Intermediate period).

MIDDLE KINGDOM

Upper and Lower Egypt were reunited under Mentuhotep II around 2040 BCE. In 1985 BCE, the throne passed to Amenemhat I, founder of the 12th dynasty, who built a new capital at Itj-tawy. The borders of the kingdom's administrative divisions (nomes) were fixed. Kings were still buried beneath pyramids, now surrounded by nobles' tombs. Substantial temples were built, and the cult of Osiris (see p.34) grew in importance.

To gain better control of Nubia's gold deposits, fortresses were built and a canal constructed. The early 17th century BCE saw a decline in royal authority, and the usurpation of power in the delta by the Semitic Hyksos dynasty in 1650 BCE began the Second Intermediate period. Itj-tawy was abandoned, but an Egyptian dynasty still controlled Upper Egypt.

NEW KINGDOM

Around 1550 BCE, the native dynasty drove out the Hyksos and founded the New Kingdom. Egyptian domination of Nubia was extended southward. Pharaohs were now buried in rock-cut tombs in the Valley of the Kings. The Theban god Amun was preeminent, and large temple complexes were built, particularly at Luxor.

In the 14th century BCE, the pharaoh Akhenaten broke with tradition, instituting worship of a single god, the Aten, and building a new capital at Amarna. Neither survived his death, the status quo being restored under his youthful successor, Tutankhamun. International trade flourished, and the Egyptians expanded their rule eastward.

By the 11th century BCE, political control was disintegrating. A general of Libyan origin seized control of Upper Egypt in 1069 BCE, ushering in the Third Intermediate period during which Upper and Lower Egypt were ruled by separate, although related, dynasties. Egypt was reunited in the late 8th century BCE by the Kushite (Nubian) 25th dynasty.

> " **Enjoy yourself** while you live… follow your heart's command **on earth,** be joyful and make merry."
>
> Harper's Song, inscribed on the tomb of King Inyotef *c.*2125–2055 BCE

POLITICS AND POWER

The mythical first king of Egypt was the god Osiris, followed by his son Horus. From Horus, both kingship and divinity were passed on to his male successors, making the Egyptian pharaoh an absolute monarch. Under royal authority, Egypt's administration was in the hands of state officials and provincial governors.

stela inscribed with hymn to Sun god

Meryptah praising rising Sun

Meryptah, priest of Amun
As Amun-Re, Egypt's principal deity Amun represented the Sun. His chief priest wielded considerable political power, particularly under weak pharaohs.

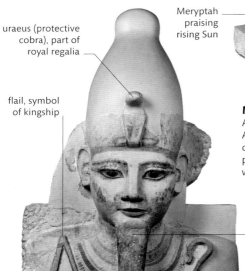

uraeus (protective cobra), part of royal regalia

flail, symbol of kingship

beard, symbolizing divinity

Ramses II
Ramses the Great was one of Egypt's most powerful and long-lived rulers. In the 13th century BCE, he built many temples, monuments, and statues, and a new city, Pi-Ramesse.

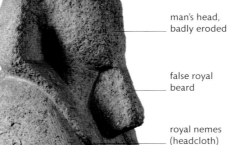

lion's body

man's head, badly eroded

false royal beard

royal nemes (headcloth)

cartouche of Ramses' son Merenptah added after his father's death

cartouche, line and oval enclosing royal name

Middle Kingdom sphinx
Sphinxes symbolized both the Sun god and royal power. In the New Kingdom, processional avenues of sphinxes were built as the approaches to many temples. This sphinx was recarved with the five royal names of Ramses II.

Royal name
This cartouche gives the throne name adopted by Ramses II on his accession, Usermaatre, which means "the Justice of Re is Powerful."

Hieroglyphs
The hieroglyphic script included logograms (signs representing a word or idea) but was mainly composed of phonetic signs signifying one, two, or three consonants.

PYRAMIDS

King Djoser constructed the first pyramid, the step pyramid at Saqqara, in the 27th century BCE. In the following two centuries, Sneferu at Dahshur and his successors at Giza (shown above) built smooth-sided pyramids, along with mortuary temples, subsidiary pyramids for their wives, and other monuments.

ART AND CULTURE

Despite its conventions—which dictated, for example, that human faces, arms, and legs be depicted in profile, while torsos be shown from the front—Egyptian artworks give a wonderfully detailed and realistic picture of Egyptian life. They include paintings, reliefs, models of people and scenes, and stone sculptures.

black pigment on wig and eyes

pleated kilt

traces of red pigment on body

Standing scribe
The self-confident pose reflects the advantages a scribe enjoyed, including potential access to high office and freedom from the backbreaking work endured by the majority.

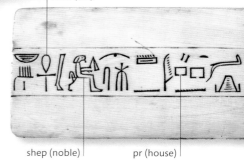

ankh (life)

shep (noble)   pr (house)

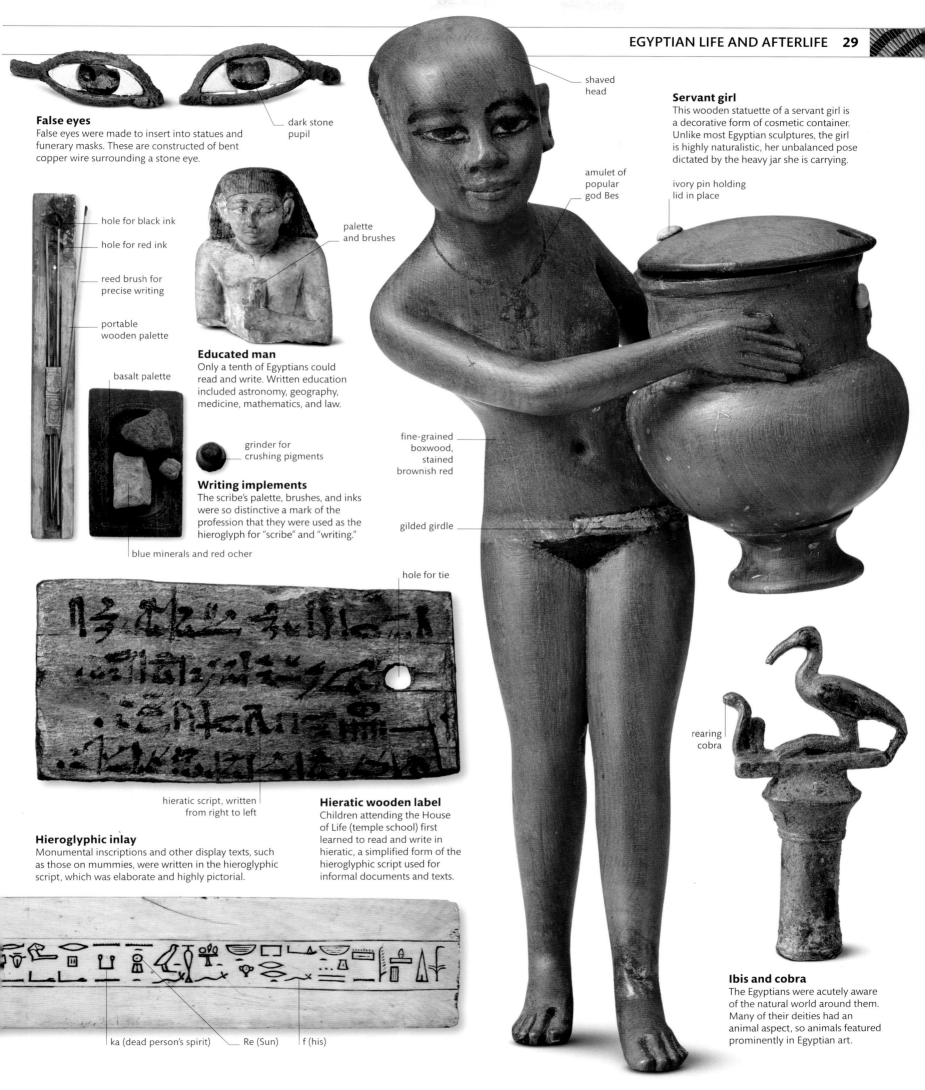

False eyes
False eyes were made to insert into statues and funerary masks. These are constructed of bent copper wire surrounding a stone eye.

dark stone pupil

hole for black ink

hole for red ink

reed brush for precise writing

portable wooden palette

basalt palette

palette and brushes

Educated man
Only a tenth of Egyptians could read and write. Written education included astronomy, geography, medicine, mathematics, and law.

grinder for crushing pigments

Writing implements
The scribe's palette, brushes, and inks were so distinctive a mark of the profession that they were used as the hieroglyph for "scribe" and "writing."

blue minerals and red ocher

shaved head

Servant girl
This wooden statuette of a servant girl is a decorative form of cosmetic container. Unlike most Egyptian sculptures, the girl is highly naturalistic, her unbalanced pose dictated by the heavy jar she is carrying.

amulet of popular god Bes

ivory pin holding lid in place

fine-grained boxwood, stained brownish red

gilded girdle

hole for tie

hieratic script, written from right to left

Hieratic wooden label
Children attending the House of Life (temple school) first learned to read and write in hieratic, a simplified form of the hieroglyphic script used for informal documents and texts.

Hieroglyphic inlay
Monumental inscriptions and other display texts, such as those on mummies, were written in the hieroglyphic script, which was elaborate and highly pictorial.

ka (dead person's spirit)   Re (Sun)   f (his)

rearing cobra

Ibis and cobra
The Egyptians were acutely aware of the natural world around them. Many of their deities had an animal aspect, so animals featured prominently in Egyptian art.

CLOTHING AND ADORNMENT

Egyptian clothing was made from white linen, and the best pieces were very finely woven. Men wore a kilt, with or without a shirt, or a loincloth for manual work. Women wore a long, straight dress, with one or two shoulder straps. Children usually went naked (see p.29), although some children's clothes were found in Tutankhamun's tomb.

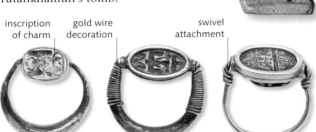

faience pig, symbol of the god Seth

faience cat, symbol of the goddess Bastet

cowrie shell

falcon's head terminal

lotus blossom

carnelian bead

amulet of protective goddess Taweret

inscription of charm

gold wire decoration

swivel attachment

Amulet bracelet
Protective cowrie shell amulets were worn by women from Predynastic times. Pigs were associated with the violent god Seth who, surprisingly, also had a protective aspect.

Finger rings
These rings all held a swiveling bevel in the shape of a protective scarab beetle, its underside inscribed with a good luck charm.

Collar and necklace
Faience, a glazed ceramic colored blue or green with copper ore, was a cheaper artificial substitute for turquoise or lapis lazuli. Wide collars of many strands of cylindrical beads, known as wesekh, were worn by noble men and women.

HOME LIFE

Paintings and models in tombs vividly document both nobles' enjoyment of the good things in life and the daily toil of those supporting them. Egypt's arid conditions have also preserved many everyday objects made of organic materials, such as basketry, and documents in perishable materials, such as papyrus, which also describe many aspects of daily life.

inscription of Queen Hatshepsut, principal wife of Thutmose II, her half-brother

scribe writing on papyrus

official clad in robe

one of four workers

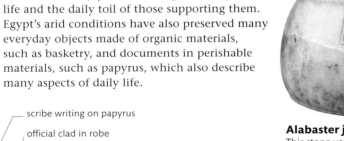

Alabaster jar
This stone vessel, inscribed with the name and titles of Queen Hatshepsut, may have been a gift to place in the tomb of a favored royal official.

Badarian culture bowl
This handmade Predynastic bowl, with a characteristic black rim, shows the great skill achieved by Egyptian potters even before 3000 BCE.

Drinking vessels
Most Egyptian pottery is basic red-brown coarse ware, for everyday use. It is known as "Nile Silt ware" after the material from which it was made.

linen cloth

coiled plant fibers

granary chamber door

Model granary
Models of real-life activities enabled the deceased to continue a normal life after death. Here, an official interviews four workmen while a scribe records the details.

Linen basket
Egypt is unusual in preserving ancient matting and basketry, used in many cultures for everyday containers. Dom-palm leaves and grasses were used in making these objects.

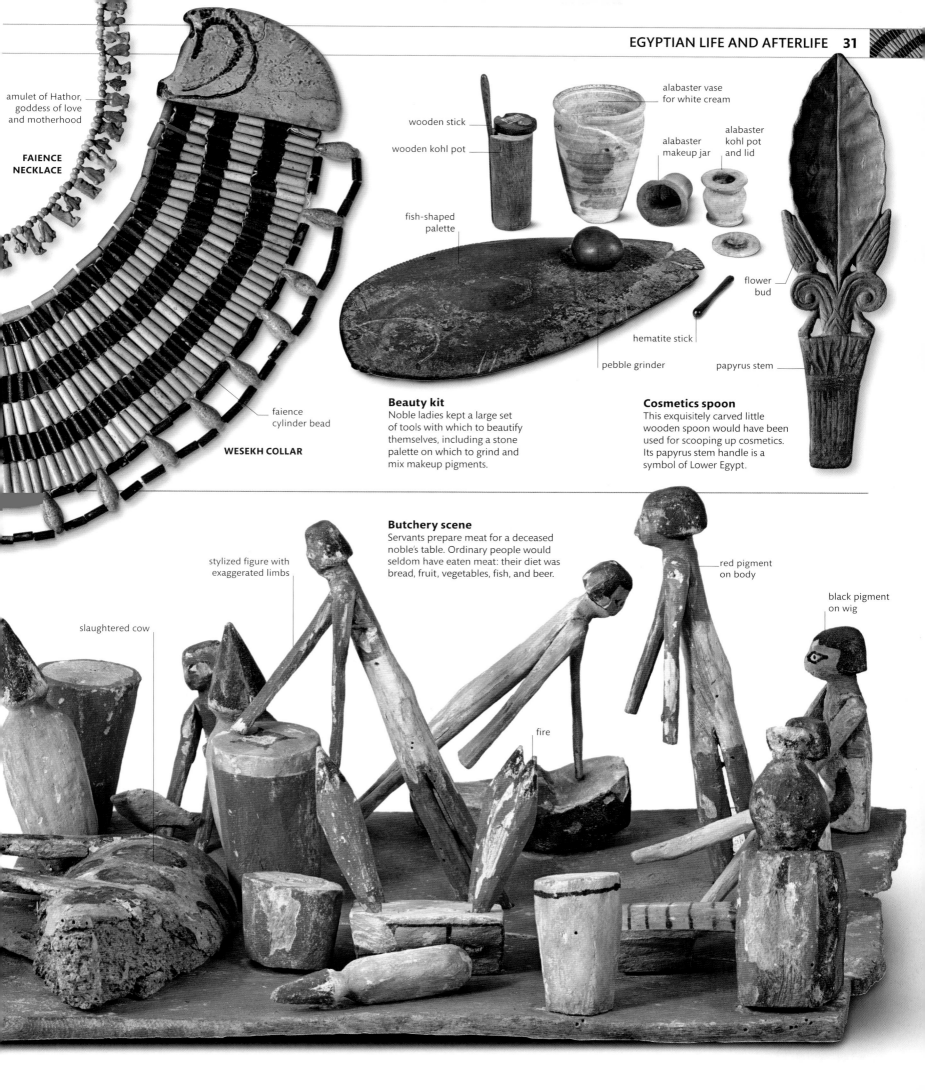

amulet of Hathor, goddess of love and motherhood

FAIENCE NECKLACE

faience cylinder bead

WESEKH COLLAR

wooden stick

wooden kohl pot

fish-shaped palette

alabaster vase for white cream

alabaster makeup jar

alabaster kohl pot and lid

flower bud

hematite stick

pebble grinder

papyrus stem

Beauty kit
Noble ladies kept a large set of tools with which to beautify themselves, including a stone palette on which to grind and mix makeup pigments.

Cosmetics spoon
This exquisitely carved little wooden spoon would have been used for scooping up cosmetics. Its papyrus stem handle is a symbol of Lower Egypt.

Butchery scene
Servants prepare meat for a deceased noble's table. Ordinary people would seldom have eaten meat: their diet was bread, fruit, vegetables, fish, and beer.

stylized figure with exaggerated limbs

slaughtered cow

red pigment on body

black pigment on wig

fire

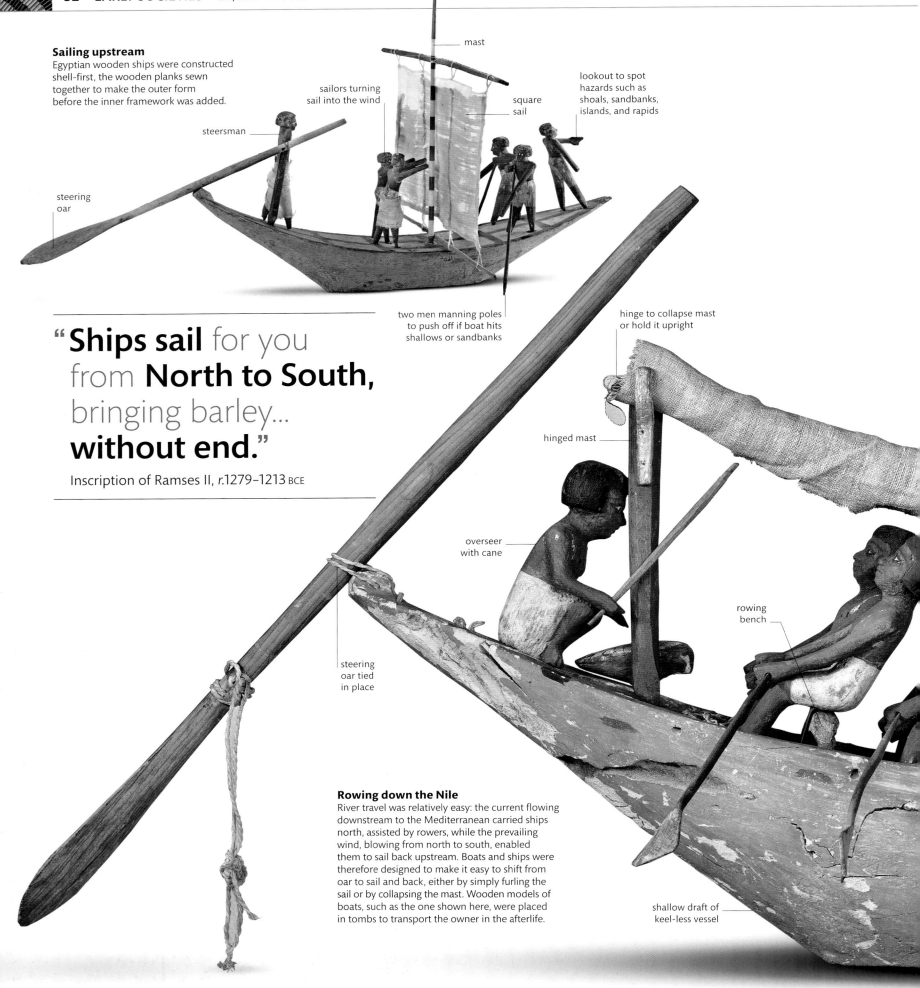

Sailing upstream
Egyptian wooden ships were constructed shell-first, the wooden planks sewn together to make the outer form before the inner framework was added.

mast

sailors turning sail into the wind

square sail

lookout to spot hazards such as shoals, sandbanks, islands, and rapids

steersman

steering oar

two men manning poles to push off if boat hits shallows or sandbanks

hinge to collapse mast or hold it upright

hinged mast

overseer with cane

rowing bench

steering oar tied in place

" **Ships sail** for you from **North to South,** bringing barley... **without end.**"

Inscription of Ramses II, *r*.1279–1213 BCE

Rowing down the Nile
River travel was relatively easy: the current flowing downstream to the Mediterranean carried ships north, assisted by rowers, while the prevailing wind, blowing from north to south, enabled them to sail back upstream. Boats and ships were therefore designed to make it easy to shift from oar to sail and back, either by simply furling the sail or by collapsing the mast. Wooden models of boats, such as the one shown here, were placed in tombs to transport the owner in the afterlife.

shallow draft of keel-less vessel

THE LURE OF THE EXOTIC

RIVER CRAFT

Simple craft for fishing, hunting wildfowl, or crossing the Nile were made of papyrus reeds bound in bundles, but most long-distance river traffic was in wooden boats, ideally of Lebanese cedar. Some had cabins, in the center of the vessel or at one or both ends. Substantial ships were required to transport stone from quarries, and for trade in the Mediterranean and the Red Sea.

Boats were essential for moving the goods and materials on which Egypt depended. Copper, stone, and semiprecious stones came from the desert east of the Nile. Copper was also sourced from Sinai farther east.

To the south, the lands around the Nile cataracts provided Egypt's seemingly limitless supplies of gold, along with ebony, ivory, and copper, and a route to the exotic produce of sub-Saharan Africa.

African exotica were also obtained from the land of Punt, reached by sailing down the Red Sea as well as overland. Its chief attraction was incense, much used by the Egyptians for religious ceremonies and mummification. In the 15th century BCE, Queen Hatshepsut even sent an expedition to Punt to obtain incense trees. Punt also yielded gold, ebony, blackwood, ivory, slaves, and wild

animals. Pygmies skilled in dance were imported from sub-Saharan Africa. The tomb of Harkhuf, an Egyptian governor, contains a copy of an excited letter from the 8-year-old King Pepy II in about 2276 BCE, urging that every possible care be taken of the pygmy dancer that Harkhuf was bringing him.

Egypt also imported timber and copper from its eastern neighbors, and Minoan and Mycenaean pottery and military equipment. Egypt's own exports included grain, wine, Egyptian caviar, dried fish, linen cloth, and luxury goods such as faience vessels.

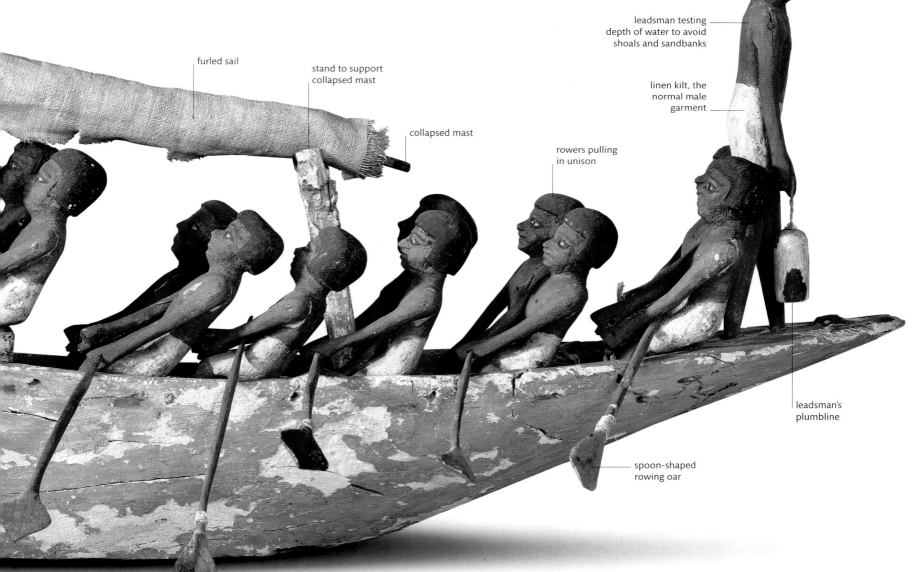

leadsman testing depth of water to avoid shoals and sandbanks

linen kilt, the normal male garment

furled sail

stand to support collapsed mast

collapsed mast

rowers pulling in unison

leadsman's plumbline

spoon-shaped rowing oar

BELIEFS AND RITUALS

Egyptian religion had a rich mythology, and the story of Osiris, by which he became god of the afterlife, was particularly important. Religious and secular life were intertwined. Nobles acted as priests or temple officials for short stints of three months, returning to ordinary life for the rest of the year.

■ GODS AND GODDESSES

tall plumes, representing the wind

feet resting on footstool

Amun
Amun ("the hidden one") was king of the gods, the creator of the cosmos, responsible for all fertility. As Amun-Re, he represented the Sun.

ibis bill

Thoth
In his role as god of scribes, Thoth was both the keeper of all kinds of knowledge and the recorder when Osiris judged the dead.

lioness head

long wig

Sekhmet
A daughter of the Sun god Re, Sekhmet was both the goddess of war and a protective deity associated with healing.

twin plumes

lotus flower headdress

Nefertem
Often seen as the son of Ptah and Sekhmet, Nefertem was the god of the lotus blossom and the Sun rising from it. He was more feared than worshipped.

jackal head

Anubis
Anubis was called "lord of the sacred land" (the desert where tombs were situated). He was responsible for mummification and protecting the dead.

Atef (feathered crown)

flail

crook

Osiris
Murdered by his jealous brother Seth but brought back to life, Osiris was the ruler of the afterlife and judge of the dead. He symbolized fertility and resurrection.

horns

solar disk

Isis and Horus
Isis, wife of the murdered god Osiris, was regarded as mourner and protector of the dead. As the mother of Osiris' son Horus, she was venerated as the divine mother and as mother to the pharaohs.

baby Horus nursing

long skirt

■ SHABTIS

false beard secured by cord

mummy, the usual shape for a shabti

carved hieroglyphic text

Early shabti
In Old Kingdom times, models of workers who would perform specific tasks for the deceased were placed in tombs. By 2000 BCE, these were replaced by all-purpose shabti ("answerer") figures.

Faience shabtis
Shabtis were made in many materials but faience was the most common. Later tombs might contain several hundred shabtis.

mass-produced shabti

kohl-painted eyes

heavy wig

elaborate collar

painted detail on wooden body

inscribed hieroglyphic text

Wooden shabti
Later shabtis were sometimes depicted with tools, and this figure wears a basket on her back. She is inscribed "Of the Lady Maya," referring to the owner of the tomb.

■ AMULETS

Sons of Horus amulets
Each of the four Sons of Horus—Qebehsenuef, Imsety, Hapy, and Duamutef—protected one of the four canopic jars in which were stored the liver, lungs, stomach, and intestines, which were removed when the deceased was mummified (see p.39).

solar disk

Pectoral amulet
From New Kingdom times, amulets frequently portrayed deities. This amulet depicts a god between two birds, all wearing the horns and solar disk of Isis or Hathor.

FALCON-HEADED QEBEHSENUEF

HUMAN-HEADED IMSETY

BABOON-HEADED HAPY

JACKAL-HEADED DUAMUTEF

faience pectoral scarab amulet

open loop

girdle tied in a bow

Scarab
The Egyptian dung beetle, patiently rolling a ball of dung many times its size, came to symbolize resurrection. It was popular in amulets.

Wedjat amulet
The left eye of Horus, plucked out by his uncle Seth but magically restored, symbolized healing, wholeness, strength, and protection.

Djed amulet
Originally seen as a pillar, the djed was later taken to represent the backbone of Osiris, symbolizing stability and his resurrection.

Tyet amulet
The tyet was an early sacred symbol. The tyet amulet became popular in New Kingdom times, when it was described as the knot of Isis.

Bes amulet
The aggression of the dwarf god Bes was all directed toward external threats. He was the protector of the family, particularly women in childbirth.

Fish-shaped amulet
Amulets were worn in life to give general protection or to ward against specific threats. They were placed in mummy wrappings for protection in the afterlife.

chased (engraved) details

gold molded around a core

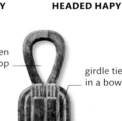

suspension loop in fish's mouth

■ GRAVE GOODS

Chapter 181

gate guardians

one of series of gates through which deceased must pass to reach afterlife

Osiris

individual named Pashed kneeling in worship

text written in hieroglyphs and arranged in chapters

Chapter 180

vertical lines separating chapters

Extract from the Book of the Dead of Neferrenpet
The Book of the Dead was written on papyrus scrolls that were placed within the bandages wrapping the mummy. It gave the deceased invaluable guidance on how best to behave at the final judgment in the underworld (see p.39).

■ MUMMY CASE

Pasenhor's mummy case
A human-shaped coffin not only housed the mummy, but could also replace it if the mummy were destroyed or damaged. Symbolic texts and images painted inside and out protected the deceased and provided help at his or her final judgment.

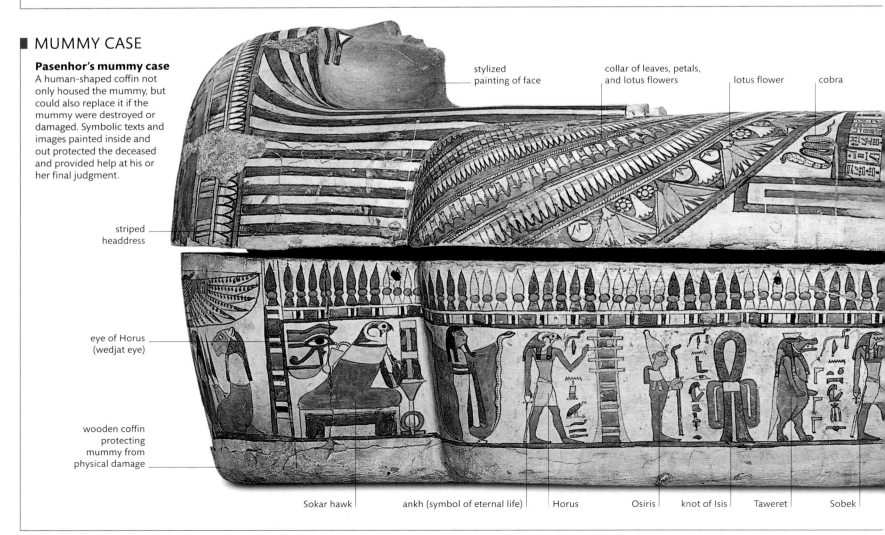

stylized painting of face

collar of leaves, petals, and lotus flowers

lotus flower

cobra

striped headdress

eye of Horus (wedjat eye)

wooden coffin protecting mummy from physical damage

Sokar hawk

ankh (symbol of eternal life)

Horus

Osiris

knot of Isis

Taweret

Sobek

cartouche of
Amenhotep II
(1427–1400 BCE)

painted
floral band

description
of wine

gold leaf
on eyes

human
face

headcloth

bird's
body

inscription naming
tomb owner
Hekay, a noble
court official

Water jar
Water was regarded as the
source of creation. It symbolized
life, regeneration, and purity,
so faience water jars were an
important burial offering.

Wine jar
Wine, made from grapes and
mixed with honey and spices,
was important in the Egyptian
diet. This large wine amphora
is from a rich woman's tomb.

Bronze cat
Cats were kept as household
pets and as animals sacred to
Re and to the fertility goddess
Bastet. This hollow figure may
have held a cat mummy.

Ba
The Ba (personality spirit) was
one of the five elements making
up a person. Its bird form helped
it return nightly from the
underworld to the deceased.

Headrest
Instead of pillows, the Egyptians
slept with their heads on a
headrest, usually of wood. This
luxury alabaster version was
placed in an Old Kingdom tomb.

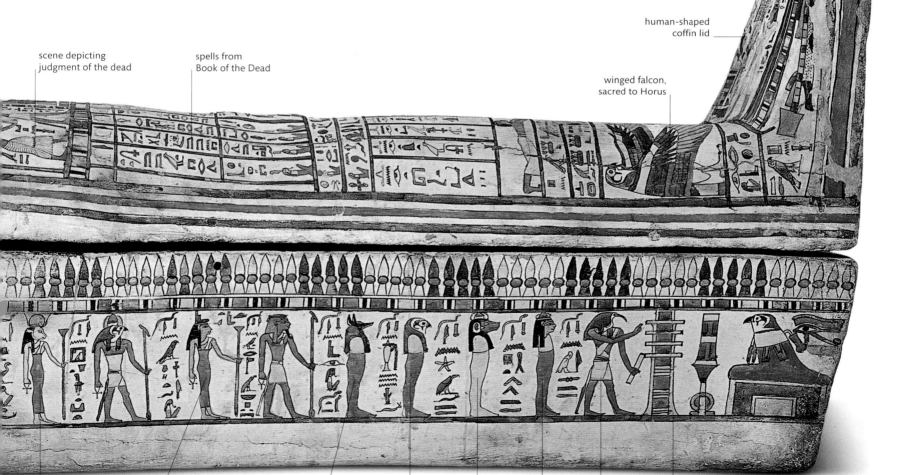

scene depicting
judgment of the dead

spells from
Book of the Dead

human-shaped
coffin lid

winged falcon,
sacred to Horus

Hathor   Isis   Duamutef   Qebehsenuef   Hapy   Imsety   Thoth   djed pillar (symbol of resurrection)

Nefersefekhy

geese, bred for meat, were sometimes force-fed

leopard-skin robe of sem-priest, who undertook the final rites of resurrection on a mummy

staff symbolizes Nefersefekhy's authority

baskets of food offerings

leg of beef

servant carrying calf carcass

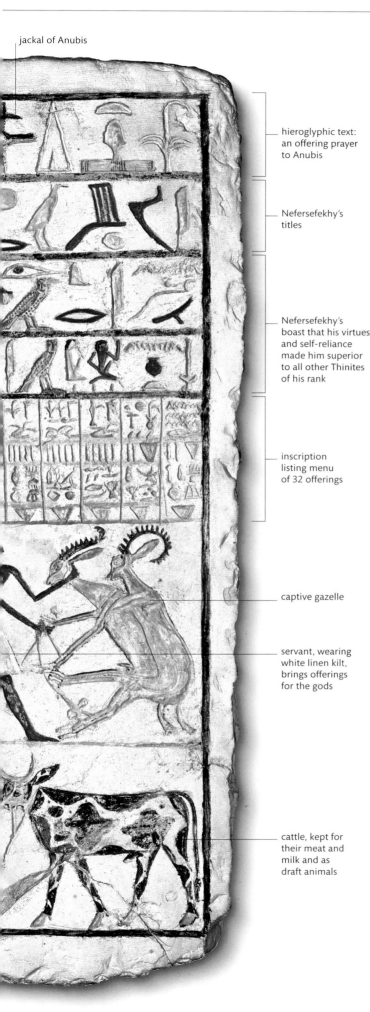

jackal of Anubis

hieroglyphic text: an offering prayer to Anubis

Nefersefekhy's titles

Nefersefekhy's boast that his virtues and self-reliance made him superior to all other Thinites of his rank

inscription listing menu of 32 offerings

captive gazelle

servant, wearing white linen kilt, brings offerings for the gods

cattle, kept for their meat and milk and as draft animals

■ PREPARING FOR JUDGMENT

FUNERARY STELA

The Egyptians considered that death was just an interruption in a life that continued from birth to eternity. In order to enjoy the afterlife, however, it was necessary that the body should be preserved and sustained. It was therefore mummified: the internal organs were removed and stored in canopic jars, and the flesh was dehydrated by packing natron (soda salts) within and around the body. When the process was complete, the body was repacked with fresh natron and resin-soaked bandages, to restore its natural shape. Layers of linen bandages were wrapped around the body, and amulets set among them to protect the deceased from spiritual harm.

OPENING THE MOUTH

The mummy was placed in its coffin, and an elaborate ritual, called the "Opening of the Mouth," was enacted by the deceased's heir. This restored the senses to the deceased, enabling him or her again to see, hear, speak, eat, and behave as in life. The mummy was now placed in the tomb, where funerary offerings of food, furniture, clothing, jewelry, and other objects, as well as shabtis (see p.34) and reliefs or paintings, provided it with all the necessities of continued existence. A memorial stela to the deceased, like the one shown here, was sometimes erected outside the tomb.

WEIGHING THE HEART

In the netherworld, the deceased was held to account by Osiris and the 42 judges of Maat (truth and justice). His or her heart (seat of the human intellect) was weighed on the divine scales against the feather of Maat.

The Book of the Dead, included in the mummy wrappings, prepared the deceased for this judgment and gave advice on how to act. Benevolent Anubis, standing by, might adjust the scales in the deceased's favor. If not, the crocodile-headed demon Ammut sat ready to eat the heart and destroy the dead person's eternal life. For the majority who passed the test, eternity beckoned. But it could only be enjoyed if the Ba (see p.36) was reunited every night with the mummified body, in order to sustain the Akh, the union in the afterlife of the Ba and Ka (life-force spirit, another of the elements making up a person).

" It is better to be **praised for neighborly love** than to have riches in your storeroom."

*Instruction of Amenemope, c.*1300–1075 BCE

Nefersefekhy's memorial
As well as decorating the inside of their tombs, wealthy Egyptians often erected memorial stelae outside. These bore their name and titles and a funerary prayer, along with offering scenes involving the deceased and often their family. This stela belonged to Nefersefekhy, an official who also served as a priest, in the town of Thinis near Abydos, around 2175 BCE.

EUROPE'S BRONZE AGE WARRIORS

Metalworking began with soft metals, such as gold or copper, used to make prestige objects. Later, people discovered that alloying copper with tin produced bronze, a metal strong enough for tools and weapons. As bronze-working spread across Europe, the need for tin (a rare metal) promoted international trade.

Status symbol
Ordinary axes were made in large numbers as bronze became more common, but prestige decorated versions were also produced.

Monumental achievement ▽
Built of massive sandstone blocks and smaller Welsh bluestones, Stonehenge is the most impressive of a series of interconnected monuments on England's Salisbury Plain. It achieved its final form by 1900 BCE.

By the Early Bronze Age (from the late 3rd millennium BCE), weapons in burials reflect a society in which status depended on prowess in combat. Horse-drawn chariots with spoked wheels, introduced from the steppes on Europe's eastern fringes after 2000 BCE, were elite fighting vehicles. Increasing demand for metals, and for other prestige and practical materials, such as amber and salt, stimulated international trade, changing the direction of existing routes and promoting the rise of a continent-wide trading system.

Societies that were rich in metal ores benefited especially from the shift in trading patterns. Ships now plied long-distance trade routes around the Atlantic seaboard of Europe and along rivers. Warmer climatic conditions allowed farming to spread into previously uncultivable areas. Arable farming intensified, and livestock were particularly important.

THE LATE BRONZE AGE

By around 1300 BCE bronze was used for everyday tools. Cremation burials, often in vast urnfields and usually with few grave goods, were now the norm over most of Europe. The onset of colder, wetter conditions around 1100 BCE brought harsher times, increasing conflict between neighbors and offerings to the gods.

Fortified settlements now became common, providing a place of refuge for rural farmers and a high-status residence for local chiefs and their entourage. These settlements developed particularly at key places along trade routes, where chiefs could enhance their power and wealth by controlling the passage of goods.

TECHNOLOGY

As craftsmen came to appreciate the potential of metals, they developed new technologies, producing elaborate jewelry, weapons, and figures. By 1300 BCE they were using multiple-piece molds and lost-wax casting, and creating large sheet-bronze objects. Other crafts also flourished, including textile production, now using wool as well as plant fibers.

one-piece mold for two axes

Mold and axes
The first, simplest bronzes were cast in one-piece molds, consisting of a shape cut into stone: this produced objects with a flat, horizontal upper surface.

one identical half of two-piece mold

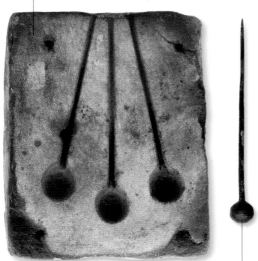

Pin mold
Two-piece molds allowed the production of more complex three-dimensional objects. The two halves were bound together and molten metal poured in at the top.

pin with spherical head, made in this mold

BATTLE AND CONFLICT

Bronze Age burials and art reflect a warrior society, engaged in cattle rustling and raids rather than mass pitched battles. Swords made their first appearance and rapidly became a vehicle for fashion and display. Late Bronze Age elite warrior equipment comprised a slashing sword and spear, a helmet, shield, greaves (shin armor), and cuirass (breastplate).

Swiss knife
Knives would have served many purposes: in daily life for tasks such as butchery, but also as weapons, particularly for casual defense or attack.

hole for securing wooden or bone handle

flame-shaped spearhead

loop for securing spear to shaft

socket

Spearheads
Spears appeared after the Early Bronze Age, and most seem designed for throwing rather than thrusting. Early forms have a tang to attach the head to the shaft; later ones are socketed.

Urnfield helmet
In the Late Bronze Age crested helmets became popular in Western Europe and especially Italy, while Eastern Europeans preferred a dome-shaped bell helmet.

crest covering join

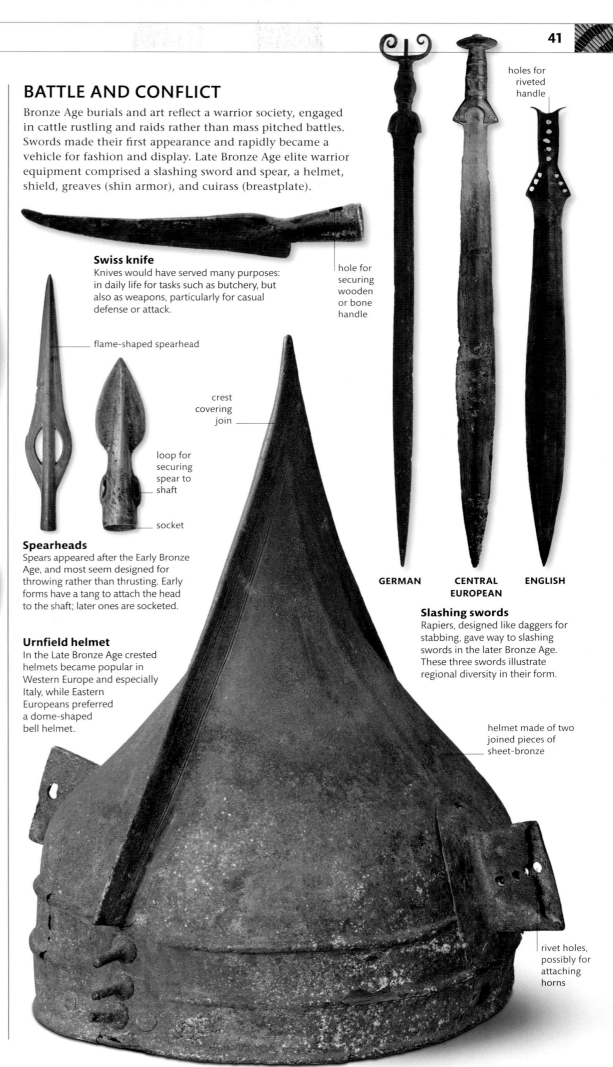

holes for riveted handle

GERMAN   CENTRAL EUROPEAN   ENGLISH

Slashing swords
Rapiers, designed like daggers for stabbing, gave way to slashing swords in the later Bronze Age. These three swords illustrate regional diversity in their form.

helmet made of two joined pieces of sheet-bronze

rivet holes, possibly for attaching horns

CLOTHING AND ADORNMENT

Bronze Age women enjoyed a growing range of designs in jewelry, such as brooches, pins, earrings, and bracelets. In Scandinavia, coffins made from oak trees preserve a rare glimpse of woolen clothing. Women were buried in long-sleeved blouses and skirts, the men in shirts and kilts. Both sexes had hats and cloaks.

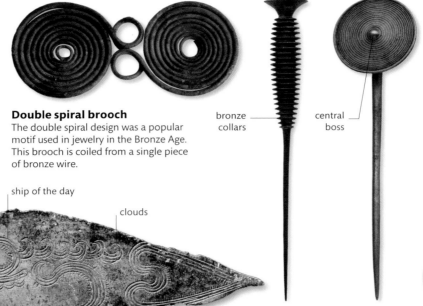

Double spiral brooch
The double spiral design was a popular motif used in jewelry in the Bronze Age. This brooch is coiled from a single piece of bronze wire.

bronze collars

central boss

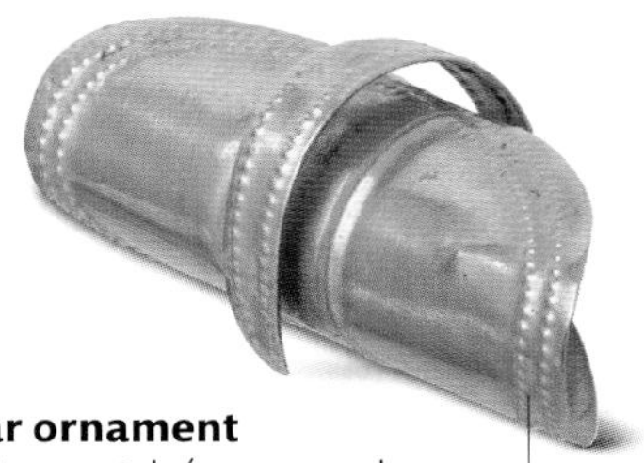

Ear ornament
When metals (copper and gold) were first used in Britain, experimentation produced distinctive ornaments, including basket-shaped earrings.

rolled-up sheet-gold

ship of the day

clouds

fish towing the Sun between ships

ship of the night

Scandinavian razor
Personal equipment such as razors reflects male concern with their appearance in the Bronze Age. Razors included both lunate and triangular forms, as shown here.

COLLARED PIN

FLOWER-HEADED PIN

Elaborate pins
Bronze jewelry provided a vehicle for metalworkers to display their versatility. Pin designs were particularly open to flights of fancy.

Irish tress ring
Gold hair ornaments made in Ireland were widely traded during the Late Bronze Age. Gold was mined in the Wicklow Mountains from around 2200 BCE.

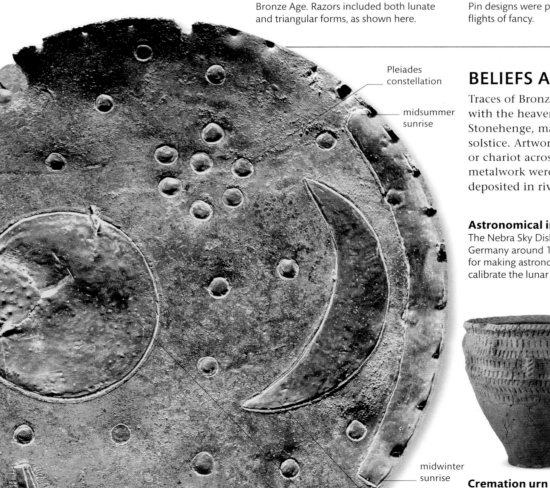

Pleiades constellation

midsummer sunrise

midwinter sunrise

waxing Moon

Sun or full Moon

Sun boat

BELIEFS AND RITUALS

Traces of Bronze Age religion show a preoccupation with the heavens. Some monuments, including Stonehenge, mark moments such as the summer solstice. Artworks depict the Sun carried by a boat or chariot across the sky. Many ritual offerings of metalwork were buried in significant places or deposited in rivers, lakes, or bogs.

Astronomical instrument
The Nebra Sky Disk was used in central Germany around 1600 BCE as an instrument for making astronomical observations, to calibrate the lunar and solar calendars.

small container for food offering

Cremation urn
Early Bronze Age British burials were often accompanied by a so-called "Food Vessel," containing a special drink. Later, Food Vessels were used as cremation urns.

Kernos
Libation tables, stone disks with a number of hollows to take offerings, were used in Early Bronze Age Aegean rituals. This rare ceramic vessel, called a kernos, served the same purpose.

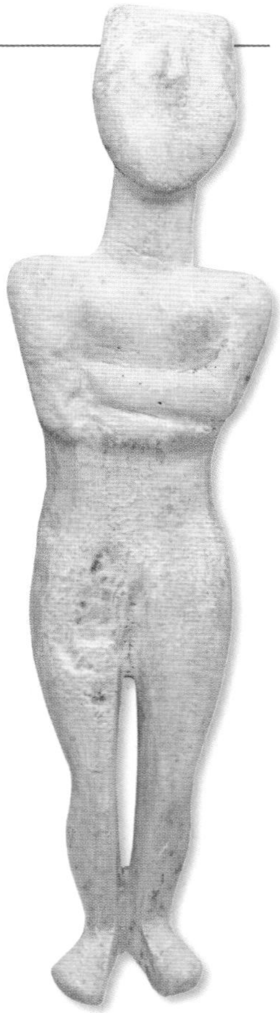

Marble figurine
3rd-millennium BCE figurines from the Cyclades, Greece, probably represented both gods and individual humans. Some were deposited in graves, others may have been placed in shrines.

THE MIGHTY HITTITES

Around 1650 BCE, central Anatolia's city-states were united by conquest into a kingdom with its capital at Hattusa. Vigorous rulers of this Hittite Old Kingdom campaigned into Syria and even sacked Babylon in 1595 BCE. However, the series of succession disputes that followed reduced their dominions.

Guarded gateway ▷
The massive defenses of city gateways were enhanced by carved figures of deities and spiritually powerful creatures, giving divine protection. This sphinx guarded Alacahöyük, a city north of Hattusa (present-day Bogazkale, Turkey).

From the 14th century BCE on, strong Hittite kings regained previously lost territories, expanded into western Anatolia (part of modern Turkey) and destroyed the Mitanni Empire in Syria, thus bringing them into direct territorial competition with the Egyptians. After the inconclusive Battle of Qadesh around 1274 BCE, Egypt accepted Hittite control over Syria, which the Hittites governed through viceroys. Widespread human and natural troubles in the eastern Mediterranean around 1200 BCE destroyed the Hittite Empire, but a number of small Neo-Hittite kingdoms sprang up in southern Anatolia and Syria, prospering until the Assyrians conquered them by 700 BCE.

Barbarian raiders ever present to their north and a tradition of armed conflict made the Hittites invest heavily in defense. Massive and complex city fortifications included towers, huge stone gateways with difficult approaches, and long tunnels under the walls to secret exits. Often a citadel and inner defensive walls protected the palace and other key buildings.

ART AND CULTURE

Hittite art included both miniature designs on seals and monumental sculptured reliefs, mainly of deities and kings. The designs incorporated inscriptions: the Hittites used both cuneiform and a hieroglyphic script; the Neo-Hittites used just hieroglyphs. Huge surviving archives of Hittite texts include diplomatic and administrative correspondence, descriptions of rituals, annals, literature, and mythology.

beaked spout

tall pedestal

hieroglyphic script

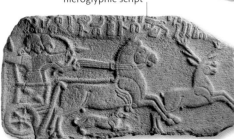

Hunting chariot
Neo-Hittite sculptured reliefs included narrative scenes, such as this deer hunt from Arslantepe (present-day Malatya). Chariots were also used effectively by the Hittites in warfare, as mobile fighting platforms.

Beaked pitcher
In Hittite times, the traditional Anatolian pitcher took on a slim form. Pottery was made on a wheel and by hand and standardized. Forms included bowls, flasks, wide-rimmed plates, and miniature vessels.

head made separately from body

ring joining head and body

battle ax, wielded to smite foe

lightning

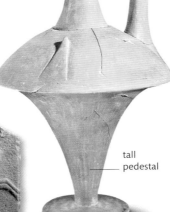

Storm god
The principal deity was the storm god, Teshub. He leads a procession of gods carved at Hattusa's shrine, Yazilikaya. This Neo-Hittite relief of Teshub is from Sam'al (present-day Zinjirli).

BELIEFS AND RITUALS

Religion permeated Hittite life. Every natural feature was imbued with a divine spirit. Individual cities had local variants of major deities, and cosmopolitan Hittite society embraced deities from every community. Temples were prominent in towns and cities, and reliefs of deities were carved at key places in the landscape.

male god holding falcon and staff

falcon held by goddess

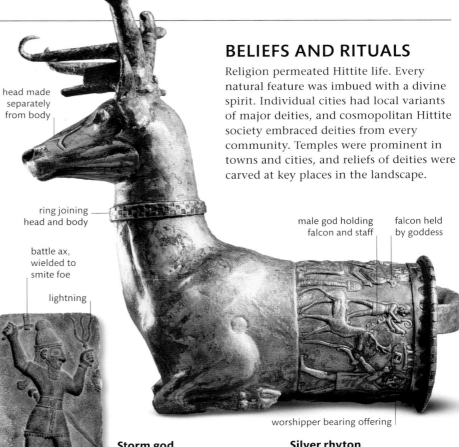

worshipper bearing offering

Silver rhyton
Probably made as an offering to the stag god, this rhyton (drinking vessel) depicts two deities, a procession of three worshippers, and (on the reverse) sacred trees and a sacrificed stag.

PALACE SOCIETIES OF THE AEGEAN

Discoveries at Mycenae in the 1870s and at Knossos in the 1900s showed that the heroic world described by Homer in the *Iliad* and *Odyssey* was not mere legend but a record of Greece's first civilizations, the Mycenaeans and Minoans: adventurous sea traders, skilled craftsmen, and painters of exquisite frescoes.

Cultural influence
Many Mycenaean seals, like this carnelian example, bore animal designs, a style inspired by Minoan art. They were often worn on the wrist or neck as talismans.

The 3rd millennium BCE saw changes that revolutionized life in the Aegean, including vine and olive cultivation and wooly sheep. Wine and olive oil could be stored as insurance against agriculturally poor years and accumulated as wealth by those with growing power; and wine played an important role in feasting. In the 2nd millennium BCE, sailing ships spurred participation in international trade. Exports included colorful woolen textiles, while metal ores were a major import, as bronze became increasingly part of life.

Palace ritual ▽
Bull-leaping, often shown in Minoan art, probably actually took place, as a ritual. Bull iconography also permeates Minoan religion, and bulls may have been linked, as in later times, to the god held responsible for Crete's frequent earthquakes.

Around 2000 BCE, Minoan palaces appeared across the island of Crete. With large central courtyards and magazines of huge pottery storage jars, they originally hosted religious and public events, including processions and feasts. After an earthquake around 1750 BCE, the palaces were quickly rebuilt, but political changes saw the rise of increasingly powerful new elites. Widespread destruction of unknown origin around 1500 BCE left Knossos as the only functioning palace. A change in the language of official records reveals that it was now Mycenaeans from the southern Greek mainland who began to control Crete.

The Mycenaeans were already familiar with Minoan culture and craftsmanship, but theirs was a very different society, in which warfare between rival palace-states played a major role. Their palaces were built on citadels, surrounded by defensive walls of massive stone blocks. Artisans lived within or near the citadel, their products including bronze swords and boar's tusk helmets. Palace society collapsed around 1200 BCE.

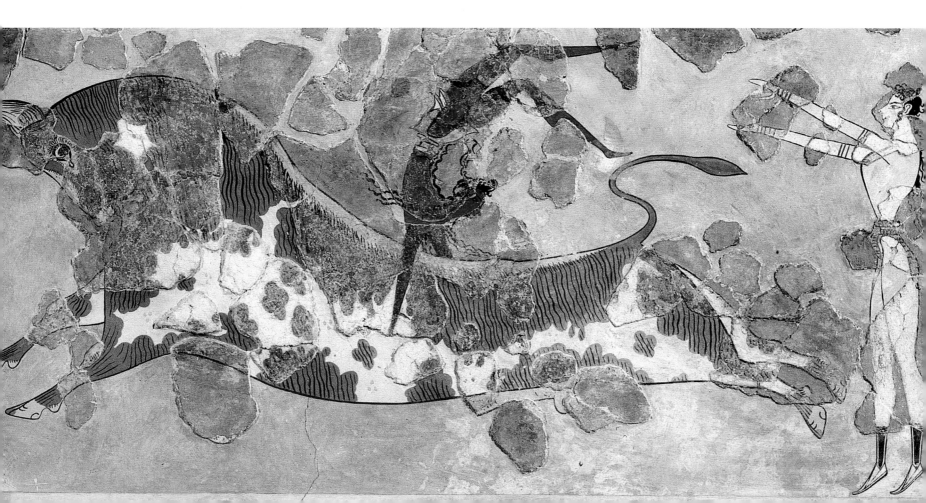

ART AND CULTURE

The Minoans and the Mycenaeans were skilled artisans, manufacturing perfumed oils, luxury pottery, fine miniature bronze, faience (a glazed ceramic), and ivory sculptures, and jewelry, particularly of gold. Like the Minoans, the Mycenaeans participated in the flourishing eastern Mediterranean trade networks, but they also sailed as far west as Sardinia and Italy to obtain metal ores.

spill-free spout

stirrup-shaped handle

stopper missing from spout

Perfume jar
Mycenaean stirrup jars were popular exports to western Asia. They were used to transport perfumed oils, a major Mycenaean product, but were also valued as attractive pottery.

Mycenaean octopus pot
Fine Minoan pottery was often beautifully decorated with a realistic octopus, its tentacles wrapping around the vessel. Later Mycenaean potters produced lifeless imitations.

POLITICS AND POWER

Minoan and Mycenaean palaces were the administrative centers of a stratified society, exercising political and economic control over associated towns and extensive territories. Minoan palaces also fulfilled a major religious role. The hinterland of Mycenaean citadels often encompassed agricultural land, hills for pasture, and access to the sea for communications and trade.

Death mask
Early Mycenaean warrior kings were buried with considerable finery in shaft graves at Mycenae, five with gold masks, dated to around 1600–1500 BCE.

beaten gold chin

embossed gold beard and mustache

BELIEFS AND RITUALS

Minoan palaces were linked with peak sanctuaries, holy places on adjacent mountains where offerings were made. The Mycenaeans had shrines within their citadels. Both cultures had gods and goddesses. The Minoan deities were associated with animals and the countryside, while Mycenaean texts include some deities later worshipped in Classical Greece.

Ritual vessel
Perforated vessels were used as sprinklers in Minoan rituals. Some were made of pottery; others of fine stone or metal. Shapes included vases and animal heads.

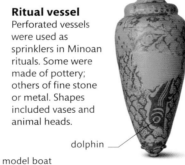

dolphin

HOME LIFE

Fascinating insights into daily life are provided by beautiful frescoes. These show musicians playing lyres and boys boxing, Minoan fishermen carrying their catch and ladies gathering crocuses, and Mycenaeans riding in chariots, hunting boar, or sitting on folding stools drinking from elegant cups. Faience plaques from Knossos depict town houses several stories high that mirror surviving houses.

Minoan cooking pot
Valuable bronze tripod cauldrons used in feasting appear in frescoes and are listed in texts. This smaller pottery version was used by ordinary people for cooking and heating food.

groove in rim for wick

simple spout

blood draining through bucket

harpist

real or model sacrificial animals

model boat offering

the deceased

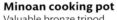

Haghia Triadha sarcophagus
This painted sarcophagus comes from a Cretan chamber tomb and shows the deceased receiving offerings. On the left is a shrine with two double axes, where a woman pours an offering of blood from a sacrificed bull (depicted on the reverse).

Steatite pedestalled lamp
Minoan and Mycenaean craftsmen produced stone seals and jewelry, as well as larger objects including elite domestic vessels, such as this Minoan lamp.

Spouted cup
The Minoans used a range of plain domestic pottery, including cups, jugs, bowls, and storage jars. By later Minoan times, even domestic wares were often of high quality.

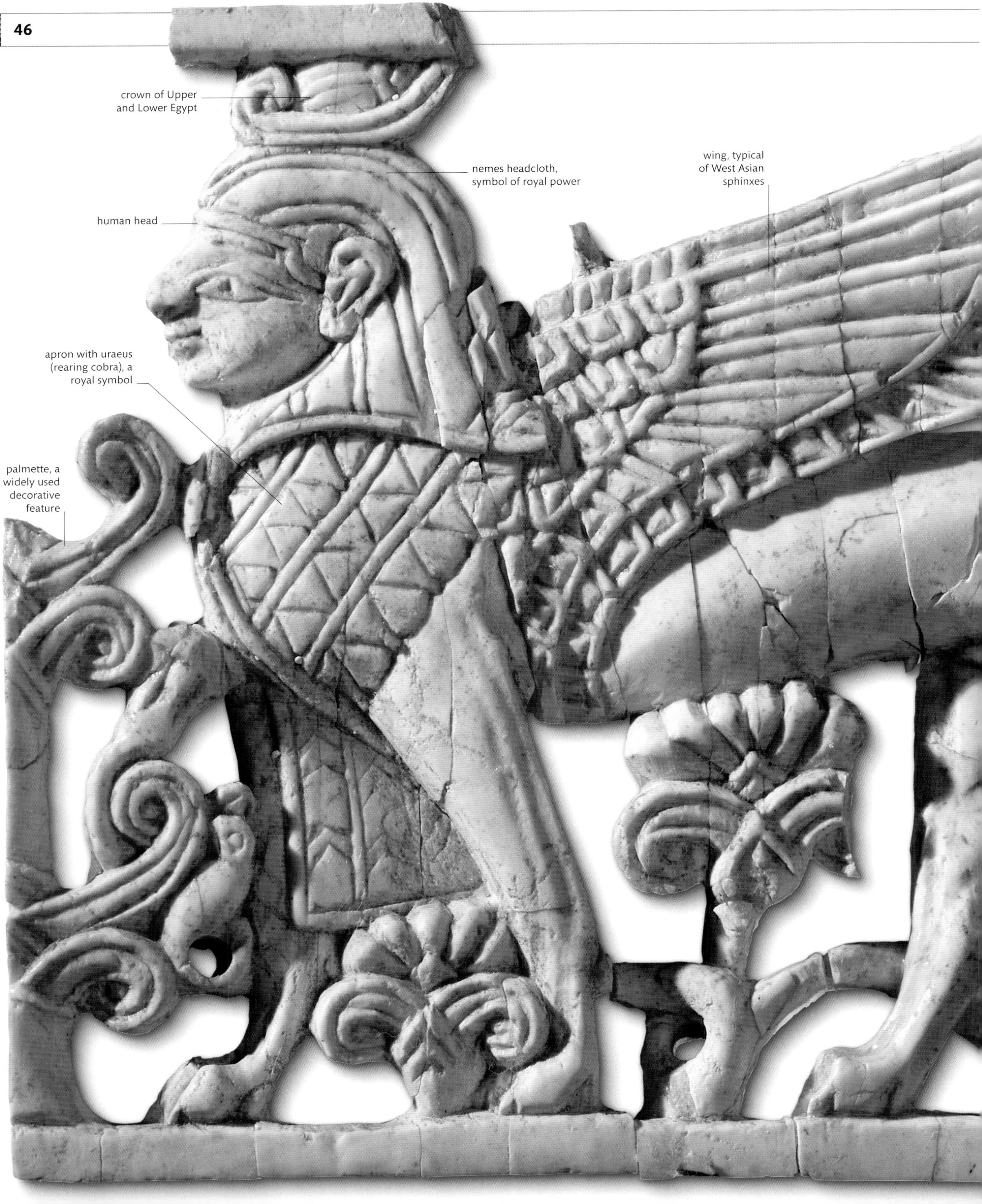

crown of Upper
and Lower Egypt

nemes headcloth,
symbol of royal power

wing, typical
of West Asian
sphinxes

human head

apron with uraeus
(rearing cobra), a
royal symbol

palmette, a
widely used
decorative
feature

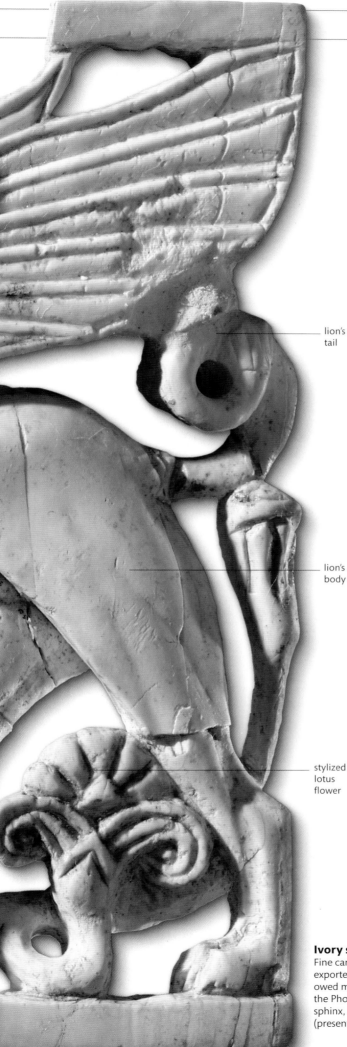

lion's tail

lion's body

stylized lotus flower

Ivory sphinx
Fine carved ivory panels for decorating wooden furniture were exported widely or made on location for foreign rulers. These owed much in style and subject matter to Egypt, with which the Phoenicians had enjoyed long, close relations. This winged sphinx, recovered from the Assyrian royal palace at Kalhu (present-day Nimrud, Iraq), is a typical example.

THE INTREPID PHOENICIANS

Canaan (the region between Egypt and Anatolia) was home to coastal city-states whose prosperity depended on trade and industry. Their inhabitants were known to the Classical Greeks as Phoenicians, after their fabulously expensive purple (*phoinix*) dye.

Exporting timber from their region's mountains to timber-poor neighbors enabled the city-states of Phoenicia (roughly, modern Lebanon) to obtain the grain, oil, and wool that their narrow coastal territories could not produce in sufficient quantity. Byblos, in the center, traded with Egypt by 1900 BCE. Others, especially Arwad in the north and Tyre and Sidon in the south, joined this trade later in the same millennium.

A ship wrecked off Anatolia around 1300 BCE gives a vivid picture of trade at this time. It was carrying copper ingots and fine pottery from Cyprus; tin, probably from Afghanistan; African ivory and ostrich eggs; and terebinth resin (for making perfume), glass ingots, and gold jewelry from Canaan. It had probably plied a circular route from Canaan via Cyprus and the Aegean to Egypt and home to Canaan.

PHOENICIAN FORTUNES

The Phoenician city-states experienced a checkered history—the region was fought over and often controlled by the surrounding major powers, including the Egyptians, Hittites, Assyrians, and Persians. The Phoenicians' value as traders and skilled artisans, however, ensured that they retained a large degree of independence under foreign domination. The city-states were often bitter rivals, particularly Tyre and Sidon. To facilitate trade, obtain raw materials, particularly metals, and gain other economic benefits, some city-states established overseas colonies. Foremost was Tyre, which had colonies in the eastern Mediterranean, such as Kition on Cyprus, but also Carthage in Tunisia and Gadir (Cadiz) in Atlantic Spain. As seafarers, the Phoenicians were in demand by inland states such as Assyria and Persia to provide ships, ship-building and navigational know-how, and sailors and navies. King Solomon engaged Phoenicians from Tyre for his expedition to Ophir (probably the Horn of Africa).

PHOENICIAN INGENUITY

The Phoenicians were skilled artisans. Among their finest creations were purple textiles, bronze bowls, and gold jewelry. In faience (a glazed ceramic) they produced both exquisite cosmetic jars, like the hedgehog shown below, and mass-market trinkets. Masters of glass manufacture, they developed new technologies, for example making transparent glass that imitated expensive rock crystal (quartz).

copper oxide glaze

HEDGEHOG KOHL POT

CHINA'S FIRST CELESTIAL EMPIRE

Northern China's Shang dynasty is famously associated with oracle bone divination, bronze and jade craftsmanship, warfare and human sacrifice, and walled settlements. However, many of these cultural features began with their predecessors, the Xia culture, traditionally the first kings of northern China, or their 3rd-millennium BCE ancestors, the Longshan culture.

Ask the ancestors
The earliest Chinese script, ancestral to that of today, appears on Shang oracle bones. Used to divine the future, they were inscribed with questions to the ancestors.

Towers in the mist ▷
China's Great Wall reached its present form under the Ming dynasty (14th–16th centuries CE), but its early beginnings were in the Zhou period, when rival states constructed stretches of rammed-earth ramparts to defend their borders.

Around 1500 BCE, the Shang succeeded the Xia culture. Work at Zhengzhou has revealed a city that was probably the first Shang capital. Its center, containing buildings that may have been palaces and elite burials, was surrounded by a massive wall of rammed earth. Outside lay a distillery, pottery, bone, and bronze workshops, and the artisans' houses.

Recent excavations have revealed the remains of another Shang city at modern Huanbei, which was probably a later capital, Xi'ang. After 50 years of occupation, however, its rulers appear to have deliberately destroyed it. The city was stripped of all its goods before being burned to the ground.

Around 1300 BCE, the final Shang capital, Anyang, was built just across the Huan River at Yinxu. Excavations here have uncovered a palace and temple complex, with pits containing chariot burials, complete with horses and charioteers. Suburbs contained the homes of both the elite and ordinary people; industrial workshops, where artisans created prestige goods for the royal family and their entourage; and several cemeteries.

In one was the richly furnished grave of Fu Hao, consort of King Wu Ding, who died around 1200 BCE. Her burial chamber lay at the bottom of a huge pit, above which were many regal grave goods, including ivory vessels inlaid with turquoise, jade items, and the sacrificed remains of 16 people and six dogs.

Texts written on oracle bones reveal the numerous concerns of the Shang dynasty. These included many aspects of warfare, harvests, rainfall, hunting, settlement construction, and general good fortune. The Shang had conflicts with a number of their neighbors, such as the people inhabiting the area near the Yangtze (Changjiang) River to the south.

ZHOU DYNASTY

Another Shang enemy were the Zhou in the west, whose ruler overthrew the Shang king around 1027 BCE and established a new kingdom. Western Zhou kings were strong rulers, backed by a large, well-organized army. They pursued a policy of expansion, settling conquered areas under the rule of members of the royal clan.

Around 771 BCE, however, the Zhou kings were forced by invaders from the north to flee from their capital Zongzhou (near modern Xi'an) eastward to Luoyang, initiating the Eastern Zhou period. Centralized Zhou authority had declined and regional power had grown. The kingdom began slowly to disintegrate, with the rulers of the small states often fighting either the Zhou king or each other.

The situation declined throughout this "Spring and Autumn period," turning into all-out war for supremacy between the states after 481 BCE (see p.101). By this time Zhou had shrunk to a small state itself.

The Zhou period saw the extension of many of the technological and social developments of the Shang period. These included bronze casting and other crafts, and trade and city life. It also included warfare, with more organized and larger armies, new weapons, and the growth of defensive architecture, including the rammed-earth border defenses that were eventually developed into the Great Wall.

> **"**It is **through fear** that **goodwill and harmony** reign between **superiors and inferiors."**
>
> Zi Han, Song ruler in the Spring and Autumn period (771–476 BCE)

TRADE

In Shang times, trade brought in cowrie shells (used as currency) and turtle shells, jade, tin, and copper, and Chinese silk was exchanged with steppe nomads. The invention of cast-bronze coinage, in various denominations, in Middle Zhou times reflects the beginning of a market economy.

coin shaped like a spade, an essential tool

inscription in early Chinese script

Spade money
Chinese coinage was invented in the 7th century BCE. In the north and central states of the Zhou region, this took the form of miniature spades.

Knife money
Each state made its own form of coinage in the Middle Zhou period. Knife-shaped coins were made by states in the east (Shandong peninsula).

BATTLE AND CONFLICT

Warfare was regularly mentioned on oracle bones, and enemy prisoners were often sacrificed in rituals—1,200 were found in 12 Shang royal graves. Horse-drawn chariots, introduced from the steppes, were originally used for ceremonial purposes. Over time, they were increasingly used as elite fighting platforms, but during the Eastern Zhou period, infantry became more important.

cutting edge of bronze ax

Axes
Blades mounted on long shafts were the usual weapon of foot soldiers. Through time, these evolved from simple axes to halberds (see p.51).

Decorated dagger
This dagger would have belonged to a member of the elite. Swords were introduced in the Zhou period, but did not become widely used until later.

turquoise inlay

ritual ax blade made from valuable white jade

dagger blade

tang for inserting into wooden haft

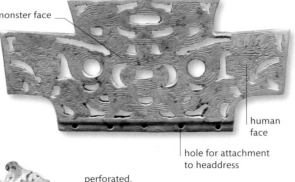

Ge dagger-ax
The dagger-ax was the characteristic weapon of the Zhou warrior. It was a developed form of the simpler halberd, mounted and wielded in the same way.

holes for binding to haft

cast bronze blade

decorative pommel

CLOTHING AND ADORNMENT

Later Neolithic, Shang, and Zhou people made textiles from hemp and ramie (a type of nettle). The elite also had garments of silk and high-quality jade jewelry. Fu Hao, consort of a Shang king, had many jade ornaments among her grave furnishings, some of which were antiques from the Neolithic Longshan and Shijiahe cultures.

monster face

polished stone

Stone earrings
These slit earrings were made by the Majiabang culture of the Yangtze river estuary in the 4th millennium BCE. Such earrings were still popular in the Zhou period.

human face

Neolithic head ornament
In the Liangzhu culture of southern China, specialized craftsmen created many jade objects. Headdress plaques were decorated with a human-and-monster face.

hole for attachment to headdress

perforated, creamy white jade head

gray-green jade pin

inlaid turquoise bead

Longshan hair pin
This beautiful jade pin comes from a rich burial, perhaps of a local ruler, around 2000 BCE. It may have been worn in the hair or with a scarf.

HOME LIFE

Shang and Zhou kings were surrounded by nobles, officials, and priests—the elite who enjoyed luxuries such as jade, bronze, and lacquerware. However, most people lived in villages, farming millet, rice, fruit, and vegetables, and raising pigs and chickens. They used everyday items such as pottery.

red and dark-brown painted decoration

Painted pot
Fine painted pottery, such as this 3rd-millennium BCE Neolithic Majiayao culture jar, may have been made to place in burials rather than for everyday use.

characteristic patterns

loop handle

Majiayao jar
Neolithic people used pots to store water and food. A rope secured round the middle of a large, heavy storage jar made it easier to grip the vessel when lifting.

distinctive decoration

Xindian pot
Groups in different regions had their own characteristic styles of pottery decoration. This vessel was made by the Xindian culture, neighbors of the Shang to their northwest.

cord-impressed decoration

turned out rim

hollow legs allow heat to be transmitted to cooking liquid

Zhou tripod pot
The tripod vessel, used to heat liquids, was a standard pottery form from Neolithic times. A perforated bowl set in the top could be used to steam rice.

BELIEFS AND RITUALS

The Shang recognized a supreme deity, Di, and during the Zhou dynasty, Tian took on this role. However, most rituals were concerned with honoring the ancestral spirits, who were consulted by oracle bone divination (see p.48). Ritual objects, many of which were made of jade, were placed in elite burials.

Jade cong
Tubular jade objects called cong were used in Neolithic elite burials and ritual contexts after 3000 BCE. Their shape echoes later cosmology, and is meant to symbolize heaven and earth.

elaborately decorated hilt

Decorated Shang halberd
Shang royalty were buried with many fine grave goods including weaponry such as this bronze halberd, which would have been mounted at right angles to a long wooden haft.

strong broad blade

hafted portion

suspension loop

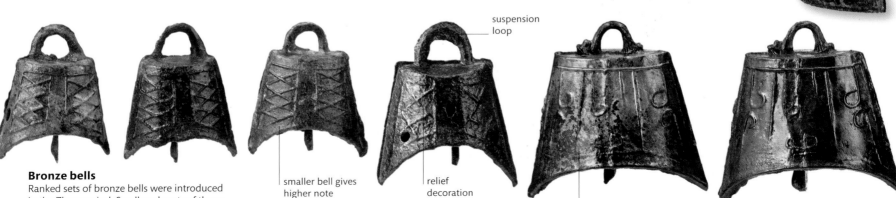

Bronze bells
Ranked sets of bronze bells were introduced in the Zhou period. Small-scale sets of these bells, such as the ones shown here, were often placed in elite graves.

smaller bell gives higher note

relief decoration

larger bell gives lower note

Shang guang

The guang was used for storing and serving wine. Once the lid was removed, the lower portion became a spouted pitcher from which to pour the wine. This clever and attractive design combines two significant animals, the tiger and the owl, placed back to back. Although the guang continued into Western Zhou times, the tiger-owl form was a short-lived Shang design.

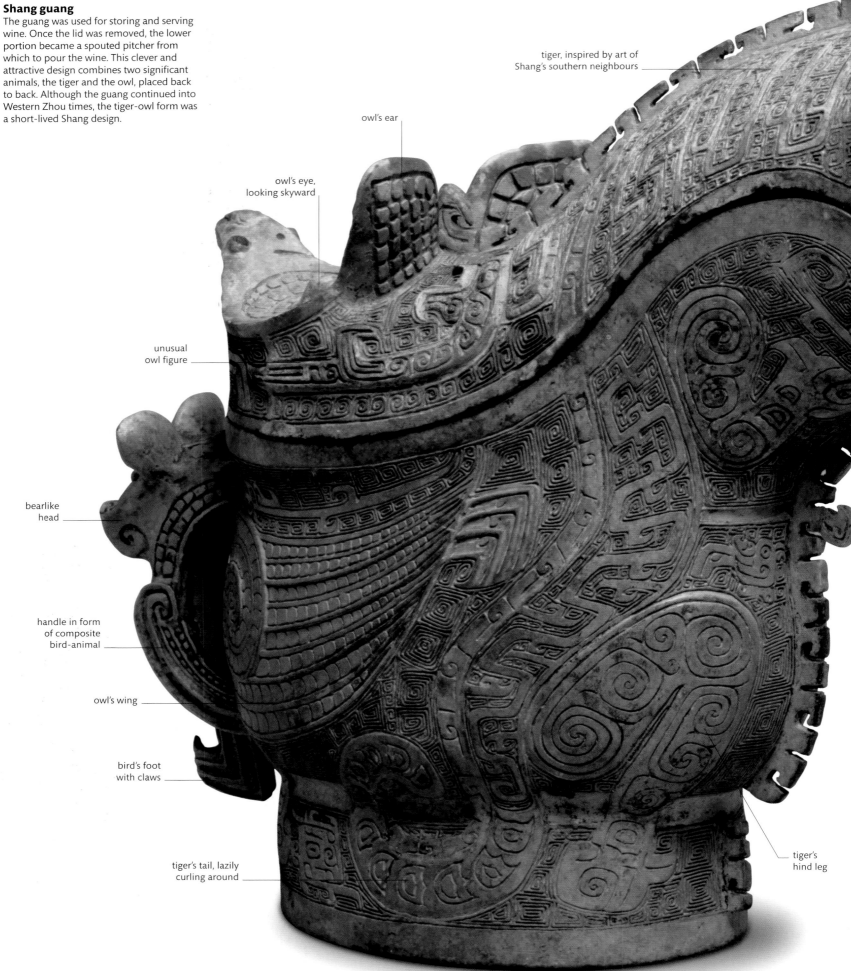

tiger, inspired by art of Shang's southern neighbours

owl's ear

owl's eye, looking skyward

unusual owl figure

bearlike head

handle in form of composite bird-animal

owl's wing

bird's foot with claws

tiger's tail, lazily curling around

tiger's hind leg

tiger's ear

tiger's eye

guang lid

tiger's open teeth through which wine could breathe while lid kept it from cooling down

RITUAL VESSEL

Like many features of Shang culture, the use of special vessels for pouring and serving liquids began in earlier cultures. Vying for prestige with the splendor of their ritual feasts, Neolithic leaders would serve drinks in ritual vessels made of pottery. By Shang and Zhou times, such cult practices had become embedded in tradition, except the vessels were now made of bronze and the designs had become more elaborate.

FOOD AND DRINK

Sets of ritual vessels were used in ceremonial banquets at which food and drink were offered to honor and placate the ancestors, who could influence the fate of their descendants, for good or ill. The make up of Shang ritual vessel sets reflects the elaborate formality of the ceremony, each vessel having its own specific purpose. The Zhou abandoned some Shang vessel types but introduced many new ones.

Social status was now reflected in the composition of an individual's ritual vessel set. Many bronze ritual vessels bear a dedication. These generally name the donor and the ancestor to whom the vessel is dedicated, and often express a hope that the vessel, placed in the clan ritual hall, would be treasured by future generations of descendants.

SHANG TECHNOLOGY

The Shang developed advanced casting technology to produce these elaborate bronze ritual vessels. A plain ceramic model of the vessel was prepared and a ceramic mold created around it. This was then cut off in sections and the fine detail added by incising the decoration into the mold pieces. When cast, these designs would appear on the vessel in relief. The mold and core were kept separate by inserting small metal spacers, which melted into the molten metal of the vessel during casting. Designs often included projecting flanges to disguise the casting seams at connections between pieces of the mold.

Unlike lost-wax casting, in which the mold has to be broken to remove the cast bronze object, the Chinese piece-mold casting allowed repeated mold use. It facilitated mass production, undertaken in large-scale official workshops rather than by individual craftsmen.

TAOTIE

vertical casting seam disguised as a flange

knobbed handle on lid

buffalo head

animal handle

high rounded relief, typical of Zhou decoration

ring foot

Western Zhou gui
The gui was one of the most important types of vessel used in the rituals. It was designed to serve grain and sacrificial meat. Many are decorated with a taotie, a mythical monster.

Shang bronze gu
A small amount of wine was heated in a tripod jue before being served in the elegant gu. Both types of vessel went out of fashion after the Shang period.

Western Zhou lei
A lei is a lidded jar with a widening base. It was used, along with the gu and the jue, in making libations of wine during ancestor ceremonies.

THE AWE-INSPIRING GODS OF THE ANDES

The first great civilization of South America was the Chavín, a culture named after their shrine at Chavín de Huantar, built high in the Peruvian Andes around 900 BCE. The Chavín influenced many cultures in the Andean region, including the Paracas.

Grim warrior ▷
Carved slabs around a pre-Chavín shrine at Cerro Sechin in Peru show a procession of warriors and defeated, mutilated enemies. Rituals involving prisoner sacrifice featured prominently in some Andean cultures.

By 2600 BCE, Andean lowland communities were supported by rich marine resources and crops grown inland. Caral, in the Supe Valley in Peru, became a flourishing city, with elite residences, craft workshops, and shrines. After its decline around 1800 BCE, other lowland communities constructed vast temple complexes. After 900 BCE, these ceremonial centers were abandoned. The remains of small settlements, some of them fortified, suggest that conditions became harsher.

Chavín de Huantar in the highlands combined lowland architecture with iconography focused on Amazonian animals, perhaps a deliberate blending of regional religions. Controlling north–south and west–east trade routes, the shrine flourished as a pilgrimage center and oracle until 200 BCE. The adoption of Chavín iconography shows that the religion gained followers over most of Peru, including the Paracas culture to the south. Later, the Paracas developed new beliefs and practices.

ART AND CULTURE

Early Andean art is rich in symbolism and formally composed, making use of symmetry, faces and bodies that can be inverted, and other compositional techniques to weave together images of gods, knives, trophy heads, sacred creatures, and plants. Chavín and Paracas artists created textiles, goldwork, pottery, and engraved gourds. The Chavín also carved stone.

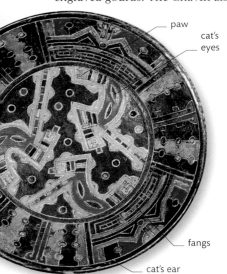

paw
cat's eyes
fangs
cat's ear

Paracas dish
The distinctive Paracas pottery was decorated with geometric and symbolic patterns sharply defined by incised borders, each section colored, after firing, with thick resin paint.

face of the Oculate Being, the Paracas god

arm with hand holding trophy-head

divided tongue, represented as two snakes

one of two birds flanking the god's legs

Paracas textile
Elaborate Paracas mummy bundles were wrapped in a mantle and contained many fine textiles made from cotton embroidered with alpaca wool.

BELIEFS AND RITUALS

Chavín de Huantar was the religion's major ceremonial center. Its two U-shaped temple mounds concealed a maze of dark galleries leading to the inner sanctum, which housed the image of the terrifying supreme deity, the Staff God, which had claws and fangs, a feline face, and snakes for hair. The sunken outside courtyards were decorated with symbolic carvings, including shamans transforming into jaguars, harpy eagles, and monkeys.

shallow mortar for grinding
symbolic jaguar form
flared nostrils
bilateral symmetry of design

Chavín jaguar stone mortar
Hallucinogenic snuff ground in this stone mortar was taken by a shaman to induce a trance in which he felt himself transforming into an animal, to communicate with the spirit world.

Shamanic transformation
Shaman heads with bulbous eyes and streaming noses depict the consequences of taking hallucinogenic snuff. Heads like this reveal the shaman's final transformation into a jaguar.

THE MYSTICAL LAND OF THE OLMEC

The Olmec are often considered the "Mother Culture" of Mesoamerican civilization, displaying many features that were typical of later societies. These included ball courts, pyramid mounds, shamanism, and ritual blood-letting.

Ceremonial center ▷
La Venta's many monuments included this huge mound, fronted by a plaza accommodating thousands of spectators. The site also contains other mounds, courtyards, colossal heads, and many ritual deposits.

The land and rivers of the Olmec's tropical lowland home in the south of the Gulf of Mexico produced abundant food. By 1200 BCE, a major ceremonial center had developed at San Lorenzo, dominating a large region. Its layout demonstrates its rulers' power to command a huge labor force: terraces bearing houses and workshops, a vast plaza, and arrangements of massive stone monuments carved from basalt quarried 50 miles (80 km) away. Around 900 BCE, San Lorenzo's dominance passed to La Venta. Much of the region was abandoned around 400 BCE, although Olmec-related culture continued further north.

Distinctive Olmec objects, art, and architecture are known from many regions of Mesoamerica. They were probably introduced by Olmec traders seeking materials such as obsidian for tools and ritually significant goods such as magnetite mirrors from Oaxaca, stingray spines for blood-letting, greenstone from Guerrero and Guatemala, and exotic feathers.

BELIEFS AND RITUALS

Olmec sculptures, stone relief carvings, and ritual deposits give many clues to their religion. The major deities—representing sky or air, earth and the underworld, water and corn (the staple crop)—had features of animals from the Olmec world, notably the caiman, jaguar, harpy eagle, and snake. Olmec rulers probably acted as mediators between the human and supernatural worlds.

loincloth

Jadeite figurines
In a ritual deposit at La Venta, jadeite figurines were arranged in a scene, with celts (axes) as pillars around them. Small human figures were traded in or locally made by many contemporary cultures, indicating the spread of Olmec religion.

Were-jaguar mask
Jadeite from Guatemala was highly valued by the Olmec and their contemporaries for making figurines and other objects to deposit in offerings, shrines, and burials.

cleft head
slanted, almond-shaped eyes
broad nose
enlarged upper lip
downturned mouth
helmet for ritual ball game
club or scepter
feet with toes

Were-jaguar celt
Probably the Olmec water god, the "were-jaguar" (perhaps the offspring of a jaguar and a human) was often depicted, shown as a dwarf or a floppy baby with a cleft head.

personal features of ruler

Colossal head
Massive basalt heads probably portray individual Olmec rulers wearing protective headgear for the Mesoamerican ball game, which had ritual, political, and ceremonial importance, both then and later.

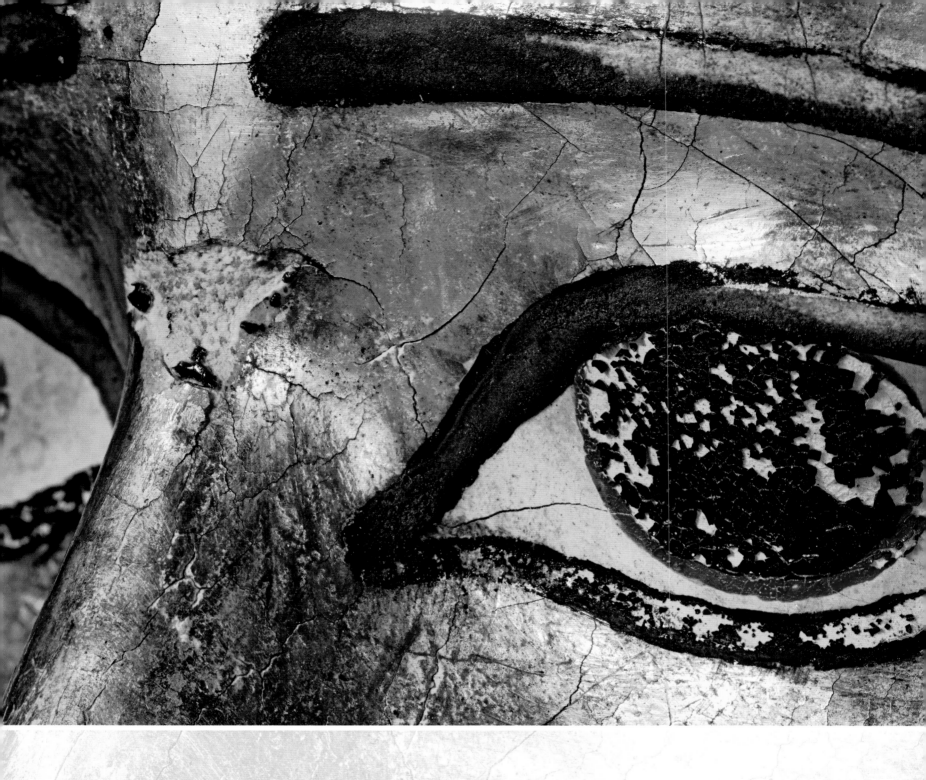

The millennium following 700 BCE is known as the Classical Age of Eurasian history. The Greek, Roman, Persian, Indian, and Chinese empires united large areas of Europe and Asia. These empires provided stable government and encouraged trade and the exchange of ideas. One result was the emergence of three world religions: Christianity, Buddhism, and Zoroastrianism. In South America and Mesoamaerica, sophisticated civilizations also developed, but these had few contacts with the wider world.

ANCIENT CIVILIZATIONS

700 BCE–600 CE

THE CITY-STATES OF ANCIENT GREECE

The civilization of ancient Greece, at its peak between the sixth and fourth centuries BCE, was one of the most influential the world has ever seen. The Greeks introduced the alphabet to Europe and changed politics, science, philosophy, theater, and the study of history, among many other achievements. The influence of Greek art and architecture, passed on by the Romans, is still visible all around us.

Armor of the warring states
Greek warriors wore many styles of helmet. The most popular among these was the Corinthian helmet, which covered most of the face.

Home of the divine ▷
The Greeks believed that at holy places, such as Delphi, the gods would give them advice through oracles. So before making any important decision, such as whether to go to war, a *polis* would send messengers to Delphi to ask the god Apollo's priestess for advice.

After the fall of the Bronze Age civilizations, there was a long "Dark Age." Not much is known about Greek history during this period, but we know more about the later Archaic ("old") Age, from 800 to 500 BCE. Overseas trade flourished and the Greeks founded many settlements around the Mediterranean. A new alphabet was introduced, and Homer composed his epic poems about the Trojan War.

THE CLASSICAL AGE

In the Classical Age, between the 6th and 4th centuries BCE, Greek civilization was at its height. Architects built stone temples with tall columns, which were decorated with magnificent sculptures, as well as theaters.

This was the age of many great thinkers, such as Herodotus, the first historian; Pythagoras, the founder of mathematics; and Hippocrates, who pioneered a new scientific approach to medicine. The philosophers Thales and Heraclitus questioned the basic substance of the universe, and

Socrates raised the all-important philosophical question, "What is the right way to live?"

THE GREAT WARS

The Greeks did not belong to a single state, living instead in hundreds of rival *poleis*, or city-states, which were often at war with each other. Each *polis*, which included the city and surrounding countryside, had its own calendar, laws, public assemblies, and coins. There was also an area, called an acropolis, where the chief temples of the *polis* were located. The most powerful *poleis* were Athens and Sparta.

Although divided and competitive, the Greeks felt they had a shared identity. They were united by their worship of the same gods and shared religious festivals, such as the Olympic Games. The Greeks looked down on foreigners, calling them barbarians—because to Greeks, foreign languages sounded like meaningless "bar-bar" noises.

In the 5th century BCE, the Persians made two attempts to conquer Greece, but the Spartans and Athenians,

leading an alliance of Greek *poleis*, defeated both invasions. Athens then led a league of seafaring *poleis* to free those Greeks who were under Persian control. Gradually, the Athenians turned the league into their own empire. The rise of Athenian power alarmed the Spartans, and in 431 BCE a war broke out between the two *poleis*. It was difficult for either side to win, for Sparta was stronger on land and Athens at sea. The war lasted a long 27 years, ending in a Spartan victory.

THE HELLENISTIC AGE

In the late 4th century BCE, the Greeks were finally united under the rule of King Alexander the Great of Macedon. He also conquered the Persian Empire, spreading the Greek way of life from Egypt to Afghanistan. His successors founded large kingdoms, such as the Ptolemaic Kingdom of Egypt. This period, until about 146 BCE, is known as the Hellenistic (Greek) Age. At the end of this time, the Romans conquered all the Greek kingdoms. But Greek remained the common language of the eastern Mediterranean.

> "**Like frogs** around a pond, we have **settled down** upon the **shores of this sea.**"
>
> Plato, *Phaedo, c.*360 BCE

BATTLE AND CONFLICT

The fiercely competitive Greeks saw constant warfare as a normal way of life. Fighting provided men with an opportunity to win glory and fame. Warriors mostly fought as hoplites—named after the large *hoplon*, or shield, they carried. Armed with thrusting spears and with their shields locked together, they would advance in a tight formation called a *phalanx*.

broken tip

Leaf-shaped blade
This is the iron blade of a hoplite's thrusting spear, which would have been about 7.5 ft (2.3 m) long. Such leaf-shaped blades are also depicted in vase paintings.

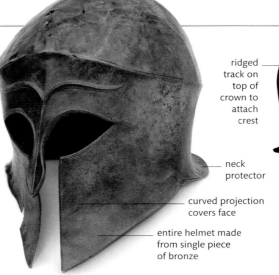

ridged track on top of crown to attach crest

neck protector

curved projection covers face

entire helmet made from single piece of bronze

Narrow blade
A hoplite would hold his spear above his head and thrust it repeatedly down at the enemy lines. The narrow blade shown here is less common than the leaf-shaped variety.

Corinthian helmet
The Corinthian was the most effective type of Greek helmet. It was named after Corinth but was worn by hoplites from many *poleis*. Some Corinthian helmets had horsehair crests.

Illyrian helmet
This open-faced helmet offered less protection than a Corinthian. It is called an Illyrian, after the Balkan area where some of these helmets were first found.

POWER AND POLITICS

The word "politics" comes from the Greek word *polis*, meaning city-state. While most ancient societies were governed by kings, Greek *poleis* were run by assemblies of male citizens. In most *poleis*, only the richest citizens wielded political power. The Athenians invented the world's first democracy (meaning "the rule of the people"), in which every citizen could vote on important decisions.

Aphrodite, goddess of Corinth, or Athena wearing Corinthian helmet

Pericles had a high forehead, which sculptors concealed beneath a helmet

Pegasus, a mythical winged horse

FRONT   **BACK**

Corinthian coin
One side of this Corinthian coin shows Pegasus, who was tamed by King Bellerophon using a bridle given to him by the goddess Athena.

Athena's helmet adorned with wreath of olive leaves and decorated scroll

owl and olive branch

FRONT   **BACK**

Athenian coin
The Athenians believed that their *polis* was named after, and belonged to the goddess Athena. She was shown on their coins, along with her sacred bird, the owl.

Marble bust of Pericles
Pericles, the most famous Athenian political leader, made Athens into an imperial power and persuaded his fellow citizens to build magnificent temples. Yet, he also led Athens into a disastrous war with Sparta, which the Athenians eventually lost.

bust would have been mounted on square stone plinth

ARCHITECTURE

The word architecture comes from the Greek words *arche* and *tekton* (meaning "rule" and "builder"). The main styles of temple building were the Doric style from the mainland; the more slender Ionic style from the coast of Anatolia in modern Turkey, and the Corinthian style with plant decoration.

egg-and-dart molding

Ionic capital
This capital (top part of a column) was made in the Ionic style. Its main features were a pair of scrolls at the top and vertical ridges on the column.

gorgon, a mythical female monster

Gorgon's head
This terra-cotta figure of a grinning gorgon's head is an antefix that decorated a temple roof. It was a protective emblem to ward off evil.

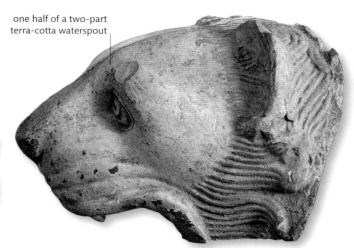

one half of a two-part terra-cotta waterspout

Lion waterspout
Waterspouts in the form of lions' heads were used by Greeks for centuries as decorations. They stood at the corners of temple roofs, draining away water.

ART AND CULTURE

Greek artists worked in various media, yet it is mostly stone sculptures, painted vases, and some metal vessels that survive today. Vase painters first used the black figure style, in which figures were painted in black silhouette, using watered-down clay, or slip, on a red background. Athenian artists invented the red figure style around 530 BCE, leaving the figures red against a black background.

EXTERIOR SHOWING DRINKING PARTY

painted figure of youth with wine bag

two handles for the vessel to be held or hung on the wall, revealing the scene on the base

Kylix
The *kylix*, a wide-bowled drinking vessel, was used by men at drinking parties called symposia. The scene on the interior was revealed as the wine was drunk.

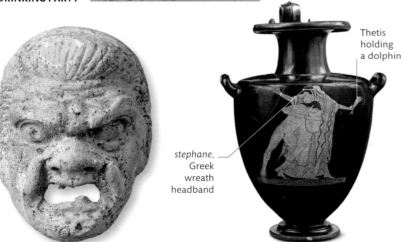

Theater mask
Many theatrical terms, including "tragedy" and "comedy" were Greek in origin. This terracotta decoration shows a mask that would have been worn by an actor in a Greek comedy.

Thetis holding a dolphin

stephane, Greek wreath headband

Hydria
Greek women used a *hydria*, or pitcher, to carry water from public fountains to their homes. This one appropriately portrays Thetis, the goddess of water.

bull-headed Minotaur

Black figure amphora
This 6th-century BCE amphora, or wine vessel, is decorated in the black figure style. It depicts the Athenian hero Theseus killing the mythical Minotaur.

maenad, a female follower of Dionysus

satyr—part goat and part man

Krater
The *krater* was used for mixing wine with water at drinking parties. This *krater* shows a *maenad* and a *satyr*, both followers of Dionysus, the god of wine.

OLYMPIAN MYTHS

THE CAWDOR VASE

The most important Greek festival was the Olympic Games, a great sports event held every four years at Olympia in southern Greece. It was staged in honor of Zeus, king of the gods, and attended by men from all over the Greek world. It was so important that warfare was suspended while the games took place, to allow Greeks to travel safely to Olympia. The games, established in 776 BCE, gave the Greeks a common dating system and a shared sense of identity.

MYTHS

The Greeks created hundreds of myths, or traditional stories, to explain the relationship between gods and humans, how cities were founded, and why religious rituals were performed. The Cawdor vase seen here features a myth invented by the Greeks to explain the origin of the Olympic Games.

KING OENOMAUS

Oenomaus, son of the war god Ares, was the ruler of Elis in southern Greece. A great charioteer and lover of horses, he named his daughter Hippodamia (horse tamer). Fearful of a prophecy that he would be killed by his son-in-law, he found a way to prevent Hippodamia from marrying. Every time a suitor arrived, King Oenomaus would challenge the young man to a chariot race across southern Greece. The suitor was given a head start, while Oenomaus sacrificed a ram to Zeus, the ruler of the Olympian gods, at Elis. The king would go on to win the race, thanks to a pair of divine horses given to him by Ares, the god of war. Oenomaus would kill the defeated suitor with a magical spear, another gift from Ares, and cut off his victim's head, nailing it above the palace gates.

THE VICTORY OF PELOPS

Oenomaus was eventually defeated by Pelops, with the help of divine horses given to him by Poseidon, the sea god. Pelops also bribed Oenomaus's charioteer, Myrtilus, to replace the bronze axle pins on Oenomaus's chariot with wax ones. Just as Oenomaus was catching up with his rival in the race, his chariot wheels flew off, and he was dragged to his death. Pelops became the king of Elis, married Hippodamia, and established the Olympic Games to celebrate his victory.

THE OLYMPIC PENTATHLON

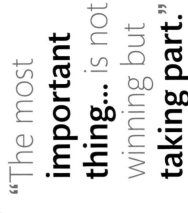

The pentathlon was an Olympic event in which athletes threw the discus and javelin, wrestled, ran races, and competed at the long jump. This discus was used in the 6th century BCE by a victorious pentathlete called Exoidas. He was so proud of his victory that he had the discus inscribed with his name and dedicated it to Castor and Pollux–twin heroes from Greek mythology.

face on end of handle

winged figure of Eros, god of love, driving four-horse chariot

scene from myth in which Zeus's sons, Castor and Pollux, carry away daughters of King Leucippus

> "The most **important thing...** is not winning but **taking part.**"
> Epictetus, Greek philosopher

three large
palmettes on
neck of vase

NAISKOS SCENE

magical spear,
a gift from Ares

King Oenomaus
pours libation (wine
offering) at altar

Fury, one of
the goddesses
of vengeance

youth seated on
cuirass (armored
breastplate)

youth sitting inside
naiskos, or small
shrine—a scene often
depicted on tombs

naiskos with
ionic columns

female
attendant
brings basket
of offerings

statue of
Zeus holding
thunderbolt
and spare
wheel for
Oenomaus's
chariot

king's
charioteer,
Myrtilus,
carries ram to
be sacrificed

altar of
Zeus at Elis

attendant brings
horses for race

Iconographic vase

The Cawdor vase is a large *krater*—
a vessel for mixing wine with water
at drinking parties. It was painted
in the late 4th century BCE by a
Greek artist in southern Italy. After
its discovery in 1790, it belonged to
the King of Naples, a French general,
and the British Baron Cawdor,
from whom it takes its name.

BELIEFS AND RITUALS

The Greeks worshipped many different gods, each of whom ruled over a specific area of life. The most important gods formed a family group headed by Zeus, the sky god. Most Greeks believed in the power of the gods and feared angering them. But some Greek philosophers doubted the very existence of the gods.

Powerful god
This statue shows either Zeus, the god of sky and thunder, or Poseidon, the sea god. Zeus would have held a thunderbolt in his right hand and Poseidon a trident. Few Greek bronzes have survived; this one was recovered from a shipwreck.

fine white marble from Mt. Pentelikon, north of Athens

arms outstreched horizontally, with right hand about to hurl object

woman's face

bird body

Horse offering
The Greeks tried to win the help of the gods by sacrificing animals to them and offering gifts at their temples. This terra-cotta horse is a votive, a gift for the gods.

Guardian herm
A herm was a head of the god Hermes, placed as a guardian figure on street corners and in gateways. This god was thought to ward off evil.

Siren bottle
This bottle in the shape of a siren was used for oil. Sirens were mythical creatures, part bird and part woman. They were believed to lure sailors to their death.

horse seen through window

deceased with family or attendants

powerful stance, with weight falling on left, forward leg

Dining scene
The Greeks believed the dead could receive offerings at their tombs. This sculpted relief shows the deceased reclining to dine.

HOME LIFE

Greek men spent their days outside, meeting their fellow men in the *agora* (marketplace) or in the gymnasium, where they exercised. Women spent most of their time at home, caring for children, cooking, and spinning and weaving wool. In the evening, men relaxed separately from women at all-male drinking parties held at home.

Swan jar
This vessel, used to store olive oil, is shaped as a swan. Olive oil was used in cooking and cosmetics, and in oil lamps in Greek homes.

vessel neck and trefoil lip rising from top of head

Ionian helmet

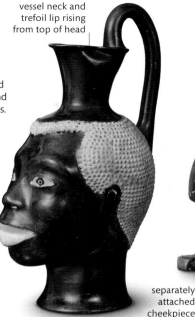

geometric pattern

hole in center to hold sauce

Fish plate
This dish shows two striped perch and an electric ray. Fish formed an important part of the Greek diet.

Feeding cup
This spouted cup was used to feed babies or the sick. The Greeks also made pottery dolls and pull-along animals on wheels for their children.

African vase
Around 40 Greek vases have been found in the form of black Africans. The Greeks had trading posts and colonies in North Africa.

separately attached cheekpiece

Ceramic jar
After bathing, Greeks would rub their skin with olive oil. This little jar, in the form of a hoplite, is an *aryballos*, a container for perfumed oil.

CLOTHING AND ADORNMENT

Most Greeks dressed in clothes made at home by the women of the family. Even wealthy women were expected to know how to spin and weave wool and linen. The Hellenistic period was a time of increased luxury, when women wore beautiful gold jewelry.

interlinked chain pattern

upper body decorated with chevrons

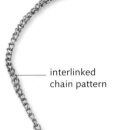

Terra-cotta figurine
Traces of color remain on this pottery statuette that dates from the 4th century BCE. The woman wears an ankle-length dress, called a *peplos*, beneath a *himation*, or mantle.

Necklace with pendant
Greek women wore several types of necklaces, such as this Hellenistic gold-chain necklace from the period 323–31 BC.

Corinthian *pyxis*
This small *pyxis*, with animal figures on it, could have been used by women to store trinkets or cosmetics. It was made in Corinth, around 600 BCE.

Perfume containers
This pair of small glass containers was made in Rhodes in the 6th century BCE. Vessels such as these were called *amphoriskos*.

garnet pendant

Horse *pyxis*
Greek women stored their jewelry in a pottery contained called a *pyxis*. This large *pyxis* from around 750 BCE has horses on the lid.

horse, symbol of wealth and nobility

himation thrown over one shoulder and wrapped around body

bull's head at one end

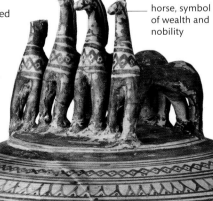

decorative swastika pattern

an ankle-length dress

Gold earring
This Hellenistic earring is made of twisted gold wire. Jewelry is often found in Greek tombs.

CELTIC KINGDOMS

From the 6th century BCE, a great Iron Age civilization stretched across Europe, from Spain to the Balkans. Its warlike people, the Celts, shared common religious beliefs and spoke related languages that survive today as Scottish Gaelic, Welsh, Irish, and Breton. Skilled metalworkers, they made distinctive art with rich, swirling patterns.

Stylized imagery
This Celtic gold coin is a distant copy of a Macedonian one showing a horse and chariot. Horses played a vital part in Celts' lives.

Tower of defense ▽
In Scotland, Celtic chieftains built more than 500 stone towers such as the Don Carloway Broch seen here. These towers could be up to 42 ft (13 m) high. They served both as strongholds and stately homes, displaying the power and wealth of the chieftains who lived in them.

The Celts lived as hundreds of different tribes and did not think of themselves as a single people. Yet they were seen as distinctive by their southern neighbors, the Greeks and Romans. The term Celt comes from *Keltoi*—the name that the Greeks used for these people. The Greeks and Romans were shocked by many Celtic practices, such as head-hunting and human sacrifice.

WARFARE

Celtic tribes were often at war with each other, and evidence for conflict survives in the form of their many defensive structures, including hill forts and Scottish brochs (towers).

Celtic armies also threatened the lands of the Mediterranean, sacking Rome in 391 BCE and invading Greece in 279 BCE. Some of the invaders of Greece then crossed into Anatolia (modern Turkey), settling in an area called Galatia. Celtic was spoken in Galatia until the 5th century CE.

TOWNS

Contact with the Mediterranean world brought changes to Celtic society. From the 3rd century BCE, the Celts built fortified towns, which the Romans called *oppida*—a term derived from the Latin word *ob-pedum*, which means "enclosed space." The largest of

these towns was built at Manching (modern Germany). The town covered 940 acres (380 hectares) and had a population of 5,000 to 10,000 people. *Oppida* were great centers for manufacturing and trade, where the Celts minted their own coins, modeled on Greek examples.

ROMAN CONQUEST

Most of the Celtic lands were eventually absorbed into the Roman Empire, and the Celtic way of life disappeared. Many Celtic languages survived, however, and in Ireland and Scotland, which were never conquered, Celtic traditions continued until recent times.

WARFARE

Unlike the Romans, who fought in tightly disciplined groups, the Celts battled as individual warriors, each seeking personal glory. Celtic warriors fought on foot or on horseback, or they stood on two-horse chariots to throw javelins into the enemy ranks. To show their bravery, many warriors went into battle naked.

■ ARMOR

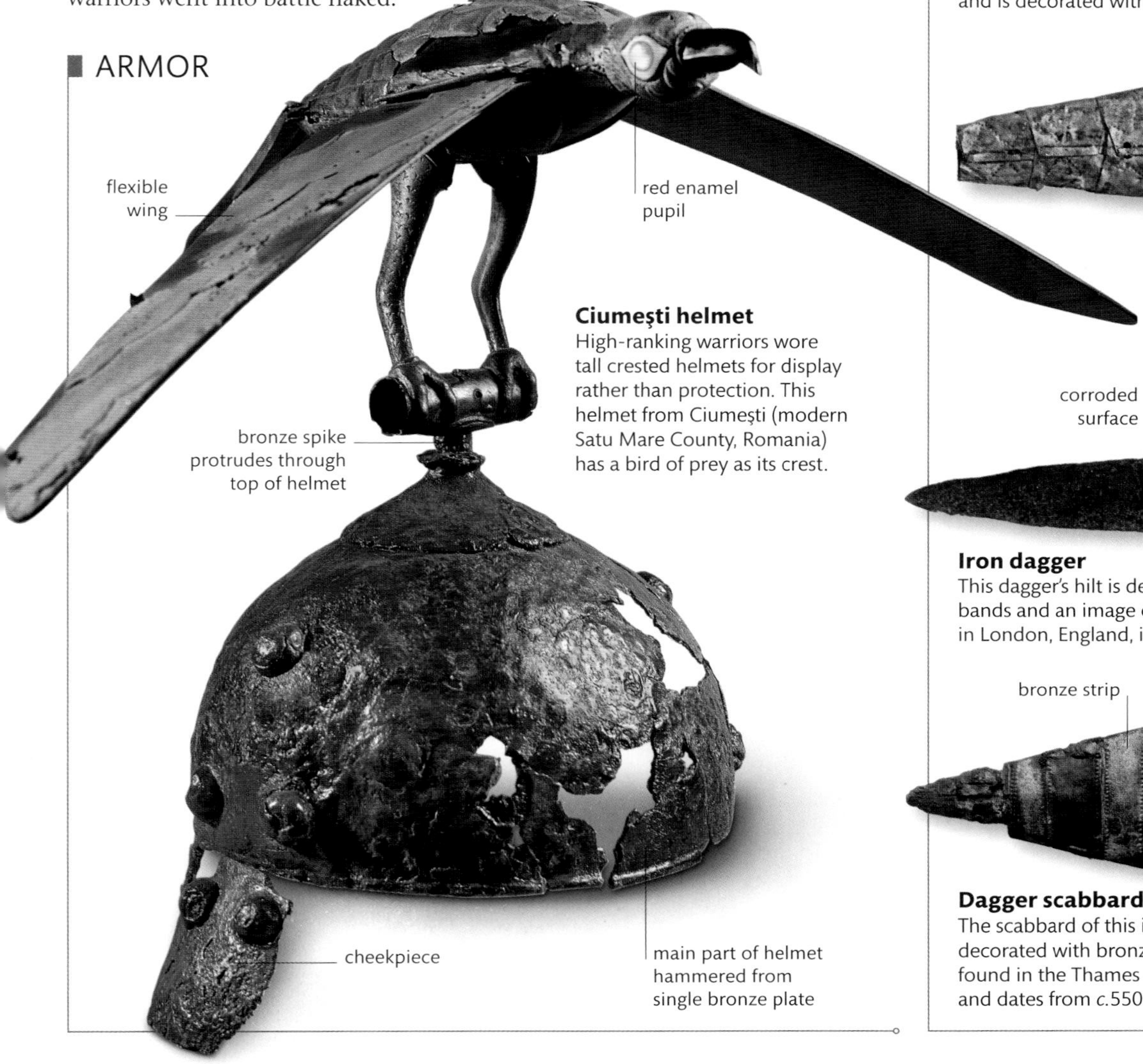

flexible wing

bronze spike protrudes through top of helmet

red enamel pupil

cheekpiece

main part of helmet hammered from single bronze plate

Ciumeşti helmet
High-ranking warriors wore tall crested helmets for display rather than protection. This helmet from Ciumeşti (modern Satu Mare County, Romania) has a bird of prey as its crest.

■ SWORDS AND DAGGERS

intricate scroll pattern

The Kirkburn sword
This 27½ in- (70 cm-) long iron sword comes from a warrior's grave in Kirkburn, England. The handle is made from 37 pieces of iron, bronze, and horn and is decorated with red glass.

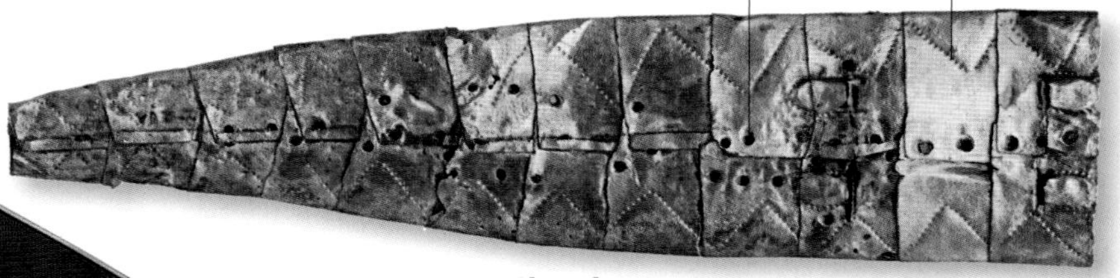

rivet holes

triangle border

Sheath
This sheath was built to cover a short sword or dagger. It is made of sheets of bronze with a bark lining. When new, the sheath would have shone brightly in the sunlight.

corroded surface

Iron dagger
This dagger's hilt is decorated with incised bands and an image of a bearded man. Found in London, England, it dates from 100 BCE to 50 CE.

hilt resembles bearded man

bronze strip

grip was originally wooden

Dagger scabbard
The scabbard of this iron dagger is decorated with bronze strips. It was found in the Thames River, England, and dates from c.550 BCE.

indentations near hilt guard

■ CHARIOT FITTINGS

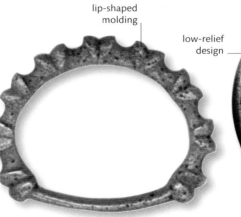

Bronze horse fittings
These fittings adorned the chariots of high-ranking horsemen and were made by cutting a pattern in the surface and pouring in molten red glass.

fine metalwork decorated with enamel

lip-shaped molding

Bronze terret
Fitted to the yoke of a chariot, a terret like this was used by the Celts to guide the reins of each horse.

low-relief design

Axle decoration
This beautiful bronze decoration, fitted to a chariot axle, shows that chariots were designed for display as much as for their function in battle.

BELIEFS AND RITUALS

Among the hundreds of Celtic gods, one of the most commonly represented is a horned male god associated with wild animals. The Celts worshipped their gods by offering them precious objects thrown into rivers, lakes, and pools—entrances to the world of the gods. People and animals were also killed as sacrifices.

BASE OF CAULDRON

scene of ritual slaying of a bull

Gundestrup Cauldron

This silver bowl, called the Gundestrup Cauldron, was found in a Danish bog. Made up of 13 separate panels, it is 27 in (69 cm) in diameter and is decorated with scenes of warfare, gods, and sacrifice. The bowl itself was an offering to the gods.

giant figure, probably a god, plunges a dead man into a cauldron

Celtic warriors ride into battle on horseback

Celtic foot soldiers with long shields

warriors carrying carnyxes—animal-headed war trumpets

god with horns of stag, holding a torc and a serpent

boy on dolphin

Celtic god

sacrificial victims

carefully worked
bronze rivets —

Headdress
This horned helmet was thrown into the Thames River, England, as an offering. Although called a helmet, it is really a ceremonial headdress, perhaps worn by a statue of a god.

Ragstone head
This male head in the La Tène style is from Bohemia, Czech Republic. A 2nd century BCE talisman found within a sacred enclosure, it could represent a warrior or a Celtic deity.

Plaque
This bronze-layered plaque dates from the 4th century BCE. It was recovered from the tomb at Waldalgesheim, Germany.

spoon divided
into quarters

Divination spoons
This pair of bronze spoons was found in Wales. It is likely that a liquid, such as blood or water, was dripped through the hole in the first spoon onto the second spoon, in order to predict the future.

eyes would
have been
inlaid with
glass —

Bronze bucket mount
A horned god, also seen on the Gundestrup Cauldron, is shown in this bucket mount from Kent, England. The horns have broken off.

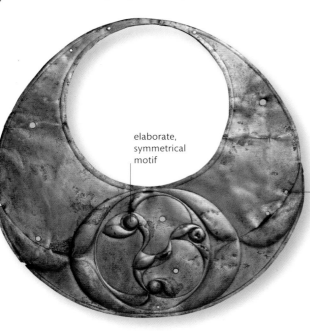

elaborate,
symmetrical
motif

rivet
hole

shield made of four
sheets of bronze
riveted together

Crescent plaque
This bronze plaque is one of 150 precious metal items dropped into a Welsh lake as an offering. The holes suggest it had been attached to something, but its function is unknown.

red glass
enamel studs

Battersea Shield
Like the headdress above, this shield, made of bronze with 27 red enamel studs, was thrown into the Thames River as an offering. It was made for display rather than for real warfare.

CLOTHING AND ADORNMENT

Greek and Roman writers record that the Celts wore brightly colored, patterned clothing—probably resembling Scottish tartans. Men wore baggy pants, called bracae, and leather belts with bronze buckles. They shaved their chins but grew long moustaches. Both men and women wore jewelry, including bracelets, brooches, and torcs (neck rings).

Torcs
Gold torcs were worn by both men and women as a mark of high status. Warriors wore torcs in battle, perhaps believing that they offered magical protection.

multiple gold threads twisted together

warrior's sword blade has broken

wolf clawing at shield

animal represented on applique

symmetrical cloverleaf pattern

Warrior and wolf
This is a 3rd-century BCE gold fibula, a brooch used for a cloak closure. It shows a naked warrior, with a shield and helmet, being attacked by a fierce wolf.

Bronze mirror
The back of this bronze mirror is decorated with intricate patterns, typical of Celtic art.

Gold applique work
This object decorated with animal forms comes from Baiceni, Romania. Skilled Romanian craftsmen excelled at applique work.

decorated catch plate

Fibula
Brooches, or fibulas, such as this bronze and silver one, were used by Celts for garment closures. They worked on the safety pin principle.

cast-iron handle

POLITICS AND POWER

The larger Celtic tribes were ruled by kings and queens, for women could hold power in their own right. Celtic society had different classes, and the warrior aristocracy owned most land. The majority of the population lived as poor farmers. There were also bards (poets), priests, merchants, specialized craftsmen, and slaves captured in warfare.

Slave chains
Slavery was accepted in Celtic society. These chains, found at Bigbury hillfort in Kent, England, were part of a slave chain with six iron collars.

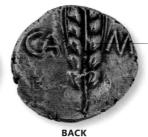

figure-eight shaped links

Gold coin
Coins were minted by King Cunobelin of the Catuvellauni—the most powerful tribe in southern Britain. The letters CAMU stand for Camulodonum (Colchester), and CUNO is short for Cunobelin. The king adopted the Roman alphabet for his coins and used the Latin title *rex* (king).

ear of corn

FRONT

BACK

THE GREAT PERSIAN EMPIRE

The Persian Empire, the world's first superpower, spanned three continents, stretching from Egypt to Afghanistan at its height. It respected foreign customs allowing different peoples to preserve their laws, languages, and religions.

The royal guards ▷
King Darius's palace at Susa had a huge *apadana*, or audience hall, decorated with a glazed brick frieze showing the king's guards, armed with spears and bows, on parade.

The Persian Empire is also known as the Achaemenid dynasty, after Achaemenes, the earliest known Persian king, who ruled in what is now southern Iran around 700 BCE. But the real founder of the empire was King Cyrus the Great, who conquered the rest of Iran, Anatolia, and the Babylonian Empire in the early 6th century BCE.

Persian power peaked in the late 6th and early 5th centuries under the fourth ruler, Darius I. He divided the empire into 20 provinces, or *satrapies*, each with a satrap, or governor. His subjects paid taxes and tribute to the king, but they were free to manage their own affairs.

In 330 BCE, Alexander the Great of Macedon conquered the Persian Empire. But the Achaemenid lineage was not forgotten, the rulers of two later Persian empires, the Parthians (247 BCE–224 CE) and the Sasanian Persians (224–651 CE), both claimed to be heirs of the Achaemenids.

POWER AND POLITICS

Achaemenid, Parthian, and Sasanian rulers all styled themselves "King of Kings," yet their empires were very different. Unlike the Achaemenids, who ruled through satraps, the Parthians let local kings govern, as long as they accepted the Parthian king as overlord. The Sasanian Empire had a strong central government.

large headdress

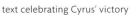

text celebrating Cyrus' victory

Clay cylinder
This cylinder seal carries an inscription that records King Cyrus's conquest of Babylon and his decree allowing those exiled by the Babylonians, such as the Jews, to return to their homelands.

Parthian rider
This statuette represents a Parthian rider. The Parthians had large cavalry armies, including mounted archers and men and horses in chain mail.

hair tied in a bun, a *korymbos*

elaborate crown

body of fallen stag covered with furlike dots

Sasanian dish
This dish shows the Sasanian King Shapur II killing a stag. Hunting was a royal sport, and Persian rulers were often shown hunting wild animals.

King Darius in his chariot

SEAL   **IMPRESSION**

Darius's seal
This seal shows King Darius I on a hunt, protected by the powerful god Ahura Mazda. The Achaemenids claimed the right to universal rule, on behalf of Ahura Mazda.

TRAVELING THE ROYAL ROAD

THE OXUS CHARIOT

In 1880, a collection of around 180 Achaemenid gold and silver objects was discovered on the banks of the Oxus River in modern-day Afghanistan. Now known as the Oxus Treasure, it includes vessels, armlets, animal figurines, and dedicatory plaques that were probably presented as offerings to a temple.

ROADS AND CHARIOTS

The finest piece is a model of a four-horse chariot. The front of the chariot is decorated with the face of the Egyptian dwarf god Bes, whose image was believed to offer protection. The Persians adopted several foreign customs. The figurines in the chariot are wearing the dress of the Medes, a northern Iranian people conquered by the Persians. Chariots like this were used by high-ranking Persians in battle and for hunting. An empty chariot, representing the presence of the god Ahura Mazda, also accompanied Persian armies into battle.

The Persian Empire was the first to use a network of roads as a means of governance and communication. Provincial nobles (or satraps) used chariots to travel quickly along these roads. The most important among them was the 1,550-mile- (2,500-km-) long Royal Road built by King Darius I, which linked the coast of Anatolia with his capital, Susa. At regular intervals along this long road, 111 posting stations were distributed, where officials and messengers could find fresh horses. Riding in relay, messengers could cover the whole distance in a week. The king also had many spies, called the "King's Ears" and the "King's Eyes," who kept watch on the satraps and reported back to him. All rebellions in the land were swiftly punished.

> "There is **nothing** in the world that travels **faster** than **Persian messengers.**"
>
> Herodotus, Greek historian, *The Histories*, 440 BCE

reins made from twisted wires

horses are long-bodied, with thick necks and heavy crests

legs were made separately and then soldered to body of horse

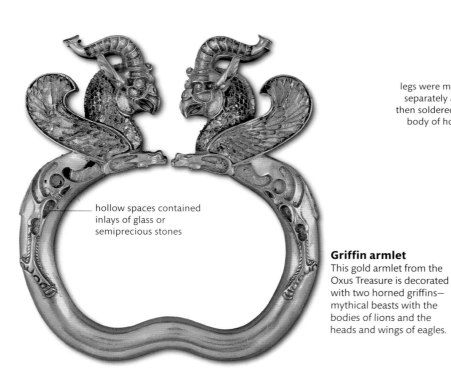

hollow spaces contained inlays of glass or semiprecious stones

Griffin armlet
This gold armlet from the Oxus Treasure is decorated with two horned griffins— mythical beasts with the bodies of lions and the heads and wings of eagles.

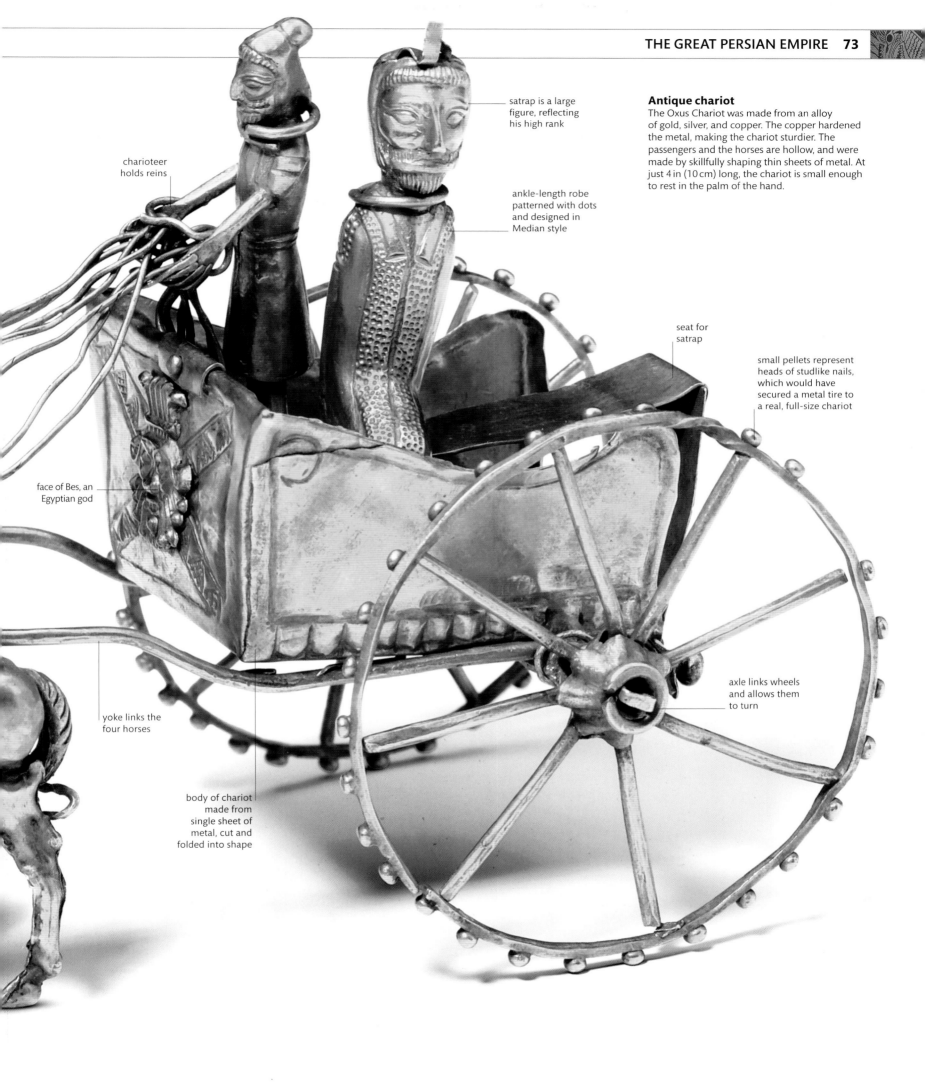

satrap is a large
figure, reflecting
his high rank

charioteer
holds reins

Antique chariot
The Oxus Chariot was made from an alloy
of gold, silver, and copper. The copper hardened
the metal, making the chariot sturdier. The
passengers and the horses are hollow, and were
made by skillfully shaping thin sheets of metal. At
just 4 in (10 cm) long, the chariot is small enough
to rest in the palm of the hand.

ankle-length robe
patterned with dots
and designed in
Median style

seat for
satrap

small pellets represent
heads of studlike nails,
which would have
secured a metal tire to
a real, full-size chariot

face of Bes, an
Egyptian god

axle links wheels
and allows them
to turn

yoke links the
four horses

body of chariot
made from
single sheet of
metal, cut and
folded into shape

THE ARTISTIC ETRUSCANS

From the 8th century BCE, the Etruscans created a major civilization in northwest and central Italy. They were skilled artists, sculpting in bronze and terra-cotta. They were also celebrated for their divination skills, which involved interpreting the will of the gods by reading lightning or examining the livers of sacrificed animals.

Independent woman
This statue depicts an Etruscan woman. Etruscan women could acheive considerable wealth.

The Etruscan language was unrelated to any other in Europe. This led the Greek historian Herodotus to argue that the Etruscans had migrated to Italy from Anatolia. More recent investigations, however, reveal that the Etruscans were the original inhabitants of northwest Italy and their language developed from an ancient Italian one.

Greek style ▽
Most of what is known about the Etruscans comes from their tombs. This painting, in a tomb in Tarquinia, Italy, shows Etruscan dancers and musicians playing an *aulos* (pipe) and lyre, both Greek inventions.

The Etruscan homeland lies in the modern-day region of Tuscany in central Italy. This area is rich in tin and copper, which were used to make bronze. The Etruscans grew wealthy through trading bronze and other goods with the Phoenicians and Greeks. They were strongly influenced by the Greeks, adopting their alphabet around 700 BCE, and embracing Greek art and clothing.

POWER AND INFLUENCE

There were 12 independent Etruscan city-states, each ruled by a king. In the 6th century BCE, with Etruscan power at its peak, these city-states formed a loose alliance. At the time, the civilization dominated Italy from the Po plain in the north, south to the Bay of Naples. The Etruscans influenced their Latin-speaking neighbors, including the Romans, who were originally ruled by Etruscan kings. In the 3rd century BCE, the Romans conquered and absorbed the Etruscan civilization into their growing empire. Nevertheless, the Romans continued to respect Etruscan expertise in religious matters. Whenever lightning struck any public building in Rome, the Etruscan haruspices, or diviners, would be summoned to interpret the significance of the event.

BATTLE AND CONFLICT

As well as admiring Greek art, the Etruscans adopted Greek military tactics. Etruscan warriors fought as hoplites, heavily armed foot soldiers, marching in a rectangular military formation called a phalanx, with overlapping shields. Their main weapons were spears. Helmets were based on Greek and Celtic designs.

ART AND CULTURE

Hundreds of Greek vases have been found in Etruscan tombs. Many were imported but others were made by Greek artists working in Etruscan cities, or by Etruscans imitating them. Etruscan potters developed a technique for making glossy black pottery, called *bucchero*. Reducing the oxygen supply in the firing process turns clay black.

Greek helmet with tall crest

right hand raised to thrust spear

raised cheek guards

lowered shield arm

ropelike edge of armor

Black-figured amphora
This Greek-style vessel was made by an Etruscan artist in the 6th century BCE. It depicts a hunting scene.

Standard design
Like most Etruscan amphoras, this one has a patterned neck, figures on the shoulder, a decorative band, and an animal frieze.

rosettes used as a decorative motif to fill spaces between lions and sphinxes

mythical sphinx painted in red and black

surface has silvery sheen

Celtic-style helmet
This bronze helmet follows the design of those worn by the Celts of northern Italy. It is called a Montefortino helmet, after the place where the first example was found.

Wine ladle
This *kyathos*, used to ladle wine from large vessels into drinking cups, was made using the characteristic *bucchero* method.

Perfume vase
This alabastron, or perfume vase, is thought to have been made by a Greek artist in the Etruscan city of Vulci. It is decorated with lions and a sphinx.

prominent beak

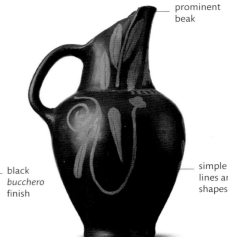

black *bucchero* finish

simple lines and shapes

Bronze hoplite
This bronze figurine is a foot soldier (hoplite), his right arm raised to thrust a spear at the enemy. On his other arm, he would have carried a round shield.

Griffin handles
The griffin, with a lion's body and eagle's head, was often depicted in Greek art. Etruscan artists made vessels with handles in the shape of griffins in bronze and *bucchero*.

Beaked jug
From around 500 BCE, Etruscan potters began to use their own styles. The decoration and shape of this jug are unlike anything made by Greeks.

BATTLEDRESS OF THE NARCE WARRIOR

VILLANOVAN ARMOR

The tombs of the Etruscans and neighbouring peoples often contain armor and weapons, indicating how common warfare was in the 1st millennium BCE. Weapons were often deliberately bent or broken, as if they were being ritually "killed" to enter the next world with their owners.

NARCE TOMBS

Some beautiful examples of armor have been found in a warrior's tomb at Narce in central Italy, dating from 725–700 BCE. Along with his military equipment, the warrior was buried with vases, razors, and horse fittings. The owner was not an Etruscan but belonged to the Falisci, a Latin-speaking people, who lived alongside the Etruscans. The Falisci allied themselves with the Etruscans, and

often fought with them against the Romans. After their conquest by Rome, in 359 BCE, the Falisci rebelled twice against their rulers. The uprisings were crushed and in 241 BCE their city, Falerii, was destroyed.

The Narce tomb dates from a period before Italians copied Greek armor. The equipment is in an earlier native style, known as Villanovan, which was in use from 900 to 700 BCE. The most distinctive item is a helmet with a tall crest. About 30 such helmets have been found in tombs. One odd feature of Villanovan armor is the use of bronze shields without wooden backings, which would have bent in battle. It is likely that they were made as tomb offerings rather than for use in combat. Functional shields were more likely to be wooden and covered with oxhide.

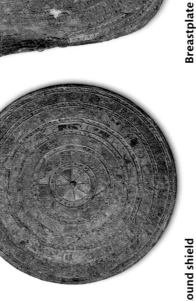

Round shield
The Narce warrior had a bronze shield, measuring 22 in (57 cm) in diameter. Some 80 bronze shields like this one have been discovered in Villanovan tombs.

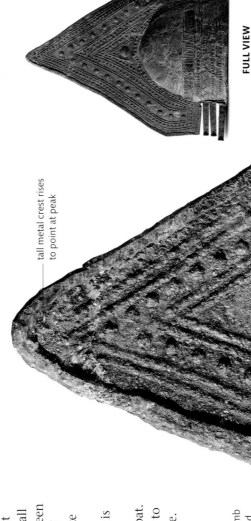

Breastplate
On his torso, the warrior wore a bronze cuirass, or breastplate, which fitted over his shoulders. Like the helmet, it is patterned with zigzag lines and studs.

FULL VIEW

tall metal crest rises to point at peak

rows of studs for decoration

Crested helmet
This warrior's crested helmet from the Narce tomb was made from two sheets of bronze, hammered into shape, and held together by small plates at the front and rear. Helmets in this style are unusually large, at about 16 in (40 cm) tall and across. The warrior probably wore a padded felt undercap to cushion his head.

PAINTED ARMOR

Some tombs, like this example from the 4th century BCE in Tarquinia, had paintings of armor on the walls as a substitute for real equipment. There are two circular shields, one carrying the Greek letter "alpha," on either side of a bronze helmet with cheek pieces. The helmet is a Greek type known as Attic.

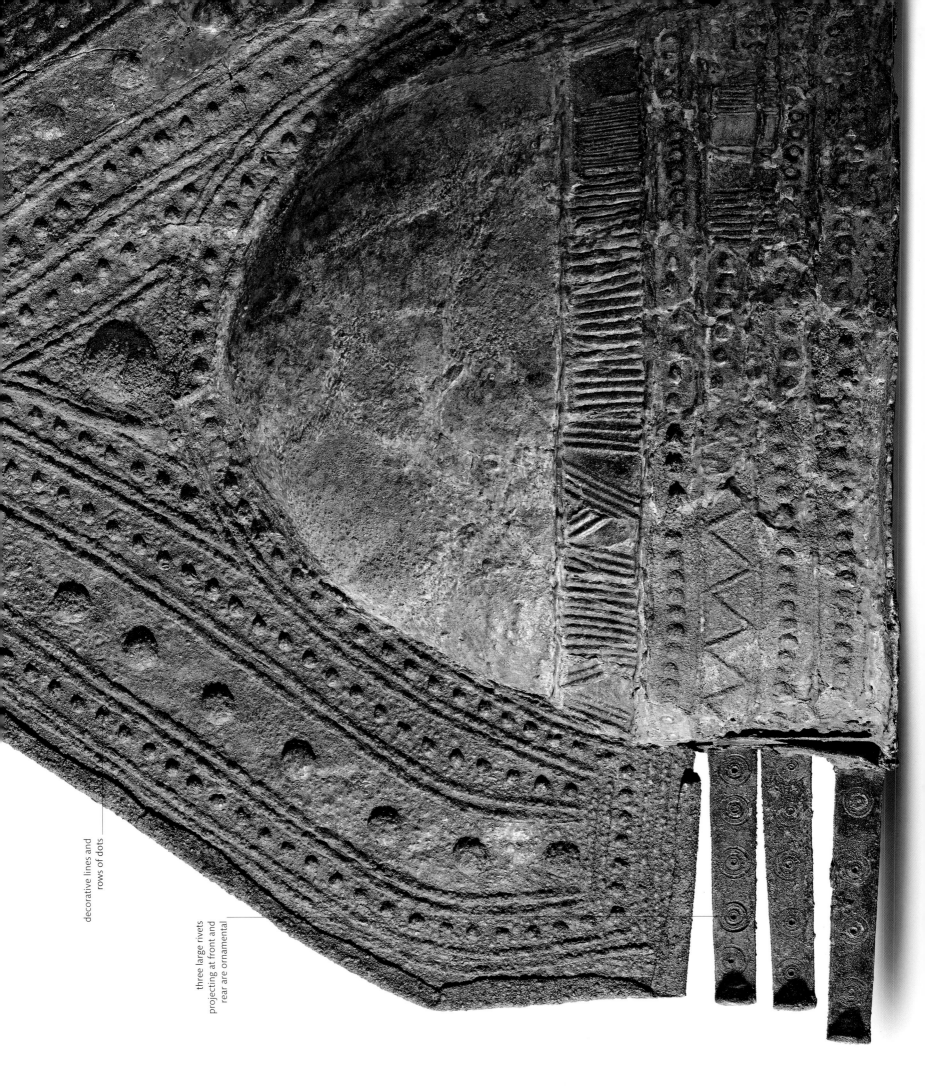

decorative lines and
rows of dots

three large rivets
projecting at front and
rear are ornamental

Bronze oxen
These bronze figures were found in a warrior's tomb. Priests divined gods' wishes by sacrificing oxen and studying the animals' livers for omens.

BELIEFS AND RITUALS

The Etruscan and Greek religions were similar in many ways. While we know less about city state and personal Greek religion, the Etruscans possessed sacred scriptures, believed to have been revealed by the gods to a legendary prophet called Tages. These contained religious laws, as well as instructions on how to interpret signs from nature.

Temple roof decoration
This terracotta antefix, or roof decoration, from a temple displays the face of a satyr. Part-man and part-goat, satyrs were associated with the Greek god of wine and fertility, Dionysus.

large diadem or headpiece

goat-like pointed ears

elaborate earrings

Maenad
The Etruscans often alternated satyr roof decorations, see left, with those depicting Dionysus' female followers, *maenads*, who performed ecstatic dances in the countryside.

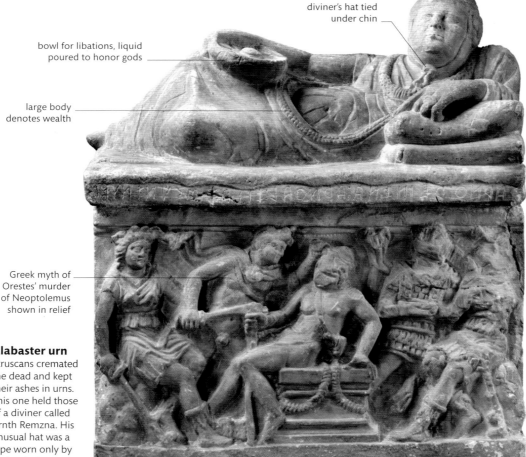

diviner's hat tied under chin

bowl for libations, liquid poured to honor gods

large body denotes wealth

Greek myth of Orestes' murder of Neoptolemus shown in relief

Alabaster urn
Etruscans cremated the dead and kept their ashes in urns. This one held those of a diviner called Arnth Remzna. His unusual hat was a type worn only by such priests.

CLOTHING AND ADORNMENT

Both men and women wore a long woolen robe, the toga, which was later adopted by Roman men. This covered the left shoulder but left the right arm free. The Etruscans were expert at making gold jewelry. They used a technique called granulation, in which they soldered minute gold granules onto a gold surface. The technique of granulation had been practiced in the Near East since the early 1st millenium BCE.

Vase necklace
Etruscan goldworkers made very elaborate jewelry. This necklace is strung with pendants in the shape of vases from which female heads emerge.

grape clusters

winged figure on reverse

engraved surface

Bronze mirror
Etruscan women dressed using polished bronze mirrors, whose backs were elaborately decorated. This type of mirror is Celtic in origin.

narrows to handle

twisted gold wire

Granulated gold
These gold earrings are made of twisted wires covered with granulation. They show the rich surface texture created by granulation.

Goddess antefix
Pottery antefixes like this one show Etruscan women's hairstyles and jewelry. Gold earrings were popular and fashions changed rapidly. This goddess is wearing a large crown.

head on vase-shaped bead

granulated texture

gold wire is tightly curved to form loops

Acorn clasps
This gold necklace clasp is in the form of two sets of acorns, one with a hook, the other with a loop.

gold beaded edge

gold foil surface

horseshoe earring

Horsehoe earring
Horshoe earrings as worn by the goddess, right, have been found in many Etruscan tombs. This gold foil piece dates from the 4th century BCE.

large round bead

leaf detail

Tubular gold earrings
These earrings are made from hollow tubes. They fasten by forcing the narrow end of the tube into the wider end.

THE SPLENDOR OF ROME

Rome was one of the biggest and best-organized empires in history. At its height in 117 CE, the empire stretched 2,300 miles (3,700 km) from north to south and 2,500 miles (4,000 km) from east to west. it included all the lands around the Mediterranean Sea, which the Romans called Mare Nostrum, or "Our Sea." Many aspects of this formidable empire have remained in the modern world.

Gladiator helmet
This bronze helmet with a tall crest was worn by gladiators—trained combatants who fought in public games. Emperors usually paid for the popular entertainment.

Spectacular site ▷
The Colosseum, Rome's great amphitheater, was built in 70–80 CE. Gladiator shows were staged there for free to entertain the public. The Colosseum could seat 50,000 spectators. who would watch the shows together with their emperor, who sat in a special box at the front. Many Roman towns had amphitheaters.

The Romans became so powerful that they even created a myth to describe the founding of their city. They claimed that Romulus, the son of the war god Mars, established Rome in 753 BCE. Archaeology shows that Rome actually began as a small farming settlement in western central Italy in the 9th century BCE, growing into a town by the late 7th century BCE.

Rome was ruled by kings until 509 BCE, when the last king, Tarquin the Proud, was driven out in a coup mounted by the aristocrats. The Romans then set up a Republic ("affair of the people"). Instead of a king, Rome was governed by annually elected magistrates, with two consuls who were the heads of state and commanders of the army. They ruled with the advice of the Senate, an assembly of serving and former magistrates. The Senate became the ultimate decision-making authority of the Republic. Roman republican society was divided into the free and the nonfree (slaves).

CONQUESTS

The Republic made allies with, or conquered, first the plain of Latium, and then the whole of Italy. This gave Rome great wealth and vast reserves of manpower for further wars of conquest. Rome's rise to power in Italy led to conflict with the rival Empire of Carthage, which controlled western Sicily, Sardinia, Corsica, and southern Spain. Between 246 and 146 BCE, Rome fought and won three wars against Carthage, becoming a formidable naval power in the process. Victory in the second war (218–201 BCE) turned Rome into a Mediterranean superpower. The Romans then began to intervene in wars between the Hellenistic Greek kingdoms of the east. By 146 BCE, they had conquered Greece. As a result of these conquests, a vast number of slaves were brought to Italy. Slave labor was used on an extensive scale for building projects.

CIVIL WARS

Warfare gave ambitious Roman generals the opportunities to win great wealth, power, and glory. Eventually, leading generals wanted more power in Rome: in the 1st century BCE, the rivalry between the generals led to a series of civil wars that destroyed the republican system. The final victor of these conflicts, Octavian, became Rome's first emperor, Augustus, in 27 BCE. The Roman Empire left a far-reaching legacy. One of the reasons behind the success of the Romans was that, unlike other ancient empires, they welcomed foreigners, offering them citizenship. At first, this was only given as a reward for loyalty, or for serving as auxiliaries in the Roman army. But under Emperor Caracalla (211–217 CE), citizenship was given to every free male inhabitant of the empire. Apart from slaves, all men could now call themselves Romans. Slaves could also earn their freedom, and their children could go on to become citizens.

THE LASTING LEGACY

Although the Roman Empire finally fell in 476, its influence is still felt today. The Roman calendar, alphabet, and hundreds of words derived from Latin are still in use. Our coins are modeled on Roman coins, and Roman law is the basis of many modern legal systems. The US political system is based on that of the Roman Republic. Christianity, a late Roman religion, is followed by 2.1 billion people worldwide. The Pope is called the Pontifex Maximus, the title of Rome's chief priest.

"Great **empires** are **not maintained** by **timidity.**"

Tacitus, Roman historian, 56–117 CE

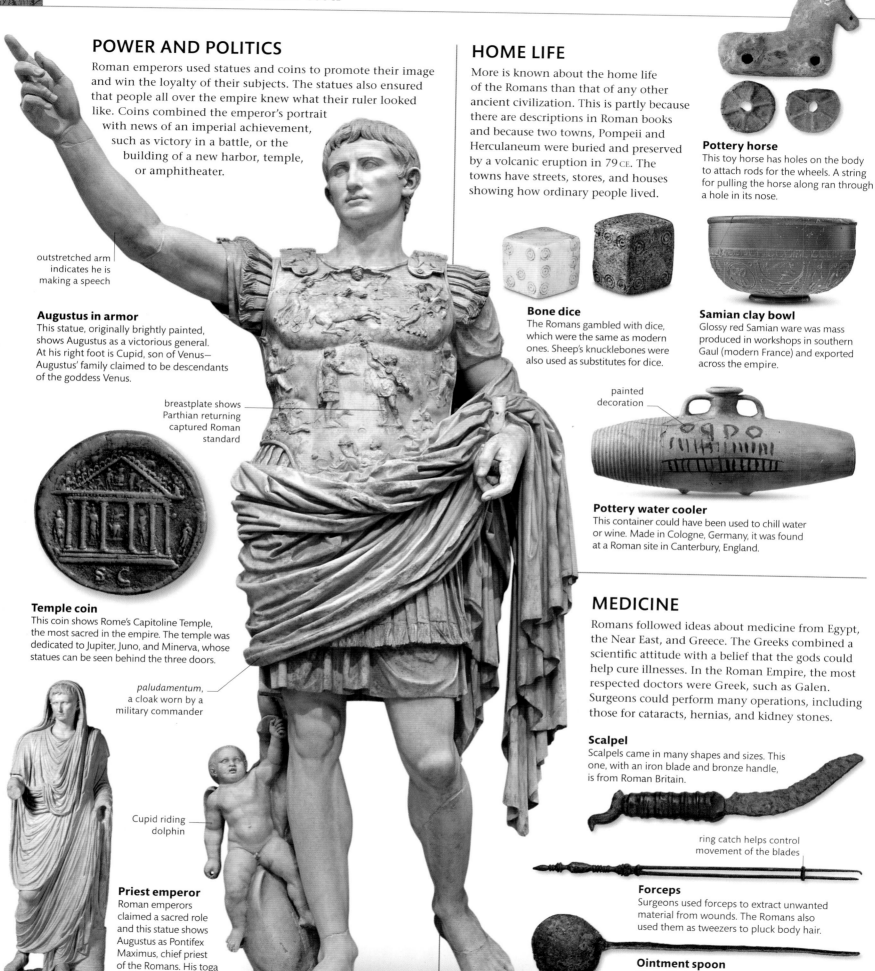

POWER AND POLITICS

Roman emperors used statues and coins to promote their image and win the loyalty of their subjects. The statues also ensured that people all over the empire knew what their ruler looked like. Coins combined the emperor's portrait with news of an imperial achievement, such as victory in a battle, or the building of a new harbor, temple, or amphitheater.

outstretched arm indicates he is making a speech

Augustus in armor
This statue, originally brightly painted, shows Augustus as a victorious general. At his right foot is Cupid, son of Venus—Augustus' family claimed to be descendants of the goddess Venus.

breastplate shows Parthian returning captured Roman standard

Temple coin
This coin shows Rome's Capitoline Temple, the most sacred in the empire. The temple was dedicated to Jupiter, Juno, and Minerva, whose statues can be seen behind the three doors.

paludamentum, a cloak worn by a military commander

Cupid riding dolphin

Priest emperor
Roman emperors claimed a sacred role and this statue shows Augustus as Pontifex Maximus, chief priest of the Romans. His toga covers his head as a mark of respect to the gods.

HOME LIFE

More is known about the home life of the Romans than that of any other ancient civilization. This is partly because there are descriptions in Roman books and because two towns, Pompeii and Herculaneum were buried and preserved by a volcanic eruption in 79 CE. The towns have streets, stores, and houses showing how ordinary people lived.

Pottery horse
This toy horse has holes on the body to attach rods for the wheels. A string for pulling the horse along ran through a hole in its nose.

Bone dice
The Romans gambled with dice, which were the same as modern ones. Sheep's knucklebones were also used as substitutes for dice.

Samian clay bowl
Glossy red Samian ware was mass produced in workshops in southern Gaul (modern France) and exported across the empire.

painted decoration

Pottery water cooler
This container could have been used to chill water or wine. Made in Cologne, Germany, it was found at a Roman site in Canterbury, England.

MEDICINE

Romans followed ideas about medicine from Egypt, the Near East, and Greece. The Greeks combined a scientific attitude with a belief that the gods could help cure illnesses. In the Roman Empire, the most respected doctors were Greek, such as Galen. Surgeons could perform many operations, including those for cataracts, hernias, and kidney stones.

Scalpel
Scalpels came in many shapes and sizes. This one, with an iron blade and bronze handle, is from Roman Britain.

ring catch helps control movement of the blades

Forceps
Surgeons used forceps to extract unwanted material from wounds. The Romans also used them as tweezers to pluck body hair.

Ointment spoon
Medical instruments were mostly made of durable, well-finished bronze. Ointment spoons could be used for both medical and cosmetic purposes.

TRADE

Roman rule was a time of peace, when trade flourished. Merchants crossed the Mediterranean safe from pirates, who were hunted down by the Roman navy. The rich empire was also a market for luxury goods from distant lands, including Chinese silk and Indian spices.

stamped inscription names Leo's workshop in Trier

pointed base acts as shock absorber

Silver ingot
This silver ingot, found in Canterbury, England, was produced in Germany. New emperors distributed ingots to their soldiers to win their loyalty.

Amphora
Wine, olive oil, and fish sauce were transported in amphorae in merchant ships. Amphorae have been found beneath the Mediterranean Sea and in relics of shipwrecks.

BELIEFS AND RITUALS

The Romans had hundreds of gods and goddesses, but they also adopted foreign gods, who they identified with Roman deities. However, Christians, who refused to worship the Roman deities, were persecuted until the reign of Emperor Constantine I (306–337 CE).

Glass urn
Until the 2nd century CE, in the western empire, many dead were cremated and their ashes buried in urns.

cremated remains in urn

Mithras along with two torchbearers

Roman Christ
This mosaic shows Christ as a Roman. The Greek letters *chi* and *rho* (XP), the first two letters in "Christ," are superimposed over each other as an early Christian symbol.

Mithras
Mithras, the Persian god of light, was incorporated into the Roman religion. Sculptures show him killing a sacred bull, an act believed to bring life to the Universe.

Bacchus in chariot, accompanied by centaur

Bacchus worshippers play drums and pipes

Bacchus
This marble relief from a tomb in Rome shows Bacchus, the god of wine and ecstasy, riding a chariot. The Romans adopted Bacchus from the Greeks and often called him Dionysus.

BATTLE AND CONFLICT

Rome's success in warfare was due to the discipline and skill of the Roman army. The heavily armed legionaries—Roman citizens who fought on foot— were the finest soldiers. Serving alongside them were noncitizen soldiers, called auxiliaries, who fought as cavalrymen, slingers, and archers.

Centurial stone
This stone records the two centuries (military units) that built a stretch of Hadrian's Wall— a boundary that ran right across northern Britain.

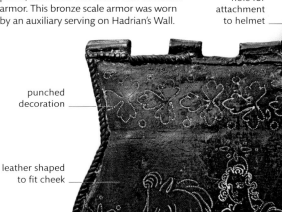

Scale armor
While legionaries wore armor of overlapping plates, auxiliaries had chain-mail and scale armor. This bronze scale armor was worn by an auxiliary serving on Hadrian's Wall.

scales protected soldier's neck

Gladius and scabbard
Each legionary was armed with two javelins and a *gladius*—a short stabbing sword for fighting at close quarters.

hole for attachment to helmet

punched decoration

leather shaped to fit cheek

Cheekpiece
This highly decorated cheek piece comes from a Roman cavalry helmet. Cheekpieces were often decorated with images of Castor and Pollux—the divine twins, who were famed for their horsemanship.

Newstead shaffron (replica)

This is a reconstruction of a shaffron—a horse's protective head cover—that was found at the Newstead (Trimontium) Roman fort in Scotland. It dates from about 80 CE, when the Romans invaded Scotland, a province they later abandoned. The archaeologist James Curle discovered this shaffron, along with other cavalry equipment, while excavating the fort in 1905–10.

ear flaps

brass-headed studs gave extra protection

Protection and display

Worn over the horse's head, the shaffron provided protection against enemy missiles. For display exercises, horses wore silvered metal shaffrons, decorated with images of gods and scenes from myths. This shaffron is adorned with bronze studs in the form of leaves.

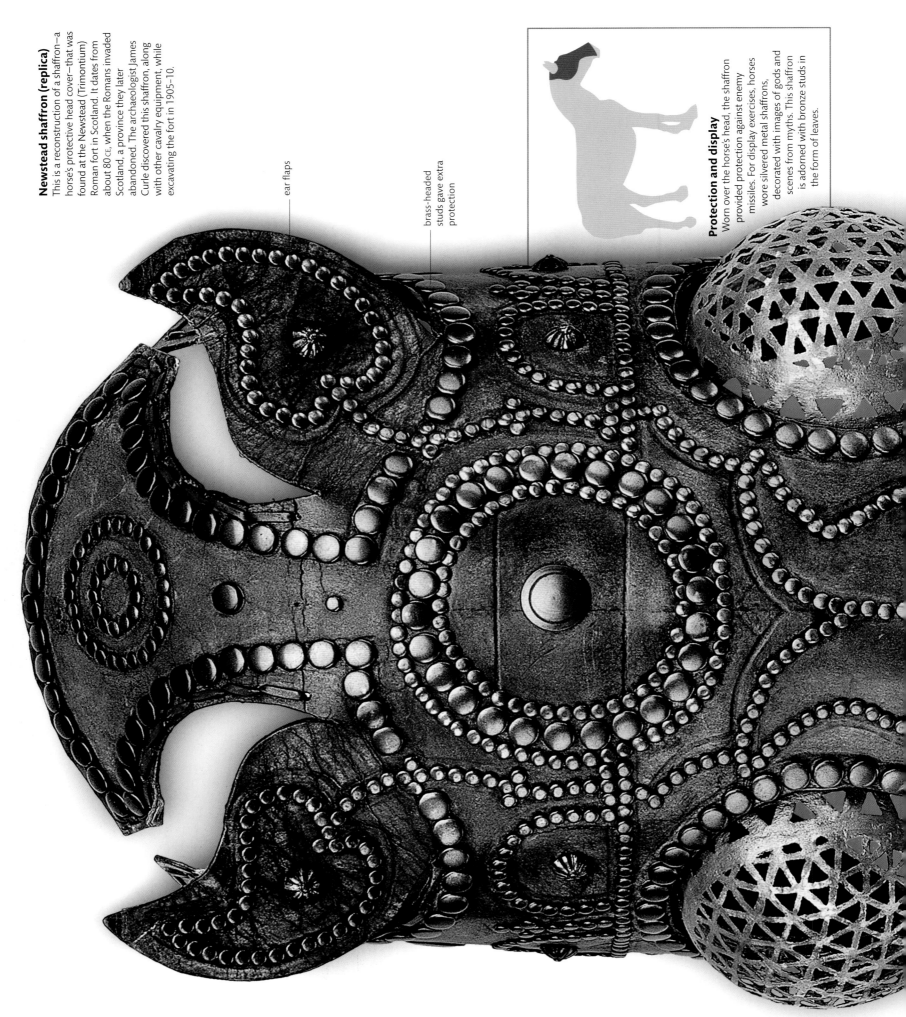

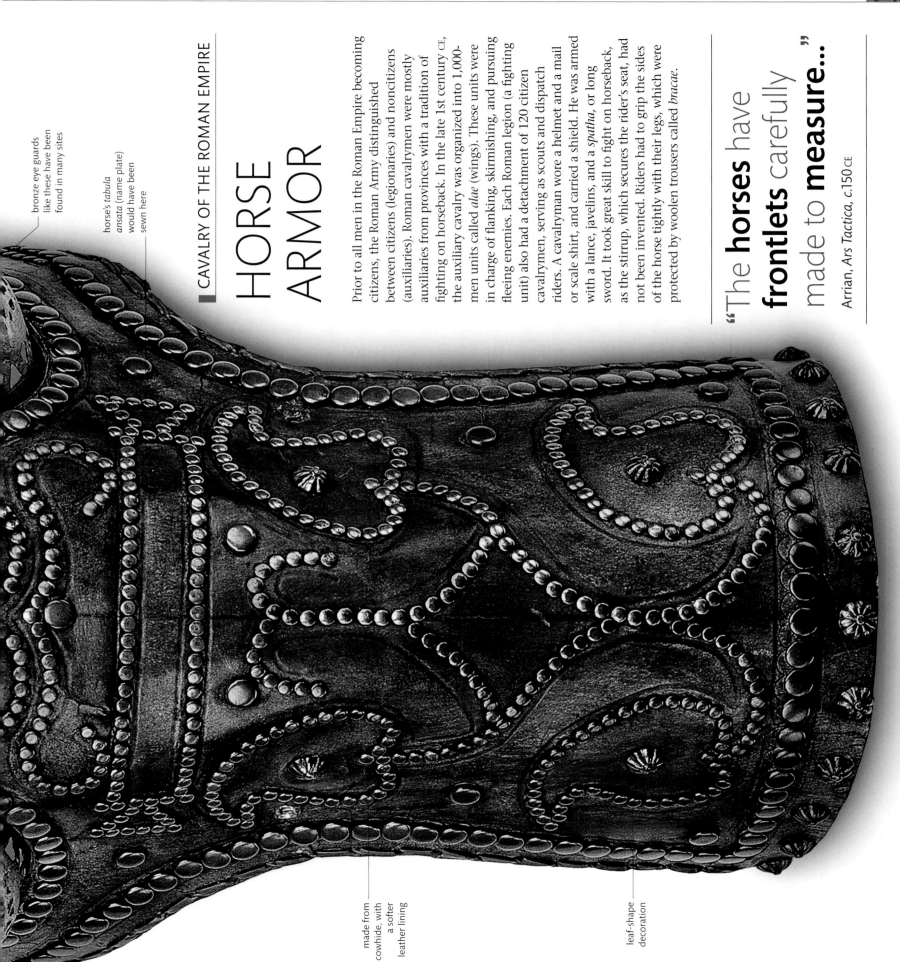

bronze eye guards like these have been found in many sites

horse's *tabula ansata* (name plate) would have been sewn here

made from cowhide, with a softer leather lining

leaf-shape decoration

CAVALRY OF THE ROMAN EMPIRE

HORSE ARMOR

Prior to all men in the Roman Empire becoming citizens, the Roman Army distinguished between citizens (legionaries) and noncitizens (auxiliaries). Roman cavalrymen were mostly auxiliaries from provinces with a tradition of fighting on horseback. In the late 1st century CE, the auxiliary cavalry was organized into 1,000-men units called *alae* (wings). These units were in charge of flanking, skirmishing, and pursuing fleeing enemies. Each Roman legion (a fighting unit) also had a detachment of 120 citizen cavalrymen, serving as scouts and dispatch riders. A cavalryman wore a helmet and a mail or scale shirt, and carried a shield. He was armed with a lance, javelins, and a *spatha*, or long sword. It took great skill to fight on horseback, as the stirrup, which secures the rider's seat, had not been invented. Riders had to grip the sides of the horse tightly with their legs, which were protected by woolen trousers called *bracae*.

"The horses have **frontlets** carefully made to **measure..."**

*Arrian, Ars Tactica, c.150*CE

BUILDING

Roman builders mostly used concrete, a Roman invention, and brick. These relatively light and cheap materials enabled the Romans to build large structures, including bathhouses, aqueducts, and domes. Yet, the Romans admired Greek architecture, so Roman temples, built of brick and concrete, were faced with stone to resemble Greek buildings.

Set square
The Romans used set squares to check right angles when building or cutting stone. The hole is for suspending a weight, used to check horizontal levels.

Roof tile
Two shapes of tile fit together to make a waterproof roof: a curved tile, or *imbrex*, and a flat tile called a *tegula*.

curved *imbrex* covered join between two flat *tegulae*

hollow brick allows hot air to pass through wall

gaping mouth through which water flowed

River god
This marble mask comes from an Italian bathhouse. It represents a river god, and was used as the spout of a fountain.

Warm walls
This Roman brick, shown in a section of a wall, is hollow. Heated surfaces in bathhouses were so hot that bathers had to wear wooden shoes to protect their feet.

pottery sections joined together to make long pipes

Water pipe
Romans used both lead, and pottery pipes, such as these, to transport water to baths, houses, and street fountains. The word "plumber" comes from *plumbum*, the Roman word for lead.

UNDERFLOOR HEATING

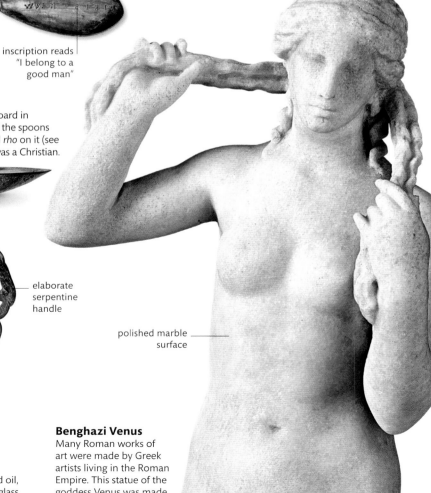

Bathhouses and some private houses used a heating system called a hypocaust. Floors rested on columns of brick or stone, leaving a space for hot air from a furnace to pass through. Public bathhouses often included steam baths and rooms providing dry heat, like a sauna.

ART AND CULTURE

The Romans were great admirers of Greek sculpture, and many of the best-known surviving Greek-style statues are actually Roman copies. The main Roman contribution to art was the development of the mosaic—a picture made from tiny tiles, or *tesserae*. Mosaics were mostly used to decorate floors.

Snail spoon
This silver spoon, known as a *cochlearium*, was used to get snails out of their shells. The name comes from *cochlea*, meaning snail.

inscription reads "I belong to a good man"

swan-shaped handle

Silver swan spoon
This spoon was found in a hoard in Canterbury, England. One of the spoons had the Greek letters *chi* and *rho* on it (see p.83), suggesting its owner was a Christian.

Mosaic
Roman mosaics often featured scenes from Greek myths. This one, from Tunisia, features the legendary Greek hero Theseus.

combed and marvered decoration

Patterned glass
Glassmakers in Libya produced this multicolored pattern by combing the surface while it was malleable.

elaborate serpentine handle

Oil jar
This *balsamarium*, a container for perfumed oil, was made by blowing glass. The Romans invented glass-blowing in the 1st century BCE, probably in Syria.

polished marble surface

Benghazi Venus
Many Roman works of art were made by Greek artists living in the Roman Empire. This statue of the goddess Venus was made by a Greek sculptor in Benghazi, Libya around 150–100 BCE.

CLOTHING AND ADORNMENT

Roman men and women wore a tunic as a basic item of clothing, beneath a variety of cloaks and shawls. Male citizens displayed their status as citizens of the Roman Empire by wearing a toga. The poet Virgil described his fellow Romans as "the race that wears the toga."

one of a pair of trumpets

splayed fantail shape

Snake bracelet
Bracelets such as this bronze one in the form of a snake, were commonly worn by Roman women. Snakes represented fertility, and were also intended to ward off evil.

Glass bangle
Women often wore several bracelets on each arm. This glass bangle or bracelet is one of a pair found in Kent, England.

mottled surface

turban beneath veil

Gold brooch
This gold brooch, 4 in (10 cm) high, would have been one of a pair worn at each shoulder and linked by a chain. Part of the Aesica hoard, its decoration is Celtic in style.

Cameo bear
This cameo of a bear is made from sardonyx, a gemstone from India. The jeweler made the picture of a bear by cutting away the white surface to reveal the brown stone beneath.

Statue
This mortuary statue (originally painted) of a woman comes from Palmyra in Syria, where there was a distinctive local style of dress and jewelry.

stick for applying makeup

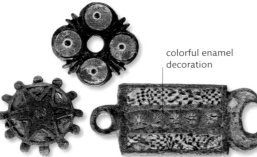

colorful enamel decoration

decoration carved into sard stone

enamel decoration on copper alloy

side handle

undulating threads

ear scoop

Celtic brooches
This type of enameled brooch was invented by the Iron Age Celts (see p.70), and continued to be made under Roman rule.

Intaglio ring
This 2nd-century carved ring shows a procession in which an elephant pulls a decorated cart containing the statue of a Roman goddess.

Chatelaine
This *chatelaine*, or decorative attachment hung from a woman's belt. It came with a variety of useful items, such as nail and ear cleaners.

Glass vessel and kohl stick
Roman women used a variety of cosmetics, including face whiteners, made from chalk or lead. This glass kohl vessel contained black eye makeup.

Hoard necklace
This silver necklace comprises a cabochon cornelian set in an oval silver bezel. It was part of a hoard, found at a Roman fort on Hadrian's Wall, England.

linked silver chains

cable molding

boxlike clasp

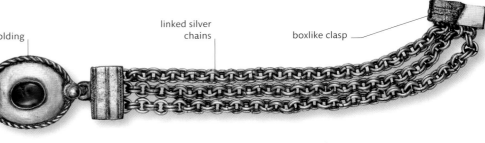

Architectural feat

Trajan's column is made of 20 drums of white Italian marble. After the column was erected, the sculptors carved the frieze, working from the base up, using scaffolding. The column is hollow, with 40 slit windows on the sides and a spiral staircase leading to a balcony at the top. It was probably built under the supervision of the Greek architect Apollodorus of Damascus, who also designed Trajan's forum.

slain soldiers

column depicts about 2,600 figures

Roman soldiers building stone fort

Roman standard

Trajan speaks to his men

auxiliary cavalrymen pursue fleeing Dacians

Dacians surrender, laying down their shields

Roman legionaries in *testudo* (tortoise-shell formation)

carroballista— device for shootin, bolts, mounted or a mule cart

original column was painted and included metal attachments such as weapons

one of 40 slit windows that allow light into column's interior

frieze is 623 ft (190 m) long and winds 23 times around Trajan's column

ROMAN MIGHT

TRAJAN'S COLUMN

The Roman Empire was at its largest under Emperor Trajan, who ruled from 98 to 117 CE. A great general, Trajan spent most of his career in the army. As emperor, he led two successful invasions of Dacia (modern Romania and Moldovia) in 101–02 and 105–06 CE. He used the vast wealth gained from the conquest of Dacia, an area rich in gold mines, to build a grand new forum in Rome. At the center, Trajan built a 125-ft- (38-m-) high structure decorated with scenes (originally painted) from the Dacian wars, with a gilded statue of the emperor on the top. This column would also be Trajan's tomb, for his ashes were later placed in the base. The

column served to commemorate Trajan's achievement in building the forum. The area, which had been previously hilly, was excavated and leveled to a depth equal to the column's height. An inscription at the column's base records that it was built "to demonstrate of what great height the hill was and the place that was removed for such great works."

A GRAND TRIBUTE

Trajan's column is a monument both to the emperor and to his soldiers, who are shown marching and fighting their way up the sides, in a continuous frieze. Before any major undertaking, such as crossing

the Danube River, the army would sacrifice animals to win the favor of the gods—many such scenes of sacrifice are depicted in the carvings. As chief priest, Trajan is often shown overseeing the sacrifices. The carvings also show how Roman soldiers were armed, how they carried their equipment, and how they fought. Roman legionaries, in their plate armor, can be distinguished from the auxiliaries by their oval shields. Rome's Dacian enemies can also be seen—the sculptors knew what they looked like, since many Dacian prisoners had been brought to Rome, together with their arms and armor, for Trajan's triumphal procession.

"My **excellent** and most **loyal fellow soldiers...**"

Trajan, letter to governors, quoted in the *Digest of Roman Law*, 6th century CE

The hero
Trajan appears frequently in the carvings, making rousing speeches, receiving messengers, and awarding prizes for bravery. Here, he steers a troop ship across the Danube.

River crossing
In this scene, Roman legionaries cross the Danube River on a bridge of boats. They are led by an officer and standard bearers in animal-skin headdresses.

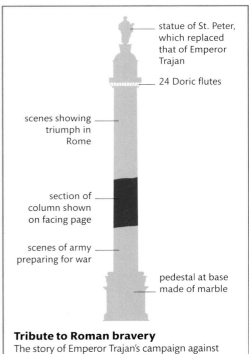

statue of St. Peter, which replaced that of Emperor Trajan

24 Doric flutes

scenes showing triumph in Rome

section of column shown on facing page

scenes of army preparing for war

pedestal at base made of marble

Tribute to Roman bravery
The story of Emperor Trajan's campaign against the Dacians is told in a continuous frieze that spirals up the column. Near the base are scenes of preparations for warfare, while the highest sections show Trajan's triumph. The area colored red on the diagram shows the approximate position of the section in the photograph on the facing page.

Securing the base
Here, legionaries, still wearing their plate armor, are shown building a fort—a secure base in enemy territory. Two auxiliaries, who carry oval shields, stand guard.

FOREIGN RULE IN EGYPT

After two periods of Persian rule, between the 6th and 4th centuries BCE, Egypt was conquered by Alexander the Great of Macedon in 332 BCE. One of Alexander's generals, Ptolemy, then founded a dynasty that governed Egypt until 30 BCE, when the Romans arrived.

Sacred ibis
In Ptolemaic times, vast numbers of ibises were mummified as offerings to Thoth, the god of wisdom.

Riverside shrine for the gods ▽
Like the Ptolemies, the Romans supported Egyptian religion. The Roman emperor Trajan built this kiosk on the island of Philae. A sacred barque (boat) carrying statues would stop at the kiosk during religious processions.

Alexander spent six months in Egypt, where he founded the city of Alexandria, named after himself. Following his death in 323 BCE, Ptolemy seized Egypt. Although the Ptolemies were Macedonian, they presented themselves to their subjects as traditional pharaohs, even following the Egyptian royal custom of marrying their sisters.

Ptolemaic Egypt was a part of the Greek-speaking world of the eastern Mediterranean. Alexandria had a mixed population of Greeks, Jews, and Egyptians, with each group living in its own district. Ptolemy I built a famous library, and the city became a great center of learning, home to Euclid, the father of geometry, as well as the geographer Eratosthenes. Ptolemy also commissioned a lighthouse, which was completed by his son and became one of the Seven Wonders of the Ancient World.

ROMAN RULE

In the 1st century BCE, the Ptolemies allied with the Romans, who began to play an increasing role in Egyptian affairs. The last Ptolemaic ruler, Cleopatra VII, was drawn into a war between her lover, Mark Antony, and Octavian (the future emperor Augustus). Octavian won, and Egypt became a Roman province following the defeat of Mark Antony and Cleopatra in 30 BCE.

Roman Egypt was an early center of Christianity—St. Mark's Gospel was written there in Greek in the late 1st century BCE. When Christianity became the official religion of the empire in the 4th century, the worship of Egyptian gods was banned. The knowledge needed to use hieroglyphs was also eventually forgotten.

POLITICS AND POWER

The Ptolemies drew prestige from Alexander the Great. Egyptian priests had greeted Alexander as the son of the ram-headed god, Amun, and Ptolemy I's coins showed Alexander with ram horns. Both Ptolemaic and Roman coins used Greek, the official language of government.

Alexander the Great
Dating from the reign of Ptolemy I, this coin shows Alexander wearing an elephant scalp, a reference to his Indian conquests. Amun's horns can also be seen on his head.

Zeus's eagle
The Ptolemies identified the Egyptian god Amun with the Greek god of thunder and the sky, Zeus. The eagle, Zeus's sacred bird, decorated many Ptolemaic coins.

Cleopatra
This coin of Cleopatra VII, the last of the Ptolemies, shows her with a Greek hairstyle. The Ptolemies were only depicted wearing Egyptian dress in temples.

Mark Anthony
This coin was struck by Mark Antony when he ruled the Greek-speaking eastern half of the Roman Empire. Defeated by Octavian, he killed himself in Alexandria.

Hadrian
The Roman Emperor Hadrian issued this coin depicting a canopic jar with the head of Isis. He had visited Egypt in 130 CE and was fascinated by Egyptian customs.

HOME LIFE

While the wealthy Greeks of Alexandria lived a life of luxury, Egyptian peasants along the Nile River carried on as they had for thousands of years. They continued to live in houses made of mud bricks, and to wear white linen clothes and reed sandals.

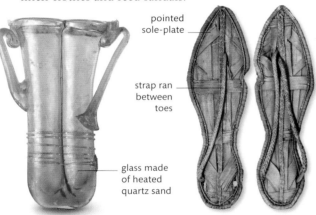

pointed sole-plate

strap ran between toes

glass made of heated quartz sand

Cosmetic jar
Dating from Egypt's Roman period, this cosmetic jar is made of glass. It has two separate tubes, probably used to hold black and green eye makeup.

Plant-fiber sandals
These Roman-era Egyptian sandals are almost 2,000 years old, yet they are perfectly preserved thanks to Egypt's dry climate.

face of Bes

Bes jars
The dwarf god Bes was seen as the protector of family life, and Egyptians placed his face on jars such as the ones seen here for protection. His fierce expression was thought to ward off evil.

WRITING

Different writing systems were used under the Ptolemies and Romans. Hieratic script and hieroglyphs continued to be used mainly for religious purposes. Egyptians also used a simpler script called demotic for everyday use. The Greek script was used by the Greek-speaking population and for official purposes. Papyrus or fragments of pottery were used for writing.

text written in Greek

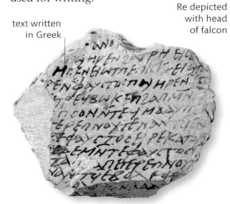

Ostracon
Fragments of pottery or stone that were used for writing or drawing are called ostracons. These were cheaper than papyrus, and were used for letters, business records, and to practice writing.

piece of pottery with hieratic writing

Hieratic
The text on this Roman-period ostracon was written in hieratic script using a pen carved from reed, which was probably cut from papyrus plants or bamboo.

Re depicted with head of falcon

Hieroglyphs
Retrieved from a tomb, this wooden stela has a hieroglyphic text naming the deceased as Nehemsumut, son of Khonsuemsaf and Ruru. He is shown worshipping the Sun God Re (centre left) and the god of creation Atum (centre right).

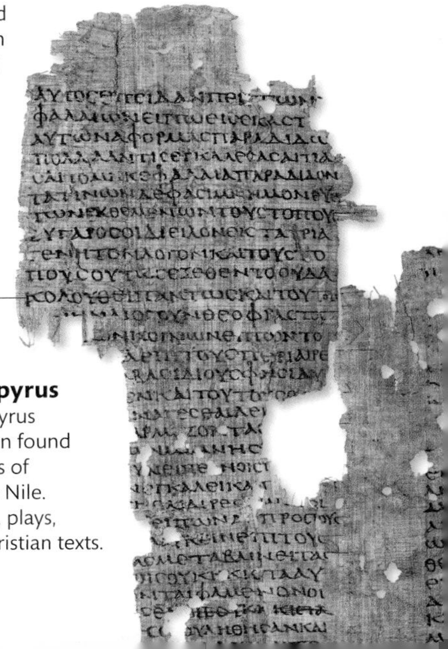

text is hymn to the Sun

Greek script

Oxyrhynchus papyrus
Vast numbers of papyrus documents have been found in the rubbish dumps of Oxyrhynchus, on the Nile. These include letters, plays, poems, and early Christian texts.

THE BEGINNING OF EGYPTOLOGY

THE ROSETTA STONE

In 1799, French soldiers campaigning in Egypt discovered the Rosetta Stone, a section of broken black basalt inscribed with writing which became the key to unlocking the mystery of ancient Egyptian hieroglyphics. After the Egyptian sacred writing system of hieroglyphics went out of use in the 4th century CE, the ability to read it was lost for 1,400 years. The Rosetta Stone's inscription was written in three scripts—hieroglyphics, Demotic (an Egyptian script used for everyday writing), and ancient Greek. European scholars realized they could use their knowledge of Greek to decipher the hieroglyphics, and raced to break the code.

In 1819, Dr. Thomas Young, an English polymath, found the name Ptolemy six times in the hieroglyphics (see panel below). The Rosetta Stone followed the Egyptian custom of placing a royal name in a cartouche, an image of a knotted coil of rope that represented "enclosing protection" and "eternity." Young argued that each hieroglyph in the cartouche was a sound sign spelling the Greek name "Ptolemaios."

CRACKING THE SYSTEM

Jean-Francois Champollion, a French linguist, cracked the system in 1822, showing that hieroglyphs combined sound signs and ideograms—signs standing for ideas. His knowledge of

Coptic—a late version of the Egyptian language preserved by the Christian church—helped him identify the sound signs. For example, he identified a sign showing the Sun as the sound "re," because this was the Coptic word for the Sun. The Rosetta Stone's inscription was a decree written by a council of priests on March 27, 196 BCE, honoring their 13-year-old king, Ptolemy V. The pharaohs valued the priests' support, which was secured by donations to temples, a fact mentioned in the decree. Thanks to Champollion, Egyptian texts written over a period of 3,500 years could be read again. This was the beginning of Egyptology, the study of ancient Egypt.

DECIPHERING THE CARTOUCHE OF PTOLEMY V

S	I or Y	M	L	O	T		P

Thomas Young set out to decipher a group of hieroglyphs surrounded by a loop called a cartouche. He guessed that these highlighted hieroglyphs represented the name of the pharaoh Ptolemy, which he knew was repeated several times in the Greek text. Young managed to correlate most of the hieroglyphs with spoken sounds (as shown in the examples above).

Three scripts
Discovered near the town of Rosetta, this black basalt block is 3.9 ft (114 cm) high and 2 ft (72 cm) wide and was damaged in ancient times. Three inscribed scripts are easily identified, with the section in hieroglyphics most badly damaged.

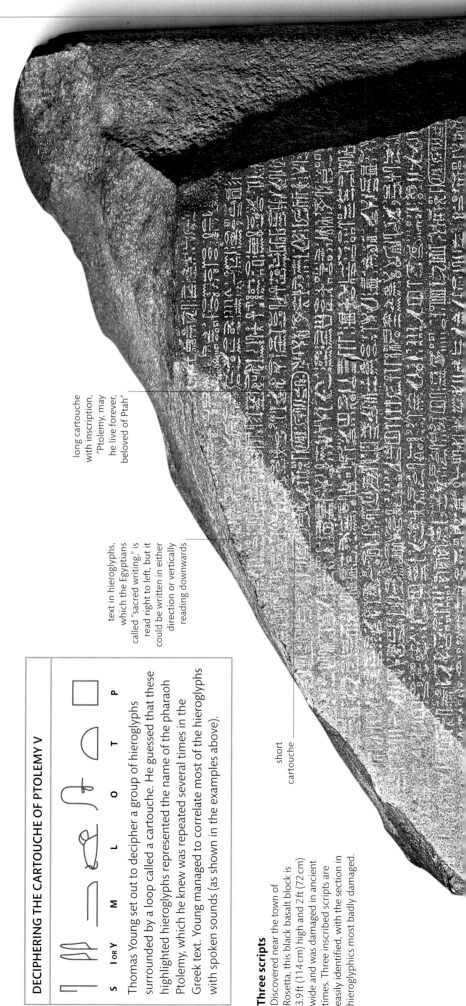

long cartouche with inscription, "Ptolemy, may he live forever, beloved of Ptah"

text in hieroglyphs, which the Egyptians called "sacred writing," is read right to left, but it could be written in either direction or vertically reading downwards

short cartouche

text in Demotic, which the Egyptians called "document writing." Demotic was always written from right to left

text in ancient Greek, the language of administration

BELIEFS AND RITUALS

The Ptolemies enthusiastically adopted Egyptian religion. As pharaohs, they were seen as living gods, which brought the royal dynasty great prestige. The Greeks identified many Egyptian gods with their own. For example, Inhert, the Egyptian god of war and hunting, was called Onuris by the Greeks and was identified with the Greek god Ares.

tripartite wig and horned sun disk

Isis seated on throne

disk may represent Sun or Sun God

rising cobra on forehead

curled wig topped by two tall feathers

raised spear to strike enemy

Isis and Horus
Isis was identified with the Greek gods Demeter and Aphrodite. From 30 BCE, her worship spread throughout the Roman Empire. This amulet shows Isis nursing her son, Horus.

Montu
This gold amulet depicts Montu, an Egyptian war god, wearing a crown with two tall plumes. Soldiers wore such amulets to protect themselves in battle.

Onuris
Amulets of deities were thought to imbue the wearer with the god's qualities. This one, showing Onuris, the war god, was worn as a source of strength.

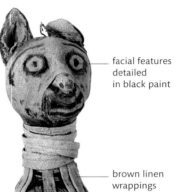

facial features detailed in black paint

brown linen wrappings

Mummified cat
During the Ptolemaic and Roman periods, cats were left as offerings to Bastet, the cat goddess. They were specially bred to be mummified and sold to Bastet's worshippers.

cobra refers to Sun God, Re

face of Ptolemaic king

style of features is Greek

striped Royal Nemes headcloth

body of a lion, representing strength

FRONT VIEW

Sphinx
Like pharaohs, the Ptolemies were depicted as sphinxes—mythical creatures with the bodies of lions. The Egyptian sphinx was an embodiment of royal authority. However, the Greek word "sphinx" means "strangler," and in Greek mythology sphinxes were terrifying monsters.

Mummy mask
This gilded mask belongs to the mummy of a wealthy Egyptian man Padineferhotep, who died in the 3rd century BCE. The mask was made from cartonnage, a material consisting of layers of linen or papyrus covered in plaster. Cartonnage mummy cases were cheap to make. They became common in the Ptolemaic and Roman periods, when ordinary people were being mummified.

mask represented new immortal face for the deceased, who would be able to look out through painted eyes

gold was seen as flesh of gods

lappet wig, hairstyle of Egyptian gods

goddess Isis, the special protector of mummies, created the very first mummy—of her husband, Osiris, the god of the dead

Sun God
Covered with protective deities, this mask has a winged scarab and a winged sun disk on top. Both these images represent the Sun God, Re.

mask was slipped over the wrapped head of the mummy

SIDE VIEW

goddess Nepthys, identified by house on her headdress

gold leaf covering the cartonnage mask

painted cartonnage beneath gilding

◼ BURIAL

wig with
thick stripes
of blue
and gold

painted to
resemble
beadwork

Egyptian mask
In the Ptolemaic period, Egyptians continued using traditional mummy masks, in which features were idealized and the skin was painted gold.

Greek mummy
The Greeks who settled in Egypt welcomed the Egyptian idea of a happy afterlife. Like the Egyptians, they had themselves mummified in order to live again. Egyptians and Greeks were sometimes depicted in Greek dress, as on this cartonnage mummy case of a woman.

Egyptian-style wig
with two lappets
(hanging folds)

white face, unlike
traditional gold of
Egyptian mummies

colorful Greek
dress (*chiton*)

arms and
hands covered
in jewelry

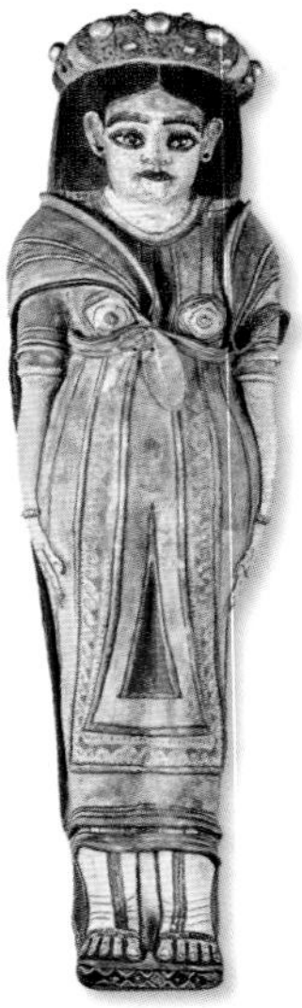

owner of
mask with
idealized
golden face

Woman's mask
In the Ptolemaic period, some mummies were less well preserved than during earlier periods. But masks were still beautifully decorated.

FULL VIEW

realistic features of young man

molded face

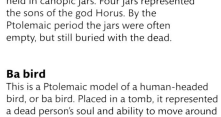

lid in form of human-headed guardian, Imsety

lid in form of jackal-headed guardian, Duamutef

lid in form of falcon-headed guardian, Qebehsenuef

lid in form of baboon-headed guardian, Hapy

LIVER

STOMACH

INTESTINES

LUNGS

Molded face
While the rich could afford gilded masks, the poor had to make do with features modeled in clay on coffins or masks. These clay covers show that in Egypt, even the poor looked forward to an afterlife.

Portrait mask
During this period mummies often had realistic portraits of the deceased, placed over the face. These are the finest portrait paintings to survive from the ancient World.

Canopic jars
Organs from mummified corpses were held in canopic jars. Four jars represented the sons of the god Horus. By the Ptolemaic period the jars were often empty, but still buried with the dead.

Ba bird
This is a Ptolemaic model of a human-headed bird, or ba bird. Placed in a tomb, it represented a dead person's soul and ability to move around and be changed into other forms.

Isis

Osiris

the deceased

altar with sacrifice

hieroglyph

blue wig with lappets on chest

band of decoration relating to sun god

base in form of lotus flower

bird feet

Mummy case portion
Part of this cartonnage mummy case shows the deceased worshipping Osiris, the god of the dead. Isis, sister-wife of Osiris, stands behind his throne.

Situla
As part of the funeral ceremony, priests made offerings to the dead. This bronze situla (bucket-shaped vessel), decorated with religious scenes, was used to pour milk.

INDIA'S FIRST EMPIRES

Between 321 BCE and 554 CE, three great empires rose in India under the Mauryans, the Kushans, and the Guptas. For the first time in history, India was united. The period also saw the rise of two new world religions—Buddhism and Jainism.

Place of prayer ▷
The Great Stupa at Sanchi was commissioned by Emperor Ashoka. A stupa is a sacred mound, holding relics of the Buddha, great Buddhist teachers, and his first followers. Stupas are places of pilgrimage, inspiring meditation and prayer.

The Mauryan Empire (321–185 BCE) was founded by Chandragupta Maurya. This empire expanded until the third emperor, Ashoka the Great, respected Buddhist teachings and called a halt to further wars of conquest. He then went on to spread Buddhism throughout India.

Another powerful empire was founded by the Buddhist Kushans (c.30–240 CE), nomads from Central Asia who conquered northwest India and much of modern Afghanistan.

During this time, a new form of the religion called Mayahana Buddhism emerged.

From 320 to 554 CE, the Gupta emperors provided stable rule. During this period, known as India's Golden Age, arts and sciences flourished. Indian mathematicians invented a decimal number system, that included the concept of zero. Buddhism thrived, but there was also a revival of Hinduism, promoted by the Guptas, who built temples to the Hindu gods.

TRADE AND TRANSPORT

Under the Kushans and the Guptas, trade flourished, thanks to the Silk Road—the overland route across Asia. Indian spices and gems were carried west to the Roman Empire and east to China. Indian merchants also sailed across the seas to Arabia and Southeast Asia.

Winged Atlas
The Silk Road brought the Kushans into contact with many different peoples, whose influences they absorbed. This winged figure is based on Atlas, the Greek mythical giant.

Gupta dinara
Vast amounts of Roman coinage flowed into India through trade. The Guptas named their own gold coin, shown here, a "dinara," after the Roman denarius.

BELIEFS AND RITUALS

The 5th century BCE saw the rise of Buddhism, founded by Gautama Siddhartha, called the Buddha, the "Enlightened One." The Mauryan emperor Ashoka and the Kushans spread Buddhism. The Guptas built the first stone temples to Hindu gods such as Vishnu and Shiva.

ART AND CULTURE

In the northern part of the Kushan empire, Indian artists were greatly influenced by Greek and Roman sculpture. They went on to carve statues of the Buddha wearing a Greco-Roman style toga. Some of the finest Indian art dates from the Gupta period, including stone temples with lofty spires dedicated to the Hindu gods.

musician's lyre

young bride in wedding cart

Kushan wedding relief
This relief of a bridal procession includes ivy leaves and a cart pulled by panthers. These features were associated with Dionysus, the Greek god of wine.

Musician with lyre
Gupta temples were built of brick or stone and richly decorated with sculpture. This terracotta tile, showing a musician, was once part of a brick temple.

Prince Siddhartha leaves his horse and groom

Kanthaka, Siddhartha's horse

The birth of the Buddha

This relief from the stupa at Amaravati captures momentous events in the history of Buddhism. Prominent figures featured in the relief include the seers who prophesied the greatness of the Buddha, Queen Maya and King Suddhodhana (the Buddha's parents), and an infant Buddha.

King Suddhodhana, Buddha's father

seers prophesy the birth of a great being

sacred tree

Queen Maya presents her child

Buddha, symbolized by footprints on a long cloth

a tree spirit worships the baby

Queen Maya dreams a white elephant, a sign of greatness, has entered her side

sleeping attendants

Queen Maya grips the branch of a sal tree

Queen Maya gives birth from her right hip

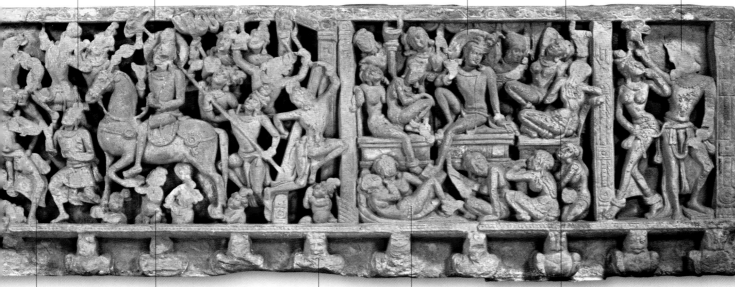

Chandaka, the groom

Siddhartha secretly leaves his palace by night

Siddhartha creeps out of bed

The royal palace at Kapilavastu

mithuna, or affectionate couple

attendant spirits watch over Siddhartha

ganas, dwarf spirits, muffle the horse's hooves

lion head bracket

sleeping attendants

Siddhartha leaves his sleeping wife, Yashodhara

The Great Departure

This frieze from the stupa at Amaravati, Andhra Pradesh, depicts scenes of Prince Siddhartha's departure from his palace in order to lead the life of an ascetic. The stupa is decorated with carved panels, which tell the story of the Buddha's journey to enlightenment.

THE UNIFIED KINGDOMS OF CHINA

In 221 BCE, six warring states were conquered and unified with a seventh under the rule of the King of Qin. He declared himself First August Divine Emperor of Qin. It is from Qin, pronounced "chin," that the name China is probably derived.

The Silk Road ▷
During the Han dynasty, an overland trade route opened up between China and the West. It was called The Silk Road, after the most valuable Chinese export. Camel caravans traveled west across Asia, carrying Chinese silk and other goods.

During a period known as the Warring States era (475–221 BCE), there were seven powerful kingdoms in constant conflict. The need to wage wars meant that these states mobilized resources on a great scale. Kings appointed civil servants to govern the states in place of rule by the hereditary nobility.

Between 230 and 221 BCE, King Ying Zheng of Qin gained control of all seven kingdoms and created a totalitarian state. Using forced labor, he built roads, canals, a great wall, and a vast tomb. Standard weights and measures, and a single currency and script were introduced.

The First Emperor's death, in 210 BCE was followed by widespread rebellions. In 206 BCE, one of the successful rebels, Liu Bang, founded the Han Dynasty, which lasted from 206 BCE to 220 CE. Literature, history, and philosophy flourished in the Han period and trade routes increased contact across Asia.

BELIEFS AND RITUALS

The supreme Chinese deity was Tian (heaven), under whose authority the emperor ruled on Earth. People also believed in the close relationship between the living and their ancestors, who required regular offerings to keep them happy in the afterlife. During the Han period, a new religion, Buddhism, was introduced.

central mountain connects to heaven

Mountain jar
The lid of this Han dynasty jar is shaped like a mountain range. In Chinese belief, mountains were sacred places. Their minerals and plants were believed to bestow immortality.

incense sticks placed here

Incense burner
This pottery jar held sticks of incense, burned as an offering to the ancestors. The dead were thought to belong to the same community as the living.

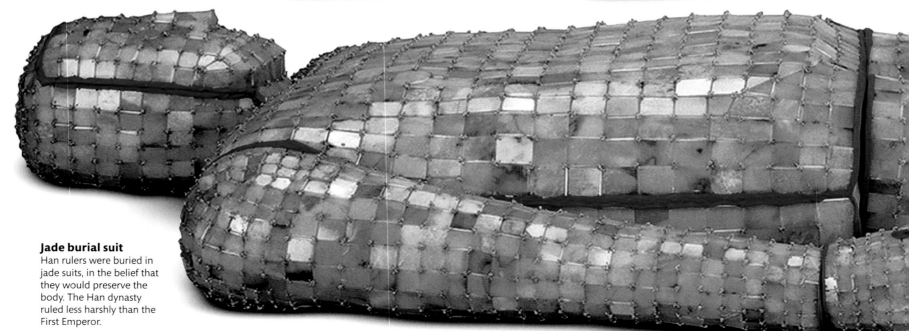

Jade burial suit
Han rulers were buried in jade suits, in the belief that they would preserve the body. The Han dynasty ruled less harshly than the First Emperor.

Jade protector
This piece of jade, carved with the face of a monster, may have been a body protector or part of a body suit used in a burial.

hole for sewing onto garment

serpentine body

Goose vessel
This bronze goose is a vessel for pouring wine, to be used by the dead in the next life. The dead were often buried with plentiful supplies of food and drink.

Hinged beak
The bird has a threatening pose, with an outstretched neck. At the tip is a hinged beak, for ease of pouring.

bronze ring may have been used to attach handle

vessel stands on large webbed feet

Jade dragons
In Chinese belief, the dragon was a symbol of strength and good luck. These two jade dragons may have been worn as pendants on a belt.

Bi disk
The dead were sometimes buried with ritual jade disks placed on the chest or stomach. They were circular, representing the domed heavens.

eye plaques

ear stopper

nose protector

cicada amulet

features and detail painted onto clay

Grave guardian
This ceramic tomb guardian figure is in the shape of a mythical Chinese creature, probably a *bixie*.

Stone mask
This late Han dynasty mask carries an inscription that reads: "A man's face is the precious possession of the immortals."

Face protectors
In Han China, a corpse's orifices, such as the ears and mouth, were plugged with jade. The cicada, put on the tongue, signified new life.

red silk trim

jade plaque—one of 4,000 that make up suit

gold wire threaded through holes to link plaques.

Serving woman
During the Han dynasty, often the dead were buried with small models of people to serve them in the next world.

PREPARING FOR ETERNITY

TERRA-COTTA SOLDIER

In 210 CE, the First Emperor was buried in a vast tomb beneath a man-made mountain, which has still not been excavated. According to the Han historian Sima Qian, it took 70,000 workmen to build the tomb, which contained a great model of China, with flowing mercury representing rivers and the sea. Tests on the soil have shown that the center of the tomb does indeed contain high levels of mercury. The toxic metal was mistakenly believed to confer immortality. Ironically, the emperor's early death, at the age of 40, was probably hastened by taking immortality pills, made from poisonous mercury.

and the vengeful ghosts of all the men he had killed. The emperor intended to continue ruling for eternity from his tomb, so he was buried with terra-cotta civil servants. To keep him amused, he also had an army of entertainers. There were terra-cotta acrobats, musicians, and strongmen buried alongside bronze dancing waterbirds.

AFTERLIFE ARMY

In 1974, farmers digging wells to the east of the tomb discovered the first of four pits, which together held an army of 7,000 life-size terra-cotta warriors. The warriors were accompanied by 130 bronze chariots, 520 terra-cotta chariot horses, and 150 cavalry horses. One pit contained 40,000 bronze weapons, the blades of which were still razor sharp. Another was full of sets of armor—made from stone plates rather than the usual lacquered leather. Stone was thought to offer spiritual protection against ghosts. The army's role was to protect the emperor in the afterlife from demons

Lined up

The figures stand in corridors, separated by banks of earth, lined with wooden beams which originally supported a wood roof. The warriors face east, with the tomb they are protecting behind them.

Face on

The faces of the horses and warriors were made in molds, then details such as eyes, noses, and ears were hand finished by potters.

Standing guard

The warriors stood at attention, holding weapons to protect the emperor. Most of the swords, bows, and halberds were either looted or have perished.

red ribbon secures hair knot

eyes painted white

scarf painted bright blue

red cords

brown armor with white rivets and red cords

armor covers chest and upper arms

blue trim at edge of sleeve

shallow shoes have square tips

traces of green paint visible

right hand open to hold crossbow

long jacket worn under armor

individual details, such as hairstyle, were hand finished

Kneeling warrior
The soldiers were originally painted with bright colors, which have now faded. Traces of paint are still visible on this kneeling archer. Most of the soldiers had their faces painted in realistic flesh colors, but this archer's face was painted green. The position of his hands suggests that he once held a crossbow.

REAR VIEW OF WARRIOR

BATTLE AND CONFLICT

Chinese warfare was fought using large armies of conscripted peasants. They fought mostly on foot, although armies also included chariots and cavalry. Among their weapons were halberds, spears, swords, and the crossbow, which was invented during the Warring States period.

Armor
Foot soldiers wore armor, made of plates of leather stiffened with lacquer and sewn together with colored string. These plates are from the Warring States period.

leather plate

decoration covers jar

chromium oxide coating

War booty
This bronze jar dates from the Warring States era. An inscription records that it was taken by Chen Zhang, during an attack on the state of Yin.

Bronze sword
The Chinese made swords from bronze, coated with chromium oxide to keep them sharp.

POLITICS AND GOVERNMENT

Under the Qin and Han dynasties, China was ruled by an all-powerful emperor, governing through a vast civil service. Emperor Wu, who came to power in the second century BCE introduced civil service examinations, which tested knowledge of Confucian texts.

tall hat worn by Han officials

square hole to string coins together

ink brush

inscription gives weight of coin

Qin coin
The First Emperor introduced a standard coinage. The square hole represented the Chinese view of the Earth as square and the heavens as domed.

Proofreaders
This pair of ceramic figures represents two proofreaders sitting at a table, with a pile of bamboo books. One read the text aloud, and the other searched for errors.

TECHNOLOGY

The ancient Chinese were the most technologically advanced civilization on Earth. By the 6th century CE, they had invented cast iron, porcelain manufacture, paper, the magnetic compass, and the seismometer, a device for gauging the direction of earthquakes.

decoration mimics lacquerware

bronzelike glaze

Silk cocoon jar
This early Han dynasty jar is based on a silk cocoon. Chinese silk was highly prized in the West, where nobody knew how it was made.

Hu vase
This Han dynasty vase, called a Hu, was made with a lead-based glaze, tinted green with copper oxide to mimic bronze.

DAILY LIFE

The vast majority of the Chinese lived as peasant farmers, growing rice in the south and millet in the north. Much of our knowledge of daily life comes from tomb offerings. Although these usually belonged to the wealthy, they often include models of ordinary people and humble buildings, such as pigsties and sheepfolds.

model sheep

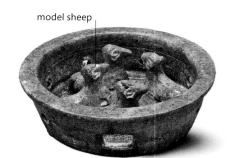

Sheepfold
This Han dynasty pottery model of a sheepfold was made as a tomb offering – a substitute for real sheep in the afterlife.

model pig

sloping path leads up to toilet

Pigsty
This tomb model shows a pigsty with a toilet above. A hole in the toilet allows the waste to fall down to be eaten by the pigs.

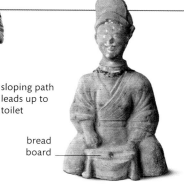

bread board

Kneeling woman
This kneeling woman is a Han dynasty tomb offering. She is probably a servant, rolling dough on a board to make bread.

YAYOI AND KOFUN JAPAN

From 300 BCE, Japanese society changed radically after the introduction of wet-rice farming fed an increased number of settled, agrarian communities. Clan nations emerged and, by the 6th century CE, the Yamato had united the country.

Resting place ▷
This aerial view of Daisen-Kofun in Sakai, shows its distinctive keyhole shape. The biggest tomb in Japan, at 1,595 ft (486 m) long, it is believed to be the burial place of Emperor Nintoku, one of the early Yamato kings.

Two new processes transformed Japanese society when they were introduced from the East Asian mainland in around 300 BCE. The method of growing rice in flooded fields and metal-working skills spread from the south to reach all of Japan. Society divided into classes and clan nations fought for dominance. Historians call this the Yayoi period, after a region of Tokyo where pottery from the time was first discovered.

The most powerful clan nation was the Yamato, which conquered all of Japan by the 5th century BCE. Yamato rulers claimed to be descendants of the Sun goddess, Amaterasu. They were buried beneath huge keyhole-shaped burial mounds, surrounded by moats, called *kofun*. Rulers had close links with China and Korea. The Korean kings sent missionaries to Japan, introducing Chinese script in 405 CE and Buddhism in 552 CE.

BELIEFS AND RITUALS

The Japanese believed in spirits, *kami*, which were thought to reside in objects, such as trees and rocks and in natural forces, such as lightning. The word Shinto, meaning "way of the spirits" was introduced in the 6th century CE to describe this native belief system and to distinguish it from Buddhism.

characteristically thin sheet of bronze

Dotaku bell
Bronze-workers made richly decorated bronze bells, called *dotaku*. These were probably rung during ceremonies to ensure good harvests.

mizura hairstyle, worn by men in ancient Japan

head has broken from the body

Haniwa head
The Yamato kings had pottery figures of men, animals, and horses buried around their *kofun* mound tombs. These models, called *haniwa*, were believed to offer magical protection.

TECHNOLOGY AND INNOVATION

Rice farmers used wooden hoes and stone-bladed reaping knives. The technique of making bronze was introduced in the Yayoi period, but was reserved for ceremonial items, such as *dotaku* bells. Iron working also developed and was used to make weapons. Innovations in ceramics included the creation of wheel-thrown kiln fired pots.

clean, functional shape

Yayoi bowl
Until the Yayoi period, Japanese pottery was made by coiling tubes of clay. But this Yayoi bowl was made on a potter's wheel, allowing a regular shape.

typical combed design

Burial vase
This tall Yayoi vase is decorated with lines made with a stick. It was buried as a grave offering and probably held rice wine.

THE FIRST CITIES OF MESOAMERICA

In the late first millennium BCE, sophisticated urban societies appeared across Mesoamerica. An important common feature was the building of temple pyramids. People worshipped similar gods and played a similar ritual ballgame. Mesoamericans also invented writing systems and complex calendars.

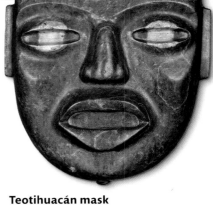

Teotihuacán mask
Mesoamerican peoples made stone masks, which they attached to the bodies of the dead to represent an immortal face.

Teotihuacán ▽
At its height, in 500 CE, Teotihuacán was one of the largest cities in the world. It was dominated by two vast temple pyramids and was laid out on a grid, with straight, wide streets and open plazas for ceremonies.

The first true city in Mesoamerica was Monte Albán, founded by the Zapotecs in about 500 BCE. Like the Olmec, the Zapotec devised an early writing system, using glyphs (signs) to name sacrificed enemies portrayed on stone stelae. Later monuments name enemy places in and around the south Mexican Oaxaca Valley that the kings of Monte Albán defeated, to create an empire that lasted until c.700 CE.

The biggest city in Mesoamerica was Teotihuacán, founded around 100 BCE and lasting until the 7th or 8th century CE. The city may have begun as a sacred center. A cave beneath the Pyramid of the Sun was regarded as the place where humanity emerged into the world and as the entrance to the underworld. Some of the buildings were painted with mythical scenes. The ceremonial center of the city was the Avenue of the Dead, with the Pyramid of the Sun and the Pyramid of the Moon.

The city of Teotihuacán was the center of a state that influenced the whole of Mesoamerica, including the Maya city-states. It was a great manufacturing center, importing raw materials and exporting jewelry, pottery, and obsidian tools.

THE MAYA

From around 200 BCE, the Maya began to build temple pyramids in the rain forests of eastern Mesoamerica. They lived in city-states that were ruled by kings who were their mediators with the gods. Wars between rival kingdoms aimed to capture kings for sacrifice to the gods. The Maya also devised the only complete writing system used in Mesoamerica.

BELIEFS AND RITUALS

Across Mesoamerica, there was a belief that the gods needed to be fed in order to maintain the Universe. People offered their own blood and sacrificed prisoners of war. Ceremonies were performed by kings and priests, who were also shamans—people believed to contact the gods through trance and spirit possession induced by hallucinogens.

cloth headband
earspool
bird's head
hourglass-shaped base of censer

Maya toad
This Mayan bowl is in the form of a giant toad. Some toad species produce a poison, called bufotenine, which shamans took to induce visions.

hole for carrying
conch shell

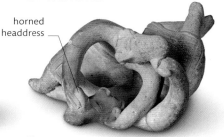
horned headdress

Conch trumpet
Throughout Mesoamerica, conch shells were blown as trumpets and used in ceremonies to announce the presence of gods. This Zapotec one has holes bored into it.

Man with conch
This pottery figure of a man has a conch shell at his navel. The figure was a tomb offering and is from the Nayarit people of western Mexico.

Incense burner
All Mesoamerican peoples burned incense, made of copal (tree resin), as an offering to the gods. In Teotihuacán, the incense was burned in richly decorated ceramic censers.

Shamans
This figurine from Colima in Mexico shows two wrestlers, whose horned headdresses identify them as shamans. It may show them being possessed by spirit beings.

jester god wears an elaborate headdress
Zapotec symbol for water
snakelike forked tongue represents lightning bolt

Mayan writing
These two jaguar femurs, from a Mayan tomb, are carved with writing and images of kings wearing the headdresses of gods. They may have been used as drumsticks in ceremonies.

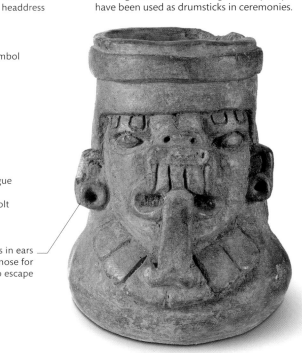
holes in ears and nose for smoke to escape

Lightning god
This clay urn depicts Cocijo, the Zapotec rain god. A similar rain god was worshipped by many Mesoamerican peoples, who called him different names.

Zapotec symbol for cornfield

Zapotec censer
This incense burner would have been used in ceremonies to bring rain. The face on the front is the Zapotec rain god, Cocijo.

Offering vessel

Zapotec rulers and nobles were buried with effigy urns, which depict gods and royal ancestors, who were consulted as oracles. Pots like this were placed in tombs beside the bodies of the dead or in niches on the walls. They held food or drink offerings, which would sustain the dead in the next world. This urn is in the form of an old man.

SIDE VIEW

FRONT VIEW

wrinkled face shows traces of original black paint

large ear flare

only four toes

Headdress

Animal heads on headdresses represent gods or supernatural forces. This old man wears the head of a peccary, a wild pig that lives in the Mesoamerican rain forest.

traces of red paint remain

beaded necklace with a large pendant

pot to hold food and drink

Seated man
This Zapotec effigy urn is in the shape of a seated man. Offerings were placed in the urn through an opening in the head.

Zapotec owl beaker
This beaker is incised with an image of an owl. Associated with night and the underworld, owls were seen as messengers from the gods.

owl incised in low relief

tail forms the spout

Dog effigy urn
Dogs were believed to help the dead travel to the underworld, and pottery dogs were often placed in tombs. Dogs were raised for meat and eaten at feasts.

CLOTHING AND ADORNMENT

Across Mesoamerica, nobles wore colorful cotton while the poor dressed in coarser textiles woven from the fibers of the maguey plant. Both men and women wore jewelry, in the form of necklaces, bracelets, ear spools, and pectorals. Nobles also wore tall, elaborate headdresses, decorated with the feathers of tropical birds.

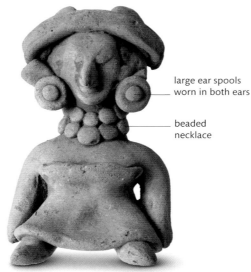

large ear spools worn in both ears

beaded necklace

Figure of a woman
Mesoamerican clothing was made by draping material around the body instead of cutting and tailoring cloth, as this pottery figurine shows.

drilled eye hole

Squirrel pendant
This squirrel pendant from Teotihuacán is carved from jadeite, which was the most prized mineral in Mesoamerica.

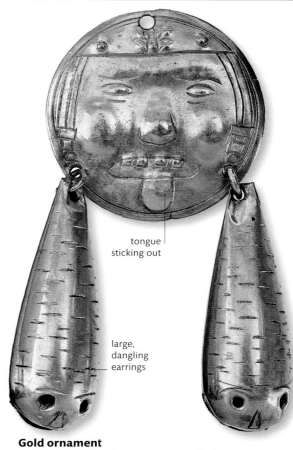

tongue sticking out

large, dangling earrings

Gold ornament
Metallurgy was introduced to Mesoamerica from South America, where gold was highly prized. This gold ornament was made by the Zapotec.

Clay ear spool
Men and women wore ear spools made of obsidian and other materials. This one, from Teotihuacán, is made of black clay.

Jadeite ear flare
Teotihuacán was a jewelry manufacturing center and jadeite, used to make this ear flare, came from Oaxaca, Guatemala, and Costa Rica.

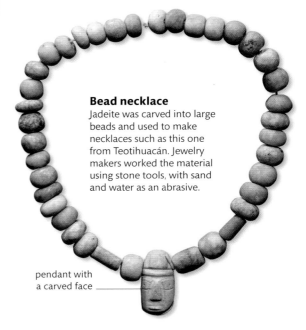

Bead necklace
Jadeite was carved into large beads and used to make necklaces such as this one from Teotihuacán. Jewelry makers worked the material using stone tools, with sand and water as an abrasive.

pendant with a carved face

THE MYSTERIOUS NAZCA AND MOCHE

After the decline of Peru's earliest civilization, the Chavin (see p.55), two regional cultures evolved: the Nazca, who made large, enigmatic drawings in the southern desert; and the Moche—northerners who created beautiful ceramics.

Nazca Lines ▷
Clearing away dark surface stones to reveal the lighter soil beneath, the Nazca drew huge pictures of birds, whales, and other creatures. This spider is 148 ft (45 m) long. The purpose of these images is not known, although they may have been offerings to the gods.

The Nazca civilization was at its height from around 200 BCE to 650 CE. The Nazca mummified their dead, dressing them in magnificent textiles woven from llama, alpaca, and vicuña wool. They also produced pottery decorated with motifs of animals and supernatural beings. The same figures appear in their geoglyphs—huge drawings made in the desert. These were discovered by the Peruvian archaeologist Toribio Mejia Xesspe while hiking through the region in

1927. From the 1940s, they were studied and preserved by the German mathematician Maria Reiche.

The Moche civilization developed later, lasting from around 200 to 800 CE. This society was ruled by warrior nobles who went to war to seize captives for torture and sacrifice. The Moche built large mud-brick pyramid tombs for their rulers and buried them surrounded by treasures. This culture is best known for its fine ceramics.

BELIEFS AND RITUALS

Evidence for religious beliefs comes from painted pottery. Both the Nazca and the Moche depicted scenes of human sacrifice. Moche vases show bound prisoners being killed. Nazca vases often portray a supernatural being holding severed human heads. Both peoples worshipped nature gods, which took on the form of animals.

conical spout at back of vessel

whiskers on cheek

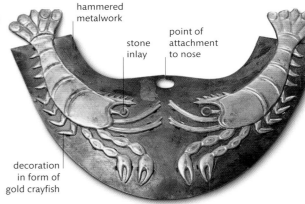

hammered metalwork

point of attachment to nose

stone inlay

decoration in form of gold crayfish

Moche nosepiece
Moche lords pierced the septums of their noses in order to wear elaborate nosepieces. This 5-in- (13-cm-) wide silver and gold nosepiece was found in a Moche tomb.

Nazca fisherman pot
Nazca pots often illustrate scenes from everyday life. This pot is shaped like a fisherman, with a net and a large fish caught on a line.

Nazca animal head
Both Moche and Nazca pots depict men dressed as animals. They represent shamans contacting animal spirits or gods. This pot is in the form of a man wearing an animal headdress, with painted whiskers.

Moche earspools
These earspools show an eagle-headed warrior holding a shield and club in one hand and a sling in the other. They are made of turquoise, coral, lapis lazuli, and gold.

Bean-shaped bottle

bottle opening

The Moche people made pots in the form of their staple foods—potatoes, corn, and beans. This red clay bottle is shaped like a bean.

decoration of bands with diagonal lines and dots

Trumpet

Many Moche pots were in the form of trumpets, which would have been played during ceremonies. Vases also show Moche warriors playing drums, flutes, and panpipes.

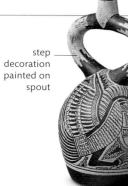

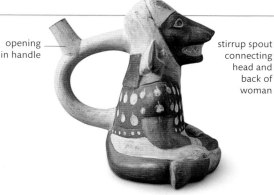

step decoration painted on spout

opening in handle

Stirrup pot

This Moche vessel, called a stirrup pot, shows a bird feeding from a bowl. The spout of the pot allowed air to enter through one side so that the liquid could pour smoothly out through the other.

Clay pot

Another Moche pot shows a seated figure with the head of a dog, perhaps an animal spirit. Pots like this were made by pressing clay into molds.

stirrup spout connecting head and back of woman

Potato-shaped vessel

This Moche pot is in the form of a potato. It has the head of a woman and a smaller head bursting out of the side, just as shoots spring from a potato.

part of decapitator's body shaped like snake

SIDE VIEW

knife held in left hand

decapitator with trophy heads

BACK VIEW

Nazca decapitator pot

The Nazca collected trophy heads for public display. Many skulls have been found with holes made in them, so they could be hung from ropes. This pot shows a supernatural being holding a knife and severed heads.

spouted pot

decapitator

large headdress with snakes

nose ornament

By the start of the 6th century, the old classical empires of Rome and Han China had fallen. China recovered under the Tang and the Song, while the new Islamic world preserved much classical learning and produced a vibrant culture that spanned much of the Middle East and North Africa. At the same time, distinctive cultures flourished across India and Southeast Asia and in the Americas. By the late 15th century, Europe had become a preeminent technical and military superpower.

TRADE AND EMPIRE

600–1450

EUROPE'S GERMANIC KINGDOMS

After the Roman Empire collapsed in the 5th century CE, many Germanic invaders, groups who had lived in Europe beyond the borders of the Empire, set up kingdoms across its former territory. These Germanic peoples had a distinctive culture and artistic tradition. Initially pagan, they gradually converted to Christianity.

Anglo-Saxon Christianity
This garnet, gold, and enamel pendant has a cross shape in the middle and probably dates from the very early days of Christianity in modern Kent, England.

Moutier-Grandval Bible ▽
This Bible formed part of the early 9th-century campaign by the Frankish ruler Charlemagne to revive classical learning. Known as the Moutier-Grandval Bible, it features beautifully illuminated pages, including this frontispiece of *Genesis* showing the story of Adam and Eve.

The last Roman soldiers left England in 410 CE. After their departure, war-bands who crossed the North Sea from present-day Germany, Frisia, and Jutland pushed the Celtic kingdoms back towards the western and northern fringes of England and into Wales.

The barbarian raiders—Angles, Saxons, and Jutes, collectively known as Anglo-Saxons—established kingdoms. These groups controlled much of England by the mid-7th century. The Anglo-Saxons brought a Germanic language, the distant ancestor of modern English, which displaced Latin, and followed their own pagan religion instead of the Christianity of the Roman Empire. Gradually, four Anglo-Saxon kingdoms absorbed the rest. As their rulers consolidated power, their courts developed the rudiments of a royal administration, issuing law-codes and charters.

In 597, the king of Kent converted to Christianity and, as the religion spread across the Anglo-Saxon kingdoms, artists produced fine illuminated manuscripts, especially Gospels and other devotional objects.

FRANKS AND GOTHS

In other parts of the former Roman Empire in the west, new groups filled the political void, but retained much of Roman culture. Germanic peoples such as the Franks (in modern France and Belgium), the Visigoths (in Spain), and the Ostrogoths and Lombards (in Italy), set up kingdoms. In these areas the influence of Roman culture meant that cities were not abandoned and the invaders began to speak a variant of Latin rather than imposing their own language.

BATTLE AND CONFLICT

The Anglo-Saxons did not have standing armies, but rulers could summon a levy, the *fyrd*, to supplement their household retainers if conflict broke out—as it often did—with neighboring kingdoms. Most warriors were lightly armed, with axes or the scramasax, a type of knife. Few had metal armor, and only the elite were able to afford swords.

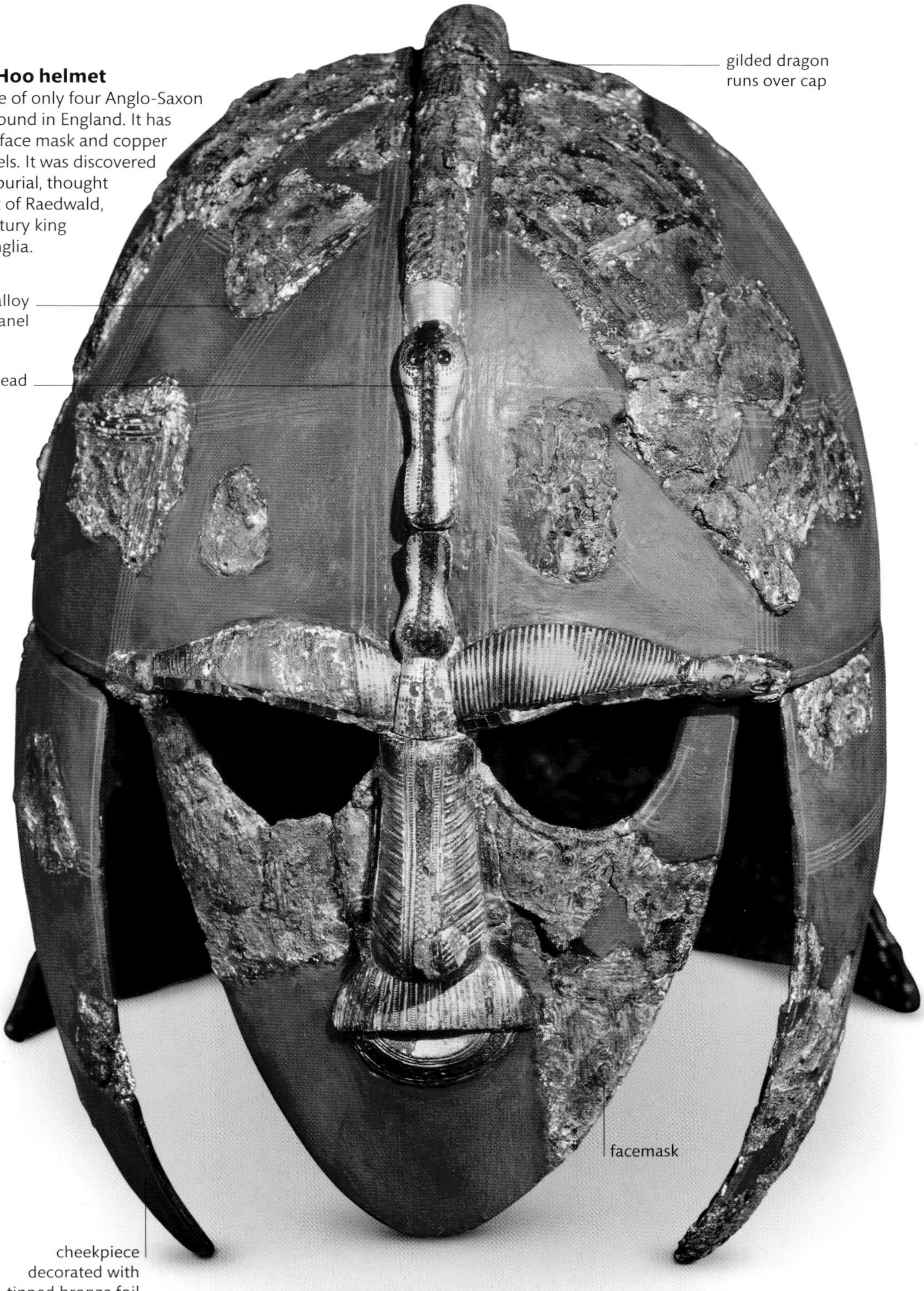

Chain-mail shirt (replica)
The hundreds of tiny metal rings in chain mail offered good protection against sword or dagger thrusts. These shirts were too expensive for common warriors, who could only afford leather.

gold and enamel pendant

Sword bead
Warriors believed this type of pendant could heal wounds, so they attached it to a scabbard as a good luck charm.

Sutton Hoo helmet
This is one of only four Anglo-Saxon helmets found in England. It has a striking face mask and copper alloy panels. It was discovered in a ship burial, thought to be that of Raedwald, a 7th-century king of East Anglia.

gilded dragon runs over cap

copper alloy panel

dragon's head

facemask

cheekpiece decorated with tinned bronze foil

protruding metal boss

Trilby shield
Anglo-Saxon shields were normally round, composed of wooden strips and covered in leather, but this example is in bronze.

tough single-edged blade

Scramasax
Also known as seax, this small, single-edged knife was used by an Anglo-Saxon warrior as a secondary weapon in hand-to-hand fighting. The blades were 3 in (8 cm) to over 19½ in (50 cm) long.

double-edged blade

Sword
Anglo-Saxon swords were owned only by the richest warriors. Generally double-edged with a broad blade, swords sometimes had an elaborate pommel to indicate the bearer's wealth.

BELIEFS AND RITUALS

The Germanic invaders of the Roman Empire were largely pagan, although some Goths had already accepted Christianity. By the late 5th century, most of the Germanic rulers were at least notionally Christian, but the Anglo-Saxons took a century longer to convert. Churches and cathedrals were widespread, and much Christian art from the period has survived.

image of figure holding two floral-headed scepters

interlinked oval medallions around cup

applied silver plates engraved and filled with niello

The Alfred Jewel
This object may have been commissioned by King Alfred, the 9th-century ruler of Wessex, England, for use as a pointer to read manuscripts. The image is in cloisonné enamel covered with rock crystal, all encased in gold.

Incense cover (replica)
Cast in copper alloy, this object was used as a cover for an incense bowl in Christian services. The decoration of entwined animals and birds is typically Germanic.

rock crystal

applied silver triangles engraved and filled with niello

CRYSTAL BALL — silver ring attachment

PERFORATED SPOON

Grave goods
This silver-gilt spoon set with garnets and a rock crystal ball were found in the grave of an Anglo-Saxon woman. Many precious objects were placed in the graves of wealthy people.

Anglo-Saxon cross
Dating from the mid-9th century, this Anglo-Saxon cross is made of copper alloy and decorated with silver and niello (an alloy of silver, copper, and lead).

silver and gold inlay

chalice cast in bronze

figures from Germanic mythology

inscription of Duke's name

King David orders the psalms to be written down

St. Jerome receives the Pope's orders to edit the psalms

Tassilo Chalice
This chalice was made for Duke Tassilo of Bavaria (in modern Germany) between 768 and 788 CE. The cup of the chalice is adorned with portraits of Christ and the Evangelists. On the base are images of the Virgin Mary, John the Baptist, and possibly a Lombard queen.

seated figure of a goddess

Gothic *patera*
This 4th-century gold dish, or *patera*, is part of the Pietrosale Treasure, probably a Gothic ruler's hoard. The *patera* may have been used in sacrificial rites.

The Dagulf Psalter
With its lavish ivory book cover, *The Dagulf Psalter* was produced in *c.*780 on the orders of the Frankish ruler Charlemagne as a gift for Pope Hadrian I.

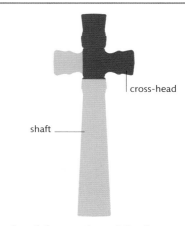

The Rothbury Cross

As Christianity became more firmly established in the 8th century, the Anglo-Saxons began to build religious monuments, notably huge standing-stone crosses, which were particularly common in Northumbria, England. The shafts were decorated with elaborate plant and animal ornaments, often combined with scenes from the Gospels. The Rothbury Cross dates from about 800 CE and depicts the crucifixion.

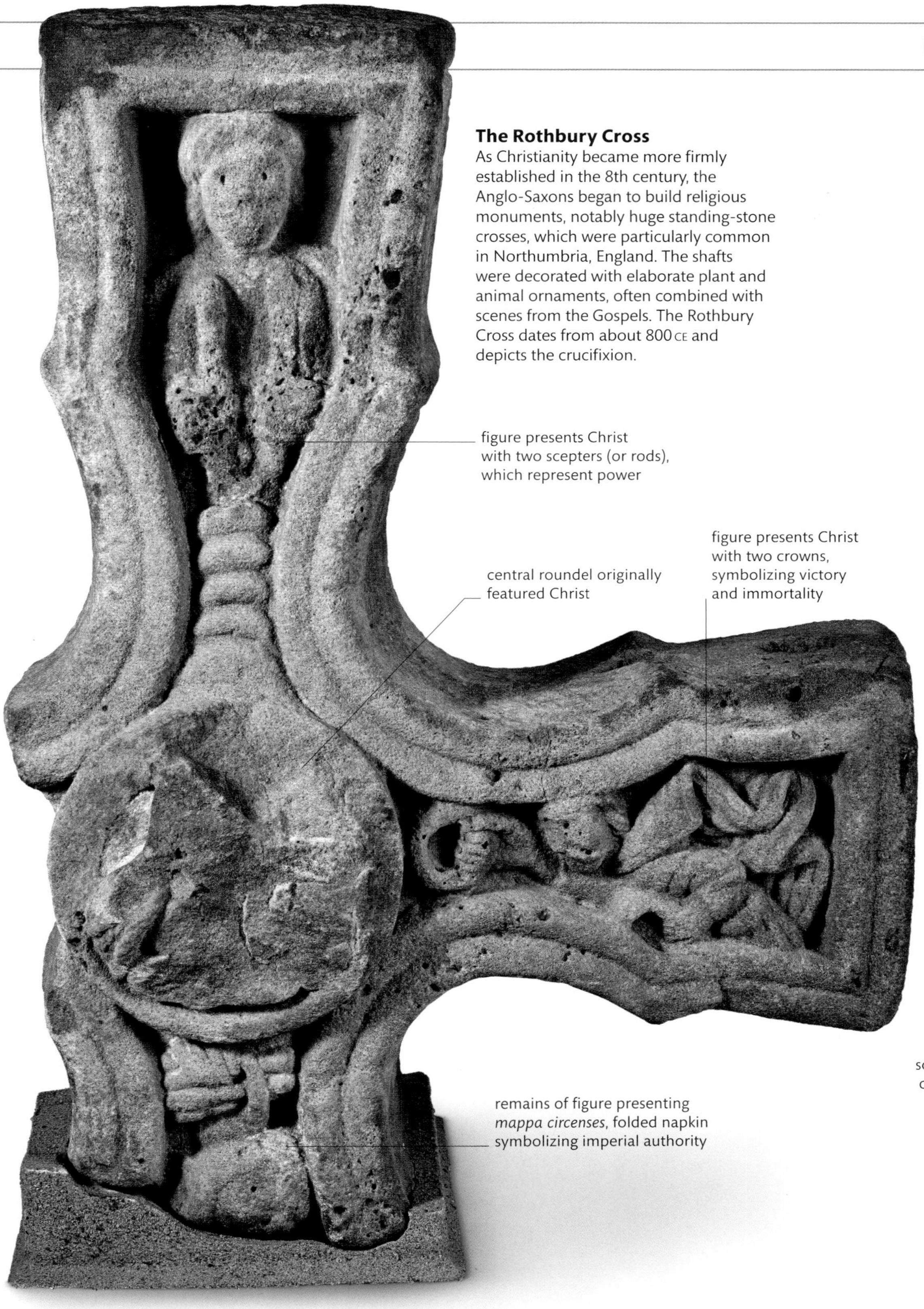

cross-head

shaft

Surviving section of the Cross

Only parts of the Rothbury Cross have survived. The part of the cross-head shown here would have been supported on a tall shaft.

figure presents Christ with two scepters (or rods), which represent power

figure presents Christ with two crowns, symbolizing victory and immortality

central roundel originally featured Christ

geometric interlace or knot pattern

socket with cross-shaft

remains of figure presenting *mappa circenses*, folded napkin symbolizing imperial authority

SIDE VIEW OF THE CROSS

animal shown nibbling vegetation

Christ raising Lazarus from the dead, four days after his burial

crowd looks on as Lazarus is brought back to life

Lazarus rises from the dead

Miracle of Lazarus

Each of the four sides of one section of the shaft shows a different scene. This section focuses on the gospel account of the miracle of Lazarus rising from the dead. Lazarus was a follower of Jesus who died and was laid to rest in a tomb. Four days later, Jesus raised Lazarus from the dead.

CURVING BRANCHES

RAISING THE DEAD

THRONG OF ONLOOKERS

THE MIRACLE

CLOTHING AND ADORNMENT

In a style typical of Germanic dress, early Anglo-Saxon women wore a long-sleeved undergarment with a tubular dress on top, generally fastened at the shoulder by a pair of brooches. Long bead necklaces and leather pouches, worn on belts and containing precious heirlooms, were also common. Men, too, wore brooches as cloak fasteners and prized elaborate belt buckles.

■ CLASPS AND PINS

long, straight pin

Brooch pin
Used to secure head coverings or clothing on the body, the most elaborate pins were of gold or silver, sometimes adorned with garnets.

precious stone

Visigoth eagle fibula
The eagle, a symbol of the Roman Empire, was taken up by the Goths and adorns this 6th-century fibula, or garment fastener, from Visigothic Spain.

■ NECKLACES

BEAD NECKLACE

AMETHYST NECKLACE

stone, glass, and paste beads

Necklaces
Gold and silver necklaces were worn only by women of high status. But necklaces were made of less expensive materials, too. Stones such as amethyst and amber, as well as glass beads, were used to make simple necklaces.

■ BROOCHES

Round brooch
This circular brooch, from 7th- to 9th-century Kent, UK, is particularly finely worked. Set with garnets and decorated with cloisonné and gold filigree, it may have belonged to a woman of high status, but is incomplete—four of the roundels on the front are empty.

gold wire filigree

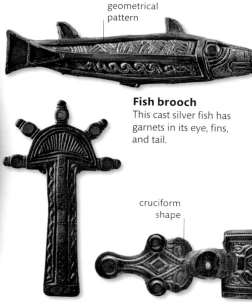

garnet inlay

Bird brooches
The shape of the bronze brooch (left) from Kent resembles others found in northern France, indicating links between the two areas in the early Anglo-Saxon period. The 5th- to 8th-century gold brooch (right) was found in a cemetery in Kent.

geometrical pattern

Fish brooch
This cast silver fish has garnets in its eye, fins, and tail.

cruciform shape

Radiate brooch
This strikingly shaped radiate brooch was used to fasten garments. Fragments of textile were found where they had been crushed by the brooch's spring.

Square-headed brooch
Set with nine garnets, this brooch dates from the 6th century, but its crosslike shape may show Christian influence.

TECHNOLOGY

Much scientific and technical knowledge had been lost after the fall of the Roman Empire, and, although the Germanic peoples were skilled craftsmen, they made limited scientific advances. Most of the ancient technical manuscripts that had survived were only accessible in monasteries, and literacy was not widespread among the general population.

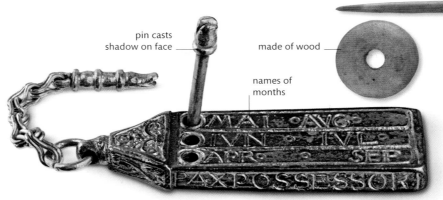

pin casts shadow on face

made of wood

names of months

Anglo-Saxon spinning whorl and spindle
Spinning and weaving were generally done by women. Spinning whorls and spindles like these are commonly found in Anglo-Saxon settlement sites.

Anglo-Saxon portable sundial (replica)
Knowing the time was important for monks who had a regular daily prayer cycle. In this portable sundial, the pin's shadow falls onto the face marked out with hours.

HOME LIFE

The early Anglo-Saxons lived in large communal timber halls, up to 66 ft (25 m) long. Household goods and personal possessions were kept in chests around the sides of the hall. The most commonly found items include pottery and glass vessels, both useful for holding perishable foodstuffs and liquids.

glazed surface

Anglo-Saxon jar
Early Anglo-Saxon pots were handmade in local settlements. Later, specialized kilns were set up, creating pieces such as this fine jar.

nail cleaner

ear cleaner

tooth cleaner

Anglo-Saxon grooming set
Although Anglo-Saxon hygiene was rudimentary, tweezers and more elaborate kits, such as this bronze example, have been found.

▌ GLASSWARE

lattice decoration

Blue glass vase
This squat vase with an interlace pattern was made around 600 by a potter whose work has been found across southern England.

simple form

Pale green jar
Glass-making techniques became simpler after Rome fell. Most vessels were light green, blue, or brown, produced when no extra colorant is added to the glass.

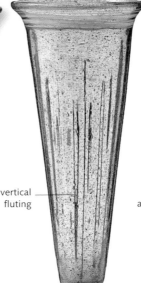

bell-like shape

Bell beaker
Few Anglo-Saxon vessels could stand up on a flat surface. This clear-glass beaker, used for drinking at feasts, was held in the hand.

vertical fluting

Clear-glass beaker
Cone-shaped vessels, such as this one from southeast England, may have been used for toasts: they could not stand upright and had to be drained in a single draught.

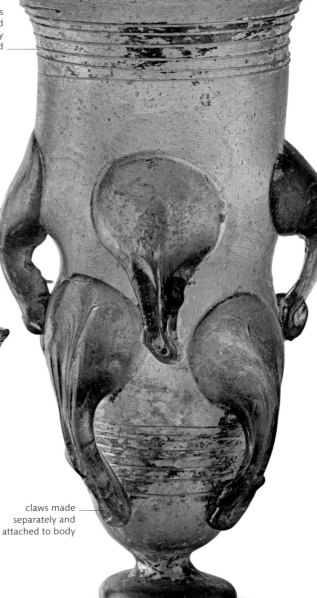

fine glass strips added after body had cooled

claws made separately and attached to body

Green claw beaker
Named after its elaborate clawlike projections, this beaker is typical of a type common in 5th- to 7th-century Kent and France, and provides evidence of close links between the two areas.

VIKING TRADERS AND RAIDERS

The Vikings were raiders from Scandinavia who terrorized the coastlines of northwestern Europe for three centuries, starting around 790. They attacked monasteries and exacted tributes, eventually seizing and setting up kingdoms of their own. The Vikings traded too, and explored the North Atlantic as far as Canada. They also produced art and literature of astounding beauty and power.

Supreme god
This bronze figurine depicts Odin—the principal Norse god, or all-father. He was usually portrayed as a tall, elderly, bearded man.

The Great Army ▷
This 12th-century manuscript shows Viking raiders led by Ingvar and Ubba, two of the leaders of the "Great Army" that invaded England in 865. This band of raiders defeated the Anglo-Saxon kingdoms of Northumbria, Mercia, and East Anglia within five years. They were ultimately beaten by Alfred the Great of Wessex in 878.

Exactly why the Vikings erupted with such ferocity from modern Denmark, Sweden, and Norway is unclear. The tyranny of newly powerful kings, such as Harald Finehair of Norway (c.870–933), could have prompted young men to become raiders. Technical developments in shipbuilding and problems of overpopulation might also have played a part.

The Vikings sailed in sleek longships that could land in harbors without the need for beaches, and allowed them to penetrate far inland up rivers. They used longships in 793 to raid the monastery of Lindisfarne in the Anglo-Saxon kingdom of Northumbria. Within a few years, the Vikings were raiding Scotland, Ireland, and France. Attacking with only a few ships at the start, the Vikings mustered bigger armies by the middle of the 9th century. These forces conquered much of Anglo-Saxon England and threatened to do the same to France for a time.

THE VIKING EXPANSION

Adept sailors, the Vikings used the seaways as conduits for raids, exploration, and trade. Using the Faroe islands and Orkney and Shetland in Scotland as jumping-off points to explore the North Atlantic, they set up colonies in Iceland, Greenland, and even Newfoundland. They reached North America around 1000, almost five centuries before the Italian explorer Christopher Columbus. To the east, the Vikings traveled down the great rivers of Ukraine and Russia, establishing trading outposts and attacking the Byzantine capital, Constantinople.

GODS AND SAGAS

The Vikings were at first pagan, worshipping a pantheon of gods headed by Odin, the all-father. This one-eyed god sacrificed his sight in exchange for knowledge of runes— the ancient Viking script. Thor was popular among young men. The sound of his hammer—*Mjölnir*— striking home was said to be the cause of thunder. His T-shaped amulets adorned the necks of Viking warriors as they fought in the hope of a glorious mention in a saga or a seat in the afterlife at Odin's heavenly hall of *Ragnarök*.

Most of the surviving sagas are from Iceland. Evoking a world where a person's honor was all, they are one of the glories of medieval literature. They also describe how Viking society was organized and how the laws were implemented. Viking warriors lived in systems of surprising complexity, which gave rise to institutions such as the Althing in Iceland, the world's oldest parliament, founded in 930.

ART AND CHRISTIANITY

Living largely in isolated farmsteads, with very few towns until the later Middle Ages, the Vikings were a largely agricultural people. They depended on pastoral farming in large parts of Scandinavia and Iceland. The Vikings also developed sophisticated artistic styles, often portraying snakes, or "gripping beasts," intertwined in complex patterns. Around 1000, the Viking lands became Christian. Churches were built and artists produced beautiful crucifixes and illuminated manuscripts. Scandinavian kings grew more powerful too, and they began to unite what would become the kingdoms of Denmark, Sweden, and Norway. By the middle of the 11th century, this increase in royal authority led to the cessation of the raids. The Viking Age was over.

"Let another's wounds be your warning."
Njal's Saga, c.37

BATTLE AND CONFLICT

Most Viking warriors were armed with axes, spears, and knives. Only the richest could afford swords, which were often family heirlooms. A few warriors also wore an armour formed of an interlinked mesh of metal rings. The warriors relied on the strength and bravery of their companions as they stood side-by-side in the interlocking formation that the Vikings called a *skjaldborg*—a shield wall.

■ ARROWHEADS

sharp iron arrowhead

broad blade

Viking arrows (replicas)
Bows and arrows were used both for hunting and in battle. However, they were not regarded as an honourable weapon by many Vikings, as they killed at a distance. Arrowheads were typically made from iron and produced in various shapes and sizes.

Arrowhead
This arrowhead from Greenland was carved from reindeer antler. It was probably used for hunting reindeer.

■ SPEARHEADS

blade strengthened by rib

Lozenge-shaped spearhead
Spears were among the most common weapons, useful both for thrusting in close combat and for throwing at enemies a few metres away.

Winged spearhead
This spearhead from the 8th century dates from the period just before the Viking raids got underway.

long blade used for thrusting

■ AXES

iron axehead

Iron axehead
This axehead from northern Europe has a convex blade and a hardened edge, welded on separately. It was attached to a wooden handle.

inlays of gold and silver

Mammen axehead
Some axeheads were elaborately decorated with inlays of precious metals, such as this example found in a wealthy man's grave dating from around 970 in Mammen, Jutland.

■ SWORDS

Danish sword
Viking swords, such as this one from Denmark, were normally up to 3 ft 3 in (1 m) long, and blunt-ended, making them more suitable for slashing than for thrusting.

guard formed of large metal plate

Viking sword
This 8th- or 9th-century sword had the simple crossguard and pommel typical of Viking swords. The blades were forged by twisting blocks of iron together and then welding, making them very strong.

rounded pommel

gold inlay

pommel top held in place by rivets

Sword hilt
This ornate Viking sword hilt is inlaid with gold. The hilt was the only part of a sheathed sword that could be seen and was often highly decorated.

■ ARMOR

iron plates welded together over leather cap

typical double-edged iron blade

edge covered in rawhide

Wooden shield (replica)
Typical Viking shields were wooden, around 3¼ ft (1 m) in diameter, with a central metal boss in front of a hand-grip. The boss could be used to strike opponents.

Helmet
This late 10th-century helmet is one of the few Viking helmets ever found. Contrary to the traditional stereotype, the Vikings did not have horns on their helmets.

face-guard

spectacle visor protected eyes and nose

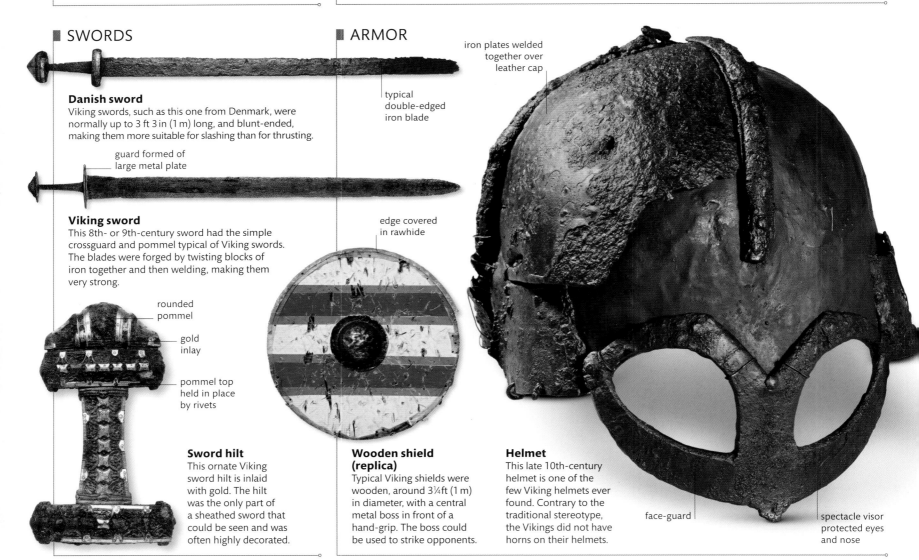

BELIEFS AND RITUALS

The Vikings were initially pagan, believing in a pantheon of gods who lived in great halls in Asgard. Viking warriors who died in battle were believed to go to Odin's hall in Valhalla, their souls taken there by Valkyries—warrior-maidens who served the gods. Around the 11th century, the Viking rulers converted to Christianity, and gradually the old beliefs withered away.

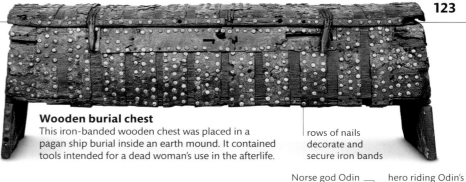

Wooden burial chest
This iron-banded wooden chest was placed in a pagan ship burial inside an earth mound. It contained tools intended for a dead woman's use in the afterlife.

rows of nails decorate and secure iron bands

■ NORSE GODS

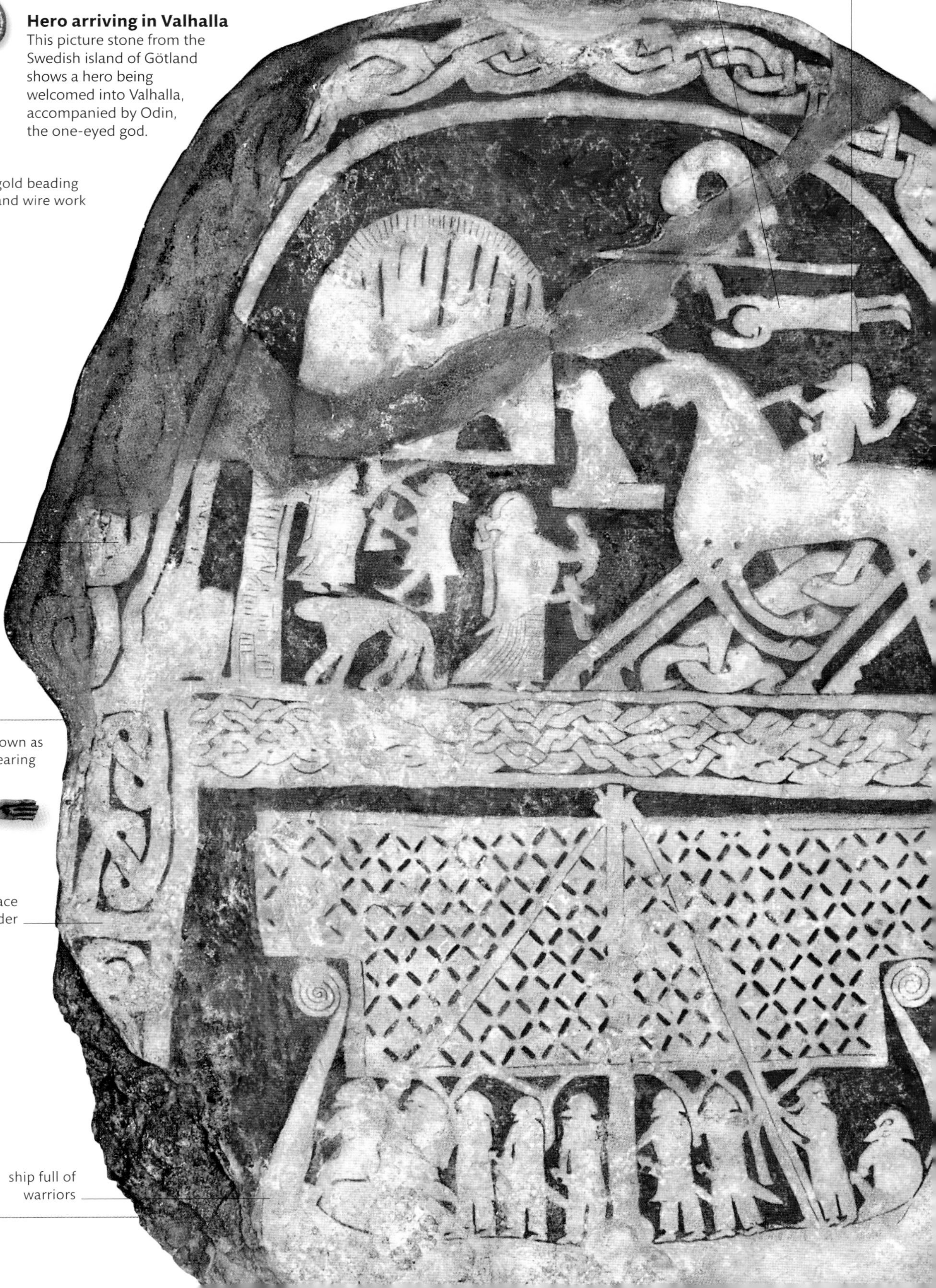

Hero arriving in Valhalla
This picture stone from the Swedish island of Götland shows a hero being welcomed into Valhalla, accompanied by Odin, the one-eyed god.

gold beading and wire work

Stone with hammer and crosses
Used for making pendants, this 10th-century mold has two crosses and an image of the pagan god Thor's hammer on it. It shows that paganism and Christianity coexisted, at least for some time.

Amulet
T-shaped amulets, such as this Thor's hammer amulet from East Gotland, Sweden, are the most widely found archaeological pieces of evidence of Viking pagan belief.

beard symbolizes fertility

piece of limestone carved and painted in 8th century

Statue of the god Frey
This is a small statuette of the god Frey—one of the most widely revered of the Viking deities. He was associated with strength and fertility.

Norse god Odin   hero riding Odin's horse, Sleipnir

■ CHRISTIANITY

Christ shown as a king wearing a crown

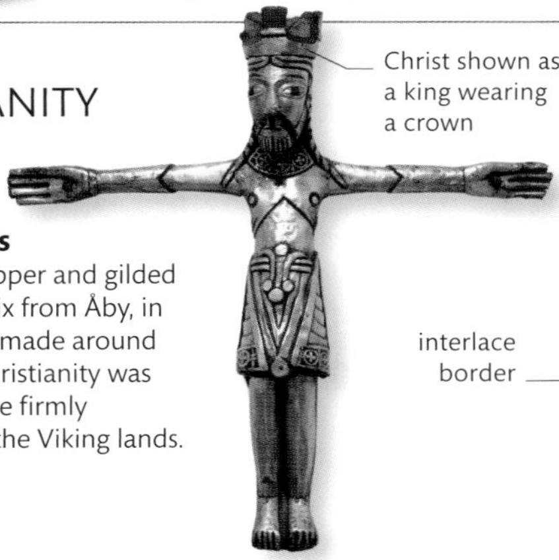

Carved cross
Made from copper and gilded oak, this crucifix from Åby, in Denmark, was made around 1100, when Christianity was becoming more firmly established in the Viking lands.

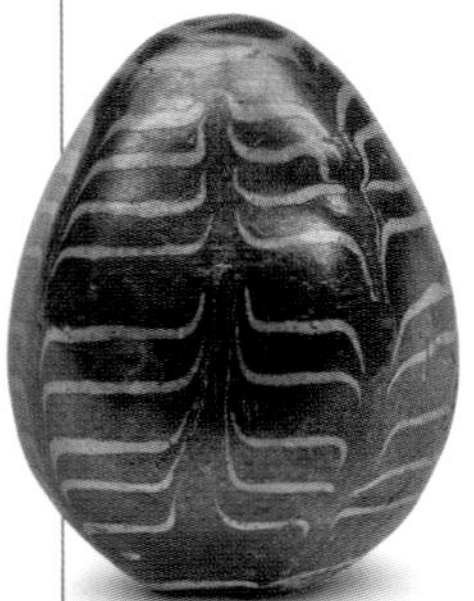

interlace border

Resurrection egg
Eggs such as this one were a symbol of Christ's resurrection. They typically came from cities such as Kiev, on the eastern fringes of the Viking world.

ship full of warriors

TRADE AND TRANSPORT

The first towns established in Scandinavia, such as Birka in Sweden and Hedeby in Denmark, were essentially trading settlements. Cargo from across the Viking world passed through these towns, from walrus tusks acquired in Greenland to Baltic amber and furs gathered along the rivers of the Russian interior.

spruce-wood stick

Axeheads
These unfinished axeheads were found on the shore in Denmark. The spruce to which they are attached came from Sweden or Norway, indicating that these were probably trade items.

copper wire

symbol indicates weight

bronze bowl

lion figure indicates wind direction

Early Danish coins
These coins from the 9th century represent some of the first Viking-issued currency. As royal authority grew, kings issued more coins as a symbol of their power.

Die for striking coins
The Vikings struck coins using dies like the one shown above. Prior to this, they were dependent on coins they gained through tribute or plunder, or on cut-up silver objects (known as hack-silver).

Trader's scales and weight
Viking traders took portable scales and trading weights wherever they went. Their trade routes extended from the British Isles to Russia, and even as far as Baghdad in the Islamic world and Arctic North America.

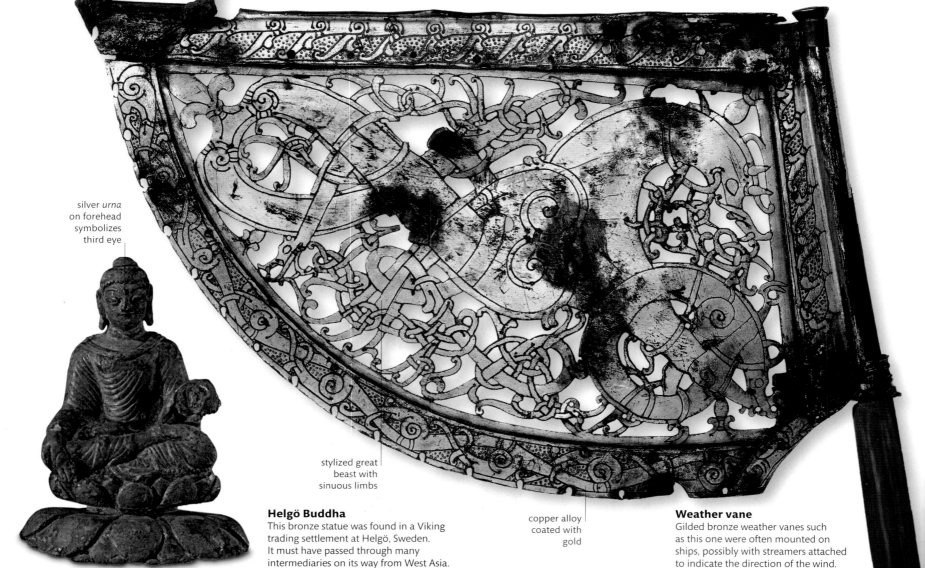

silver *urna* on forehead symbolizes third eye

stylized great beast with sinuous limbs

Helgö Buddha
This bronze statue was found in a Viking trading settlement at Helgö, Sweden. It must have passed through many intermediaries on its way from West Asia.

copper alloy coated with gold

Weather vane
Gilded bronze weather vanes such as this one were often mounted on ships, possibly with streamers attached to indicate the direction of the wind.

TECHNOLOGY

The Vikings were expert craftsmen, whether in creating gold and silver jewelry or using mundane tools to shape the longships with which they plied the oceans. Their main innovations were in shipbuilding, in particular the creation of clinker-built vessels made from overlapping wooden planks, with shallow drafts, which could sail up rivers.

T-shaped adze-head
The Vikings used adzes to smooth wood after felling. They worked with the wood grain, retaining its strength, while axes tended to cut across the grain.

sharp edge could cut through bone and metal

Small hacksaw
This hacksaw was useful for trimming edges off wood and working on fine details.

iron-toothed blade

wooden handle

Wood saw
This saw was used to cut and make grooves, or indentations in planks. It could also be used to add extra carving or ornamentation to ships or to the walls of wooden buildings.

HOME LIFE

The typical Viking dwelling was a longhouse, up to 66 ft (20 m) in length. Rows of posts supported a high roof, and people slept on benches set against the walls. A number of families lived together, with the animals housed in a byre at the end.

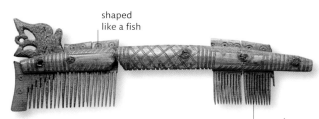

shaped like a fish

Wooden comb
Combs carved from wood or bone are found in almost every Viking settlement. They display the care that the Vikings took over their appearance.

carved teeth

Smoothing board
This bone plaque, decorated with dragon heads, was used with a smooth stone to "iron" wrinkles out of clothes.

fine dragon head with curly mane

openwork decoration, including four gripping beasts

Decorated key
Keys were used to lock the chests in which Vikings kept their valuables. Keys were generally entrusted to the women, as a symbol of their responsibility for the household.

lightweight metal protects clothes from fraying

Clothes pin
Pins are a common find at Viking settlements. Almost all clothes were homemade and were fastened using pins such as these.

carved animal head with open jaws

Animal head post
This dragon head was created in a stone mold, by heating bronze in a crucible over a fire until it melted. The head may have been used to decorate a fancy box.

human figure holding his beard in both hands

two entwined, ribbonlike animals

trailed decoration

Glass cup
Found in a grave, this cup was made in Rhineland, Germany. It could have been traded or plundered by the Viking in whose grave it was found in Sweden.

Silver cup
Known as the Jelling Cup, this cup is no bigger than an egg cup. It is decorated with animals depicted in the Jellinge style of Viking art.

IVORY GAMING PIECE

AMBER GAMING PIECE

Gaming pieces
These pieces from Denmark and Greenland may have been used in *hnefatafl*, a popular Viking board game. The larger amber piece may be the king, which the players tried to capture during the game.

The cache
Ninety-three chess pieces survive from the cache found in the 19th century, but they do not make up complete sets. There are eight kings and queens, 15 knights, 12 rooks, and 19 pawns. Fourteen pieces are plain round tokens, and may have been *hnefatafl* pieces. Some pieces were originally stained red (rather than the black of a modern chess set).

conical helmet typical of Viking warriors

bishop carved with liturgical headdress, staff, and Bible

long spear useful for thrusting at opponents from horseback

bowl-shaped helmet

warder carries long sword

plain piece probably for use in *hnefatafl* game

king holds a scabbard

kite-shaped shield typical of the later Viking period

knight carries kite-shaped shield, ready for battle

berserker bites his shield, a sign of aggression

queen with ornate gown and decorated throne, whose pose resembles that of the Virgin Mary grieving over Christ on the cross

pawn carved with interlocking geometric design

GAME OF KINGS

THE LEWIS CHESSMEN

Made of walrus ivory and whalebone, the Lewis Chessmen are the most remarkable surviving pieces of evidence indicating the pastimes of the 12th-century Vikings. The chess pieces, made around 1150 or 1200, were found in 1831 on a beach at Uig on the Scottish island of Lewis. The Vikings settled in this area in the 9th century. It remained under Scandinavian control until the territory was ceded to Scotland by the Treaty of Perth in 1266.

THE PIECES

The chessmen were buried in a dry-stone chamber inside a sand dune, but exactly why the owner concealed it there is not known. When found, the pieces showed very little sign of wear, indicating that they had not seen extensive use. The chessmen depict figures from the upper levels of most European medieval feudal societies, such as king, bishop, and knight. They also portray typically Viking characters, most notably berserkers—soldiers who would work themselves up into a battle frenzy and rush into combat virtually

unprotected by armor. The chessmen represent the feudal order of society. The pieces were probably made in Scandinavia—possibly at Trondheim, Norway. They may have formed part of the trading stock of an itinerant merchant. Chess had become very popular among the European aristocracy by the 11th century. The fact that Viking chieftains in the Scottish islands were also enjoying the game is a sign of their gradual integration into mainstream European feudal culture.

OTHER POPULAR GAMES

The Vikings played other board games as well. One of the favorites was *hnefatafl,* and boards used to play it have been found throughout the Viking world. In this game, one side had 12 pieces, plus a king, and would try to get the king to escape to the edges of the board. The other side, with double the number of pieces, would try to surround and "capture" the king. After the main phase of the Viking raids ended in the mid-11th century, *hnefatafl* gradually lost its popularity to chess.

THE ORIGINS OF CHESS

Chess originated around 500 CE in India. It spread westward to what is now Iran, and after the country's conquest by Arabic-speaking Muslims in the mid-7th century, chess became popular in the Islamic world. The rules gradually changed, and the Indian war elephant became a bishop. By the 10th century, the game had reached southern Europe and it spread gradually northward from there.

CLOTHING AND ADORNMENT

Viking women generally wore a long overdress with a dresslike pinafore attached to it by two ornate brooches. A shawl could be added for extra warmth. Men wore pants with a long overtunic, and a cloak, which was also fastened with brooches. Men and women also wore various types of jewelry.

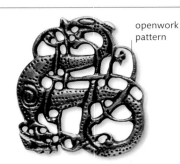

openwork pattern

Gripping beast brooch
This silver brooch portrays a gripping beast—a typical motif of Viking art. The imaginary animal seems to grip its own body with sharp claws.

entwined animal and snake in combat

Urnes-style brooch
This 11th-century brooch follows a relatively late artistic style. A snakelike creature forms its main decorative element.

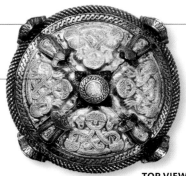

silver and gold inlay

TOP VIEW

FRONT VIEW

Box brooch
In addition to being a closure, this drumlike brooch could also contain small objects. This style was particularly popular on the island of Gotland, Sweden.

plant decoration shows Western European influences, but the technique is Scandinavian

twisted gold wire forms heart-shaped patterns

granules of gold

Gold brooch
This brooch from Hornelund, Denmark, was made by pressing a sheet of gold into a lead die. The surface was then decorated by the jeweler using delicate gold wire to create a sumptuous object, which only the very rich could afford.

BEAD NECKLACE

SILVER NECKLACE

Oriental plant ornamentation

Necklaces
The Oriental-style decoration on this silver necklace shows that Viking trading centers were open to eastern influences from Russia and beyond. The bead necklace is from Gotland, a thriving Viking trading center.

grooves filled with niello, a black compound, to make details stand out

four double-twisted gold rods braided together

Gold neck ring
Twisted gold neck rings such as this one were a favorite Viking adornment. They could be very large, weighing as much as 4½ lb (2 kg)

Pendant cross
This cross-shaped pendant from Birka is evidence of the Christianization of Sweden. Its complex, decorative pattern of dots also includes crosses.

Gold arm ring
Dating from the Christian Viking period, this arm ring bears a design of a mound with three crosses on it, which represents Christ's crucifixion on the hill of Golgotha.

patterns made by stamping, beading, and engraving

ornate engraving

Buckle plate
Made from metal, this plate would have been attached to a leather belt so that it could be buckled. It has two sections, one for each end of the belt.

ART AND CULTURE
Between the 8th and the 12th centuries, Viking art followed a number of different styles, all of which were characterized by the use of interlocking animal figures and gripping beasts, sometimes also with complex patterns of vegetation. From jewelry to wooden panel carvings and runestones, these motifs appear in a wide range of artistic forms.

horned headdress

Swedish warrior with sword

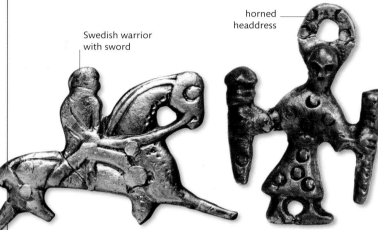

Equestrian silver figure
This silver equestrian figure shows the importance of horses in Viking culture, as evident from their portrayal on such a valuable object.

Silver figurine
This small figurine from Sweden may represent a dancing god. It carries a stave in one hand and a sword in the other.

Bone flute
Made from sheep bone, this musical instrument from Sweden was played like a recorder by blowing into one end while covering one or more of the holes.

sound is produced as air passes through this hole

Calendar stave
This Viking calendar stick or *primstav* from Denmark was engraved with runic inscriptions to indicate the passing of the seasons. These sticks remained in use until 1753.

carved with 657 different marks

RUNES

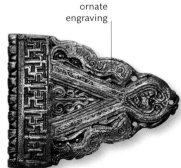

F U THAR K H N I A S T B M L R

The Vikings developed a system of writing using angular symbols called runes, which were easy to carve on wood or stone. The earliest version, developed around 200, had 24 letters, but by about 700, eight of these letters had been dropped. The runic alphabet is called the *futhark* (from its first six letters), but it was never widely used in Viking-age manuscripts, in which the Latin alphabet became universal.

THE GLORY OF BYZANTIUM

The Byzantine Empire was the eastern part of the Roman Empire, which survived after the western provinces fell to Germanic barbarians in the 5th century. It endured for over a thousand years, weathering many invasions and producing beautiful art, until it finally fell to the Ottoman Turks in 1453.

Plundered liturgy
This 9th-century liturgical book, bound in gold and with enamel and pearl decoration, may have been looted by soldiers of the Fourth Crusade in 1204 at Constantinople.

Offerings to god ▽
Empress Theodora (wife of Justinian I) is shown in this mosaic in the church of San Vitale, Ravenna, Italy. She holds a chalice representing Christ's sacrificial blood. Lavishly attired, her dress shows the three Magi presenting gold, frankincense, and myrrh to Christ.

In 330, Constantine the Great, the first Christian ruler of the Roman Empire, moved the capital from Rome to Byzantium, where he founded Constantinople. As Rome withered, Constantinople became the center of a new Christian culture, which drew heavily on classical Greek and Roman precedent. After 451, Byzantine Christianity split from its western counterpart, giving rise to the tradition of Eastern Orthodoxy.

After a resurgence in the 6th century under Emperor Justinian I, who reorganized the laws and reconquered some of the western provinces, the Byzantine Empire was shorn of most of its African and Middle Eastern lands by invading Arab Muslim armies. It almost lost the Balkans to invading Slavs.

The empire reinvented itself to meet these challenges, replacing Roman-style legions with levies raised from large landowners and the judicious use of mercenaries. It was weakened by the advances of the Seljuk Turks in Anatolia from the 11th century, and crusaders who seized Constantinople in 1204 and held it for more than 50 years. The Byzantine Empire was finally destroyed by the Ottoman Turks in the 15th century.

A LASTING TRADITION

The Byzantines produced several imposing buildings, such as the great domed cathedral of Hagia Sophia, constructed under Justinian I. They also produced beautiful religious icons, mosaics, frescoes, and jewelry. Even after Constantinople's fall, the city's artistic and religious tradition exerted a profound influence on the Balkans and Russia.

ADORNMENT

The basis of Byzantine costume, both for rich and poor, was a knee-length tunic. Jewelry continued in the Roman tradition and was an important means of expressing status. In 529, Emperor Justinian passed a law stating that sapphires, emeralds, and pearls were reserved for the emperor, but every free man could wear a gold ring.

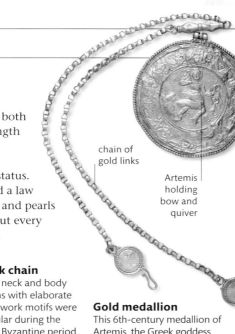

chain of gold links

Artemis holding bow and quiver

chain has 32 links with openwork motifs and a circular pendant

Neck chain
Gold neck and body chains with elaborate openwork motifs were popular during the early Byzantine period. This 6th-century chain was found in a hoard at Scythopolis (now Beth Shean, Israel).

Gold medallion
This 6th-century medallion of Artemis, the Greek goddess of hunting and the Moon, shows that pagan gods were still worshipped after the empire became Christian.

TRADE AND TRANSPORTATION

Coinage was the most common means for ordinary Byzantines to come in contact with the government and the main coin was the gold solidus. Trade was controlled by the imperial government; the most important commodities were grain from Egypt and Tunisia, followed by textiles and metalwork.

FRONT   **BACK**

Gold coin
This early 7th-century gold solidus was found in a hoard of over 3,000 coins buried at Beth Shean. One side depicts Emperor Phocas wearing an imperial diadem.

HOME LIFE

The teeming city of Constantinople had more than 500,000 inhabitants—the rich lived in large houses built around courtyards, and the poor in crowded, basic dwellings. Artisan guilds, such as potters, coppersmiths, and bakers, regulated the commercial life of the cities, while in the countryside most peasants were farmers.

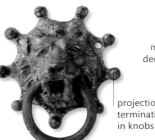

menorah decoration

Oil lamp
In Byzantine homes, light was provided by lamps such as this one. The menorah decoration on one side suggests that it may have belonged to a Jewish family.

projections terminating in knobs

Door knocker
This Byzantine knocker is shaped like a lion and would have stood on the main door of a house.

Silver cup
This intricately decorated Byzantine drinking cup ended up in a hoard in Sweden, looted or traded by Vikings.

BELIEFS AND RITUALS

Religious beliefs lay at the heart of Byzantine life. However, religious disputes also weakened it, with non-Orthodox Christian churches, such as the Monophysites, gaining many adherents in the empire's Middle Eastern and North African provinces. A belief in miraculous intervention and the power of religious icons to aid worshippers were pronounced features of Byzantine Christianity.

Ivory triptych
Ivory carving was a widely practiced luxury trade in Byzantium. This 10th-century triptych was intended for private devotional use.

Cross pendant
This gold and enamel chain and reliquary cross is typical of the religious objects owned by the rich in the Byzantine Empire.

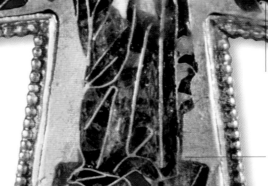

hinge enables cross to open and reveal relic inside

Virgin Mary

Greek inscriptions identify the figures

bust of St. Basil the Great

bust of St. Gregory Thaumaturge

"sunken enamel" style where figures are silhouetted against bare metal

THE TRIUMPH OF ORTHODOXY

Since its earliest times, the Christian Church had been subject to disputes over what constituted orthodoxy—a claim to be the true Church with an unbroken link to the faith, doctrine, and practices of the ancient Church. Within the Byzantine Church a rift

developed over the use of icons—painted images of Christ, the saints, and the Virgin Mary. Veneration of icons occupied a central role in Byzantine Christianity, and especially in popular devotion. However, some theologians were uneasy about prayers

being directed toward the icons, claiming it verged on worship and therefore amounted to idolatry. In 726, Emperor Leo III issued an edict forbidding the veneration of images, a measure confirmed by his successor, Constantine V, at the Church council in Hieria in 754. For a century, the Byzantine Church was torn apart by the doctrinal dispute between those who were opposed to the icons (the iconoclasts) and those who favored their use (the iconodules). There were violent episodes of icon-smashing and persecution of iconodules in the army. The icons were restored in the 780s, but opposition to icons (iconoclasm) returned in 815. Only the accession of Michael III in 843, with his mother

the iconodule Theodora as regent, led to the restoration of the icons, an occasion celebrated in the Eastern Orthodox churches as the Triumph of Orthodoxy. Icons came to occupy an even more important position in Byzantine Christianity, with images of the saints and episodes from the life of the Virgin Mary adorning every church. Smaller icons also found an honored place in every household.

THE DEFEAT OF ICONOCLASM

This 15th-century icon of the Triumph of Orthodoxy commemorates Empress Theodora's restoration of the icons in 843. It reaffirms icon-veneration at a time when the Ottomans, who were followers of Islam, a religion without images, threatened the Byzantine borders.

> " He who **venerates the icon,** venerated in it the **reality for which it stands.** "

Second Council of Nicea, which declared iconoclasm a heresy, 787 CE

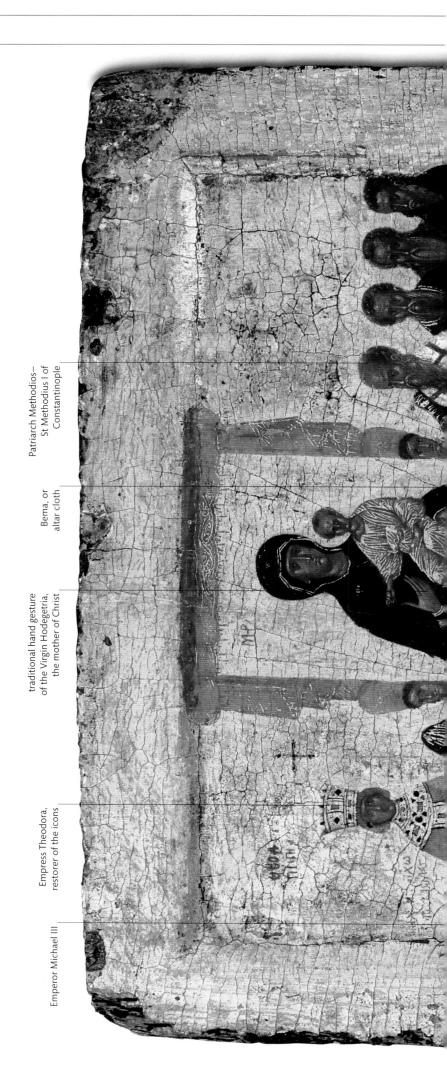

Patriarch Methodios— St Methodius I of Constantinople

Bema, or altar cloth

traditional hand gesture of the Virgin Hodegetria, the mother of Christ

Empress Theodora, restorer of the icons

Emperor Michael III

wooden panel covered in gesso, linen, and gold leaf

St. Theodore

St. Theodosia, holding the icon of Christ

ISLAMIC COURTS AND CALIPHATES

The armies of Islam conquered much of the Middle East and North Africa in the 7th and 8th centuries. This mixing of cultures created a powerful fusion of new religious ideas and existing traditions, producing original political and artistic visions.

An exquisite storehouse ▷
The treasury in Umayyad Mosque, Damascus, was built in 789 as a storehouse for the local governor's valuables. The walls of the treasury are decorated with delicate green and gold mosaic.

A caliphate was an Islamic state ruled by a caliph—a religious and political leader who was a successor to Muhammed and other prophets. The Umayyad caliphate was based in Damascus, from where its power extended west to Morocco. As they moved into areas that had been controlled by the Byzantines, local craftsmen built mosques for the Umayyads in a style following Byzantine architectural traditions. In 750, the Abbasids overthrew the Umayyads and created Baghdad as the new capital. They were patrons of the arts and also cultivated scientific knowledge. Meanwhile, in 909, the Fatimid dynasty established itself in Tunisia, and went on to conquer Egypt, making Cairo their capital. Internal revolts and the Crusades weakened their empire, which ended in 1171. In 1258, Baghdad was sacked by the Mongols, by which point Abbasid power had already waned in the Islamic World.

POLITICS AND POWER

The courts of the first Muslim rulers, or caliphs, were simple encampments on the outskirts of towns, or traveling structures that shifted from place to place. By the time of the Abbasids, the caliphs had large courts and splendid palaces, from which they ruled as autocrats in a similar style to Persian shahs or Byzantine emperors.

tarnished copper surface

Court musician figurine
This figurine from the Fatimid caliphate in Egypt depicts an Islamic lute (*oud*) player. The *oud* was key to the classical Islamic style of music that emerged at the Umayyad courts.

ivory inlay

trained falcon used for hunting wild quarry

Wooden fragment
This piece of wood from Fatimid Egypt depicts a hunting scene. Hunting was a favorite pastime of the Umayyad rulers, who built hunting lodges in the Syrian desert.

engraved with image of courtier

Fatimid glass
Under the patronage of the Fatimid court, there was a renaissance of the decorative arts, notably glass production.

TRADE AND TRANSPORT

The Umayyad Empire was a vast territory within which a single authority regulated and protected trade. The coins of the Umayyad rulers, as well as those of the Abbasids and the Fatimids, were valued within their domains and beyond. At the local level, trade in markets was controlled by officially appointed inspectors.

Silver dirham
For religious reasons, Islamic coins did not bear the ruler's image. Ornate calligraphy was used instead to proclaim the ruler's name or the Islamic credo, as seen on this Abbasid coin.

Gold coin
Fatimid coins such as this one were designed in a distinctive style, with three circular bands of calligraphy instead of regular horizontal writing.

ISLAMIC CULTURES OF SPAIN AND AFRICA

The Islamic lands of southern Spain and Maghreb (northwest Africa) developed distinctive political and artistic traditions. The fusion of Islamic, Jewish, and Christian ideas in southern Spain led to great scientific and cultural achievements.

Lions at the fountain ▷
Nasrid architecture was a hybrid of Maghreb and Christian influences. This courtyard from the Palace of the Lions in Alhambra, Granada, exhibits skilled carving and stonework.

Islamic rule was established in Spain in 711. In 929, Abd ar-Rahman III of the Umayyad dynasty (see p.134) set up a caliphate there. The caliphs patronized art and literature, especially poetry, and built a number of mosques. Jewish and Christian communities were tolerated in the Umayyad Empire, and this combination of traditions produced the unique culture of Islamic Spain, or al-Andalus. In 1031, civil war destroyed the Umayyad caliphate. It was replaced by the Almoravids and Almohads—more austere dynasties from Morocco (part of Maghreb).

Meanwhile, Christian Spanish kingdoms made steady progress in their campaigns to reclaim the peninsula. By 1238, only the Nasrids of Granada survived to build the great Alhambra, before they were conquered by the rulers of Castile and Aragon in 1492.

BELIEFS AND RITUALS

North Africa and Spain had been bastions of Christianity, but while the former was almost entirely Islamized, Jewish and Christian communities persisted in Spain. They were referred to as the Mozarabs, and they adopted many elements of Arab culture.

gold circle serves as verse marker

text in cursive Maghrebi

Koran folio
This page from the Koran is written in the Maghrebi script, which developed in northwest Africa in the 10th century and then spread to southern Spain.

ART AND ARCHITECTURE

Southern Spain and Maghreb were the westernmost frontiers of Islamic art. In Spain, Visigothic influence (see p.114) in architecture was important. Ivory carving and fine stuccos became an Umayyad speciality, to be replaced by a more conservative ethos under the Almohads in the 12th century.

winglike handle

Wooden frieze
The architecture of the Marinids, who succeeded the Almohads, shared many characteristics with that of Islamic Spain, including carved friezes such as this one.

Alhambra vase
Vases such as this glazed model from the Nasrid dynasty are known as Alhambra vases. They are usually painted gold and cobalt and are pear shaped.

seated musician playing a harp

14th-century casket
Sicilian Muslim craftsmen produced works such as this casket for wealthy patrons. Southern Spain was also a major center of ivory carving during the 10th and 11th centuries.

cusped arch

painted cedar

NORMAN CRUSADERS AND CONQUERORS

Europe saw two major upheavals in the 11th century. The first was the conquest of England by the Normans—a people of Viking descent. The second was the launch of the First Crusade in 1096, marking the beginning of a series of military expeditions from Christian Europe to wrest Palestine from Islamic rule.

Knight-shaped ewer
This 13th-century jug, in the form of a horse and rider, exemplifies the courtly ideals of knighthood that pervaded Western culture in the medieval era.

Embarking on a Crusade ▽
This page from the French illuminated manuscript *Order of the Holy Spirit* depicts crusaders departing for the Holy Land. The banners include the papal arms, alongside those of the Holy Roman Emperor and the kings of England, France, and Sicily.

In 911, Charles III of France gave a portion of northern France to the Viking raiders who had settled there. They founded the duchy of Normandy and came to be known as the Normans, later adopting French as their language and Christianity as their religion. From their settlements in Normandy, the Vikings embarked on several expeditions of conquest and colonization elsewhere in Europe.

Duke William of Normandy defeated the Anglo-Saxon ruler Harold Godwinson at Hastings in 1066, ushering in an era of Norman rule that strengthened England's ties with northwest Europe. Norman adventurers also began to invade parts of southern Italy and Sicily. The Normans brought a feudal system to England in which the king allowed the nobility to hold land in exchange for military service, and the nobles let the peasants occupy their land in return for their labor.

RELIGIOUS FERVOR

In the 11th century, religious devotion and the power of the Church grew in Normandy and spread to England.

Many Normans made pilgrimages to Rome and the Holy Land. Initiated by Pope Urban II in 1095, the First Crusade began as a holy pilgrimage and ended as a military expedition to regain the Holy Lands by Roman Catholic Europe. France and England, along with the Holy Roman Empire, seized Jerusalem and set up Crusader states that survived until 1291. Successive Crusades provided reinforcements to these enclaves. The Crusades helped transmit knowledge from the East, such as advances in the art of fortification.

BATTLE AND CONFLICT

Knights were the principal fighting force of medieval monarchies. The charge of these heavily armored troops was almost impossible for infantry to resist. However, such armies were expensive to maintain in the field, and foot soldiers, particularly archers, came to play a more prominent role in the later Middle Ages.

- pommel curves backward around rivet, mirroring crossguard

Curly quillon dagger
This 15th-century English dagger has a crossguard formed by unusual quillons that curve back toward the blade.

- inlaid geometric design

Quillon dagger
Dating from *c.*1400, this English dagger has a distinctive brass pommel. Such daggers were often carried by men of rank when not bearing swords.

■ SWORDS

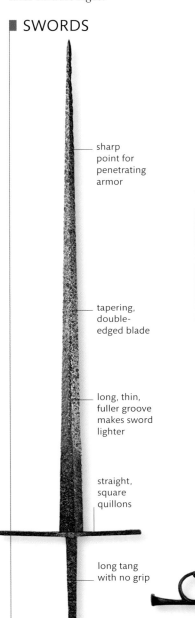

- sharp point for penetrating armor
- tapering, double-edged blade
- long, thin, fuller groove makes sword lighter
- straight, square quillons
- long tang with no grip
- octagonal pommel

- double-edged blade of hexagonal cross section
- double looping finger-guards
- wheel pommel

- double-edged cutting blade
- flattened, diamond-shaped blade in cross section
- straight crossguard
- round pommel

- straight, double-edged blade
- wheel pommel with cap

Hand-and-a-half sword
This 15th-century English sword was mainly used for thrusting. Its extra-long grip allowed the bearer to hold it in both hands.

Transitional sword
This early 16th-century sword was produced during a transitional phase between the heavy medieval blades and the lighter Renaissance rapiers.

Crusader sword
With its broad blade, simple crossguard, and nut-shaped pommel, this sword is typical of the 12th century and the central part of the crusading era.

French sword
The long, tapering point of this 14th-century sword could pierce vulnerable joints in plate armor. Swords like this were becoming widespread at the time.

SIEGE TACTICS

Sieges were more common than field battles in the Middle Ages, and attackers would often try to starve a garrison. Siege engines such as towers were placed against walls, and catapults were used to hurl heavy projectiles. Primitive cannons, like the one shown here, could weaken defenders in advance of an all-out assault.

■ HELMETS

- typical conical shape

Norman helmet
This replica Norman helmet has a downward projecting nose guard. Similar types remained in use from the 7th to the 12th centuries.

Great helm
By the late 12th century, the conical Norman helmets had evolved into models such as this, providing greater all-round protection, at the cost of extra weight.

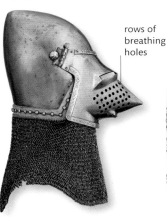
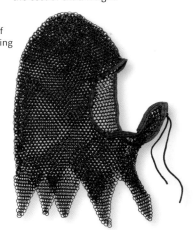

- rows of breathing holes

Italian basinet
This 14th-century helmet has an elongated skull, a visor, and an aventail, or mail neck-guard. Such helmets were nicknamed "dog-faced" or "hounskull" because of their distinct shape.

Chain-mail hood
Hoods, or coifs, could be worn under a helmet for extra protection. They also served as a safeguard when worn without a helmet.

Funeral procession
The body of Edward the Confessor, who died on January 5, 1066, is carried in an elaborate bier, behind which walk a group of tonsured monks.

The diplomat
The tapestry shows Harold Godwinson sailing across the English Channel on a diplomatic mission to Normandy in 1064. He was met by the knights of Guy of Ponthieu, who arrested him.

The wounded king
The figure in this scene with the arrow in his eye may be King Harold. The Latin inscription reads, "Here King Harold was killed." His death caused the collapse of the Anglo-Saxon army.

" **Fight your best** and put everyone to death. What I gain, you gain... We will **never return** to Normandy **disgraced...** with God's aid **we shall conquer.**"

William the Conqueror

embroidery in wool yarn on linen

bird figure on decorative border

Story of the Norman conquest
The Bayeux Tapestry is a piece of embroidery that was made around 1080. First recorded in the inventory of the Bayeux Cathedral, France, in 1476, it begins with Harold's alleged oath to Duke William in 1064 and concludes with the Norman victory at Hastings two years later.

Latin inscriptions describe key moments

tapestry contains more than 200 horses

interlocked shields used to form wall

Anglo-Saxons depicted carrying spears or javelins

NORMAN VICTORY

THE BAYEUX TAPESTRY

Despite its name, the Bayeux Tapestry is actually an embroidered strip of linen more than 230 ft (70 m) long that tells the story of Duke William of Normandy's conquest of Anglo-Saxon England in 1066. Although thought to have been created in England, the narration of the story is from a Norman perspective, depicting scenes of the Norman conquest in a series of episodes. Along the top and bottom run decorative borders with figures of animals, scenes from the fables of Aesop and Phaedrus, and some scenes related to the main pictorial narrative.

This extraordinary work of art provides information about the events that led up to William's expedition to England and his victory at the Battle of Hastings on October 14, 1066. It recounts King Edward the Confessor's despatch of Harold Godwinson—his

successor-to-be—to Normandy, where Harold is shown swearing an oath of fealty to Duke William, promising to uphold his candidacy for the English throne on Edward's death. It goes on to show the Norman duke's expedition to England to uphold that claim after Harold seizes the throne.

BATTLE TACTICS

The Bayeux Tapestry provides valuable contemporary evidence for the military equipment and tactics of mid-11th-century armies. It is by far the best pictorial source of information about the arms and armor of the Normans and Anglo-Saxons.

The men-at-arms on both sides are depicted wearing conical helmets with metal nose guards. The warriors bear kite-shaped shields and a mixture of lances, swords, and battle-axes.

The Norman side is shown to have a contingent of archers, while the Anglo-Saxons have very few. This disparity, together with William's astute use of feigned flight to draw the Anglo-Saxons out of the shield wall and render them vulnerable, ultimately played a crucial role in his victory.

The Anglo-Saxons are depicted forming a protective wall with their shields and spears. The Normans adopted a more fluid approach, with repeated cavalry charges and volleys of arrows to thin the shield-wall. The climax of the battle shows Harold's fall, apparently struck in the eye by an arrow. The final surviving panels of the tapestry show the inevitable end of a medieval battle: the massacre of the fleeing enemy and the ruthless looting of corpses on the battlefield.

Bishop Odo of Bayeux rallies the Normans with his staff; clergymen were not permitted to spill blood

diamond-shaped shield

mail armor made of thousands of interlocking metal rings

Latin text reads, "Here, Odo the Bishop holding a club strengthens the boys"

Norman men-at-arms used bows and arrows

Duke William throws back his helmet to reassure his knights that he is still alive

POLITICS AND POWER

In the late 11th century, kings in England and elsewhere in Western Europe relied on their position as the head of the feudal hierarchy. Gradually, royal courts grew more sophisticated and rudimentary administrations evolved. This enabled the courts to enforce royal justice and collect the taxes needed to engage in long campaigns, such as the Hundred Years War.

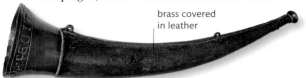

brass covered in leather

Moot horn

Moot horns, such as this one from Faversham in England, were used to summon townsfolk to the moot or assembly. These gatherings had a limited role in local decision making and the election of officials such as the mayor.

inscription of Duke's name

Medallion

The image on a coin or medal was often the only time the common people saw the face of their ruler. This 15th-century medallion shows Charles the Bold, duke of Burgundy.

■ COINS

King Edward III holds a sword and shield

Edward III gold coin

Known as a noble, this was the first gold coin minted in England on a large scale and was produced from the 1340s. It was worth a third of a pound.

Silver coins

These four silver coins span four centuries of English kings, from Cnut (1016–35) to Offa of Mercia (757–96), to Edward the Confessor (1042–66), and Aethelred the Unready (979–1016).

BELIEFS AND RITUALS

The Christian Church played a central role in European life. It grew extremely wealthy and became a patron of specific types of art and literature. Christianity also inspired popular piety, motivating arduous pilgrimages as well as the more militant fervor of the crusading movement.

in Medieval times, green glass was made by adding copper ore or filings to glass

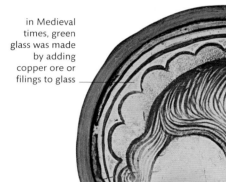

Stained-glass fragment

Part of a stained-glass window, this piece bears the image of the head of a saint. With comparatively low levels of literacy, imagery was an important way of communicating religious messages in medieval Europe.

image of interior of the hospital

Hospitaller seal

This medieval seal belonged to Raymond de Berenger, the Grand Master of the Knights Hospitaller in 1365–74. By this time, Jerusalem had fallen back under Islamic control and the knights were based in Rhodes.

Medicine mortar

Used for grinding medical ingredients, this 12th-century mortar was used by the Knights Hospitaller. Although they were a military order, originally the Knights Hospitaller had been set up to administer a hospital in Jerusalem.

jewels on cuff

Pilgrim badge

Badges such as this one shaped as the hands of St. Thomas Becket were worn by pilgrims as a sign that they had visited a particular holy site, in this case Canterbury, UK.

Pilgrim bell

Miniature bells were another popular souvenir for pilgrims to Canterbury in the 14th and 15th centuries. They were designed to be worn around the neck.

Holy Land pilgrim flask

This water bottle is decorated with the cross of the Order of St. John, or Knights Hospitaller, a charitable religious order established in 1048 to care for pilgrims to Jerusalem.

brightly colored Majolica decoration

Monk's medicine jar

This decorated jar was used by monks to hold medicines. Monasteries and religious orders were the principal repositories of medical knowledge during the early Middle Ages.

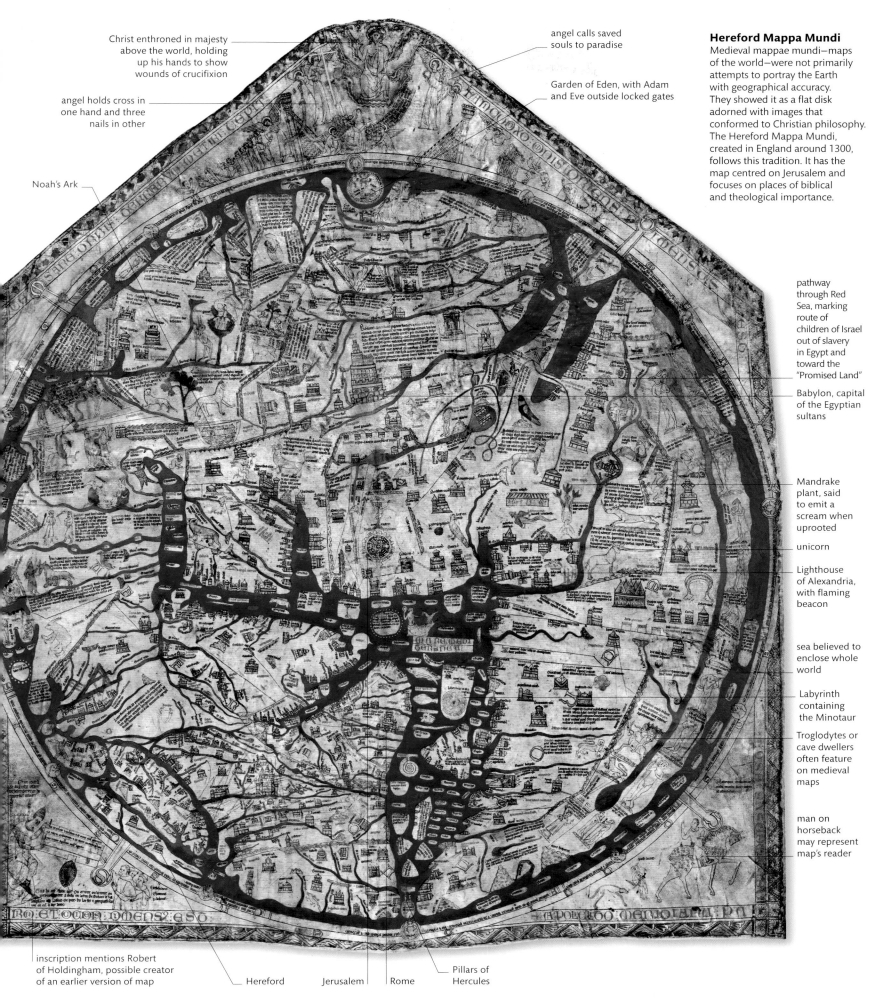

Christ enthroned in majesty above the world, holding up his hands to show wounds of crucifixion

angel holds cross in one hand and three nails in other

Noah's Ark

angel calls saved souls to paradise

Garden of Eden, with Adam and Eve outside locked gates

Hereford Mappa Mundi
Medieval mappae mundi—maps of the world—were not primarily attempts to portray the Earth with geographical accuracy. They showed it as a flat disk adorned with images that conformed to Christian philosophy. The Hereford Mappa Mundi, created in England around 1300, follows this tradition. It has the map centred on Jerusalem and focuses on places of biblical and theological importance.

pathway through Red Sea, marking route of children of Israel out of slavery in Egypt and toward the "Promised Land"

Babylon, capital of the Egyptian sultans

Mandrake plant, said to emit a scream when uprooted

unicorn

Lighthouse of Alexandria, with flaming beacon

sea believed to enclose whole world

Labyrinth containing the Minotaur

Troglodytes or cave dwellers often feature on medieval maps

man on horseback may represent map's reader

inscription mentions Robert of Holdingham, possible creator of an earlier version of map

Hereford

Jerusalem

Rome

Pillars of Hercules

chalice, symbol of St. John the Evangelist

decorative floral border

St. James, wearing broad-brimmed pilgrim's hat

closed book, symbol of St. Peter's two letters

sword, symbolizing St. Paul's execution

elaborate initial capital letter

ILLUMINATED CAPITAL LETTER

English *Book of Hours*

This 14th century *Book of Hours* is less lavish than the French example above, making it affordable to people of more modest means. With the advent of printing in the 16th century, these books became even more widely available and were even owned by people who were unable to read.

Book of Hours

From the 13th century onward, the *Book of Hours* became common. Intended for the layman, it contained a collection of psalms, prayers, and other readings. Organized around the daily cycle of the Divine Office (canonical hours), it was recited throughout the day in monasteries. This 15th-century French example is lavishly illustrated and would have been commissioned by a wealthy patron.

clasp used to fasten covers when closed

CLOTHING AND ADORNMENT

Clothing styles varied significantly between 1000 and 1500. However, the basic male garment remained a tunic, sometimes worn with an overtunic, which was belted at the waist. The decoration and quality of the cloth varied according to rank. Women wore a longer tunic or dress, which was closely fitted after the 12th century, with a variety of headdresses. Rings and other jewelry also helped determine a person's social status.

inscription engraved into gold

bezel in form of clasped hands

SILVER SEAL RING

inscription on bezel

double-faceted bezel

GOLD SIGNET RING   **GOLD ICONOGRAPHIC RING**

engraved angel and Virgin Mary

Silver pendant
This exquisite diamond-shaped 15th-or 16th-century pendant was found at Barham, England. The images engraved on it probably represent the Annunciation.

Gold brooch
The clasped hands on this 15th-century "fede ring" brooch symbolize fidelity. This type of brooch was often presented at a wedding.

Gold and silver rings
Inscriptions and motifs were often added to medieval rings. The silver ring is inscribed with an image of Jupiter with a thunderbolt, while the iconographic ring follows the medieval fashion for devotional images. The signet ring is engraved with a sheep head—a medieval pun—because it was from Sheppey, in England.

HOME LIFE

Daily life for the poor in rural areas was very conservative. It changed little for centuries, apart from external shocks such as the Black Death in 1348–50, which killed over a third of Europe's population. The rich and those living in towns had access to a much greater range of luxury goods, many of which were imported from abroad.

Gaming counter
Made from a cow's jawbone, this gaming counter was probably used to play a forerunner of backgammon known as tabula, which was, in turn, derived from a Roman game.

decorated with concentric circles

bearded face, common motif on bellarmine jars

blue trailing

anglular handle

Medieval cauldron
Made from copper alloy, medieval cauldrons such as this one had a handle that enabled them to be easily removed from over a cooking fire.

salt-glazed ceramic jar

splayed foot

Stemmed goblet
This rare, late-13th century stemmed goblet is made of colorless soda glass. Similar goblets have been found in southern England and northern Germany, but most that have survived do not have a stem.

SILVER SEAL RING

14th-century mazer
Mazers are a special type of drinking vessel. These shallow drinking cups without handles are made of maple, with a characteristic mottled effect.

Bellarmine jar
Jars such as this one contained wine exported from Germany. They were then often reused as "witches' bottles" to hold hair, nails, urine, and other items believed to protect against witchcraft.

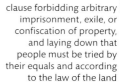

Barons of Faversham

This inscription states that the indenture was issued to the "barons of the port of Faversham." The charter was granted to the leading men of the town, who held the courtesy title of "baron" but were not the aristocracy.

Great Seal of Edward I, originally showed the king enthroned, with an orb and scepter

fragment of original medieval parchment tag

clause forbidding arbitrary imprisonment, exile, or confiscation of property, and laying down that people must be tried by their equals and according to the law of the land

Magna Carta
This copy of Magna Carta was specially obtained by the barons of Faversham, which belonged to a confederation of port towns known as Cinque Ports. In 1301, the barons cited it in a court case against the Lord Warden of the Cinque Ports for his alleged usurpation of ancient liberties guaranteed to Faversham by Magna Carta.

clause forbidding forced marriage of widows—earlier widows with substantial domains had been forced to marry royal supporters, and so would forfeit their property to their new husbands

section establishing uniform weights and measures across the realm, giving merchants and customers confidence that they would not be cheated

article lays down that royal officials must have witnesses to back up their evidence, protecting the public from arbitrary and unfair judgements

Royal approval
The charter carried a confirmation that it had been examined by Master Edward of London, a royal clerk. This indicated that the charter had royal approval.

◼ CHARTER OF LIBERTIES

MAGNA CARTA

The financial strains caused by English monarch King John's unsuccessful war against France in the early 13th century led to discontent among the kingdom's leading nobles—the barons. By feudal law, the barons held lands "in fee" from the monarch, in return for their sworn loyalty and a commitment to provide the king with knights to fight his wars. By the time John succeeded to the throne in 1199, the barons' obligation had taken the form of a cash payment, or "scutage." which was used to raise an army. A demand for scutage in 1215 sparked a rebellion. The barons insisted that John uphold the coronation charter of Henry I. They claimed it guaranteed them protection from royal injustices such as unfair taxation.

The barons marched on the royal castle at Northampton on May 5, 1215, before occupying London. On June 15, 1215, King John was forced to meet the barons at Runnymede on the banks of the Thames River to negotiate peace. Their demand for a charter was the first time in English history that influential people had collectively protested about bad government. The negotiations were mediated by Stephen Langton, the Archbishop of Canterbury, and ended with agreement on a number of issues known as the Articles of the Barons. This document was sealed in the presence of John and converted into a charter by the king's clerks. It was reissued in 1216 by Henry III, John's son, and again in 1225, when it became known as Magna Carta ("Great Charter").

RESTORING LIBERTIES

Much of Magna Carta referred to specific grievances relating to feudal taxes, the regulation of the justice system, and the ownership of land. It also established general principles and reestablished privileges that had been lost. For example, it claimed no taxes could be demanded without the "general consent of the realm."

Although it was written to resolve differences between John and his strongest subjects, Magna Carta also acknowledged laws, rights, and freedoms. It became an icon for liberty throughout the world. The rights in Magna Carta were evoked by American revolutionaries in the late 18th century during their struggle against British rule.

> "The **democratic aspiration** is no mere recent phase in human history… it was written in the **Magna Carta.**"
>
> Franklin Delano Roosevelt, President of America, 1941

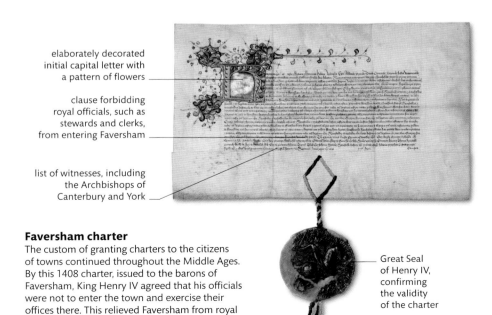

elaborately decorated initial capital letter with a pattern of flowers

clause forbidding royal officials, such as stewards and clerks, from entering Faversham

list of witnesses, including the Archbishops of Canterbury and York

Great Seal of Henry IV, confirming the validity of the charter

Faversham charter
The custom of granting charters to the citizens of towns continued throughout the Middle Ages. By this 1408 charter, issued to the barons of Faversham, King Henry IV agreed that his officials were not to enter the town and exercise their offices there. This relieved Faversham from royal interference and the imposition of illegal taxes.

THE RISE OF THE HOLY ROMAN EMPIRE

The coronation of the Frankish ruler Charlemagne as Emperor by Pope Leo III in 800 marked the emergence of a new empire in Western Europe, the first since the fall of Rome. The Holy Roman Empire survived for more than 1,000 years, weathering various setbacks such as invasion, plague, and religious strife.

Head of Barbarossa
Shaped like a bust of Emperor Frederick I Barbarossa, this reliquary contains remains of St. John. It was probably a gift from the Emperor's godfather, Otto of Capenberg.

Crowned by the Pope ▽
This 15th-century French illuminated manuscript depicts the coronation of Frederick II by Pope Honorius III in 1220. Frederick needed Papal recognition since the pope had deposed his predecessor.

After the Frankish Empire fragmented, in the later part of the 9th century, the seat of the Holy Roman Empire moved eastward into modern Germany. The Holy Roman Emperor derived his authority both from his status as a feudal overlord and from his recognition by the Church through Papal coronation.

The Holy Roman Empire lasted until 1806, when Francis II, the last emperor, abdicated. The Empire did not have a single center of political power. Instead, it evolved as a patchwork of petty principalities, church domains, and free towns, with a few large territories controlled by landowners such as the Welfs, the Wittelsbachs, the Hohenstaufen, and the Habsburgs.

CHURCH AND STATE

The church remained powerful and conflicts sometimes arose between the emperor and the pope, such as over the right to appoint bishops (investiture). The revival of monastic orders, beginning with the foundation of the Abbey of Cluny in 909, saw periodic renewals in church life, but secular culture also grew, rooting itself first in the elaborate code of "chivalry" of the martial classes and strengthening later as the influence of the Italian Renaissance spread northward.

Much effort was lavished on items meant for religious use, for example, paintings, crosses, and sumptuous manuscripts, including the *Gospel Book of Otto III*. Yet as towns grew—many of them forming leagues, such as the mercantile Hanseatic League—a class of secular patrons arose with the money and motivation to commission their own works of art.

POLITICS AND POWER

After the coronation of Otto I in Rome in 962, the Holy Roman Emperor was always the king of Germany. This revived the concept of a Christian emperor in the West and the beginning of an unbroken line of emperors lasting more than eight centuries. Gradually a system of Imperial Diets, in which the chief nobility of the empire decided federal issues, evolved. By the 19th century, the emperor had very little power over his theoretical domain.

double-headed eagle, symbol of the Emperor's authority

larger shields at top are those of the Prince Electors

Heraldry
This illuminated manuscript of the Quaternionenadler, the double-headed eagle symbol of the empire, contains the coats of arms of all its member states.

crest of Charlemagne

Charlemagne period coins
These two coins are from the period of Charlemagne. His coronation in 800 brought him the title of Imperator (Emperor). This was the first time a Germanic ruler had claimed the title since Rome's fall in 476.

view of city of Rome

Seal of Louis IV
This is the golden seal of Louis IV, who was crowned Emperor in 1328 after a bloody struggle with the Austrian Frederick the Fair that saw Louis being excommunicated and also deposing Pope John XXII.

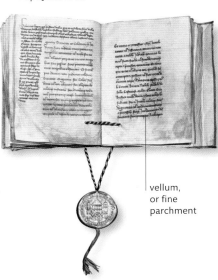

vellum, or fine parchment

Golden Bull of Charles IV
This decree issued by the Imperial Diet at Nuremberg and Metz in 1356, which was headed by Emperor Charles IV, contained legislation about the constitutional structure of the Holy Roman Empire.

crown is ornamented with 144 precious stones and more than 100 pearls

Imperial Crown
The imperial crown of the Holy Roman Empire, dating from the 10th or 11th century, has a unique octagonal shape. This work of art from the Romanesque era is made of eight hinged panels decorated with Biblical scenes.

jeweled cross, originally a pectoral cross that may have belonged to Emperor Henry II

one of eight plates of 22 carat gold that make up crown

one of four cloisonné enamel pictures in Byzantine style showing scenes from the Bible

■ DIVINE AUTHORITY

THE ELIZABETH RELIQUARY

St. Elizabeth was a Hungarian princess canonized in 1235, just four years after her death. Her skull was placed in this magnificent agate reliquary. Elizabeth's rapid elevation to sainthood exemplifies the striking interplay between Christian piety and political power in the Middle Ages. The royal houses that could claim a saint among their number were able to claim divine authority for their rule. The cult of saintly ancestors, such as Louis IX of France, King Olaf Haraldsson of Norway, and Queen Jadwiga of Poland, was vigorously promoted by their successors.

THE LIFE OF ELIZABETH

Elizabeth had been married to Louis IV, the Margrave of Thuringia—a German nobleman above the rank of count. When her husband died in 1227, on his way to join the Sixth Crusade, Elizabeth refused to remarry. She took a vow of celibacy and devoted herself to charitable works, establishing a hospital at Marburg where she personally ministered to the sick. Soon after her death in 1231, miracles began to be reported. Elizabeth's canonization by Pope Gregory IX was helped considerably by the Hungarian royal house of Arpad, which was eager to have a saint among its number. Her body was laid to rest in a golden shrine in Marburg.

MEDIEVAL RELIQUARIES

The hunger for saints' relics was intense in the Middle Ages, because they were said to heal sickness or grant remission of sins. The altar of every new church required a relic. The richest monasteries and cathedrals had huge collections of artifacts associated with the saints or with Christ himself. To honor these relics, they were placed in reliquaries—housings made of precious metal and often encased in jewels. Reliquaries holding the most prestigious relics, such as the remains of St. Elizabeth, were very lavish—a sign of the power and the sanctity of the religious institution that owned them.

DOME-SHAPED SILVER COVER

RELIQUARY CROWN

RELIQUARY BASE

Carved gemstone
A carved piece of agate shows two passengers and a driver in a carriage. The work is typical of the Roman provincial style of the 4th and 5th century CE.

Overhead view
Four golden bands forming a cross shape and set with emeralds, sapphires, and amethysts adorn the bowl-shaped silver cover to the reliquary.

Crucifixion
A golden image of the crucified Christ, with two saints by his side, decorates the stem of the reliquary. The gems set on either side dramatically highlight the shape of the cross.

Golden lion
A golden lion, also the symbol of Mark the Evangelist, was one of the symbols of the Arpad dynasty, which ruled Hungary from 1000 to 1301.

filigree ornamentation on crown is work of an expert goldsmith

reliquary crown, gifted by Emperor Frederick II

wide border of gold inset with gemstones

hammered gold handles on side of cup

ancient agate bowl at base of reliquary was a drinking vessel originally used at Roman and Byzantine banquets

bowl contained skull of St. Elizabeth

Jeweled reliquary

The Elizabeth reliquary was created from a Byzantine drinking cup. A jewel-studded golden band was added to the cup in the 11th century. After Elizabeth's canonization, the Holy Roman Emperor Frederick II ordered the base of the cup to be replaced with a new, studded one. The addition of a royal crown and a bejeweled cover completed the reliquary, which remained in Germany until Swedish troops looted it in the 1630s during the Thirty Years War.

Byzantine bowl

The bowl of the crown, lit from within, shows dramatic firelike patterns within the silicate microcrystals that make up the agate.

stem of cup decorated with images of saints

BATTLE AND CONFLICT

The Holy Roman Empire emerged at a time when mounted knights were becoming the dominant force on European battlefields. But by the 14th century, infantry were rising to prominence, winning victories such as that by the Swiss over the imperial cavalry at Morgarten in 1315. By this time, armor had become extremely elaborate, often with highly decorated overlapping plates.

gorget, or collar-guard

Emperor's helmet
German armorer Lorenz made this helmet for Emperor Maximilian I in c.1490. It is a variation of the sallet helmet popular at the time.

long, sloping tail

Sallet helmet
This German helmet has a single sight visor and a tail (designed to protect the neck), both key features of the sallet helmet.

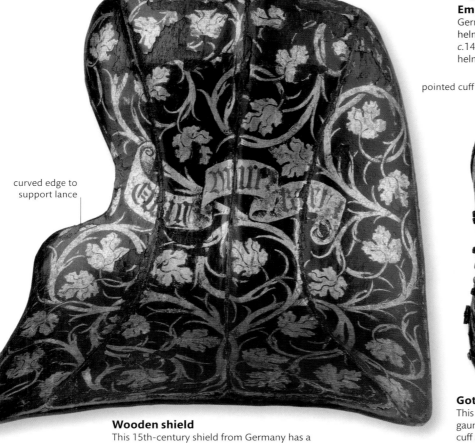

curved edge to support lance

pointed cuff

German shaffron
Equine armor, or barding, prevented a knight's horse from being killed, rendering him vulnerable to attack by infantry. This mid-16th century shaffron was used to protect a horse's face.

center plate

articulated plates

shaped knuckle plate

rivets originally held internal lining

flanged nose-guard

Wooden shield
This 15th-century shield from Germany has a notch on one side that was probably used to couch a lance in a tournament or on the battlefield.

Gothic gauntlet
This late 15th-century armored gauntlet has the sharply pointed cuff and the radiating embossed ribs characteristic of German armor of the time.

HOME LIFE

Most people in the empire lived in isolated farmsteads or villages, although towns grew steadily in number and importance. There were around 3,000 towns in Germany by the 13th century. As elsewhere in Western Europe, feudal burdens lessened after the Black Death, a deadly plague that killed a third of the population and created labor shortages.

rider on lion pulling its ears

spout in form of man opening lion's mouth

hollow body for water

partly glazed to add color

flat, broad blade

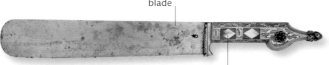

uneven bottom of pitcher

Serving knife
Broad-bladed knives, such as this German example from the 15th century, were used for serving, rather than cutting food.

grip of handle has mahogany panels with plaques of stag horn

Water pitcher
The aquamanile was a type of water pitcher with a spout. This bronze version from Germany was used to cleanse hands, either by a priest before Mass or before eating.

German pottery
Germany's Rhineland had a long tradition of pottery dating back to Roman times. Plain pieces, such as these, would have been used in relatively humble households.

EARLY KINGDOMS OF EASTERN EUROPE

From the 9th century, states began to coalesce in eastern central Europe, forming the core of future countries such as Russia. By 1000, most had become Christian, strengthening their ties to Byzantium or Western European monarchies.

Triple-domed splendor ▷
The magnificent Cathedral of St. Sophia in Novgorod is nearly 130 ft (40 m) high. It is northern Russia's oldest stone building, dating from around 1050, only 60 years after the country became Christian.

The fortunes of states in eastern central Europe varied greatly between 800 and 1500. As Byzantine power waned, new states asserted themselves in the southeast—first Bulgaria, and then Serbia. Hungary, founded by Magyar raiders in the 10th century, became an established monarchy under a Christian king around 1000. By the 14th century, it had grown into eastern central Europe's strongest country. To the north, Poland was one of the last areas to adopt a centralized kingship. It was plagued by political instability, but an alliance with Lithuania in 1385 created a regional superpower.

To the east, Russia had its origins in the interplay of Viking settlers and Slav tribes in the 9th century. Surviving devastating Mongol raids in the early 1240s, it prospered in the form of the Grand Duchy of Moscow, which became a cultural powerhouse and the precursor to the modern Russian state.

POLITICS AND POWER

Although strong monarchies began to emerge from the early 11th century, the region saw a tendency to resist control from the center, and regional landowners, such as the Serbian leader Župan, remained important. Assemblies such as the Polish Sejm had the right to elect the king and also acted as a brake on royal power.

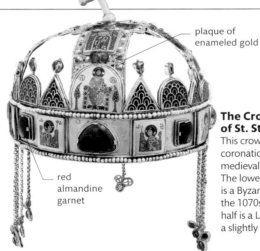

plaque of enameled gold

red almandine garnet

The Crown of St. Stephen
This crown was used in the coronation of most medieval Hungarian kings. The lower half of this crown is a Byzantine crown from the 1070s, while the upper half is a Latin crown from a slightly later period.

fine filigree work

remains of pearl border

Ceremonial necklace
This gold necklace with medallions dates from the 12th or 13th century. It was used by the nobility of Kievan Rus—the first state to emerge in Ukraine and Russia.

BELIEFS AND RITUALS

By 1000, most of the states of the region had become Christian. A divide emerged when some rulers—such as Mieszko I of Poland and Stephen of Hungary—looked to the Papacy of Rome, while others—such as Boris of Bulgaria and Vladimir of Kiev—turned instead to the Greek Orthodox Patriarch in Constantinople (modern Istanbul).

Silver reliquary
This 12th-century box is decorated with chivalric scenes. It was adapted for use as a reliquary for the remains of St. Stanislaus, the Bishop of Krakow, who was martyred by Polish King Boleslaw II in 1079.

warrior spearing a fallen enemy

guilded and embossed surface

expression indicates tenderness and maternal love

lion symbolizes strength

The Virgin and Child
The Virgin of Vladimir, or *Theotokos*, arrived in Russia in 1130 and became one of the most venerated icons. It was credited with saving Russia from the invading Mongols.

EMPIRES OF THE MONGOL KHANS

The Mongols, a nomadic people of Central Asia, were united in the early 13th century by the warrior Genghis Khan. Over the next 30 years, they conquered a vast land-based empire straddling Asia and Europe but it had fragmented by 1300.

Shahnameh ▷
This page is from *The Book of Kings*, a traditional Iranian epic poem. Produced in 1330, during the reign of the Mongol Ilkhanid ruler Sultan Abu Sa'id, this version shows the main characters in typical Mongol dress.

In 1209, Genghis Khan was chosen to lead the fractious Mongol tribes. He built a huge army, which first conquered Kara Khitai in Central Asia and part of northern China. He then turned west, devastating the lands of the Khwarazm Shah, in Central Asia and modern-day Iran. In 1220, he is said to have massacred the 30,000 defenders of Samarkand, the capital. His successors expanded his empire, conquering Iran, Russia, and China. The Mongols struck as far west as

Hungary and Poland. But the death of Ögodei Khan, the second Great Khan, in 1241 forestalled further conquest. A defeat at Ain Jalut, Palestine, in 1260 prevented the conquest of Egypt. The Mongol Empire fragmented, with separate khans ruling in Iran (the Ilkhans), in Russia (the Golden Horde), and in China (the Yuan dynasty). Yet they created stable political conditions, and set up a postal system in which messages could travel from Beijing to Tabriz (in Iran) in just a month.

BATTLE AND CONFLICT

All Mongol boys over 14 years of age were expected to take up military service. The army was organized into *tumans* of 10,000 men and was largely mounted, giving it a big advantage in mobility. The elite Mongol troops were armed with bows that could decimate the enemy at a distance, and protected by leather scale armor, leather helmets, and wicker shields.

elaborately decorated head

wooden shaft covered with polished ray skin

Iron mace
This 14th-century decorated mace is from China, during the reign of the Mongol Yuan dynasty. Maces were carried by heavy cavalry and used when closing in on the enemy for hand-to-hand combat.

leather wrist loop

short, articulated sleeves allowed full range of arm movement

Quiver
A Mongol quiver could contain up to 60 arrows. Some arrows had specialized arrowheads, such as heavy ones for piercing armor and curved blade shapes for severing limbs.

silver inlaid crest

helmet bowl of iron plates

steel neck protector

Leather armor
Mongol armor provided good protection from glancing blows or arrow strikes. Underneath, the warriors wore silk shirts, which caught arrowheads and allowed them to be removed more easily.

Mongol helmet
The helmet worn by Mongol warriors had a traditional conical shape, trimmed with a padded roll of fur for a snug fit and protection against extreme cold.

Nogai helmet
This metal helmet from the Nogai Horde, a Mongol group from north of the Caspian Sea, has a chainmail neck guard to protect one of a warrior's most vulnerable areas.

ART AND CULTURE

The Mongol conquests helped artists—along with their techniques and motifs—to travel freely in the entire area between China and Iran. The Mongol Khans also drew craftsmen from across the empire to their palaces. As the Mongol Empire fragmented, regional variations emerged and the conversion of the Ilkhanid Khans to Islam created a Mongol-Islamic style.

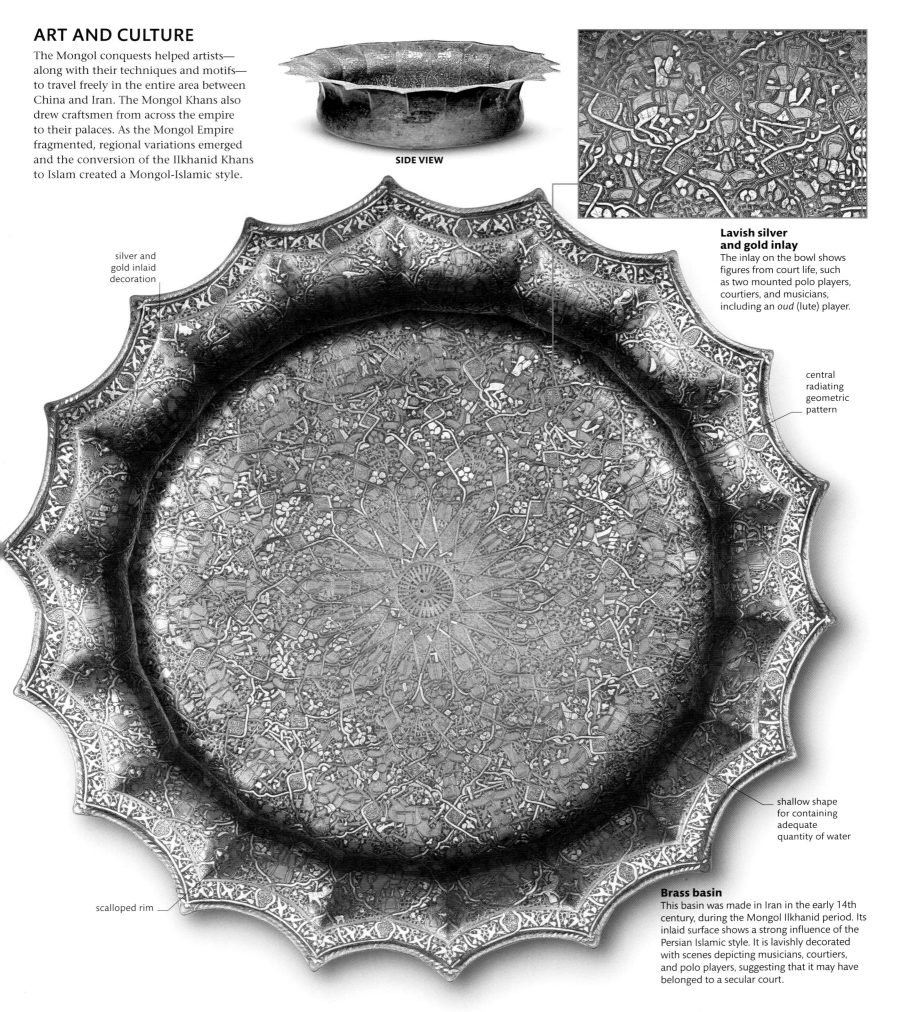

SIDE VIEW

silver and gold inlaid decoration

Lavish silver and gold inlay
The inlay on the bowl shows figures from court life, such as two mounted polo players, courtiers, and musicians, including an *oud* (lute) player.

central radiating geometric pattern

shallow shape for containing adequate quantity of water

scalloped rim

Brass basin
This basin was made in Iran in the early 14th century, during the Mongol Ilkhanid period. Its inlaid surface shows a strong influence of the Persian Islamic style. It is lavishly decorated with scenes depicting musicians, courtiers, and polo players, suggesting that it may have belonged to a secular court.

ART AND DEVOTION IN CLASSICAL INDIA

After the Gupta Empire collapsed in the late 5th century (see p.98), India broke up into regional states. From time to time, one or other of these exerted dominance over large parts of the subcontinent. But their dominance was always short-lived, because rival dynasties soon reasserted themselves.

Warrior's shield
Decorated with a solar emblem, this shield belonged to the warrior Rajput clans. The Rajputs set up independent kingdoms in north-central India from the 9th and 10th centuries.

Epic city ▽

The earliest shrines at the site of this Hindu temple in Hampi, Karnataka, date from the 7th century. The site was added to over time, becoming a key religious center of the mighty Vijayanagara empire, who made Hampi their capital. The interior of the temple is richly carved with episodes from the Ramayana.

Around 467 CE, the Huns invaded India and overpowered the forces of Skandagupta, the last significant Gupta ruler of the country. After this, the empire fragmented into smaller kingdoms. King Harsha, a member of the ruling family of one of these kingdoms, conquered much of India. Some dynasties, such as the mighty Cholas in the early 10th century, managed to assert supremacy over southern India, while others, such as the Pratiharas and Rashtrakutas, dominated the northern part of the country at around the same time.

RELIGIOUS CHANGES

Between 500 and 1100, Buddhist monasteries were the major centers of education and manuscript production; monks from as far as China visited these holy places to pray and study. The worship of Shiva, Vishnu, and Devi-Ma (or the Great Goddess Mother), who took on many forms including Durga and Kali, became ever more popular. The religious map of India became still more diverse with the advent of Islam, whose spread began with the Arab conquest of Sind in 712. It

continued with the establishment of Mahmud of Ghazni's empire across much of northwestern India.

During this time, India saw many notable achievements in art and architecture. Fabulous cave paintings were added to the walls of the stone-cut temples of Ajanta in the south. The Hindu temple style was further developed, culminating in iconic temples such as the Brihadisvara, built by the Cholas around 1000, and the 11th-century complexes at Khajuraho, 400 miles (600 km) southeast of Delhi.

RULERS AND CONQUEST

Medieval India was characterized by intense competition between dynasties, whose focus tended to be either the north or the south. Only occasionally did rulers such as Harsha in the 7th century or dynasties such as the Rashtrakutas in the 9th century straddle this divide.

Palla dynasty coin
The Palla dynasty dominated northwestern India for two centuries. This silver coin with animal figures was issued in the 11th century by Madana Palla Deva (1145–67), one of the last Palla rulers.

figure on horseback

Islamic Sultanate coin
This large silver coin, or *tanka*, with Persian inscriptions, dates back to the rule of Shams ad-Din Ilyas over the Islamic Sultanate of Delhi in the 14th century.

BELIEFS AND RITUALS

In 500 CE, Buddhism was still a major force in India. Hinduism was in its "temple phase," which meant more and more people practised a temple-based form of worship. By the beginning of the 8th century, Islam had entered the subcontinent and established itself in northern India, while Buddhism had been pushed to the margins.

intense color palette unusual for Islamic painting

intense blue color derived from lapis lazuli

Islamic illustration
During this period in northern India, art began to reflect stories from Islamic cultures in Central Asia and Iran. This illustration shows Rustam, the hero of the Persian epic *Shahnameh*, killing his rival, Alkus.

Jain folio
The *Kalpasutra* details the lives of 24 *Jinas* (victors) who have achieved enlightenment. This folio shows the mother of the founder of Jainism, Mahavira, being foretold of his birth in "14 auspicious dreams."

war discus, or *chakra*, in raised right hand

Bronze Vishnu
During the 7th century, forms of worship dedicated to a personal relationship with Vishnu, Shiva, and the Great Goddess were gaining popularity in southern India.

tirthankara meditates on a stone cushion

Tirthankara statue
This 11th-century statue depicts a tirthankara, one of Jainism's 24 "liberated souls," or *Jinas*, believed to have reached the ideal state of spiritual knowledge.

wide sleeve, with rectangular profile

lines and circles separate sections of text

gold script translates to "God is the merciful, the compassionate"

gold, orange, and blue medallions

band contains 99 names for God in Islam

Talismanic shirt
The entire Quran is inscribed on the panels of this 15th-century cotton shirt from northern India. The *shuhada*, or the profession of faith, has been given a prominent place in the central lozenge.

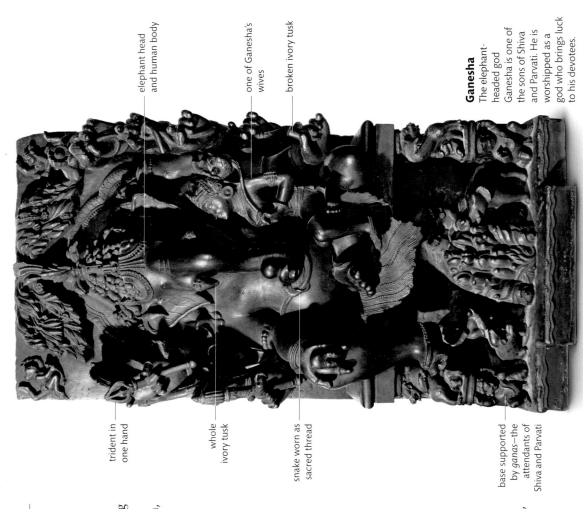

trident in
one hand

whole
ivory tusk

snake worn as
sacred thread

base supported
by *ganas*—the
attendants of
Shiva and Parvati

elephant head
and human body

one of Ganesha's
wives

broken ivory tusk

Ganesha
The elephant-
headed god
Ganesha is one of
the sons of Shiva
and Parvati. He is
worshipped as a
god who brings luck
to his devotees.

divine garland bearer

trident symbolizes
Shiva's sovereignty

decorative
architectural
throne-back

fly-whisk
bearer

matted hair
wound in
a crown

EULOGIES TO THE GODS

SHIVA AND PARVATI

Early forms of the Hindu religion emphasized the performance of elaborate rituals and offerings in honor of the gods. Hindu rituals were carried out by Brahmins, highly trained priests who devoted their lives to these sacred practices.

Around 300 CE, new ways of worship became popular, especially in southern India. Later known as *Bhakti* traditions, they emphasized a loving relationship between the worshipper and the god. By the 6th century, these practices had profoundly transformed Hinduism. The teachers, or saints of the Bhakti movement, believed that an individual might have a role in striving for liberation from the cycle of rebirth, which could be achieved without the aid of a Brahmin's sacred rituals. According to *Bhakti* traditions, love for god was considered to be more important than rituals and sacrifices.

FORMS OF BHAKTI

There are different forms of *Bhakti*. Saivism stressed the worship of Shiva, who as both the creator and destroyer

of all things, represents the contrasting values of peace and destruction. Another prominent form, Vaishnavism, focuses on the devotee's worship of the god Vishnu and the various avatars in which he has manifested himself on Earth during times of crisis and struggle. Goddess worship venerated Devi-Ma in her many forms, from fierce warrior to loving mother.

As the Bhakti movement grew, the building of temples, which had previously not been a feature of Hinduism, began. These were, at first, mainly dedicated to Shiva, Vishnu, Parvati, or Durga, deities featured in the *Puranas*—cycles of devotional poems eulogizing the Hindu gods.

The early temples were centered around an inner sanctum, the *garbha-griha*, or "womb chamber," in which the main image of the deity was placed. By the 13th century, most of these beautifully decorated temples, had developed into huge complexes in which many hundreds of devotees could worship.

Parvati

jeweled belt

donor carving
represents a husband
and wife who gave
money for the temple

lotus throne of
Shiva and Parvati

lion, the animal
vehicle of Parvati

Shiva and Parvati
Shiva and his wife,
Parvati, are depicted
in this statue from
Orissa, India. Shiva
was worshipped in
many forms, including
as the slayer of
demons, the creator
and destroyer of the
cosmos, a loving
husband, and a great
yogi. Parvati is one of
the many aspects
of Devi-Ma, the Great
Goddess Mother,
who can appear to
her devotees in a
multitude of forms.

Shiva

rosary
symbolizes the
contemplative
side of Shiva

lotus is a
symbol of
purity

Nandi the
bull, the
animal
vehicle of
Shiva

floral pattern

stylized floral designs flank central panel

Mahamayuri, three-headed, four-armed goddess

page number 44 inscribed in letters

lotus pedestal, with aureole beyond

Sanskrit text

colored lozenge shapes flank central panel

Mahapatisa, eight-armed, four-headed goddess

right hand holds jewel

left hand makes *varadamudra* gesture, indicating compassion

opaque watercolors and ink on palm leaves

circular loop shapes flank central panel

Mahamantranusarini, twelve-armed, three-headed goddess

thumb and index finger form circle in *dharmachakramudra*, symbolic of Buddha's teaching

page number 44
inscribed in
Sanskrit numerals

page number 115
inscribed in
Sanskrit numerals

page number 155
inscribed in
Sanskrit numerals

▮ THE PURSUIT OF WISDOM

PANCHARAKSHA MANUSCRIPT

In the 5th century BCE, Buddhism arose out of dissent with traditional Vedic Hinduism. Following the teachings of Siddhartha Gautama (c.483-400 BCE), known as the Buddha, the religion gained a firm foothold in the Ganges Basin and in the courts of north Indian rulers.

By the early 1st century CE, Buddhism had diverged into two main traditions known as Theravada and Mahayana. The Theravada tradition adhered more closely to the original tenets of Buddhism and became the dominant form in Sri Lanka and Southeast Asia. The Mahayana tradition stressed the role of the *Bodhisattava*—one who is on the path to enlightenment and liberation from worldly cares, but who has delayed reaching this state of nirvana in order to help mankind.

PERFECTING WISDOM

Mahayana Buddhism stressed the notion of *prajna*, or wisdom, a heightened state brought about by the analysis of religious truths. The perfection of wisdom was known as *Prajnaparamita*. An adept Mahayana Buddhist had to master the perfections of giving, morality, exertion, endurance, meditation, and *prajna* itself. A series of *Prajnaparamita* texts were assembled to offer guidance to those pursuing wisdom. The most famous of these is the *Vajracchedika*, or *Diamond Sutra*, which was particularly revered in China and Japan. These were supplemented by other texts that focused more on ritual, such as the *Pancharaksha* (shown here)—a set of *sutras* (scriptures) concerning the five protective goddesses of Buddhism.

THE DECLINE

The Mahayana tradition became dominant in China, Japan, and those parts of north India where Buddhism resisted a tide of Hindu revival the longest. Buddhism was on the retreat in the mid-7th century when the Chinese monk Xuanzang, who visited India in search of sacred texts, noted a decline in sacred sites such as Sarnath. Some rulers—including Harsha in the early 7th century and the Pala dynasty in northern India in the 8th century—patronized Buddhism and Hinduism. By the 11th century, Buddhism was reduced to a minority tradition in eastern India.

***Pancharaksha* text**
These three leaves from a *Pancharaksha* text date from the 11th to 12th century CE. They show three of the five protective Hindu goddesses, each one regarded as a personification of an early Buddhist *sutra* and each having a special power to protect worshippers. The *sutras* are written on palm leaves, a traditional form of manuscript material used as early as the 5th century BCE, during the very early days of Buddhism.

THE SANSKRIT LANGUAGE

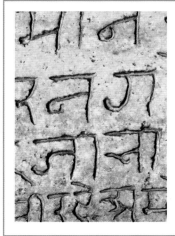

Sanskrit is an Indian language in which the earliest Hindu scriptures, the *vedas*, were composed. Most later Indian texts, such as the inscriptions on the walls of the Jain temple at Adinathas, Ranakpur, were also penned in it. It was the language of court culture and political administration until Persian and regional languages became more popular.

THE DRAGON THRONE OF IMPERIAL CHINA

Under the Tang and Song dynasties, China enjoyed over six centuries of relative stability and powerful central control, occasionally punctuated by revolts and incursions by nomads, from the north and west, and by the Mongols. A strong bureaucracy ensured equitable governing of the provinces, while the emperors facilitated a flowering of literature and of the arts, especially painting and sculpture.

Beast of burden
Camels were the main means of transportation along the Silk Road and elaborate glazed figurines such as this were placed in the tombs of the elite during the Tang dynasty.

In memoriam ▷
This painted hand scroll by the well-known artist Qian Xuan is inspired by the concept of *fugu* (the restoration of antiquity), a nostalgic yearning invoked by the fall of Hangzhou, the Southern Song capital, to the Mongols in 1276.

The final collapse of the Han dynasty in 220 CE led to three centuries of disunity until China was finally reunified in 581 by Yang Jian, the first emperor of the Sui dynasty. In 618, the Tang toppled the Sui during a brief civil war. The Tang pushed the borders of China deep into central Asia under the great reformer Emperor Taizong. He restructured the bureaucracy, reestablished formal examinations for entry into the civil service, and set up an official records bureau. He was also a generous patron of the arts. Literature, painting, and ceramics flourished during the early Tang dynasty and Emperor Xuanzong founded an Imperial Academy of Literature. Since the dragon was the emblem of imperial power, the throne of the Emperor of China was known as the "Dragon Throne."

THE SONG DYNASTY

Tang expansion toward what is now Iran was halted when the Chinese were defeated by forces of the Abbasid Caliphate at the River Talas in 751. This left the central Asian outposts beleaguered as the dynasty began to decline, leading to a rebellion against the Tang led by the military general An Lushan between 755 and 763. In 907, China again descended into a time of chaos known as the "Five Dynasties and Ten Kingdoms" period, which only ended with the rise of the Song dynasty in 960. The first Song ruler, Taizu, a former general, ushered in a glorious period in Chinese cultural history. Taizu and his four successors strengthened the administration, encouraged the arts, and exercised moderation in their rule. They were guided by the secular philosophy of neo-Confucianism, which rejected the mythical elements of Buddhism and Taoism that had influenced Han dynasty Confucianism.

The civil service examination was broadened to include engineering, law, geography, and medicine. Economic reforms included the spread of paper money known as "flying money." In the 1070s, the minster Wang Anshi built government grain warehouses in the provinces. He also instituted official loans to farmers so they could purchase seeds and tools.

The arts flourished under the Song dynasty. Particularly important was the development of block printing in the 9th century, which led to the widespread dissemination of literary and scientific texts. Song emperor Huizong presided over a brilliant court and also collected over 6,000 paintings. But the Song's military weakness let Jin nomads from the north breach the empire's borders. The invaders sacked the capital, Kaifeng, in 1126, and occupied all of northern China. A branch of the Song survived in southern China, but the Mongol armies of Kublai Khan deposed the last Song emperor in 1279.

THE RISE OF THE MING

The Mongols ruled China as the Yüan dynasty, adopting many Chinese practices. They were overthrown by the Ming—the last native Chinese dynasty—in 1368. The Ming emperors built the Forbidden City, a new palace complex in Beijing, and strengthened the Great Wall of China. Civil service exams were reintroduced in 1384, and the civil service hierarchy came to dominate the military. Meanwhile, traditional Chinese drama, originating in the Song dynasty and banned under Mongol rule, was restored. Chinese culture flourished once again.

"**Painters** are... to **depict** objects **as they are.**"

Emperor Huizong, instruction to artists, 1082–1135

POLITICS AND POWER

Although the Tang and Song emperors set up efficient bureaucracies, the stability of the state still depended on the personality of the emperor. Strong rulers such as the second Tang Emperor Taizong could weather crises, but weak ones such as Xizong aggravated long-standing social tensions and provoked bloody revolts.

design created by hammering from reverse

Dragon crown
This 10th- or 11th-century crown was presented by the Song court to the ruler of the Liao, north of the Chinese frontier.

five-clawed dragon used in artifacts of the Ming imperial family

Glazed spittoon
This spittoon belonged to a Ming dynasty imperial concubine. The color and pattern of ceramics were dictated by the owner's rank.

rider wears trousers and boots, unusual for a Chinese woman

ceramic with traces of pigment

Polo player
Polo was a popular game among the Tang elite. This tomb model depicts a woman playing the sport.

TECHNOLOGY AND INNOVATION

China made great scientific advances at this time, particularly under the Song. The field of hydraulics saw key developments, such as polymath Su Song's water-powered model of the heavens. Mathematics and cartography were also very advanced. The spread of printing from the late 9th century aided the dissemination of knowledge.

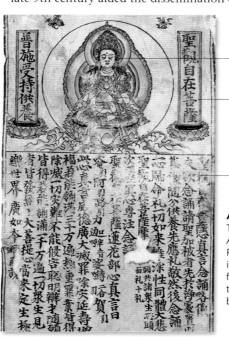

Avalokiteshvara, the Bodhisattva (enlightened being) of compassion

color added by hand to enhance image

layout with image on top and text below typical of Chinese illustrated books of the 9th century

Avalokiteshvara
This woodblock depicting *Avalokiteshvara*, dating from the Five Dynasties period, was found in a cave. Many other prints were found in the same cave, including the world's earliest dated printed book, the *Diamond Sutra*, from 868.

BELIEFS AND RITUALS

Buddhism entered China during the Han period and received imperial sponsorship under the Tang. During the Song era, a modified version of Confucianism received strong support from the court. The interplay of this stream with Buddhism and native Daoist beliefs created a complex religious landscape.

Taizong's horses
Emperor Taizong had six reliefs made commemorating his favorite horses. They were placed outside his tomb mound and worshipped.

low relief in limestone

glazed earthenware hipped roof

Model granary
This model of a granary was deposited in a Tang dynasty tomb in the belief that it would provide sustenance to the dead person.

raised arm would have originally held a weapon

fierce, warrior-like expression

delicate features beaten into shape from heavy sheet of metal

Death mask
Made from silver, this death mask is from the Liao dynasty of the Kitan people, who ruled the area to the north of China from 900 to 1125.

Tang dynasty *lokapalas*
This pair represents two of the Four Heavenly Kings Chinese Buddhists consider the guardians of the cardinal directions.

candleholder

Guardian lion
This glazed Ming dynasty figurine depicts the Buddhist guardian lion *Suanni*. There is a candleholder on the back, indicating it was made for use in a temple.

green and amber splashes

buff-cream body

Candleholder
This candleholder is an example of three-color glazed ceramics, or *sancai*. These were primarily made for depositing in aristocratic tombs during the Tang dynasty.

hair drawn up tightly into double bun, one of main hairstyles of Tang dynasty women

thin black eyebrows painted on figurine in style that was popular with Tang women

color may represent remains of yellow face makeup powder, often used by Tang women to paint their foreheads

red lips in style of Tang women, who whitened them and then applied rouge so they resembled a cherry

Chinese wind instrument known as *sheng*

pear-shaped, four-stringed lute, called pipa, with flat back

MUSICIAN WITH HARP

MUSICIAN WITH PIPES

Chinese harp, or konghou, played solo or as an accompanying instrument

whirling circular motion of dance conveyed by draped sleeves

long sleeves appear to be billowing with dancer's movement

figures all depicted wearing pleated, high-waisted dress tired with sash

DANCER

DANCER

clay figurine originally decorated with striking colors

Musicians and dancers

These models were placed in a Tang dynasty tomb to provide entertainment for the deceased in the afterlife. Music was an important part of life in imperial China, and at the royal palace the court orchestra performed for the emperor. Ceremonial music also accompanied religious rituals. These figurines provide realistic representations of various Chinese musical instruments.

TANG BURIAL HORSE

People in ancient China believed that life in the afterworld was as important as life on Earth. In traditional Chinese religion, the earthly soul, or *po*, remained present in the grave and was dependent on offerings presented by the living to nourish it. This belief led to the creation of elaborate burials for the dead in tombs that replicated earthly dwellings. During the Han dynasty, the practice of furnishing tombs with ceramic figurines flourished. The figurines were substitutes for real objects because the dead were thought to need possessions and, if rich, servants, to sustain them in the afterlife.

By the beginning of the Tang dynasty, burial goods had become so lavish that emperors were issuing laws restricting the types, sizes, and numbers of grave goods that people could have, according to their rank and status.

MASS PRODUCTION

By the 7th century, one of the most important uses of ceramic material in China was the manufacture of intricate funerary figurines of humans, animals, and fierce lion-headed tomb guardians.

Funerary goods were so popular during the Tang dynasty that workshops were forced to use molds in order to keep up with the demand.

Sometimes lead glazes were applied to the figurines and three-color glazes, or *sancai*, were popular during the 7th and 8th centuries. The oxides needed for this type of glaze were expensive commodities, and so *sancai* glazed figurines were items of great prestige found only in imperial and elite tombs.

HORSES

The masterpieces of Tang funerary figurines are undoubtedly the horses, which were created in a naturalistic style with a high level of detail, giving them a sense of animation. Horses were revered in China, especially the mythical "celestial horses"—flying beasts with dragonlike features. They were imported at great expense from the Central Asian territory of Ferghana. In 608, the emperor received a large number of horses in tribute from the region. Symbols of access to exotic trade goods, such horse figurines are frequently found in Tang dynasty tombs.

Painted eye
Traces of paint that were used to decorate the figurine have survived. The eyes were originally painted in black.

Horseshoe
Like the horses themselves, horseshoes originated from central Asia. The horse's delicate pose allows the shoe to be seen.

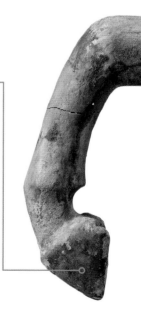

RIGHT SIDE

FRONT VIEW

LEFT SIDE

Tang horse figurine
In addition to symbols of the wealth of the departed, pottery horse figurines may also originally have been a substitute for the sacrifice of the animal during the funeral rituals. The models could be up to 20 in (50 cm) high, and the horses were generally depicted with small heads, strong necks, high shoulders, and low rumps.

closely trimmed
mane painted
in red

saddle with
curved seat
to give rider
greater stability

" Later, the **emperor** obtained the **blood-sweating horses** from **Daiyuan** [Ferghana]. **"**

Sima Qian, *Records of the Grand Historian, c.*100 BCE

medallion-like
ornaments added
for decoration

saddle cloth with
hanging tassels

bulging leg muscles
convey sense of
movement

Tail end
Tang horses were elaborately groomed.
They generally had their tails clipped
short and tightly bound in bandages.

ART AND CULTURE

Chinese art, particularly sculpture, took on more naturalistic aspects under the Tang dynasty than in previous dynasties. This trend continued during the Song period, when realism was highly prized. While much sculpture was religious, tomb figurines portrayed secular themes, and a tradition of landscape painting, which began in the Tang period, achieved an exquisite refinement under Song rule.

Wucai box
Five-colors style, or *wucai*, developed and flourished during the time of the Ming dynasty. It combined enamel colors with a blue underglaze.

dragon motif on porcelain, with overglaze of red, yellow, and green

dancing horse

Silver flask
This gilded flask emulates the shape of a conventional leather bag, showcasing the advanced techniques used by the Tang to craft gold and silverware.

pair of mandarin ducks symbolizing happy matrimony

Porcelain bowl
This bowl with ivory-white glaze is from the Northern Song dynasty. It was made at the Ding kiln in Dingzhou, which is famous for its distinctive porcelain.

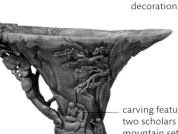

streaky splashes of color on dark background create opalescent effect

Flower ware bowl
Under the Tang, monochrome glazes gave way to flowing shades. This bowl was made by splashing colors onto a black glaze—a style known as *huaci* (flower ware).

eight-petal lotus as central decoration

carving features two scholars in mountain setting

Libation cup
This Ming dynasty cup is carved from rhino horn, which was believed to have important medicinal qualities.

Earthenware dish
This plate in the three-colors style has a baoxiang floral pattern. The lotus, a symbol of purity, became a popular motif as Buddhism spread in China under the early Tang.

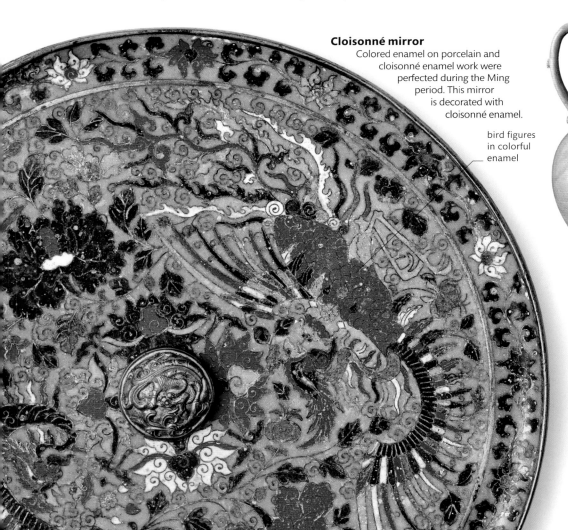

Cloisonné mirror
Colored enamel on porcelain and cloisonné enamel work were perfected during the Ming period. This mirror is decorated with cloisonné enamel.

bird figures in colorful enamel

handle terminates with dragon heads

Stoneware vase
The dragon head handles on this Tang vase are traditionally Chinese, but the bulbous shape was probably derived from Persian models, which were traded along the Silk Road.

dragon trying to reach sacred pearl of wisdom

two-shaded elephant with saddle

Jade carvings
In ancient China, jade was used for ritual and ceremonial objects but later pieces show the increasing popularity of sculpture and other tabletop items of display.

warping in kiln caused tilt in both vases

handles shaped like elephant heads

Phoenix in flight associated with long life

floral pattern in thick rim below neck of vase

four-clawed dragon signifies wisdom and benevolence

blue color on blue-and-white porcelain comes from cobalt

flaming pearls and crossed swords thought to be symbols of good luck

David vases
This pair of vases was made during the Mongol Yüan Dynasty, when trade between China and the Middle East flourished. They were originally altar vases presented by a man called Zhang Wenjin to a Daoist temple. Blue-and-white porcelains such as these continued to be popular under the Ming and Qing.

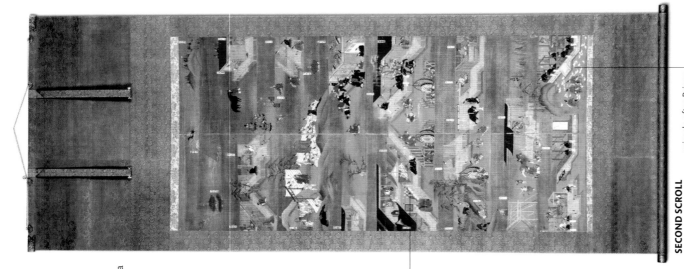

SECOND SCROLL

miracle after Prince lectures on Buddhist *Shomangyo* scripture

Shotoku's mother, Empress Anahobe, dreams of Bodhisattva in form of golden monk entering her mouth and making her pregnant

empress gives birth in Imperial stables

prince three years old, with parents, Emperor Yomei and Empress Anahobe

court life scenes with nobles reading letters and composing calligraphy while Buddhist monks worship image of the Buddha

Prince Shotoku usually depicted in orange

Soga chapel, built in 585 with permission of Emperor Bidatsu, burned down by warriors of rebel lord Mononobe no Moriya

Mononobe no Moriya's warrior throws Buddha image, which was brought over by Korean monks in 585 as endowment for Soga family's new Buddhist temple, into canal

death of Moriya on walls of his castle with arrow in his neck marks victory of Buddhism in Japan

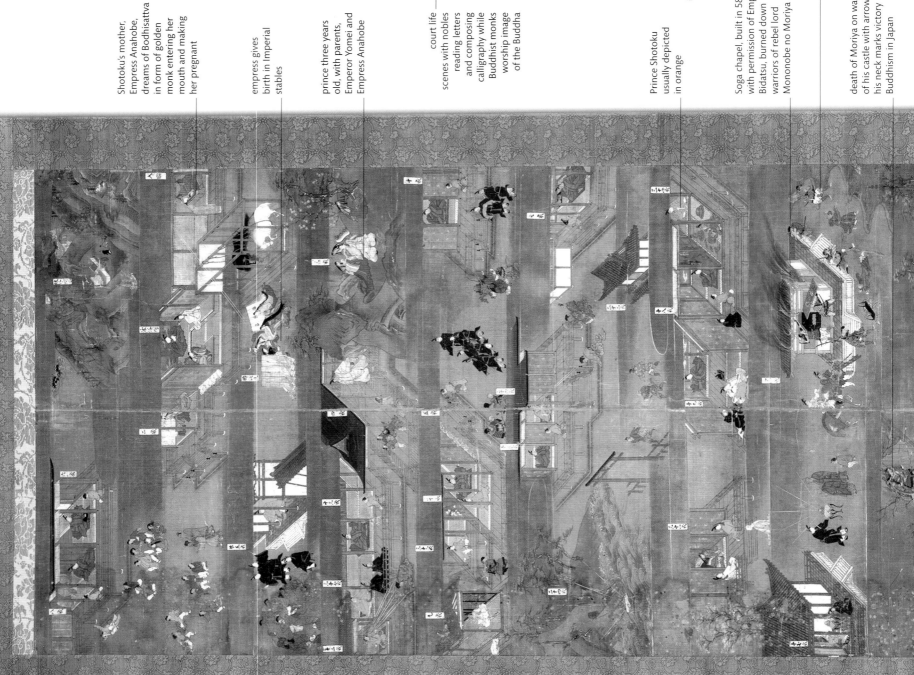

Shintoism, the traditional religion of Japan, is based on reverence for the *kami* or spiritual essence, which resides in objects such as mountains, trees, and waterfalls. Shrines were built to worship the *kami*. Shintoism lost ground to Buddhism in the 7th century, but later emperors protected Shinto shrines. Under the shogunates it became influential again.

BUDDHISM IN MEDIEVAL JAPAN

Japan, a unified state under the Yamato emperors from the 3rd century CE, imported cultural influences from Korea and China, but also retained a strong native tradition. The interplay between these cultures produced unique and rich artistic, political, and religious traditions.

The arrival of Buddhism in Japan—signaled by the sending of an image of the Buddha by the king of Paekche in Korea in 552—marked the beginning of the Asuka period (552–646) in which the country opened itself to cultural influences from the east Asian mainland. The Imperial administration became more formalized, notably under the influence of Prince Shotoku, regent for the Empress Suiko (592–628). In addition to being a talented Buddhist scholar, in 604 he issued the Seventeen Articles. They established

principles for the government based on Chinese Confucian ethics and were consolidated in 702 by the Taiho Code, which set up government ministries along Chinese lines but allowed tax exemptions for the nobility that gradually undermined imperial rule.

The art of the Asuka and the succeeding Heian (794–1185) periods was heavily influenced by Buddhism, particularly the sculpture and architecture of temples (such as Todaiji in the city of Nara). A strong tradition of landscape painting

emerged alongside the beginnings of a long-lasting literary culture, which culminated in such masterpieces as the *Tales of Genji* in the 11th century.

RISE OF THE SAMURAI

During the 8th century, power devolved into the hands of a series of dominant families, first the Fujiwara, then the Taira and Minamoto. Regional nobles held power bases largely outside central control. A damaging civil war resulted, from which Minamoto no Yoritomo

emerged victorious in 1185. He established the Kamakura shogunate, which was the first of a series of military dictatorships to rule Japan.

A new militarized society developed in Japan. The samurai, the new warrior elite, served the *shugo*, the regional aristocracy, who had taken most of the power from the shogunate itself by the 15th century. The rise of the samurai was accompanied by a new strengthening of Shintoism, the traditional Japanese religion, as outside influences were rejected.

Prince Shotoku scroll
This *kakemono*, or hanging scroll, is the first of a pair depicting the life of the 7th-century Prince Shotoku in 62 episodes. He was a fervent champion of Buddhism against the opposition of hereditary clans who practiced Shinto ritual. Tales of his life draw parallels with the life of the Buddha, and they aided the spread of popular Buddhism in medieval Japan.

battle for Buddhism between pro-Buddhist Soga clan, led by Soga no Umako, and anti-Buddhist Mononobe clan, led by Mononobe no Moriya. Shotoku, 16 years old, rides into battle against Moriya

Shotoku prays to images of Guardian Kings of Buddhism, and asks for help to defeat Moriya

KOREA'S GOLDEN KINGDOMS

The unification of Korea in the mid-7th century led to its rule by a succession of dynasties, starting with the Silla and the Goryeo. These dynasties held sway over the peninsula for more than a thousand years. Long periods of relative stability allowed the flourishing of a culture steeped in Buddhist belief.

Silla crown
This jeweled gold crown was found in a Three Kingdoms period tomb. Shaped like three trees, it may show artistic influence from Eurasia rather than China.

Sacred Buddhist scripture ▽
This 14th-century frontispiece of the *Lotus Sutra* expounds key elements of Mahayana Buddhism—the main form of the religion in Korea. Produced on mulberry paper dyed indigo blue, it is an example of the high quality of Goryeo illuminated manuscripts.

The weakening of the Three Kingdoms of ancient Korea, aggravated by a series of invasions from Tang China in the mid-7th century, led to the unification of Korea under the Silla dynasty in the 670s. Chinese influence remained extremely strong and the Silla capital Kyong-ju was modeled on the Tang capital, Gyeongju. Buddhism became so widespread that by 806 King Aejong was forced to ban the building of any further Buddhist temples to check their proliferation. The collapse of the Tang in 907 in China had a secondary effect on

Korea. Silla control fragmented during a series of civil wars, ending with the establishment of the Goryeo dynasty under Wang Geon in 918. His will, encapsulated in what became known as the Ten Admonitions, urged his subjects to maintain a separate culture from China.

Despite upheaval in China, strong artistic and cultural ties between the two countries continued. An examination mirroring the Chinese system was introduced for Korean civil servants in 950. Meanwhile, Buddhism became the de facto state religion.

Artistically, this period is noted for its high-quality celadon ceramics and woodblock printing.

GORYEO COLLAPSES

Goryeo rule was affected by wars with the Khitan and Jurchen nomads from Manchuria in the 11th century, military revolts in the 1170s, and Mongol raids in the 1230s. Korea stayed under Mongol influence until the reign of King Gongmin from 1351–74. But the Goryeo collapsed and was replaced in 1392 by the Joseon dynasty, founded by Taejo—a former Goryeo general.

BELIEFS AND RITUALS

Buddhism played a central role in both Silla and Goryeo Korea. In 1807, the Goryeo ruler ordered the creation of a complete woodblock set of the *tripitaka* (Buddhist scriptures), a task that demonstrated the intimate connection between religion and political authority. They were destroyed during the Mongol invasion of 1232 but a new set was produced by 1251.

Spoons
Incense spoons such as these mid- to late-Goryeo dynasty ones were used to offer incense before statues of the Buddha.

magpie-tail handle

design of tiny concentric circles

Funerary urn
This early Silla urn contained the cremated remains of a Buddhist devotee. Cremation was also used in the Goryeo dynasty, while the Joseon preferred burial.

Demon tile
Roof tiles, such as this one, became widespread around 680 and were placed on houses, palaces, and Buddhist temples. They were intended to scare away evil spirits as well as being signs of wealth.

FRONT   Buddha seated on lotus flower

BACK   decorated, nonreflective back

Decorated mirror
This Goryeo dynasty mirror shows the high level of craftsmanship devoted to polished bronze pieces largely destined to become grave goods.

face resembles dragon, an animal associated with water because buildings were at risk from fires

---

HOME LIFE

Society in Silla and Goryeo Korea was hierarchical. The Silla system of hereditary social ranks was simplified to six classes under the Goryeo. Strict laws laid down what people of each rank could wear or be named. Rich households often contained celadon ware—ceramics with a distinctive gray-green glaze. These were decorated with a series of delicate inlaid designs.

elongated double gourd form

gold lacquer repair work

inlaid with colored slips

Inlaid bowl
The black and white details on this bowl were made using *sanggam*—a typical mid-Goryeo dynasty technique in which designs were incised in clay before firing.

grayish blue-green tint from iron oxide in glaze

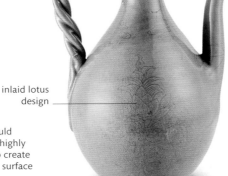

inlaid lotus design

bronze would have been highly polished to create a reflective surface

incised vertical ribbing

Bronze mirror
Mirrors such as this 12th-century one first appeared in Goryeo dynasty tombs. They were used as everyday objects by the wealthy.

Lotus pitcher
A common Buddhist symbol, lotus flowers were also a common motif on Goryeo ceramics. This pitcher may have been used to pour wine.

Oil bottle
Dating from the 12th or 13th century, this ceramic bottle was probably used to store hair oil. The rim has been repaired with gold lacquer, indicating the owner's high status.

Stem cup
The raised base of this 14th-century cup shows Mongol influence—a sign of the profound impact of the Mongol invasions on Korean society.

TEMPLE CITIES OF CAMBODIA

The Angkor kingdom flourished in modern Cambodia and extended across much of southeast Asia from the 9th to the 15th centuries. Its rulers built a series of capitals at Angkor around monumental temple complexes. The greatest of these was adorned with spectacular shrines.

During the 9th century, a series of great kingdoms emerged in southeast Asia. They were influenced by Indian culture and religion, particularly Buddhism and Hinduism. Their rulers also built magnificent temples, such as Borobudur in modern Java and Pagan in Myanmar.

One of the most spectacular sites was built at Angkor, in modern Cambodia, by the Khmers, a dynasty founded by King Jayavarman II in 802. The Khmer monarchs believed they had a divine right to rule and were called *devarajas,* or supreme kings. At times, the Angkor kingdom extended to modern Vietnam, Laos, and Thailand. Angkor became the Khmer capital and it was built over centuries. It contains beautiful palaces, pools, sculptures, and temples.

ARCHITECTURAL WONDERS

The largest temple complex at Angkor is Angkor Wat. It was built by King Suryavarman II at the start of the 12th century. Dedicated to Vishnu, the walls and galleries of the temples and walkways of Angkor Wat are adorned with intricate reliefs showing scenes of everyday life, battles, and stories from the Hindu epics, *the Mahabharata* and *the Ramayana*. A five-towered temple stands at the center of the complex, which was built to represent Mount Meru, the mythical home of the Hindu gods and the center of the Universe.

From the reign of King Jayavarman VII, starting in 1181, the Angkor kingdom began a long decline. Jayavarman VII made Buddhism the new state religion and converted the Hindu shrines at Angkor Wat. He built a new capital at Angkor Thom and the Bayon temple, dedicated to Buddha. Many of his Buddhist sites were destroyed by his Hindu successor, Jayavarman VIII. From the 13th century, drought and threats from neighboring peoples kept the Angkor kingdom from ever regaining its former glory.

fingers bent backward to form gesture known as *sandamsa*

Hall of dancers
This relief from the Preah Khan temple at Angkor, built by Jayavarman VII, shows a group of flexed dancers that may represent *yoginis* (female masters of yoga). Another interpretation is that they depict *asparas*—female divinities shown in dancing poses and associated with water. *Asparas* are also depicted on the walls of Angkor Wat.

apsaras or *yoginis* dance on lotus flowers

Home of the gods

Angkor Wat is the largest religious monument in the world. The outer walls represent the edge of the world and the moat is the cosmic ocean. The central temple complex has towers topped with lotus bud flowers—an important symbol in Hinduism.

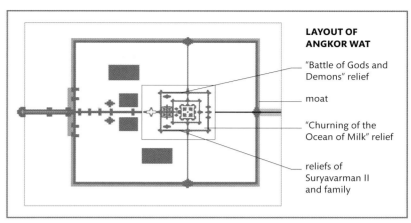

LAYOUT OF ANGKOR WAT

"Battle of Gods and Demons" relief

moat

"Churning of the Ocean of Milk" relief

reliefs of Suryavarman II and family

War scene

This relief depicts the Khmer army going to battle against the Chams from modern Vietnam. The soldiers carry spears and ride war elephants.

Hanuman

This scene from the Hindu poem, *the Ramayana*, shows Hanuman, the monkey god who traveled to the Himalayas to find herbs to heal Lord Rama's brother, wounded in battle.

Churning the Ocean

This relief from Angkor 's "Churning of the Ocean of Milk" section, shows the mythical Hindu serpent Vasuki being pulled back and forth by demons and gods to make amrita, the milk of immortality.

central figure, probably Mera, a mythological celestial maiden

outstretched arms pose, used in modern traditional Cambodian dance, derives postures from reliefs like this

feet depicted in profile

bas relief carving in sandstone

SELJUK AND EARLY OTTOMAN REALMS

From the 11th century, many Turkish tribes dominated Mesopotamia, Anatolia, and other parts of western Asia (in modern-day Iraq, Turkey, and Iran). Two of these tribes, the Seljuks and Ottomans, built vast empires that became centers of power and vibrant Islamic culture.

The Seljuks, originally nomadic Oğuz Turks, reached the Samarkand area early in the 11th century. They converted to Islam and continued to push west, conquering Khorasan (in modern-day Iran) after a victory against the Ghaznavids in 1040 that marked the real foundation of the empire.

The Seljuk Emir Tuğrul Beg captured Baghdad in 1055, placing the Abbasid Caliph under his protection. But it was the victory of his son Alp Arslan against the Byzantine emperor, at Manzikert in 1071 that enabled the empire to overrun vast swathes of land in Anatolia, even threatening Constantinople (modern Istanbul).

THE SULTANATE

Now known as the Sultanate of Rum (Rome), the Seljuk capital at Konya became the center of a glittering court. One of Alp Arslan's viziers (advisors), Nizam al Mulk, set up a university in Baghdad and endowed many educational institutions. Mosques were built throughout the sultanate, many showcasing elaborate, lacelike tracery that included floral designs and interlocking patterns. Caravanserais, or roadside inns for travelers, were established along the trade routes crossing the empire. The sultan's officials levied a tax of 2.5 percent on most goods to fund expenditure.

The Seljuks also retained their nomadic warrior tradition. They withstood the crusaders in the 11th and 12th centuries and prevented a Byzantine renaissance in 1176. But, the sultanate was beginning to fragment, and Mongol invasions of the Middle East in the late 1250s broke its power.

THE OTTOMANS

Western Anatolia was divided between competing Turkmen tribes, such as the Ottomans, who established emirates on abandoned Seljuk territory. One emirate was led by Osman I, from which the name Ottoman is derived. By 1331, the Ottomans had captured Nicaea. Within half a century, they had surged into Europe, capturing Constantinople in 1453. Inheritors of much of the Seljuk artistic tradition, their mosques and *medrese* (religious schools) sprang up in the areas they captured. The wealth they gained from their conquests let the sultans become significant patrons of the arts by 1500.

multicolored glaze and gilding added on top of opaque single-colored glaze

middle band contains birds and mounted horsemen

thick band of geometric pattern

Persian inscription in *kufic* script

> "Here below are many **sovereigns** who... **reached the Pleiades** with the tips of their **lances.**"

Inscription on the mausoleum of the Seljuk Sultan Kaykavus I in Sivas, Turkey

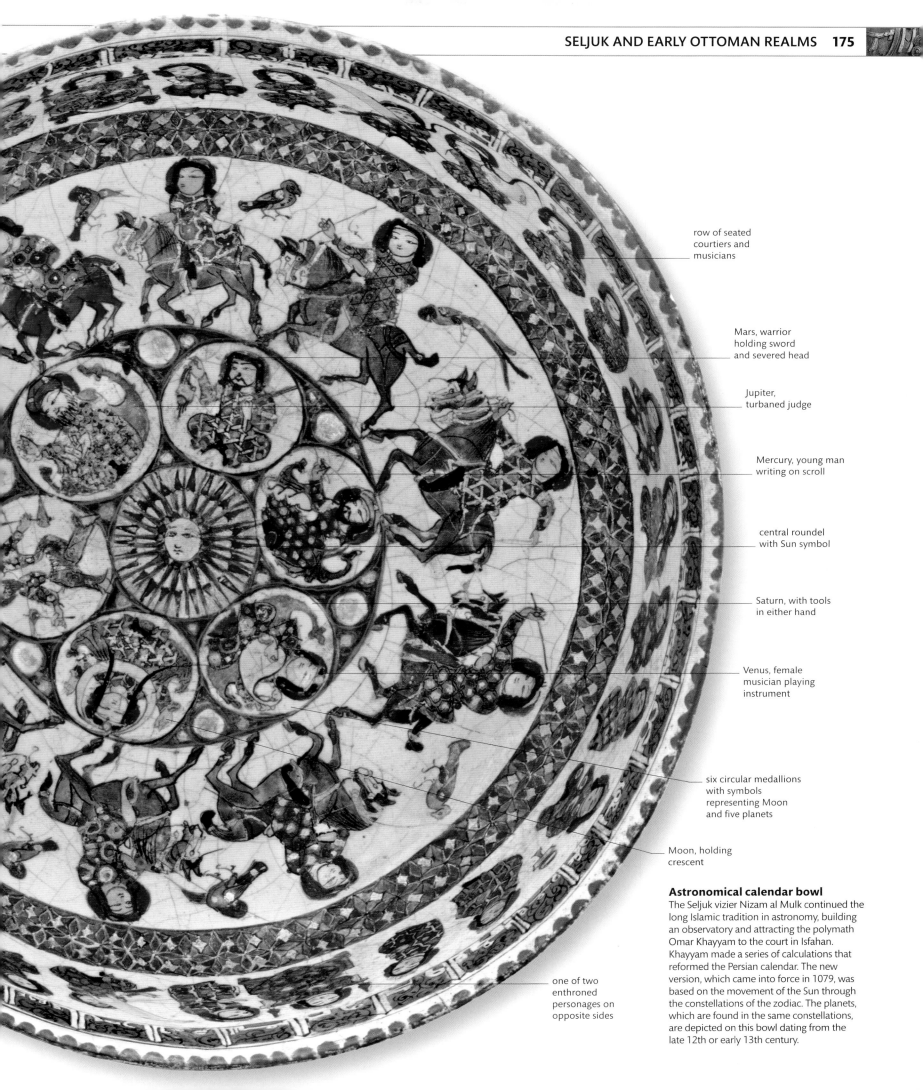

row of seated
courtiers and
musicians

Mars, warrior
holding sword
and severed head

Jupiter,
turbaned judge

Mercury, young man
writing on scroll

central roundel
with Sun symbol

Saturn, with tools
in either hand

Venus, female
musician playing
instrument

six circular medallions
with symbols
representing Moon
and five planets

Moon, holding
crescent

one of two
enthroned
personages on
opposite sides

Astronomical calendar bowl

The Seljuk vizier Nizam al Mulk continued the
long Islamic tradition in astronomy, building
an observatory and attracting the polymath
Omar Khayyam to the court in Isfahan.
Khayyam made a series of calculations that
reformed the Persian calendar. The new
version, which came into force in 1079, was
based on the movement of the Sun through
the constellations of the zodiac. The planets,
which are found in the same constellations,
are depicted on this bowl dating from the
late 12th or early 13th century.

SPIRIT OF THE GREATER SOUTHWEST

From the 9th century, the semiarid and desert regions of the American Southwest and northern Mexico gave rise to a series of cultures. These were characterized by large complexes of adobe dwellings known as pueblos, which became important centers for trade, craft, and agriculture.

Mogollon bowl
It is thought that the Mogollon drilled holes in bowls, as seen here, to kill the object and let a spirit escape into the next world.

Carving on stone ▽
The engravings on this sandstone panel at Newspaper Rock in southeastern Utah were made over a long period, starting 2,000 years ago. They include markings made by the Ancestral Pueblo, as well as the later Fremont and Navajo. Their exact purpose is unknown.

As the 1st millennium CE came to an end, settlements in the American Southwest grew larger, and a number of complex cultures emerged. These included the Ancestral Pueblo in New Mexico, the Hohokam in Arizona, and the Mogollon in western New Mexico and northern Chihuaha (part of modern Mexico).

THE CULTURES

From around 900, the Ancestral Pueblo built a number of large, well-planned towns in Chaco Canyon, New Mexico, with long, straight roads linking the settlements. By 1100, the population of these towns had swelled to 6,000, subsisting on a diet of cultivated corn and squash at the center of trade routes in precious turquoise. The culture collapsed within 50 years, possibly due to variable rainfall causing a decline in food production.

The Hohokam culture flourished around the Gila and Salt River basins in Arizona, reaching its height in 1100–1450. The largest settlement, Snaketown, had around 1,000 people living in subterranean pit dwellings and above-ground adobe houses. Ball courts and platform mounds found in the Hohokam area suggest a significant cultural influence from Mesoamerica. The Hohokam culture, too, declined in the 15th century, and its trade networks were abandoned.

The Mogollon culture (and a subculture, the Mimbres) was centered in the mountains of western New Mexico. Noted for their fine red and brown ceramics, the Mogollon also built settlements with up to 150 rooms centered around a plaza. The main settlements had declined by about 1450.

HUNTING

Although the peoples of the American Southwest relied on crops such as corn and squash for food (and domesticated turkeys), they supplemented their diet by hunting. Larger animals such as deer or, close to grasslands, buffalo, were hunted in late fall or early spring, while rabbits were the target of communal hunts throughout the colder months.

HOHOKAM ARROWHEAD

tang to attach arrowhead to shaft

ANCESTRAL PUEBLO ARROWHEAD

notched point

MOGOLLON ARROWHEAD

Arrowheads
The bow and arrow reached the American Southwest in the first three centuries CE. Arrows allowed hunters to hunt in wooded country and strike their prey at greater range.

angled surface to allow flight

wood stained with red pigment

Spear thrower
This spear thrower from the pre-Ancestral Pueblo Basketmaker culture could hurl a spear with greater force than with the arm alone.

CLOTHING AND ADORNMENT

People of the Pueblo cultures wore clothes woven—largely by men—from cotton, which was imported from areas to the south. Some items, such as kilts and blankets, were woven from native yucca fiber, while shoes were made from braided yucca. Jewelry made of shell or turquoise is a common find at Pueblo sites.

Ancestral Pueblo sandal
Made from yucca fiber, early Ancestral Pueblo sandals were square-shaped. Sandals were important as clothing and marking social identity.

dyed yucca fiber

made from shells

Ancestral Pueblo pendant
The turquoise and shell of this Ancestral Pueblo culture pendant are likely to have been imported.

shell bracelets fashioned using stone tools

Bracelets
The raw material for this pair of Hohokam bracelets was probably imported. Marine shells came from the Pacific coast and freshwater shells from Texas and California.

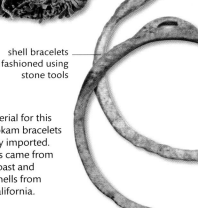

HOME LIFE

The Pueblo peoples of the Four Corners region, where the states of Arizona, New Mexico, Colorado, and Utah intersect, created great cliff dwellings that were similar to the adobe houses and villages they had built centuries ago. At the site of Paquimé at Casas Grandes in Mexico, a multi-storey complex with over 2,000 rooms was developed.

Paquimé jar
The serpent decoration on this Paquimé jar is a typical image from farther south in Mesoamerica. It indicates the transmission of cultural ideas across the region.

banded, geometric design on white background

vessel shaped like body of pregnant woman

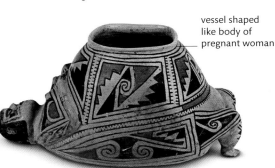

Painted Paquimé vessel
The Casas Grandes, or Paquimé, culture is marked by the creation of distinctive polychrome pottery, such as this vessel.

painted decoration of frog

Ancestral Pueblo cup
This cup from Mesa Verde was made by the Ancestral Pueblo in the 13th century. The Ancestral Pueblo perfected a distinctive style of black-on-white pottery.

Ladle
Pottery reached the Four Corners region around 300–400 CE. Within a century, items such as this ladle from the pre-Ancestral Pueblo Basketmaker culture were being produced.

zigzag geometric pattern

Ancestral Pueblo *olla*
This jar from the early 12th century would have been used for storage. Such jars are often found as grave goods.

THE MYTH-MAKERS OF MESOAMERICA

A succession of cultures occupied Mesoamerica—the area from northern Mexico to El Salvador and Belize—from 600 CE to the arrival of Europeans in 1519. Although very diverse, these cultures shared key features, including city-states and empires with monumental centers, the worship of a common set of gods, and the playing of a ceremonial ball game.

Aztec calendar stone
This carved calendar stone from 1427 has the Sun in the middle. It records the four "suns," or creations, that the Aztecs believed had preceded the present "fifth sun."

Set in stone ▷
This *chacmool*, or reclining male statue, from the Mayan city of Chichén Itzá in Yucatán, Mexico, may represent a sacrificed war captive or the rain god Tlaloc. It is thought that the flat plate on the stomach was used to hold offerings or as an altar.

The Late Classic Period (c.600–900) saw a flowering of Mayan culture. The city-states of Palenque, Yaxchilan, and Tikal were remodeled to create stone temples, pyramids, palaces, ball courts, and plazas. At its height, the Mayan civilization consisted of over 40 cities, each governed by a noble ruler. The Maya were renowned not only for their stone buildings but also for their agricultural techniques of irrigation and raised fields, as well as their sophisticated writing, calendar, and astronomy systems.

The lowland cities began to decline during the 9th century due to drought, deforestation, and warfare. Meanwhile, the Putun Maya, sea traders and warriors from the Gulf lowlands, rose to prominence. They created a state centered on Chichén Itzá in the highlands of the Yucatán. Another city, Mayapán, conquered Chichén Itzá around 1221 but collapsed by 1450.

THE TOLTECS
In the central highlands of Mexico, the warlike Toltecs founded the city of Tula, which reached the height of its power between 900 and 1150, when the population may have reached over 40,000. Tula's buildings included two massive pyramids. As well as being masters of architecture, the Toltecs also produced colossal sculptures of warriors, reflecting their militaristic ethos. They marked a rise of militarism in Mesoamerica and their influence was wide. The Toltec military orders—the Coyote, the Jaguar, and the Eagle—were introduced into Mayan cities such as Chichén Itzá and Mayapán.

THE RISE OF THE AZTECS
As the Toltecs declined, possibly because of a change to a more arid climate, the Aztecs came to dominate the Valley of Mexico. In 1325, they settled on the islands in Lake Texcoco and founded their capital—Tenochtitlán—by creating canals through the lake and heaping up the earth to make artificial islands on which they could grow crops. This ability to cultivate any available land, create complex systems of irrigation, and reclaim swampland was key to the empire's success.

The Aztecs created a dynasty of *tlataoni*, or supreme rulers, who lived in lavish palaces and controlled a large empire through might. They demanded tribute from the peoples they conquered and set up a large trading network to accumulate great wealth. By the start of the reign of Moctezuma I, in 1440, much of Mexico was either controlled by the Aztecs or owed tribute to them.

The Aztecs had a complex belief system based on the need to sustain the Sun. They thought it was necessary to offer human sacrifices to keep the Sun in the sky and prevent it from destroying the Earth. To gather victims to sacrifice, the Aztecs fought ritualized combats, known as flower wars, against the peoples they had conquered.

In 1519 Spanish explorers, led by Hernán Cortés, arrived in Mexico. Moctezuma II underestimated the Spanish and, after treating them as guests, he was taken captive. Deprived of leadership, decimated by smallpox, which the Spanish had carried with them, and attacked by their former allies, the Aztecs' empire crumbled.

" If we **do not achieve** what **we intend...** you will have **your vengeance.**"

Itzcoatl, Aztec ruler, before the war with the Tepanecs, late 1420s

BATTLE AND CONFLICT

Warfare was at the center of Aztec society, and young men were trained as warriors from an early age in eagle houses. The Aztec armies numbered as many as 200,000 men. Their battle tactic involved confronting opponents with volleys of stones and spears, followed by hand-to-hand combat using clubs.

helmet shaped like an eagle's head

modeled in clay, with mother-of-pearl inlay

Toltec jar
This plumbate effigy jar from the Toltec capital of Tula is shaped like a helmet. It depicts a coyote warrior emerging from the jaws of a coyote.

stucco paint remains in patches, showing figurine was once covered with white feathers

Eagle warrior
The most prestigious Aztec military orders were the Eagle and the Jaguar. The warriors wore costumes to match their order.

legs adorned with claws

Obsidian arrowhead
The Aztecs and other Mesoamericans made weapons and tools from obsidian, which produces a sharper edge than metal.

jaguar skin

band of dyed feathers

Aztec shield
All Aztec warriors carried a shield for protection. There were prescribed rules for military wear, based on the number of captives a warrior had taken, and only nobles wore feathered armor.

CLOTHING AND ADORNMENT

Cotton formed the basis of Aztec and Mayan clothing. The men wore a loincloth and the women dressed in a *huipil*, or a square-cut tunic. The common man wore plain clothes. Decorated styles and featherwork garments were reserved for the nobility, who also wore obsidian ear spools, necklaces, and pendants of jade and gold.

Pendants
These small 11th- or 12th-century pendants with mother-of-pearl and jadeite inlay show the virtuosity of Mayan craftsmen.

obsidian earspool decorated with a glyph

Earspool
Aztec nobles wore earspools like earrings. They were frequently made from rock crystal, amber, or obsidian.

monkey decoration

stamp with floral pattern used to decorate cheek

geometric design

Body stamps
These ceramic stamps were used by the Aztecs to decorate their bodies as well as their clothes. The stamps would be dipped in paint or dye and pressed onto the skin or cloth to imprint the pattern.

effigy pendant

beads of jadeite and greenstone

Pendant necklace
Jewelry making was considered a prestigious craft and Aztec jewelers had their own guilds. This necklace has a pendant carved like a human figurine.

Toltec figurine
Elaborate feather headdresses, such as the one on this figurine, were worn by the Toltec nobility as well as the elites of other Mesoamerican cultures.

HOME LIFE

The vast majority of Mesoamerican people worked on communal farmlands. Women spent much of their time weaving cotton and grinding corn for tortillas, while the men worked the fields, often also serving the nobility or performing military service. Many of the artifacts of Mesoamerican daily life that have survived belonged to the elite.

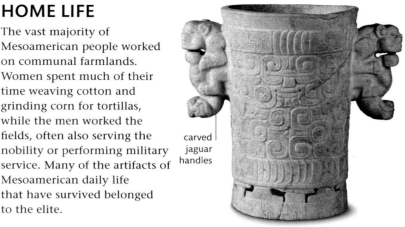

carved jaguar handles

Cylindrical vase
Marble vases from Honduras's Ulua valley, such as this one, were used by elites and traded as far as Belize, indicating the extensive trade networks of the Mayan world.

face shows signs of scarring

ear spools

large beaded necklace

off-shoulder blouse

large bracelet

Mayan woman
This 9th-century figurine illustrates a Mayan woman in attire typical of the time. She also has the crossed eyes and flattened forehead that the Maya prized.

rectilinear geometric patterns characteristic of early Aztec pottery

Aztec bowl
Ceramic workshops in four main areas of the Aztec Empire—Texcoco, Chalco, Ixtapalapa, and Tenochtitlán—crafted pottery in this characteristic black-on-orange style.

glazed ceramic turkey-head handle

Pacific pot
Plumbate effigy vessels, such as this one, were an important type of commercial ware during the Toltec civilization. They were produced on the Pacific Coast.

brazier on head

one leg forms pipestem and back of bowl

Aztec pottery pipe
The figure on this pipe represents Huehueteotl (the old god). He was believed to guard the hearth, the place where many household religious rites took place.

figurine may represent Ix Chebel Yax, goddess of weaving

back-strap loom used throughout Mesoamerica

Mayan figurine
This figurine depicts a seated woman operating a back-strap loom. Women weaving were a common theme in Mayan art.

ART AND CULTURE

Mesoamerican craftsmen were skilled stoneworkers, particularly adept at carving stone reliefs. Jewelry and decorated metalwork were also highly prized art forms. Mesoamerican cultures excelled at architecture, creating planned cities with huge temples and palaces grouped around central plazas.

INNER SURFACE WITH SUPERNATURAL FIGURE

three-legged dish

figure wears ear spools

Aztec figure

This figure has delicate detailing on the hair and face. The Aztecs did not use metal tools to work the hard jadeite. They used tools of jadeite or other hard materials.

Polychrome dish

This dish is from Greater Nicoya, Nicaragua, a region at the farthest southern extent of Mesoamerican influence.

frog associated with rain god Tlaloc

Frog figure

Frogs were associated with water and rain, as well as with fertility. They often appear in Aztec art, although they were also eaten as a delicacy.

depiction of seated Mayan lord

Carved jadeite

Mesoamerican jadeite carvings showed fine symmetry and balance, as well as delicate surface detailing, as seen in these two Mayan jadeite plaques.

FRONT VIEW   **SIDE VIEW**

Stone skull

Made during the high point of the Aztec Empire, between the mid-15th and early 16th centuries, this skull shows the Aztec preoccupation with death. It may have been mounted into a wall socket.

Temple model

This pottery model of a temple is Toltec, but its high pyramidal sides and the high roof comb suggest a strong influence from Mayan architectural practice.

steep stairs to reach temple platform

THE BALL GAME

The Aztecs, the Maya, and many other Mesoamerican civilizations all played a ritual ball game based on religious beliefs. It had a cosmological significance as well as being a competitive game and a form of ritualized warfare. Some cultures sacrificed the captain of the losing team.

CINNABAR PIGMENT ON YOKE

Greenstone yoke

This yoke is probably a ceremonial stone replica of the wicker or leather yolks that ball-game players wore around their waists as a form of protection.

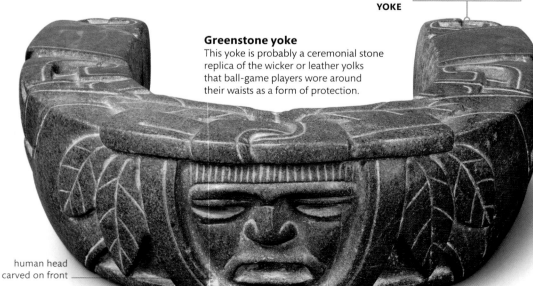

human head carved on front

Stone skull

The ball game was strongly associated with death. This skull may have been worn on a player's yoke or used to mark off sections of the ball court.

Mayan vase

This cylindrical vase depicts a ball-game player wearing his yoke and other forms of protective padding. Players also wore deerskin suits and elaborate helmets.

Ball-game courts

Courts for the ball game can be found throughout Mesoamerica. Players had to keep the ball in the air by hitting it with their hips, shoulders, and knees, and scored by propelling the rubber ball through a ring embedded in the court's wall.

ball-court ring

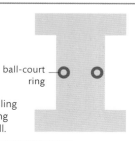

BELIEFS AND RITUALS

Mesoamerican religion was focused on the cosmos and the natural world, including agricultural fertility and deities such as the Sun. Blood sacrifice was practiced by most Mesoamerican cultures to nourish the gods. The Aztecs, in turn, believed that the gods had sacrificed themselves to create the world.

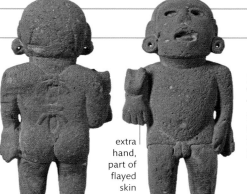

statue shows him wearing freshly flayed skin

extra hand, part of flayed skin

Fertility god
The Aztec fertility god Xipe Totec was referred to as "the flayed god." The skins of those sacrificed to him were flayed, treated, and worn by this deity's priest.

made from turquoise, jadeite, shell, and mother-of-pearl

Aztec mask
This mosaic mask depicts Quetzalcoatl, who was worshipped across ancient Mesoamerica as a creator deity, the god of nature and the wind, and the god of knowledge.

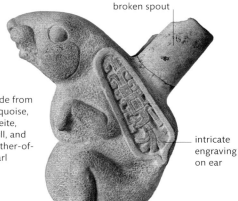

broken spout

intricate engraving on ear

Effigy vessel
This vessel depicts a rabbit. In the creation myth of the Guatemalan Highland Maya, a rabbit aids the Hero Twins in a ball game against the gods of the underworld.

corn, attached to headdress

elaborate headdress

Chac often depicted with large eyes and protruding fangs

mosaic of small pieces of turquoise

teeth inlaid with white and red shells

Serpent pectoral
Worn by a high priest, this double-headed serpent pectoral may have formed part of the treasure sent to Cortés by Moctezuma, who believed Cortés was the returning god Quetzalcoatl.

bowl of smoking incense in one hand

animal head headdress

tail of animal costume serves as a third leg

Standing figure
This figure with elaborate jewelry and arms outstretched, from Mexico's Gulf coast, may represent a shaman.

animal effigy represents porcupine with raised quills

Censer
This Mayan censer was used to burn incense made of copal (tree resin), which was an essential part of most Mayan religious ceremonies.

Rain god
Chac, the Mayan rain god, was believed to protect corn fields. Facades of buildings were often covered with masks of Chac.

■ THE FAVOR OF THE GODS

YAXCHILAN LINTEL

During the Late Classic Period (c.600–900)—the high point of Mayan culture—the Mayan world consisted of a series of competing city-states, with various dynasties vying for supremacy over others. The kings raised great carved stelae (tall stone shafts) and lintels (horizontal beams) to mark their victories and other important events.

Lying on a bend in Mexico's Usumacinta River, Yaxchilan was at first a relatively minor city-state. From 359, it was ruled by the same dynasty,

but it was engaged in constant struggles with its neighbors, such as Calakmul, Bonampak, and Piedras Negras. Yaxchilan flourished under Shield Jaguar II (681–742), whose long reign saw a string of victories, elevating the state into a position of regional dominance. Power was further consolidated under the rule of his son Bird Jaguar IV (752–68).

SACRIFICE OF BLOOD

A number of temples and monuments were built during Shield Jaguar II's reign in honor of his successes. These included Temple 23, said to have been commissioned by his principal queen, Lady K'ab'al Xook. The temple's Lintel 25 marks the king's accession in 681,

with the image of the rain god Tlaloc springing from the jaws of a giant serpent. The lintel that follows shows Lady K'ab'al Xook presenting her husband with a jaguar helmet.

On Lintel 24 (below), she is shown engaging in a blood-letting ceremony, one of the many rituals required of the Mayan rulers. The sacrifice of blood to gods and other supernatural beings was believed to repeat the primeval sacrifice that had caused the creation of the universe. Blood-letting was carried out on particularly auspicious dates, such as the anniversary of the accession of a ruler, or on dates in the Mayan calendar that marked the end of a period—such as the end of a 20-year epoch known as a *katun*.

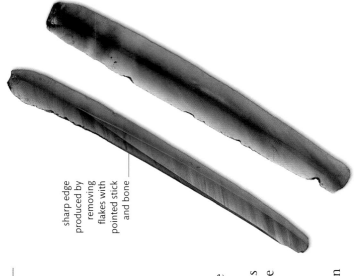

Obsidian blades
These blades are typical of the tools used in Mayan blood-letting ceremonies. Stingray spines and snail shells were also used for this purpose.

sharp edge produced by removing flakes with pointed stick and bone

Blood-letting relief
Lintel 24 depicts a ceremony from 709. In it, Shield Jaguar II stands to the left, while his wife, Lady Xook, pulls a thorny rope through her tongue. The relief also marks the capture of Ah Ahual, a foreign ruler.

glyph with name of Ah Ahual, the captive

flaming torch of Shield Jaguar II

name glyph of Shield Jaguar II

shrunken head of sacrificial victim

glyph indicating blood-letting

glyph indicating date of event—October 24, 709

mosaic head of the rain god Tlaloc

sun god pectoral strung with beads

brooch representing the Mayan sun god

red pigment

thorn-studded rope used for blood-letting

intricately carved *huipil*, or tunic

traces of blue pigment

woven basket to collect drops of blood

THE DRESDEN CODEX

The Dresden Codex is one of only four verified Mayan books that survived the Spanish conquest of Mesoamerica in the 16th century, the other three being the Madrid, Paris, and Grolier codices. These books were named after the European cities to which they were eventually taken.

The Dresden Codex is 11.5 ft (3.5 m) long and consists of 39 painted leaves (pages) that can be folded into a book. Most of its pages feature a mixture of symbols and pictures, mainly of the Mayan gods. The codex contains almanacs detailing astronomical and calendric information.

MARKING TIME

The Mayan calendar was highly complex and it was also used by other Mesoamerican peoples. It was based on a series of recurring cycles governed by the interaction between the sacred year of 260 days (13 months of 20 days each) and the *haab* or "vague year" of 365 days. The 52-year period in which the two cycles reached the same point was known as the calendar round.

The Maya believed that time was cyclical, with events repeating, so the future could be predicted from the past. The movement of the heavens was thought to relate to the activities of the gods, and astronomical knowledge was essential to determine which days were propitious or dangerous. The Maya used a calendrical system known as the long count, which had its origins in earlier times. This was based on counting forward from August 13, 3114 BCE in units of *kins* (one day), *uinals* (20 days), *tuns* (360 days), *katuns* (7,200 days or about 20 years), and *baktuns* (394 years). The Dresden Codex was compiled after 1210, which is the latest long count date recorded in it.

MAYAN ASTRONOMY

Mayan astronomers tracked the cycles of the Moon and calculated that 149 lunar cycles were equal to 4,400 days. The cycles of the planet Venus were especially important to the Maya, who called it *Noh Ek* ("the great star"). The codex contains five pages of Venus tables, of which panel 53 is one. The Maya regarded Venus and the Sun as sons of the corn god, who were responsible for his resurrection, after outwitting and killing the gods of the underworld.

The Maya calculated that five Venusian years (of nearly 584 days) were equal to almost eight Earth years. Their sophisticated astronomers realized that the true Venusian year was around one-twelfth of a day shorter than this, and they included corrections in their astronomical codices to compensate.

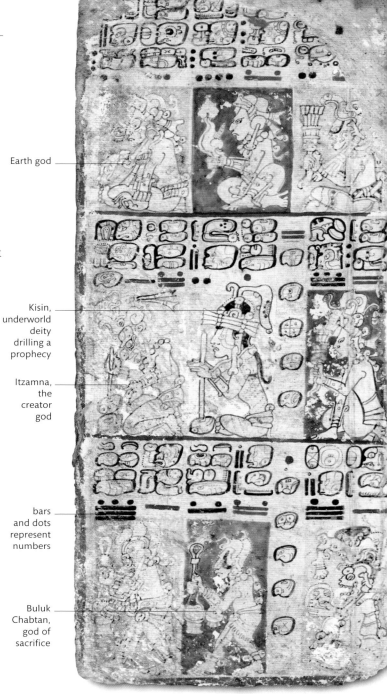

Earth god

Kisin, underworld deity drilling a prophecy

Itzamna, the creator god

bars and dots represent numbers

Buluk Chabtan, god of sacrifice

PANEL 6

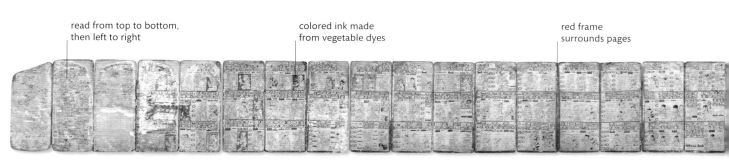

The complete codex
The codex begins with multiplication tables that were useful in Mayan calendar calculations. These are followed by a series of 260-day almanacs detailing the properties of each day. It also includes tables for the planet Venus, the Moon, and a set of prophecies relating to 20-year *katuns*.

read from top to bottom, then left to right

colored ink made from vegetable dyes

red frame surrounds pages

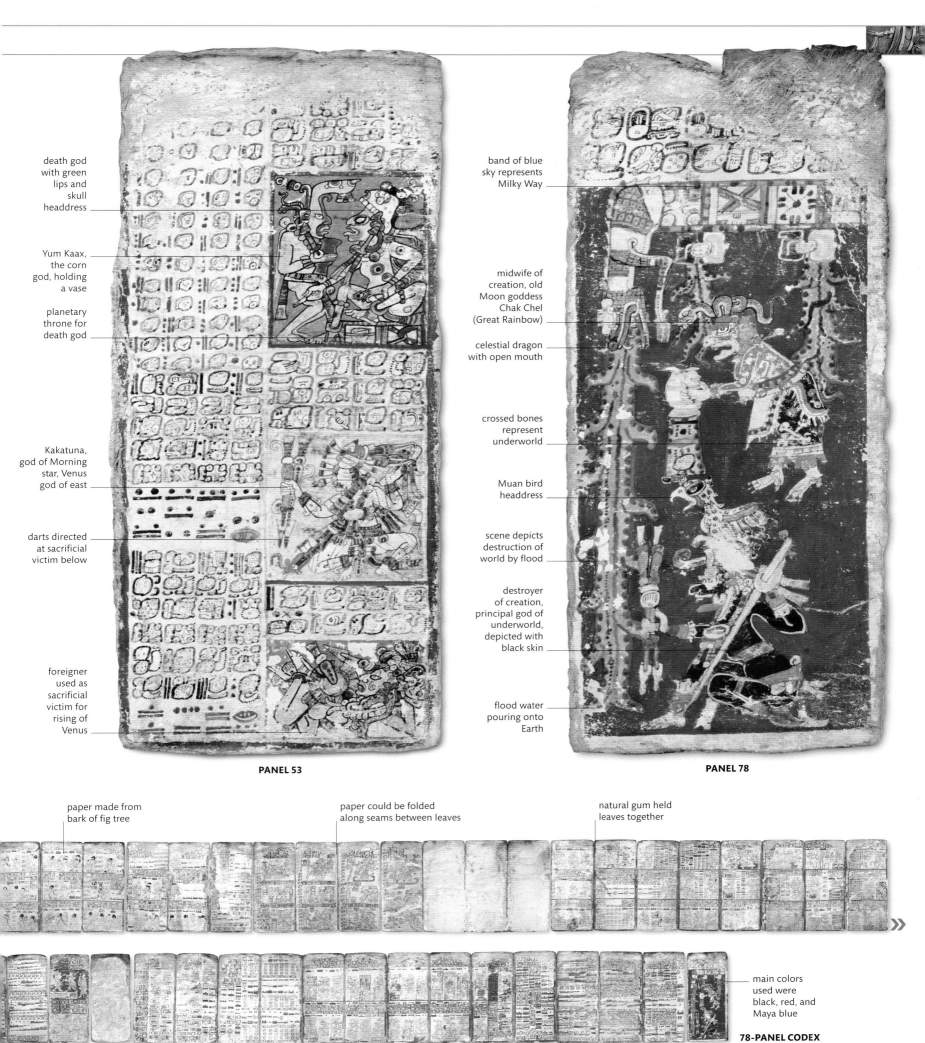

death god with green lips and skull headdress

Yum Kaax, the corn god, holding a vase

planetary throne for death god

Kakatuna, god of Morning star, Venus god of east

darts directed at sacrificial victim below

foreigner used as sacrificial victim for rising of Venus

PANEL 53

band of blue sky represents Milky Way

midwife of creation, old Moon goddess Chak Chel (Great Rainbow)

celestial dragon with open mouth

crossed bones represent underworld

Muan bird headdress

scene depicts destruction of world by flood

destroyer of creation, principal god of underworld, depicted with black skin

flood water pouring onto Earth

PANEL 78

paper made from bark of fig tree

paper could be folded along seams between leaves

natural gum held leaves together

main colors used were black, red, and Maya blue

78-PANEL CODEX

TREASURES OF THE ANDES

A series of imperial cultures emerged in the highlands of Peru from the 4th century CE, each of which built large monumental centers. The last of these cultures, the Inca, conquered much of the Andean highlands and coastal regions by the 15th century only to fall to Spanish invaders by 1532.

decorated with geometric, embossed design

Burial offering
Gold was associated with the Sun in Andean religious belief. These Chimú funerary gloves are made from beaten gold.

Paradise lost ▽
Built high in the Andes around the end of the 15th century, the city of Machu Picchu is an outstanding example of Inca architecture. This natural fortress had 143 buildings, 80 of which were houses and the rest ceremonial buildings such as temples.

Around 600, political power in Peru shifted to two states originating in the Andean highlands. The city of Tiwanaku on the shores of Lake Titicaca had magnificent temples and ceremonial precincts. Its influence spread to southern lowland areas.

The Wari people, centered on the Ayacucho Basin, built a highly organized state with an advanced irrigation system, dominating highland and lowland regions far to the north. Wari and Tiwakanu art shared many elements. Both states declined by c.1100.

During the 8th century, the Sicán culture developed in the Lambayeque Valley on the north coast. They built cities with funerary-religious precincts in which pyramids housed elite tombs, containing many gold objects.

The Sicán were defeated by the neighboring Chimú state of Chimor in 1375. A succession of Chimú kings conquered most of the central Peruvian lowlands. The Chimú were skilled architects and their capital Chan Chan housed around 10,000 inhabitants, including nine successive *ciudadelas* (royal compounds).

Around 1470, Chan Chan was captured by the Inca. The last great Andean civilization, the Inca originated in the Peruvian highlands and grew in the mid-15th century under a series of great conqueror-rulers. Their empire was called *Tawantinsuyu* (the "Land of the Four Quarters"). Rapid communications via more than 24,855 miles (40,000 km) of roads and way stations helped the Inca to conquer most of the Andean region. Smallpox, introduced by the Spanish in the 1520s, played a central role in their decline.

CLOTHING AND ADORNMENT

The production of cloth was highly developed in ancient Peru, where the different cultures created a wealth of woven textiles. In the Andean highlands, most clothing was made from wool, while in the lowlands cotton was the main material. The Chimú and the Inca also had expert feather-workers.

Tabard
A variety of colored bird feathers—from species found in the Amazon rain forest and the coast of Peru—were used to decorate tabards (short-sleeved jackets).

handspun threads decorated with feathers

Inca coca pouch
Pouches like this one contained coca leaves, which were traditionally chewed to fight off fatigue and the effects of altitude sickness.

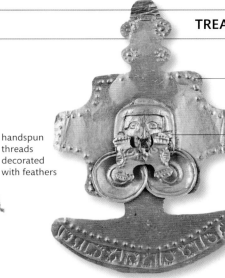

embossed and hammered sheet gold

nose ornament

Gold breastplate
This 10th-century breastplate from the Calima culture of modern Colombia is decorated with a human face wearing a nose ornament, similar to ones worn by people at the time.

Inca armlets
Warriors who distinguished themselves in battle were rewarded with fine textiles, gold, and jewelry, such as this pair of gold armlets.

made from shell and turquoise

Disk
These disks may have been worn as earrings or attached to clothing. They are decorated with alternating representations of a bird and a feline.

heavy crown ornament may have been made for funerary purposes

eyes and headbands would have been inlaid with semi-precious stones

figure stands on balsa raft

decorated with anthropomorphic figure of a man surrounded by zoomorphic figures

Chimú crown
Religious and political leaders adorned themselves with metal jewelry, such as this gold crown. Sicán craftsmen deported to Chan Chan made a lot of gold work after the Chimú defeated the Sicán.

fringe of gold and feathers

Chimú headdress
In ancient Peru feathers, like gold, were highly prized items. They were used on ceremonial objects and garments for people of high-ranking status, such as this 14th-century headdress.

human figure wearing headdress

carved from a single piece of fine-grained wood

Mirror frame
This Chimú wooden mirror frame shows influences from the Wari culture. It was probably once covered with thin sheet gold or silver attached with tiny nails.

HOME LIFE

For most people, life in the Andes was harsh and strictly regulated, with little social mobility. The Chimú city of Chan Chan had residential compounds reserved for the elite. In Inca society, people remained bound to the clan they were born into. Ordinary people lived in small, rectangular houses that were made from stone and had only one room.

burnished finish

flared body with inward sloping rim

Inca plate
This clay plate is from the Pachacamac Sun Temple. It is decorated with a bird-head handle and concentric geometric patterns with images of frogs.

human face carved in relief

color created by use of pigmented gum

Colonial period Inca *keros*
These post-Spanish-conquest cups are based on earlier ceremonial bowls. The human figures on them are much larger than in traditional examples.

spoutlike protrusion

Inca pitcher
The Inca made ceramics for either ritual or domestic use, including different-sized pitchers painted with geometric patterns. They were frequently decorated with a leaf pattern, as seen on this pitcher.

BELIEFS AND RITUALS

Andean religions venerated ancestors, as well as complex pantheons of gods. For the Chimú, the chief deity was the Moon goddess, Si. The Incas viewed Inti, the Sun god, as supreme; gold was said to be his sweat, and silver was believed to be the tears of his wife, the Moon goddess Mama-Quilla.

striped cloak and several belts cover body

bag hanging from belt contains cotton and coca leaves

Chimú mummy
Corpses of important people were mummified by the Chimú. The mummies were placed in funerary monuments and worshipped.

Mummy figure
Colorful figures such as this one were sometimes buried along with mummies. They were placed with the deceased to serve them in the afterlife.

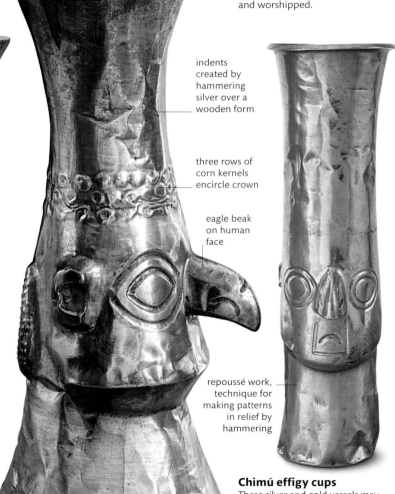

indents created by hammering silver over a wooden form

three rows of corn kernels encircle crown

eagle beak on human face

repoussé work, technique for making patterns in relief by hammering

Chimú effigy cups
These silver and gold vessels may have contained *chicha*, or corn beer, which was often consumed during sacrifices and rituals or used as an offering to the gods. Such offerings were considered neccesary to ensure a good harvest.

hollow body

Silver figurine
The Inca made figurines, such as this one of a woman, and placed them in human burials as offerings. They were originally clothed in woven garments.

Gold cup
This Sicán cup has an elaborate turquoise inlay and a flat base. It may have contained liquids such as sacrificial blood used in rituals and sacrifices.

made from hammered gold

granulation around inlaid stone

Llama figurine
Llamas were the most common animals used for religious sacrifices. Miniature figures of llamas were also given as offerings alongside human sacrifices.

Naymlap, the Sicán ancestor deity

painted bird on front of body

inscribed Sun figure

Effigy vessel
Shaped like a jaguar, this Wari vessel dates from 600–800 CE. The cult of jaguars and other cats played an important role in Andean religions.

turquoise inlay

forked bone with incised design

Gold *tumi*
In Andean temples, many sacrifices and rituals were performed using ceremonial knives, or *tumi*. This *tumi* is from the Sicán-Lambayeque culture of Peru.

Snuff pipe
This pipe from Tiwanaku is made from llama bone. It was used to store the crushed seed of a hallucinogenic plant that was inhaled in order to produce a vision-inducing trance.

Snuff tablet
This engraved tablet from Tiwanaku would have contained snuff in the rectangular depression, which was then cosnumed directly off a spoon.

snake decoration

Inca mortar
This stone mortar was sculpted from a single block of volcanic basalt from the Inca capital of Cusco. It may have been used in religious ceremonies to hold liquid offerings.

half-moon shaped blade

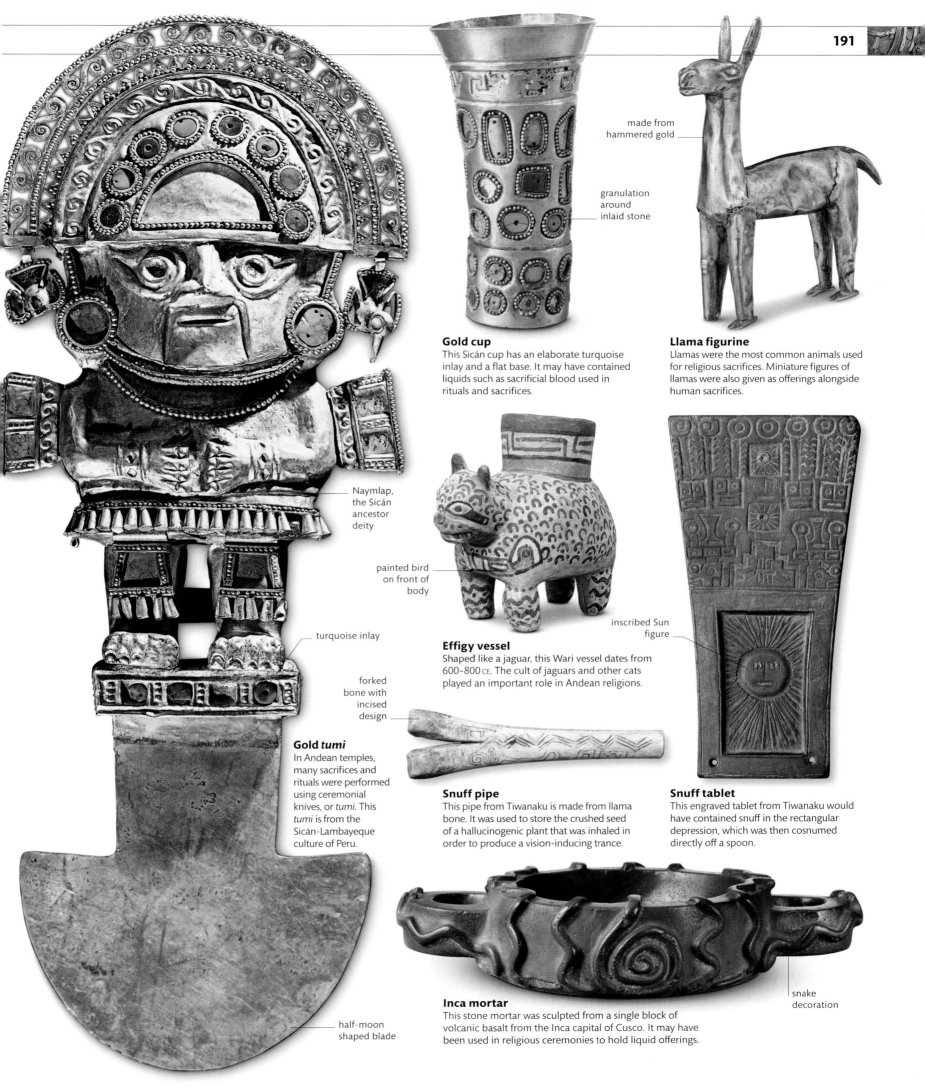

pukao, warrior's stylized headdress

THE SCULPTORS OF EASTER ISLAND

The extreme isolation of Rapa Nui, or Easter Island, saw the development of a unique culture that featured a religion honoring ancestors. This led the island's inhabitants to erect hundreds of massive monumental stone statues, mainly along its shorelines.

Thousands of kilometers from the nearest land, Rapa Nui was first settled around 1200 by voyaging migrants from other Polynesian islands who sailed there on double-hulled canoes. According to legend, the settlers were led by a chief named Hotu Matu`a.

The Easter Islanders lived on subsistence agriculture, supplemented by shore fishing and the collection of shellfish. Their population grew rapidly, and by 1350 it may have reached over 3,000. It remained stable until the arrival of Europeans nearly four centuries later.

THE SOCIETY

The class structure of the society that developed was hierarchical. All economic activity was controlled by the Miru lineage, who were supposedly the descendants of Hotu Matu`a, and led by the *Ariki Henua,* or hereditary chief. Settlements were small, some of them consisting of just two or three houses. Village complexes with houses for priests acted as ceremonial centers.

Much effort was devoted to ritual activity, notably the quarrying of stone to build the *Moai*—monumental stone statues that are thought to be deified ancestors—and to build the *ahu*—platforms on which the *Moai*

stood. Many of the *moai* were set up in rows along the island's shorelines. By the beginning of the 18th century, deforestation and erosion compelled the islanders to develop new agricultural methods. Food became scarce, aggravated by the lack of wood for canoes, which made offshore fishing difficult. Warfare broke out between clans, and warriors became more important. The traditional ancestral religion was augmented and replaced with the establishment of a ritual contest that decided which of two rival clans would rule the island each year.

THE END OF RAPA NUI

It was the arrival of Europeans in 1722 that led to downfall of Rapa Nui. The next century and a half saw conflict with European invaders and enslavement, as well as newly introduced diseases that decimated the population. In 1774, when British navigator Captain James Cook arrived on the island, the Englishmen with him observed that the *Moai* were no longer venerated. Many of them had been deliberately toppled from their platforms. They were rejected in favor of a creator god—*Makemake*—chief of the religious activity centered around the birdman (see panel, below).

arms carved
in bas-relief

Moai statues
This row of *Moai* are situated on an *ahu* facing inland. Originally, Easter Island had 250–300 such platforms. It is thought that the statues were positioned in this way in order to watch over the villages.

THE BIRDMAN

Makemake was the chief god of the religious activity centered around the birdman. From around 1760, an annual competition developed in which champions of the competing military clans swam to the island of Motu Nui to find a speckled tern egg. The winner was proclaimed the *tangata manu*, the birdman, and his chief became the island's ruler for a year.

Moai
The 800–1000 *Moai*, or monumental statues, of Rapa Nui were erected between 1200 and 1600. They probably formed part of a protective ancestor religion. Made of Rano Raraku tuff (a volcanic rock), the largest erected statue is 33 ft (10 m) high and weighs over 88 tons (80 tonnes). Some of the statues originally had *pukao* headdresses of red scoria stone. During rituals, white coral was placed in their eye sockets.

The world became more connected in 1492, after Europeans reached the shores of the Americas. At the same time in Europe, a profound transition had been taking place during the Renaissance, which transformed artistic output and scientific inquiry, but it was followed by the violent religious warfare of the Reformation. Mighty Eastern empires, such as the Qing and Ottoman, grew in stature, but other peoples in the Americas and Africa were unable to prevent encroaching European colonization.

ENLIGHTENMENT AND IMPERIALISM

1450-1750

ART AND SCIENCE IN RENAISSANCE EUROPE

The Renaissance was a cultural movement, which began in the thriving city-states of Italy. The prospering social elite started spending their acquired wealth on artistic pursuits. This prosperity, combined with a burgeoning interest in learning, spread throughout Western Europe, giving rise to scientific inquiry, maritime voyages to new lands, and revolutionizing the visual arts and architecture.

Exploring the world
Globes became more accurate as navigational devices after the Portuguese explorer Ferdinand Magellan's crew traveled around the world in 1519–22.

Sistine masterpiece ▷
This chapel in the Vatican Palace was built in the 1470s for Pope Sixtus IV, but was decorated in stages. In 1508, Michelangelo was commissioned to paint the ceiling. His frescos depict scenes from the Old Testament, including the much-reproduced *The Creation of Adam*.

The Renaissance—literally meaning "rebirth"—emerged through a series of gradual, and sometimes subtle, changes, which began around the 1300s. It pulled Europe out of the Middle Ages and into the start of a cultural revolution, gathering momentum by the 17th century.

This rebirth began in Italy, where artists and scholars began to find inspiration in the works and aesthetics of ancient Roman and Greek ruins. This was aided by the arrival of Greek scholars fleeing Constantinople, which fell to the Ottoman Turks in 1453. Meanwhile, the growth of trading centers in Italy—which, at the time, did not exist as a country but was composed of small kingdoms and city-states, such as Florence, Venice, and Genoa—encouraged urbanization.

Soon, translations of ancient texts were circulating through communities of scholars in these growing urban centers and beyond. Inquiring minds were reading Plato's philosophical ideas from the 4th century BCE or pondering Ptolemy's calculations from the 2nd century CE. This led to the emergence of humanism, a drive to develop human virtues through arts such as philosophy, rhetoric, and poetry. It was a distinct step away from the Christian worldview that had dominated the medieval age. This cultural revival spilled over into many facets of life, from the production of art to the development of new styles of architecture. Technological and scientific changes also abounded, including key advances in maritime navigation, which enlarged the world and worldview of Europeans.

OVERSEAS EXPANSION

Before Genoese sailor Christopher Columbus encountered the Americas in 1492—all the while believing he had found a sea route to Japan—Europeans' knowledge of the world was confined to the Mediterranean basin, reaching northward to the North Sea and Baltic, and southward to Muslim North Africa and the Middle East. A few traders and travelers had made the journey to the Far East, including the Venetian Marco Polo, whose 13th-century account of his time in Asia was eagerly re-read throughout Western Europe some 200 years later. However, little was known about the world west of the Mediterranean until Columbus's voyage. Exploration then began in earnest, and ships set out to find their own passages to these new worlds. John Cabot (also known as Giovanni Caboto) found a northern sea route to Canada in 1497, while Portuguese Vasco da Gama reached India by sea in 1498. These men and thousands of other sailors brought back knowledge of the Americas, southern Africa, and India, and this too fed the imagination of Europeans.

PATRONS OF ART

The intellectual and cultural passions of the Renaissance particularly manifested themselves in art. The wealth brought by expanding trade meant that merchants and nobles, like the Medici family, could fund the work of talented individuals. Artists such as Leonardo da Vinci and Michelangelo Buonarroti flourished under this system and made a deep and lasting impact on Western art.

"Where the **spirit** does not work with the **hand,** there is no **art.**"

Leonardo da Vinci, 1452–1519

EXPLORATION AND TRADE

Columbus's journey to the Americas did not just map out a route across the Atlantic, it accelerated the development of exploration and great technological changes in ships and the science of navigation. This period also fostered global trade, with goods being bought and sold around the world.

New World coins
These coins were made with gold brought back by Columbus from his voyages. They depict King Ferdinand and Queen Isabella of Spain.

metal rim

outer pockets for coins

Merchant's bag
This style of bag was often used by traveling merchants. It would usually carry samples of their goods as well as keep their silver and gold coins safe.

Damask (woven design)

Florentine silk
One of the most important trade items was cloth, such as silk brought from the East, although it was also produced around the Mediterranean.

mater, or main body, with degree scale engraved around limb, or edge

scale of hours engraved around limb

Astrolabe
This 15th-century astronomical device was used to help measure latitude and steer a ship's course. The first astrolabes were used as early as the 6th century for sighting stars.

zodiac belt divided into 12 months of the calendar

coat of Arms from 1631

VENETIAN GLASS   **GERMAN GLASS**

Export glasses
Glass making became popular in the Renaissance, especially in Venice, and these glasses would have been typical of the kind made for export.

names of stars labeled on astrolabe

decoration includes ships and nautical instruments

rule (rotating bar) used to locate stars

Frontispiece of first sea atlas
This frontispiece comes from one of the earliest sea atlases, compiled by Dutch sailor and cartographer Lucas Wagenaer and published in 1582.

circles in corners
of map depict
wider universe

text discusses
cosmology

African continent, which became
important for trade after Portuguese
exploration of the western coast

inscriptions include latest
travelers' reports from
Africa and Asia

the biblical paradise showing
Adam and Eve in the Garden of
Eden, and the rocky, inhospitable
world they are about to enter

China and Asia

map drawn on vellum
parchment using gold
and pigments

Fra Mauro map
Produced in 1450 by the Venetian monk Fra Mauro, this map of the
world is thought to be one of the earliest "modern maps." Influenced
by the south-pointing compasses of the time, he drew his map with
south at the top—rather than east, which was common at the time.

MODELLING THE HEAVENS

ARMILLARY SPHERE

The armillary sphere was a device used by early astronomers to represent the circles of the heavens—the rings are known as armillaries, from the Latin *armilla*, meaning ring or bracelet. They represent celestial bands—such as the horizon, equator, and zodiac—and circles of latitude and longitude on Earth. The angles between the different rings were used to measure the location of various heavenly bodies, enabling astronomers to further their understanding of the movements of celestial objects. These devices varied in design but were mostly used during the Renaissance to illustrate the difference between two astronomical models of the Solar System: the geocentric model and the heliocentric model. The geocentric theory, developed by Greek polymath Ptolemy in the second century CE, argued that the planets and Sun moved around Earth, while the heliocentric theory, revived by Renaissance astronomer Nicolaus

Copernicus in the 16th century, contended that Earth actually moves around a central Sun. Earlier Earth-centered versions of the spheres predate Copernicus, going as far back as the ancient Greeks. They were also popular with Islamic astronomers, and the use of similar apparatus has also been traced to China.

LEARNING AID

During the 18th century, the sphere shown here was primarily used as a teaching aid, but it could also be used as a type of sundial, called an equatorial sundial, to measure the longitude of the Sun. Armillary spheres were often found in the homes of the wealthy.

Terrestrial globe
This model of the celestial sphere depicts Earth orbiting the Sun. Early spheres were constructed with Earth in the center.

Compass
Points from the compass are built into the base of the sphere to enable its spin axis to be aligned with that of Earth.

Horizon ring
The position of the shadows falling onto this band, which represents the horizon, helps determine the Sun's position at different times of the day.

longitude measured along this band

rings divided into degrees to aid measurement of positions of celestial bodies

marker representing north celestial pole

latitude measured along this band

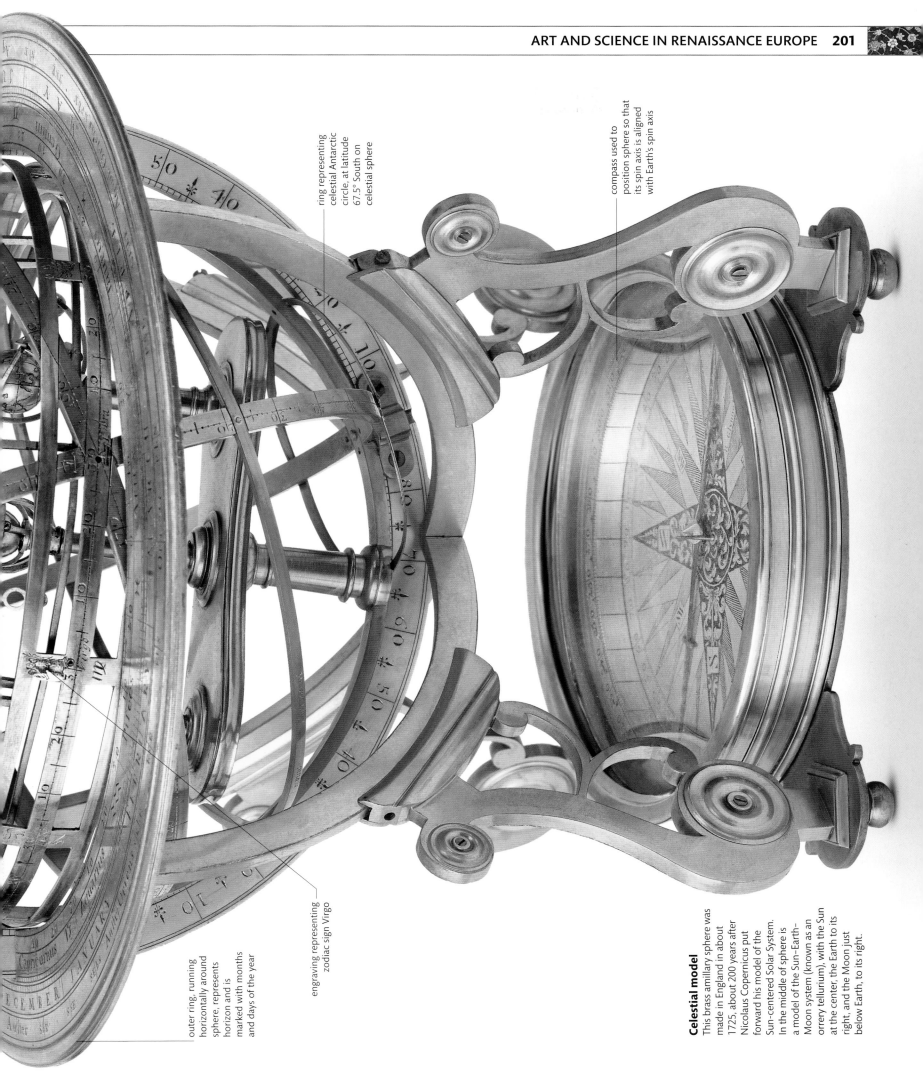

ring representing
celestial Antarctic
circle, at latitude
67.5° South on
celestial sphere

compass used to
position sphere so that
its spin axis is aligned
with Earth's spin axis

outer ring, running
horizontally around
sphere, represents
horizon and is
marked with months
and days of the year

engraving representing
zodiac sign Virgo

Celestial model

This brass armillary sphere was
made in England in about
1725, about 200 years after
Nicolaus Copernicus put
forward his model of the
Sun-centered Solar System.
In the middle of sphere is
a model of the Sun–Earth–
Moon system (known as an
orrery tellurium), with the Sun
at the center, the Earth to its
right, and the Moon just
below Earth, to its right.

MUSIC AT COURT

Musicians depended on both the church and the aristocracy for employment and patronage. The courts of European monarchs were vibrant centers of musical life, in particular the French court during the reign of Louis XIV (pictured below). In Paris, and later Versailles, music accompanied firework displays, feasts, and balls. In Tudor England, the court masque developed, with its combination of dialogue, songs, and instrumental music.

Ornate sound hole
The sound hole of this Matteo Sellas guitar is decorated with an elaborate four-tiered rose of parchment, paper, and red-stained and partially gilded leather. It is surrounded by a geometric inlay of ebony and ivory.

Elaborate decoration
The Sellas family of instrument-makers were noted for their ornate guitars and lutes. The neck of this guitar has an elaborate vine decoration of ebony and ivory, both costly materials.

Ivory plaque
Plaques of ivory or bone inlay are found on several Matteo Sellas guitars. His father, Domenico Sellas, created equally lavish guitars with plaques of mother-of-pearl inlay. The ones on this guitar depict rural scenes.

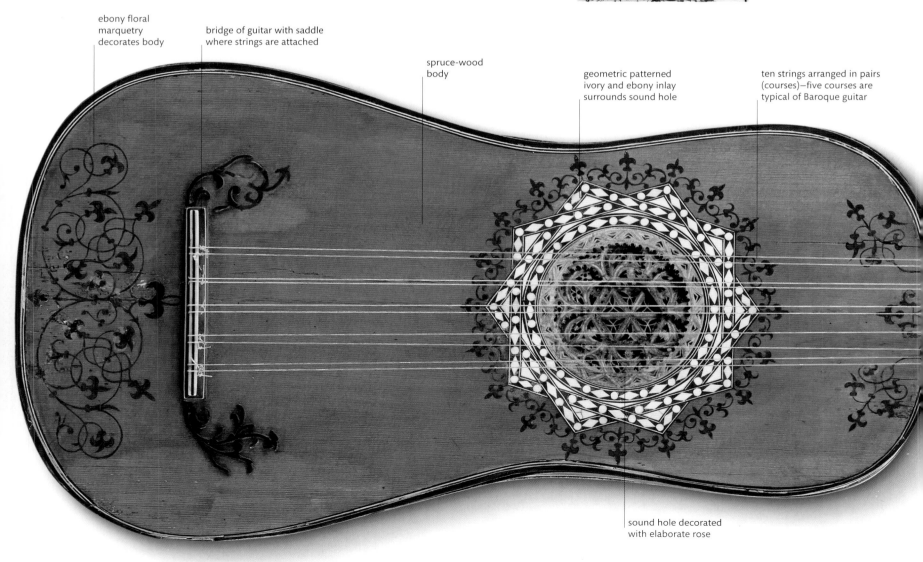

ebony floral marquetry decorates body

bridge of guitar with saddle where strings are attached

spruce-wood body

geometric patterned ivory and ebony inlay surrounds sound hole

ten strings arranged in pairs (courses)—five courses are typical of Baroque guitar

sound hole decorated with elaborate rose

MUSIC AND MUSIC MAKERS

BAROQUE GUITAR

The Baroque style is thought to have emerged in 16th-century Italy, from where it quickly spread, particularly to Germany and Austria. The term "Baroque" came from the Portuguese name for a misshapen pearl and was initially used to describe something elaborate or unnatural. Now it is used to refer to a period and style in art and architecture characterized by a mixture of sensuousness, grandeur, and exuberant ornamentation, all of which were intended to stimulate the senses and evoke spiritual feelings and a sense of drama.

In music, the term Baroque has another meaning. It describes a period of music production from around 1600 to the mid-1700s when harmonies grew more complex. One of the hallmarks of Baroque music is counterpoint—several independent melodies woven together, often to produce an elaborate, multivoiced work. Another is continuo, in which a soloist is accompanied by "basso continuo" or "figured bass." This was a continuous bass line played on a stringed instrument, such as a lute or guitar, or a keyboard instrument. The bass line was reinforced by a low instrument such as a violincello, bass viol, or bassoon.

New musical forms developed, such as the Italianate sonata and concerto, exemplified in the compositions of Archangelo Corelli and Antonio Vivaldi, and the French and Germanic suite, as practiced by François Couperin, George Frideric Handel, and Johann Sebastian Bach. Composers also began to write music for specific instruments based on their unique sound qualities.

While religious music continued to flourish, secular works emerged as a form of entertainment, becoming popular in royal courts, among the European nobility, and with the populace as a whole after the 17th-century rise of the public concert.

NEW INSTRUMENTS

Instrument-makers achieved technical advances that increased the expressive powers of instruments. Harpsichords became popular and were used in continuo. The guitar developed a fifth course (each course being a set of two strings), but by 1790 courses were gradually being replaced with six single strings, as seen on the modern acoustic guitar. The Baroque guitar was played with the fingers or a plectrum. It was used to accompany songs or to play solo music.

"Musica Donum Dei" (Music is a gift from God)...

Inscription by Andreas Ruckers, instrument maker, 1651

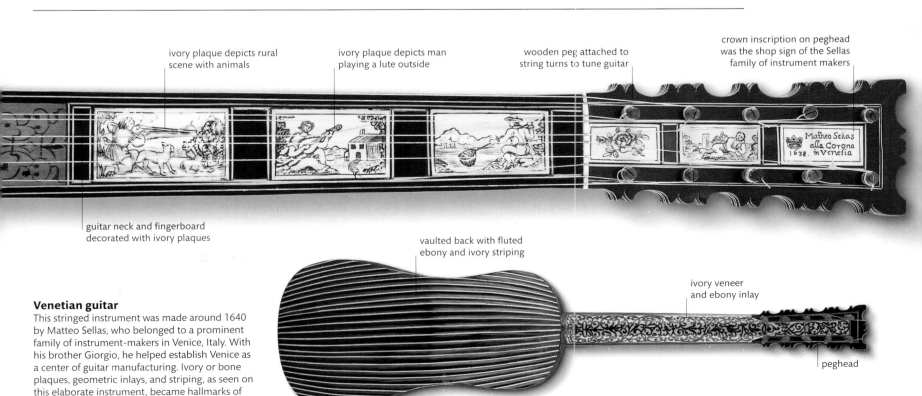

ivory plaque depicts rural scene with animals

ivory plaque depicts man playing a lute outside

wooden peg attached to string turns to tune guitar

crown inscription on peghead was the shop sign of the Sellas family of instrument makers

guitar neck and fingerboard decorated with ivory plaques

vaulted back with fluted ebony and ivory striping

ivory veneer and ebony inlay

peghead

BACK VIEW

Venetian guitar
This stringed instrument was made around 1640 by Matteo Sellas, who belonged to a prominent family of instrument-makers in Venice, Italy. With his brother Giorgio, he helped establish Venice as a center of guitar manufacturing. Ivory or bone plaques, geometric inlays, and striping, as seen on this elaborate instrument, became hallmarks of the Venetian tradition of lute and guitar making.

MUSIC

During the Renaissance period in music (1450–1600), instruments were often constructed in families of various sizes. Preexisting instruments, such as the trumpet, organ, flute, and recorder, were updated, and entirely new families, such as those of the violins, the violas da gamba, and the sackbuts (trombones), were created. The Baroque era (1600–1750) saw further development, including the invention of the oboe, bassoon, and early piano.

Carved head
Violas da gamba often had intricately carved heads at the top of the peg box. This one has a female head.

tuning pegs

openwork scroll

ebony fingerboard inlaid with ivory

nine ivory pegs

ivory veneer neck

pear wood peg head

pear wood rosette in gothic-style tracery

fruitwood bridge

carved from single piece of wood

mouthpiece

copper tubing

engraved silver bell

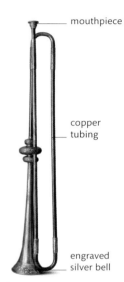

Stradivarius mandolin
Although the Italian Antonio Stradivari is usually associated with making violins, this 1680 choral mandolin also came from his Cremona workshop.

Treble lute
Although stringed instruments date back to ancient times, the lute is closely associated with Renaissance music. This version was made in northern Italy, *c.*1500.

Cittern
The cittern was a popular Renaissance stringed instrument that became fashionable throughout Italy and central Europe after 1574.

Tenor viola da gamba
This east Prussian six-stringed viola da gamba dates from 1693 and would usually have been played as part of a group of violas da gamba.

Natural trumpet
According to an inscription, this trumpet was made in 1666 by Simon Beale, state trumpeter to both Oliver Cromwell and Charles II of England.

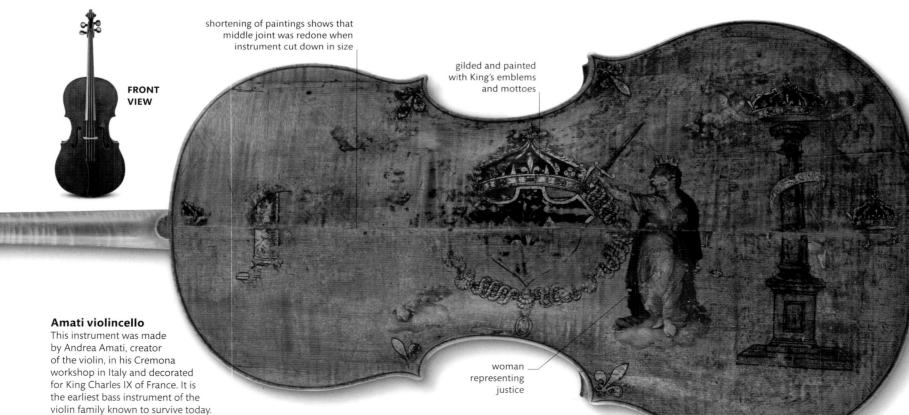

FRONT VIEW

shortening of paintings shows that middle joint was redone when instrument cut down in size

gilded and painted with King's emblems and mottoes

woman representing justice

Amati violincello
This instrument was made by Andrea Amati, creator of the violin, in his Cremona workshop in Italy and decorated for King Charles IX of France. It is the earliest bass instrument of the violin family known to survive today.

ART

The Renaissance is often associated with changes in painting, but other art forms also saw dramatic transformations. Art, architecture, and sculpture were heavily influenced by improved knowledge about the human form and proportions. Writers, too, flourished, as printing presses first appeared and facilitated the wide circulation of their work.

"Cantoria" detail
Sculptor Luca della Robbia's *Cantoria* (singing gallery) from 1481, is a 10-piece marble frieze depicting verses from Psalm 150 of the Bible.

children dancing and playing music

gift for infant Jesus

King of Spain
The 16th-century Habsburg king and Holy Roman Emperor Charles I is depicted here as Gaspar, one of the three wise men in the Bible's New Testament. It was made by Felipe Bigarny, a leading sculptor of the Spanish Renaissance.

RENAISSANCE PAINTING

The importance of rationalism over faith during the Renaissance brought new meaning to portraits, such as *The Ambassadors*, painted by the Flemish artist Hans Holbein the Younger in 1533. It depicts French ambassador to England Jean de Dinteville, on the left, with George de Selve, the Bishop of Lavaur. The objects on the table, such as the books and globe, symbolize their learning and intelligence.

whole statue carved from single block of marble

figures divided into sections

three intertwined figures demonstrate artist's ability to create complex sculptural group

figures are in proportion from all angles

older man overpowered by strength of youth

spread-eagled figure forms circle

Rape of the Sabine women
This 1582 work by Flemish-born sculptor Giambologna, who spent most of his career in Florence, depicts the abduction of the Sabine women by the neighboring founders of Rome—a legend from classical antiquity.

Dürer's proportions
These pages are from the 1532 *Four Books on Human Proportion* by the German artist Albrecht Dürer, who applied the principles of geometry to understanding the human form.

Vitruvian man
Leonardo da Vinci's anatomical study from *c.*1509 was based on the classical formula of the ideal proportions of the human figure and their relationship to geometry, as proposed by the ancient Roman author Vitruvius.

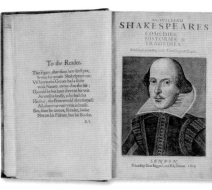

Shakespeare plays
This 1623 publication of *Comedies, Histories, and Tragedies* was written by the English playwright and poet William Shakespeare, who transformed English literature.

■ RENAISSANCE NATURALISM

MICHELANGELO'S PIETÀ

The Pietà is the name given to a depiction of the Virgin Mary holding the body of a dead Christ following his crucifixion. Mary is sometimes flanked by angels or biblical figures, such as St. John or Mary Magdalene. The Pietà became a common theme in Renaissance art, appearing in sculptures and paintings throughout Europe, having first shown up in a German work sometime around the 13th century. The scene it represents, known as a lamentation, is not explicitly described in the Bible but rather comes from medieval texts that discussed Mary's empathy and her ability to act as an intermediary between humans and God—the Italian word pietà means "pity."

RENAISSANCE MAN

One of the most famous depictions of the Pietà scene, and the first Italian version, is a sculpture by Michelangelo Buonarroti. Born in 1475, the Florentine artist was one of the original embodiments of a Renaissance man, his talents stretching not only to sculpture but also to painting, architecture, and even poetry.

He established his reputation early on in his careeer, and became a dominant figure in his own lifetime. He was only 24 years old when he finished the Pietà, which was commissioned by a French cardinal, Jean Bilhères de Lagraulas, originally for his funeral monument. He specified that it should be "the most beautiful work in marble that exists today in Rome." The sculpture was later moved to St. Peter's Basilica in the Vatican City, where it remains today.

The sculpture made an immediate impact, since it is not only a deeply expressive work but also embodied the idealistic human form that artists of this period were striving for. It also exhibited Michelangelo's technical expertise—multifigured sculptures were rare, and exceptional skill was needed to carve one.

POPULAR FORM

Mary and Christ represented in this form continued to be the subject of paintings and sculptures in Italy, France, and elsewhere in Europe. Despite the overall declining use of religious themes in art by the 18th century, the Pietà continued to inspire artists into the 1800s.

> "The more the **marble wastes,** the more the **statue grows."**
>
> Michelangelo, 1475–1564 CE

Jesus
The humanism of this period is evident in Michelangelo's flawless execution of the painful and serene beauty of Christ shown after his death on the cross.

evidence of crucifixion just visible from nail marks on hands and feet

David's hands are carved exceptionally large

the statue is unusually slender in comparison to its height

rock of Golgotha forms the base of the statue

David
Completed in Florence, this sculpture of the biblical hero David is another of Michelangelo's most famous works of art. It came to embody the Renaissance idea of the perfect human form.

Mother and Christ
The Pietà is a symbolic devotional representation designed to inspire prayers and contemplation. Although it appeared often in art of this period, Michelangelo's version stood apart. His ability to carve two subjects from one block of marble displayed his technical mastery and helped cement his reputation.

Mary depicted
considerably taller
than Jesus

entire sculpture carved
from single block of
Carrera marble

Mary
Michelangelo's portrayal of Mary as
a beautiful young woman is thought
to have been criticized by some people
at the time as being unrealistic.

folds in Mary's
clothing illustrate
Michelangelo's
dexterity

balance of figures
embodies Renaissance
ideals about harmony

HOME LIFE

The Renaissance brought changes to many aspects of daily life. The revolution in the arts inlcuded improvements in the design of everyday items. As trade increased and disposable income grew, a broader spectrum of consumers was able to acquire items previously associated only with patronage, and objects from other lands.

parchment covered with horn

Alphabet table
Most 16th-century children of the merchant and upper classes would have learnt to read at home, probably in Latin, using devices similar to this one.

wooden board carved to be held in hand

decorated with mythological figures

Baby's crib
This italian crib dates from the 16th century. Children died young in this period—about a quarter to one half of all babies died in their first year.

features creatures from classical mythology

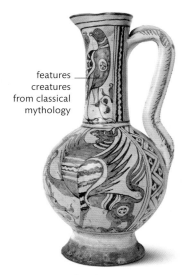

winged cherubs, grotesques, and animals depicted on border

open design allows smoke to escape

Ceramic pitcher
This 16th-century vessel was used to store wine, which Europeans drank in large quantities due to the poor quality of drinking water.

Majolica dish
This plate from Urbino, Italy, dates from around 1570 and depicts a tale of jealousy between the Roman god Jupiter and his wife Juno.

central chamber contained candle

gilt and enamel decoration

burned and carved wood

English chest
Sailing ships are carved into this 16th-century wooden chest from England, which was probably used for storage in a home.

Venetian glass

gilded bronze and enamel

Engagement present
This enamel-decorated, green glass goblet is an example of the type of gift a couple might have received upon their betrothal or marriage.

Decorative nightlight
In the Middle Ages, lights were simple and functional in design, but around the 15th century they became more elaborate and highly decorated, like this 16th-century Venetian lantern.

CLOTHING AND ADORNMENT

Traveling ships brought back new fabrics and trends that were quickly assimilated into Renaissance fashion. Clothing began to be used as a symbol of wealth, and luxury materials such as silk were in high demand. Dresses and suits became more detailed and elaborate as people tried to display their riches and social position.

intricately carved design

Ivory comb
Ivory, like silk, was a highly valued luxury material. It was used in many grooming implements, such as this Italian comb.

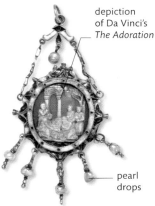

depiction of Da Vinci's *The Adoration*

pearl drops

Pearl pendant
A law was passed in Siena forbidding women to wear pearls. However, the ban had to be reversed when the women protested.

Belt buckle
This silver gilt buckle was a betrothal gift. It portrays an imaginary ideal couple. Similar buckles often showed the actual engaged couple.

angels carved into ivory frame

wooden platform soles

Carved mirror
Luxury grooming devices and accessories were also ornate during this time, such as this carved octagonal mirror with convex glass.

Platform shoes
These elevated platforms started out as practical footwear designed to keep feet dry on flooded Venice streets, but they soon became fashionable.

MEDICINE

Medicine and health improved as scientific inquiry lead to better medical techniques and understanding of the human body. The rise in sea travel meant that sailors and scientists also looked at ways to prevent disease from wiping out the crew of a ship, which was a real risk in this period.

Apothecary's jars
These tin-glazed, earthenware jars from Faenza, Italy, were used to store medicinal mixtures by apothecaries.

name of drug, Roman philonium, written on jar in Italian

spout in shape of dragon

winged cherubs sitting on either side of spout

frontispiece with portrait of author Nicholas Culpeper

London Pharmacopoeia
This book, published in 1618, listed instructions on how to prepare a wide range of medicines. In England, it became mandatory for apothecaries.

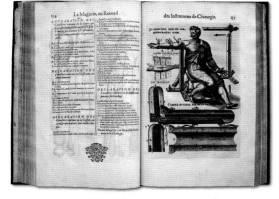

French surgery manual
Renowned surgeon Jacques Guillemeau wrote this book published in 1598. The increasing knowledge of human anatomy greatly helped to improve operations.

long handle to increase leverage

head shaped like crow's bill

Crow's bill forceps
Dentistry often involved using dental forceps, like these English ones from 1550, to pull out bad teeth—without painkillers.

wooden handles

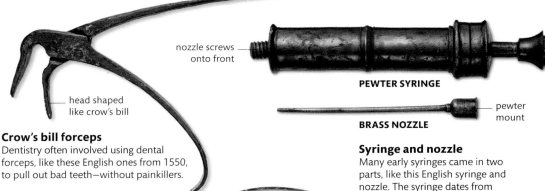

nozzle screws onto front

PEWTER SYRINGE

pewter mount

BRASS NOZZLE

Syringe and nozzle
Many early syringes came in two parts, like this English syringe and nozzle. The syringe dates from c.1650 and the nozzle from c.1725.

blades made from carbon steel

Delivery forceps
This obstetric device was used to help deliver babies in the 18th century. Childbirth was potentially very dangerous for women in this period.

REFORMATION, WAR, AND ENLIGHTENMENT

Marked by great changes—such as the rise of Protestantism and the proliferation of scientific discoveries—the 250 years between the Reformation and the Enlightenment in Europe were a time of upheaval and violence. As the 18th century drew to a close, it was clear that the political and intellectual transformations that had taken place had irrevocably changed European society.

Navigating the oceans
The first chronometer was invented in 1728 by Englishman John Harrison. It could be used to accurately determine longitude, which greatly improved the safety of sea travel.

Ruthless massacre ▷
This painting by French artist François Dubois depicts the St. Bartholomew's Day massacre, which took place on August 24, 1572. Catholic nobles attacked and killed thousands of French Huguenot Protestants. Starting in Paris, and despite royal orders to stop the next day, the killings spread as far as Rouen and Bordeaux.

In 1517, acting out of dissatisfaction with the Catholic Church, a German theologian called Martin Luther nailed 95 theses (or propositions for debate) to the door of a church in Wittenberg, Germany. His actions ignited a radical social transformation that led to the emergence of Protestant Christianity, as well as decades of war throughout Europe. This period also saw a transition from the medieval world to a more modern society, eventually resulting in the republican and secular ideas of the mid-18th century Enlightenment.

Protestantism was not a single united movement. Over the course of the Reformation, a number of different sects emerged. These included the Lutherans, Baptists, Puritans, and Calvinists. All of them broke with Catholic theology and rejected the infallibility of the pope, embracing unorthodox ideas such as predestination. In England, King Henry VIII cut off relations with Rome and established the Church of England in the 1530s. The Catholic Church was forced into self-examination, resulting in the reforms of the Council of Trent (1545–63)

during the Counter-Reformation, which took place around the same time. Catholic religious orders, however, were looking outward, spreading Catholicism through the Americas, which Spain had begun to colonize after the Italian explorer Christopher Columbus had set sail and claimed the West Indies in 1492.

A TIME OF STRIFE

The Reformation sparked a series of conflicts—the Wars of Religion (1562–98) in France, as well as the wider Thirty Years War (1618–48), which affected much of Europe. As these conflicts drew to a close, another was beginning in England. Tension between the parliament and the monarchy of Charles I—who later dissolved the parliament—hit a crisis point in the 1640s. In 1642, a battle erupted between the supporters of the king (Royalists, or Cavaliers) and those who supported the parliament (known as Roundheads for their short hair). This continued over a series of wars until 1651.

In 1653, Oliver Cromwell, who had led the forces against Charles I, set himself up as Lord Protector of the Commonwealth of England. After

Cromwell's death in 1658, the Commonwealth faltered, and by 1660, Charles II had reclaimed the throne.

THE ENLIGHTENMENT

Although the 17th and 18th centuries continued to be plagued by warfare and violence, another transformation was taking place. Driven by reason rather than religion, new intellectual currents started circulating around Europe by the mid-1700s—a period generally known as the Enlightenment.

Scientific enquiry and philosophical discourse—often inspired by classical Greek and Roman works—became the order of the day. Thinkers of the time eschewed the extreme religious mentality that had dominated the preceeding century. These new insights and intellectual freedoms led to the proliferation of ground-breaking works. Englishman Isaac Newton's formulation of the universal law of gravitation, the satirical writings of France's Voltaire, and the economic theory of Scotland's Adam Smith were all born at this time. This period marked a decisive break with the past and laid the foundation for the era of revolution that followed.

"I always admired virtue—but I could never imitate it."

King Charles II of England, the "Merry Monarch," who banished Puritan sobriety during his reign

ARMS AND ARMOR

The antagonism between Catholics and Protestants led to numerous wars and conflicts throughout Europe in the 16th and 17th centuries. Firearms were now part of the artillery for most European armies. Swords and other traditional weapons continued to be used, although their style had become increasingly elaborate.

decoration shows hunting scene

Powder flask
Guns of the 16th and 17th centuries required powder to fire. The powder was carried in flasks like this example from England, which was carved from animal horn.

■ MILITARY FIREARMS

serpentine, or match holder

trigger guard

iron lock plate anchors firing mechanism

octagonal barrel

Matchlock musket
The mechanically firing matchlock, as seen on this English 17th-century musket, was a major improvement on previous models of guns.

steel

serpentine, or match holder

ramrod pipe

jaw-clamp screw to grip flint

Combination long gun
This 17th-century Dutch musket is fitted with a flintlock and a matchlock mechanism that gave the user a firm grip at the time of firing.

striking steel attached to pan cover

round barrel

simple wooden grip allows single- or double-handed use

Flintlock pistol
This ornate pistol from c.1680 is inlaid with stag horn. It is from Silesia (straddling modern Poland and the Czech Republic).

Flintlock pistol
The hearts engraved on this Scottish gun from c.1700–30 symbolize support for the Jacobites, who wanted to restore the Catholic monarch James II to the thrones of England and Scotland.

trigger with finial ball at end

ramrod for pushing projectile down barrel

■ HUNTING

cocking ring

bull horn tube

Hunting rifle
This German wheel lock from 1640, with elaborate bone inlay, has an externally mounted serrated wheel that ignites gunpowder. These guns were used to hunt small game.

squared shaft for winding mechanism

trigger

steel lath or prod

decorative foliage

brass mouthpiece

Hunting crossbow
This 1526 crossbow from Germany was inlaid with ivory plaques and decorated with two coats of arms. Crossbows slowly vanished from battlefields but continued to be used in hunting.

TRIGGER DETAIL

rope binds lath to tiller

Hunting horn
Hunting was a popular pastime among royals and nobles. Hunters used horns such as this one to round up the hounds that assisted in hunting.

■ EDGED WEAPONS

Execution sword
The punishment for religious dissent could sometimes be beheading. This German weapon depicts scenes of execution on its blade.

impalement by spike

impalement by hook

religious exhortation

blade etched with scenes of execution

curves on quillons could trap opponent's blade

FRONT OF SWORD

BACK OF SWORD

bound, nonslip grip

heavy pommel balances the weapon

cup provides protection for hand

Cup-hilt rapier
A light sword, the cup-hilt rapier was the weapon of choice for most gentlemen. This rapier from c.1650 shows the Spanish design with a fully enclosed guard.

grip

shell guard

knuckle-bow or guard

Small sword
Dating from c.1720, this French example of a small sword has a steel blade and a decorated golden hilt. A light weapon, it was designed to be used with one hand.

single fuller (groove) imparted greater strength to blade

ornate scrollwork

Cavalry sword
This long sword with a straight blade would have been used by English heavy cavalry. The scrollwork on the guard is an example of the mid-18th century style.

carved inscription

blades were often decorated with religious icons

·LVOG·VND·SITH·DITH·EBEN·FIR·VOR·AIM·

Infantry sword
The design of some weapons was particularly intricate, and could include carved inscriptions, such as the one on this Swiss sword from c.1500.

FULL VIEW

decorated grip

three-sided blade with numbered scale for measurement of gun bore

Gunner's stiletto
This 18th-century Italian dagger would have been used on the battlefield for tasks such as tearing open paper gun cartridges rather than for hand-to-hand combat.

■ POLEARMS

shaped steel flange

decorated steel shaft

Decorated mace
This mace's steel flange made it a simple but effective weapon. A wrist loop helped a mounted soldier keep hold of it.

axe blade

one of two cocks

FULL VIEW

Halberd wheel lock
This German weapon from c.1590 has an ornate axe and fluke at the front and is fitted with a double-barrelled wheel lock pistol.

balancing fluke

safety catch

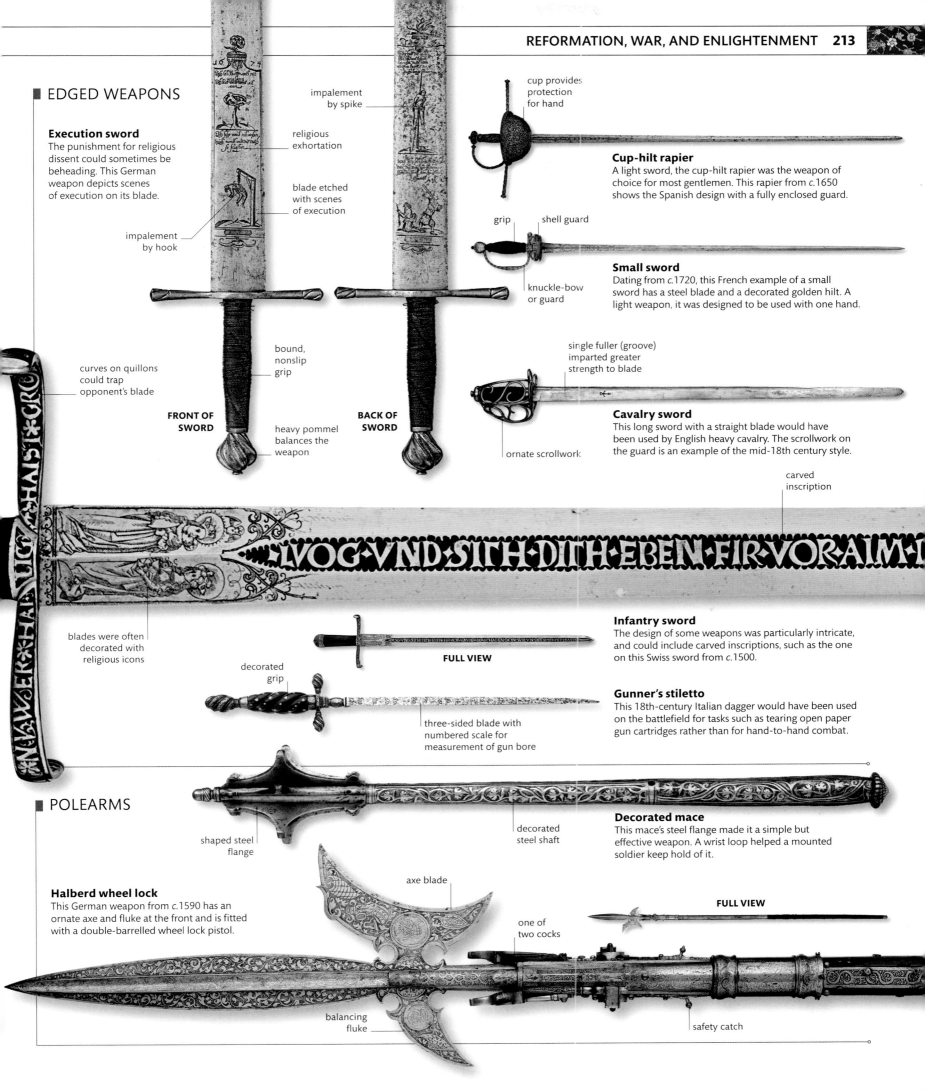

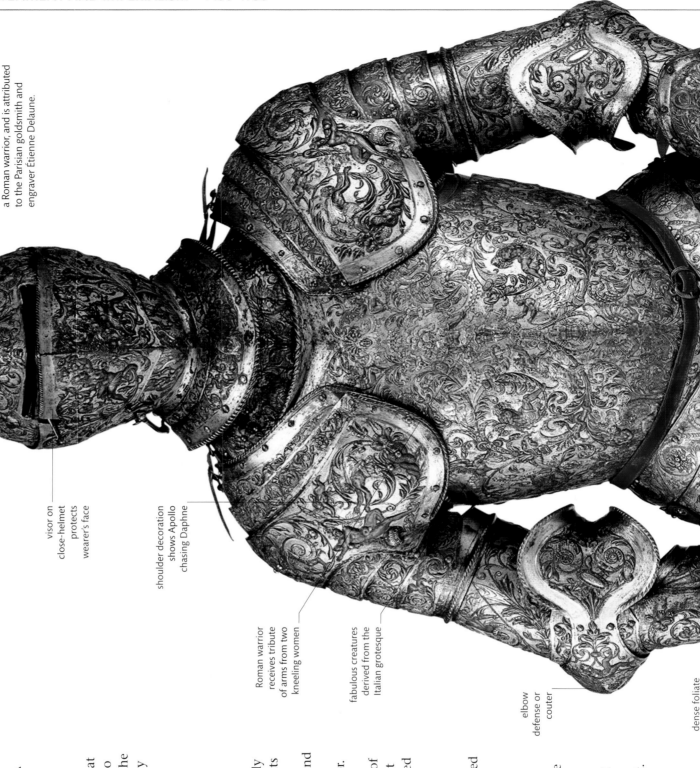

Ceremonial armor
This elaborate suit of armor was intended for ceremonial use, as a declaration of King Henry II's military and political successes by associating the French monarchy with the triumphant Roman Empire. The decoration includes a Roman warrior, and is attributed to the Parisian goldsmith and engraver Étienne Delaune.

visor on close-helmet protects wearer's face

shoulder decoration shows Apollo chasing Daphne

Roman warrior receives tribute of arms from two kneeling women

fabulous creatures derived from the Italian grotesque

elbow defense or couter

dense foliate scrolls on surface

ROYAL SPLENDOR

HENRY II'S SUIT OF ARMOR

The reign of King Henry II of France, from 1547 to 1559, was a time of near-constant conflict. Not only was France at war with its neighbors, but the king also faced unrest and revolts at home over the taxes levied to pay for these wars. Henry was also fiercely Catholic and in 1559 outlawed Protestantism within France in his Edict of Écouen.

RENAISSANCE ARMOR

At the same time, gunpowder weapons and new military technologies eventually changed warfare and the need for knights in shining armor on the battlefield diminished. However, the Renaissance and Baroque periods saw the production of elaborate, richly decorated suits of armor.

These were worn for ceremonial purposes, and armor became a symbol of status. Men in armor were an important part of the ceremonies that accompanied military parades, royal weddings, coronations, funerals, canonizations, diplomatic visits, and carnivals. For example, when Henry II of France entered Lyons he was accompanied by infantrymen dressed in uniforms that resembled those of Roman soldiers.

Armor was also used during jousts and tournaments (see panel, below). The Treaty of Cateau-Cambrésis established peace between the Holy Roman Empire and France in 1559. It was accompanied by festivities, including a joust and a tournament in which Henry II took part. During a joust between Henry and the captain of the Scottish Guards, a large splinter from the guard captain's lance entered through the sight of Henry's helmet, and he died just 10 days later.

gilded surface

whole surface is embossed, blued, silvered

embossed steel

human faces depicted on knees

greaves to guard lower leg are more decorative than protective on this ceremonial suit

small plates on gauntlet allow greater freedom of movement

peg for lifting visor

hook attaches upper and lower bevors to close helmet

comb with roped edge

Henry's helmet
Covered in foliate scrolls and human figures, the king's helmet matches the rest of the armor in its intricate design.

JOUSTING

The joust, a contest in which two armored men on horseback charge each other in order with lances, was a popular training exercise and pastime in medieval and Renaissance Europe. Due to changes in warfare, as well as King Henry II's death, the practice declined during the late 16th century and was replaced with other festivities, such as shooting contests.

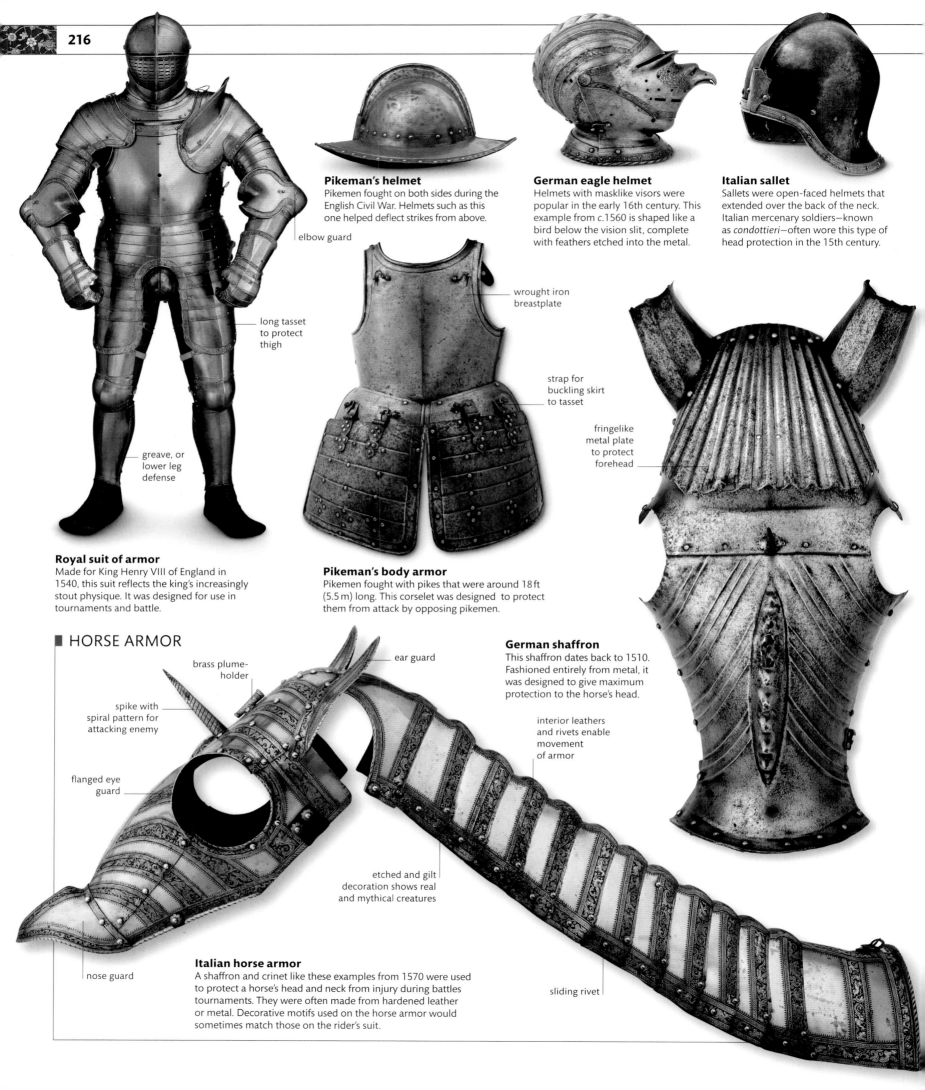

Pikeman's helmet
Pikemen fought on both sides during the English Civil War. Helmets such as this one helped deflect strikes from above.

German eagle helmet
Helmets with masklike visors were popular in the early 16th century. This example from *c.*1560 is shaped like a bird below the vision slit, complete with feathers etched into the metal.

Italian sallet
Sallets were open-faced helmets that extended over the back of the neck. Italian mercenary soldiers—known as *condottieri*—often wore this type of head protection in the 15th century.

elbow guard

long tasset to protect thigh

greave, or lower leg defense

wrought iron breastplate

strap for buckling skirt to tasset

fringelike metal plate to protect forehead

Royal suit of armor
Made for King Henry VIII of England in 1540, this suit reflects the king's increasingly stout physique. It was designed for use in tournaments and battle.

Pikeman's body armor
Pikemen fought with pikes that were around 18 ft (5.5 m) long. This corselet was designed to protect them from attack by opposing pikemen.

■ HORSE ARMOR

brass plume-holder

ear guard

spike with spiral pattern for attacking enemy

flanged eye guard

German shaffron
This shaffron dates back to 1510. Fashioned entirely from metal, it was designed to give maximum protection to the horse's head.

interior leathers and rivets enable movement of armor

etched and gilt decoration shows real and mythical creatures

nose guard

Italian horse armor
A shaffron and crinet like these examples from 1570 were used to protect a horse's head and neck from injury during battles tournaments. They were often made from hardened leather or metal. Decorative motifs used on the horse armor would sometimes match those on the rider's suit.

sliding rivet

CHURCH AND RELIGION

The division of the Church was reflected in religious objects as well as everyday ones. Images of heroes, martyrs, and saints were incorporated into medals and coins. Catholic devotional objects, such as crucifixes, continued to be elaborate and made of expensive materials such as silver. Protestantism embraced a simpler, more austere style.

oak cross covered with silver plate

Processional cross
Ornate crosses such as this one were typically used to lead a procession into a Catholic mass in the 16th century.

tapering cup above a spreading shaft with two disks

Candlestick
Used in a Catholic church, this candlestick dates from the 1500s. Candles were placed on or beside the altar, especially during the Mass.

St. George and the dragon
This English piece of carved ivory depicts St George, the patron saint of England. He was a Christian martyr famed for having slain a dragon.

castle battlements in background

St. George dressed as a knight

dragon represents the devil

elaborate decoration

medallion shows head of saint

Catholic chalice
Protestant critics of the Catholic Church often criticized it for its opulence, as embodied in this silver chalice that would have held wine during the Mass.

Huguenot Bible
This Bible belonged to French Huguenots—Protestants who emigrated from France throughout the 1500s to avoid religious persecution.

Latin inscription, "I believe in one Holy Catholic Church"

FACE OF CARDINAL ROBERTO BELLARMINO

Gold medal
This medal shows a bust of Johann Huss (also known as Jan Hus)—a Czech reformer who was burned at the stake in 1415 for heresy against the doctrines of the Catholic Church.

Stoneware jug
Dating from the 17th century, this jug depicts Cardinal Roberto Bellarmino, a critic of Protestant doctrine who rejected Nicolaus Copernicus's model of the Solar System. Jugs such as this one were probably made to ridicule the Catholic cardinal.

POLITICS AND POWER

The Reformation had a profound influence on the nature of European warfare and statehood, and it became far more than a religious division. This was a time of dramatic events, such as England's defeat of the Spanish Armada in 1588, but more subtle social changes also spread across Europe's diverse landscape.

Latin inscription around edge

OLD SEAL

Canterbury Seal
The original seal of the English city of Canterbury depicted the murder of Archbishop Thomas Becket in its cathedral in 1170. After the Reformation the seal was changed to an image of the city's crest.

Dutch medal
The Protestant Netherlands launched a revolt against their Spanish rulers in 1566. This medal commemorates the support of the English for the Dutch in their war against Spain.

Altered mace
The mayor's mace from Faversham, England, was amended to reflect the restoration of Charles II in 1660. Royal arms of the four countries—England, Scotland, France, and Ireland—were placed on the head.

shield bearing Canterbury's arms—a lion and three choughs

CR stands for Charles II

NEW SEAL

Spanish ships with crew jumping overboard

Armada glory
This medal commemorates the English victory over the Spanish Armada in 1588, which ended Spanish plans to conquer England and reintroduce Catholicism.

decoration shows William on horseback

German stoneware jar
Made for export to England, this jar shows William of Orange of the Netherlands, who became William III of England and was regarded as a champion of the Protestant faith.

Royal stumpwork
A form of needlework in which the ornament is raised on a foundation, this stumpwork depicts Charles II, the Stuart monarch, with his Portugese wife, Catherine of Braganza.

FASHION

Despite the unrest and violence in Europe, global commerce continued to grow unabated. The cloth trade prospered as new materials were used for making clothes, while different fashions spread from city to city. Technological innovations also improved the techniques that were used to make clothing and accessories.

fabric arranged in box pleats

Floral dress
Silk was considered a luxury item because it was often imported from Asia. It was used to make clothes, such as this brocade dress from the 1770s.

tassle to compliment outfit

Lace parasol
Parasols became fashionable in the 1600s. By the 18th century, it was common to see women using parasols to protect their skin from the sun.

Fabric shoe
This delicately embroidered cloth shoe from the 1740s shows how fashion triumphed over function, as consumers became more concerned about style.

Painted fan
By the 1700s, fans had become a popular fashion accessory in Europe. They were usually imported from China and Japan for eager European consumers.

folding fan with carved ivory sticks

Collar detail
Short stand collars were a popular feature on men's coats in the 1790s, and were often worn with Jabot frills. The collar on this coat is small but has exquisite embroidery.

embroidered design on one side mirrors that on other

narrow-wristed, slim sleeves contribute to elegant shape

Waistcoat pocket detail
Made of ivory satin, the front section of this waistcoat is richly embroidered with colored silks. The pocket has three-pointed flaps, with tiny flowers embroidered in silk.

breeches were tight fitting, like coats and waistcoats of the time

Rococo court suit
The lavish Rococo style started in 18th-century Paris and spread to other European countries. Its hallmarks included curving, elegant forms intended to be a reaction to the heavier Baroque style. Rococo influenced the fine arts, architecture, and fashion. This court suit from 1780 is typical of Rococo clothing, with its floral embellishments and embroidery.

coat fabric is black velvet with pink stripes

Cuff detail
Smaller than in previous eras, cuffs were designed as extra decoration on coats. They were narrow-wristed and lavishly decorated with sequins, glass pieces, and embroidered buttons.

narrow, cutaway sides reveal decorated waistcoat

SIDE VIEW   BACK VIEW

PRINTING

By the time of the Reformation, printing using ink and woodblocks had already been in use for hundreds of years. But it took the development of the printing press and moveable type in the 1450s to change the way knowledge could be disseminated. German inventor Johannes Gutenberg is commonly credited with the invention of the printing press.

Gutenberg Bible
The Bible produced by Johannes Gutenberg around 1455 is the earliest known book printed from moveable type. It is acknowledged as a 42-line Bible after the number of lines in each column.

Composing stick
Early printers lined up individual letters into words using a composing stick before pressing them onto paper. Moveable type facilitated the easy and rapid movement of individual letters to form words.

Printing press
By the 18th century, printing presses were being used to produce books and pamphlets. Even newspapers were beginning to be printed.

— plate for laying moveable type

Type plane
This tool was used to shave the backs of the metal type to make sure that letters were placed at exactly the same height.

— screw to secure blade

Propaganda
Pamphlets addressing a vast range of social and political issues were abundant during the 18th and 19th centuries. This pamphlet, for example, was part of a campaign against the consumption of alcohol.

— beverages are compared to work of the devil and his demons

— apostles Peter and Paul seated above central text

King James Bible
Commonly known as the Authorized Version, this translation of the Bible into English began in 1604 under King James I of England. The book was completed in 1611, and was considered to be the standard for some 300 years.

— roller

— lever to turn roller

SCIENCE

By the 18th century, there was a growing interest in the sciences. This was fueled by the secular climate in which Enlightenment ideas circulated. One aspect of the transformation was a new passion for scientific inquiry and experimentation, which resulted in many discoveries in areas such as mathematics, biology, and astronomy.

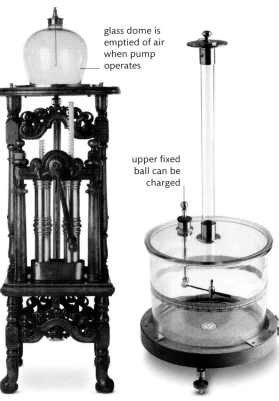

— glass dome is emptied of air when pump operates

— upper fixed ball can be charged

Air pump
English scientist and inventor Francis Hauksbee created this two-cylinder air pump. It is regarded as the forerunner of the modern vacuum pump.

Torsion balance
The French physicist Charles-Augustin de Coulomb developed this sensitive apparatus based on the pendulum to investigate the attraction and repulsion of the electric charge between two objects.

■ ASTRONOMY

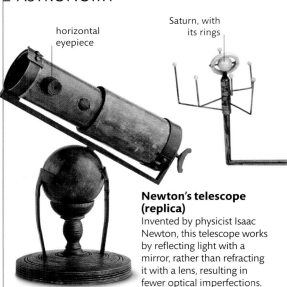

— horizontal eyepiece

— Saturn, with its rings

Newton's telescope (replica)
Invented by physicist Isaac Newton, this telescope works by reflecting light with a mirror, rather than refracting it with a lens, resulting in fewer optical imperfections.

Eyeglasses

open design allowed watch to be read through lid

These 17th-century glasses were the forerunner of modern optical lenses. They had existed in Europe since the late 1200s but improved in the 1700s.

single (hour) hand

gilded fretwork design

Brass pocket watch

Early pocket watches did not keep accurate time until the invention of the coiled spring in the 16th century. These watches were often worn as jewelry.

MICROSCOPES

lens

screw moves specimen up or down

Leeuwenhoek's microscope

This is a replica of an early microscope built by Antonie van Leeuwenhoek around 1674. The tiny spherical lens helped the Dutch scientist observe bacteria and protozoa.

howing contains eyepiece lens

inner body tube

sliding tube used to adjust focus

glass jar prevents electric charge from leaking out

glass dish contained liquid compound

metal coating

terminal linked to battery

Leyden jar

An early type of capacitor, this device was used to store static electricity. It was accidentally developed by Pieter van Musschenbroek at the University of Leiden, Netherlands, in 1746.

Salt apparatus

British scientist Humphry Davy discovered and separated the elements sodium and potassium by electrolyzing molten salt in this apparatus.

Culpeper's microscope

English scientist Edmund Culpeper was the first to use a concave mirror on a microscope to help illuminate the object being studied. Made of wood and brass, his microscopes had an upright design that made them uncomfortable to use.

stage holds specimen

Mars

Sun at center of Solar System

Mercury

Venus

Earth

Uranus

Jupiter, with four Galilean moons

brass tripod legs support stage and microscope body

mirror

Orrery

This 18th-century mechanical astronomical model is known as an orrery. It could be used to demonstrate the orbits of planets around the Sun.

THE HEIGHT OF OTTOMAN POWER

From its beginnings in 15th-century Anatolia (in modern Turkey), the Ottoman Empire grew to control a vast territory, stretching eastwards to Iraq and the western borders of Iran. The sultans inspired respect and fear throughout Christian Europe.

Moment of triumph ▷
This miniature depicts the decisive victory at the battle of Mohács of about 100,000 Turkish troops in Hungary on August 29, 1526. This resulted in Ottoman administration of Hungary's eastern provinces.

After the creation of the Ottoman Empire under the northern Anatolian ruler Osman I (see p.174), the empire expanded under his successors. Constantinople (modern Istanbul) was captured in 1453 under Sultan Mehmet II. Egypt, the Hejaz region in Arabia with its holy cities of Mecca and Medina, as well as Iraq fell to the Ottomans soon after. The empire was at its peak in the 16th century, during the reign of Suleyman the Magnificent. At this time, the

Ottomans were famed for their wealth, much of which was built on trade, and their military prowess.

Although the Ottoman Empire existed in some form until the early 20th century, its decline began during the rule of Suleyman's son, Selim. His weak leadership encouraged corruption within the government. Public support diminished and the empire lost land to encroaching European powers. By the end of World War I it had ceased to exist.

BELIEFS AND RITUALS

The religion of Islam predominated in the Ottoman Empire. However, because the empire encompassed a wide geographical area, it also absorbed diverse cultures and beliefs, including Christianity and Judaism, which flourished there. Islam still prevailed, however, and this was reflected in the art and architecture of the Ottoman period.

Tombstone
This grave marker has a turban-style top and an inscription, part of which reads, "Here lies the pilgrim Ali L'il Sudan who died in the year of the Hegira, 998."

Arabic inscription

clear glaze

Blue tile
This brightly colored 17th-century tile is from an Ottoman mosque. The Arabic inscription contains the names of Allah, the Prophet Muhammad, and the first four Caliphs.

depiction of Ka'aba in Mecca

Geography box
The *kiblenüma*, or *qibla numâ*, was used to find the direction of Mecca, as the person has to be facing Mecca during prayer.

HOME LIFE

The Ottoman period, in particular the lifestyles of its sultans and other members of the ruling class, are associated with wealth and luxury. Household objects were often ornate and highly decorative, and artisanal trades flourished. In addition to being used throughout the empire, Ottoman goods were in demand across Europe and Asia.

candle holder

applied rosette

Ceramic jar
Dating from 19th-century Turkey, this glazed jar has a twisted handle. It is adorned with dotted rosettes and a painted floral pattern.

Candlestick
This late 15th-century brass Islamic candlestick is delicately inlaid with precious metal. Such candlesticks were commonly found in homes and mosques.

ART AND CULTURE

The arts flourished under the Ottoman Empire. The transformation of the Byzantine church Hagia Sophia into an imperial mosque inspired architects, and many impressive buildings were constructed. Manuscript painting and calligraphy also thrived. Expansion and trade made carpet weaving a large-scale operation, and various Ottoman cities were established for artistic production.

Iznik plate
Floral designs, such as the one on this 17th-century plate, were a hallmark of ceramics made in Iznik, Turkey, which were highly prized in the empire.

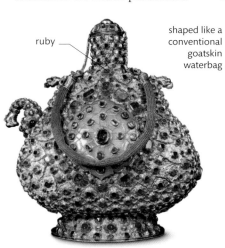

Gold bottle
Crafted from gold and studded with precious stones, including emeralds and diamonds, this decorative bottle is from the late 16th-century.

Rock crystal bottle
Intricately engraved, this bottle is from the late 1500s. It has gold stoppers and is embellished with rubies.

Wall panel
Colorful panels made from glazed tiles manufactured at the ceramic production center of Iznik were often used to cover or decorate walls and columns.

Page from a *muraqqa'*
This lavishly illustrated *muraqqa'* (album) is a history of the greatest Ottoman calligraphers from the 15th to 18th centuries.

Silver pen and ink case
Turkish calligraphers used pens known as *qalam*, which were made of reed. Pens and ink were stored in holders like this 18th-century case.

CLOTHING AND ADORNMENT

The wide variety of cultures across the empire influenced the development of Ottoman fashion. Some of the clothing from Central Asia and North Africa, such as loose trousers, tunics, and the fez hat, became associated with Turkish style. Status was displayed through the types of materials used, as well as the kinds of jewelry worn.

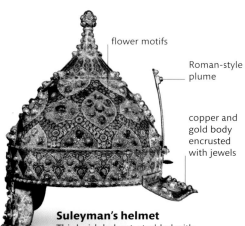

Suleyman's helmet
This lavish helmet, studded with turquoise and rubies, belonged to Suleyman the Magnificent, one of the longest-reigning Ottoman sultans.

Jeweled aigrette
This late 17th-century aigrette-style headdress (imitating an egret's plume) is decorated with pearls, diamonds, emeralds, and feathers.

Lady's robe
Cut from pink silk and delicately embroidered, this luxurious *anteri* (robe) is lined around the hem and cuffs with gilt braid.

WEAPONS AND ARMOR

The peak of Ottoman expansion lasted from the 1450s until the early 1600s, and it was fueled by a need to fend off encroaching Europeans and protect trade routes. At its height, the empire stretched from Hungary to Iran and the Crimea to North Africa, but the price was near-continual warfare during this period.

Mace

An Ottoman *gurz*, or mace, such as this one had a heavy round end. It was used by soldiers on horseback or on the ground to bludgeon the enemy.

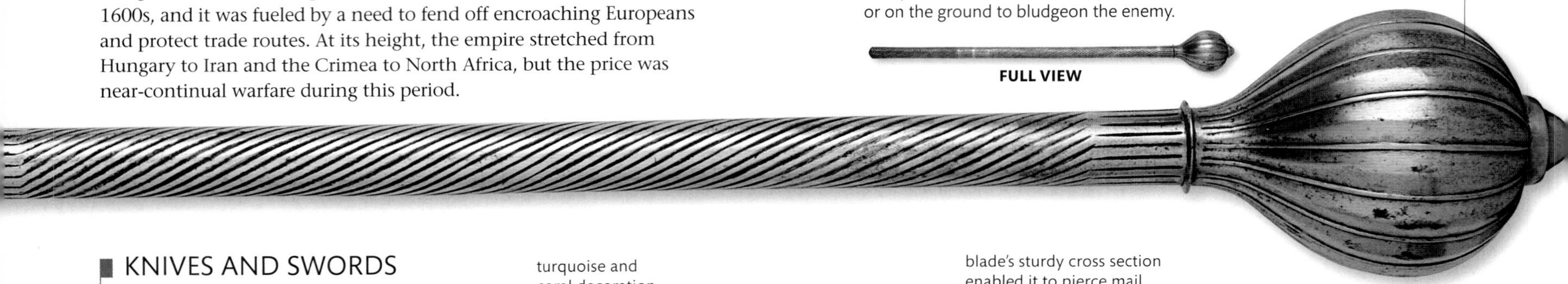

hollow, onion-shaped head

FULL VIEW

■ KNIVES AND SWORDS

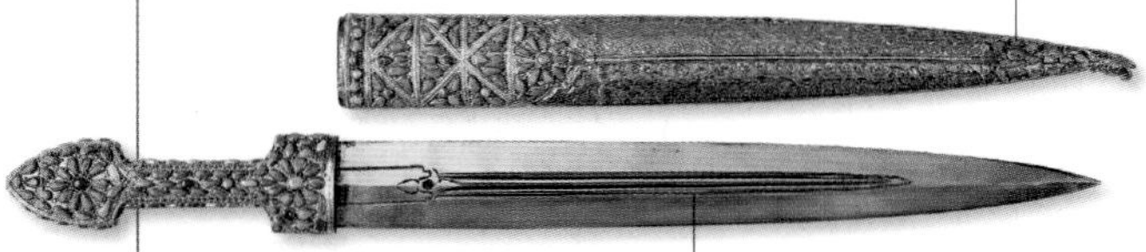

turquoise and coral decoration

blade's sturdy cross section enabled it to pierce mail

Khanjar

This small dagger, or *khanjar*, has an ivory handle. The unsharpened blade near the quillons, or finger-guard, allowed the soldier to have greater control over the weapon.

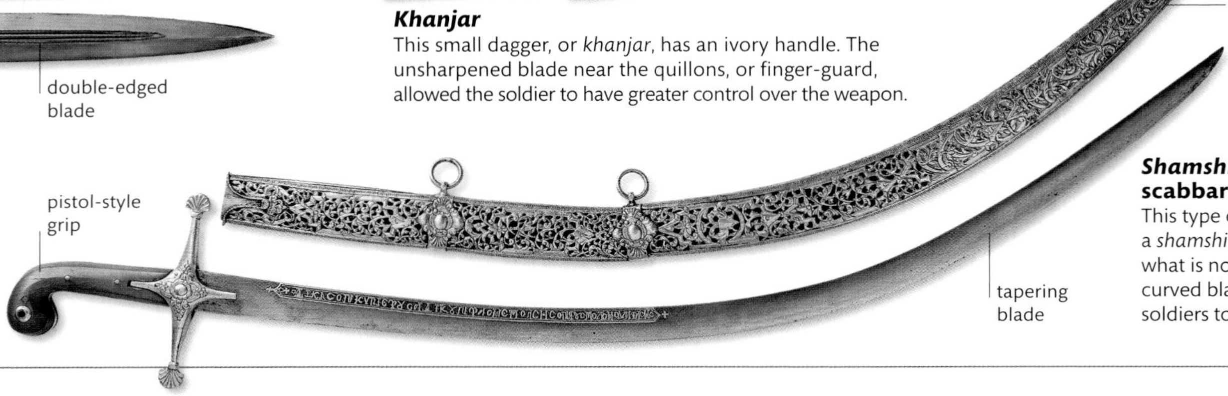

highly decorated scabbard

Quarma and scabbard

Known as a cossack dagger, this weapon comes from Georgia in the Caucasus region. It has an elaborately decorated hilt and scabbard, indicating the wealth of its owner.

double-edged blade

pistol-style grip

Shamshir and scabbard

This type of saber, called a *shamshir*, originated in what is now Iran. It has a curved blade that allowed soldiers to slash the enemy.

tapering blade

■ FIREARMS

engraved spherical pommel

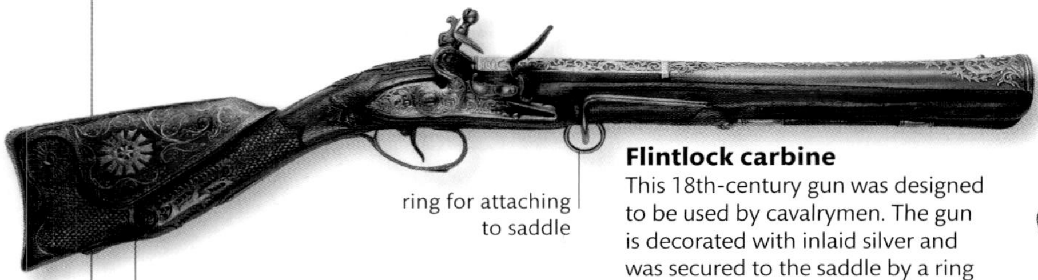

Flintlock carbine

This 18th-century gun was designed to be used by cavalrymen. The gun is decorated with inlaid silver and was secured to the saddle by a ring on its underside.

ring for attaching to saddle

carved shoulder stock

Flintlock pistol

Ottoman arms were often lavishly decorated. This late 18th-century flintlock pistol has an intricate gilded design that extends from the pommel to the muzzle.

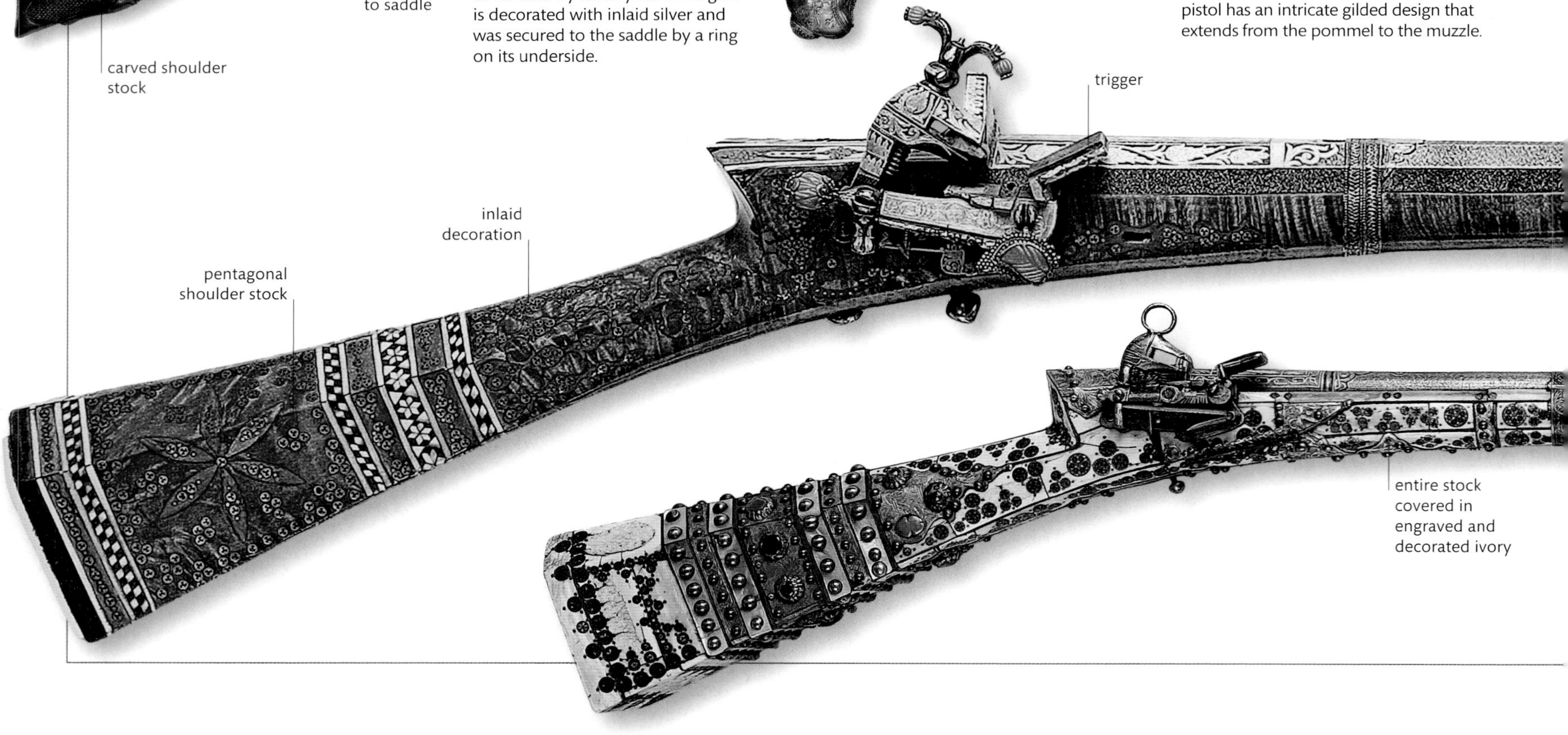

trigger

inlaid decoration

pentagonal shoulder stock

entire stock covered in engraved and decorated ivory

■ ARMOR

Steel helmet
Ottoman soldiers in the 16th century would have worn this type of steel helmet, which has ear, neck, and nose guards.

concave neck guard

nose guard

chainmail

Rawhide helmet
This pointed helmet is known as a chichak helmet. It is based on the headgear worn by janissaries.

copper gilt decoration

handgrip rivets

Shield
This 17th-century *kalkan*, or small shield, consists of a central boss of iron surrounded by silk-covered strips of cane.

plates

large plates joined together by chainmail

buckles join plates together

four linked plates protect toes

Chainmail armor
Known as *zirh gomlek*, this Ottoman cavalry armor was made of ferrous metal, copper alloy, and leather. It consists of rows of riveted links, with inserted overlapping plates.

Breastplate
A cuirass from the 1500s, this body armor bears the mark of the St. Irene arsenal in Constantinople, which had been a church prior to the 1453 conquest of the city.

Cavalry boot
These steel boots were heavy—weighing 6.2 lb (2.8 kg) each—but they offered vital protection. They are made of several plates of metal and columns of mail.

CHAINMAIL SOLE

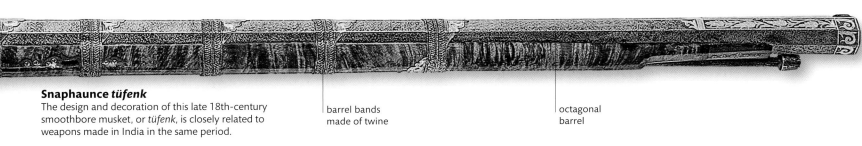

Snaphaunce *tüfenk*
The design and decoration of this late 18th-century smoothbore musket, or *tüfenk*, is closely related to weapons made in India in the same period.

barrel bands made of twine

octagonal barrel

Miquelet *tüfenk*
The name of this weapon comes from the miquelet lock on it, which was commonly used in Spain and Italy.

embellished with inlay of precious stones and brass

barrel band

ramrod

OTTOMAN CARTOGRAPHY

PIRI RE'IS MAP

Dating from 1513, this remnant of a map drawn by Turkish mariner Piri Re'is is one of the earliest cartographic depictions of the Americas. Historians have long been fascinated by many aspects of the map, such as its level of accuracy. The route to the New World was at first a secret closely guarded by the Spanish and Portuguese navigators who were exploring the Atlantic—not least the Genoese explorer Christopher Columbus, who was working under the sponsorship of the Spanish monarchy. Re'is surprisingly placed the New World on the correct longitudinal meridian in relation to the African continent, and this was the earliest known map to do so. The scale of the map is inconsistent, with the Americas drawn much larger than Africa or Asia. However, this was similar to many maps of the time.

SEA WARRIOR

Re'is means "captain," and Piri Re'is spent most of his life on ships, learning to sail under his famous corsair uncle, Gazi Kemal. He spent years sailing the coasts of the Mediterranean and North Africa and fought in many battles with the Ottoman navy. He recorded his navigational knowledge, resulting in this extraordinary map. He also wrote the *Book of Navigation (Kitab-i Bahriye)* in 1521, which gave nautical instructions for the Mediterranean and the Persian Gulf, and included a number of maps.

CARTOGRAPHIC LEGACY

The map drawn by Re'is is known as a portolan sailing chart, which uses lines to show distances between points. Piri Re'is wrote on the map itself that he had consulted other maps in Arabic—including some classical sources. He also referred to four contemporary Portuguese maps, as well as one by Qulunbu, or Columbus. Some historians think this may be the closest map to the one Columbus made of his early discoveries, a theory supported by numerous aspects of the map.

For example, the island of Hispaniola seems to be, to modern eyes, upside down. When discovered by Columbus, he believed it to be Japan (known as Cipangu)—Piri Re'is seems to have reproduced this mistake in the shape of the island. The mystery remains, however, as to how Piri Re'is gained access to all this information.

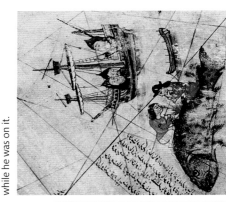

St. Brendan
The travels of this Irish abbot and saint were legendary. He was said to have confused a large fish, or in some versions a whale, for an island until it moved while he was on it.

Hispaniola
One of the surprising features of this map is its depiction of some of the West Indian islands discovered by Christopher Columbus, including Hispaniola, labeled as "Izle despanya," or Spanish island.

North Africa
The kingdoms of North Africa were well known to the Ottomans, and the illustrations of people and animals on the map display a great degree of accuracy.

South America
This map of South America shows fantastic creatures and a man with his face on his chest, who also appeared on the European mappae mundi.

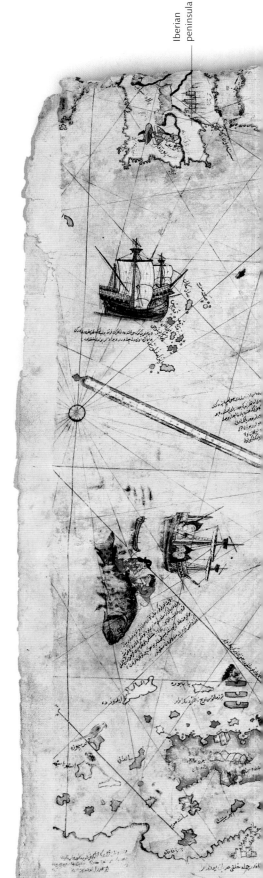

Iberian peninsula

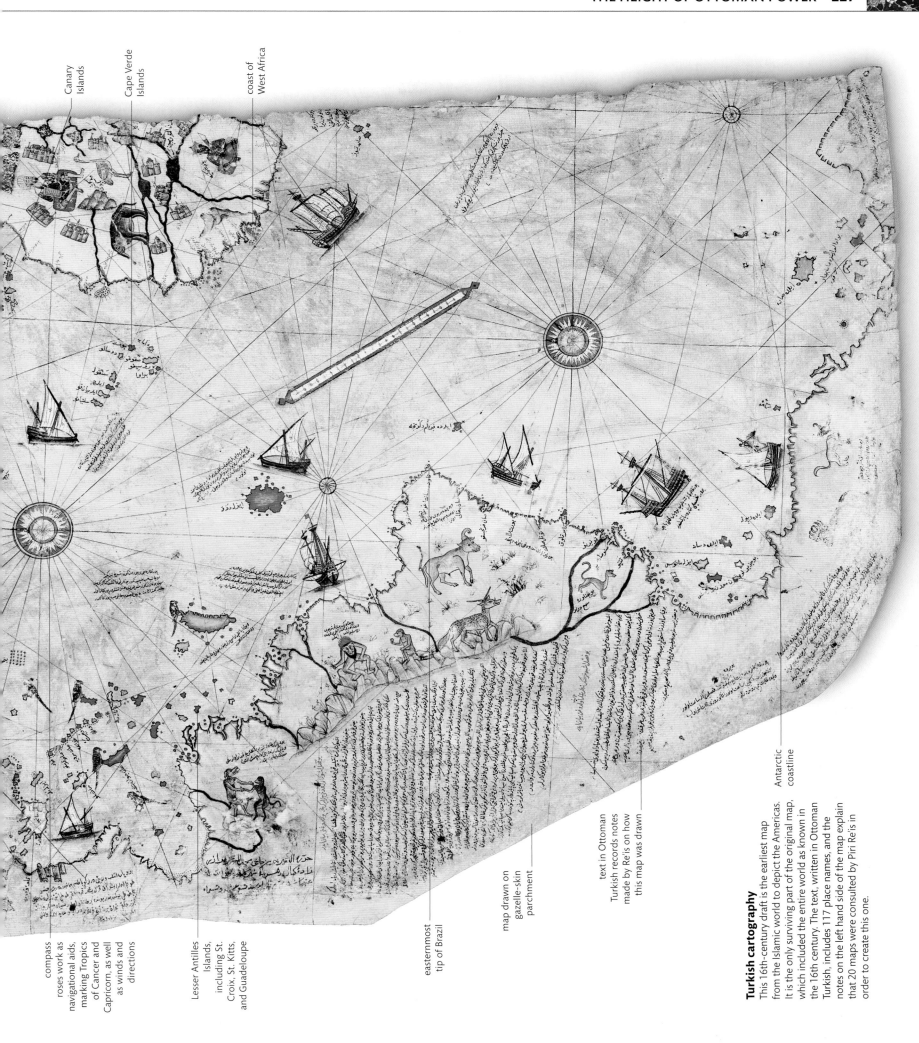

Canary
Islands

Cape Verde
Islands

coast of
West Africa

compass
roses work as
navigational aids,
marking Tropics
of Cancer and
Capricorn, as well
as winds and
directions

Lesser Antilles
Islands,
including St.
Croix, St. Kitts,
and Guadeloupe

easternmost
tip of Brazil

map drawn on
gazelle-skin
parchment

text in Ottoman
Turkish records notes
made by Re'is on how
this map was drawn

Antarctic
coastline

Turkish cartography

This 16th-century draft is the earliest map
from the Islamic world to depict the Americas.
It is the only surviving part of the original map,
which included the entire world as known in
the 16th century. The text, written in Ottoman
Turkish, includes 117 place names, and the
notes on the left hand side of the map explain
that 20 maps were consulted by Piri Re'is in
order to create this one.

POETRY AND POWER IN THE SAFAVID EMPIRE

inscribed
Shia prayer

Standard
This standard would have been used in a military or religious ceremony. The surviving fingers display verses from the Koran.

Lasting for more than 200 years, the Persian Safavid Empire was known for its fine arts and crafts—especially its poetry and architecture. However, the Safavid era was also a time of religious transformation, as Shia Islam was implemented in Iran.

The Safavid dynasty laid the foundation of modern Iran. Although it was named for the descendants of Sufi leader Safi al-Din, the dynasty began with the rule of Isma'il I, who came to power in 1501. He brought all of Iran under his control, and the territory grew to encompass parts of modern Iraq, including Baghdad.

A new capital was established at Isfahan, replacing the two previous capitals of Tabriz and Qazvin. Isfahan became a thriving city renowned for its beautiful architecture. At the same time, there was growing wealth, much of it related to silk. This was produced by the local Armenian community, which held a monopoly on the trade. Arts, such as manuscript painting and poetry, also flourished.

ROLE OF ISLAM

It was in the realm of religion that Isma'il made the longest-lasting impact. He decreed that the Shia form of Islam should be the established religion at a time when this variant was a smaller sect in a largely Sunni area, although he was not the first to do so; Shia had been the official religion in Fatimid Egypt around the 10th century. However, Isma'il's policy was unpopular in other parts of the Muslim world. At the same time, the Safavids were under pressure from the Ottoman Turks, who mounted an invasion in 1514, leading to more than a century of intermittent warfare. The Safavids also had to fight against the Uzbeks, who were attacking from the northeast.

Shah Abbas I came to power in 1588. He made an uneven peace with the Ottomans in 1590 by giving away territory in order to focus on fighting the Uzbeks. The Safavids eventually defeated the Uzbeks, and then the Turks once again in 1603, who were forced to renounce all the territory they had seized, keeping the Safavid Empire intact for another century.

Decorative vault ▽
Completed around 1630, the *Masjid-i-Shah* (or Shah Mosque) soon became famous for its impressive vaulting and colorful tiling.

TRADE

Iran had enjoyed a prominent position along the long-established overland trade route known as the Silk Road, which connected Europe to the Far East. It was an important commercial corridor along which Persian merchants prospered, and demand for Armenian silk helped add to the empire's wealth.

bold flower motif in Timurid style

blue-glazed pot

Persian script replaced Arabic on coins

Decorated plate
The Chinese influence on this decorated Persian ceramic plate shows that the Silk Road also continued to be important for Safavid trade.

Silver coins
As international trade grew, Persian silver, as found in these 17th-century coins, came to be considered more valuable.

ART AND CULTURE

Calligraphy and painting were considered to be important arts during the Safavid period. The wealthy urban elite could afford to commission manuscripts or works of art, and some calligraphers gained great fame and were paid large sums for their creations. The manuscripts produced ranged from the holy Koran to works of poetry, history, and science.

Silk rug
The Kashan province in modern-day Iran produced this woven silk rug, or *kilim* in the 16th century. Initially, such textiles were only available to the very wealthy. Popular designs included flower patterns and animals, as well as scenes from popular literature.

Decorative tile
Made in Kubachi, in the Caucasus region, this colorful tile was produced using a technique that involved firing tiles at a low temperature, which often led to a distinctive crackle developing on the glaze.

adorned with animals

distinctive flower motif arranged in rows

■ CALLIGRAPHY

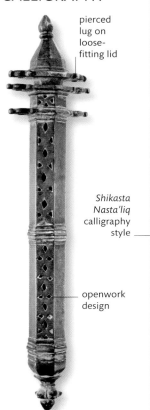

pierced lug on loose-fitting lid

Shikasta Nasta'liq calligraphy style

openwork design

Pen case
This hexagonal gold pen case would have held calligraphy tools. The geometric pattern is a typical feature of Islamic design.

Shahnameh page
Seen here is a page from a 17th-century copy of the epic poem, *The Book of Kings*, or *Shahnameh*, by the Persian poet Ferdowsi, also called Firdawsi.

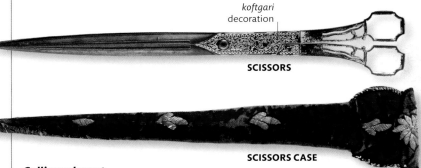

koftgari decoration

SCISSORS

SCISSORS CASE

Calligraphy set
These steel scissors and case would have been part of a calligraphy set. They are decorated with gold inlay in an ornamental pattern known as *koftgari*.

■ PERSIAN CLASSICAL POETRY

KHAMSA ILLUMINATED MANUSCRIPT

Although the work of the 12th-century Persian poet Nizami Ganjawi, popularly known as Nizami, predated the establishment of the Safavid dynasty, it remained an important part of Iran's written culture for hundreds of years. His writings in Persian synthesized many earlier poetic traditions, while setting a new standard that ensured his work became influential across Iran and beyond.

The respect Nizami garnered is evident from the fact that many illuminated manuscript versions were made of his greatest work, *Khamsa*, or *The Five Poems*. The earliest surviving copy dates from 1362, while the manuscript shown here dates from 1584. The poems in this version are illustrated with 39 full pages of paintings and illuminations—these were both highly prized visual art forms and continued to be during the Safavid period. The text itself consists of five long *masnavi*, or poems, which are made up of around 30,000 couplets. These poems are animated by vivid imagery and innovative use of language.

THE LIFE OF THE POET

Believed to have been born into a prosperous family, Nizami was orphaned at an early age. He spent most of his life in the town of Ganja (in modern Azerbaijan), in the Caucasus. Nizami drew inspiration from the extensive and rich Persian poetic traditions as well as tales from folklore. Azerbaijani oral folk literature, including *dastans* (stories), legends, and proverbs are skillfully used in Nizami's creations. Though Nizami was not a court poet, he dedicated his poems to the rulers of the time, as was the custom. Refusing royal patronage gave him greater freedom to express himself as a storyteller.

MYSTIC QUALITY

The first work in the *Khamsa*, which is called "The Treasure of Mysteries," is a philosophical poem, though it is inspired by mysticism. The other four poems, love stories, are also mystically inspired and serve as mystical allegories. Many scholars believe that Nizami may have been a Sufi—a form of Islamic mystic—and his abiding interest in this mystical aspect of the religion is often reflected in his work.

intricate geometric design

Khusraw watching Shirin bathing

outdoor setting

FRONTISPIECE

SCENE FROM THE POEM "KHUSRAW AND SHIRIN"

SCENE FROM THE POEM "THE TREASURE OF MYSTERIES"

buildings with intricate patterned tiles

architectural depiction may portray ruins

Illuminated scenes
The ornate front cover and these scenes from two different poems in the *Khamsa* reflect some of the artistic styles of the Safavid period, including the use of brilliant colors.

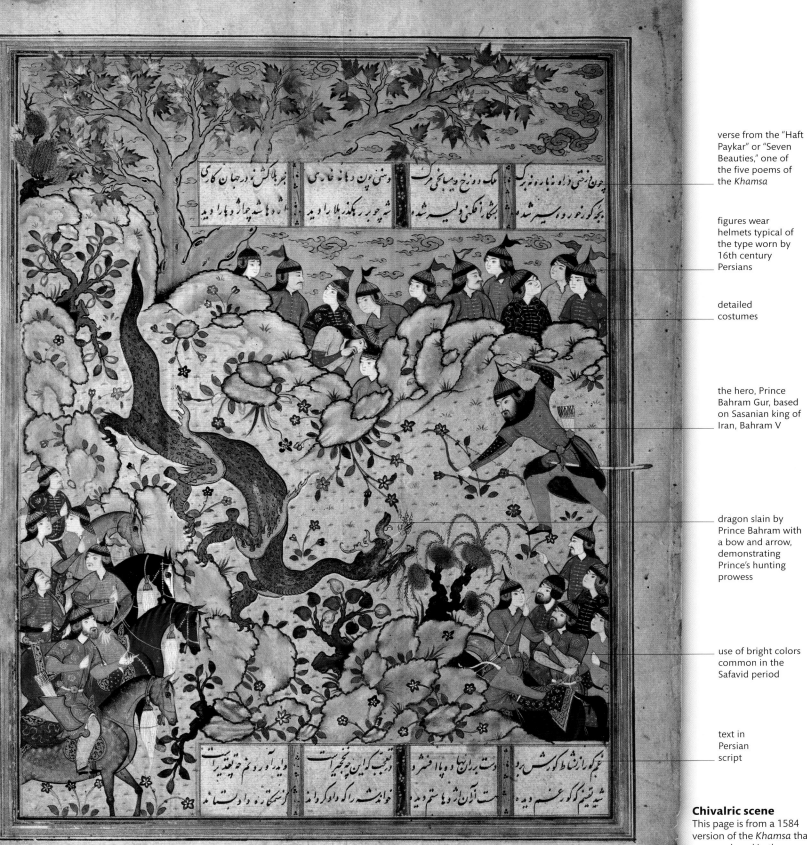

verse from the "Haft Paykar" or "Seven Beauties," one of the five poems of the *Khamsa*

figures wear helmets typical of the type worn by 16th century Persians

detailed costumes

the hero, Prince Bahram Gur, based on Sasanian king of Iran, Bahram V

dragon slain by Prince Bahram with a bow and arrow, demonstrating Prince's hunting prowess

use of bright colors common in the Safavid period

text in Persian script

Chivalric scene
This page is from a 1584 version of the *Khamsa* that was produced in the busiest commercial manuscript atelier of early modern Iran, Shiraz. This poem narrates the exploits of Sasanian king Bahram Gur, who was thought to represent the ideal king. The *Khamsa* was influential and its style inspired other illustrated manuscripts.

CULTURE IN KOREA'S LAST DYNASTY

The Joseon dynasty, established in 1392, ruled Korea for more than 500 years. Although intially inspired by Ming China, this period saw the emergence of distinct Korean cultural forms and a Korean phonetic alphabet.

Sign of rank ▷
Members of the Joseon military and civil service wore a *hyungbe*, or patch, such as this one to show their rank. This *hyungbe*, depicting two leopards, would have been worn by military officials of 1st, 2nd, or 3rd rank.

After military leader Yi Song-gye defeated the reigning Goryeo king in 1392, he established his own dynasty, which he called Joseon. Yi, later known as King T'aejo, moved the capital to Hanyang (modern Seoul). His successors stayed in power for more than 500 years, until Korea was annexed by Japan in 1910.

The Joseon had a close relationship with the Chinese Ming dynasty (1368–1644), and China considered Joseon Korea to be a subordinate state. There is much evidence showing the cultural influence of the Chinese in this period, including the replacement of Buddhism with a form of Confucianism as the official ideology. Koreans did bring their own traditions to some artistic fields. The creation of a royal kiln in 1392 greatly increased porcelain production, and many ceramics borrowed indigenous forms. This period also saw the development of a phonetic, written Korean alphabet in the 1440s called *Hangul*.

WRITING AND LANGUAGE

Under the ruler Sejong, *Hangul* was devised since Chinese characters were difficult to learn and could not fully express the Korean spoken language. *Hangul* was based on pronunciation and therefore, better suited for everyday use. However, Chinese characters were still used in all official documents and much literature.

Chinese characters

Writing desk
This table was designed to hold all the instruments a scholar would need, including seals, ink sticks and stones, and red seal paste. There is also a drawer to hold brushes. Paper and scrolls were placed at the base.

Soapstone seals
These seals are carved out of soapstone. Although Korea developed its own alphabet, Chinese characters were still used.

Wooden seal
This seal depicts four characters from the *Hangul* alphabet. The remnants of red paste can be seen on the base.

circular, hard stone ink-paste pot

porcelain with cobalt blue pigment

Water dropper
This 19th-century container would have been part of a scholar's writing set. It is in the shape of a peach, which is a symbol of longevity in Korea.

SLATE INKSTONE

BAMBOO BRUSH

Brush and inkstone
These tools were meant for writing. The brush could also be used for painting, while the inkstone was designed to mix ink for writing.

ART AND CULTURE

Elite culture in Joseon Korea, such as poetry, painting, and porcelain production, was influenced by Chinese forms, whereas folk traditions were favored by common people. The palace patronized the best craftsmen, while others worked for the open market. Less popular among the elite were forms of theater, which was considered a lower-class pursuit.

CLOTHING AND ADORNMENT

Personal fashions often followed the same Confucian precepts of simplicity that dominated other aspects of social life in Korea, with well-designed objects depicting little lavish ornamentation. Porcelain played an important role in everyday life as well, and its use spread beyond the royal household and into the general public.

brighter blue pigment was probably imported

painted paper stretched over split bamboo frame

"cloud" design in blue glaze

metal pin attaches handle to fan

three hawks painted in red

base shaped like a tortoise

Dance mask
This wooden mask, called a *maldduki*, depicts the face of a servant. It would have been used in a *talchum* —a satirical, masked dance drama—which was often held outdoors in villages.

Porcelain vase
The use of cobalt in glazes for porcelain was introduced in this period. At first, objects made with this type of glaze were for royal use only.

Perfume bottle
This 19th-century bottle has a blue decorative glaze under popular white porcelain. The duller blue-gray finish indicates that a local mineral was used.

Hand fan
Men and women both used fans, but there were distinct styles for each. This paper and bamboo fan was designed for a woman.

Paper charm
Dating from the late Joseon period, this *Sam ma*, or paper charm, was meant to be worn inside clothing or placed under a pillow for good luck.

HOME LIFE

Although Korean objects were often embellished with decoration that drew inspiration from the natural world, their attributes also continued to draw heavily from the Chinese influence, sometimes mirroring Ming trends. Domestic goods were no exception, although many objects combined both influences, resulting in a unique Joseon-period style.

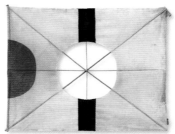

Kite
This *Bangpae yeon*, or shield kite, has a circle in the center, which was typical of the simple design in the late Joseon period.

Wooden ducks
Marriage ducks symbolized fidelity and were placed in the marital home. When arranged beak-to-beak, they represented happiness, but when placed tail-to-tail, it meant the couple was arguing.

Home screen
This wood, paper, ink, and pigment screen depicts a story called "A Nine Cloud Dream"—a symbolic tale concerning the conflicting Confucian and Buddhist ideals about what constitutes a successful life. Such screens were used as dividers in large rooms or displayed against the wall.

start of story, which reads from right to left

Buddhist monk begins journey to meditation, but is stopped by beautiful women representing earthly temptations

■ MAPPING THE KNOWN WORLD

THE KANGNIDO MAP

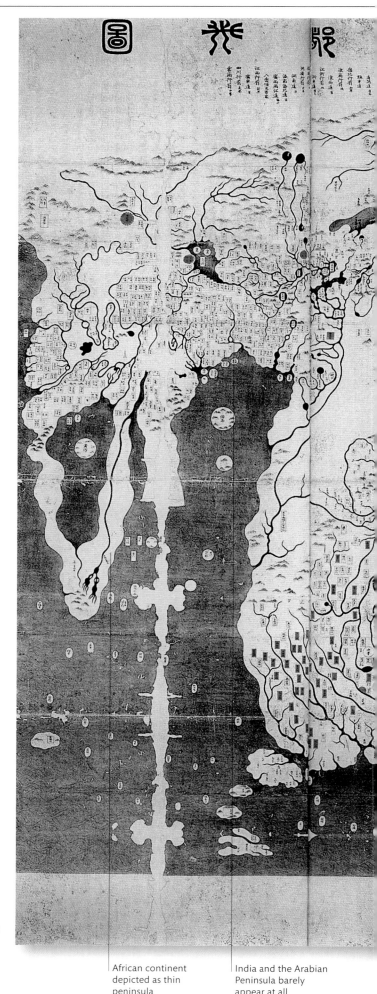

This famous map is one of the most valuable artifacts from Korea's Joseon period. Usually known as the *Kangnido*, its full title means "Map of Integrated Lands and Regions and of Historical Countries and Capitals." The original version, completed in 1402, was lost, but several copies have survived. The *Kangnido* is the earliest map known to come from East Asia. It is also the first to provide a geographical depiction of the boundaries of Korea as established by the previous Goryeo regime.

CHINESE INFLUENCE

The map, which was drawn a century before the western voyages to the Americas, depicts the world as known to Korea at the time. One of its most striking features is the scale of China in relation to the rest of the world. Maps drawn in Europe at the time were often oriented toward where the cartographer believed Jerusalem to be, because it was considered the spiritual center of the known world. In the East, however, China's Ming dynasty was clearly the focal point and the dominant power. But one aspect that is common to both types of maps is their basis in the work of the ancient Greek astronomer Ptolemy, whose influential studies of astronomy and cartography

spread around the world. Ptolemy's writings from the 2nd century CE were translated by Islamic scholars hundreds of years later, and eventually passed into China as well. The Chinese, however, also had a rich body of their own scientific knowledge to draw from, including works on astronomy.

THE TWO FUNCTIONS

Kwon Kun, a respected Korean scholar, was involved in drafting the *Kangnido* map and overseeing a team of the king's astronomers. For most of his career he was an important administrator, and often travelled to China (where he had spent time studying). The final years of his life, however, were devoted to the development of this map.

Although it was intended to be a practical aid for government administration, the *Kangnido* map also served a larger symbolic function that helped underpin the ancient Chinese philosophical concept of "Mandate from Heaven," which argued that the right to rule was granted to emperors by the gods. This legitimized their right to exercise power. The Joseon also adopted this idea, and the *Kangnido* map gave it a physical manifestation.

> "One can indeed **know the world without going out** of his door!"
>
> Kwon Kun, from the text under the *Kangnido* map

East Asian cartography
The detailed *Kangnido* map dates from 1402. It is the earliest known cartographic work of this kind from East Asia and the first to depict the borders of Korea. The original version was lost, but the map had proven so popular at the time that many copies were made, some of which survived—including this replica from *c.*1560.

African continent depicted as thin peninsula

India and the Arabian Peninsula barely appear at all

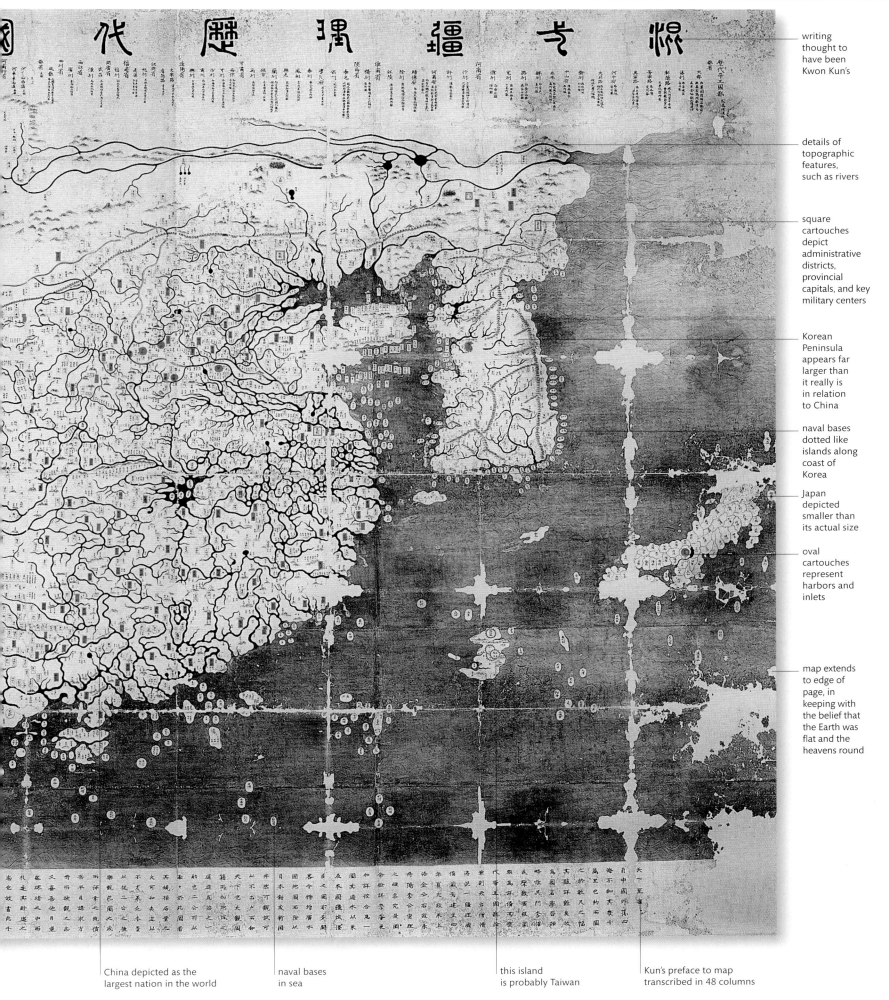

writing thought to have been Kwon Kun's

details of topographic features, such as rivers

square cartouches depict administrative districts, provincial capitals, and key military centers

Korean Peninsula appears far larger than it really is in relation to China

naval bases dotted like islands along coast of Korea

Japan depicted smaller than its actual size

oval cartouches represent harbors and inlets

map extends to edge of page, in keeping with the belief that the Earth was flat and the heavens round

China depicted as the largest nation in the world

naval bases in sea

this island is probably Taiwan

Kun's preface to map transcribed in 48 columns

CHINA'S AGE OF PROSPERITY

The Qing dynasty transformed China not only by adding significantly to its size and population but also by spending vast sums of money on its cultural life. The empire's first two centuries were marked by strong leadership, such as that of Emperor Kangxi, who was in power for 61 years. It was also well known for the production of luxury goods, such as silks and fine porcelain.

Royal helmet
The early years of the Qing dynasty were marked by intense warfare. This gold-inlaid helmet with a dragon frieze was intended for use by a member of the imperial family.

Gateway to heaven ▷
The Hall of Prayer for Good Harvests is part of the Temple of Heaven complex in Beijing, which was built under the Ming dynasty and expanded by the Qing. The Hall's three roofs have three levels of columns supporting them, and the entire structure was built without the use of a single nail.

The Qing dynasty ruled over China from 1644 until the start of the 20th century. It was founded by the Manchus, from Manchuria in northeast China. The preceding Ming dynasty had entered a troubled period by the 1600s, and in 1644 the rebel leader Li Zicheng captured the capital of Beijing. The Ming emperor asked the Manchus to help fight this invader—a disastrous move, as the Manchus had ambitions of their own and eventually took control of the Ming Empire.

THE REIGN OF KANGXI
China's longest-serving emperor, Kangxi, was one of the best-known and greatest rulers of this period. He began his reign at the age of six in 1661, initially with the help of regents, and stayed in power until his death. The size and population of Qing China grew significantly during his reign. He consolidated control of other parts of China while also quelling internal revolts. In addition, he managed to extend Chinese power to Siberai, Central Asia, and Tibet, assimilating people who

were not Manchu or Chinese. This period was marked by conservative attitudes infused with the Confucian principals of hierarchy. Although Qing society was guided by Confucian philosophy, it was not the only prevalent belief system. Many people followed the principles of Taoism (or Daoism) and Buddhism, both of which had existed in China for more than 1,500 years. Kangxi also welcomed members of the Catholic Jesuit order to enter China, and took a keen interest in their knowledge of astronomy, map-making, and other scientific pursuits.

CULTURAL RICHES
Kangxi was willing to open up a few ports, including Canton, for trade with foreigners. Ships from Britain and the Netherlands, among others, soon arrived, bringing foreign merchants eager to buy goods such as silk, porcelain, and especially tea. This beverage had long been popular in China—some estimates date its use as a drink to around 600 CE, although it had been used for medicinal purposes for at least 2,000 years before

that. Once traders had their first taste of tea, they were keen to take it to their home countries, and Great Britain became one of the biggest markets for this product.

THE EMPIRE FLOURISHES
The growing international trade added to the prosperity of this period, which continued under Kangxi's son Yongzheng, and Yongzheng's son, Qianlong. Kangxi's son and grandson were both great patrons of the arts; Qianlong himself painted and was a poet. Their interest and patronage meant that art and culture flourished during the period. But at the same time, the regime harshly censored any writings deemed to be subversive.

The financial stability of the empire encouraged elites to fund painters and poets. Painting was considered an important art in early Qing China, and European influences were seen in paintings for the first time during this period. There was also a growth of traditional handicrafts, such as porcelain-making, which was partly driven by international demand for Chinese wares.

" Esteem… **filial piety** and **brotherly submission…** give due importance to **human moral relations.**"

Emperor Kangxi, Sacred Edict, 1670

ART AND CULTURE

The early Qing period was a time of remarkable innovation in Chinese arts and crafts, especially in porcelain-making. New forms of colored, opaque glazes were used, and lacquerwork was also popular. Much of the work of this time featured natural motifs, or depicted religious symbols.

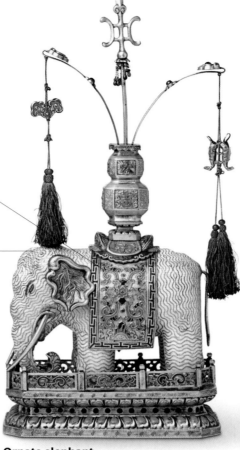

saddle cloth finely enameled with stylized lotus flower and scrolling leaves

gilded cloisonné to represent wrinkled hide

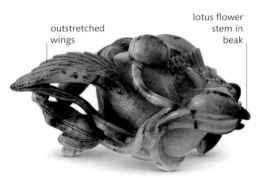

outstretched wings

lotus flower stem in beak

Water dropper
Chinese calligraphy flourished during the early Qing dynasty. This elaborate water dropper is carved in the shape of a squat goose.

Ornate elephant
This elaborately decorated elephant was part of the palace collection of the Emperor Qianlong. Elephants were considered to be lucky, and they symbolized strength.

decorated stand to hold candle

cloisonné enamel inlay

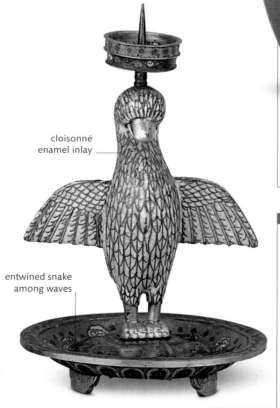

entwined snake among waves

Bird candlestick
Cloisonné enamel reached great levels of sophistication and complexity over the centuries. This pair of 18th-century decorated candlesticks are shaped like a bird with outstretched wings, standing on a tortoise.

■ CERAMICS

egg yolk lead glaze on surface

flask-shaped bottle with intricate decoration

four-clawed dragon

Dragon bowl
This bowl from the mid-17th century shows a dragon chasing a luminous pearl, which was often used to symbolize wisdom.

Pilgrim bottle
Bottles such as this one were designed to be carried by pilgrim travelers. Later versions were too ornamental for such use, but retained the round form.

gilt around the mouth

rose-pink glaze

Stem cup
The elegant and brilliant shade of blue on this bowl was produced by firing cobalt at a high temperature of around 2,372°F (1,300°C).

Buddhist vase
The shape of this vase is meant to represent the bottle of Bodhisattva Guanyin, who, according to legend, used a bottle to carry water to save people from drought.

Ritual bowl
Red monochromes were the most important type of ritual vessel. They were called "sacrificial red" after their use in sacrifices at the Altar of the Sun in Beijing.

■ MUSIC

Bronze bell
Sets of bells were initially employed as instruments for performing rituals, often in a court or temple.

Jade flute
Music was an important part of social and religious life. This flute, carved out of jade, could have been played on a variety of occasions.

Lioness with cub

Lions were a popular decorative motif during the Qing dynasty. These animals were believed to have powerful male and female protective qualities. Imposing pairs were often found at the entrances of temples, homes, and imperial palaces. This 17th-century cloisonné statue depicts a mother with her male cub at her feet.

number of bumps on head sometimes signified status of house owner

gaping mouth

lions were often shown with their mouths open to symbolize the sacred Buddhist sound "om," a mantra commonly used in prayers

hook used to secure bell or tassles

collar decorated with chrysanthemums

enameled design constructed out of wires and soldered to metal surface

Intricate design

The use of cloisonné on a figure of this size indicates that it might have been produced in an imperial factory, possibly under the emperor's patronage.

pedestal intricately decorated with lotus flowers on fine scrollwork background

Cub

The young cub is curled around his mother's foot. The mother and cub were often depicted together in statues.

animal heads on legs of pedestal

Playing dragons

The elaborate base has a motif of two dragons playing. Dragons were thought to represent heaven and were also symbols of the imperial family.

PILGRIMS

MOUNTAINS

ANIMAL SYMBOLS

SACRED STONE

JADE BOULDER

Widely used and valued across Asia, jade has a special and long-running association with Chinese culture. In China, some of the earliest carvings made from this stone date back to the Neolithic period (c.3000 BCE). Through its long history, jade became a symbol of power and wealth to the Chinese, but it also developed moral dimensions.

Jade was famously praised by the philosopher Confucius (551–479 BCE), who likened the virtues of honorable people to jade, describing the stone as "fine, compact, and strong—like intelligence." It was also the subject of poems and songs, and even today there are idiomatic expressions in the Chinese language that invoke jade to describe purity or brilliance.

HARD PROPERTIES

Jade—known in Mandarin as *yu*—is commonly thought of as being green. Historically, the type of stone carved over centuries was the mineral nephrite, although jadeite began to be used in the past 300 years.

Although jadeite and nephrite are mostly green, both have a wide range of colors and tones, from white to purple to black, and are very hard to shape. Jade could not easily be cut or chopped with the tools available in China at the time where the boulder shown here was made. Instead, it had

to be shaped using techniques such as sanding. Although jade is tough, it is brittle rather than malleable and cannot be hardened like steel, so it was unsuitable for making swords and was instead often used to craft ornamental weaponry.

SPIRITUAL POWER

Jade is considered to have important spiritual dimensions. It was thought to have healing powers and to bring people closer to the deities of Taoism and Buddhism. Many carved objects made of jade have been found in the ancient tombs of nobles, indicating that this stone had some sort of religious or ritualistic use. Later Chinese pieces often depicted deities or certain symbolic animals, and related images from folk tales and myths.

Imperial jade

This nephrite boulder dates from the Qing Dynasty, during the reign of emperor Qianlong (r.1735–96), who was an enthusiastic collector of elaborate engraved objects. The period is considered to be one of the high points of jade output, partly driven by Qianlong's passion for the stone.

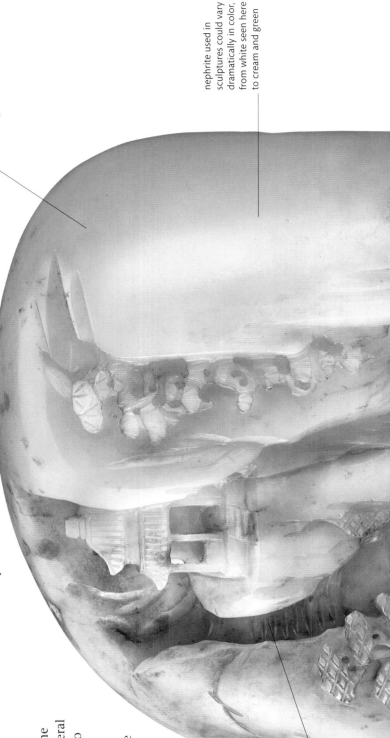

rounded shape achieved using techniques such as sanding

nephrite used in sculptures could vary dramatically in color, from white seen here to cream and green

steps up mountain represent spiritual journey undertaken by pilgrims and other devoted followers

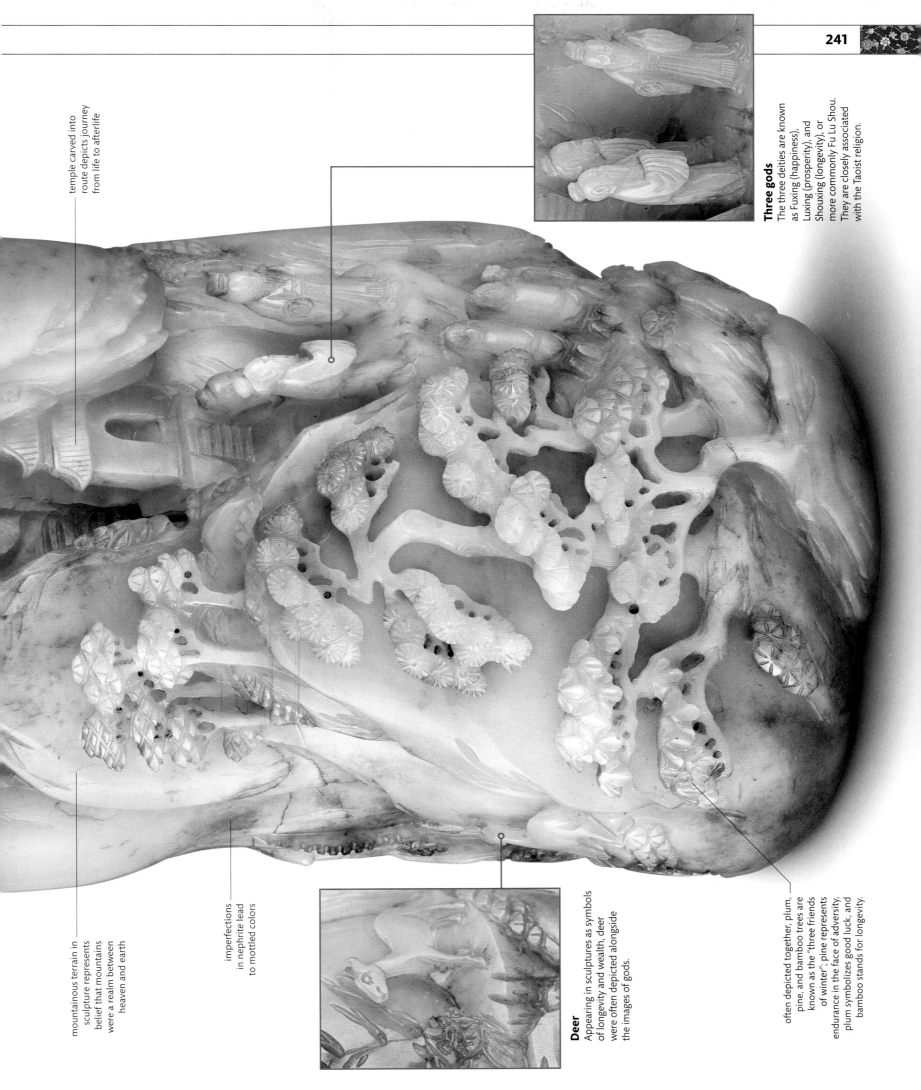

temple carved into route depicts journey from life to afterlife

Three gods
The three deities are known as Fuxing (happiness), Luxing (prosperity), and Shouxing (longevity), or more commonly Fu Lu Shou. They are closely associated with the Taoist religion.

mountainous terrain in sculpture represents belief that mountains were a realm between heaven and earth

imperfections in nephrite lead to mottled colors

Deer
Appearing in sculptures as symbols of longevity and wealth, deer were often depicted alongside the images of gods.

often depicted together, plum, pine, and bamboo trees are known as the "three friends of winter"; pine represents endurance in the face of adversity, plum symbolizes good luck, and bamboo stands for longevity.

CLOTHING AND ADORNMENT

Fashion in the Qing period often reflected the wearer's status. The dynasty had a dress code, and there were restrictions on what the general population was permitted to wear. Official court clothing included ceremonial robes, which were often decorated with symbols indicating rank and status.

Dragon jacket
This brightly colored jacket, decorated with a dragon, a symbol for the emperor that was often found on court robes. Commoners were forbidden from wearing clothes with this symbol.

yellow could only be worn by the imperial family and high-ranking officials

fur lining facing outward was fashionable during Qing period

Hairpins
Whilst the accessories and jewels women wore were meant to reflect their husband's position, hairpins like these could be worn by anyone who could afford them.

BACK VIEW

FRONT VIEW

HOME LIFE

The early Qing period was a time of prosperity, and people enjoyed a relatively high standard of living. The splendor of the dynasty was also reflected in the domestic life of the wider public. Utilitarian household objects including teapots, teacups, and other related wares, became more and more decorative, although their designs varied widely from simple to ornate.

brass lid

Traveling kit
Travelers would have used this lacquered case to carry eating utensils such as ivory chopsticks and a sharp knife.

TRADE

Europeans were especially eager to buy Qing dynasty porcelain; in fact, porcelain was one of the earliest traded Qing commodities. Chinese wares were prized for their design as well as for their durability, and some porcelain styles were eventually developed especially for the overseas market.

inscription with title of emperor

CHINESE SIDE   **MANCHU SIDE**

Qing coin
The engravings on Qing coins consisted of Chinese characters on one side and the Manchu script on the other.

■ **EXPORT CERAMICS**

lack of pattern enhances pure ivory tone of white glaze

porcelain with blue underglaze decoration

Dehua lamp
The style of this lamp is typical of the kilns in Dehua. Popular with Europeans, it was called Blanc de Chine by the French.

sancai decoration, which uses a mix of three colors to create patterns

engraved with Chinese script

Tea caddy
This simple pewter tea caddy from the 18th century features floral designs as well as some calligraphy on its sides.

Teapot
Shaped like a well, this rectangular teapot represents the seasons on its four sides.

overglaze enamel decoration on white porcelain

Punch bowl
The colorful English hunting scene depicted on this bowl was intended to appeal to British customers.

Porcelain plate
This 18th-century plate has an English mansion and garden painted on it, and may have been specially ordered by a British buyer.

BELIEFS AND RITUALS

Confucian philosophy provided the foundation of Chinese social morality. It remained a guiding force and its values were promoted by the Qing. The native Daoist religion and philosophy remained popular. By the Qing dynasty, Buddhism had existed in China for centuries and many continued to follow its principles. Folk beliefs and rituals also persisted.

Shou Lao

dragons on either side of Shou Lao

Peach-shaped box
Shaped like a peach, which represents long life, this box depicts Shou Lao, the Daoist god of longevity, enclosed by *Chun*, the Chinese character for spring.

elaborately carved lid

Incense burner
The top of the lid and the feet of this incense burner depict mice or rats. Burners such as this one were sometimes given as gifts to people born in the year of the rat.

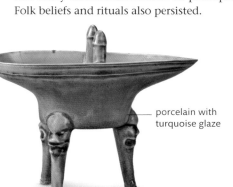

porcelain with turquoise glaze

Porcelain vessel
All metal vessels used in ritual ceremonies were replaced by ceramics during the Qing period.

decorated with brown, green, yellow, blue, and aubergine glaze

dragon at base

Guanyin
The bodhisattva Guanyin was revered by Buddhists and Daoists. In this statue, she is shown with a book of dharma on her left, containing teachings of the Budhha and the underlying order of the universe.

red spot of divinity on its crown

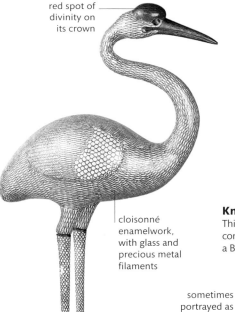

cloisonné enamelwork, with glass and precious metal filaments

intricate floral pattern

hollow, molded porcelain

Kneeling Bodhisattva
This figure represents Bodhisattva, a person committed to following the path to becoming a Buddha through self-awakening.

sometimes portrayed as scratching his ear, symbolizing purification of the sense of hearing

Sacred bird
Next to the phoenix, the Chinese considered the crane to be the most important winged animal. It was thought to symbolize wisdom and longevity.

Reclining Lohan
When a Buddhist attains nirvana and has freed himself from desire and thus no longer needs to be reborn, he is said to be a Lohan.

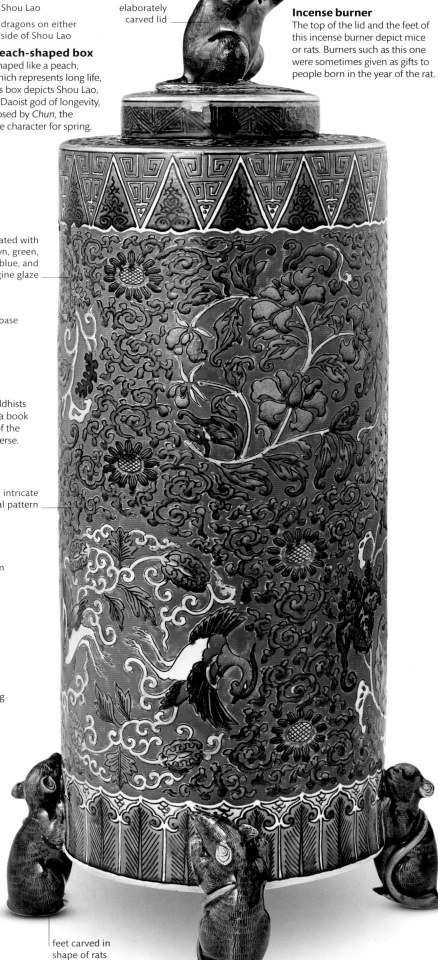

feet carved in shape of rats

LAST DAYS OF THE SAMURAI

The Edo period in Japan (1603–1868) was a time of peace and stability. The economy grew, and there was a great artistic flourishing that saw the development of forms such as woodblock printing, kabuki theater, and haiku poetry. Social changes also took place, as the wealth of middle-class merchants increased and the power of the mighty samurai warriors declined.

made of leather, wood, or paper, covered in lacquer

netsuke decorated with a floral pattern

Kyoto *inro*
Inro, like this one depicting Kyoto, were designed to store small objects. They were worn hung from a sash around the waist and secured by a *netsuke*.

Battle triptych ▷
The center panel of *The Fording of the Uji River* (1847–48), a color woodblock triptych by Utagawa Kuniyoshi, depicts a famous incident during a 12th-century war in which two generals raced to cross the river and attack the enemy.

Lasting more than 250 years, the Edo period differed significantly from the decades that preceded it, during which Japan had been a mostly feudal society divided by civil war between rural lords. These conflicts were gradually brought to an end, culminating in the shogunate—or military rule— founded by Tokugawa Ieyasu. The country's capital was moved from Kyoto to Edo, which is today's Tokyo (the city was renamed in 1868). Although the static social order remained, with the samurai at the top of the hierarchy, by the end of the period the merchant classes had made significant social and economic gains, while the samurai warriors saw their fortunes and power decline. However, the relative stability of the period helped open the way for a wide range of other economic and cultural changes.

FORTRESS MENTALITY
Despite the many internal changes, Japan was fiercely isolationist when it came to external matters. European explorers began to arrive in the

1500s—they were already navigating the globe and trading with China. Christian missionaries, especially Jesuits from Portugal, were among the first to land. They gained some access, but the shogunate considered them and their religion to be a threat to order. Most were expelled from Japan in the early 1600s.

At the same time, merchants who sailed to Japan had hoped to access the silver from its mines, as well as goods for trade, but they too were seen as potentially destabilizing. The nation adopted a fortress mentality, but not before these foreigners had introduced firearms, which the Japanese soon began to produce themselves. By the 1630s, Japan's citizens were forbidden to trade with outsiders, or to travel abroad, on pain of death. The one exception was a small settlement of Dutch merchants, who managed to keep their trading post in Nagasaki, a port to the south of Tokyo.

However, this isolation was no barrier to internal economic and cultural changes. Japanese arts thrived as the economy grew in the 18th century. Urbanization had

begun, and cities such as Tokyo became centers for the manufacture of products such as silks. The merchant class sought to display the wealth gained through trading these goods, becoming patrons of the arts and spending their money on new leisure activities. Professional female entertainers (geisha) prospered, music and literature flourished, and the visual arts embraced woodblock printing. Kabuki, a type of theater involving highly stylized singing, dancing, and costumes, emerged.

NEW SOCIAL ORDER
These social changes undermined the position of the samurai classes. They were usually stationed in rural palaces, connected to the local ruler, and dependent on land tax for their earnings. The growing urbanization meant their power was waning. Many samurai found themselves heavily in debt at the end of the Edo period, while the middle-class merchants enjoyed their wealth, climbing the social ladder to positions of prominence previously denied to them.

> **"Adepts** of [martial art] do not use the **sword to kill;** they use it to let **people live."**
>
> Takuan Soho, Zen master, 1573–1645

佐々木四郎高綱

BATTLE AND CONFLICT

Even though the Edo period was marked by peace, life under the shogunate meant maintaining a strong military. Weapons used in this period included swords, bows and arrows, and spears, although guns were later introduced. Samurai warriors were also expected to be proficient in martial arts, and to be constantly fit for battle.

silk braid

hand guard

■ POLEARMS

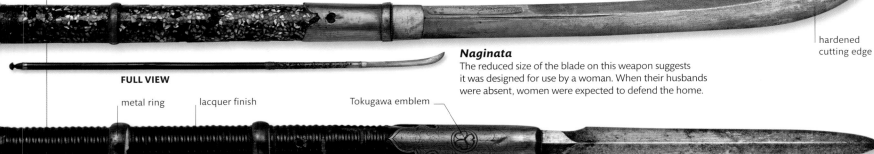

hardened cutting edge

FULL VIEW

Naginata
The reduced size of the blade on this weapon suggests it was designed for use by a woman. When their husbands were absent, women were expected to defend the home.

metal ring   lacquer finish   Tokugawa emblem

FULL VIEW   SCABBARD

Su yari with scabbard
This straight spear, made of wood, lacquer, steel, and copper, was used by samurai warriors to stab their opponents.

copper cover

FULL VIEW

Su yari with hadome
Made of steel, wood, and copper, this spear has cross blades, which were often used to drag a samurai from his horse.

mother-of-pearl embellishment

sharp cutting edge

Jumonji yari
Made of steel, wood, copper, and mother-of-pearl, this spear had a diamond-shaped cross section so it could be easily thrust through animals.

cross bar

FULL VIEW

■ GUNS

rear sight

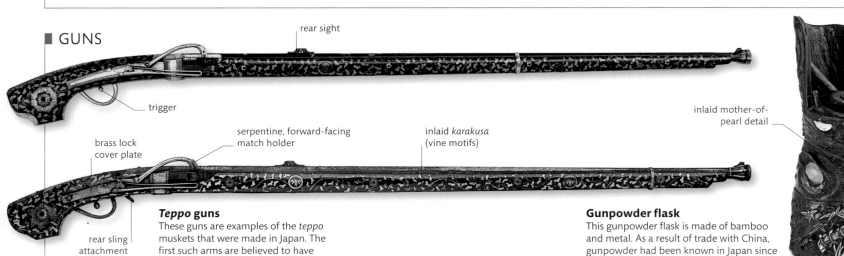

trigger

brass lock cover plate

serpentine, forward-facing match holder

inlaid karakusa (vine motifs)

inlaid mother-of-pearl detail

Teppo guns
These guns are examples of the teppo muskets that were made in Japan. The first such arms are believed to have been brought by the Portuguese.

rear sling attachment

Gunpowder flask
This gunpowder flask is made of bamboo and metal. As a result of trade with China, gunpowder had been known in Japan since the 13th century.

■ SWORDS

Long sword
In addition to the short sword, or *wakizashi*, the samurai sometimes wore a large sword, known as a *katana*, thrust through their sash. When both swords were carried, this was called *daisho*, meaning one long, one short. Samurai weapons were often displayed on stands in the warrior's home as a status symbol.

aoi-mon (emblem) of the Tokugawa shogun

lacquer stand decorated with gold foliage, fruit, and peonies

cloisonné enamel

monkey swinging on a tree

Decorative fittings
Often decorated with elaborate motifs, *fuchi* and *kashira* were ornamental fittings on the hilt (handle) of a sword.

fisherman and cormorant

Sword handles
These decorative handles, called *kodzuka*, were used on the large *katana* swords, with the designs often showing scenes from the natural world.

tsuba chiseled out of an iron plate

gold overlay

Tsuba
These guards were placed on swords to protect the warriors by preventing their hands from slipping onto the blade during battle or being cut by an opponent.

kogai (grooming implement)

sageo (cord for tying scabbard to belt)

SCABBARD (SAYA)

kissaki (point)

Sword and *kogai*
The samurai's short *wakizashi* sword was the companion to the larger *katana* sword. This 17th-century example is also fitted with a *kogai* grooming implement.

petals made of inlaid silver and brass

buckle

footplate inlaid with mother-of-pearl

Abumi
These 18th-century cast iron stirrups were designed to allow the warrior to stand while riding, to shoot arrows or use a sword.

Moon

Sun

War fans
These fans could be used as signaling devices to send commands, or as weapons of last resort in war. A legend claims that a samurai who was fanning himself used the fan to fend off an attack.

when closed, point was used in close combat

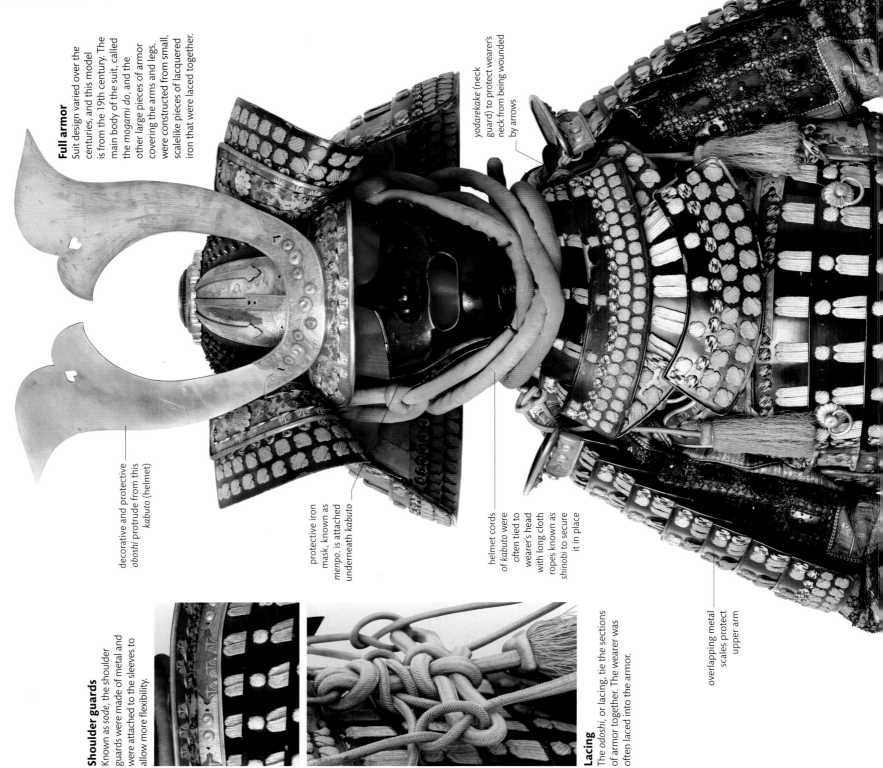

Full armor
Suit design varied over the centuries, and this model is from the 19th century. The main body of the suit, called the *mogami dō*, and the other large pieces of armor covering the arms and legs, were constructed from small, scalelike pieces of lacquered iron that were laced together.

decorative and protective *oboshi* protrude from this *kabuto* (helmet)

protective iron mask, known as *menpo*, is attached underneath *kabuto*

helmet cords of *kabuto* were often tied to wearer's head with long cloth ropes known as *shinobi* to secure it in place

yodarekake (neck guard) to protect wearer's neck from being wounded by arrows

overlapping metal scales protect upper arm

Shoulder guards
Known as *sode*, the shoulder guards were made of metal and were attached to the sleeves to allow more flexibility.

Lacing
The *odoshi*, or lacing, tie the sections of armor together. The wearer was often laced into the armor.

Helmet
Elaborate designs adorned the helmets. Some soldiers decorated their helmets with familial symbols, while others used animal motifs or other natural themes.

Leg protection
These *suneate* protect the shins, while another piece of armor, called the *haidate*, fits over the thighs.

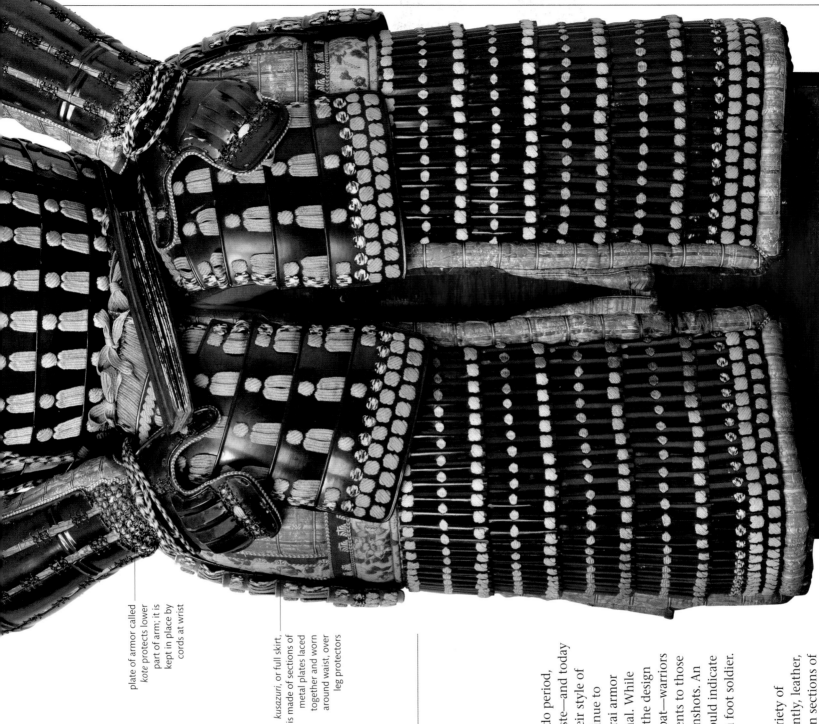

plate of armor called *kote* protects lower part of arm; it is kept in place by cords at wrist

kusazuri, or full skirt, is made of sections of metal plates laced together and worn around waist, over leg protectors

wooden box for storing armor

BACK VIEW

SIDE VIEW

■ MILITARY NOBILITY

SAMURAI ARMOR

Although their fortunes declined during the Edo period, the samurai were a privileged and powerful caste—and today their history, which dates back to the 700s, their style of battle, and the intricate armor they wore continue to generate much interest and admiration. Samurai armor was highly decorative, yet necessarily functional. While the armor remained colorful and well crafted, the design changed to reflect the evolving trends in combat—warriors fighting hand to hand had different requirements to those who were mounted on horseback or facing gunshots. An elaborate suit, such as the one shown here, would indicate a wearer of high status, rather than a common foot soldier.

CRAFTSMANSHIP

These complex garments were made from a variety of materials. Although metals figured predominantly, leather, lacquer, and even silk were also used. The main sections of the cuirass (which protected the torso) were generally forged from iron and steel that were then tied together to make plates of protective mail.

HOME LIFE

Tea has long played an honored role in the home life and social customs of the Japanese. The tea ceremony involves going to a specially designed room or tea house, where the drink is prepared and served to guests according to principles rooted in the country's Zen Buddhist tradition.

irregular outline and rough surface create rustic feel

Water jar
This vessel would have been used to hold cold water for the tea ceremony. Made in the 16th or 17th century, its rustic design embodies the influence of Zen Buddhism.

entire whisk made from single piece of bamboo

Tea whisk
An important part of making the tea is mixing the powdered leaves with hot water, which is done with a bamboo whisk.

Cake bowl
Guests at a tea ceremony would have been offered pieces of cake from a round, shallow pottery bowl like this one.

■ TEA CEREMONY

Iron kettle
Used only for heating water, kettles were not an official part of the tea ceremony. They were made from iron because the metal was thought to enhance the flavor of the tea.

ivory lid

cover protects jar

Tea powder jar
This brown pottery jar once held powdered green tea. During the ceremony, the tea is stirred in hot water but not prepared with a strong flavor.

flower motif

Hachi sweet bowl
This porcelain hachi bowl would have been used to present sweets eaten as part of the meal served during the tea ceremony.

peonies in white slip

Tea bowl
This rounded bowl would have been offered to participants in a tea ceremony. It follows a simple and popular style.

decorative dragon

light brown crackle glaze

Hagi Ware teapot
This teapot, with a spout but no handle, is an example of a style known as Hagi Ware.

vessel shaped like a sparrow

Incense burner
This sparrow-shaped censer, dating from c.1830, was used to burn incense in the home.

glazed surface

Sake teapot
In a longer version of the ceremony, the fermented rice drink sake might also be served, alongside a meal, before the tea.

Edo vase
The simple white and brown decoration of this vase is typical of the style found in homes during this period.

surface intricately carved with animal motifs

Brass lantern
Designed to be mounted on a wooden pole, this monumental and elaborate 19th-century lantern disassembles into five parts. It was intended for exterior use, probably at an entrance approach.

top piece emphasizes height

bamboo and silver pipe

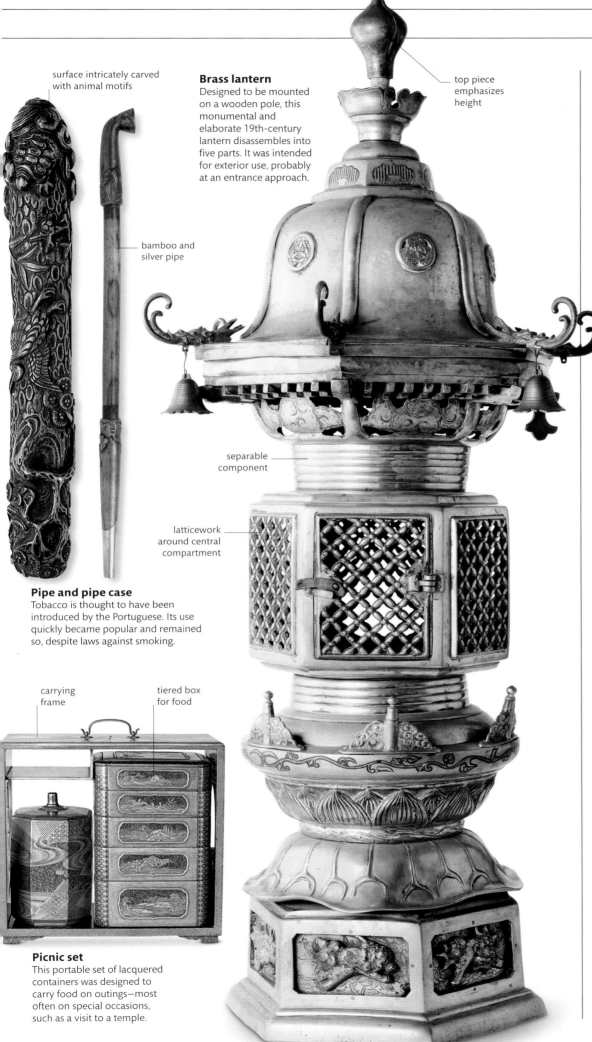

separable component

latticework around central compartment

Pipe and pipe case
Tobacco is thought to have been introduced by the Portuguese. Its use quickly became popular and remained so, despite laws against smoking.

carrying frame

tiered box for food

Picnic set
This portable set of lacquered containers was designed to carry food on outings—most often on special occasions, such as a visit to a temple.

CLOTHING AND ADORNMENT
The growing wealth of the merchant class gave them money to spend on elaborate outfits and accessories. Clothing styles changed too and the classic kimono became more lavish in design and bolder in the use of color.

carved ivory *netsuke*

netsuke

inro

Inro and *netsuke*
This decorative box, dated c.1765–90, was worn attached to a sash. The *inro*, which was used to carry objects, was secured by the *netsuke*.

Netsuke
Objects such as this *netsuke* depicting an old man and a boy became popular accessories with the affluent merchant class in the Edo period.

flock of cranes

small boats

Kimono design
This 19th-century print shows a design for a kimono, with branches of early budding trees and a pale blue river running diagonally from shoulder to hem.

lacquered wood

Combs
These Japanese combs made from shell, coral, and wood depict scenes from the natural world. Their designs include a river scene with boats, and a fish with other sea life.

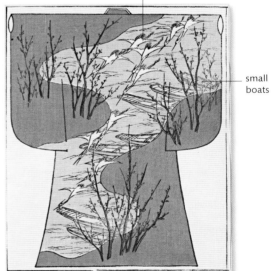

BELIEFS AND RITUALS

Buddhism remained the prevailing religion in Edo Japan, having been introduced around 552 CE. At the same time, the practices of Shinto, an indigenous religion incorporating folk beliefs and many deities, continued to be embraced. It was common for people to have shrines for both religions in their homes.

loop in form of opposed dragons

phoenix-headed dragon on neck

tripod feet support round body

decoration shows Kirin, a mythical creature

gold leaf

lacquered surface

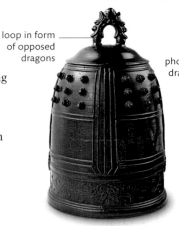

Temple bell
An inscription on this bell explains that it was dedicated to the Zen Buddhist Korinji Temple in Shinjo in 1841.

Incense burner
This incense burner reflects the influence of China in Japan: the shape is taken from a Chinese vessel known as a *ding*.

Buddha statue
The gold finish of this statue suggests it was made for a wealthy household or for use in a small temple or shrine.

ART AND CULTURE

Increasing urbanization and generous funding from the wealthy merchant classes led to innovation across the arts. Painters began to focus on themes of city life, while new techniques led to the production of woodblock prints. Haiku poetry appeared in this period, as did new forms of theater, including popular *bunraku* puppetry.

brush and inkstone in hand

Bunshosei, demon patron of written thought

dragon-headed winged carp

inlaid eyes

bamboo mount gives fan rigidity

Screen fan
Fans have long had an important place in Japanese culture. This screen fan has a scene by the famed woodblock print designer and ukiyo-e artist Hiroshige II.

narrow, deep overlapping lid

cord attached to each side

Bronze sculpture
This bronze *okimono* sculpture depicts a man riding a carp. *Okimono* sculptures were purely decorative objects that were displayed in the home.

Letter box
This elongated box, called a *fubako*, was used to send and receive letters or documents, and was often part of a wedding trousseau.

three volumes bound together

water pot   seal block

bamboo brush

wooden cube contains penknife and a needle

grinding block

detail drawn from nature

Woodblock prints
This volume of woodblock prints is bound with a single cover. Woodblocks were often carved from cherry wood, and each color usually needed its own block.

Writing set
This wooden box contains compartments to hold writing tools, such as a water-holder, penknife, needle, black ink block, reed seal block, and brushes and grinding blocks.

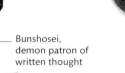

disheveled hair gives grisly appearance

horns reinforce demonic identity

hair emphasizes wild movement

gaping mouth contains demonic teeth

light skin coloring typical of an aristocrat

JAPANESE THEATER

Kabuki theater is one of the best-known cultural legacies of the Edo period. It is a type of performance that uses stylized singing and dancing alongside elaborate costumes and staging—as illustrated by the scene on this panel from an 1872 woodblock print triptych. This form of theater was the first in Japan to be aimed at a nonelite, popular audience.

Theater mask
This dramatic mask depicts the female demon Hannya, who was associated with jealousy and hatred. It is part of the Noh theater tradition, which is a form of storytelling that was often performed only for the elites during the Edo period.

THE MAJESTY OF MUGHAL INDIA

The Mughal Empire was founded by Babur, a descendant of the Turkic and Mongol conquerors Tamerlaine and Genghis Khan. The empire lasted for more than 300 years, spreading Islam through India while also fostering a climate of religious tolerance. The Mughals were famed for their riches and celebrated for their cultural output, including visual art, poetry, and architecture.

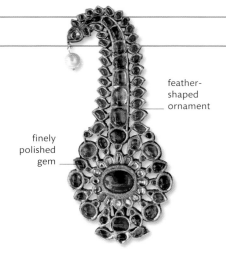

feather-shaped ornament

finely polished gem

Exquisite riches
This *sarpech*, a decorated turban ornament from India, is made from gold set with emeralds, rubies, diamonds, sapphires, and pearls.

Monument of love ▷
The iconic Taj Mahal, is perhaps the finest example of Mughal architecture. It was built as a mausoleum for Mumtaz Mahal, beloved wife of the Mughal emperor Shah Jahan (c.1628–58), who commissioned it to house the queen's remains after her death in 1631.

The Mughal Empire ruled over most of India for more than 300 years, reaching the peak of its powers in the 16th to the mid-18th centuries. In addition to controlling almost all of northern and central India, it also extended into modern-day Pakistan, Afghanistan, and parts of Iran, with its population reaching 100–150 million by the late 1600s.

The empire was founded by a prince named Babur (Zahir al-Din Muhammas Babur), who was a descendant of two great conquerors: Tamerlaine (also Timur) and Genghis Khan. Babur was born within Central Asia, but he extended his territory beyond its borders, seizing Kabul (in present-day Afghanistan) in 1504. He spent the following years making raids on India. In 1526, he captured the Delhi sultanate, and northern India fell under his rule.

THE EXPANSION
The Mughal Empire grew by consolidating smaller kingdoms. This was often a violent process, because not all kingdoms were willing to acquiesce to Babur or his descendants. At the same time, various internal rebellions and family rivalries broke out in the empire, making the Mughal period a time of constant warfare.

The Mughals were Muslims, and they spread Islam in India. Islam had existed in the country since the 8th century on a very small scale, but it grew under the influence of the Mughals. There was a great degree of religious tolerance initially. However, this changed under the reign of Aurangzeb in the 17th and 18th centuries. Some believed that his strict interpretation of Islam and subsequent policies, such as the reimposition of *jizya*, or poll tax, offended his Hindu subjects.

ART AND CULTURE
The centuries of Mughal rule became associated with luxury and wealth, and the empire's riches also allowed for the flowering of the arts. Babur had written his autobiography, and many of the Mughal leaders who followed were concerned with cultivating an active cultural life throughout the empire. Especially important in this process were the Persians, who contributed their famed literary and scientific traditions to Mughal culture. It was under the rule of Akbar—who is often considered to be the greatest Mughal ruler—in the late 16th century that the empire scaled new cultural heights.

Art, handicrafts, and architecture flourished during his time. Akbar spent lavishly on poets, painters, historians, and musicians. This growth, however, did not end with Akbar—perhaps the most enduring monument of Mughal culture is the stunning Taj Mahal, built under Shah Jahan's supervision.

THE DECLINE AND END
A number of factors led to the decline of the Mughals. The empire had grown during the reign of Aurangzeb, but his successors failed to control the vast territory. Warring factions and family rivalries weakened it from the inside, while constant warfare was a drain on money and manpower. Aurangzeb's religious intolerance angered non-Muslims. The growing Hindu Maratha Empire in southern India capitalized on Mughal weakness and made conquests in the northern territory. By the time the British deposed the last emperor, Bahadur Shah Zafar, in 1858, the Mughal Empire consisted of little more than the Red Fort in Delhi.

> "**Hindustan** is... a country with **lots of gold.**"
>
> *The Baburnama*, the memoirs of Babur

ARMS AND ARMOR

Battle and conflict were part of Mughal life as a succession of rulers pushed the empire's frontiers north into Afghanistan and farther into central and South India. The Mughals applied their ideas about beauty to weapon-making, producing arms that were both formidable and highly decorated.

Early *talwar*
The blade of this *talwar* is made of wootz steel. Made using a technology that originated in India several centuries earlier, this type of steel was both strong and of uniform composition.

Later *talwar*
This weapon was probably made in Lahore, in modern Pakistan. It has a decorated hilt, and a bilingual inscription inside the finger-guard.

Firangi sword
This style of weapon was fashioned after a type of European sword. The hilt has a spike at the end of the pommel.

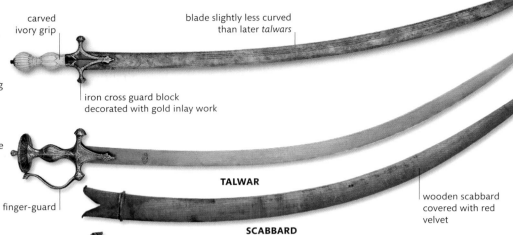

carved ivory grip

blade slightly less curved than later *talwars*

iron cross guard block decorated with gold inlay work

TALWAR

finger-guard

wooden scabbard covered with red velvet

SCABBARD

double-edged blade

tubular iron shaft, with sheet-silver decoration

FULL VIEW

Axe
With embellishment, basic models could be turned into ornate objects, such as this battle ax from Lahore. Unscrewing the knob at the base revealed a slim knife.

elaborate decoration on head

hollow shaft

FULL VIEW

Spiked mace
Used to crush an enemy's skull, this mace is a version of the "morning star" design found in Europe. Its elaborate decoration was meant to show the wealth and status of its owner.

curved cutting edge

ART AND LITERATURE

The Mughal period was a time of great literary output, in various languages. Poetry was especially popular, and the writings of Persian and Indian poets were enjoyed in the imperial court. Emperors had the means and interest to fund writers and historians, and many rulers amassed large libraries.

Illuminated anthology
This *divan*, or anthology, contains the works of the Persian poet Hafiz (Hafez), whose writings were popular during the Mughal period. People often opened his book of poems at random to seek advice or inspiration.

ink and opaque watercolor

painted lacquer cover, typical of Kashmiri work

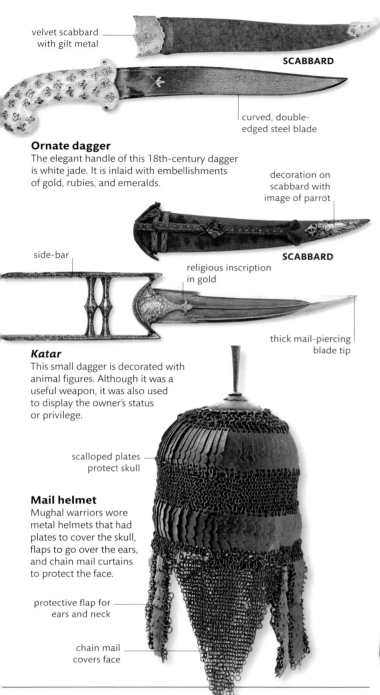

velvet scabbard with gilt metal

SCABBARD

curved, double-edged steel blade

Ornate dagger
The elegant handle of this 18th-century dagger is white jade. It is inlaid with embellishments of gold, rubies, and emeralds.

decoration on scabbard with image of parrot

side-bar

SCABBARD

religious inscription in gold

thick mail-piercing blade tip

Katar
This small dagger is decorated with animal figures. Although it was a useful weapon, it was also used to display the owner's status or privilege.

scalloped plates protect skull

Mail helmet
Mughal warriors wore metal helmets that had plates to cover the skull, flaps to go over the ears, and chain mail curtains to protect the face.

protective flap for ears and neck

chain mail covers face

COURT LIFE

The Mughal Empire was famed around the world for its riches. In addition to its natural resources, the growing trade of the 16th and 17th centuries brought more wealth. Foreigners were often dazzled by the scale of the jewels and objects they saw, as well as the size and elaborate decoration of the royal palaces.

small, domed cover

Jade ewer
Fashioned from elegant green jade, this ewer, or jug, is designed in the Mughal style. It shows trademark fluting and carved floral designs.

Pendant
This decorative piece of jewelry dates from the late Mughal period. It is made of jade inlaid with gold, pearls, and precious stones.

decorated with delicate pink flowers

Mughal robe
Mughal rulers took an interest in fashion and textiles. Made of cotton, this colorful 17th-century robe, called a *jama*, would have been worn by a wealthy nobleman.

Dragon drinking cup
This 17th-century jade drinking cup was probably made to be exported as a diplomatic gift, possibly for a French king.

gold tendrils

collar painted with gold leaf

■ MAPPING THE STARS

CELESTIAL GLOBE

The Mughal period was a time of great cultural and scientific development, which was influenced by the traditions of various peoples and lands under the empire's control. These peoples included the Persians, who had a long history of scientific inquiry. Made in the 1790s, the celestial globe shown here demonstrates the importance of astronomy to the Persians, as well as the intricate workmanship of the Mughals.

SCIENTIFIC LEGACY

Although this globe dates from the end of the 18th century, its influence is much older. It draws from *Zij-i-Ilkhani*, an astronomical work compiled by 13th-century Persian polymath Nasir al-Din Tusi. He served as a scientific adviser to the Mongols, who had invaded what is now Iran, which was under the rule of the grandson of Genghis Khan at the time.

As well as translating the works of classical thinkers such as the second-century Greek mathematician and astronomer Ptolemy into Arabic,

Tusi also became involved in the construction of a fine observatory and was one of the most advanced astronomers of his time.

Tusi's observations included a description of the Milky Way. He wrote that it is "made up of a very large number of small, tightly clustered stars, which, on account of their concentration and smallness, seemed to be cloudy patches; because of this, it was likened to milk in color." Tusi's supposition that the Milky Way is made up of stars was proven to be correct in the 16th century by the Italian astronomer and mathematician Galileo.

STAR-CROSSING

Globes like the one shown here were often decorative objects, but they could also be used, in a crude way, to measure time by estimating how long it took a particular constellation to move a certain distance in relation to the horizon. Similar globes were made in ancient Greece and Rome, and later in the Arab world. Evidence also points to their use in the Pacific islands.

script on globe is *naskh*, a form of writing that dates back to around 9th century

globe is made of brass, but earlier examples were constructed from materials such as marble

stars and constellations omitted from region around south celestial pole

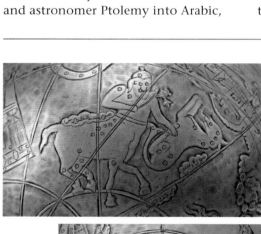

Sagittarius
The half-man, half-horse figure corresponds to the zodiac sign Sagittarius, who is depicted aiming his bow at neighboring Scorpius.

Artistic influence
The globe's design and decorative motifs draw on ancient knowledge but also reflect Mughal tastes of the time.

The far south
Few stars are shown in the far south of the sky. Tusi would have been able to see much of the Southern Hemisphere sky, but not the region around the pole.

constellation Ursa Major,
the Great Bear, which
contains the Big Dipper

axis of globe passes
through north and
south celestial poles

longitude
markings

lionlike creature
illustrates zodiacal
constellation Leo

band
respresenting
zodiac

band
respresenting
celestial equator

constellation
Hydrus, the water
snake

Celestial globe
Like all celestial spheres, this version is a map of the
visible night sky, with stars grouped into constellations.
The band around the center sits on the celestial equator,
a projection into the sky of Earth's own equator. This band
is crossed at an angle by another band called the zodiac,
which is divided into 12 constellations that correspond
to astrological signs.

THE RISE OF THE MARATHA EMPIRE

The Marathas began to fight for supremacy against the Mughals in the 1640s, led by the warrior Shivaji. They eventually controlled much of India until the early 19th century.

The last leader ▷
This painting depicts Serfoji II—the last Maharaja of Tanjore, or Thanjavur, in the western province of Tamil Nadu. He was famed for establishing printing presses in south India.

The Marathas were based in the west of India, primarily in Maharashtra. Under the leadership of Shivaji—crowned king in 1674—they grew into a powerful kingdom. Shivaji wanted to challenge the ruling Mughals because of their religious persecution and oppression. He organized a group of willing soldiers, who attacked and raided less-protected outposts throughout the 1640s and 1650s. A decisive victory in 1659 helped to pave the way for the eventual toppling of the Mughal Empire. This left much of India under the control of Maratha chiefs, who sometimes quarreled among themselves, from about 1674 to 1818.

The Marathas practiced the ancient Hindu religion. This influenced everything from their style of literature to architecture and ornamental items in the home. Maratha society was structured along a caste-based hierarchy as set down by Hinduism.

BELIEFS AND RITUALS

Embraced by the Marathas, Hinduism is an ancient belief system dating back to at least 2000 BCE. Over millennia, a complex and diverse set of practices has emerged around the religion, varying across south Asia. Hinduism has many gods and goddesses. Many Hindus believe that the deities are all manifestations of a single divine power.

Lakshmi's son Kamadeva, god of love and desire

mouse serves as Ganesha's mount

COURT LIFE

Artists at the Maratha court brought elements of Mughal and European styles, including British and French, to their work. This was also reflected in the architecture of the period, as well as in the more decorative arts, which embodied lavish design and bright colors.

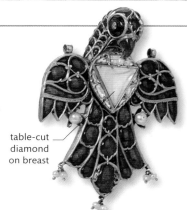

table-cut diamond on breast

Eagle pendant
The Marathas made opulent jewels such as this pendant, which was cast from gold and decorated with rubies, emeralds, and sapphires.

openwork top and sides

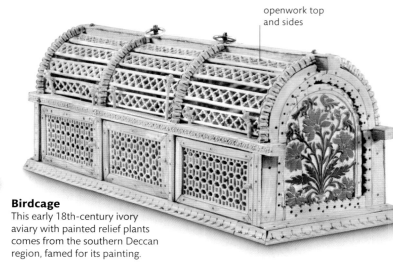

Lakshmi
Wife of the four-armed god Vishnu, Lakshmi symbolizes creative energy and prosperity. A lotus flower usually appears with her image, representing purity.

Ganesha
One of the best-known Hindu gods, Ganesha has an elephant head, which symbolizes wisdom. He is worshipped as a god of learning and is believed to help remove life's obstacles.

Birdcage
This early 18th-century ivory aviary with painted relief plants comes from the southern Deccan region, famed for its painting.

ARMS AND ARMOR

The power of the Maratha rulers had to be constantly enforced with arms. Enemies included the Mughals in the north, as well as smaller kingdoms in the south of India. Alliances were constantly changing, and the entry of the British into Maratha politics and warfare eventually led to the empire's demise.

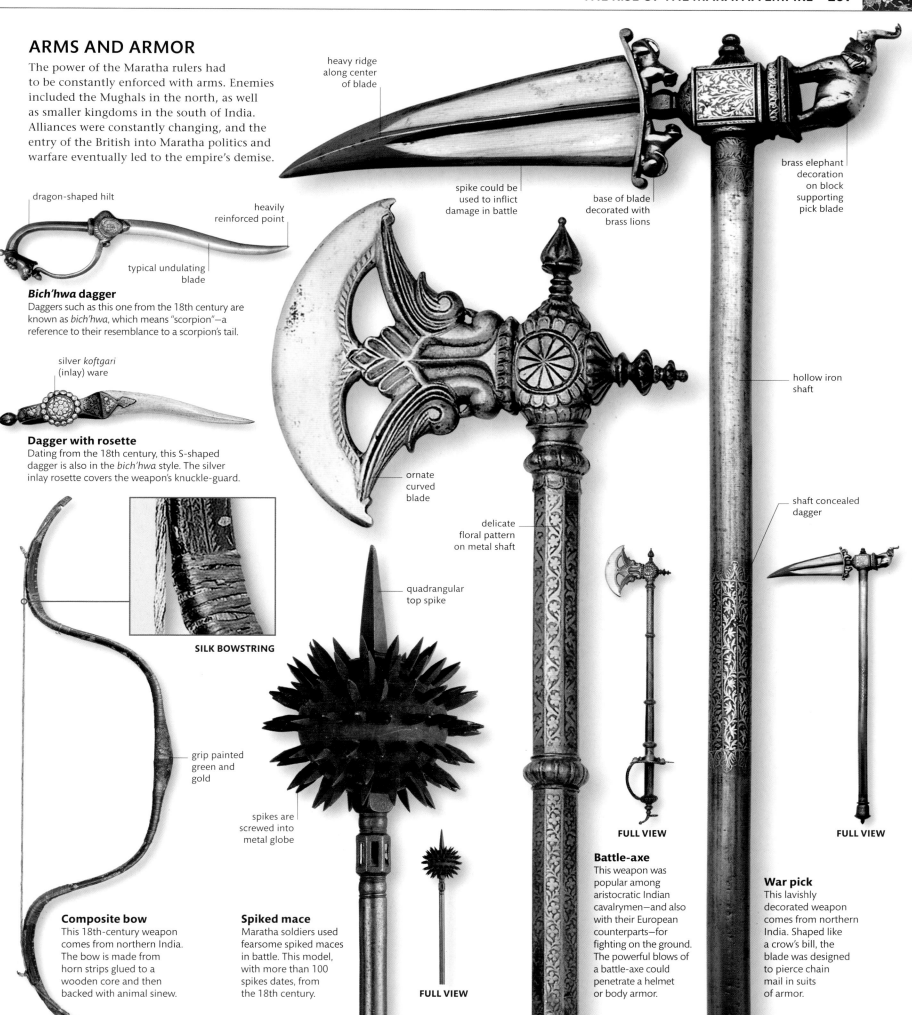

heavy ridge along center of blade

spike could be used to inflict damage in battle

base of blade decorated with brass lions

brass elephant decoration on block supporting pick blade

dragon-shaped hilt

heavily reinforced point

typical undulating blade

Bich'hwa dagger
Daggers such as this one from the 18th century are known as *bich'hwa*, which means "scorpion"—a reference to their resemblance to a scorpion's tail.

silver *koftgari* (inlay) ware

Dagger with rosette
Dating from the 18th century, this S-shaped dagger is also in the *bich'hwa* style. The silver inlay rosette covers the weapon's knuckle-guard.

ornate curved blade

delicate floral pattern on metal shaft

hollow iron shaft

shaft concealed dagger

SILK BOWSTRING

quadrangular top spike

grip painted green and gold

spikes are screwed into metal globe

FULL VIEW

FULL VIEW

Composite bow
This 18th-century weapon comes from northern India. The bow is made from horn strips glued to a wooden core and then backed with animal sinew.

Spiked mace
Maratha soldiers used fearsome spiked maces in battle. This model, with more than 100 spikes dates, from the 18th century.

FULL VIEW

Battle-axe
This weapon was popular among aristocratic Indian cavalrymen—and also with their European counterparts—for fighting on the ground. The powerful blows of a battle-axe could penetrate a helmet or body armor.

War pick
This lavishly decorated weapon comes from northern India. Shaped like a crow's bill, the blade was designed to pierce chain mail in suits of armor.

THE MERCHANT EMPIRE OF BENIN

Bronze head
Idealized portrait busts of deceased Bini kings, such as the one shown here, were placed on royal altars.

Between the 13th and 19th centuries, the kingdom of Benin was one of the most powerful in the southern part of present-day Nigeria. It grew increasingly wealthy on trade, starting with the Portuguese in the 15th century and later the Dutch and the British. Bini craftsmen became renowned for their bronze work and ivory carvings.

Festival ▽
This early 19th-century lithograph by Italian artist Angelo Biasioli shows a festival celebrating the king of Benin, with the royal palace in the background. The procession includes leopards, which were symbols of the king's power and were often paraded as mascots.

Although little is known about the early days of Benin, its first king or *oba*, is thought to be Eweka, who ruled in the late 13th century. In the centuries that followed, Benin expanded, stretching from the Niger River delta to present-day Lagos in Nigeria by the time of the rule of Oba Ewuare in the mid-15th century. A capital had been built in Benin City, complete with a vast royal palace complex. When the Portuguese first arrived, they were surprised by the grandeur and size of the palace, which occupied a third of the city.

ARTISTIC PRODUCTION

Ivory carving and metalwork were important art forms; Benin was famed for its bronzes, but they were actually cast of brass. Artists were organized into guilds and apprentices studied with masters. Ivory was used in the royal household, while bronze plaques glorified the kings's achievements. West Africans had developed the technique of smelting metal as early as the 10th century, and the production of these works was further expanded after Europeans brought metals in the 15th century.

EUROPEANS AND SLAVERY

Benin participated in the transatlantic slave trade, providing Europeans with prisoners of war in exchange for manufactured goods, including metal and cloth, as well as coral beads. By the late 19th century, Benin had weakened due to conflict with neighboring kingdoms and pressure from the British, who wanted to take control of its lucrative trade. They invaded Benin City in 1897, and although the kingdom continued to exist, the king was exiled for a number of years.

POWER AND POLITICS

The kings of Benin wielded absolute power over their subjects and were considered to be divine. The rest of Bini society was also organized along highly stratified lines. The king used ceremonies to display his power and wealth, and this was embodied in the objects used by the royal household.

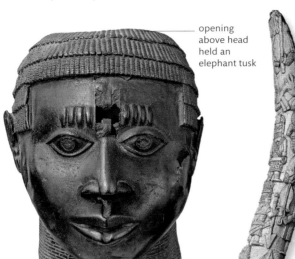

opening above head held an elephant tusk

King's head
A captured foreign king is the subject of this 16th-century bronze piece. The layered hairstyle indicates he was an outsider.

symbolic figures carved into ivory

Ancestral ivory
This 19th-century carved elephant tusk, thought to record the achievements of the *oba*, was mounted on top of an idealized bronze head of the deceased *oba*, and displayed at a royal ancestral altar.

cross pendant

Bronze figure
This figure is wearing a cross, which suggests that he was a royal prince who was educated in Portugal, where many sons of nobles were sent. The cross became popular among the Bini people, who saw the Portuguese wearing them.

cockerel was associated with the queen mother

Bronze cockerel
The cockerel was a symbol of strong leadership and authority. Bronze casts such as this one were placed on palace altars as a tribute to the deceased queen mother.

Leopard's head pendant
Leopards were symbols of power, and Bini kings often kept them in the royal household; one of the king's metaphorical names was "ekpen," meaning leopard. Sometimes the animals were killed as sacrifices to the gods.

emblem may have denoted rank

Warrior plaque
A bronze relief from the 16th century shows a Bini warrior and two frogs, which represent the ability to live in water and on land.

Queen's head
This early 17th-century commemorative bust is of a queen mother, called an *iyoba*, an important figure in the royal court. Such bronze casts were placed in the palace altar after her death.

conical headdress was made of coral beads, a symbol of nobility

coral neck ring

Bronze plaque

This mid-16th-century plaque displays Bini warriors. A high-ranking chief stands in the center dressed in ceremonial regalia, holding a dance sword in his right hand and a spear in his left, while his lieutenants flank him carrying shields and spears. During this period, such plaques were attached to the columns in the king's palace.

high-ranking
war chief

elaborate headdress
indicates high status

holes used
to attach
plaque to
column

lieutenants
flank the chief

shield
denotes
warrior

attendants in the
background

TRADE

The Bini were in a position to profit from and control the commerce between Europeans and Africans that took place along the coast of West Africa. Europeans arrived initially looking for a source of gold, but they found instead ivory, pepper, and palm oil—as well as people to send into slavery.

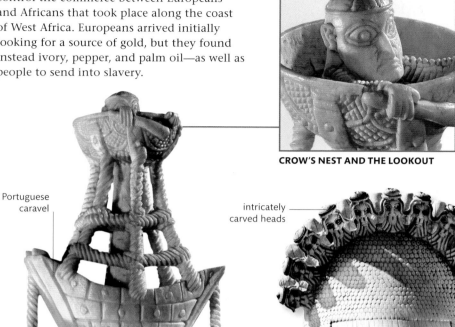

CROW'S NEST AND THE LOOKOUT

Portuguese caravel

intricately carved heads

Portuguese noblemen decorate base

Mask pendant
Around the top of this 16th-century ivory pendant are the heads of Portuguese traders, symbolizing the Bini's relationship with Europeans.

Ivory salt cellar
The long hair, clothing, and beads indicate that the figures on this 16th-century salt cellar are Europeans. Objects such as these were often made for the overseas traders who became eager consumers of ivory. A Portuguese caravel, complete with a crow's nest and a lookout, is carved on top of the cellar.

ART AND CULTURE

Bini bronze and ivory objects were created to use at shrines of deities or in ceremonies, while some everyday goods were carved from wood. Benin became famed for intricate ivory work, and the carvers often sat at the top of the guild hierarchy.

clothing indicates possible European

figure holds carved gun

long, decorative, pointed teeth

coral necklaces

Comb
Carved out of wood, this elaborate 19th-century comb shows a man with a gun and powder flask, suggesting that he might be European.

Ivory woman
This late 18th- or early 19th-century statue depicts a woman wearing valuable coral jewelry, which indicates that she may be a princess.

mold

polished object

cast bronze face

Bronze casting
An intricate method known as lost wax casting was used for creating the bronze objects. A clay model of the object was made and then covered with a layer of wax. Melted bronze was poured into the mold, and once it had cooled, the clay was chipped away to reveal a rough cast, which was then filed and smoothed.

bright and striking colors are
hallmark of Ethiopian style

leather straps hold
panels together

Virgin Mary is an important
icon and appears frequently

Triptych
This 17th-century triptych depicts Jesus, Mary, and Joseph.
On the right panel are images of Jesus's crucifixion and
ascension, while on the left are a group of saints, with
St George slaying the dragon below.

triptych was painted on cotton
canvas stretched over a wood panel

story of Jesus is shown on this panel

heads of angels with wings were a common motif

ETHIOPIA AND THE CHRISTIAN WORLD

The ancient kingdom of Ethiopia was one of the earliest Christian nations in Africa. It adopted the Orthodox Christianity found in Egypt, later resisting incursions from Islam and from Roman Catholicism, and its unique religious art reflects the influences of east and west.

Christianity arrived from the Middle East, first with traders and later with monks, and it took root around the 4th century. Eastern orthodoxy and the Egyptian Copts were both influential in the establishment and development of the Ethiopian Orthodox Church. Christianity also underpinned the kingdom; by 1270, a new ruling dynasty had emerged, claiming to be descended from Menelik I, the son of the biblical King Solomon and the Queen of Sheba. A book known as the *Kebra Nagast*, or Glory of the Kings, that attempted to trace this genealogy was produced around this time. The Solomonic dynasty ruled into the later decades of the 20th century.

FIGHT AGAINST ISLAM

As Islam later spread through North Africa and around the Red Sea and Persian Gulf, it also made its way toward Ethiopia. Although there were Muslims in the country, Ethiopian emperors were often locked into battles against Islamic invaders. Following a declaration of a holy war against Ethiopia in the early 16th

century, Islamic invaders were finally driven out in 1543 with the help of the Portuguese. However, many churches and manuscripts were destroyed in the decades of fighting.

CATHOLIC CONFRONTATION

The Portuguese missionaries who arrived in the 1600s were eager to convert the country to Roman Catholicism. In the early 17th century, Emperor Susenyos eventually relented by accepting some of the theological precepts, but the ensuing outrage among his people forced him to abdicate. In 1632, his son Fasilides, who kept close to the Ethiopian Orthodox Church, took power. He moved the capital to Gonder, which became a hub of cultural activity, including the copying of religious manuscripts and panel painting. However, by 1769, this time of artistic output and relative peace were brought to an end after several conflicts erupted, resulting in the empire being split and ruled by various factions. This period, known as the Age of Princes, destabilized the country until 1855.

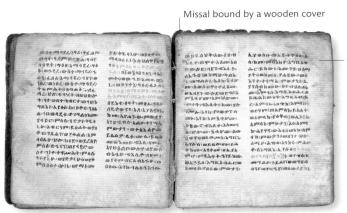

Missal bound by a wooden cover

pages made from vellum

Missal

Written in the Ge'ez language, this late 17th- or early 18th-century missal would have been used to celebrate the mass in accordance with Ethiopian rites.

EUROPEAN SETTLERS IN THE NEW WORLD

Columbus's journey to the Americas in 1492 led Spain to establish a colony on the island of Hispaniola. Soon after, settlers from all over Europe followed suit. They transformed the vast American continents, bringing diseases that wiped out much of the native population and importing Africans to work as slaves.

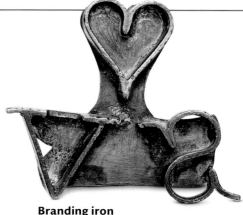

Branding iron
Slaves were often branded with their master's sign to prevent escape. Brazil was the last country to abolish slavery, in 1888.

Spain tried to claim ownership of the "new" lands found by Christopher Columbus in 1492, but other European countries were eager to establish their own colonies. Inspired by the Spanish riches found in Central America, ships from England, Holland, Denmark, and France brought people eager to seek their fortunes. Others came to escape religious persecution back at home. Thousands of settlers arrived in the 16th and 17th centuries, spreading from the eastern seaboard of North America, down to the islands of the West Indies, and as far as the coastal regions of South America. In doing so, however, they destroyed much of the existing indigenous society.

Founding fathers ▽
This 19th-century painting depicts a meeting of English Puritan dissenters on the *Speedwell* in 1620 on the eve of their voyage from Holland to England. From there, they set sail on the *Mayflower* to settle in North America.

NATIVE DEATHS

The Americas were home to a diverse number of indigenous peoples, such as the Cherokees, Arawaks, and Aztecs. Europeans brought diseases that the natives had little resistance to, which led to millions of deaths. Other indigenous peoples were displaced from their land, leading to constant conflict with the colonists.

THE SLAVE TRADE

Upon arrival, Europeans set up plantations and initially used enslaved indigenous people, as well as indentured servants from Europe, as laborers. Eventually, however, they turned to Africans. By the 1500s, millions of Africans were being taken to the Americas and forced to live in slavery. The settlers sold their crops to Europe and bought manufactured goods with the profits. These could then be used to purchase more slaves in Africa. This brutal triangular trade lasted for around 400 years.

TRADE

As plantations prospered in North America, merchants arrived in the growing cities of the Atlantic seaboard, exporting commodities and importing manufactured goods, such as furniture and clothing. At the same time, people in the colonies also traded with Native Americans and learned how to grow indigenous crops, such as corn.

detachable cover imitating chinese ceramics

arms of a wealthy merchant family from colonial New York

Teapot
Although the design of this early 18th-century teapot emulates Chinese ceramics, the engraving exemplifies New York silver work in this period.

Knife and Sheath
This knife and its cover, made of deerskin and embellished with beads, would have been made by Europeans to trade with the Sioux people.

decorative beaded tassels

Virginia money
Hard currency was in short supply in colonial America so some colonies started issuing their own paper currency—but they were easily counterfeited. This Virginia note is from 1755.

POLITICS AND POWER

By the 17th century, England and France had a firm foothold in North America, with the French claiming most of what is now Canada and the Great Lakes region of the US. English colonies were set up along the coastline. Spain stayed in control of Florida and the surrounding area, and farther west.

North America map
This map shows the division between English (yellow), French (pink), and Spanish (blue) territory c.1721. By the end of the century, the boundaries would be significantly different.

BELIEFS AND RITUALS

The Europeans introduced Christianity in its various forms. Catholic colonies were established by the Spaniards and Portuguese, while different sects of Protestantism were introduced by the English, Dutch, and French Huguenots.

central panel depicts crucifixion of Christ

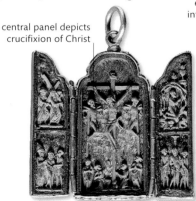

Bay psalm book
This translation of biblical psalms was published by English Protestants in 1640, making it the first printed book in British North America.

Mexican triptych
This pendant was crafted by indigenous people, who were taught by Franciscan missionaries to make tiny carvings using specialized Flemish techniques.

emeralds set into radiating pattern

angel holding up a sun

Monstrance
This 18th-century gold receptacle, known as a monstrance, was used to display the communion host. It took seven years to complete, and weighs almost 11 lb (5 kg).

golden stand

BATTLE AND CONFLICT

North America in the 18th century was rife with conflict—from ongoing battles between settlers and American Indians to wars between European powers, notably the French and Indian War (1754–63), which turned into the Seven Years' War (1756–63). The century ended with the American Revolution (1776–83).

Powder horn
Engraved powder horns were considered a trophy of service in the French and Indian wars. The 1759 siege of Quebec is depicted here.

powder dispensed from narrow end of horn

carving shows upper and lower towns making up city of Quebec

ships belonging to British fleets deployed in siege

The late 18th and 19th centuries were a time of rapid change. Large-scale factory production and the use of steam power transformed work and transportation. Revolution in France left monarchies and empires on the defensive against popular forces. European powers still held much of the globe, but in the Americas, countries won their independence. The United States, born of revolt against British colonial rule, grew within a century into a major power.

INDUSTRY AND INDEPENDENCE

1750-1900

THE BIRTH OF THE INDUSTRIAL AGE

Around 1750, a sustained, accelerating growth in human productivity, often referred to as the Industrial Revolution, began. The use of technology and intensive exploitation of labor in factories was accompanied by increased farm output and improvements in health, allowing a steep rise in population. The rapid movement of people, goods, and information across oceans and continents created a truly global economy.

Engine of change
The Valiant steam fire pump, manufactured in Britain from 1863, was a typical product of its era. Sturdy and efficient, it could pump 100 gallons (450l) a minute.

Technology showcase ▷
In 1851, Britain mounted the Great Exhibition in the steel-and-glass Crystal Palace to show off the nation's achievements in industry and invention. It was the first of many "universal expositions" held across the world to celebrate the triumphs of economic and scientific progress.

The Industrial Revolution began in Britain, a country that, by the mid-18th century, had achieved mild prosperity through trade and commercially oriented farming. It had plenty of coal—the essential fuel of industrialization. There was also a burgeoning market for consumer goods, both domestically and in its overseas empire.

Britain's government was inclined to encourage business enterprise. From around 1780, the British textile industry was transformed by the adoption of large-scale factory production and new machinery for cotton spinning and weaving. British output of cotton goods increased 50-fold between the 1780s and 1850. Britain also pioneered new techniques in iron founding and development of steam engines. These advances were driven by the efforts of practical inventors and entrepreneurs.

THE RAILROAD AGE

Outside the textile industry, the impact of factories was limited until large-scale railroad building, from the 1830s and 1840s, changed the scale of industrialization. Building and operating railroads generated an immense demand for steel and coal. This stimulated the growth of heavy industry and mining, not only in Britain but also in parts of continental Europe and the northern United States. By the 1850s, progress in precision engineering facilitated the mass production of highly efficient machines, including printing presses. The expansion of output created a new economy with permanent growth as its essential principle.

By the late 19th century, chemicals, electricity, and gasoline engines were opening up new areas of innovation. Scientists worked for industrial companies, while inventors, such as Thomas Edison, set the pace for developing ingenious gadgetry. Meanwhile, Germany and the United States surpassed Britain as centers of industrial production, and Japan emerged as an important new player.

The impact of industrialization and other economic and technological changes on people's lives was extensive. The vast majority of the world's population had always lived in rural areas, but the second half of the 19th century witnessed a change, with Britain and Belgium becoming the first countries to have more of their people living in towns and cities than on the land. In the short term, many communities in the world experienced industrialization as a catastrophe because it overthrew established ways of life and demanded excessive regimented toil in grim conditions.

Environmental degradation was an automatic consequence of economic expansion based on coal and steel. The impact was felt by those far from the industrial centers—by Zulu who toiled in southern African mines, or slaves in the American South harvesting cotton for textile mills. But statistics show a remarkable rise in living standards during this period in the industrializing zones. Life expectancy increased, partly through medical advances and the decline of epidemic diseases but also because of improved food supply. The more privileged social classes enjoyed unprecedented wealth and luxury.

> **"The bourgeoisie...** has created more **colossal productive forces** than all preceding generations..."
>
> Karl Marx and Friedrich Engels, *The Communist Manifesto*, 1848

AGRICULTURE

Increasing agricultural output from the mid-18th century was achieved through improved practices such as crop rotation, but also through factory-made machinery and new inventions. Although quite simple and cheap, new equipment helped produce the food to supply a growing urban population and released surplus farm workers to take up jobs in factories.

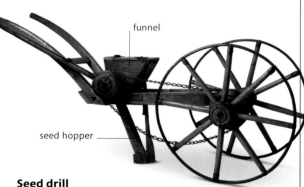

funnel

seed hopper

Seed drill

This is a 19th-century model of the seed drill introduced by English agriculturalist Jethro Tull in 1701. The seed drill planted seeds more quickly and accurately could be done by hand.

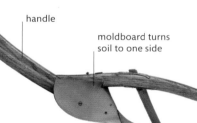

handle

moldboard turns soil to one side

Rotherham plow

This light and efficient plow, made of wood and iron, came into use in Britain around 1730. It became the first agricultural implement to be mass-produced in factories.

flywheel   centrifugal governor

Aveling and Porter traction engine

Traction engines were a mobile source of steam power, driving to farms where they would hook up to agricultural machinery. This engine dating from 1871 was the first in Britain.

POWER AND INDUSTRY

The Industrial Revolution was driven first by water power and then by steam. Large-scale factory production spread from textiles to steel-making and other heavy industries. Railroad steam locomotives provided the first land transport that was faster than a horse. By the late 19th century, gasoline engines were ushering in a new phase of development.

■ TEXTILES

wooden frame

spindles twist cotton fiber

Arkwright frame

In 1769, the British industrialist and inventor Richard Arkwright patented a machine for turning raw cotton into thread. Driven by water power, it equipped the first textile mill in England in 1774.

heddle divides threads

punched cards

loom frame

Jacquard loom

Invented by Joseph Marie Jacquard in France in 1801, the loom used a system of punched cards to automatically control the weaving of textiles with complex patterns.

handle

metal funnel

wick covered by a mesh

Davy lamp

In 1815, English chemist Sir Humphry Davy invented a safety lamp for coal miners. Its flame was enclosed in a mesh that stopped it from igniting flammable gases found in mines.

egg-shaped convertor turns iron to steel

tilting mechanism for pouring out molten steel

Bessemer converter

English engineer Henry Bessemer patented a large-scale process for turning molten iron into steel in 1855. The converter made steel a relatively cheap, mass-produced material that transformed the railroads in the United States.

shackle for attaching rope

trail stabilizes gun in firing

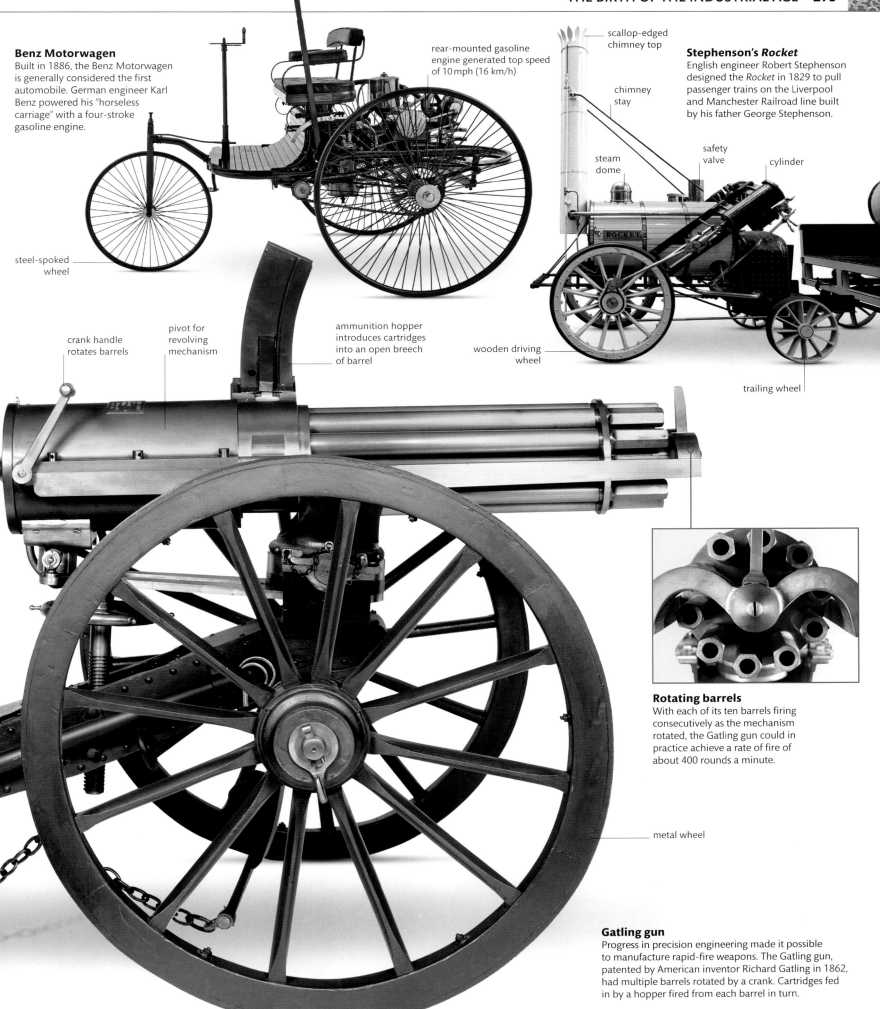

Benz Motorwagen
Built in 1886, the Benz Motorwagen is generally considered the first automobile. German engineer Karl Benz powered his "horseless carriage" with a four-stroke gasoline engine.

rear-mounted gasoline engine generated top speed of 10 mph (16 km/h)

Stephenson's *Rocket*
English engineer Robert Stephenson designed the *Rocket* in 1829 to pull passenger trains on the Liverpool and Manchester Railroad line built by his father George Stephenson.

scallop-edged chimney top

chimney stay

steam dome

safety valve

cylinder

steel-spoked wheel

wooden driving wheel

trailing wheel

crank handle rotates barrels

pivot for revolving mechanism

ammunition hopper introduces cartridges into an open breech of barrel

Rotating barrels
With each of its ten barrels firing consecutively as the mechanism rotated, the Gatling gun could in practice achieve a rate of fire of about 400 rounds a minute.

metal wheel

Gatling gun
Progress in precision engineering made it possible to manufacture rapid-fire weapons. The Gatling gun, patented by American inventor Richard Gatling in 1862, had multiple barrels rotated by a crank. Cartridges fed in by a hopper fired from each barrel in turn.

UNIVERSAL WORKHORSE

JAMES WATT'S ENGINE

Scottish inventor James Watt (1736–1819) transformed the steam engine from a pumping machine of limited usefulness into the universal workhorse of the Industrial Revolution. Watt was a maker of mathematical instruments at Glasgow University when, in 1764, he became interested in the Newcomen steam engine. Invented by the Englishman Thomas Newcomen around 1712, this machine was widely used to pump water out of mines, but it was inefficient and unreliable. In 1769, Watt set out to improve it, patenting his version, which employed a condenser. Four years later, Watt met Birmingham businessman Matthew Boulton and the two formed a partnership. Located at Soho, Birmingham, the firm of Boulton & Watt manufactured their first steam pumping engines in 1776. Since these were three times as efficient as the Newcomen engines, the product was an instant success.

CHALLENGES

The next hurdle for Watt was to make a steam engine that would drive rotary motion. However, his first attempt to create a "steam wheel" did not build upon the success of his pumping engine and was a failure.

It was Boulton who, for commercial reasons, pushed Watt to adapt the steam engine's reciprocating linear motion into rotary motion. Since a crank, which would have achieved this effect, was under patent elsewhere, Watt solved the problem with a sun-and-planet gear system. Rotative engines could be used for a much wider range of tasks, powering workshops and factories, and eventually allowing steam-powered vehicles to be built.

IMPROVEMENTS

Watt went on to make further improvements to the steam engine, including the introduction of a centrifugal governor, an ingenious feedback system to slow the engine automatically when it threatened to "run away." It was also Watt who established horsepower as a measure of an engine's output, a unit that is still in use today. The exploitation of patents, as well as direct sale of their products, made Watt and Boulton wealthy men.

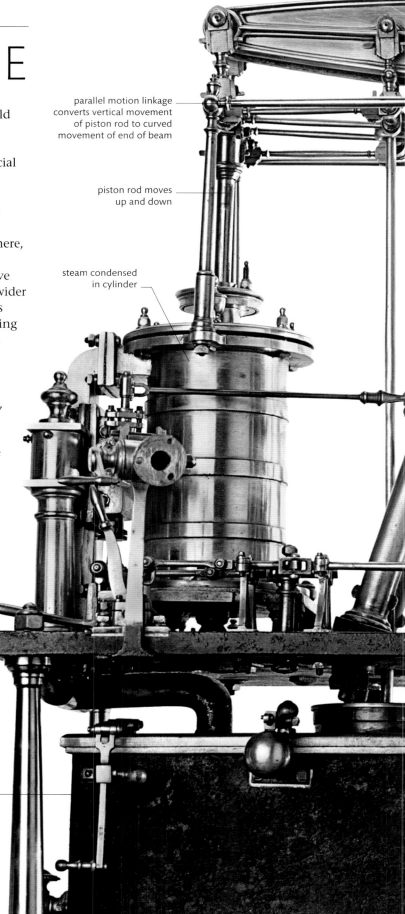

parallel motion linkage converts vertical movement of piston rod to curved movement of end of beam

piston rod moves up and down

steam condensed in cylinder

cistern full of cold water holds condenser and pump; condenser cools steam back into water, which is removed by pump

---

STEAM AND THE FACTORY

During the course of the 19th century, steam power largely eclipsed water power as a source of energy for large-scale manufacturing. Since coal provided the fuel for steam engines, industrial development took place near coal-mining districts. By 1870, the annual output of the steam engines powering factories worldwide totaled around four million horsepower.

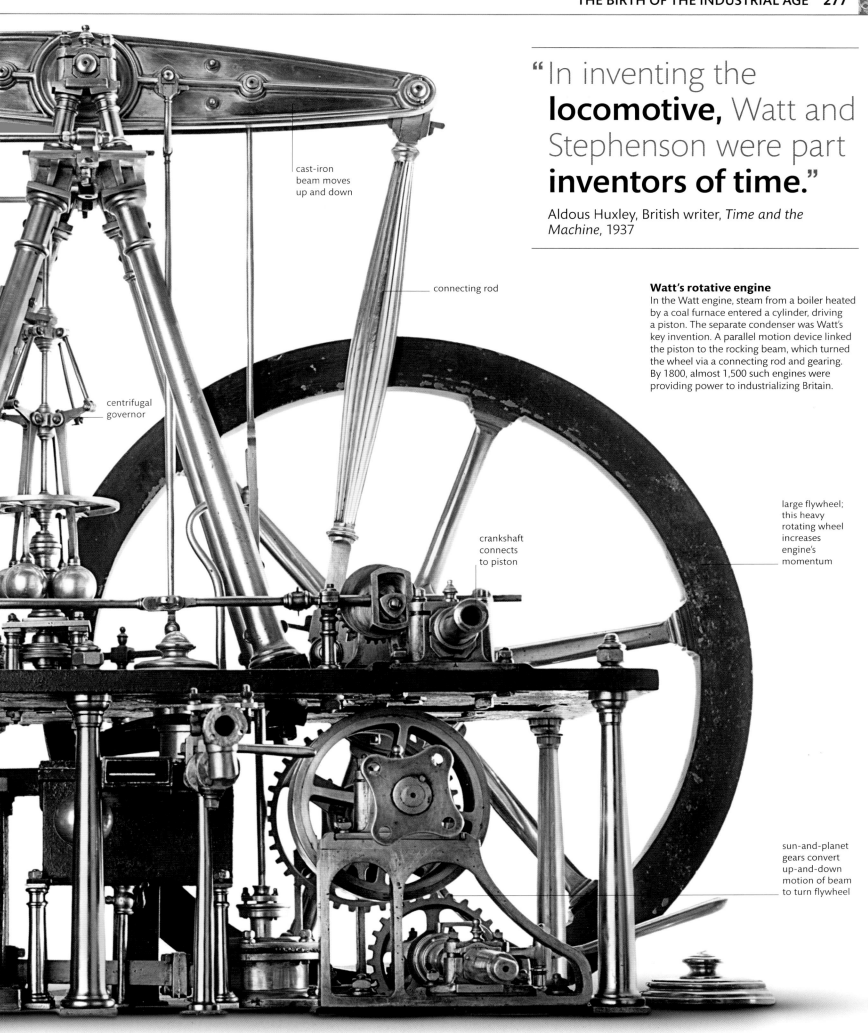

cast-iron beam moves up and down

connecting rod

centrifugal governor

crankshaft connects to piston

"In inventing the **locomotive,** Watt and Stephenson were part **inventors of time.**"

Aldous Huxley, British writer, *Time and the Machine*, 1937

Watt's rotative engine
In the Watt engine, steam from a boiler heated by a coal furnace entered a cylinder, driving a piston. The separate condenser was Watt's key invention. A parallel motion device linked the piston to the rocking beam, which turned the wheel via a connecting rod and gearing. By 1800, almost 1,500 such engines were providing power to industrializing Britain.

large flywheel; this heavy rotating wheel increases engine's momentum

sun-and-planet gears convert up-and-down motion of beam to turn flywheel

ELECTRICITY AND COMMUNICATION

In 1750, no message could be carried faster than a horse could gallop. But by 1858, the electric telegraph could transmit a message via an undersea cable from Europe to North America in a few minutes. Electricity was at the heart of many 19th-century innovations, from the light bulb to the telephone.

zinc and copper disks

Voltaic pile
Italian physicist Alessandro Volta invented the first electric battery in 1800. The voltaic pile stacked alternating copper and zinc disks separated by brine-soaked cloth, generating a continuous current.

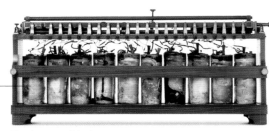

row of cells connected to terminals

Rechargeable battery
The first lead-acid rechargeable battery was invented by French physicist Gaston Planté in 1859. Another Frenchman, Camille Faure, developed a commercially viable version in the 1880s.

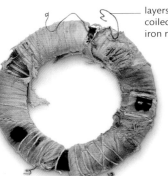

layers of copper coiled around iron ring

Faraday's induction ring
In 1831, British scientist Michael Faraday created an electric transformer with two copper wires wrapped around an iron ring. Ten years earlier, he had also invented the first electric motor.

filament

Electric light bulb
Many inventors worked on developing an incandescent light bulb, which became practical technology around 1879. British scientist Joseph Swan and American inventor Thomas Edison shared the credit for this.

telegraph key

Morse transmitter
Invented in 1837, the electric telegraph transformed the speed of long-distance communication. The system developed by American Samuel Morse used a code tapped out by the operator.

profile of Queen Victoria

Penny Black stamp
The Penny Black, the first postage stamp, in Britain in 1840, was part of a broad improvement in postal services worldwide that made written communication quicker and cheaper.

■ RECORDING SOUND

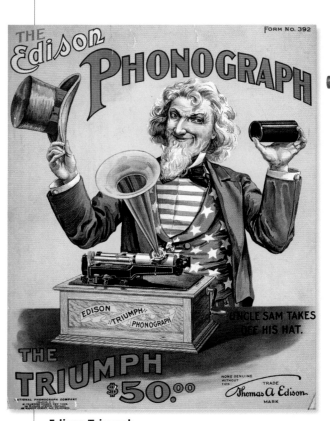

FORM NO. 392

Edison Triumph Phonograph poster
From the 1880s, phonographs—also known as gramophones—and cylinders, with recorded music to play on them, were marketed as novelty entertainment.

tin cylinder with sound recorded as indentations

combined stylus and loudspeaker apparatus

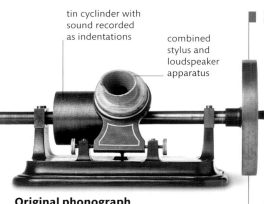

Original phonograph
This is a model of Thomas Edison's original phonograph, invented in 1877. It recorded speech by transcribing sound vibrations onto a rotating cylinder with a needle.

apparatus support

needle

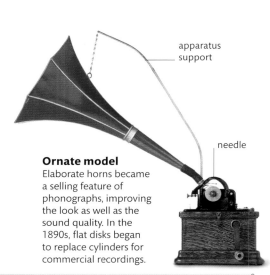

Ornate model
Elaborate horns became a selling feature of phonographs, improving the look as well as the sound quality. In the 1890s, flat disks began to replace cylinders for commercial recordings.

■ PHOTOGRAPHY

glass plate coated in light-sensitive emulsion

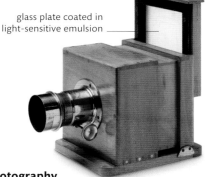

Early photography
In 1839, French inventor Louis Daguerre made public his daguerreotype photographic process. By 1860, cameras using practical methods, such as the dry collodion process, were widely used.

daguerrotype image in frame

Portrait photos
In the 1840s and 50s, photo-portrait studios using the daguerreotype process opened in cities across Europe and North America. Each "daguerreotype" was a unique image—there was no negative from which further prints could be made.

TELEPHONE

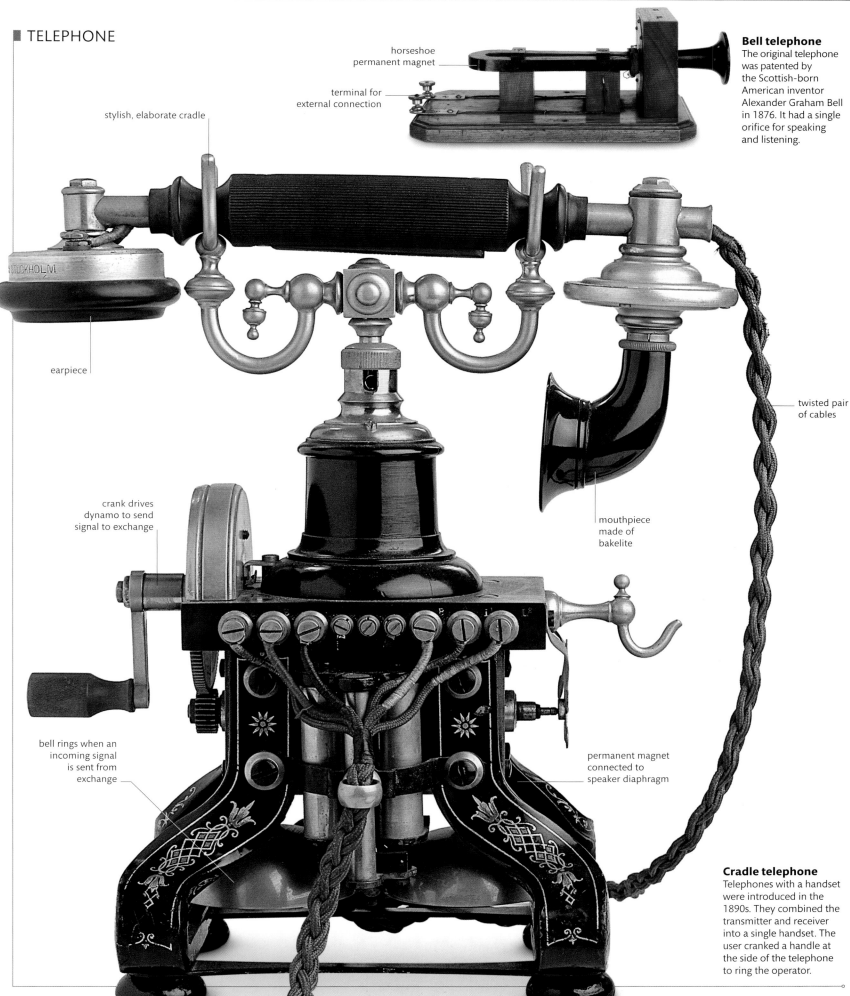

horseshoe permanent magnet

terminal for external connection

Bell telephone
The original telephone was patented by the Scottish-born American inventor Alexander Graham Bell in 1876. It had a single orifice for speaking and listening.

stylish, elaborate cradle

earpiece

twisted pair of cables

crank drives dynamo to send signal to exchange

mouthpiece made of bakelite

bell rings when an incoming signal is sent from exchange

permanent magnet connected to speaker diaphragm

Cradle telephone
Telephones with a handset were introduced in the 1890s. They combined the transmitter and receiver into a single handset. The user cranked a handle at the side of the telephone to ring the operator.

HOME LIFE AND LEISURE

In the countries where the Industrial Revolution took place, domestic life was transformed by a flood of cheap, factory-produced consumer goods. Department stores opened to sell these goods, which were sold first to the middle classes but later also to the more prosperous members of the working class. By 1900, the advertising industry was also growing rapidly.

Canned food
The process of sealing food in airtight cans was patented in 1810. The introduction of smaller, lighter cans in the 1860s brought canned food into the mass market.

wooden handle

flat, metal base

Early electric iron
Almost all 19th-century households had flat irons that could be heated in a variety of ways. The first flat iron heated by electricity was patented in the United States in 1882.

Doll's house
Children's toys became consumer products in the 19th century. This Tiffany-Platt House, made in the 1860s, offers a detailed model of a contemporary domestic interior.

simulated limestone block

full canopy bed with silk hangings

wooden chimney

Corset
Corsets were standard wear for women. This model from the 1890s has a flat front, avoiding excessive compression of the waist but emphasizing the hips.

rooms decorated in 1860s American style

electric and kerosene parlor lamp

compact frame designed to be placed against wall

Upright piano
Invented in 1827, upright pianos were mass produced in factories. They made the piano an affordable form of entertainment, found even in better-off working-class homes.

Pears soap advertisement
The British Pears company produced the first mass-market soap. Pears pioneered advertising during the 1880s, using posters and slogans to establish a brand image.

Facile safety bicycle
The hobbyhorse, a proto-bicycle driven by the feet, was demonstrated in 1817. By the 1880s, mid-century "penny farthing" designs were evolving into popular "safety bicycles."

large front wheel

decorated front board

MEDICINE

Despite great efforts made to improve medical care, until the late 19th century progress was limited by lack of scientific understanding of diseases. Advances in anesthetics from the 1830s did reduce the travails of surgery, but it was improved hygiene and food supply that made the largest contribution to public health.

cupping glass

leather case

Cupping set
Bloodletting was widely used as a medical treatment until the late 19th century. These glass cups were heated to create a vacuum and applied to the skin to draw blood.

bladed scarificator

wooden tube

single earpiece

LAENNEC'S STETHOSCOPE **FERGUSSON'S STETHOSCOPE**

Stethoscope
Invented in 1816 by Rene Laennec, the first stethoscope was a wooden tube. Dating from around 1890, the Fergusson stethoscope was finely crafted from tulip wood.

handle made from tortoiseshell scale

Vaccination lancet
In the 19th century, deaths from smallpox were sharply reduced by vaccination. Through the work of Louis Pasteur in France, rabies and anthrax vaccines were produced in the 1880s.

horn bell shape

Queen Victoria's hearing aid
Acoustic hearing aids, or "ear trumpets," were common in the 19th century. This model was made for Queen Victoria. The first portable electronic hearing aid dates from 1898.

■ SURGERY

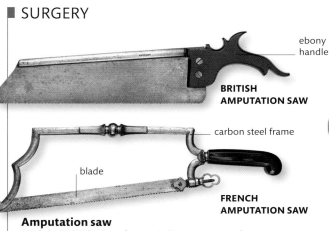

ebony handle

BRITISH AMPUTATION SAW

carbon steel frame

blade

FRENCH AMPUTATION SAW

Amputation saw
Made in 1780, the French amputation saw was used on patients without the benefit of anesthesia. By 1860, the British version of this saw could cut through flesh and bone more easily than the 18th-century models.

sprayer

steam chamber

nozzle

Carbolic steam spray
By the 1860s, surgeons had discovered that carbolic acid could reduce post-operative infection. Operating rooms were sprayed with carbolic steam before surgery was carried out.

■ MEDICATION

grooves cut medicine into equal-sized pills

PILL-MAKING BOARD

Aspirin
Marketed by German company Bayer from the late 1890s, aspirin was one of a host of medicines sold unregulated in shops. Aspirin was unusual in that it worked.

Pills
In the 18th century, pills were rolled into spheres on a pill tile. A pill-making board was used to roll and cut medicine into equal-sized pieces, which were then rolled into spheres by hand.

PILL TILE

REVOLUTION AND REPUBLIC IN FRANCE

The French Revolution of 1789 overthrew the monarchy and instituted a republic based on the tenets of "Liberty, Equality, and Fraternity." Although the French general Napoleon Bonaparte eventually seized power to proclaim himself emperor, this revolt had a lasting impact far beyond the country's borders.

Keeping time
This traveling clock was used by Napoleon to synchronize the movements of his forces at the Battle of Waterloo in 1815. It was found in his carriage after his defeat.

Power to the people ▽
Used as a prison, the Bastille in Paris was a symbol of the authority of the French monarchy. On July 14, 1789, a mob stormed the fortress and seized and killed its governor. This event marked the start of the historic French Revolution.

Facing chronic financial crises and political unrest, King Louis XVI called a meeting of the Estates General—an archaic form of parliament—in 1789. Amid mounting popular disturbances, the Estates General grew into a National Assembly that took control over of the government. The privileges of the aristocracy and the Church were abolished. A document called the *Declaration of the Rights of Man* proclaimed all men free and equal. Women, however, were not mentioned. This revolution soon underwent radicalization—a Reign of Terror condemned thousands of royalists to death by the guillotine, and the king himself was executed in 1793. Led by Maximilien de Robespierre, the Jacobin party tried to rebuild France from scratch, with the "Cult of the Supreme Being" replacing Catholicism. This was an attempt to introduce a nationalistic religion based on the belief that God does not interfere in the destinies of men.

From 1792, revolutionary France was at war. Raised by mass conscription, large French armies repeatedly defeated the more conventional forces of European monarchies. General Napoleon Bonaparte staged a military coup in 1799 and proclaimed himself emperor in 1804. Although his rule restored order, it maintained and formalized the innovations of the revolution. His armies dominated Europe, but Britain offered strong resistance. It deployed naval and financial power to support Russia, Austria, and Prussia, enabling Napoleon's defeat. However, the ideas introduced in the revolutionary period—such as the concept of human rights—have endured over time.

BATTLE AND CONFLICT

The French Revolutionary Wars (1792–1802) and the Napoleonic Wars (1803–15) pitted France against various coalitions of other European powers. French conscript armies won many victories on land, but Britain's Royal Navy was dominant at sea. Napoleon was finally defeated after a disastrous invasion of Russia in 1812.

grooves lighten blade without compromising strength

Model An IV cavalry sword
This single-edged sword is named after the fact that it was introduced in Year Four of the Revolution. Used by French heavy cavalry—the Cuirassiers—it was equally effective in slashing and stabbing.

D-shaped langet to hold sword in scabbard

Flintlock pistol
In the Napoleonic Wars, pistols were primarily carried by officers as a status symbol. This British weapon was used in the Peninsular War in Portugal and Spain.

brass-bound butt

heavy blade, broader at tip than hilt

British light cavalry sword
Curve-bladed sabers such as this one were widely used by cavalry in the Napoleonic Wars. This model was adopted by the British light cavalry in 1796.

protective cover for cock and steel

tubular housing for ramrod

RIFLE

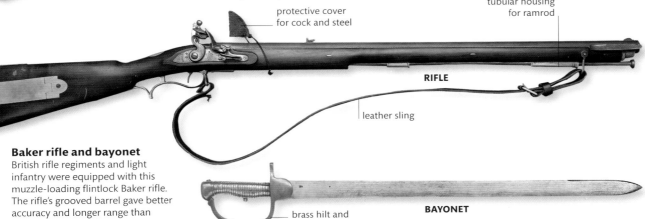

leather sling

Baker rifle and bayonet
British rifle regiments and light infantry were equipped with this muzzle-loading flintlock Baker rifle. The rifle's grooved barrel gave better accuracy and longer range than a smoothbore musket.

brass hilt and knuckle guard

BAYONET

Ball bullets
Round lead balls were the standard bullets for flintlock muskets and rifles. The ball was often wrapped in greased cloth to grip the grooves in rifle barrels.

striker steel

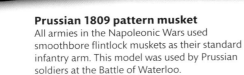

Prussian 1809 pattern musket
All armies in the Napoleonic Wars used smoothbore flintlock muskets as their standard infantry arm. This model was used by Prussian soldiers at the Battle of Waterloo.

barrel band

Rifle cartridge
Cartridges such as this one were used to load flintlock weapons. The gunpowder was poured into the barrel and then the paper and ball were pushed in with a ramrod.

gunpowder and lead ball wrapped in paper

long barrel shows battle damage

holes to position cannon for traveling

vent for igniting powder charge

French 12-pounder cannon
A smoothbore cannon, the 12-pounder was the largest field gun employed by Napoleon's armies. It was used at long range against infantry and cavalry.

wooden gun carriage, made from elm

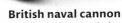

British naval cannon
British warships carried at least 74 cannons firing 24- or 32-pound shot. The cannons were mounted on wheeled wooden carriages, allowing them to run backward under recoil.

Infantryman uniform

In 1804, there were 350,000 conscripts in Napoleon's infantry, forming the backbone of his Grande Armée (Grand Army). On the battlefield, the soldiers were expected to march over open ground into enemy fire in massed columns—a tactic that made concealment impossible. Their uniform was designed for display, to raise morale, and intimidate the enemy. About a million Frenchmen were killed or wounded on military service in the Napoleonic Wars.

red collar matches cuffs

blue tunic with white turnbacks

corporal's stripes

tricolor cockade

Imperial Eagle emblem

chinstrap

brass buttons embossed with regimental number

regulation red cuff with dark blue flap

Shako hat

Most European armies adopted the cylindrical shako as the standard infantry headgear during the Napoleonic Period. The shako replaced the earlier bicorne hat of the French infantry.

knuckle guard

ribbed brass handle

curved steel blade

loose-fitting pants worn for battle over close-fitting knee breeches

FULL VIEW

Saber

Unlike his British counterpart, the French infantryman usually wore a sword. Known as a briquet, this brass-hilted short saber was most commonly issued to Napoleon's foot soldiers.

POLITICS AND POWER

Inspired by the ideas of the 18th-century Enlightenment, the leaders of the French Revolution sought to remake the world from scratch, on rational principles. Liberating notions, such as universal citizenship, released popular enthusiasm and energy. However, the opposition of conservative elements of the population was suppressed with savagery at the same time.

Napoleon's face surrounded by inscription "Napoleon Emperor of France"

wreath of oak and laurel leaves

depiction of phases of Moon

Decimal clock
The French government decreed a new decimal time system in 1793 that divided the day into 10 hours of 100 minutes. This clock shows both the traditional 24-hour format and the decimal time.

dial with duodecimal time system

dial with decimal time system

enamel decoration

Legion of Honour
Napoleon created the Legion of Honor in 1802 to acknowledge exceptional merit in soldiers and civilians. This award was open to all citizens, regardless of social status.

50-livre *assignat*
Paper money bills issued by French governments from 1789 were known as *assignats*. Irresponsible printing of money to pay state debts caused hyperinflation, and by 1796 the *assignats* were worthless.

turned-up portions of brim form gutter

Tricorne hat
The red, white, and blue cockade on this tricorne hat shows that its wearer supported the Revolution. The hat belonged to a member of the National Guard, a citizens' militia.

Declaration of Rights
This extract from the minutes of the National Constituent Assembly of 1789 marks the adoption of a statement of individual and collective universal human rights.

King Louis XVI

obverse with Napoleon as Emperor

Royal and imperial coins
These silver five-Franc pieces bear the images of Emperor Napoleon and King Louis XVI. The Franc was reintroduced by Napoleon to stabilize the currency.

Masonic level symbol from the Place de la Nation in Paris

caduceus—symbol of commerce and negotiation

BUNDLE OF WOODEN RODS SYMBOLIZING AUTHORITY

Sèvres pottery
After the king was deposed in 1792, the former royal porcelain factory at Sèvres turned to producing tableware decorated with Republican and Revolutionary symbols.

THE DECLINE OF THE AUSTRIAN EMPIRE

In the 19th century, Austria lost a contest with Prussia for the leadership of the German population of central Europe. United under the Prussian monarchy, the German Empire became a major industrial and military power, while the Austrian Empire slipped into terminal decline.

In 1750, the Habsburg rulers of Austria still held the title of Holy Roman Emperor, exercising control over the many small, internally autonomous states into which Germany was divided. In the Seven Years' War (1756–63), the Kingdom of Prussia fought Austria, establishing itself as an alternative power center in the Germanic world. Until the mid-19th century, Germany remained fragmented, its smaller states often characterized by the eccentricity of their rulers. The Germans were known for their Romantic poets and students, and their philosophers, musicians, craft workshops, and quaint university towns. Industry was slow to develop, lagging well behind Britain, Belgium, and France.

One of the results of the French Revolution of 1789 was the rise of the idea of the nation-state. A conservative attempt to contain this new nationalism through stability, the 1815 Treaty of Vienna put national boundaries in place that stood for more than four decades. The Habsburgs had positioned themselves as the principal opponents of nationalist ideology because it threatened their multinational empire, which included Hungarian, Italian, Slav, and German subjects. In 1848, a series of uprisings shook the Austrian Empire, including nationalist revolts in Hungary and Italy. In Germany, a national parliament assembled in Frankfurt. Austria and Prussia both took part in the suppression of the popular movements and the German parliament came to nothing, but the writing was clearly on the wall.

UNIFICATION OF GERMANY

At the time of the revolutionary agitations in 1848, the German states were a loose confederation, with Prussia most powerful among them. In the 1860s, under the direction of Prime Minister Otto von Bismarck, Prussia fought a series of wars to unify Germany under its leadership, and in 1871, King Wilhelm I of Prussia became Emperor of Germany. The rulers of states such as Bavaria and Saxony retained their titles but lost all effective political power. The German unification unleashed a tide of economic growth and urbanization, transforming a largely agricultural country into a major industrial power. The Habsburgs, meanwhile, formed an alliance with the Hungarian nationalists to hold down the Slavs. The Austro–Hungarian Empire, formed in 1867, saw the joint capital cities of Vienna and Budapest flourish as centers of culture, but a glittering surface could not hide the instability of a regime that had become a subordinate partner in an alliance with Prussian-led Germany.

"You see in me the **last monarch** of the **old school.**"

Franz Joseph, Emperor of Austria and King of Hungary, to Theodore Roosevelt, 1910

Symbol of power
This coronation mantle was made for Ferdinand, Habsburg heir to the Austrian throne, in 1830. Because the personal rule of the Habsburgs was the only cement holding together the empire's disparate peoples, it became essential to bolster imperial authority with symbols and ceremonies. However, the failings of the Habsburg autocracy could not be hidden— Ferdinand proved incapable of effective rule and his successor, Franz Joseph, presided over the empire's decline.

ermine

gold miter symbolizes
divine right to rule

rubies represent
royal wisdom

diamond squares
symbolize royal
authority

Austrian imperial crown
This crown was made for the Holy Roman Emperor Rudolf II
in 1602. It was adopted as the crown of the Austrian Empire
when the Holy Roman Empire was abolished in 1806.

Embroidery
Designed by Philipp von Stubenrauch,
the gold embroidery on the royal
mantle, showing oak and laurel
leaves, was executed by master
gold embroiderer Johann Fritz.

embroidered
laurel leaves

red velvet

Habsburg
double eagle
insignia

MUSIC AND NATIONALISM

Oppressed in the political arena, nationalism found
expression in music. The mazurkas and polonaises
of Frederic Chopin (whose *Polonaise-fantasie* of
1846 is shown above) represented the Polish cause
after a nationalist uprising was suppressed in 1830.
Composers Bedřich Smetana and Antonín Dvořák
expressed Czech opposition to Austrian rule, and the
operas of Giuseppe Verdi represented the spirit of
the Italian *risorgimento*, which led to the founding
of an Italian nation-state in 1861.

RUSSIA UNDER THE ROMANOVS

Czarist Russia was a major power, holding territory in Europe and Asia, and establishing a court with international interests. However, reform and counter-reform led to upheaval, assassinations, and political intrigue. Combined with the ravages of war, these gave rise to a revolution that ended Romanov rule.

opaque white enamelled shell

multicoloured hammered gold hen

eye made of ruby

The golden egg
The first imperial egg, made for Czar Alexander III to give his wife in 1885, was enameled in white to simulate an egg, with a gold "yolk" containing a golden hen inside.

Czar Peter the Great, the sole ruler of Russia from 1699 to 1721, laid the foundations for imperial expansion with wide-ranging reforms. These affected the armed forces, the administration, education, and social customs, and propelled his country into the mainstream of European culture. This modernizing autocrat built St. Petersburg as a new capital city oriented toward the West, unlike the more tradition-bound Moscow. The monarchy was strengthened under Catherine the Great in the later 18th century, who consolidated power and culture around her court.

In contrast, despite some early attempts at reform, many landholders continued to hold significant numbers of serfs into the 19th century. Alexander II issued a proclamation abolishing serfdom in 1861 but was assassinated soon afterward. His death brought caution and reaction from his successors, including some censorship from Alexander III. Nicholas II was not prepared for the transfer of power to his shoulders after the early death of his father Alexander III, but his reign did start an increase in industrialization, with growth in foreign investment and the expansion of the railroads to transport goods.

A GROWING EMPIRE

Russian expansion grew from the powerful armed forces established by Peter the Great. In the 19th century, the tide of expansion turned eastward, with the conquest of territory in the Caucasus and Central Asia, and the opening up of Siberia. However, the resulting acquisition of resources was not accompanied by a program to maximize their benefits for the giant empire that Russia had become.

THE ROAD TO REVOLUTION

The political demands of the late 19th century, brought about by rising numbers of industrial workers and continued agrarian reform, coexisted with great artistic ferment. By the early 20th century, St. Petersburg was a cultural center, and Russian artists were admired all over Europe. Although there was some industrialization and real economic progress, the rigidity of czarist autocracy meant Russia's future lay in violent revolution.

diamond-set imperial eagle

green-gold laurel leaf cage

imperial crown in rose-cut diamonds

platinum tire

repeating sunburst pattern

translucent lime yellow enamel

rock crystal window

Royal coach in miniature
Made to celebrate the coronation of Czar Nicholas II and Czarina Alexandra in 1896, this egg opens to reveal an exact model of the czarina's coronation coach with moving parts.

opalescent white enamel background

statue of Paul I, Emperor of Russia between 1796 and 1801

rows of identical seed pearls divide egg into 12 segments

gold trumpet in enamel

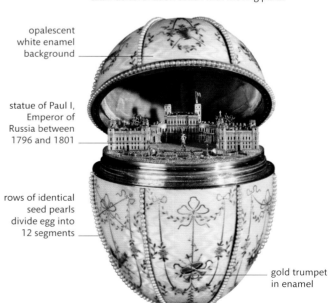

Palace of gold
This egg was a present from Nicholas II to his mother in 1901. It contained a detailed model of Gatchina Palace, which became her principal winter residence just outside St. Petersburg.

> "It is better to begin to **abolish serfdom from above** than to wait until it begins to **abolish itself from below.**"
>
> Czar Alexander II, addressing Moscow gentry, March 30, 1856

EASTER AND THE ORTHODOX CHURCH

Eggs were not eaten during Lent, the 40 days leading up to Easter, the holiest event in the Christian year. This added to their symbolism in the especially rich celebrations of Easter in the Russian Orthodox tradition observed by much of the country. From the time of Peter the Great, the Russian Orthodox Church was effectively taken under state control. Identified with and funded by the czarist regime, it lost most of its independent spiritual authority. The Church of the Savior on Spilled Blood, shown here, was built by Czar Alexander III on the site of his predecessor Alexander II's assassination in St. Petersburg.

Royal gift

Between 1885 and 1917, St. Petersburg jeweler Carl Fabergé and his workmasters produced over 50 eggs for the Russian imperial court. Involving elaborate mechanisms and miniature paintings, these vastly expensive creations were displays of outstanding craftsmanship in enamel, precious stones, and metals that revealed complicated surprises. Showing elements of Art Nouveau style in its floral design, the Lilies of the Valley Egg, shown here, was presented by Czar Nicholas II to his wife in 1898.

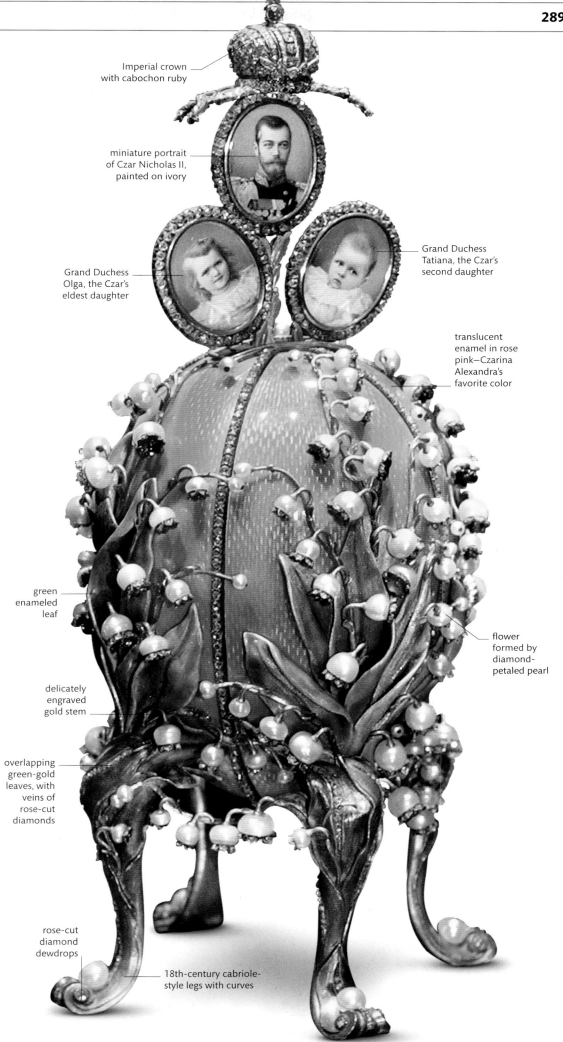

Imperial crown with cabochon ruby

miniature portrait of Czar Nicholas II, painted on ivory

Grand Duchess Tatiana, the Czar's second daughter

Grand Duchess Olga, the Czar's eldest daughter

translucent enamel in rose pink—Czarina Alexandra's favorite color

green enameled leaf

flower formed by diamond-petaled pearl

delicately engraved gold stem

overlapping green-gold leaves, with veins of rose-cut diamonds

rose-cut diamond dewdrops

18th-century cabriole-style legs with curves

THE RACE FOR AFRICAN EMPIRES

At the start of the 19th century, Africa was a continent with a wide variety of peoples living in a range of societies, from large-scale kingdoms and empires to small-scale villages and bands of hunter-gatherers. By the end of the century, almost the entire continent had been brought under direct or indirect European rule.

Asante gold
The wealthy ruler of the West African Asante kingdom sat on a golden throne decorated with symbolic carvings such as this eagle, coated in gold leaf.

Zulu Resistance ▽
The imposition of European rule in Africa often encountered fierce resistance from local peoples. In January 1879, Zulu warriors armed with spears and shields defeated a British invasion force at the battle of Isandlwana, killing almost all the British troops.

Before the colonial era, one of the major European influences on West Africa and the western coastal areas of central Africa, including Angola, was exerted through the Atlantic slave trade. By the late 18th century, around 100,000 Africans were being forcibly transported to the Americas every year to be bought by traders in Britain, France, Spain Portugal, the, Dutch Empire, and the United States. In 1807, Britain banned the slave trade, but it continued on a large scale into the second half of the 19th century. The trade generated conflict,

since kingdoms such as the Asante fought wars to obtain prisoners for sale to the Europeans. However, wars also resulted from shifts in a turbulent continent. For example, in southern Africa, from the 1820s the Zulu created a large empire by conquering neighboring peoples, and in West Africa Muslim rulers launched wars to extend the reach of Islam.

NEW MOTIVES

In the early 19th century, European explorers and missionaries began to penetrate deep into Africa. A mixture

of motives, from humanitarianism to a desire for new markets for their goods and a search for raw materials drew the European powers into a race to carve up the continent.

By the end of the century, Britain, France, Portugal, Belgium, Germany, and Italy had claimed large territories. With the exception of Ethiopia, which fought off the Italians, no African state was strong enough to keep its independence. A slow transformation of African life began, in some places brutally imposed, in others negotiated by compromise with existing rulers.

tiny colored beads

ART AND CULTURE

African craftsmen worked in varied cultural traditions using locally available materials such as wood and ivory. Much of their output was for personal adornment, from beautiful textiles to intricate beadwork. Sophisticated carvings and ceremonial objects embellished the courts of wealthy African kingdoms, including the Asante, Benin, and Kongo.

Bead necklaces
The Zulu and other peoples of southern Africa wore beads threaded to create ornate necklaces, girdles, and headgear. They were worn by both men and women.

Gold weighing spoon
Asante traders used this spoon for measuring out gold dust. The quantity of locally produced gold the Asante possessed amazed and impressed the British.

headdress

Ivory statue
Carved by a craftsman of the Kongo nation of central Africa, this ivory statuette shows two women, possibly roped together.

■ WEIGHTS

MAN WITH PIPE AND BASKET

TWO MEN SHAKING HANDS

GROUP OF FOUR BIRDS

PEANUT

OX WITH BIRDS

Dealer's weights
About 2 in (5 cm) tall, these brass objects were used as scale weights by the Asante when making and receiving payments in gold dust, the local currency.

■ SWORDS

decorative gilded handle

Asante warrior's sword
This sword, used by an Asante warrior, has a sharkskin scabbard covering its curved blade and a distinctive grip with rounded pommels.

semicircular holes

blade unsharpened, since it was not intended for war

Asante state sword
This ceremonial sword belonged to Kofi Kakari, the Asantehene (Asante king) from 1867 to 1875. The gilt seed shapes on the handle symbolize fertility.

hilt

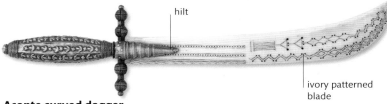

ivory patterned blade

Asante curved dagger
Working in about 1870, a skillful Asante craftsman has engraved the curved blade of this ceremonial weapon with a variety of West African decorative patterns.

Asante state dagger
Asantehene Kofi Kakari carried this pure gold dagger on state occasions. It was among booty seized by the British from the Asante capital, Kumasi, in 1874.

elaborately decorated blade

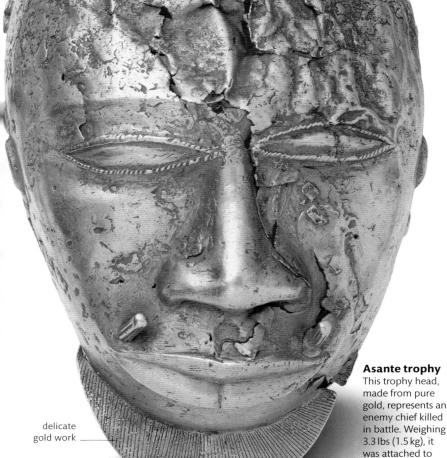

delicate gold work

Asante trophy
This trophy head, made from pure gold, represents an enemy chief killed in battle. Weighing 3.3 lbs (1.5 kg), it was attached to the Asante king's state sword.

BELIEFS AND RITUALS

North Africa and large areas of West Africa and coastal East Africa adopted Islam. There were scattered Christian outposts, as in Ethiopia (see pp.266–67). In the rest of the continent, polytheistic beliefs and ancestor worship prevailed. However, from the late 19th century, the Christian faith began to spread rapidly, becoming the dominant religion in sub-Saharan Africa.

Yoruba carving of missionary

This late 19th-century carving was made in the town of Abeokuta by a craftsman of the West African Yoruba people. The town had a number of Christian and Muslim communities. The carving shows a Christian missionary accompanied by converts and a Muslim with his retinue. The Yoruba were among the first West Africans to adopt Christianity in substantial numbers in the 19th century.

missionary mounted on horse, identifiable by his European-style hat

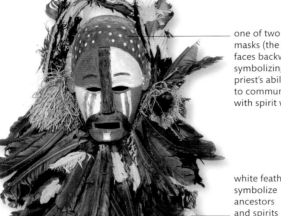

one of two masks (the other faces backward) symbolizing priest's ability to communicate with spirit world

white feathers symbolize ancestors and spirits

black feathers symbolize land of the living

Christian converts accompany missionary

headdress of figure suggests high status

retine of mounted Muslim

Kongo priest's costume

In traditional African religions, priests are powerful figures who perform rituals and channel spiritual forces. This priest's costume comes from the Kongo people of Central Africa.

Yoruba dance mask

Worn in dance rituals, this Yoruba mask has a carved superstructure showing a mounted god or king. Such masks are objects of spiritual power, kept in shrines.

decorated wooden base

Ethiopian charm
Africans traditionally put great faith in the power of amulets and charms. This charm from Ethiopia was thought to ensure successful breeding of cattle.

amulets worn around neck

animal handle for lid

elaborate wooden carving

Yoruba bowl
This Yoruba bowl was used to hold divination equipment. In traditional Yoruba religion, divination vessels are used by priests to consult the ancestors about important decisions, such as the correct date for rituals.

carved leopards

Yoruba leopard mask
This Yoruba mask was made in the late 19th century and was worn during Gelede dances in celebration of mothers in society. Although most Yoruba became Christians or Muslims, traditional beliefs remained a significant influence.

BATTLE AND CONFLICT

Africans had some firearms, but they mostly fought with traditional weapons such as spears. Determined African armies, such as the Zulu or the Sudanese Mahdists, achieved occasional victories against European forces, but ultimately modern firepower was always decisive. Only the wars between the British and the Boers (1880–1881 and 1899–1902) were fought with modern weapons on both sides.

■ ZULU WARFARE

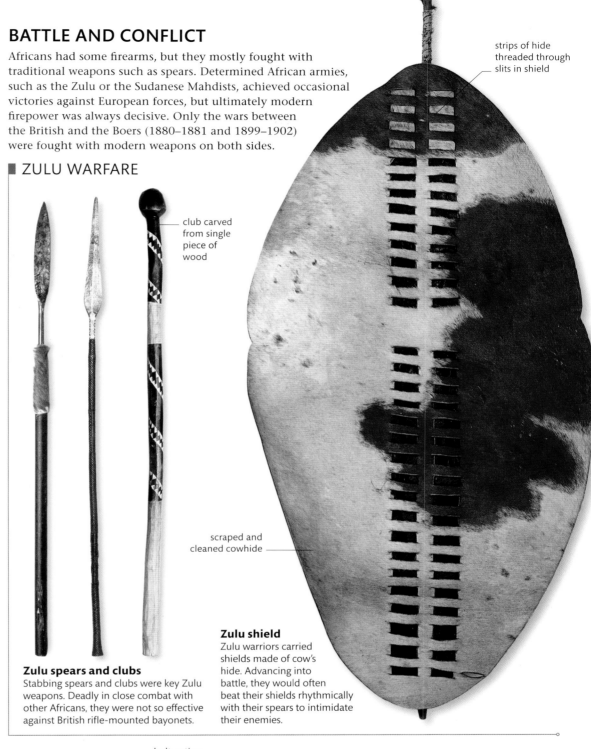

strips of hide threaded through slits in shield

club carved from single piece of wood

scraped and cleaned cowhide

Zulu shield
Zulu warriors carried shields made of cow's hide. Advancing into battle, they would often beat their shields rhythmically with their spears to intimidate their enemies.

Zulu spears and clubs
Stabbing spears and clubs were key Zulu weapons. Deadly in close combat with other Africans, they were not so effective against British rifle-mounted bayonets.

■ GUNS

bolt-action allows rapid fire

rear sight

fore sight

Mauser rifle
Fighting to prevent a British takeover of their independent Transvaal and Orange Free State republics, the Boers were equipped with the latest German Mauser rifles.

attachment

removable stock

Mauser pistol
The Mauser pistol was typical of the sophistication of Boer weaponry. However, far superior British resources had brought the Boers to defeat by 1902.

THE EMPIRE OF THE SIKHS

In the early 19th century, Sikh leader Maharajah Ranjit Singh, known as "the Lion of the Punjab," created a powerful state in northwest India. However, weakened by internal power struggles and eventually defeated in wars with external forces, the Sikh Empire did not long outlive its founder.

Royal image
This ivory carving of Ranjit Singh, made in 1830, shows him as a one-eyed figure. He was blinded in one eye during childhood.

Crafted in gold ▽
The Harmandir Sahib in Amritsar, known as the Golden Temple, is one of the most prominent Sikh places of worship. Maharajah Ranjit Singh, founder of the Sikh Empire, was responsible for embellishing it with marble and decorative gilding in the early 19th century.

The decline of the Indian Mughal Empire in the 18th century allowed competing Sikh leaders to rule areas of the Punjab. In 1799, Ranjit Singh, one of these leaders, captured Lahore, part of present-day Pakistan. In 1801, he crowned himself Maharajah of Punjab, founding a unified Sikh state. He embarked on military campaigns against the Afghans and Rajputs, extending his rule as far north as Kashmir, west to the Khyber Pass, and east to the Tibet border. Maharajah Ranjit Singh did not attempt to impose the Sikh faith, 70 percent of whom were Muslims. However, he did ban certain Muslim customs, including the call to prayer by the muezzin and the killing of cattle.

A TIME OF UNREST

A murderous conflict of succession broke out following the death of Maharajah Ranjit Singh in 1839. After a welter of assassinations, five-year-old Duleep Singh, Maharajah Ranjit Singh's youngest child, came to power in 1843. Effective control devolved to the army, which declared itself the true embodiment of the Sikh people. This turmoil within the Sikh Empire exacerbated tensions with the British, who had recently extended their control of India to include Sindh, on the empire's southern border.

In 1846, British forces were victorious in the First Anglo–Sikh War. The Sikh Empire had to cede large areas of territory and accept supervision of their government by a British Resident. A Sikh uprising led to the Second Anglo-Sikh War in 1848–49, at the end of which Punjab was absorbed into British India.

BELIEFS AND RITUALS

The Sikh religion was founded in the 16th century by Guru Nanak. It is based on his teachings and those of the nine other gurus who followed. Sikhs believe in the concept of one god and in a cycle of reincarnation. They were a minority in the Sikh Empire, which had a majority of Muslims and many Hindus.

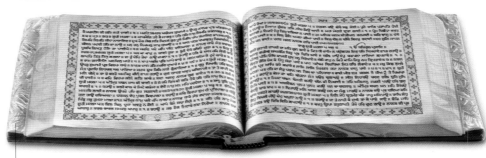

Guru Granth Sahib
Setting out the teachings of the gurus of the Sikh faith, this book known as the *Guru Granth Sahib* is the central religious text of Sikhism. The text is chanted as prayers.

decorative cloth covering

papier maché with gold leaf

Chauri
A ceremonial object of the Sikh religion, the *chauri* is a whisk that is waved over the *Guru Granth Sahib* as a sign of respect when the holy book is being read.

yak hair or artificial fiber

Qalamdan
This *qalamdan*, or pen box, was made in Kashmir in the early 19th century by one of the Sikh Empire's Muslim subjects. It once held the reed pens of a scribe copying Islamic texts.

BATTLE AND CONFLICT

Ranjit Singh employed French and other foreign consultants to train his army. They combined disciplined musket-armed infantry and modern cannons with the traditional fighting skills of the Sikh warrior class. The Sikhs were repeatedly victorious against the Afghans and other neighboring peoples, but could not ultimately withstand the organization and armament of the British forces.

green velvet embroidered in gold thread

Powder belt
Loading a flintlock firearm was a complex procedure. Musket-armed Sikh troops wore this belt with its powder flask and ammunition pouches, which made loading firearms easier.

egret feathers mounted in plume tube

barrel formed by coiling strips of steel around a mandrel

Flintlock pistol
This pistol was made in the Sikh capital, Lahore, around 1800. Local artisans had no difficulty making European-style firearms, and added their own elaborate decorations.

Dhal
Dating from the period of the Anglo-Sikh wars, this *dhal* shield bears Persian inscriptions. It may have belonged to a Muslim fighting in the Sikh army.

gold inlay

steel quoit

conical cap wrapped in silk *pagri*

breast plate

small throwing knife

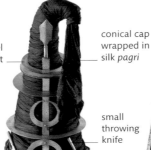

Sikh armor
This Sikh suit of armor was made in the 18th century. This type of armor was still worn by commanders in the Anglo-Sikh Wars, but was more for appearance than for protection.

Quoit turban
The sharp-edged quoit, or *chakram*, was a favorite weapon of the Sikh Akali sect, who stacked them on their tall turbans. The quoit was launched by whirling around the finger.

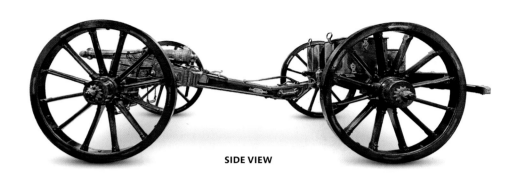

SIDE VIEW

Muzzle
This ornate, bronze tiger's-head stopper blocks the muzzle of the gun when it is not in use. Indian bronzesmiths traditionally featured motifs of tigers on guns.

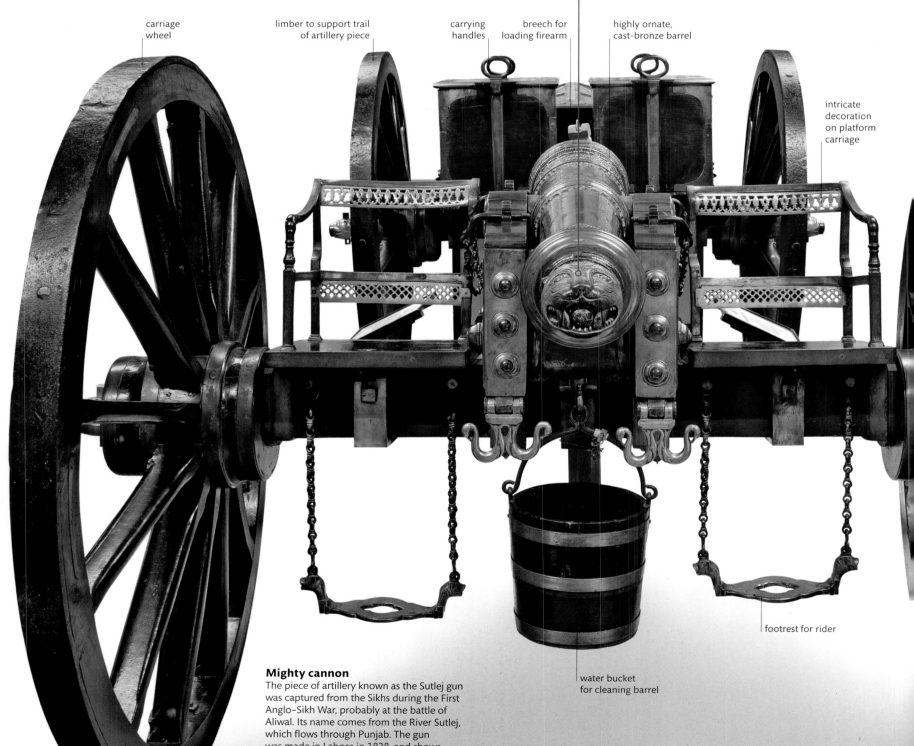

carriage wheel

limber to support trail of artillery piece

carrying handles

breech for loading firearm

highly ornate, cast-bronze barrel

intricate decoration on platform carriage

footrest for rider

water bucket for cleaning barrel

Mighty cannon
The piece of artillery known as the Sutlej gun was captured from the Sikhs during the First Anglo–Sikh War, probably at the battle of Aliwal. Its name comes from the River Sutlej, which flows through Punjab. The gun was made in Lahore in 1838, and shows the high quality of Sikh technical expertise and craftsmanship.

■ CAPTURED IN CONFLICT

SUTLEJ GUN

The death of Maharajah Ranjit Singh in 1839, and the resulting power struggle, left the Sikh Empire weakened and internally divided. Court rivalries unraveled into disorder, and the British extended their control over the Indian subcontinent, reaching the Sikh Empire's southern border. As the situation in the Punjab became more unstable, the British moved men and weapons to the frontier in open provocation. Although the Sikhs were ultimately defeated in the ensuing wars, they proved to be formidable opponents. The Sutlej gun shown here was a cannon deployed by the Sikh army against the British forces in the 1840s and it remains a reminder of the Sikh army's impressive firepower.

ON THE BATTLEFIELD

The First Anglo–Sikh War, fought in the winter of 1845–46, pitted the Sikh army against a mix of British army regiments and British-officered Indian troops of the East India Company. The Sikhs crossed the Sutlej, marking the divide between the Sikh Empire and British-controlled India, in December 1845.

On December 21, 1845, in a battle at Ferozepur, Sikh artillery of around 130 guns inflicted heavy casualties on the British, killing almost 700 men in a day. But the initial Sikh successes ended at Aliwal in January 1846. Wielding only sabers, the British cavalry charged and defeated the musket-armed Sikh infantry, which had formed defensive squares. A further defeat, at Sobraon in February, forced the Sikhs into accepting peace.

An uprising revolt, two years later, led to a second war in which the Sikhs were decisively defeated, although the British again suffered heavy losses while facing the fire of Sikh cannons at the Battle of Chillianwala.

THE EMPIRE'S END

On March 14, 1849, at the Battle of Gujrat, the Sikhs surrendered their 41 remaining guns. Within two weeks the Punjab was formally annexed by the British. They disbanded the Sikh army and deposed Maharajah Duleep Singh, only 10 years after the death of his father, Ranjit Singh.

Battle names
The rear of the barrel is engraved with the names of the battles of the First Anglo–Sikh War. These were added after the British captured the gun.

Wire cutter
Lahore craftsmen took every opportunity to add luxurious decorative details to their guns. This cutter is shaped like a peacock, the national bird of India.

Tow hook
A hook with an image of an elephant and rider connects the trail of the gun to the limber—the two-wheeled horse cart that tows the gun.

Storage chest
Chests at the front of the limber held ammunition for the cannon. Many British infantry members were killed while advancing into shots fired by such Sikh guns.

COMPANY RULE AND THE RAJ IN INDIA

Company coin
This gold coin was issued in 1819 by the British East India Company in Chennai. Until 1858, the Company administered the British-controlled areas of India.

In 1757, the British East India Company changed from a trading enterprise into the ruler of the Indian subcontinent. Eventually, India passed from the Company to the Crown, and Britain's Queen Victoria was declared Empress of the Raj, which included modern-day Pakistan, Bangladesh, Sri Lanka, and Burma, as well as India.

Pomp and splendor ▽
Held in 1877, 1903, and 1911, the Delhi Durbars were ceremonial occasions at which British monarchs were proclaimed Emperor or Empress of India. The 1903 Durbar, following the accession of Edward VII, was a spectacular display of the wealth and power of the Raj.

By 1750, the decline of the Mughal Empire had left the Indian subcontinent politically fragmented, with European traders controlling scattered coastal enclaves. The British and French fought to extend their influence, forging alliances with rival Indian rulers. A series of victories left the British dominant by 1818, with their East India Company in effect acting as the government's agent in India. After the suppression of the 1857 rebellion, which began as a revolt by Indian soldiers in the British army, India came under direct British rule.

BRITISH INVOLVEMENT

Britain's Indian Raj was politically complex. In addition to British direct rule of territories, more than 600 Indian princely states remained partially independent. Along with the recruitment of Indians into the army, police, and lower ranks of the civil service, this arrangement let Britain run its empire with very little British manpower. In 1900, some 300 million Indians were ruled by 20,000 British officials and army officers. The British believed they were bringing progress through honest administration, economic and technological development, and modern education for an Indian elite. Yet British policies left the majority of the Indian population in poverty and did nothing to prevent famines that killed millions.

Nationalist sentiment grew under the Raj. In 1885, the Indian National Congress, a pan-Indian political party, was founded. Agitation for freedom from foreign rule grew, and hostilities increased during the 20th century until Indian independence from Britain was realized in 1947.

TRADE

British traders initially went to India to buy refined, high-quality goods produced in Indian workshops. Under the British Raj, the subcontinent was flooded with cheap goods made in British factories, to the detriment of local manufacturers. Products such as raw cotton and tea, grown on British-owned estates, became India's major exports.

diamonds cut in both local and European style

Gold jewelry
India was renowned for its precious stones, often used to make jewelry for local rulers and Raj officials. These lavish 19th century examples demonstrate the meeting of Indian techniques and European tastes.

animal head with ruby eyes

ribbed, melon-shaped body

fine repoussé decoration

Silver tea set
The Indian princely states provided a haven for artisans within the British Raj. This silverware was made at the court of the ruler of Kutch, in modern Gujarat.

floral border with scattered bird motif

Decorative chintz
Finely painted and printed Indian textiles were highly prized around the world in the 18th century. This chintz drapery was designed for European sensibilities, and was imported to Britain by the East India Company.

POLITICS AND POWER

The British had to overcome determined local resistance to claim power in India—fighting four wars between 1767 and 1799 against the kingdom of Mysore. The Indian uprising of 1857, beginning with a mutiny by Indian troops in British service, was suppressed. This revolt revealed the underlying Indian hostility to British rule.

Stamp paper
The British East India Company raised revenue by charging a fee for the official stamp on legal documents. The text on this paper is written in the script of southern Indian Tamils.

British medal
The Indian Mutiny Medal was awarded to British soldiers and civilians and Indian troops who fought in the rebellion of 1857.

Britannia with wreath in right hand and union shield on left arm

Tipu's Tiger
This life-size automaton of a tiger mauling a European was owned by Tipu Sultan of Mysore. When a hidden handle is turned, the tiger roars and the victim cries out in pain.

ART AND CULTURE

As British control of the Indian subcontinent solidified, there was an increasing emphasis on perceived British superiority. The status of Indian female classical vocalists and dancers was severely diminished by Victorian standards of behavior and social roles, to the point that their performance traditions nearly disappeared entirely. However, traditional Indian music and other arts continued to flourish at the courts of Indian princes.

Company painting
Indian artists created paintings of East India Company officials enjoying an Indian lifestyle. This painting shows surgeon William Fullerton relaxing, attended by Indian servants.

Fullerton depicted in uniform, smoking a water pipe

head decorated with real peacock's beak

hollow, wooden body

Mayuri veena
Also known as a *taus*, from the Persian word for a peacock, the *mayuri veena* is a complex stringed instrument that was a favorite at Indian princely courts in the 19th century.

movable, arched metal frets

real tail feathers

CONNECTING A CONTINENT

DHR B CLASS NO.19

The Indian railroad network was a triumph of engineering that, in a practical sense, unified the subcontinent as never before. In the late 1840s, the East India Company and the British government agreed to support private companies in building railroad lines from the major coastal cities of Mumbai (Bombay), Kolkata (Calcutta), and Chennai (Madras).

The first commercial passenger railway opened in April 1853. Built by the Great Indian Peninsula Railway Company, it ran for 21 miles (34 km) between Mumbai and Thane. The first East India Railway line from Kolkata opened the following year, and the Madras Railway began operations in 1856. By 1871, the three companies had joined their railroad networks to link Mumbai, Kolkata, and Chennai. The mountainous Indian landscape and lack of skilled labor caused unprecedented challenges to railway engineers. The construction workers, mostly Indian, were paid very low wages and their use of traditional skills such as using baskets for hauling instead of wheelbarrows culminated in low productivity. Thousands of workers died during construction because of poor living conditions.

By 1880, Indian railroads extended for about 9,000 miles (14,500 km). Expansion carried on into the 20th century, with rail lines spanning 41,000 miles (66,000 km) by the end of the 1920s.

LOCAL COLOR

Located at an altitude of 7,200 ft (2,200 m), the Indian town of Darjeeling was a popular summer resort for British civil servants and army officers due to its temperate climate. In 1881, a 48 mile- (78 km-) narrow-gauge railroad line was built through tea plantations to link the hill station of Darjeeling to the North Indian plain. For many years locomotives—including the one shown here, built in 1889 in Britain—hauled passengers along the mountain railway. With a short wheelbase, it was perfectly suited to the Darjeeling Himalayan Railway's many curves. All the locomotive's weight was driven down onto the rails, helping adhesion on tricky terrain.

" ...It was thought desirable that, if possible... the **whole country** should be covered with a **network of lines** on a **uniform system.**"

Viceroy Lord Mayo, at the opening of the Mumbai–Kolkata route, March 7, 1870

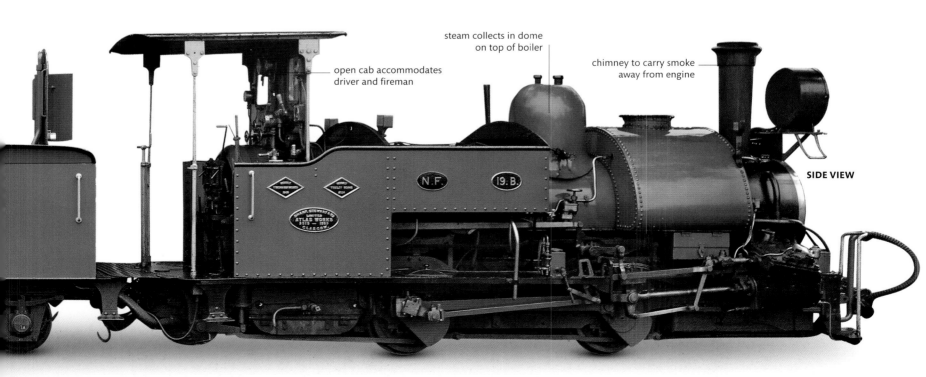

steam collects in dome on top of boiler

open cab accommodates driver and fireman

chimney to carry smoke away from engine

N.F. 19. B.

SIDE VIEW

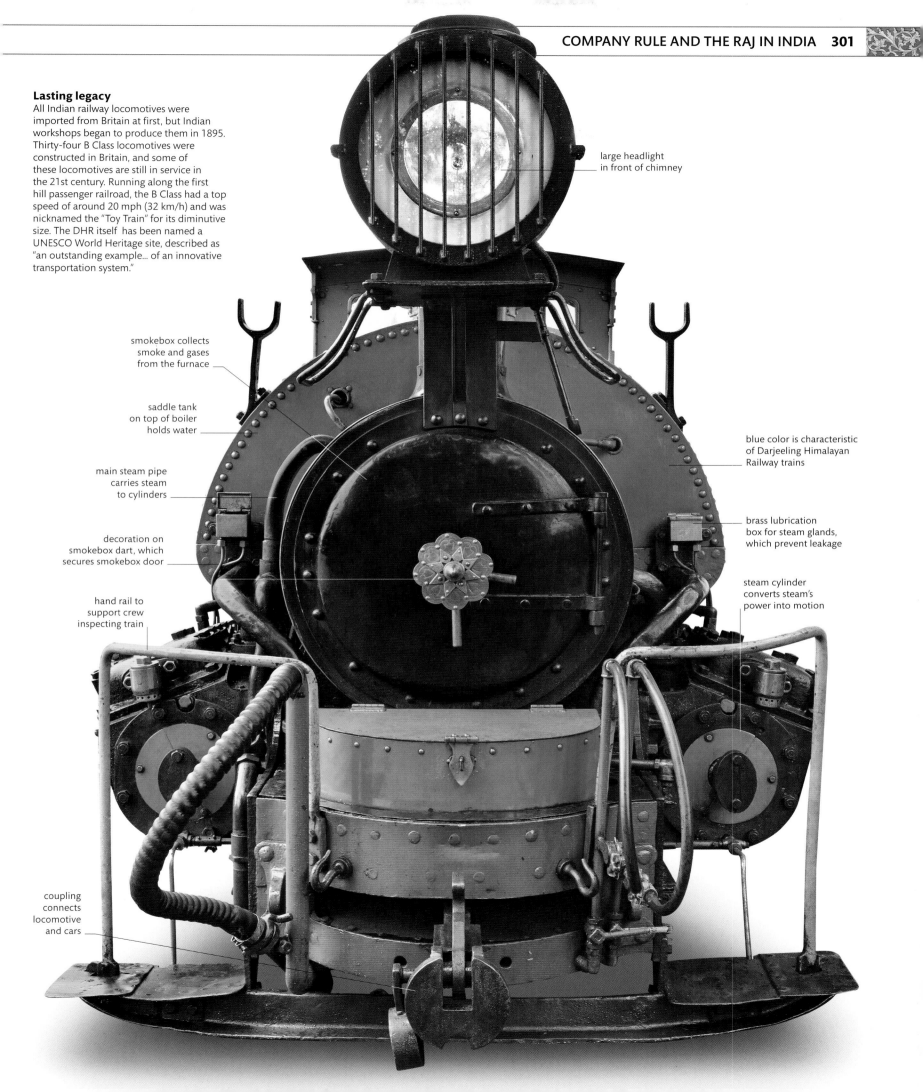

Lasting legacy

All Indian railway locomotives were imported from Britain at first, but Indian workshops began to produce them in 1895. Thirty-four B Class locomotives were constructed in Britain, and some of these locomotives are still in service in the 21st century. Running along the first hill passenger railroad, the B Class had a top speed of around 20 mph (32 km/h) and was nicknamed the "Toy Train" for its diminutive size. The DHR itself has been named a UNESCO World Heritage site, described as "an outstanding example... of an innovative transportation system."

large headlight in front of chimney

smokebox collects smoke and gases from the furnace

saddle tank on top of boiler holds water

main steam pipe carries steam to cylinders

blue color is characteristic of Darjeeling Himalayan Railway trains

decoration on smokebox dart, which secures smokebox door

brass lubrication box for steam glands, which prevent leakage

hand rail to support crew inspecting train

steam cylinder converts steam's power into motion

coupling connects locomotive and cars

THE REOPENING OF JAPAN

In the second half of the 19th century, Japan carried through a rapid modernization of its economy and society. With a strong centralized government that promoted the growth of industry, it was also able to create a powerful army and navy. Instead of falling prey to foreign imperialists, Japan became the first non-Western country to consolidate its power in the industrial age.

Reforming emperor
Coming to the throne in 1867, Emperor Meiji presided over the modernization of Japan. He adopted a Western-style uniform and haircut to set an example to his subjects.

Road to modernization ▷
This woodblock print, made in 1875, shows the Tokyo terminus of Japan's first railroad, the Tokyo–Yokahama Railroad. It was constructed by British engineers and operated with British-built locomotives. The Japanese government exercised tight supervision over such projects, ensuring that they served national needs.

From 1641 into the 1850s, the ruling Tokugawa shoguns strictly limited the flow of trade and information between Japan and the outside world. This policy was in many ways a success. At the start of the 19th century, Japan had an effective government system. The *daimyo* (feudal lords) in the provinces provided strong local government under the shogunate in Edo (Tokyo). The emperor in Kyoto was a powerless figurehead, and the numerous samurai warriors had mutated into a high-status class of officials who wore swords only as a mark of rank. A commercial class, with wealth but low status, inhabited flourishing cities. In 1800, Edo probably had a larger population than London or Paris. Entertainers, artists, and craftsmen flourished, servicing the needs of this commercial class and the samurai.

POWER STRUGGLE

In the first half of the 19th century, however, an urgent need for change was felt. There were agricultural crises, and revolts by peasants and the urban poor. The shogunate was aware that Europeans had attacked China, and worried that Japan might face the same challenge. In 1853, the arrival of an American naval squadron led by Commodore Matthew Perry triggered a political crisis, as the ruling elite debated a response to Perry's demand for the opening of Japan to foreign trade. The Tokugawa regime decided on concessions to the foreigners under duress. In reaction against this policy, a revolt led by samurai from the Satsuma region eventually overthrew the Tokugawa in 1868.

The rebels brought the emperor from Kyoto to Tokyo, claiming to restore imperial rule, although in reality they ruled themselves in the emperor's name. Instead of carrying out a conservative reaction against change, however, the leaders of the Meiji Restoration initiated a rapid program of economic growth and social reform. They realized that only by learning from foreigners could Japan become strong enough to resist foreign domination and assert its national independence.

REASSERTING TRADITION

By 1873 the Meiji government had extended equal citizenship to all Japanese, abolished the regional rule of the *daimyo*, introduced universal elementary education, established a postal system and electric telegraph service, and laid the foundations for a mass conscript army and a modern navy. In 1877, a samurai revolt against social reforms that destroyed their privileged status was crushed. Foreign experts, technology, and money were brought in to kick-start the development of a modern industrial economy, but the process was controlled and directed by the Japanese. Former samurai joined with the pre-Meiji commercial class to provide a body of entrepreneurs who developed factories and trade, with large-scale backing from the Japanese government. From the 1880s, cotton-spinning and silk manufacture grew rapidly into major export industries, alongside an armaments industry supplying the Japanese armed forces.

As the Japanese recovered confidence, they began to emphasize their distinctive national culture. Western methods were employed pragmatically, but a reassertion of Japanese traditions became central to the ideology of the Meiji era. Thus the emperor emerged both as a European-style constitutional monarch and a sacred ruler at the focus of state-sponsored Shinto religious rituals.

"Enrich the country, strengthen the military."

Japan's national slogan during the Meiji era

HOME LIFE

Japanese domestic life was on the whole resistant to Westernization. After the Meiji Restoration, a civil servant would sit on a chair at work, but probably on a floor cushion at home. Interiors were bare and sparsely furnished by Western standards. A few imported clocks or lamps coexisted with products of traditional Japanese crafts.

Porcelain cup and saucer
Part of a coffee set, this cup and saucer show people sheltering from the rain. Tea-drinking had a central place in Japanese culture, but consumption of coffee began to take off in the 1880s.

egg-shell porcelain

gold inlay

Bronze flower vase
Japanese metalworkers were skilled in producing exquisite bronze vases with colored metal inlays. Restraint, elegance, and simplicity were the essence of Japanese good taste.

Black lacquer cabinet
Made by Japanese craftsmen in the Meiji era, this black lacquer cabinet embellished with a design of fans would have been an expensive item of furniture.

doors decorated with fans

gold lacquer finish

plum blossoms and dahlias mean happiness and wealth

inlaid design

Black Meiji plate
Decorated with an image of a bird and flowers, this black lacquer plate is a fine example of Meiji domestic ware, celebrating an entirely traditional Japanese esthetic.

small fish represent parents with a child

carp symbolizes faithfulness in marriage

Porcelain plate
A dish like this would have been given as a wedding present. Its design contains a number of elements relating to married life.

BATTLE AND CONFLICT

Under the Tokugawa shogunate, Japan was largely at peace and military technology stagnated. The arrival of Western navies from 1853 on stimulated rapid adoption of imported weaponry. After the Meiji Restoration, making use of foreign expertise, Japan developed formidable modern armed forces, defeating China in 1894–95 and Russia a decade later.

steel point

IVORY THROWING ARROW

Throwing arrows
Although firearms had been in use in Japan since 1543, the samurai warriors of the Tokugawa era used hand-thrown arrows as an alternative to the bow when fighting at close range.

feather fletching

LACQUER THROWING ARROW

head cut down from longer spear

semi-pistol grip

Arisaka rifle
Introduced in 1897, the Arisaka was a state-of-the-art bolt-action repeater rifle. Designed and manufactured in Japan, it was as good as any infantry weapon equipping Western armies.

integral five-round magazine

gold cord shoulder strap

dark blue tunic

Meiji military uniform
Initially trained by French instructors, the Japanese Imperial Army adopted a uniform with a dark blue tunic, similar to that worn by the contemporary French army.

sword sash

bayonet lug

ART AND CULTURE

Traditional arts and crafts survived the modernization of Japan and exposure to Western influences from the 1850s. The Japanese even developed a fresh awareness of the unique value of their culture and the high quality of its craft products, which were celebrated as a symbol of national identity and marketed as desirable exotica to Western buyers.

bamboo frame

Japanese fan
This fan is decorated with a painting of pottery by renowned Meiji era ceramicist Tozan Ito. Such items were appreciated by wealthy Japanese and foreign collectors.

Forging
Produced from the 18th century through to the Meiji era, novelty products such as this articulated model snake and jointed crustacean were a popular creation of Japanese craftsmen working in metal. No longer required to make samurai swords and armor, metalworkers turned their skills to making such products.

posable pincer

JOINTED CRAB

pentagonal cards

fan-shaped two-tiered box

decorated black lacquer

individually joined hammered plates

ARTICULATED SNAKE

Japanese poetry game
Made in 1880, this game consisted of cards with poetry written on them. Players had to match cards to complete a poem, demonstrating knowledge of traditional literature.

■ MODERNIZING JAPAN

NOBLE LADIES WOODBLOCK PRINT

This triptych, by celebrated Japanese artist Toyohara Chikanobu (1838–1912), captures an extreme moment in the Westernization of Japan in the second half of the 19th century. As part of their program for the modernization of Japan from 1868 onward, the rulers of the Meiji era promoted the wearing of Western-style clothing in place of the traditional kimonos. In 1872, civil servants were instructed to wear Western-style suits, and the practice quickly spread to businessmen and politicians. Western-style military uniforms replaced the kimonos of the samurai.

WESTERNIZING SOCIETY

In the 1880s, women were also encouraged to adopt European fashion, which perhaps unfortunately at that moment consisted of the highly impractical bustle and elaborate bonnets. Used to going bareheaded with loose, elegant clothing, Japanese women of the elite gallantly adopted these alien and uncomfortable garments. The *sokuhatsu* style—a woman's hairstyle—was devised as a hybrid between Japanese tradition and the current European models.

Western-style clothing was, however, exclusively for use at work or at public functions. The Japanese elite reverted to their kimonos in their domestic lives. The reason for this was partly simple practicality. Western clothing, cut tight to the shape of the body, required chairs and tables if it was to be worn with any comfort at all. Such furniture was duly introduced to Japanese offices, but at home the Japanese still sat on the floor, necessarily in their looser garments.

The shift to Western clothing for women never affected more than a small minority of the population and did not prove durable. By the 1890s, a nationalist reaction had begun, calling for modernization without Westernization. Japanese women of the elite reverted to the kimonos that women of the lower orders had never abandoned. Men of the official and business classes, however, continued to wear Western-style suits and military uniforms.

Japanese maple has been bred in Japan for hundreds of years, and maple viewing remains a popular pastime

sokuhatsu hairstyle was a combination of Japanese and European looks

high-buttoned Victorian shoe styles were impractical for use around the home

accessories, such as umbrellas, were more commonly adopted than full Western dress

imperial chrysanthemum crest

Meiji Emperor

Rising Sun flag

the Emperor loved horses and horseback riding

traditional samurai swords were banned from military use in 1876

Military review
In this woodblock triptych, Toyohara Chikanobu shows the Meiji Emperor (in the center panel) reviewing his army. The new Japanese military uniforms of the post-samurai era were modeled on those of France and Prussia. The structure of the army also imitated contemporary Europe, with a mass of conscripts serving under a professionally trained corps of officers.

bustle was suited to Western furniture, not traditional tatami mats

bonnet could be worn over modern hairstyles

synthetic Western dyes allowed artists and dressmakers to produce colors such as red and purple more easily

Western-style short hair and mustache

promenade gardens were designed for strolling

modern military uniform

Noble Ladies triptych
Working in the traditional medium of the color woodblock print, Toyohara Chikanobu presents an updated image of the Japanese social elite at leisure. Such images promoted the Europeanized styles favored in the Meiji era. Changes went beyond clothing. Men learned to cut their hair short and grow mustaches and beards. Women ceased to blacken their teeth.

"We expect and intend to **reform** and **improve...** to stand upon a similar footing with the most **enlightened nations...**"

Emperor Meiji, Letter to US President Ulysses S. Grant, 1871

UNREST IN LATE IMPERIAL CHINA

The late Qing dynasty period was marked by national humiliation, breakdown, and upheaval, with the empire suffering defeat in wars and facing mass rebellions from within. The imperial regime adopted elements of Western technology and military organization, but attempted reforms failed to prevent foreign invasions.

Manchu character   Chinese character

Source of unrest
This Qing coin has Manchu script on one side and Chinese on the other. The Qing dynasty's alien Manchu (see p.236) origins drew the anger of Chinese nationalists.

Symbol of royal might ▽
Created in the 18th century, the gardens of the Summer Palace, Beijing, displayed the wealth and tastes of imperial China at its height. Yet, in 1860 the Chinese were unable to prevent the palace from being ransacked by Anglo-French soldiers.

Some of the pressures threatening imperial rule in 19th-century China were domestic. Agricultural production could not meet the needs of an expanding population. Mass emigration provided a partial solution, creating a diaspora of Chinese communities in Southeast Asia and North America. But at home, poverty and malnutrition increased, fueling discontent with inequality and government corruption. Four major rebellions shook the country in the course of the century. The largest, the Taiping Uprising, cost 20 million lives

before it was suppressed in 1864. But internal upheaval was inseparable from the issue of Western influence.

DESTRUCTIVE INFLUENCES

In 1800, China was still able to keep European and American traders under strict control, treating foreign powers as humble petitioners. But in 1839, an attempt to stop the spread of opium addiction led to a war with Britain, whose merchants ran the opium trade. China was defeated and forced to cede Hong Kong, admit Christian missionaries, and concede to British

demands for free trade. This opened the previously firmly closed floodgates to outside influence. Despite efforts to modernize its forces, China was unable to resist foreign demands. Beijing was twice occupied by European forces—in 1860 and 1900—and some areas of the country came under foreign control. Moreover, Confucianism was undermined by the teachings of Christian missionaries and by the influence of different forms of Western social and political organization. The imperial decline led to the abdication of China's last emperor in 1912.

BATTLE AND CONFLICT

In encounters with European forces from the 1830s, the Chinese Empire discovered the shortcomings of its military equipment and organization. The imperial regime made strenuous efforts to modernize its forces throughout the 19th century, creating state arsenals to manufacture modern weaponry. However, it was defeated consistently by foreign powers.

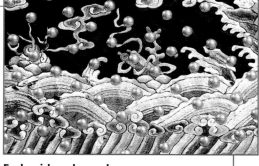

Embroidered panel
Made of blue silk, each panel features trailing clouds above crashing waves and stripe motif. The decoration includes round and diamond-shaped brass studs.

single-shot bolt mechanism

adjustable rear sight

Jingal
This long-range rifle, or wall gun, was manufactured around the time of the Boxer Rebellion. At more than 7 ft (2.1 m) long, it had to be fired from a stand.

embossed gilded panel on scabbard

ivory grip

blade decorated with silver inlay

Sword
The double-edged sword, of a traditional Chinese design, was still being produced in the 19th century. By then, swords had a limited role in warfare. The rich decoration on its scabbard suggests this sword belonged to a senior officer.

Guardsman's uniform
Imperial guardsmen protected the Forbidden City, the emperor's residence in Beijing. This satin ceremonial uniform comprises a tunic, skirt, two sleeves, shoulder cape, and underarm protectors.

POLITICS AND POWER

The Qing emperors ruled through a council of state and regional governors-general. Candidates for high office took exams on Confucian classics—exams that had been in place since the Han dynasty—and palace eunuchs played a prominent role in court life. Dowager Empress Cixi, ruling as regent from 1861 to 1908, resisted social and political reforms.

large bead, known as Buddha head

subsidiary string of ten beads

Court necklace
High-ranking officials wore jewelry, such as this ivory necklace, at the imperial court in the last years of the empire. Court dress was strictly regulated to indicate hierarchical status.

design based on Buddhist rosary

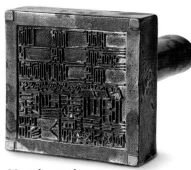

Manchu seal
This seal from the late Qing period is in Manchu, the native language of the Qing rulers. Seals authenticated documents and administrative orders.

woven brocade with embroidery and handwritten script

Official mandate
Documents such as this one were commonly used to confer titles, promotions, or appointments to office.

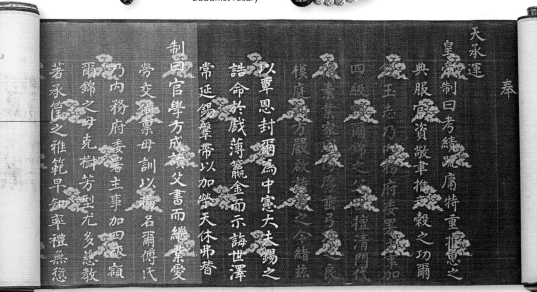

CLOTHING AND ADORNMENT

The late 18th and 19th centuries were not a time of radical change in Chinese dress, and conservative resistance to Western influence prevailed in the early 20th century. For men, a shaven forehead and ponytail, or queue, continued to symbolize acceptance of Manchu rule. Wealthy women wore sumptuous brocades and velvets embroidered with exquisite patterns.

Comb
This 19th-century comb is from the Muslim Khotan area of western China, where the population was chiefly Uyghur, with a distinctively central Asian style of dress.

flap with fringe and fur trim

enamel inlay

Nail protector
High-status Chinese grew some of their fingernails very long to show that they did not need to work. Decorative protectors were often worn over these nails.

coral decoration

green silk with colored embroidery

made from silver and copper alloy

Phoenix brooch
The *fenghuang*, or phoenix, is a symbol of female power and virtue. It was used to symbolize the empress.

gilt metal threads

delicate embroidery

Opera robe
Beijing opera, combining music, dance, and acrobatics, flourished as an art form in late Qing China. This female warrior's robe is typical of the opera's colorful costumes.

Shoes for bound feet
The feet of young Chinese girls were bound to constrict growth. Adult women wore elaborately decorated shoes to show off the resulting tiny feet, considered to be a mark of beauty.

TRADE

Until the 1830s, the Chinese severely restricted foreign imports. Foreigners had to pay for porcelain and tea with silver bullion. In opium, the British discovered a product for which there was a market. The Opium Wars in 1839–42 and 1856–60 forced China to open its ports to free trade, including the importation of opium.

valve

Water pipe
Tobacco was introduced to China in the 16th century. Under the Treaty of Tianjin of 1858, cigarettes could be imported free of duty. Water-pipe tobacco became fashionable in later Qing China.

removable tobacco holder with lid

water reservoir

globular "damper" bowl where moisture collects

scenes on ivory pipe show Daoist immortals

Opium pipe
Despite efforts to suppress it, opium addiction spread rapidly in China through the 19th century. It was fed by the importation trade from India operated by British merchants.

kylon, or lion-dog handle

molded lizard

mountainside scene with warriors

Porcelain vase
Europeans discovered the secret of making porcelain in the 18th century. However, Chinese porcelain was still highly valued. This vase was made in the 1850s for a British collector.

HOME LIFE

The Chinese of the late Qing period were the inheritors of a long tradition of domestic refinement and sophisticated pleasures. Chinese cities had several craft workshops where traditional skills were deployed for the manufacture of high-quality goods for the homes of the rich, as well as for exportation.

Snuff bottles

Taking snuff, or powdered tobacco, was common at all levels of Qing society. Finely decorated glass or lacquered snuff bottles such as these indicated the user's high social status.

decorative
lacquer
coating

painted
glass

Tea set

This porcelain bowl with lid and saucer dates from the late 19th century. It was used for drinking tea, and only the wealthy could afford such a tea set.

Enamel teapot

Tea consumption was a long-established feature of Chinese social and domestic life. This late Qing teapot from Beijing has a gilded rat on the lid.

cloisonné
enameling

▇ GAMES

Tangram set

The tangram is a puzzle game, using seven shapes, invented in China around 1100. It became a Western craze after a set was brought to America in 1816.

piece of puzzle with
carved phoenix pattern

lid of box carved
with houses and
gardens

Spillikins

The game of spillikins, or pick-up sticks, is believed to have originated in China. This 19th-century set has an elaborate ivory box to contain the bamboo sticks used in the game.

set of bamboo
spillikins

carved lid
screws shut

pattern of figures
in garden setting
carved in relief

Ivory chess set

China had its own type of chess, called *xiangqi*. European chess was only introduced there in the 1800s. This Chinese set, made around 1820, features British ruler George III as the king in the game.

finely carved
figure of King
George III as
emperor

KING GEORGE III **QUEEN CHARLOTTE** **BISHOP** **KNIGHT** **ROOK** **PAWN**

BELIEFS AND RITUALS

Confucianism was the official and dominant belief system of the Qing Empire. However, China had many Buddhist and Taoist temples and places of ancestor worship alongside shrines to Confucius. The Qing Empire also included a substantial Muslim minority, while Christian missionaries became an important and controversial influence in the country in the 19th century.

incense was
placed in
drawer in
lion's chest

Incense burner

This bronze lion from the late Qing era served as an incense burner. Statues of lions were erected at the gates of secular government buildings, private homes, as well as sacred buildings.

inscription
expressing
Buddhist
Middle Path

Monastery bell

This bell from the meditation hall of a Zen Buddhist monastery was made in 1898. It is decorated with Taoist symbols, a fusion of beliefs common in Qing China.

ASTRONOMICAL CLOCK

A British delegation headed by Lord Macartney traveled to the Imperial court at Beijing in 1793. In an attempt to interest China in opening its ports to free trade, Macartney offered Emperor Chien-lung a range of manufactured goods, including mechanical clocks. The emperor responded contemptuously, stating, "I set no value on strange and ingenious gadgets." Yet this astronomical clock, made in China at almost exactly the same moment, employed a mechanism that a Chinese clockmaker had copied

from a British design. It was made in Canton (now Guangzhou)—the port through which strictly controlled trade with British and other European merchants was exclusively conducted.

WESTERN INFLUENCE

The mechanical clock has been traced originally to China—a water-powered model was created by inventor Su Song in 1092. But over the centuries, Europe had gained a clear lead in mechanical devices such as clocks, as well as in astronomy. From the

mid-17th century, the Imperial Board of Astronomy in Beijing (see panel, right) had been placed under the control of European Jesuit missionaries, because of the accuracy of their observations and calculations.

This clock dates from a moment in Chinese history when the country had begun to absorb elements of Western technology and science in some areas, but was still proudly resistant to foreign influence and determined to defend traditional Chinese practices.

The precise calculation of the seasons through astronomical observation and measurement of time was essential to imperial rule in China. The emperor had to conduct certain rituals and ceremonies during the year to maintain celestial harmony. The Imperial Observatory in Beijing, keeping track of the movement of heavenly bodies, was a vital institution.

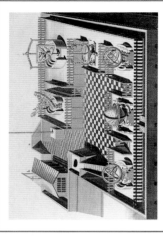

Chinese-made, British design
This astronomical clock was made in the late 18th century. Only two of its kind are known to exist, the other being in the Forbidden City in Beijing. The clock tracks the progress of the seasons and tells the time.

fixed outer brass ring is marked in minutes, quarter hours, and double hours

inner brass ring marks the seasons, completing one revolution in a year

face of clock charts stars seen from southern China

Milky Way is most prominent feature

stars, 850 in total, are indicated as small red circles

hour hand moves once around clock in 24 hours

carved wooden frame

stars are joined to form Chinese constellations

COLONIAL STRUGGLE IN SOUTHEAST ASIA

The progress of European imperialism in Southeast Asia challenged long-established societies, from Burma and Thailand to Vietnam and Java. Although they mounted determined resistance, local peoples could not prevent the European conquest.

The occupiers ▷
This painting by a local artist depicts Dutch colonial troops in an Indonesian landscape. In the 19th century, the Dutch fought a number of wars to subdue resistance to their takeover of Indonesia.

The societies of Southeast Asia, chiefly Muslim and Buddhist, had a long history of contact with Europeans. The Spanish colonized the Philippines from the 16th century, and the Dutch controlled parts of Java from the mid-17th century. The pace of European expansion quickened in the 19th century, driven partly by a need for raw materials for industry, including bauxite, rubber, and petroleum. The British founded Singapore as a trading post in 1819,

and went on to take effective control of the states of Malaya, while Burma was absorbed into British India.

The Dutch extended their hold over Java and neighboring Sumatra. From the 1860s, France, by stages, took over Indochina—Vietnam, Cambodia, and Laos. By 1900, Thailand was the only Southeast Asian state still independent. However, local elites continued to exercise a degree of power, and outside the Philippines the adoption of Christianity was rare.

BATTLE AND CONFLICT

The armies of Southeast Asia were influenced by Indian, Chinese, and Islamic military traditions, from martial arts to bladed weapons. In the 19th century, they were capable of sustained warfare against European forces—such as in the Java and Aceh Wars in Indonesia—but could not ultimately resist the superiority of European weaponry and organization.

handle carved into head of mythological eagle named Garuda

Mallay *kris*
Found throughout Southeast Asia, the *kris* is a form of dagger with a wavy blade and a decorative handle. It was considered to have magical powers, with some blades bringing good luck.

bone hilt

tang button visible at base

Curved dagger and sheath
This 18th-century dagger has sharpened edges, making it effective for slashing as well as stabbing. The sheath is made of leather and brass.

brass point (chape) with molded finial

Dha and scabbard
Used through much of Southeast Asia in the 19th century, the *dha* may have derived from the Chinese *dao*. This ornate ceremonial example is Burmese.

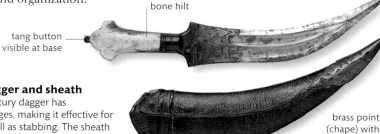

yellow gold scabbard mounting embossed and punched with decorative vines

curved sword with single-edged blade

BELIEFS AND RITUALS

Buddhism and Hinduism were the dominant faiths in Southeast Asia until challenged by the spread of Islam, which was in the ascendant in Java from the 15th century. Catholic missionaries ensured that the Spanish-ruled Philippines became predominantly Christian. In Indonesia, gamelan music was a central feature of most rituals, regardless of religious differences.

boarlike tusks

long, protruding tongue

Balinese mask
This mask represents Rangda, a demon in the mythology of Balinese Hinduism. Bali's dominant belief system combines elements of Buddhism and animism with Indian Hinduism.

Burmese Buddha
This gilded statue shows Buddha carrying an alms bowl. His long ears are a reminder that he was once a prince, with ears that were heavy with jewelry.

Gamelan

The Indonesian gamelan is an ensemble of predominantly percussion instruments—gongs, drums, metallophones, and xylophones—used to produce music that is highly complex in rhythm and melody. These gamelan instruments, part of a set, are from Java, where in the 19th-century gamelan music was played at the courts of Muslim princes and in religious ceremonies. A gamelan orchestra caused a sensation when it performed at the Paris Exposition in 1889.

GAMELAN ORCHESTRA ARRANGEMENT

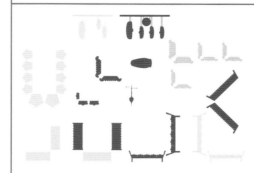

A gamelan orchestra has many instruments, including those shown below. This diagram shows the typical seating arrangement of an orchestra. The instruments pictured are colored red. The loudest are placed toward the rear and the quieter ones at the front. The drum player in the center leads the group.

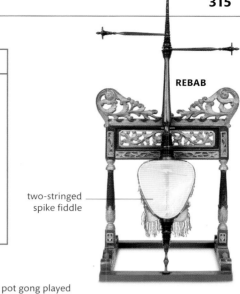

REBAB

two-stringed spike fiddle

decorated teakwood body

KENDHANG KETIPUNG

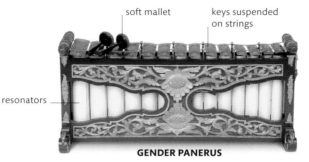

soft mallet

keys suspended on strings

resonators

GENDER PANERUS

pot gong played by one player to mark beats

KEMPYANG

KETHUK

set of pot gongs played by single player

BONANG BARUNG

hard mallet

bars used to play central melody

SARON BARUNG

horn-handled mallet

GAMBANG

wooden bars—unique feature among gamelan instruments

decorated with *nagas* (dragons) wearing crowns

flower and leaf pattern covered in gold leaf

three-piece teakwood stand

gong played to mark out structure of musical piece

GONG SUWUKAN AND GONG KEMPUL

PACIFIC EXPLORATION AND EXPANSION

The first explorers in the Pacific were ocean voyagers in outrigger canoes, who lived on the islands of Micronesia, Melanesia, and Polynesia between 1300 BCE and 1200 CE. The arrival of European sailors much later, especially from the later 18th century, posed a grave challenge to the islanders' traditional way of life.

Food hook
Carved from the tooth of a sperm whale, this hook was used to hang baskets of food to keep edibles away from rats.

Harbingers of change ▽
Captain Cook's ships *HMS Resolution* and *HMS Adventure* dropped anchor off Huahine in the Society Islands and in Tahiti during his second Pacific voyage of discovery (1771–75). The arrival of European vessels in Polynesia had many unfortunate consequences for the islanders.

Probably originating from Asia, the Oceanic peoples developed a diversity of societies and cultures on their far-flung island homes. Political organization was generally on a small scale, although some chiefs, such as the kings of Tonga and the Samoan Tui Manu'a, established control over substantial confederacies or empires.

The Polynesians first came into contact with European sailors in the 17th century. But it was not until the voyages of exploration by British Captain James Cook and French Admiral Louis-Antoine de Bougainville in the 1760s and 1770s, that links with the wider world began to affect the Polynesian way of life in a serious way.

COLONIZATION

The Europeans undermined the health and stability of Polynesian societies by trading firearms and alcohol, and by inadvertently introducing diseases that decimated the local populations. Missionaries arrived, dedicated to replacing traditional beliefs with Christianity. They were set on reforming established codes of dress and behavior. Competition between imperialist powers led to the sharing out of islands through the 19th century. Tahiti became a French protectorate in 1842, Fiji was declared a British colony in 1874, and Hawaii was annexed as a US territory in 1898. But traditional rulers sometimes retained considerable authority over internal affairs—in Tonga, the same royal line ruled from before a British protectorate was established in 1900 through to full independence in the post-imperial era.

BATTLE AND CONFLICT

Warfare played a big role in traditional Oceanic societies. Polynesian chiefs often led huge forces in attacks on neighboring groups, although weaponry was limited to clubs, daggers, and spears. The arrival of European muskets fueled armed conflicts between Polynesians in the 19th century. But acts of resistance against the Europeans were limited.

debossed shell etched with pieces of serrated ivory

Breastplate

Warriors of some Oceanic peoples wore breastplates as body armor. This one, made for a Fijian chief, is made from sections of sperm whale teeth and trochus shell.

geometrical motif

Polynesian weapon

This exquisitely decorated club or cleaver has been shaped to resemble the cutlasses that European sailors used to carry.

face of ancestral spirit

colored bark wrapping

Swords

These ornate models of swords are from the Melanesian region of the Pacific. They were made of wood, with carved sharks' teeth on the edges of the blade.

Painted shield

Painted wooden shields such as this one gave the warriors of the Sepik region of New Guinea both magical and practical protection.

BELIEFS AND RITUALS

Pacific Islanders traditionally believed in the pervasive influence of gods or spirits on every aspect of life. People or objects inhabited by positive supernatural forces had *mana*, or special powers, but such sacred people or objects might be *tabu* ("untouchable"). Rituals were designed to solicit the support of positive spirits and ward off mischievous ones.

four sharp prongs

Chief or priest's fork

A Fijian chief would have used this fork to eat with, since he was not allowed to feed himself on ritual occassions. His fork was untouchable by ordinary humans.

Mask

Men in New Ireland, off the coast of New Guinea, wore a painted malagan mask such as this one during ceremonies. The wearer took on the identity of the spirit that the mask represented.

CLOTHING AND ADORNMENT

Thoughout Oceania communities creatively used materials from their environment (feathers, plant fibres, bone, and shell) to decorate their bodies. Polynesian and Micronesian communities were renowned for tattooing their bodies, exploiting readily available natural materials such as shells and bone

Head ornament

Inhabitants of the Solomon Islands made fine head ornaments from turtle and mollusk shells. This one was worn over the forehead or the ears.

Tiki figure

In some Polynesian cultures, carved wooden or stone figures known as *tiki* were used to mark the boundaries of sacred sites. *Tiki* was an important character in Polynesian mythology.

carved wood with animal figures

painted bone

Nose clips

Warriors in the Solomon Islands traditionally pierced their nasal septum and wore objects in it. This helped to make a warrior look more fierce.

dog hair

Chest ornament

Captain James Cook brought back this ornament from his voyages to the Pacific. It was worn by a chief in the Society Islands.

SETTLERS IN AUSTRALIA AND NEW ZEALAND

Waitangi sheet damaged by both water and rodents

The first Aboriginals arrived in Australia 40,000–60,000 years ago. The peopling of New Zealand was more recent, the first Polynesian Maori probably arriving by sea around 1300 CE. In the 19th century, both Australia and New Zealand became flourishing British colonies, opening the door to extensive European settlement.

Historic agreement
The Treaty of Waitingi, drawn up between Britain and the Maori in 1840, made New Zealand a British colony but, at least in principle, guaranteed Maori land rights.

Sacred site ▽
Uluru, also known as Ayers Rock, is a natural feature in central Australia that is sacred to the Aboriginal Anangu people. When Europeans arrived in Australia, they ignored the Aboriginal people's deep-rooted relationship to the land.

European sailors had come across Australia and New Zealand in the 17th century, but it was not until 1770 that British explorer Captain James Cook, sailing along Australia's east coast, claimed it for Britain. The first European settlers were British convicts, deported to Botany Bay in New South Wales in 1788.

Free settlement began in the 19th century, especially after the discovery of gold in the 1850s, which brought with it a large influx of immigrants. No major European settlement occurred in New Zealand until 1839, but colonization gained momentum in the mid-19th century. The vast majority of early colonists, both in Australia and New Zealand, were from the British Isles.

A HOSTILE TAKEOVER

The Aboriginal population of Australia was unable to resist the British takeover and the distribution of land among settlers for sheep farming. By the end of the 19th century, newly introduced diseases, loss of vital resources, and localized violence had decimated the natives. Small numbers survived, living mostly on the margins of white Australian society. The Maori of New Zealand, on the other hand, adopted firearms and fought against colonization. Although ravaged by disease—as were the Aborigines—a series of conflicts and compromises eventually left the Maori in possession of some land and rights.

The Australian colonies and New Zealand grew into liberal democracies, forming self-governing states within the British Empire, but the treatment of their native populations remains a stigma on their histories.

BATTLE AND CONFLICT

Australian Aborigines were ill-equipped for warfare and only engaged in scattered skirmishes with European colonists. The Maori, however, had an aggressive warrior tradition. Obtaining European firearms, Maori tribes fought one another in the early 19th century and confronted the British army in a major rebellion in the 1860s.

Weapons from new materials
Australian Aborigines made use of materials introduced by the British colonists, fashioning weapons using their own traditional skills and techniques.

lancehead made of beer bottle glass

markings at ends may represent clan affiliations

Aboriginal banded shield
This shield is made of solid wood and was held by a handle at the back. It would have served to deflect throwing sticks or spears in skirmishes between rival hunting bands.

red ocher band over finely engraved design

arrowhead made from telegraph insulator

traditional *wahaika* club

markings and decorations often associated with Dreamtime myths

Aborigine club
Finely carved to a sharp angle, this weapon was used in close combat. It is decorated in red ocher and white pipe clay.

hooked edge to catch opponent's shield

made from mulga wood

Maori clubs
All Maori warriors learned to fight with clubs and spears in close-quarter conflicts. Although useful in tribal warfare, these weapons were ineffectual against modern European forces.

wooden *patu* club inlaid with haliotis shell

Hooked boomerang
Designed for curving flight, boomerangs were primarily meant for hunting, but they could also be used as weapons.

BELIEFS AND RITUALS

The beliefs of the Australian Aboriginals are centered around the "Dreamtime," a complex set of creation myths that give spiritual significance to animals, plants, and sacred places. The Polynesian culture of the Maori is similarly animist in its attitude to the natural world, attributing spiritual power to diverse animals and objects.

Maori *waka huia*
The *waka huia* is a decorated box hung from the ceiling of a Maori dwelling. It was used to house the prized tail feathers of the huia bird, a *tabu* (sacred) creature.

wood carved with stone chisel

Mourning armlet
Armlets made of tree bark were worn by Aboriginal women during dances of mourning for the dead and at the end of puberty rituals to mourn the transition of a child into adulthood.

Aboriginal painting
This painting on bark features a kangaroo. But its geometric elements have symbolic significance that may be known only to initiates.

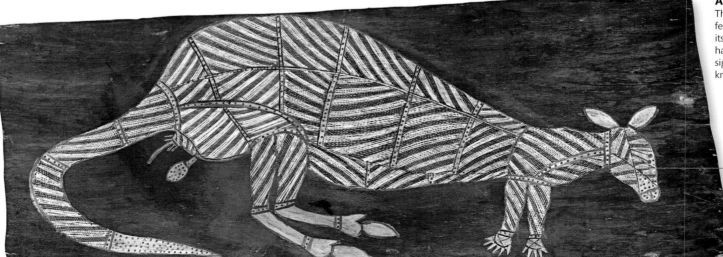

striped areas represent different clans

REVOLUTION IN LATIN AMERICA

In the 19th century, most of Central and South America—as well as Haiti in the Caribbean—achieved independence from colonial rule and slavery was abolished. But these victories left behind unsolved problems of political instability, social inequality, and economic exploitation.

The catalyst for change in the European colonies was upheaval in Europe itself. The French Revolution of 1789 triggered a slave uprising in France's West Indian colony of St. Domingue. The territory gained independence as Haiti in 1804, becoming the first black-ruled state in the Americas.

While Spain and Portugal were engulfed in the Peninsular War in Europe in 1807–08, their colonies in Central and South America were in tumult. The local elite creoles (ethnic Europeans born in the Americas) began a struggle for independence in the Spanish colonies. Simón Bolívar led the pro-independence forces in Colombia and Venezuela, and José de San Martín did the same in Argentina, Chile, and Peru. After tortuous and prolonged conflicts, all the Spanish colonies had become independent republics by 1826. Brazil split from Portugal peacefully in 1822 and appointed a scion of the Portuguese royal family as its emperor.

In Brazil and on the Caribbean islands, a large majority of the population was of African origin. Most were slaves working on plantations, producing crops such as sugar and coffee for European consumers. Although Britain outlawed trade in slaves in 1807, slavery continued in British West Indian colonies.

AN UNCERTAIN FUTURE

Slavery was abolished gradually and in a piecemeal way over the next 80 years, with Brazil being the last country to outlaw slavery, in 1888. After abolition, freed slaves often joined the lower strata of hierarchical societies in which poverty and inequality were made worse by unfair land redistribution.

In Latin America, independence did not lead to widespread prosperity or good government, merely to vacuums of power and economic inequality. Military dictatorships were common, as were wars and civil conflicts. However, there were areas of successful development—Argentina, for example, achieved rapid growth in the late 19th century, attracting a large influx of European settlers. Meanwhile, Brazil experienced a "rubber boom" from the 1880s. But development was entirely based on investment from Europe and North America, and was designed to serve the needs of the industrialized countries, not the local people.

Illustrated atlas
This atlas, in which the maps shown here appeared, was created by Mexican geographer Antonio García Cubas. He aimed to assert Mexican national identity and the country's place in the world through his creation.

chart showing gold and silver production

Mining map
Mexico was the world's leading source of silver and also mined gold, copper, and other metals. From the 1870s, US companies took over much of the Mexican mining sector, modernizing production techniques and rapidly expanding output at the expense of domestic ownership.

Miguel Hidalgo y Costilla, leader of War of Independence, alongside other heads of state and revolutionary heroes

Political map
Mexico was plagued by political instability and lawlessness. From 1876, Porfirio Díaz imposed a dictatorship that brought order and stability at the expense of freedom. While foreign investors were encouraged, hundreds of thousands of peasants were dispossessed of communal land by reforms.

> "A state too **expensive** in itself, or by virtue of its **dependencies,** ultimately **falls into decay.**"
>
> Simón Bolívar, military and political leader, *Letter from Jamaica*, 1815

built with foreign capital, transportation and communication facilities linked up productive cities, cutting off rural interior regions

Manzanillo, now Mexico's busiest port, opened the Pacific coast's first telegraph office in 1869

cross-section of railroad between Mexico City and Veracruz

railway-building in difficult terrain, such as Paso de la Mula, was a feat of British engineering

while urban life flourished, Mexican rural dwellers still lived in poverty and isolation

Transportation map

After gaining independence in the early 19th century, the countries of Central and South America suffered social and economic stagnation. This map, published in 1885, celebrates the belated takeoff of development in Mexico from the 1870s. Railroads, electric telegraph lines, and modern port facilities, built using British and American capital and expertise, tied Mexico into a rapidly expanding global economy.

TRADITION AND WAR IN NORTH AMERICA

Peace token
US governments gave medals to American Indian chiefs to encourage friendly relations. This medal was issued in 1801 under President Thomas Jefferson.

At the time of the founding of the United States, most of North America was occupied by Native peoples who sustained themselves by hunting, fishing, or farming. These American Indians reacted to the growing influx of European settlers in varied ways, from alliance to armed resistance.

By the waterfall ▷
Painted by American artist George Catlin in the 1840s, these American Indians are shown alongside the Horseshoe Falls at Table Rock, Ontario. It was a place of portage, where native traders and trappers carried their canoes on land around the Falls.

When Europeans arrived at the end of the 15th century, North America was occupied by hundreds of different tribes speaking many different languages, practicing distinctive cultural traditions. Their world was radically disrupted by the Europeans, who brought different ways of using the land and diseases such as smallpox. Introduction of the horse by the Spanish in the southwest transformed the Plains; people could travel longer distances to find bison, for their meat and hides and then transport them to trade centers. At the same time, European traders introduced firearms in the northeast, which soon became essential for hunting and defending territory. These changes brought increased warfare as tribes sought to protect their traditional lands or to gain access to trade resources. By the 18th century, the horse and gun frontiers met and overlapped, supporting new tribal ways of life.

During the colonial era, many tribes were able to negotiate successfully with the different foreign governments that needed them as trading allies. However, that all changed when the English defeated the French, followed by American independence from England. A powerful unified government was formed, interested in claiming land for white settlement. Although the sovereignty of Indian nations was legally acknowledged, most transfers were forced on tribes by this new government.

RESISTANCE AND REMOVAL

In the War of 1812, the Iroquois Confederation—the Cayuga, Mohawk, Oneida, Onondaga, and Seneca—joined together under a spiritual and political alliance to resist treaties forced upon them and forged a strategic alliance with the British. They were forced to remove to Canada following British defeat. The Shawnee Chief Tecumseh similarly sought to unite all Indian nations in the Midwest into a powerful confederacy. He was killed by American forces; the confederacy was smashed and those involved lost their lands.

Many European practices were blended into Indian cultural traditions especially by the Cherokee, Creek, Chickasaw, Choctaw, and Seminole, known as the Five Civilized Tribes. By the 1820s, the Cherokee had towns with two-story houses, a written language, a police force, a judiciary, and, from 1827, a written constitution. But this availed them nothing, as was the case with the armed resistance of the Creek and the Seminole. Under

the United States' Indian Removal Act of 1830, the Civilized Tribes were dispossessed of their lands. They were forcibly relocated in reservations far to the west, treading what was eloquently named "the Trail of Tears".

Conflicts arose with the Plains tribes, such as the Sioux, Cheyenne, Comanche, and Kiowa, as Americans pushed roads and railroads into the Great Plains. Despite notable victories, especially at Little Bighorn in 1876, these tribes were defeated by superior firepower and the destruction of the bison herds upon which they relied. Government agents continued to fear Indian resistance and forbid gatherings for ceremonies such as the Ghost Dance. When a group of Lakota gathered in 1890 for a dance at Wounded Knee, South Dakota, they were massacred.

The fate of the Canadian native peoples was less harsh than that of American Indians in the US. The tribes of the Pacific Northwest coast, such as the Haida and Tlingit, maintained effective independence through the 19th century, withstanding the effect of European diseases and pressure to adopt Christianity. Further north, the Inuit were protected to a large degree by geographical remoteness well into the 20th century.

"One does **not sell the land** people **walk on.**"
Crazy Horse, American Indian war leader, September 23, 1875

TRADE

Initially eager to acquire new goods and technologies, American Indians gained useful items such as manufactured cloth, glass beads, metal knives, and firearms through trade with Europeans. But, by the mid-19th century, reliable access to firearms and ammunition had become essential to defend tribal territory. Access to these new trade networks caused population movements and competition.

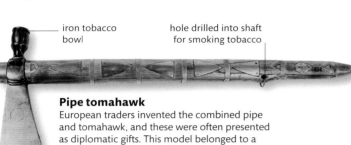

iron tobacco bowl

hole drilled into shaft for smoking tobacco

wampum means "white shell beads," but purple beads were of even higher value

animal hide fringing

Pipe tomahawk
European traders invented the combined pipe and tomahawk, and these were often presented as diplomatic gifts. This model belonged to a Miami chief.

Wampum belt
Crafted from pieces of shell, wampum became a valuable trade currency. Woven into a belt, like this Algonquin example, wampum could be used to mark a significant event or a transaction with Europeans.

Saddle bag
Saddle bags were part of the gear used by all the equestrian tribes. This example is from the Plateau, where people were strategically positioned to trade goods between the Great Plains and California.

gun rest

barrel

Flintlock rifle
The Inupiat people of Alaska obtained this musket through trade in the 1800s, demonstrating that European goods penetrated into even the remotest regions of the US.

powder horn

WARRIOR TRADITIONS

All American Indian tribes tried to defend a territory that allowed them to carry out their distinctive way of life. On the Great Plains, the warrior tradition was especially honored. All young men were expected to prove themselves in battle, raiding for horses, or by defending their own people.

bow string made of sinew

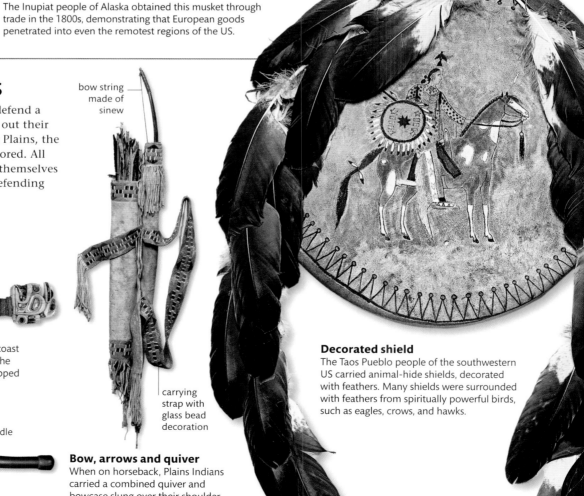

leather strap used to lash knife to wrist

Fighting knife
The Tlingit people of the Pacific Northwest coast learned to make metal-bladed knives from the Europeans. The handle of this example is topped with a totemic ivory carving.

stone blade

"rabbit's hind leg" design

handle

Stone-bladed war club
War clubs continued to be carried as an honored symbol of leadership even after they were no longer used in battle.

carrying strap with glass bead decoration

Bow, arrows and quiver
When on horseback, Plains Indians carried a combined quiver and bowcase slung over their shoulder. Some bows were made of wood backed with sinew. Arrows were tipped with stone or metal.

Decorated shield
The Taos Pueblo people of the southwestern US carried animal-hide shields, decorated with feathers. Many shields were surrounded with feathers from spiritually powerful birds, such as eagles, crows, and hawks.

eagle feathers typical of war shields

Lakota Sioux war bonnet

Warriors of the Sioux tribes of the Great Plains wore eagle-feather bonnets. The feathers represented brave battle deeds performed by the man who wore the bonnet or the people he led. The Lakota Sioux were among the tribes that defeated General George Custer and the US 7th Cavalry at the Battle of the Little Bighorn in 1876.

headdress made of 22 eagle feathers, finished with red down

tufts made of horsehair, attached to feathers with white clay

tail made of 35 eagle feathers

red woolen stroud cloth

each feather records a brave deed in battle

Forehead band

The blue-and-white glass beads used to make this band were obtained from European traders. The red woolen cloth is called "stroud," after its original place of manufacture in Gloucestershire, England.

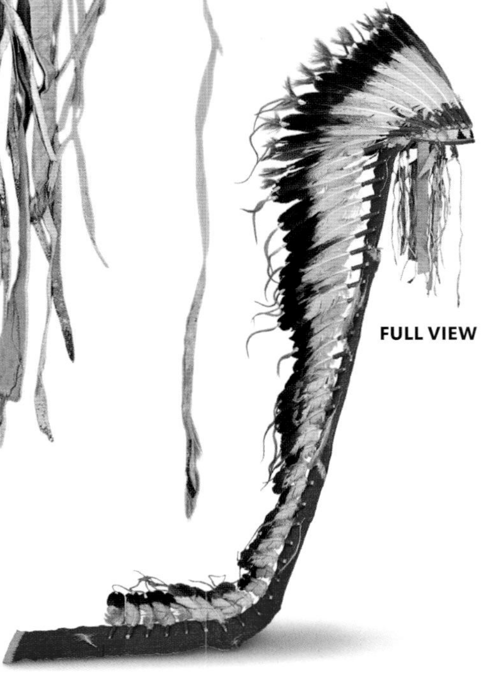

ribbons and buckskin thongs

FULL VIEW

CLOTHING AND ADORNMENT

American Indians made skillful use of available natural materials to create clothing that was both practical and decorative. Animal skins, such as deer hide, were the basis for most attire. For decoration, other animal products, such as porcupine quills and horse or moose hair, were often used, along with glass beads supplied by European traders.

QUILLWORK MOTIF

buckskin

decorative shoulder fringe

glass beading on sleeve

dyed horsehair

Chief's leggings
These leggings were worn by a chief of the Mandan people on the Missouri River around 1830. The stripes represent his various achievements.

Penobscot jacket
The Penobscot people of Maine in the northeastern US made this buckskin jacket, tailored in a European style. It is decorated with glass beads acquired through trade.

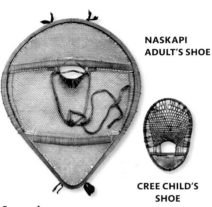

NASKAPI ADULT'S SHOE

CREE CHILD'S SHOE

Snowshoes
To help them travel during winter, American Indians in Canada made snowshoes, using a birchwood frame, rawhide netting, and moose skin.

Moccasins
Quilled with moose hair and made in Canada in the late 18th century, these moccasins are exquisite examples of American Indian craftwork.

colored moose hair

narrow slits allowing vision

Snow goggles
The Inuit of Baffin Island, northern Canada, made these wooden snow goggles. By reducing vision to narrow slits, they decreased glare and avoided temporary snow blindness.

BELIEFS AND RITUALS

American Indian tribes each had distinct spiritual beliefs. Their social life revolved around ceremonies and rituals designed to bring spiritual blessings. Spiritual leaders—priests, shamans, and healers—helped people gain access to spiritual assistance for health, hunting, and success in a wide range of activities.

Potlatch hat
The peoples of the Pacific Northwest coast held potlatches, in which accumulated goods were ceremonially distributed to guests. Each ring on this hat denotes a potlatch hosted by the wearer.

ermine pelt decoration

family crest

woven strands of spruce roots

Decorated skull
This buffalo skull was used by the Blackfeet in their Sun Dance. The ceremony was performed to bring blessings to the people through fasting prayer, and sacrifice.

eye and nose cavities were stuffed with grass and sage

real horsehair mane

backward slanting ears show fear and pain

red paint signifies blood seeping from wounds

blood runs from mouth in form of red horsehair

HOME LIFE

Gender roles were strictly organized in the life of American Indians. In most societies, women gathered berries and planted crops, cooked and preserved food, erected dwellings, and made clothes. Men mostly hunted and fished and defended their land. They also played a leading role in the rituals and ceremonies considered essential to the tribe's well-being.

Birch bark knife
The Penobscot people employed this knife for cutting the bark of birch trees into sheets to make tents and canoes.

specialized blade to create two-tone patterns in birch bark

Pestle and mortar
Iroquois women prepared corn kernels by shelling, boiling, washing, and drying them. They would then turn the kernels into meal by laboriously pounding them with a mortar and pestle.

wooden pestle

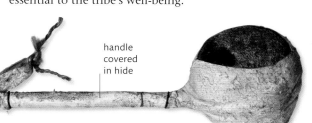

handle covered in hide

Pemmican hammer
The Hidatsa of North Dakota used a stone-headed tool to pound dried bison meat to a powder. Mixed with fat and berries, this formed a compact, high-protein food called pemmican.

side barbs to grip fish

central barb to stab fish

Fishing spear
The Micmac people of Nova Scotia made this spear to fish from canoes on lakes and rivers. They often fished at night, using torches to draw the fish to the surface.

mortar made from hollowed tree trunk

Stickball stick
Many American Indian peoples played a ball game called stickball. Northern tribes used one stick (modern lacrosse is derived from this version), while southern tribes used two, with a stick held in each hand.

hide lash held ends together

heavily woven webbing shows intricate style

Ceremonial smoking pipe
Smoking tobacco formed part of many religious ceremonies, in which it was associated with prayer. This pipe belonged to the Kaskaskia people of the Great Lakes region.

elongated pipestem

pipe with extension for attaching pipestem

elk bone with abalone inlay

small frog

Soul catchers
In ceremonies to restore health, shamans used soul catchers to capture a lost soul and return it to the sick person's body. These soul catchers belonged to the Tsimshian people.

raven head

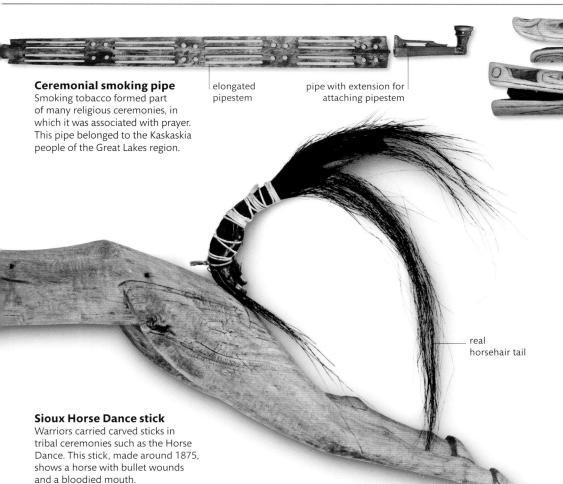

real horsehair tail

Sioux Horse Dance stick
Warriors carried carved sticks in tribal ceremonies such as the Horse Dance. This stick, made around 1875, shows a horse with bullet wounds and a bloodied mouth.

lower parts depict marriage allegiances and other important family events

Haida totem pole
The peoples of the Pacific Northwest coast, such as the Haida, sculpted totem poles out of tree trunks. The figure of Raven is seen as both the Great Creator and a rascal.

THE BIRTH OF THE UNITED STATES

Born of an uprising against British rule in 1776, the United States was a bold political experiment, a new kind of state embodying the principles of individual rights and democracy—although at first exclusively for white people. In the first century of its existence, the country experienced enormous growth in territory and population, transforming itself into the world's largest industrial power.

Symbol of protest
This tea chest was one of those thrown into the harbor by Americans protesting against the iniquities of British rule at the historic Boston Tea Party in 1773.

Bird's-eye view ▷
Made in 1874, this view of Chicago shows a town that had grown out of the prairie in 30 years to become the second largest city in the United States. The rate of expansion of the American population and economy in the 19th century was unprecedented.

North America was an arena of conflict between British and French colonialism in the mid-18th century. The British victory in the French and Indian War of 1754–63 settled this issue in Britain's favor, but disagreements between Britain and its 13 North American colonies mounted in the aftermath of the war. Colonists disputing the right of the British Parliament to impose taxes and duties on them staged rebellious acts that provoked a repressive response. Escalating conflict led the colonists to unite in declaring independence in 1776 and, with French help, they defeated British efforts to suppress the rebellion. Most colonists who had remained loyal to Britain left the country, many moving to Canada, which remained in British hands.

IN THE BEGINNING

The new US had an initial population of around 4 million, similar in size to the population of Ireland at that time. They were farmers, merchants, lawyers, seafarers, and black slaves. American society differed from that of contemporary Europe in having no mass of peasantry or formal aristocracy, as well as no monarch. This made it, in European eyes, singularly democratic long before voting rights were extended even to the entire white male population, which did not begin to happen until the 1820s. The country's reputation as a land of freedom and opportunity led to increasing immigration through the 19th century.

THE CIVIL WAR

The territorial expansion of the US more than matched its population growth. In the Louisiana Purchase of 1803, the US paid France $15 million for a vast swathe of territory from New Orleans to Montana. To the south, Florida was obtained from the Spanish, and Mexico was forced by war to cede large areas from Texas to California. Meanwhile, settlers pressed into the Midwest, with devastating effects on Native Americans.

By the mid-19th century, this territorial expansion, along with economic growth, had brought to the fore fundamental political and social divisions. While the northern states, in which slavery had been abolished, became a center of manufacturing, the cotton produced by slave labor in the South grew into a major export crop. Whereas the Founding Fathers of the US had imagined that slavery would fade away, it in fact expanded rapidly through the first half of the 19th century. In 1861, a block of southern states seceded from the Union, precipitating a Civil War. The Union victory in 1865 ensured that the country remained united. Slavery was ended nationwide.

AFTER THE WAR

The war was followed by a burst of economic growth that radically changed the nature of the US. Cities such as New York and Cincinnati were largely peopled with immigrants from non-English-speaking countries. Their poverty contrasted with the fortunes of industrialists and railroad builders. Industry and agriculture flourished everywhere except in the depressed South. By 1900, the US was the largest industrial producer in the world, with a population of 76 million.

"The whole continent of **North America** appears... destined... to be **peopled by one nation.**"

John Quincy Adams, who later became the 6th US President, in a letter to John Adams, August 31, 1811

EXPLORATION, TRADE, AND TRANSPORT

The opening up of the American West, comprising regions west of the Mississippi, began in 1803, when President Thomas Jefferson ordered a military expedition, led by Meriwether Lewis and William Clark, to cross the continent to the Pacific coast. Soon after, cheap land and gold drew increasing numbers of migrants westward. By the end of the 1860s, the railway and the telegraph had established rapid coast-to-coast communications.

Fremont stamp
Known as the Pathfinder, explorer John Charles Frémont led four expeditions across the American West between 1842 and 1848. This commemorative stamp was issued in 1898.

compass encased in mahogany box

Compass and carrying case
This pocket compass was used by army officers Lewis and Clark on their expedition from the Mississippi to the Pacific coast in 1804–06.

Propaganda poster
The government of California produced this poster in 1885 to draw immigrants to the state, promoting the availability of land and a pleasant climate as attractions.

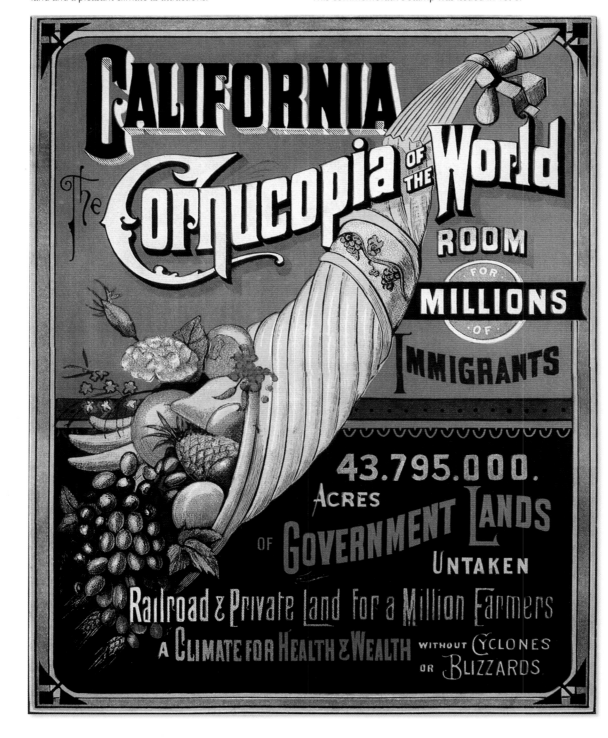

Pony Express envelope
Between April 1860 and October 1861, Pony Express riders carried mail from the westernmost railhead at St. Joseph, Missouri, to Sacramento, California. They did so in 10 days, using several relay stations.

curved wagon bed prevented cargo from sliding on mountain slopes

Conestoga wagon
The heavy, horse-drawn Conestoga wagon was widely used in North America in the 18th and 19th centuries for transporting people and goods over long distances.

Californian gold
The discovery of this flake of gold at Sutter's Mill in 1848 triggered the famous California Gold Rush. The lure of gold drew 300,000 migrants to the previously undeveloped state.

FRONT   **BACK**

Gold coin
This 20-dollar coin was minted in 1849, after the discovery of gold in California. The US adopted the gold standard in 1873, thereby pegging the value of the dollar to its gold reserves.

Confederate note
During the Civil War, the Confederacy issued its own currency. The bills rapidly lost value and had to be printed in ever higher denominations, such as the 500-dollar note shown here.

engraved names of railway officers and directors

Golden Spike
This ceremonial spike was used to mark the completion of the first transcontinental railway in 1869, when lines from the east and west met at Promontory Summit, Utah.

POLITICS AND POWER

The Founding Fathers of the US expressed lofty principles of freedom and human rights, but the reality of American life included the enslavement of African Americans, the unbridled power of money, widespread lawlessness, and unscrupulous law enforcement agencies. Even though slavery was abolished in 1865, the ideal of equal rights was far from achieved.

cameo of a kneeling slave in chains

fine-grained, unglazed stoneware known as jasperware

Anti-slavery medallion
Designed by British abolitionist Josiah Wedgwood in 1787, this medallion was adopted as a symbol by the anti-slavery movement to abolish the slave trade, and later slavery itself.

■ SLAVERY AND ABOLITION

statement mentions that map was sold for the benefit of US Army's wounded soldiers

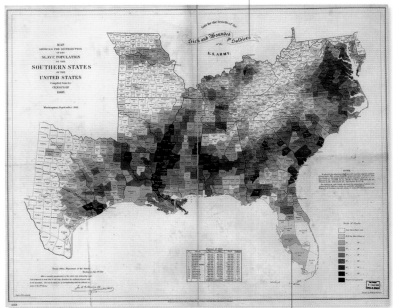

Distribution of slavery
This map, based on the 1860 census, shows the distribution of slaves in the Southern states. Cotton produced using slave labor in the South was the main export crop during the mid-19th century.

gray pattern indicates percentage of slaves in each state

Thirteenth Amendment
Passed by the US Congress on January 31, 1865, the Thirteenth Amendment to the Constitution abolished slavery within the US and in all territories under its jurisdiction.

Harper's Weekly cover
This image shows African-American males casting their votes in Virginia in 1867. This right, however, was soon widely denied in most Southern states.

■ LAW AND ORDER

Texas Ranger's badge
Founded as a self-defence force in 1823, the Texas Rangers became America's first state law-enforcement agency. It was ruthless towards American Indians and in combating outlaws.

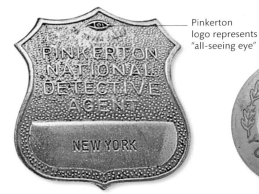

Pinkerton logo represents "all-seeing eye"

Agent's badge
Founded in 1852, the Pinkerton National Detective Agency was a formidable private organization that used unscrupulous methods to suppress bands of outlaws and break strike actions by labor unions.

Prison guard badge
Many prisons were built to reform criminals, including Arizona's Yuma Penitentiary. Prisoners were harshly treated, working in labor gangs or subjected to solitary confinement.

Preamble begins with "We the People," echoing Declaration of Independence, which spoke of "One People"

Article I describes structure and legislative powers of Congress

statement of what Constitution aims to achieve

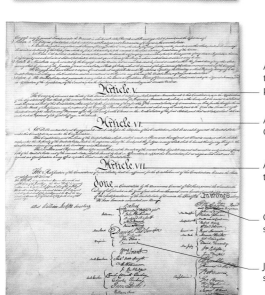

Article I, Section 8 establishes legislative powers of Congress but sets limits to its powers too

Article II refers to the President and other executive posts

Article III establishes Supreme Court as highest federal court in United States

Article IV concerns relationship between state and federal powers

Article V concerns amendments to Constitution, setting out process by which it may be altered

Article VI asserts precedence of Constitution over state laws

Article VII details necessary ratification to set proposed Constitution in action

George Washington's signature

James Madison's signature

Original Constitution
The original four-page draft of the Constitution was signed on September 17, 1787. Although it set out the political and legal arrangements for the United States, it did not define exactly who had the right to vote. Ten amendments were made to the Constitution in 1791 by the Bill of Rights, including the right to freedom of religion and speech, and the right to bear arms.

SUPREME LAW OF THE UNITED STATES

THE US CONSTITUTION

The founding of the United States of America began in 1776 through a revolt against British rule by 13 separate North American colonies (see p.328). As a necessity of the joint struggle against Britain, Articles of Confederation were agreed. These allowed the Congress that represented the former colonies to act in limited ways as a federal government. After independence was won in 1783, this makeshift arrangement remained in place. In practice, each state pursued its own interests under its own constitution.

BUILDING A GOVERNMENT

Provoked by the economic difficulties that followed the war for independence, Massachusetts faced an armed uprising called Shays' Rebellion in 1786. Although the rebellion was quelled, it impressed upon the wealthy elite who governed the states the importance of a strong central authority to resist popular revolts. In order to set up this authority, all states except Rhode Island sent delegates to a Constitutional Convention at Philadelphia in 1787.

Virginian statesman James Madison played a key role in the development of the Constitution. The process was contentious—many delegates were hostile to the idea of the loss of states' rights and a strong government. The larger states wanted representation in proportion to their populations, while the smaller ones desired equal representation. As a compromise, two houses, which together made up the Congress, were set up. A lower house, the House of Representatives, would have proportional representation, with each slave counting as three-fifths of a person. An upper house, the Senate, would have two representatives from each state. Under the Separation of Powers, the power of the executive (President) would be checked by the legislature (Congress) and the judiciary.

A NEW CONSTITUTION

The Convention came to an agreement on the Constitution in September 1787. But further concessions had to be made to quell fears of excessive government powers, including a proposal for amendments to the Constitution by a Bill of Rights. Finally ratified by 12 states, the Constitution came into force in March 1789, with Rhode Island reluctantly ratifying it the following year. Unanimously elected, George Washington became the first President of the United States in April 1789.

THE DECLARATION OF INDEPENDENCE

The Declaration of Independence, ratified on July 4, 1776, was written by the US statesman Thomas Jefferson. When setting out the reasons for the colonies' revolt against British rule, he wrote "all men are created equal" with the right to "Life, Liberty, and the pursuit of Happiness." He also stated that governments derive "their just powers from the consent of the governed."

BATTLE AND CONFLICT

The US was born in the War of Independence (1775–83), when its Continental Army, with the help of the French, defeated the British. In the Civil War of 1861–65, the Union forces of the North fought to prevent the secession of the Confederacy—the slave states of the South. This war, the bloodiest in US history, cost 600,000 lives.

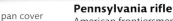

Brown Bess musket
In the American War of Independence, the flintlock musket was used as a standard weapon both by British infantry and George Washington's Continental Army.

pan cover

Pennsylvania rifle
American frontiersmen were expert marksmen with long-barrelled rifles such as this one. They were far more accurate than the muskets used by European and Continental armies.

gunpowder wrapped in paper

Paper cartridge
The Civil War infantryman's ammunition included a paper cartridge containing gunpowder and a lead bullet. The cartridge was rammed down the musket barrel using a ramrod.

hammer

lock plate

Spencer rifle
Breech-loaded repeating rifles firing metal cartridges were used in the Civil War by some Union forces, especially the cavalry. The breech is an internal chamber to the rear of the barrel. This rifle could fire seven rounds before being reloaded.

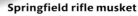

trigger guard and breech-operating lever

butt contains tubular magazine with rounds

bayonet mounting tube

retaining spring for barrel band

SPIKE BAYONET

Springfield rifle musket
The basic infantry weapon of the Civil War was a musket with a rifled barrel and a bayonet attached to the muzzle. Rifle muskets were superior to flintlock muskets in accuracy, range, and rate of fire.

bronze barrel

cardboard stabilizing fin

Solid shot
This 12-pound solid shot was the standard ammunition for the Napoleon cannon.

Ketchum grenade
These hand grenades were used by Union infantry when attacking Confederate trenches and fortifications. A percussion cap in the nose set off the main gunpowder charge.

wooden sabot with gunpowder charge

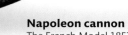

trail enabled gun to be towed

Napoleon cannon
The French Model 1857 gun-howitzer was the most widely used artillery piece in the Civil War. Known as the Napoleon cannon, it had a range of almost a mile.

forward
sling swivel

ramrod

leather grip
wrapped
in twisted
brass wire

Confederate sword
This sword belonged to a Confederate infantry officer. Often,
it would have been used as a symbol of rank or a tool to
command soldiers in battle, rather than as a weapon.

long, rifled
barrel

Union saber
Carried by Union cavalrymen in the Civil War,
sabers were of limited use on battlefields dominated
by heavy firepower. Cavalry most often fought
dismounted, firing a short rifle called a carbine.

curved,
single-edged
blade

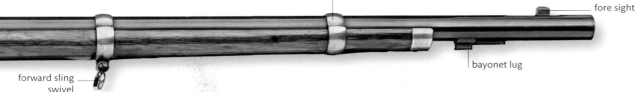

barrel band retains
barrel in stock

fore sight

bayonet lug

forward sling
swivel

upright
collar

braiding signifies
officer's rank

Civil War kepis
The kepi, a flat hat with
a visor, was issued to
officers in both Union
and Confederate armies
during the Civil War. The
wide-brimmed slouch
hat was also widely worn.

UNION OFFICER'S KEPI

CONFEDERATE OFFICER'S KEPI

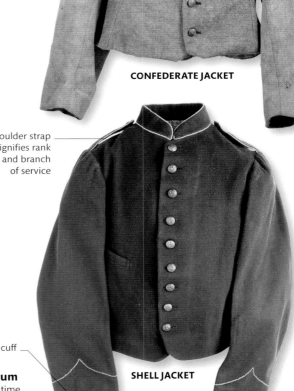

CONFEDERATE JACKET

wood shell

slider keeps
drum skin
taut

shoulder strap
signifies rank
and branch
of service

US national
symbol

French cuff

SHELL JACKET

Union army drum
As well as keeping time
on parades, drums were
used to convey orders on
the battlefield. Drummer
boys were the youngest
soldiers in the Civil War,
many under the age of 16.

Civil War jackets
The Union forces adopted blue uniforms,
efficiently manufactured in Northern factories,
while the homespun Confederate uniforms
were regulation gray or butternut in color.

stars sewn into blue background

indigo-dyed wool

space where one of original 15 stars, cut out and given away in 1800s, originally appeared

one of 37 patches used to repair flag at different times by different people

red stripes are made of wool dyed with madder, a plant pigment

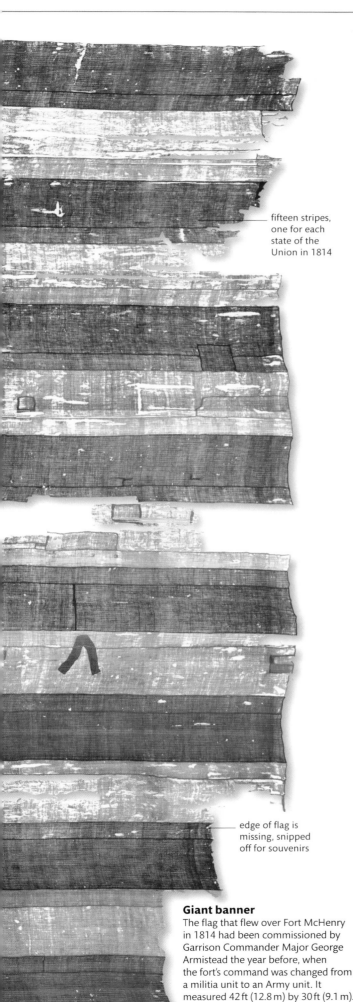

fifteen stripes, one for each state of the Union in 1814

edge of flag is missing, snipped off for souvenirs

Giant banner
The flag that flew over Fort McHenry in 1814 had been commissioned by Garrison Commander Major George Armistead the year before, when the fort's command was changed from a militia unit to an Army unit. It measured 42 ft (12.8 m) by 30 ft (9.1 m).

SYMBOL OF A NEW NATION

THE STAR-SPANGLED BANNER

The Stars and Stripes was adopted as the flag of the United States in 1777. Its original 13 stars and stripes—representing the colonies that had declared independence in 1776—were expanded to 15 each when Vermont and Kentucky became states in 1795. It was this version of the flag that became one of the most famous symbols of American patriotism in 1814.

A SECOND WAR

Between 1812 and 1815, the US fought a second war against Britain. The British, at war with France, had blockaded American trade and forced American sailors into British military service. Further motivated by the unsuccessful ambitions of some of the hawkish American politicians to take over British-held Canada by force, the US was moved to a declaration of war. The battle was fought on a small scale and had no practical consequences. In the end, both sides accepted a return to the prewar status quo. But the conflict played a vital role in confirming a sense of American national identity.

One of the key events of the war—the Battle of Baltimore—created not only a fresh sense of patriotism, but also inspiration for the country's national anthem. In 1814, the British sent a seaborne force to attack coastal America, landing at Washington in August. They burned down government buildings and moved on to attack the port of Baltimore. On September 13, Fort McHenry, defending the approach to the port, was bombarded by the Royal Navy. The solid shot, explosive shells, and Congreve rockets did only light damage to the recently fortified position and, after nightfall, British troops were ordered ashore. The following morning, the fort's garrison raised its largest flag to signal that the fort was still under American control. Unsure of the number of American soldiers defending the position, the British troops soon withdrew and the attack on Baltimore was abandoned.

THE BIRTH OF AN ANTHEM

The brief Battle of Baltimore was observed by American lawyer and poet Francis Scott Key. Inspired by the sight of the flag billowing over Fort McHenry, he jotted down the poem that later became known as "The Star-Spangled Banner." Set to music, it soon became a popular patriotic song, although it was not formally adopted as the US national anthem until 1931.

FLAGS OF THE CIVIL WAR

anchor added by owner to indicate his sea service

Old Glory
During the Civil War, a Stars and Stripes flag nicknamed "Old Glory" was hidden by its owner in rebel-held Nashville. He unfurled it to greet the Union troops in 1862.

Confederate flag
The Confederate's original "Stars and Bars" flag was easily confused with the Union's Stars and Stripes. They adopted this battle flag to make the distinction clear.

Colored troops' flag
African Americans fought on the Union side in the Civil War in segregated "colored" regiments. Flown by the 84th Regiment, this flag lists some of their battles.

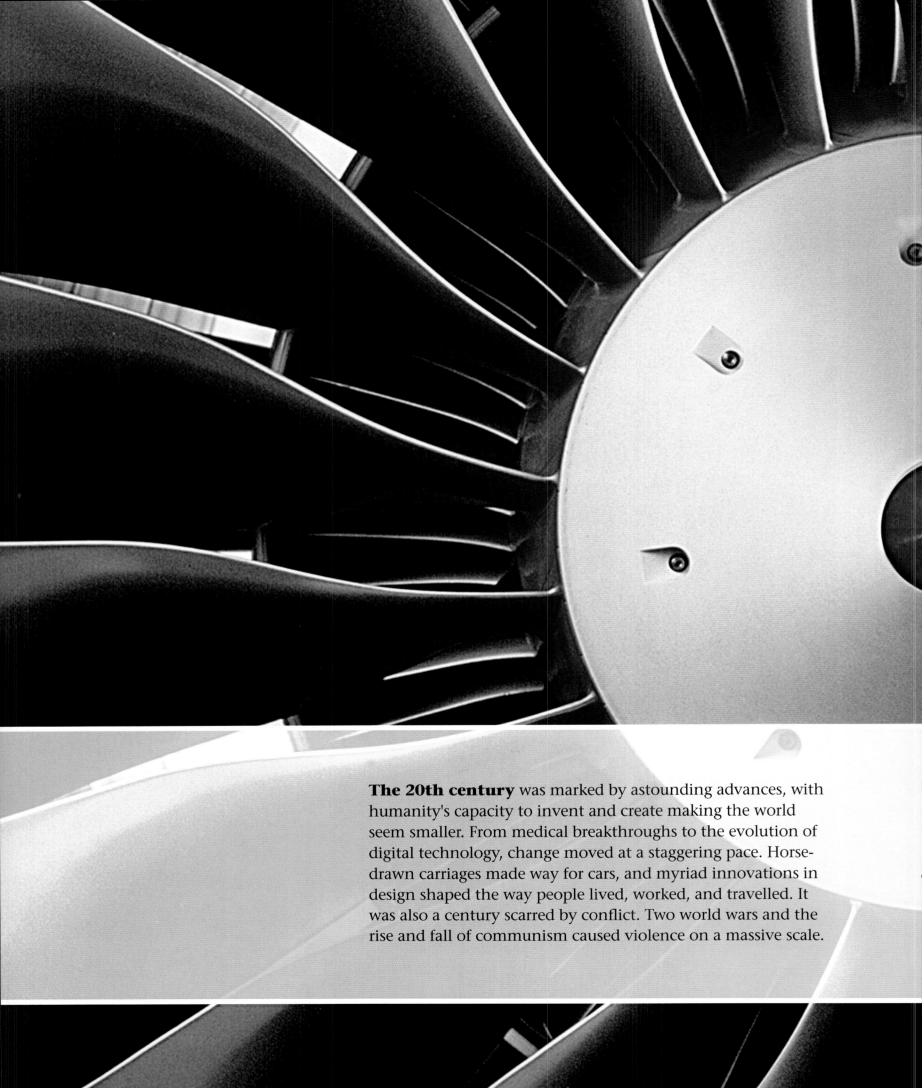

The 20th century was marked by astounding advances, with humanity's capacity to invent and create making the world seem smaller. From medical breakthroughs to the evolution of digital technology, change moved at a staggering pace. Horse-drawn carriages made way for cars, and myriad innovations in design shaped the way people lived, worked, and travelled. It was also a century scarred by conflict. Two world wars and the rise and fall of communism caused violence on a massive scale.

A SHRINKING WORLD

A CENTURY OF FLIGHT

From a faltering flight in 1903 to supersonic travel today, it has taken less than a hundred years for aircraft to transform our lives. Innovations in flight have radically changed the way we travel, explore, distribute goods, and wage war.

World tour ▷
When aircraft engines became lighter, more powerful, and reliable, it made possible the start of scheduled domestic and international flights. This 1949 poster advertised the Pan American Pacific Clipper's around-the-world flight.

The desire to fly is as old as civilization itself, but the challenge that faced engineers of the 20th century was to make a flying machine that could not only stay in the air but also be controlled. This finally happened when bicycle mechanics Wilbur and Orville Wright flew the first fixed-wing aircraft in 1903. Their breakthrough led to a plethora of planes being designed and built. Aircraft production boomed when it was

discovered that planes had uses other than recreation; they could be used as a weapon of war.

Other challenges preoccupied aviators. The Americans Charles Lindbergh and Amelia Earhart became national heroes when they crossed the Atlantic on solo flights. The fledgling airline industry took off, and aircraft were transformed from small biplanes to giant jet carriers, transporting millions of travelers all around the world.

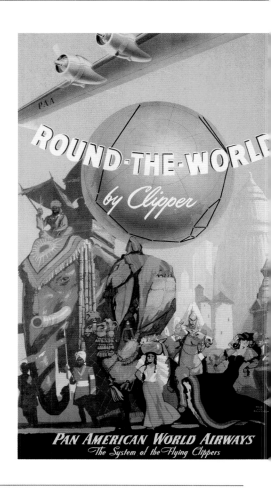

FIXED-WING AIRCRAFT

The history of flight is full of heroes who took spindly, crude, and underpowered craft and attempted to make their devices stay airborne. From gliders to boxed kites, the development of fixed-wing craft made manned flight a reality, using forward motion that generates lift as the wing moves through the air.

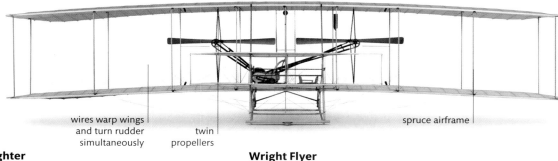

wires warp wings and turn rudder simultaneously

twin propellers

spruce airframe

Bristol F.2B Fighter
One of the most popular and versatile planes of WWI, the "Biff" was the first two-seater fighter plane used by the British Royal Flying Corps.

rear-mounted Lewis gun

fabric-covered fuselage

Wright Flyer
The first fixed-wing plane to be taken on a controlled flight, the Flyer made history on December 17, 1903, when it stayed airborne for 12 seconds at 120 ft (37 m).

exhaust pipe

LVG C.VI
Chiefly used as a reconnaissance and artillery spotting aircraft during WWI, the German C.VI continued in service as late as 1940 in Lithuania.

wooden fuselage

chimney-like exhaust

rudder controls direction of flight

bracing wires keep frame stiff

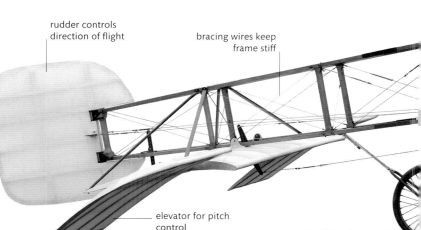

elevator for pitch control

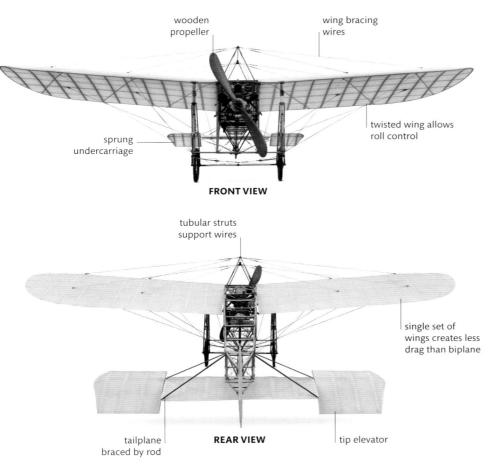

wooden propeller

wing bracing wires

sprung undercarriage

twisted wing allows roll control

FRONT VIEW

tubular struts support wires

single set of wings creates less drag than biplane

tailplane braced by rod

REAR VIEW

tip elevator

Walnut propeller
This smooth, laminated, two-blade propeller, 6½ ft (2 m) in diameter, was designed to withstand the Channel crossing without splitting.

Brass fuel tank
A small, barrel-like fuel tank was installed horizontally between the engine and the cockpit. In cramped conditions, it lay in front of the pilot's seat.

Rudder
Two foot pedals controlled the rudder, seen here. This new system helped solve the problem of controlling direction while airborne.

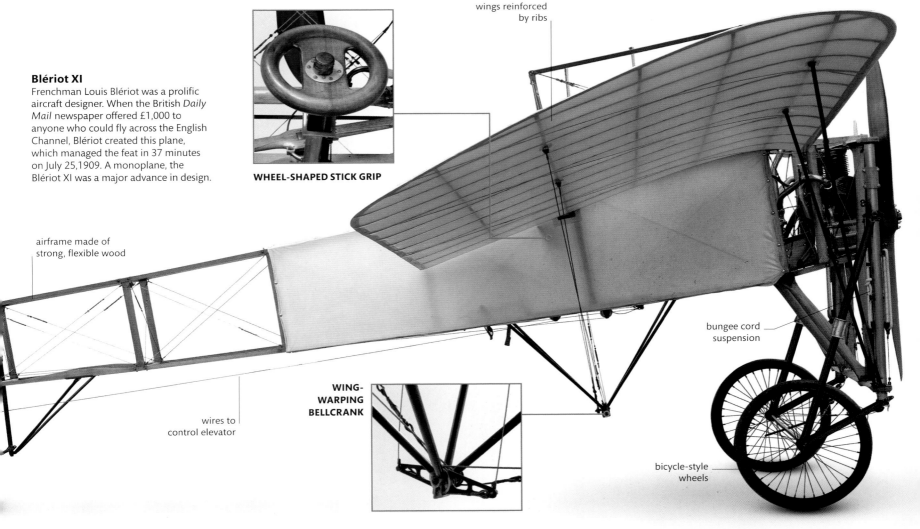

wings reinforced by ribs

Blériot XI
Frenchman Louis Blériot was a prolific aircraft designer. When the British *Daily Mail* newspaper offered £1,000 to anyone who could fly across the English Channel, Blériot created this plane, which managed the feat in 37 minutes on July 25,1909. A monoplane, the Blériot XI was a major advance in design.

WHEEL-SHAPED STICK GRIP

airframe made of strong, flexible wood

bungee cord suspension

wires to control elevator

WING-WARPING BELLCRANK

bicycle-style wheels

visible radial "Whirlwind" engine

wing-mounted engines

Spirit of St. Louis
The famous *Spirit of St. Louis*, a tiny monoplane, carried American aviator Charles Lindbergh from New York to Paris nonstop in 1927. The journey took 33.5 hours.

Dornier Do-X
A true giant, this was the largest flying boat when it was built in 1929, with 12 engines and three decks. It flew passengers in luxury on international flights before WWII.

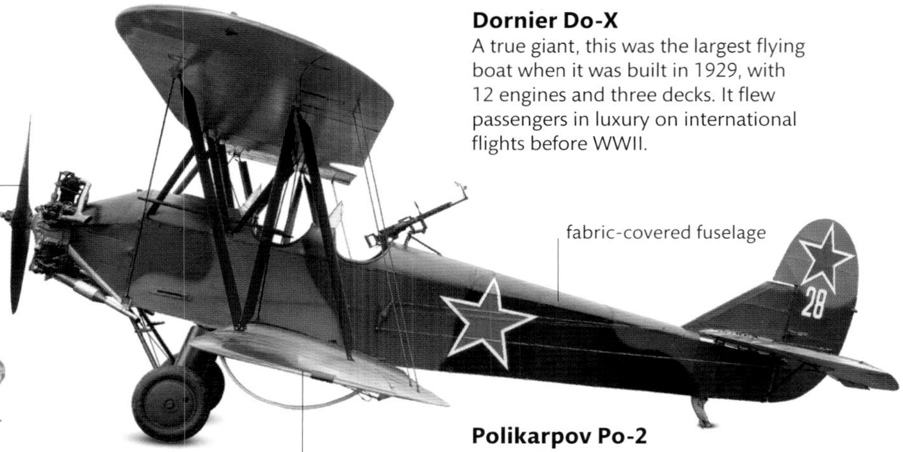

wooden two-blade propeller

fabric-covered fuselage

efficient wing section with powerful flaps

wing with rounded tip to improve altitude performance

Polikarpov Po-2
Originally designed as a trainer biplane in the 1920s, this Soviet utility aircraft soon had many uses in WWII, from light attacks and night raids, to dropping propaganda.

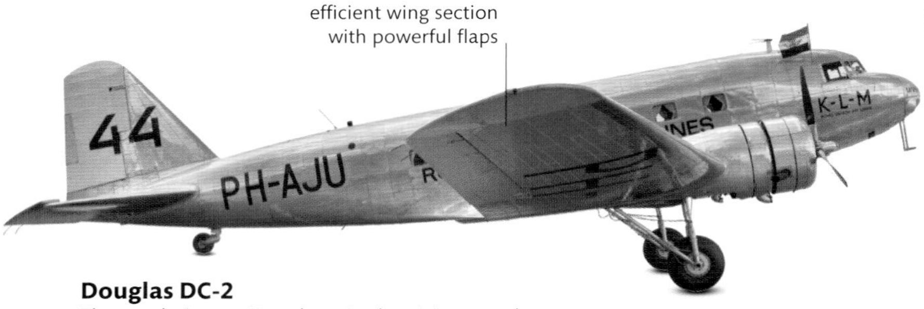

Douglas DC-2
The revolutionary Douglas raised cruising speeds, opening up new opportunities to "sell speed" in the 1930s. For the first time, commercial flights became possible.

Lockheed XC-35
In 1937, the first airplane specifically built with a pressurized cabin took to the air. Pressurization allows safe and comfortable travel, even at high altitudes.

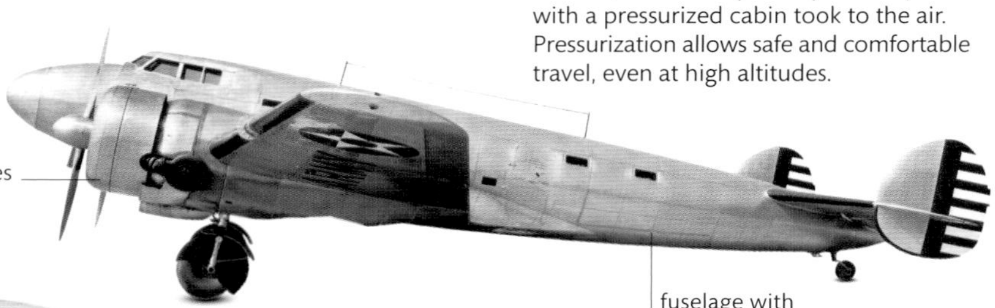

cockpit raised above main deck

twin engines

fuselage with circular cross section

nose cone

fuselage fabric over steel frame

tail braced by wires

nose gear has two wheels

Piper J3 Cub
Almost 20,000 units of this aircraft were produced during its 10-year run. Many of these were the L-4 "Grasshopper" military variant, used by the US for training during WWII.

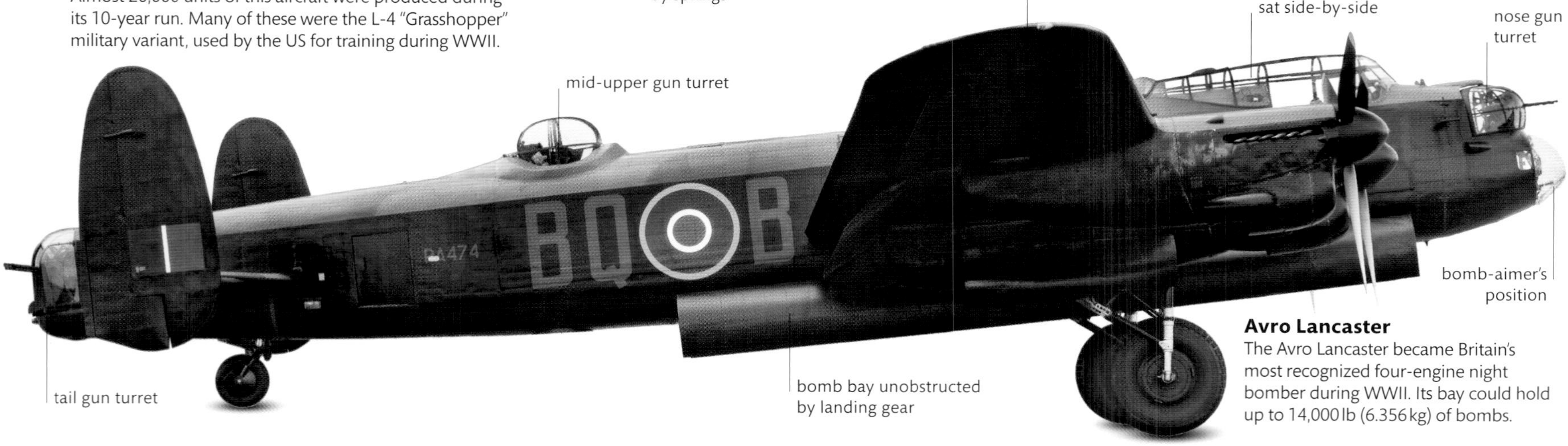

tail wheel steered by springs

all-metal construction

pilot and flight engineer sat side-by-side

nose gun turret

mid-upper gun turret

bomb-aimer's position

Avro Lancaster
The Avro Lancaster became Britain's most recognized four-engine night bomber during WWII. Its bay could hold up to 14,000 lb (6,356 kg) of bombs.

tail gun turret

bomb bay unobstructed by landing gear

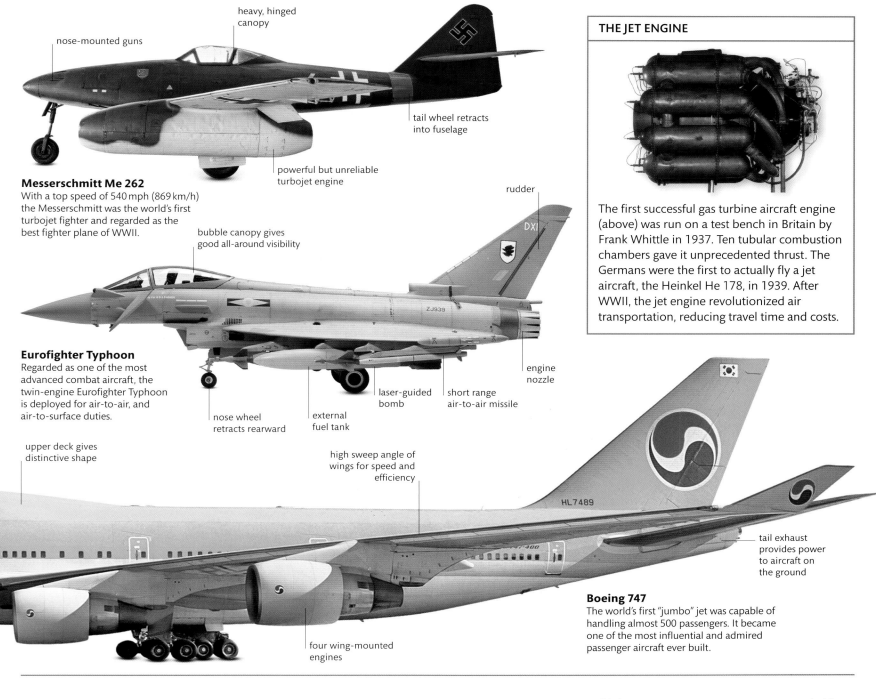

nose-mounted guns

heavy, hinged canopy

tail wheel retracts into fuselage

powerful but unreliable turbojet engine

Messerschmitt Me 262
With a top speed of 540 mph (869 km/h) the Messerschmitt was the world's first turbojet fighter and regarded as the best fighter plane of WWII.

bubble canopy gives good all-around visibility

rudder

Eurofighter Typhoon
Regarded as one of the most advanced combat aircraft, the twin-engine Eurofighter Typhoon is deployed for air-to-air, and air-to-surface duties.

nose wheel retracts rearward

external fuel tank

laser-guided bomb

short range air-to-air missile

engine nozzle

THE JET ENGINE

The first successful gas turbine aircraft engine (above) was run on a test bench in Britain by Frank Whittle in 1937. Ten tubular combustion chambers gave it unprecedented thrust. The Germans were the first to actually fly a jet aircraft, the Heinkel He 178, in 1939. After WWII, the jet engine revolutionized air transportation, reducing travel time and costs.

upper deck gives distinctive shape

high sweep angle of wings for speed and efficiency

tail exhaust provides power to aircraft on the ground

Boeing 747
The world's first "jumbo" jet was capable of handling almost 500 passengers. It became one of the most influential and admired passenger aircraft ever built.

four wing-mounted engines

HELICOPTERS

The first helicopter to raise itself in free flight was designed by Paul Cornu, a French bicycle dealer, in 1907. The establishment of the helicopter industry took off with Igor Sikorsky's development of the first practical single-rotor helicopter in 1938 in the US. It spawned hundreds of helicopter types, from tiny one-man carriers to fearsome war machines.

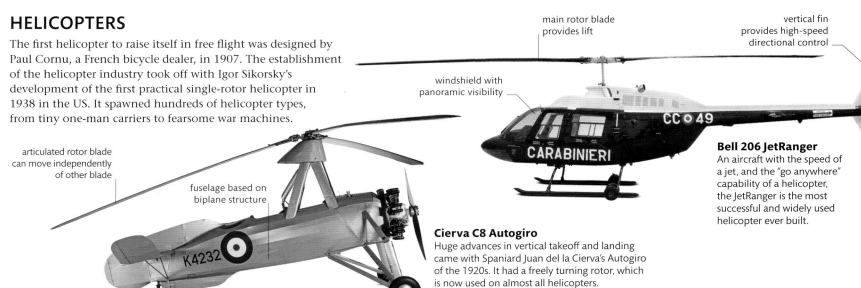

main rotor blade provides lift

vertical fin provides high-speed directional control

windshield with panoramic visibility

articulated rotor blade can move independently of other blade

fuselage based on biplane structure

Bell 206 JetRanger
An aircraft with the speed of a jet, and the "go anywhere" capability of a helicopter, the JetRanger is the most successful and widely used helicopter ever built.

Cierva C8 Autogiro
Huge advances in vertical takeoff and landing came with Spaniard Juan del la Cierva's Autogiro of the 1920s. It had a freely turning rotor, which is now used on almost all helicopters.

TRANSPORTATION FOR THE MASSES

Amazing advances in transportation took place during the 20th century. By the century's end, journeys took hours, not days, and mass travel became the norm. The evolution of automobiles and trains transformed society and everyday life.

Streamlined beauty ▷
This poster from 1941 showcases the Empire State Express, a long-haul, stainless-steel passenger train built in the Art Deco style. Powered by a huge steam engine, the train provided comfortable, affordable travel.

The invention of the internal combustion engine in the 19th century accelerated the pace of life in the 20th. At the turn of the 20th century, however, it was inconceivable that the average worker could afford to buy a car, let alone leave home to take a vacation.

This all changed with Henry Ford's groundbreaking introduction of the factory assembly line, which turned out cheaper, mass-produced vehicles. The car and the motorbike evolved together, giving people the freedom to travel when and where they wanted. Long-distance railroad lines reduced the time it took to cross entire continents. Journeys that previously took months were now completed in days. Holidays and days out at the seaside became a reality for many families. Steam engines were replaced with streamlined diesel passenger trains, and the electrification of the railroad system encouraged widespread travel.

The New **EMPIRE STATE EXPRESS**
NEW YORK CENTRAL SYSTEM

TRAINS

The train became a vibrant form of transport in the 20th century as a result of improvements to track and engines that revolutionized the railways. Although steam reigned supreme for many decades, electric and diesel trains became increasingly competitive rivals. When the first high-speed passenger service opened in Japan in 1964, it cut the journey time from Tokyo to Osaka from 6.5 to 4 hours. Today's high-speed trains are faster still and can even compete with air travel.

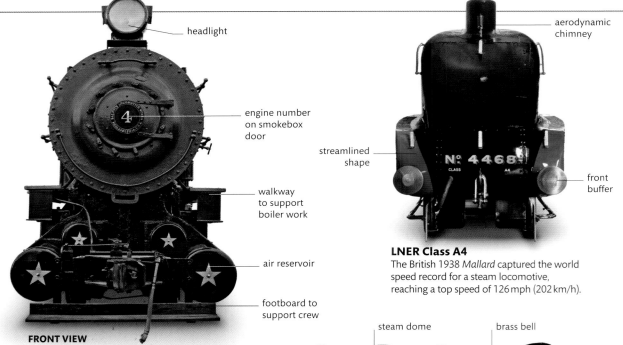

headlight

engine number on smokebox door

walkway to support boiler work

air reservoir

footboard to support crew

FRONT VIEW

aerodynamic chimney

streamlined shape

N° 4468
CLASS A4

front buffer

LNER Class A4
The British 1938 *Mallard* captured the world speed record for a steam locomotive, reaching a top speed of 126 mph (202 km/h).

VGN Class SA
Built for the Virginian Railroad in 1910, this massive steam locomotive was used for moving rail freight around, or "switching." It was retired in 1957.

light

SIDE VIEW

coal bunker

steam dome

brass bell

VIRGINIAN

MOTORCYCLES

From clumsy machines to sleek symbols of personal power, the motorcycle has evolved from a wooden bicycle fitted with a steam engine to a speedy sports vehicle. Used extensively by soldiers during wartime and by police officers now, motorcycles are regarded by many as one of the most exciting forms of transportation in the world.

single-cylinder engine

BAT 2½ HP
Made in 1904, this modified bicycle with an engine had a sprung saddle. It was used in competitive racing and set numerous records.

blackout light for night combat conditions

non-reflective, drab paint

Harley-Davidson WLC
This is one of over 90,000 Harley-Davidsons produced during WWII, spawning a postwar biker culture.

leg shield

side panel

spare wheel

Lambretta LD 150
This classic 1950s Italian scooter, the first to feature full sized leg-shields and protective side panels, became a youth fashion accessory.

traditional yet stylish fuel tank

four-cylinder engine

Honda CB750
The first Japanese superbike, this 1970 model boasted power, reliability, and performance. It was able to reach 125 mph (201 km/h).

adaptive system keeps headlight level as bike turns

heated seat

BMW K1600 GT
This modern bike has a powerful six-cylinder engine and is designed to carry two people in comfort on long-haul rides.

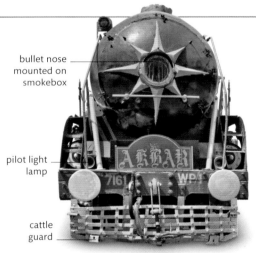

bullet nose mounted on smokebox

pilot light lamp

cattle guard

Indian Railways Class WP
After WWII, the WP became the standard Indian passenger locomotive. This engine was named *Akbar*, after the Mughal emperor.

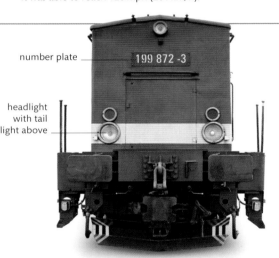

number plate

headlight with tail light above

Modified DR V100
The diesel-fuelled East German DR V100 was built as a passenger and goods train between 1966 and 1985. It was also exported to other Communist countries.

centrally positioned driver's seat

headlight with tail light below

FRONT VIEW

British Rail Class 395
The super-fast and stylish electric Javelin is Britain's fastest commuter train, with a 140 mph (225 km/h) top speed. It was designed by Japanese manufacturer Hitachi.

safety line warns crew of overhead power cables

automated sliding doors

SIDE VIEW

CARS

More than any other invention, the automobile has transformed everyday life. As inventors raced to make the first "road locomotive," German engineering was complemented by French flair and American enterprise. Innovation accelerated after WWII and the modern vehicle took shape. Cars now have more computing power than was needed to take man to the moon.

open driving compartment

Rolls-Royce Silver Ghost
One of the most famous cars of all time, the Silver Ghost was designed in 1906. With a top speed of 69 mph (110 km/h), it was silent and smooth.

wooden wheels with detachable rims

tiller steering

headlight

Benz Ideal
By 1900, when the Ideal was unveiled, Karl Benz was the world's leading car manufacturer. He had made the first successful car in 1885.

rear-wheel brakes only

Citroën Type A
Europe's first mass-produced car, the 1919 Type A was powered by a 1.3-liter four-cylinder engine with a three-speed gearbox. This French car was versatile and reliable.

extended nose

drum brakes on all four wheels

Alfa Romeo 6C 1750
The most famous Alfa Romeo model, the 1750 had separate road and racetrack versions. With a top speed of 68–106 mph (110–170 km/h) it easily outperfomed the competition in 1929.

gently curving roof

front-opening hood

full whitewall tires

long wheelbase

Lincoln-Zephyr
An American success story, the 1936 Zephyr had a sleek, streamlined body, starting a styling trend that would dominate the 1930s.

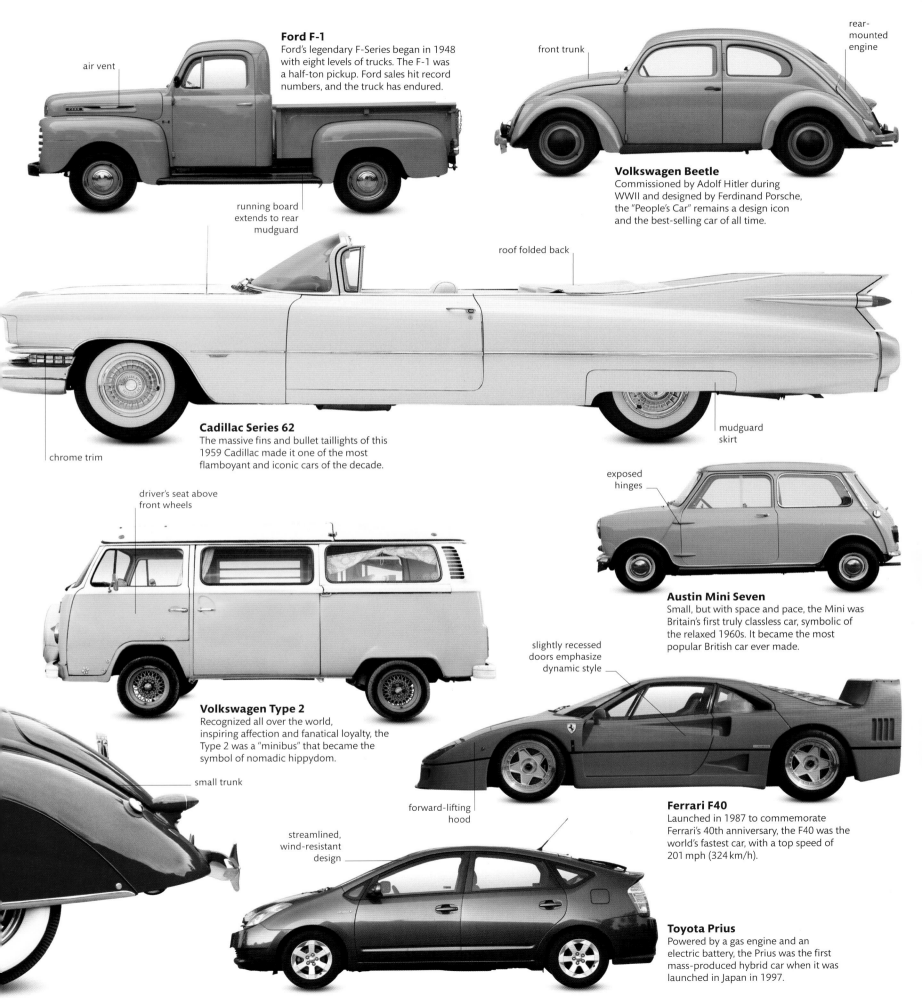

Ford F-1
Ford's legendary F-Series began in 1948 with eight levels of trucks. The F-1 was a half-ton pickup. Ford sales hit record numbers, and the truck has endured.

air vent

running board extends to rear mudguard

front trunk

rear-mounted engine

Volkswagen Beetle
Commissioned by Adolf Hitler during WWII and designed by Ferdinand Porsche, the "People's Car" remains a design icon and the best-selling car of all time.

roof folded back

Cadillac Series 62
The massive fins and bullet taillights of this 1959 Cadillac made it one of the most flamboyant and iconic cars of the decade.

chrome trim

mudguard skirt

driver's seat above front wheels

exposed hinges

Austin Mini Seven
Small, but with space and pace, the Mini was Britain's first truly classless car, symbolic of the relaxed 1960s. It became the most popular British car ever made.

slightly recessed doors emphasize dynamic style

Volkswagen Type 2
Recognized all over the world, inspiring affection and fanatical loyalty, the Type 2 was a "minibus" that became the symbol of nomadic hippydom.

small trunk

forward-lifting hood

Ferrari F40
Launched in 1987 to commemorate Ferrari's 40th anniversary, the F40 was the world's fastest car, with a top speed of 201 mph (324 km/h).

streamlined, wind-resistant design

Toyota Prius
Powered by a gas engine and an electric battery, the Prius was the first mass-produced hybrid car when it was launched in Japan in 1997.

Steering wheel

Placed on the left, this wooden steering wheel spearheaded the left-hand drive configuration. The spark and throttle levers were mounted on the steering column.

Speedometer

The speedometer was driven by a cog and a fragile cable, which often snapped. The speed restriction in 1910 was 10–12 mph (16–19 km/h) in most American towns.

Engine

The four-cylinder engine was simple and efficient. Cast in a single block, it was rated at 20 hp, giving a top speed of 45 mph (72 km/h).

Headlight

Made of brass, the headlights were fueled by acetylene gas created by a generator.

Tin Lizzie

In 1908, Henry Ford brought motoring to the masses with his Model T. He wanted a car that the average worker could afford—a car for all. Built using strong materials, raised high off the ground, and boasting three-point suspension, the Model T was able to endure the often unsurfaced, poor-quality roads of the time.

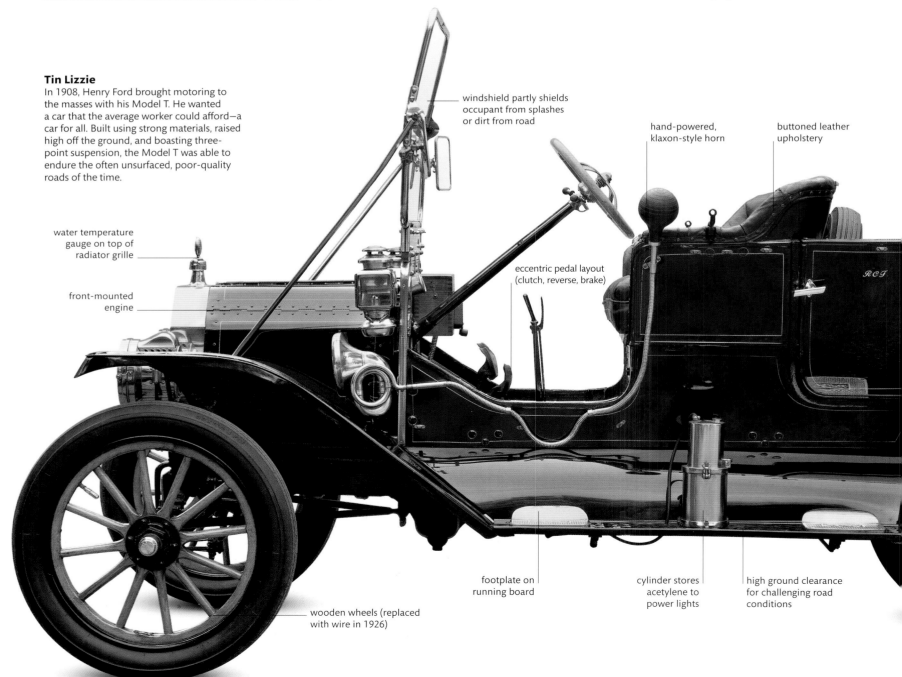

windshield partly shields occupant from splashes or dirt from road

hand-powered, klaxon-style horn

buttoned leather upholstery

water temperature gauge on top of radiator grille

front-mounted engine

eccentric pedal layout (clutch, reverse, brake)

footplate on running board

cylinder stores acetylene to power lights

high ground clearance for challenging road conditions

wooden wheels (replaced with wire in 1926)

brass-framed windshield

solid rubber tires

FRONT VIEW

adaptable chassis bends and twists

REAR VIEW

coils for ignition housed on dashboard

SIDE VIEW (CLOSED TOP)

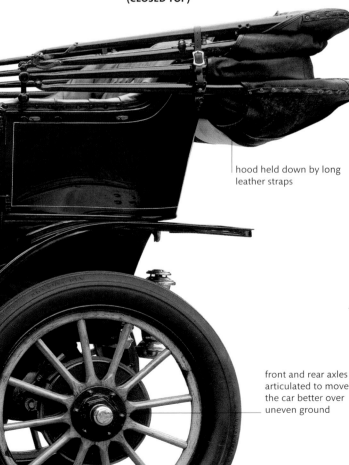

hood held down by long leather straps

front and rear axles articulated to move the car better over uneven ground

MASS PRODUCTION FOR THE AMERICAN ROADS

FORD MODEL T

The automobile industry got off to a slow start. Most of the parts of early vehicles were individually made by hand, and the motor manufacturers often bought parts from a host of different suppliers instead of making their own. Each example of a part was slightly different and fit the adjoining part only by chance. The customer could also specify bodywork. As a result, no two cars were the same and making them was laborious and expensive.

MASS PRODUCTION

A revolution in car manufacturing began in 1913, when American industrialist Henry Ford set up a plant in Highland Park, Michigan, to mass-produce his Model T Ford. The Model T "Tin Lizzie," introduced in 1908, was easy to drive, hardy, and simple to repair (a particular advantage for owners in rural areas).

The Highland Park factory used two novel principles. The first was the uniformity and interchangeability of parts. The second, a Ford innovation, was the moving assembly line. Car parts, and even the whole car, were carried past a succession of workers, who either added a part or performed one operation. One complete car left the production line every 10 seconds. This process reduced the price of the car by two-thirds, suddenly making cars affordable to the wider public.

FORD'S VISION

The car industry soon became the largest single industry in the developed world. By 1918, the Model T was selling for under $400 and accounted for half of all cars on the roads of America.

Henry Ford argued for better roads and more gas stations. He introduced the eight-hour working day, raised the minimum wage to an unprecedented $5 a day, and had his workers doing shifts. By the time the last Model T rolled off the production line in 1927, 15 million Model Ts had been built.

" A **great many things** are going to **change.** "

Henry Ford, *My Life and Work*, 1922

ASSEMBLY LINES

The concept of mass production remains a vital aspect of the modern automobile industry, although robots now often perform the tasks that were once assigned to human workers. Ford's idea of standardized parts is still alive, too. Platform sharing means that cars with similar capabilities from different, competing manufacturers use the same parts in order to save time and money.

ENTERTAINING THE WORLD

Cinema, music, television, and publishing have all evolved to create a world of pleasure and leisure. The 20th century saw the rise of global entertainment, with mass-circulation newspapers, television, best-selling novels, and movies.

Bright lights ▷
Billboards touting Broadway musicals symbolize New York's dominance of the entertainment industry, from the 1920s up to the present day, with movies, graphic artists, literature, popular music, and theater.

In the early 20th century, most people had to find their own entertainment. But as movie theaters began to appear, going to the movies became increasingly popular. By the 1930s, many people worldwide went at least once a week. Movies were in black and white until the 1930s, when the first color ones were made. At home, people could listen to the radio from the early 1920s but television only became widely available to the masses in the 1950s.

By the mid 60s, it had become the main source of entertainment, at the expense of movies.

Advances in technology allowed people to listen to music anywhere, at any time, on portable devices. Home movies came into the living room with the advent of videos in the early 1980s, and then DVDs replaced videos in the late 90s. By the early part of the 21st century, the e-reader began to transform book reading.

WORDS

Technology kept pace with the spread of literacy in the 20th century. Newspapers, comics, and magazines were illustrated with bright colored images, and printing became speedier. Typing went electronic in the 1960s, and typewriters were gradually abandoned for computers in the 1980s. With the development of electronic tablets, reading was transformed.

Books for everyone
Paperbacks brought novels to the masses. Penguin was the first British publisher to turn paperbacks into a mass-market phenomenon.

Kindle e-reader
The electronic reader dates back to 1998, but only with the launch of Amazon's Kindle in 2007 did these new devices spark a cultural revolution in how people read and access books.

inexpensive black ink rubs off

Newspapers
By WWI, technical innovation made the modern newspaper possible. As words and pictures moved ever more quickly around the world, papers grew larger and gained mass circulation.

Spider-man comic
Comic books took off with the publication of Action Comics in 1938. Since then, they have become a staple of youth culture. Spider-man is one of the most popular comics published by Marvel.

SOUND

At the start of the century using sound as a medium for mass communication was as yet a dream. But within a few years radio brought news and popular tunes to the public. The introduction of radio broadcasting created massive changes in the record industry. By the end of the century, the music and entertainment industry was a global, billion-dollar business.

Marconi radio receiver
In 1901, Guglielmo Marconi used this radio receiver to pick up a transatlantic radio transmission. Radio became the first means of mass communication.

Bakelite was the first molded plastic used to make radios

Bakelite radio
Radio took off as an entertainment medium in the 1920s and 30s. Popular music was inextricably linked with broadcasting, and radio reached its "Golden Age."

small enough to fit in pocket

Transistor radio
Radios were big and bulky until the advent of portable transistor sets in the 1950s. Anyone, anywhere could now tune in, and teenagers regularly did.

turntable with record

1920s record player
In the 1920s, record players were an expensive luxury. By the 1950s they became common in most households.

reel-to-reel recording using magnetic tape

Reel-to-reel tape
Researchers in Germany worked hard to improve magnetic tape machines during WWII, until listeners could not tell if a broadcast was live or recorded.

selection of 24 records

design inspired by WWII bomber plane

glass dome

Wurlitzer jukebox
The jukebox craze of the late 1930s marked a major boom in the youth market. Thirteen million records a year were sold to fill the machines.

large stereo speakers

Boom box
In the 1980s, "boom boxes" (huge radios with cassette players) were an important form of personal audio technology.

Sony CD Walkman
Japanese company Sony made portable devices, first to play cassette tapes and then CDs in 1984. These changed how people experienced music.

display screen

iPod
This tiny portable music player, with its vast storage capacity and lightning-quick download capability, has transformed the way we listen to music.

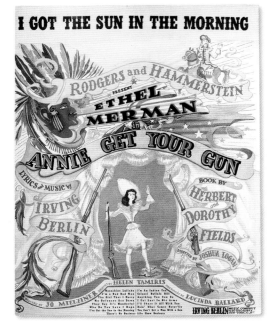

Musical sheet music
In the 1940s, Richard Rogers and Oscar Hammerstein transformed musicals with huge productions, such as *Annie Get Your Gun.*

guitar has six metal strings

fingerboard with mother-of-pearl inlay

pegs attached to strings are turned to tune guitar

solid-wood body with metallic gold veneer

pickup makes sound audible

FENDER TELECASTER

1950s electric guitars
During the 20th century, electric musical instruments, in which sound is picked up electronically and transmitted to an amplifier, was developed. Fender and Gibson created the first electric guitars.

volume control

GIBSON LES PAUL

Woodstock music festival
In 1969, over 40,000 people partied at the open-air festival at Woodstock, New York. Today numerous music festivals are held all over the world.

The Beatles tickets
British band The Beatles played to an audience of 44,000 screaming fans at Shea Stadium, New York, in 1966.

Vinyl LP
The increased playing times of the LP (long-playing record) enabled performers to produce longer albums. *Thriller* by Michael Jackson is the best-selling album of all time.

Keyboard synthesizer
Invented in 1965, the synthesizer is an electronic device that uses electrical signals to produce sound. It can imitate the sounds of a range of musical instruments.

PICTURES

Television and movies were a novelty at the start of the 20th century, but the entertainment industry was transformed by technological advances. With the introduction of shorter working hours and higher wages, more people were able to go to the movies, and televisions have made their way into most homes.

35 mm film
For over a century, movies have been shown on 35 mm film with a projector passing light through the celluloid film.

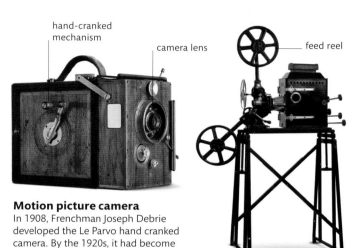

hand-cranked mechanism

camera lens

feed reel

Motion picture camera
In 1908, Frenchman Joseph Debrie developed the Le Parvo hand cranked camera. By the 1920s, it had become the most used camera in the world.

Early film projector
The first projectors were hand-cranked to advance the film. Many used gas light as a light source. Later projectionists began to use powerful electric arc lights.

Casablanca poster
In the 1930s, American cinema entered a "Golden Age" of technical innovation and creativity. The movie *Casablanca*, released in 1942, was a huge critical hit.

■ TELEVISIONS

Baird television
Designed for British television pioneer John Logie Baird in 1930, this television was the first mass-produced TV.

rotates 360 degrees on base

acrylic visor covers glass screen inside

plastic base

Flatscreen TV
Flatscreen High Definition TVs became popular for their slim build and superior quality. They can be used for DVD movies, games consoles, and the Internet.

Bakelite plastic casing

1950s Bush TV
This was one of the first televisions to use an aluminized cathode ray tube to ensure most of the picture's light came out into the room.

1970s spherical TV
Inspired by the moon landing in 1969, this popular and expensive spherical TV is shaped like an astronaut's helmet.

DVDs
The first DVD (Digital Versatile Disk) players and disks were available in 1996 in Japan to play full-length movies. They replaced the VHS tape.

FIGHTING THE WORLD WARS

Two world wars changed the battlefield forever. Conflicts were no longer short and politically decisive but involved large territories, vast armies, and new, deadly weapons. Fighting was revolutionized by the sheer scale of modern war.

Gassed ▷
In this painting, American artist John Singer Sargent captured the horror of being blinded by mustard gas on the Western Front in 1918. The scene shows a medic directing blinded soldiers toward a aid station.

World War I saw horrendous casualties as a result of the industrialization of war. Machine guns, poison gas, and aircraft created a different field of combat from earlier wars. A soldier's life was dominated by mud, barbed wire, and gunfire, while new weaponry made possible mass slaughter.

In 1939, the world was plunged into a second war, which by 1941 had become truly global in scale because the Axis states—Germany, Italy, and Japan—used armed aggression to carve out territories in Europe, the Mediterranean, and Eastern Asia. When the USSR and the US entered the war in 1941, the Axis was doomed to defeat.

Weapons were now even more destructive. Tanks and armored vehicles gave a new mobility, and huge bombers pulverized enemy cities. By the war's end, the age of jets, rockets, and atomic bombs had arrived. Civilians died in even larger numbers than soldiers in what became a true "total war".

UNIFORMS

Soldiers fighting during the world wars were not part of a single force. They served in tank divisions, the navy, or the air force, for example. In addition to distinguishing their role and nationality, uniforms, especially helmets, provided essential protection against shrapnel and artillery fire.

cartridge pouches

haversack made either of linen or hemp

overcoat is double-breasted with tails, made of iron-blue wool

hobnailed boots

regimental markings

French army uniform
This WWI uniform of the *pioupiou* (French soldier) was considered a relic of the 19th century, with its conspicuous red pants and blue overcoat.

bayonet

brass Prussian eagle

Prussian artillery helmet
Originally designed by the Prussian King Friedrich Wilhelm in 1842, this German helmet, or *Pickelhaube*, was worn by artillery soldiers in WWI.

simple steel construction

British Brodie
Designed by John Brodie, the "tommy helmet" was first used by the British in 1915. Good for overhead protection, it gave little coverage to the neck.

coating of waterproof paint

German helmet
The distinctive German *Stahlhelm*, first used in WWI, was based on a "coal scuttle" design. This example has the Luftwaffe insignia on the side.

camouflage mesh covering

US M1 helmet
The iconic steel M1 saw service with the US military from the early 1940s. It was so successful that many other countries adopted it.

EQUIPMENT

A soldier's gear was designed to keep him fed, watered, alive, and an effective member of a fighting force. Many advances were made during wartime to lighten the load and aid survival. Most items were standard issue. A few, such as photographs and letters, were far more personal.

British ration can
This WWII military-issue can was packed with five different types of candies and cookies for dessert. Cans were easily carried.

Japanese identification card
This wooden card belonged to a Japanese serviceman. It lists his military unit and gives permission to go out, perhaps after curfew.

pouch hooks to belt

M1910 wire cutters
Both sides relied on wire cutters to break through enemy defenses in WWI. This pair was part of standard issue to American soldiers.

plastic goggles

screw-on air filter

German gas mask
This was the first respirator worn by German storm troopers after both sides began to use chemical weapons during WWI.

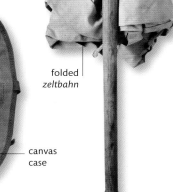

folded *zeltbahn*

lacing protects valve of interior rubber bladder

Improvised glasses
British WWII POWs held by the Japanese used items such as toothbrushes molded around lenses to create glasses like these.

Loos soccer ball
This is one of six soccer balls British troops successfully dribbled across the German front line as a show of bravado at the Battle of Loos in 1915.

forceps

tongue depressor

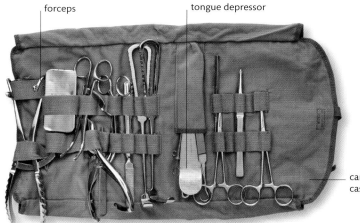

canvas case

Surgical instrument roll
This WWII British military canvas roll holds surgical instruments such as scalpels, shears, and cloth-cutting scissors for use near the frontline.

German assault pack
This WWI storm-trooper pack held rations, grenades, a *zeltbahn*, or rain cape that doubled as a tent, and a shovel, essential for digging a trench.

handlebar can be rotated

tool pouch

Michelin "war grade" tires

frame weighs less than 21 lbs (10 kg)

FOLDED BICYCLE

BSA folding bicycle
This British folding bicycle was made by the Birmingham Small Arms Company (BSA). It was a lightweight means of allowing paratroopers to regroup quickly and reach their target quietly.

crankset with BSA logo

pedals have unique design with cylindrical spindle

WEAPONS

Through the world wars, weapons became increasingly powerful and technically sophisticated. In WWI, trench warfare produced the high-firing light trench mortar while sea blockade saw the emergence of the submarine. By WWII, large tanks, aircraft, rockets, and automatic weapons transformed the way modern warfare was fought.

■ KNIVES

rudimentary iron blade

Japanese cane knife
Fighting in Burma was especially challenging in WWII. Both the Japanese and Allied troops carried a machete to hack through jungle terrain and to use as a weapon.

motto in gothic print

Nazi eagle and swastika

German Allgemeine dagger
This dagger was issued to members of the Allgemeine, Nazi Germany's SS paramilitary force, for ceremonial use. The official motto "My Honor Is Loyalty" is etched on the blade.

double-edged blade

German knife bayonet
This short, double-edged knife could be attached to a rifle as a bayonet. It was used by German infantrymen toward the end of WWI.

■ ARTILLERY

rocket inserted at rear

wooden shoulder support

M1A1 bazooka
An open-ended tube operated by two men, the bazooka was used by US forces in WWII to launch a small solid-fuel rocket, which was inserted into the back. Its main purpose was to defend against tanks.

shaped-charge warhead

M-2 ILLUMINATING PARACHUTE MORTAR

JAPANESE MILITARY SHELL

World War II projectiles
Used by US forces, the M-2 mortar fired rounds at night, illuminating the sky for 25 seconds to aid observation while drifting down on a small parachute. The shell was typical of the thousands used by the Japanese to bombard Singapore in mid-February 1942.

pig-iron body

FRANCO-ITALIAN BESOZZI

GERMAN M1915 DISC GRENADE

FRENCH P1 GRENADE

World War I grenades
The Besozzi had an exterior fuse, which had to be lit by a match, whereas the P1 "pear" grenade had a time fuse activated by a spring-loaded igniter released by a pin. The German *diskus handgranate* was thrown like a discus to make it spin, exploding on impact.

gun shield

short barrel can shoot up to 88 lb (40 kg) shells

German antitank mine
Developed in 1935, the Teller mine effectively and powerfully ripped the tracks off tanks.

flash hider

crew step

gun carriage and main body can be separated during transportation

carriage wheel has wide steel tires for crossing difficult terrain

Skoda howitzer M14/16
Howitzers could be used to decimate targets in the rear of enemy positions. This heavy Austro-Hungarian 149 mm howitzer was designed and built by Skoda.

■ GUNS

magazine port

wooden stock

M1921 submachine gun
The "Tommy Gun" began life in 1919. With its high rate of fire, it became the weapon of choice for US soldiers in WWII fighting at close quarters.

50-round magazine drum

folding spiked bayonet

Mosin-Nagant rifle
Used extensively by the Russian army in WWII, this rifle was developed for urban and confined fighting. Some versions had a bayonet attached.

rear sight

Gewehr 43
With a telescopic sight attached, the Gewehr 43 was an excellent sniper's rifle. It was adopted by the Czech Army after WWII.

10-round detachable box magazine

Berthier rifle
This bolt-action weapon fired a smokeless cartridge and was issued to French troops in WWI. It was modeled on the 1886 Lebel rifle.

hammer

Steyr 9 mm automatic pistol
This was the first automatic pistol to be part of standard military equipment, adopted by the Austro-Hungarian Empire in 1911 and later by the Chilean army.

gas cylinder

optical sight

steadying grip

pistol grip

elevation wheel

gunner's seat

Hotchkiss MLE 1914
This French gas-operated machine gun was used widely by American troops in WWI. It was reliable and fired 450 8 mm rounds per minute.

INSTRUMENTS OF WAR

In the struggle for dominance over the enemy, all nations encouraged problem solvers and code breakers to come up with new tools and gadgets. These ranged from navigation aids and cameras to radios and code machines. In many ways, the two world wars were a triumph of ingenuity.

German field telephone
Telephones were used extensively during WWI to relay orders. By May 1917, the Germans had laid 319,000 miles of cable on the Western Front.

sliding index arm

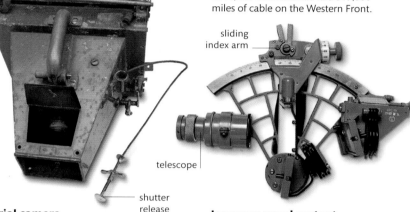

telescope

shutter release

Aerial camera
Aerial photography was used for the first time in WWI in the hope that mapping enemy trench fortifications would help break the deadlock on the Western Front.

Japanese naval sextant
In WWII, sextants were used by both sides for navigating poorly charted seas. Latitude was calculated with a scale showing degrees north or south of the equator.

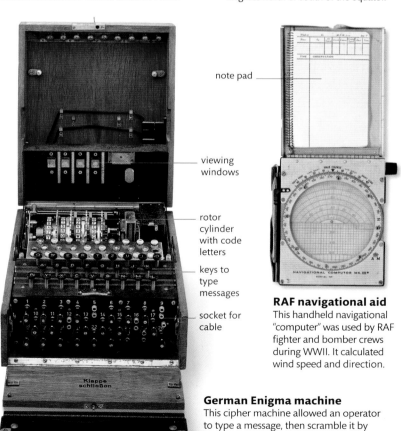

note pad

viewing windows

rotor cylinder with code letters

keys to type messages

socket for cable

RAF navigational aid
This handheld navigational "computer" was used by RAF fighter and bomber crews during WWII. It calculated wind speed and direction.

German Enigma machine
This cipher machine allowed an operator to type a message, then scramble it by using a series of notched wheels. Three Polish mathematicians were the first to break the Enigma code, in December 1932.

LIFE ON THE HOME FRONT

Those left at home during the world wars had their own battles to fight. Food and other resources were rationed, children were evacuated, cities and towns bombed, and civilians were mobilized en masse to support the war effort. The pattern of life for all fighting powers was transformed by war.

Can of dried eggs
Fresh eggs were rationed in Britain in WWII. From May 1941, dried egg powder was imported from America.

Happy families
Many British toys were made of paper and card during WWII. Traditional card games, such as Happy Families, were produced in special wartime packs.

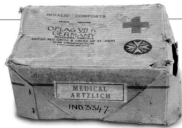

British POW parcel
The Red Cross sent over 20 million parcels to prisoners of war in WWII. The parcels contained mostly food, tobacco, and personal hygiene items. Most men got one package a week.

Cigarette cards
Put inside British cigarette packages, different cards showed how to protect the home from air raids in WWII. This example shows an inflatable "balloon" shelter.

brightly colored to appeal to children

Child's gas mask
By 1938, respirators were issued to all British families. This lightweight "Mickey Mouse" mask was designed for children from 18 months to four years old.

filter holds block of asbestos

"Jude" written in mock-Hebraic type

Jewish star
In WWII, Jews were persecuted throughout Nazi-occupied Europe. From 1941, all Jews were made to wear a six-pointed yellow star with the word Jude (German for "Jew") inscribed on it.

circular case molded from bakelite

Cabinet wireless radio
Radios such as this EKCO AD 65, designed by architect Wells Coates in 1932, were central to the WWII British home, offering vital news and much-needed entertainment.

dated and stamped July 15, 1937

Membership book
The Nazi party was the ruling political elite in Germany during WWII. Its members carried books proving their allegiance.

each square worth one portion of meat

Meat ration card
Rationing became a way of life on the home front. German WWII ration cards were printed on stiff paper with coupons to cut out.

French munitions poster
Women were a vital part of the war effort, often taking over men's roles. This 1917 poster depicts a woman working in a munitions factory.

earpiece

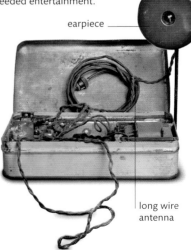

long wire antenna

Homemade wireless
Hidden in a tin, this radio was used by a Dutch family to tune into British war broadcasts during the Nazi occupation. Owning a radio was strictly prohibited.

Navy recruitment poster
Images of women were often used to shame men into enlisting in the armed forces. This WWI poster challenged men to do what women could not—join the US Navy.

SS recruitment poster
This Nazi poster encouraged men in German-occupied France to join the Waffen-SS, stating "under the sign of the SS you shall overcome!".

Chinese propaganda poster
In this poster, China celebrates American victory over enemy Japan, depicting the US as an enormous pilot crushing a Japanese soldier.

American flags adorn triumphant pilot

MEDALS AND MEMORIALS

In both world wars, countless men and women risked their lives defending their countries, showing incredible courage. All nations recognized the contribution of individuals with medals and honors. Other tokens of war are more private and personal, and exist as poignant reminders of the human cost of conflict.

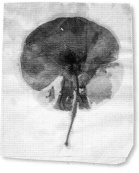

Flanders poppy
Poppies proliferated on WWI European battlefields. Some soldiers pressed and sent them home, such as this one from Passchendaele.

Croix de Guerre
Established on July 20, 1941, the Belgian Croix de Guerre with Silver Palm rewarded acts of heroism in combat by individuals and entire units.

Legion d'Honneur
France's highest award, this medal was presented to those distinguished through military valor. Towns and cities were also recipients.

name of fallen soldier

rosette in colors of Belgian flag

George Cross
This medal is the highest award for UK civilians. It was originally created during the height of the Blitz in 1940 to award civilian acts of courage.

Grave marker
Many of the graves on the Western Front were later moved to vast cemeteries. This Belgian wooden cross marked a temporary grave.

Iron Cross (2nd class)
Awarded for bravery, this 2nd class medal had to be held before gaining the 1st class. This version was issued to Germans in both wars.

COMBATTING DISEASE

The scientific advances of the 20th century have enabled doctors to make significant breakthroughs in medicine. Research into the causes of disease and new machines that can see into the body have led to a medical revolution.

New frontiers ▷
MRI technology, or magnetic resonance imagining, provides an alternative method of looking into the body without having to use potentially harmful X-rays or surgery. This scan shows the activity in different parts of the brain.

The effective treatment and prevention of disease over the past century has extended life expectancy and reduced disability more than was thought possible by early 20th-century doctors.

The injuries caused by two world wars accelerated research into treating and fighting infection. Hygiene improved, methods of surgery became more precise, and prosthetics and plastic surgery progressed significantly. Increased efforts were also made to understand and treat mental illness. Advances in medical treatment have continued apace since then. The development of vaccines to provide immunity to diseases such as smallpox and polio saved lives and reduced disability. The use of antibiotics to treat bacterial infections has also saved millions of lives. X-rays, ultrasound, and other scanning methods have made diagnosis more accurate and led to a greater understanding of the body.

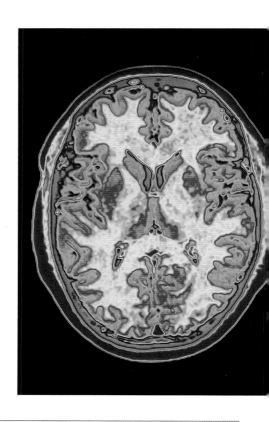

CONTRACEPTION AND CHILDBIRTH

Advances in the fields of childbirth, conception, and contraception have included the invention of oral and injectable contraceptives, *in vitro* fertilization (IVF), and microsurgery. Improved diagnostic techniques, imaging, and both surgical and nonsurgical procedures have contributed to better outcomes in childbirth.

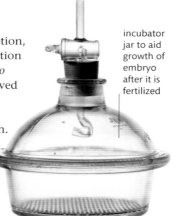

incubator jar to aid growth of embryo after it is fertilized

First IVF test tube
This glass jar incubated the fertilized egg (embryo) that became the first test-tube baby in 1978. Millions of babies have since been born by IVF.

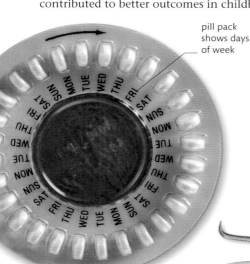

pill pack shows days of week

Contraceptive pill
Hailed as one of the most significant advances of the 20th century, the Pill was welcomed by many people. It first went on sale in 1960.

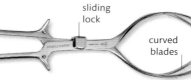

sliding lock

curved blades

Obstetric forceps
Used throughout history for delivering babies, 20th-century forceps became shorter and were designed to protect, rather than compress, the baby's head.

DIAGNOSIS

New technology allowed doctors to look inside the body without cutting it open. The discovery of X-rays in 1895 led to a medical revolution in noninvasive diagnosis. Other diagnostic methods include various types of scanning, heart monitoring, and and measuring of brainwaves.

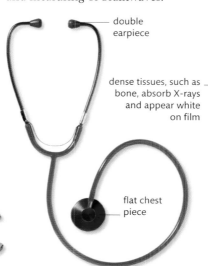

double earpiece

Stethoscope
The modern stethoscope has flexible tubes, double earpieces, and improved acoustics to hear the sounds of the heart and chest.

Ear thermometer
This digital ear thermometer is more accurate at measuring temperature than earlier models, which were put in the mouth.

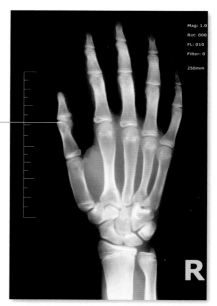

flat chest piece

dense tissues, such as bone, absorb X-rays and appear white on film

Mag: 1.0
Rot: 000
FL: 010
Filter: 0
250mm

R

Hand X-ray
X-ray machines use electromagnetic waves to photograph the inside of the body, allowing doctors to detect broken bones and other abnormalities.

PREVENTION AND CURE

The 20th century was the era of drug and vaccine development—specifically designed to treat or prevent disease. Antibiotics (first used in the 1930s), powerful cancer drugs, and antiviral medicines were introduced. Some treatments involve new ways of administering medicines and nondrug treatments.

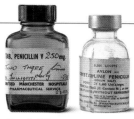

Penicillin
The antibiotic penicillin treated infections such as pneumonia and gangrene. It was made in large quantities to treat soldiers in WWII.

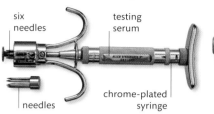

six needles — testing serum — chrome-plated syringe — needles

Heaf test kit
Testing for sensitivity to tuberculosis, this syringe delivers a tiny dose to the skin. Millions of children have been screened for tuberculosis.

Diabetes pen
The increase of diabetes has prompted a boom in technology. This device uses high pressure to send a fine spray of insulin through the skin.

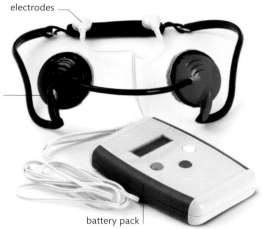

two electrodes — head piece delivers current

TDCS machine
A 21st-century phenomena, noninvasive brain stimulation techniques are being offered for a variety of conditions. Transcranial Direct Current Stimulation (TDCS) can help treat brain injuries.

battery pack

SURGERY

Attitudes to surgery evolved after WWI, aided by technological progress. New inventions enabled limb replacements, heart surgery, and wound repairs. Sterile surgical environments saved lives, and anesthetic advances enabled less painful surgery.

thin cutting blades

Rib shears
This powerful tool is used for cutting through the ribs and opening up the chest cavity during an operation.

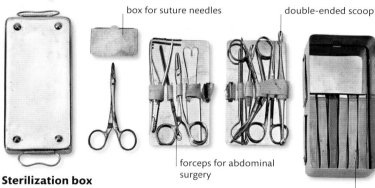

box for suture needles — double-ended scoop

forceps for abdominal surgery — scalpels in sterilizing rack

Sterilization box
Once surgeons realized that sanitization could prevent infection, they began sterilizing their tools. This sterilizer box was used in WWI.

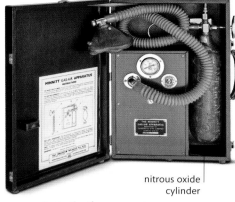

nitrous oxide cylinder

Anesthetic apparatus
Pain reduction by anesthetic was a major breakthrough. This machine delivered gas and air (Entonox) to relieve labor pain during childbirth.

LIFE-CHANGING MACHINES

Modern medicine has brought the development of assistive technologies and life-saving devices. Artificial limbs, hearing aids, wheelchairs, and contact lenses have enhanced people's quality of life, while machines supporting organs such as the heart, lungs, and kidneys have prolonged life expectancy.

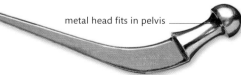

metal head fits in pelvis

Artificial hip
Hip replacement, first done in 1940, was one of the most important surgical advances of the last century, helping millions regain mobility. Artificial hips have become lighter and stronger.

openings connect to blood vessels

polyester shell

internal circuitry and batteries

Myoelectric hand
This hand is controlled by muscle sensors placed against the skin at the site of amputation. Muscles can then contract to make movements.

electrode

Heart pacemaker
This is implanted near the heart and electrical pulses regulate the heartbeat. First used in 1960, it was a breakthrough in treating heart rhythm disorders.

Jarvik-7 artificial heart
The dream of implanting an artificial heart became a reality on December 2, 1982, when the Jarvik-7 was used for the first time in a human.

left ventricle (lower chamber)

▌LIFE-SAVING TECHNOLOGY

IRON LUNG

Polio is an extremely infectious disease that can invade the nervous system and, within hours, can cause total paralysis. One of the main symptoms is the inability to breathe because muscles in the chest become paralyzed. Before polio vaccines were introduced in the 1950s and 1960s, polio patients were ensconced in a tank respirator, or "Iron Lung," a massive set of bellows that breathed for them. It became an iconic symbol of the scourge of polio.

ASSISTED RESPIRATION

Invented by Americans Phillip Drinker and Louis Agassiz Shaw, the first version, used in 1928, was known as the "Drinker Respirator." In 1931, the American inventor John Haven Emerson introduced his improved version of the machine. Emerson's respirator was more efficient, lighter, and quieter.

Both Drinker and Emerson's iron lungs worked on the same principle. The patient remained in the airtight container with only his or her head resting on a support outside the machine, with a rubber collar around the neck to provide a seal. Pressure inside the tank changed to manipulate the lungs into imitating the mechanics of breathing. Smaller machines were made for children.

POLIO EPIDEMICS

The worst epidemic of polio occurred in the 1940s and 1950s. At its height in 1952, nearly 60,000 cases were reported in the US alone. Dedicated wards were filled with people lying in the iron tubes. Patients had to learn to live with the constant "swishing" sound created by the rise and fall of the bellows. Some people were kept in the machines for weeks, months, or even years, although most were weaned off within a few weeks of a sudden, short-lived attack and as soon as they could breathe independently. Some patients described the iron lung as a salvation, but others saw it as a prison. Ultimately, it saved lives—most of those who used the machines survived.

The iron lung was replaced eventually by the positive pressure mechanical ventilator, and patients no longer had to be encased in a machine. Vaccination has virtually eradicated the disease.

Smith-Clarke "senior" cabinet respirator
In the 1950s, Captain George Smith-Clarke, who had been a car engineer, designed this British model, as well as a "junior" version for young children. He included more ports in the side of the machine, so that nurses could reach in without affecting the patient's breathing. Iron lungs were not patented, so they could be available worldwide.

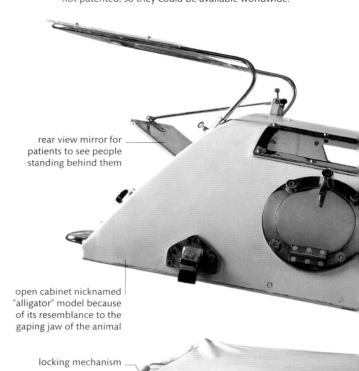

rear view mirror for patients to see people standing behind them

open cabinet nicknamed "alligator" model because of its resemblance to the gaping jaw of the animal

locking mechanism

wheel-mounted stand for easy movement

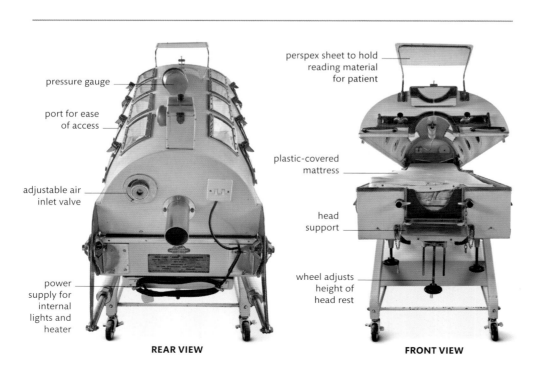

pressure gauge

port for ease of access

adjustable air inlet valve

power supply for internal lights and heater

REAR VIEW

perspex sheet to hold reading material for patient

plastic-covered mattress

head support

wheel adjusts height of head rest

FRONT VIEW

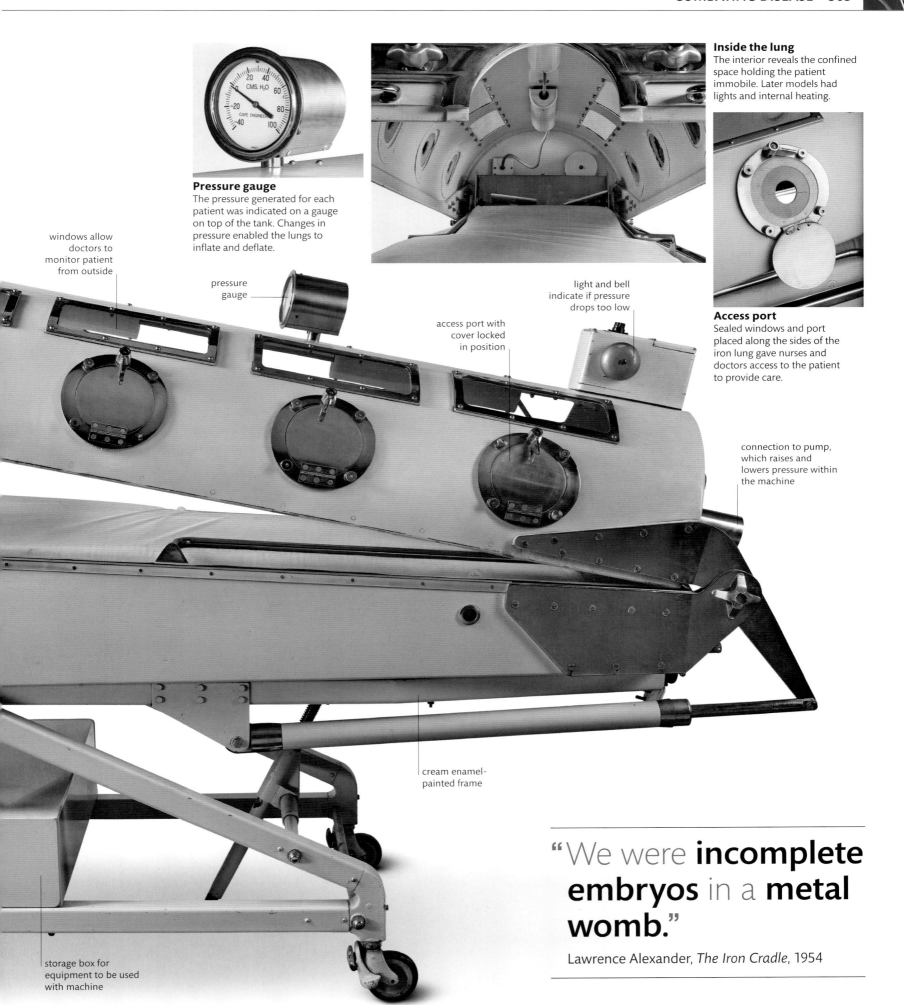

Pressure gauge
The pressure generated for each patient was indicated on a gauge on top of the tank. Changes in pressure enabled the lungs to inflate and deflate.

Inside the lung
The interior reveals the confined space holding the patient immobile. Later models had lights and internal heating.

Access port
Sealed windows and port placed along the sides of the iron lung gave nurses and doctors access to the patient to provide care.

windows allow doctors to monitor patient from outside

pressure gauge

light and bell indicate if pressure drops too low

access port with cover locked in position

connection to pump, which raises and lowers pressure within the machine

cream enamel-painted frame

storage box for equipment to be used with machine

> " We were **incomplete embryos** in a **metal womb**."
>
> Lawrence Alexander, *The Iron Cradle*, 1954

LIFE UNDER THE REVOLUTION

In 1917, Marxist revolutionaries seized power in Russia. They founded the Soviet Union, the first state ruled by a Communist Party. By the 1980s, almost one-third of the world's population was under Communist rule. Many became disillusioned when the better world promised by Communist ideology failed to materialize.

Pride of the people
This 1980 newspaper celebrates the first Cuban in space. Soviet space exploration was a major source of pride and prestige.

The Soviet Union established the model for a Communist state. The Communist Party held an absolute monopoly of political and economic power. Opposition to or criticism of the regime was ruthlessly repressed. Peasants were forced into collective farms at gunpoint. Millions of people were sent to prison camps. Belief in the revolutionary transformation of society—with an end to exploitation and the promise of future equality—ensured popular support for Communist regimes. Considerable support endured even when policies led to large-scale disasters, such as famines in the Soviet Union in the 1930s and in China in the 1950s.

SPREAD AND FADE

The success of Soviet armies in World War II brought Communist rule to Central Europe and North Korea. China joined the Communist bloc after Mao Zedong's victory in a civil war in 1949. The Communist world later expanded to include Cuba and parts of Africa and Southeast Asia. But Communism began to falter. Party rule slid into personal dictatorship, as during Joseph Stalin's rule in the Soviet Union from 1924 to 1953. The party and state officials became self-serving, privileged groups. Lack of freedom was resented.

Despite early success with rapid industrialization, state-run economies failed to keep pace with capitalism. Consumer goods were scarce and shoddy, shortages common, and living standards low. From the 1980s, the Communist project began to unravel. In most countries, Communist parties either lost power or, as happened in China, adopted some capitalist policies.

Lenin power ▽
Vladimir Ilyich Lenin, the leader of the Bolshevik party who emerged victorious after the Russian Revolution, makes a speech in Red Square, Moscow, in 1919. Three years later, Lenin founded the Soviet Union.

POLITICS

Communist states were totalitarian, with every aspect of life directed to a common goal. The state ideology was hammered home in the media and at schools and workplaces. When necessary, opposition was crushed by force. At times, as in the Chinese Cultural Revolution of the 1960s, popular activism was encouraged.

Czarist imperial badge

White Army hat
The Communist power grab in Russia sparked a civil war. The White Army, loyal to the Czar, fought the revolutionaries.

■ ARMIES AND PARTIES

party member ticket number

Party membership
In the Soviet Union, membership of the Communist Party was a privilege, giving access to top jobs, stores, and housing.

characters read
Hong Weibing
(Red Guard)

Red Guard uniform
In the mid-1960s, Chinese youths were mobilized by Chairman Mao Zedong as Red Guards. They attacked authority figures allegedly hostile to the revolution.

Little Red Book
This book of Chairman Mao's ideas was compulsory reading in factories, farms, and schools. Over a billion were printed.

■ SUPPRESSION AND CENSORSHIP

Mandelstam's poem "Stalin Epigram"

Poet's typewriter
In 1933, Osip Mandelstam wrote a poem on this typewriter satirizing Stalin. In 1938 Mandelstam was sent to a prison camp, where he died.

keys have Russian letters

■ PROPAGANDA

heroic workers from the Daqing oilfield were an example of productivity

shipyard workers are urged to be productive

cheerful comrades celebrating progress under Communism

Chinese message
This poster from the 1960s extols the virtues of Chinese industry. Such posters were used to promote desirable behavior.

five-pointed red stars are Communist symbol

Soviet worker
A Soviet poster from the mid-20th century celebrates the 1917 revolution. A worker breaks his chains, and the stars proclaim peace, democracy, and socialism.

Cuban hero
Fidel Castro led the 26th of July Movement to power in Cuba in 1959. This mid-1970s Cuban poster depicts Castro as a guerrilla fighter.

INDUSTRY

Communist regimes gave prime importance to heavy industry and mining, developed under state economic plans. High growth rates were achieved, as in the Soviet Union in the 1930s, but at the expense of pollution and poor working conditions. The creation of huge state farms was greatly resented.

headlight allows working at night

spikes prevent skidding

First Soviet tractor
The Soviet Union began manufacturing its own tractors in 1930. The tractors were held at regional centers, from which they were loaned out to vast, state-run collective farms.

wheel spokes painted revolutionary red

THE WESTERN HOME

During the 20th century, homes in the West changed dramatically. Millions of lives were transformed by increasing prosperity, technological advances, mass production, and the steady rise in ownership of household appliances.

Target audience ▷
Advertisements in the 1950s reached out to hardworking housewives, promising them devices that would give them more time to enjoy life. This German poster offers the prospect of extra storage space provided by a new generation of refrigerators.

At the turn of the 20th century, old country houses and other rich households were staffed by large teams of domestic servants, but World War I changed this. Servants became harder to find as workers found better-paid employment in industry and other vital sectors, and more people bought their own homes. This meant the housewife, whether well-off or poor, had to do many things for herself, armed with a slew of labor-saving devices.

The modern housewife needed machines that did some of the work for her. The coming of electric-powered devices brought relief from domestic drudgery. New prosperity in the postwar 1950s brought with it a new consumerism. Mass-produced goods were more affordable and were seen as the solution to modern life—or, at least, that is how they were advertised.

The boom in housebuilding also fueled demand. As soon as new houses were built, people filled them with new things: furniture, serving dishes, and stylish decorative pieces. There was limitless demand, and limitless production. Family life was transformed by the development of new toys, extra leisure time, and comfortable fixtures and fittings.

Einer der Besten!
LIEBHERR

FURNISHINGS AND DININGWARE

New woodworking technologies and cheaper, faster methods of manufacturing produced goods that appealed to the new consumer. There was little that harked back to the past; instead, furnishings appeared contemporary, stylish, and colorful, and designers looked to the future.

Homemaker dinner plate
After a decade of plain china, people fell in love with modern patterned tableware in the 1950s, such as the popular Homemaker series by Ridgway.

Plastic tableware tray
Mass production of new forms of plastic in the 1940s inundated the modern home with light, colorful, and inexpensive products, and provided the perfect storage solution for cutlery.

Clarice Cliff ceramics
British potter Clarice Cliff brought modernity to the kitchen in the 1930s with exotic, colorful Art Deco tea and coffee sets designed to be used as well as admired.

yellow band represents the Sun

brown band represents earth

Autumn Crocus pattern

fashionable 1950s furniture

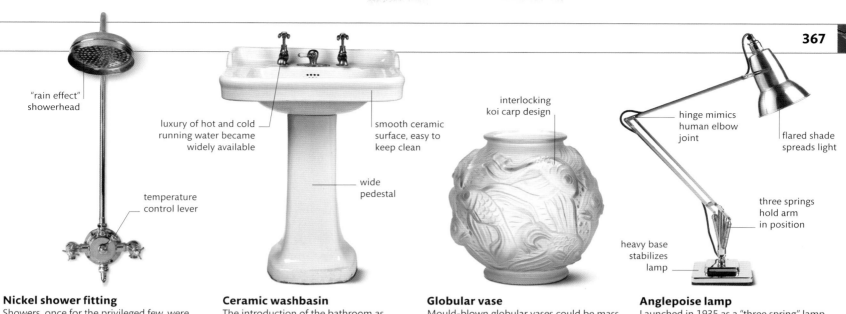

Nickel shower fitting

Showers, once for the privileged few, were common in homes by the mid-20th century. Innovations in plumbing and heating meant the reinvigorating shower upstaged the bath.

- "rain effect" showerhead
- temperature control lever

Ceramic washbasin

The introduction of the bathroom as a separate room in ordinary houses—containing a toilet, bath, and washbasin—was a revolution for personal hygiene.

- luxury of hot and cold running water became widely available
- smooth ceramic surface, easy to keep clean
- wide pedestal

Globular vase

Mould-blown globular vases could be mass produced and so were an affordable luxury. This vase imitiates the Art Deco style of the French glass designer René Lalique.

- interlocking koi carp design

Anglepoise lamp

Launched in 1935 as a "three spring" lamp, the Anglepoise could be mounted on desks, walls, and ceilings. Its versatility meant that everyone could adjust and direct light.

- hinge mimics human elbow joint
- flared shade spreads light
- three springs hold arm in position
- heavy base stabilizes lamp

Art Deco writing desk

This desk was exhibited by the British government at the Art Deco exhibition in Paris in 1925. Designed by Sir Edward Brantwood Maufe, it echoes the glamorous world of Hollywood.

- surface gilded with white gold
- haldu wood footrest
- ivory, rock crystal, and silk handle

Postwar sofa bed

Ercol, a British postwar furniture brand, became renowned for its modernist design and innovative ways of working wood. This sofa doubles up as a single bed.

- steam-bent elm arm
- removable beech back

Eames chair and ottoman

American husband-and-wife team Charles and Ray Eames created modernist furniture constructed with industrial materials, which, in the 1950s, suggested a brave new world.

- buttons emphasize comfort and luxury of leather upholstery
- cushion shape follows contours of wooden shell
- steam-bent plywood with rosewood veneer
- angled back
- cast-aluminum base with black paint finish
- chair seat swivels on base

OTTOMAN

LOUNGE CHAIR

HOME APPLIANCES

One of the main changes that technological change brought to the home during the 20th century was the proliferation of labor-saving machines that helped to relieve domestic drudgery. Running a home was likened to running a business. Devices such as vacuum cleaners, washing machines, irons, and refrigerators helped the homemaker increase efficiency and maybe save time for more creative pursuits.

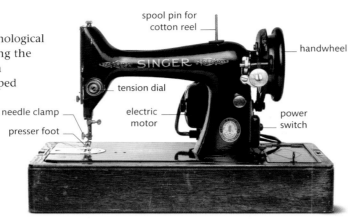

spool pin for cotton reel

handwheel

tension dial

needle clamp

electric motor

power switch

presser foot

Singer sewing machine

Since 1851, the Singer brand has been synonymous with sewing machines. The reliability and continuous stitching of its products freed women from the chore of hand sewing.

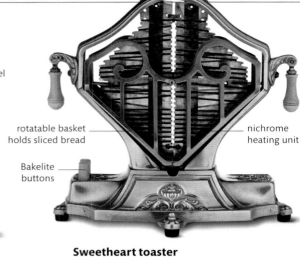

rotatable basket holds sliced bread

nichrome heating unit

Bakelite buttons

Sweetheart toaster

The heyday of the electric toaster began in the 1920s with widespread electrification and presliced bread. This striking, nickel-plated Sweetheart model was both decorative and practical.

Kenlite chrome bowl

modern square design for high-tech appeal

Kenwood food mixer

Making baking quick and easy, the food mixer soon became a "must have" item. Designed by Ken Wood, this model went on sale in Britain in 1950 and quickly sold out.

hinged lid

top chamber collects coffee

bottom chamber contains water

Moka Express

In 1933, Italian Alfonso Bialetti fashioned the first aluminium stove-top espresso coffee maker. Today, the Moka Express is found in 90 percent of Italian homes.

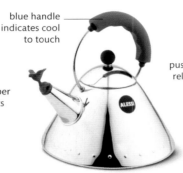

blue handle indicates cool to touch

Whistling Bird kettle

A design classic, the Alessi kettle, with its witty postmodern design by US architect Michael Graves, was immediately popular. Millions have been sold since its launch in 1985.

pushing button releases steam

Bakelite handle

Steam iron

Invented in the United States in the early 20th century, the first electric steam irons were not a commercial success, but 1930s models such as The Chief, made by American Electric Supply, soon won over the public.

large freezer compartment

rustproof aluminum shelving

Electric refrigerator

Electric fridges, which first appeared in the United States in the late 1930s, revolutionized food storage. When kitchens with large fridges were introduced in the 1950s, they transformed eating habits.

hinged burner cover

handrail

thick door insulates roasting oven

AGA heat storage stove

Throughout Europe, the AGA cooker became one of the most sought-after kitchen appliances. It is known for its iconic design which, externally, has changed little since the 1920s.

heavy cast-iron frame absorbs, stores, and radiates heat

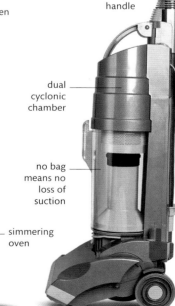

telescopic handle

dual cyclonic chamber

no bag means no loss of suction

simmering oven

Dyson Cyclone

From the 1920s, the vacuum cleaner came in two forms, the rolling canister and the upright. The design changed little until the Dyson arrived in the 1980s.

Electric washing machine

At the turn of the century, soap, hot water, and physical effort were all that could get clothes clean. The electrically powered washing tub greatly reduced the drudgery of laundry. Beatty Brothers of Ontario, Canada, was the first company to produce an agitator washing machine. The machines were not an immediate success, with problems including poor temperature control, leaking water, and the threat of electrocution.

four-pinned agitator

raising tub lid automatically stops motor

motor connected to mangle wheel via large belt

handle engages mangle drive

lowering lid starts motor

lid catch

tub handle

large wooden washing tub

SIDE VIEW

powered mangle

water drainage tap

unprotected electric motor located under tub

four-legged dolly

castors for easy movement

FRONT VIEW

LEISURE

Until the 20th century, most toys were homemade and very simple. As the developed world became more industrialized, toys began to be manufactured on a large scale. With shorter working hours, there was more time to spend in the garden, play sports, or take up a hobby. But some traditional pastimes, such as board games, never went out of fashion.

ears used as handles

adjustable height

brake

folding mechanism

ankle support

wheels all in one line

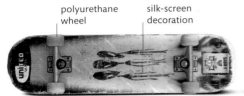

polyurethane wheel

silk-screen decoration

Skateboards
In the 1950s, Californian surfers developed the idea of "surfing" the street. By the 1970s, with new wheels and outdoor skate parks, the craze for skateboarding was born.

Micro Scooter
Heralded as a healthy way for children to get fresh air, the scooter quickly became a familiar sight. In the 21st century, the Micro Scooter appealed to adults as well.

Space Hopper
It is often the simplest of toys that start a craze. In the 1970s, every child wanted to bounce up and down on this orange ball with a friendly face.

Inline skates
Inline skates have been around since the 1700s, but in the late 1980s, aided by stronger materials, they developed into a fitness and extreme sport phenomenon.

rear hoop imitates motorcycle "sissy bar"

The Chopper
The Chopper child's bike, produced by British company Raleigh in the 1970s, was highly sought after. Famed for its angular seat and high-rise handlbars, it became a cultural icon despite being harder to ride than conventional bicycles.

rubber grip

long, padded seat with back support

high-rise (ape hanger) handlebars

brake lever

spring suspension

rear rack

Sturmey-Archer 3-speed central gear stick

smaller front wheel

named Chopper because style borrowed from customized (chopper) motorcycles

wide tire

kickstand

larger rear wheel

Steiff bear
Perhaps the most iconic of all childhood toys, teddy bears became popular from the beginning of the 20th century. Steiff bears from Germany are collector's items.

- body has five joints
- plush, furlike exterior

Windup tin robot
Before the arrival of battery-powered toys, a windup mechanism made toys move, including this robot inspired by the 1950s frenzy for science fiction.

- metal key winder

Birthday Wishes Barbie doll
The Barbie doll revolutionized play for girls. Introduced in 1959, it symbolized teenagers and consumerism. Dominating the market, it became the best-selling doll in history.

- fitted bodice
- tulle and satin skirt

Polaroid camera
In 1972, Polaroid unveiled a new "magic" camera that developed film in one minute. The SX-70 camera instantly captured the public's imagination.

- manual focus wheel
- viewfinder
- shutter release button
- picture exit slot

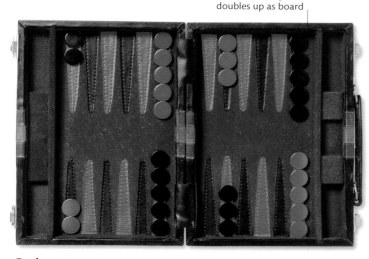

Backgammon set
Board games such as backgammon, which was first played by Persians around 5,000 years ago, have enduring appeal.

- leather carrying case doubles up as board

Rubik's cube
Invented by Hungarian design lecturer Erno Rubik in 1974, the Rubik's cube became such an addictive toy that players contracted a medical condition known as cubist's thumb.

- each face can be rotated independently

Game controller
A big hit since the late 1970s, the game controller has had several makeovers. This one for Microsoft's Xbox was popular from 2001.

- home button
- left thumb stick
- face buttons
- directional pad
- right thumb stick

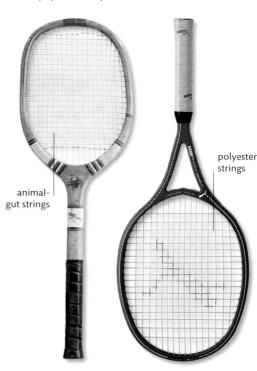

Golf bag and clubs
The rise of the middle-class professional saw golf, long held as an elite sport, emerge as a popular pastime, providing healthy outdoor activity at a relatively gentle pace.

- one of three "woods"
- cast-steel "iron" with graphite shaft
- putter

Single lens reflex (SLR) camera
Mass-market film photography enabled people with only limited means to afford a camera and film, and photography became a popular hobby from the 1970s.

- shutter release button
- film rewind crank

Tennis racket technology
Technology has played a major role in perfecting much-loved sports, transforming the heavy wooden tennis racket into its sleek modern form.

- animal-gut strings
- polyester strings

WOODEN-FRAMED RACKET

GRAPHITE-FRAMED RACKET

FASHION FOR THE PEOPLE

In the 20th century, fashion entered a world of democracy. Class hierarchies were discarded as people chose to dress up, dress down, stand out from the crowd, or blend in. Throughout, fashion's ability to reinvent itself has remained constant.

On trend ▷
Women the world over have been influenced by the latest haute couture featured in magazines such as *Vogue*. These magazines acted as a style barometer of the social and cultural changes that shaped the 20th century.

During the 20th century, it became harder to tell the rich from the poor by how they dressed. Ready-to-wear clothing became available at affordable prices, and clothes lost their class associations. Those with limited means could create a personal style, and fashion became accessible to people from all social levels. Trends changed constantly, as technology, culture, and world events influenced style. Women's hems rose and fell, clothes

emphasized femininity, then became more masculine, and comfort replaced constriction. Fashion reflected the mood of the period, from wartime austerity to political rebellion.

In recent decades, advances in man-made fibers, mass-production techniques, and the major influence of postwar subcultural styles have transformed fashion, and the choice of apparel, into a global phenomenon.

VOGUE

T
America
Ch
60 new fash

New Paris Fashions Important to

50 CENTS — Special section: Fashions

FASHION BEFORE 1945

From the turn of the century, functional, tailor-made suits slowly gave way to shorter hemlines for women and a less rigid structure. Two world wars brought with them periods of austerity. These were punctuated by the decadence of the vibrant Jazz Age in the 1920s, until the Great Depression forced fashion to focus once again on more sober practicalities.

V-neck insert with decorative buttons

Going-away outfit
With the world in economic crisis, this 1929 suit showed a "down to earth" attitude. The skirt, with side pleats, finishes just below the knee.

Fair Isle cardigan made from recycled yarn

notched lapel

high lace collar

jacket and waistcoat in matching tweed

plus fours knickerbockers reached mid-calf

Three-piece suit
The British Prince of Wales (later King Edward VIII) was a trendsetter. He popularized this plus fours suit, with roomy pants and a tweed waistcoat.

Skirt suit
This stylish French suit from 1908 moved away from the hourglass silhouette with a narrower skirt, masculine tailoring, and straighter line.

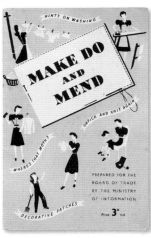

HINTS ON WASHING
MAKE DO AND MEND
PREPARED FOR THE BOARD OF TRADE BY THE MINISTRY OF INFORMATION
Price 3ᵈ net

Make Do and Mend
WWII forced people to be more resourceful in their fashion. This British Ministry of Information booklet from 1943 offers tips for recycling and repairing clothing.

only two box pleats were allowed per dress

Wartime utility clothes
During the austerity of wartime, even fabric was rationed. This dress is made from crease-resistant moygashel fiber, an artificial material.

front crease

Demob suit
After WWII, British men exchanged their wartime kit for "civvy" suits at demobilization centers after the war. The three-piece version was single breasted, in navy or brown.

Flapper dress

The 1920s was an era of extraordinary social change, as many old attitudes were swept away. Flappers were ultramodern women who embodied the new freedoms of the decade. The short, light, and skimpy flapper dress became their uniform. In this daring outfit, they could stride briskly, go to work, drive or bicycle, and, crucially, dance. This beautiful example, designed by British company Reville and Rossiter around 1925, typifies the modern Jazz era.

V-shaped neckline
emphasized by
beaded trim

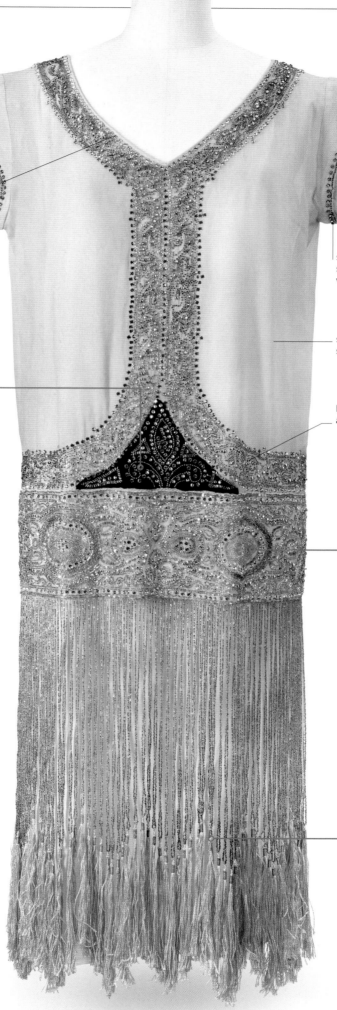

short capped
sleeves trimmed
with silver

soft and light
silk chiffon

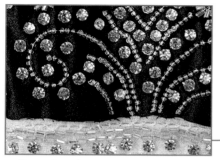

Delicate beadwork

The beadwork, stitched by hand, reflects the Art Deco style of the 1920s. It is characterized by geometric shapes and metallic, shiny beads.

heavy beading draws
attention to waist

BACK VIEW

THE JAZZ AGE

American novelist F. Scott Fitzgerald coined the phrase the Jazz Age in 1922 to describe the flamboyant, exciting era that emerged in America after WWI. It was a time of wild prosperity and decadence, and with new money came a revolution in morals and manners. However, the economic crisis of 1929 brought the fun to an abrupt end.

Drape and definition

The dropped waist is sewn with a mass of rhinestone embroidery and glass beads. This helped weigh down the light fabric and gave the dress a flattering drape.

Silk tassels

Hung at different lengths, tassels decorate the skirt and emphasize its short hem. Tassels were the perfect adornment for dancing.

FASHION AFTER 1945

Influenced by the economy, politics, and technology, clothes became less restrictive and more practical after WWII. With increasing personal freedom, women showed off their bodies, began to wear typically male clothing, and fashion shifted toward the young. Meanwhile, pop culture exerted a significant influence on the evolution of male clothing, as the old "rules" of dress were gradually relaxed.

stiff peak

Baseball cap

The modern baseball cap arrived in the 1940s, when latex rubber replaced buckram (coarse cotton) as the stiffening material inside the peak.

wide-brimmed hat

shawl collar

The New Look

Christian Dior's 1947 Bar suit is the iconic example of his New Look. Its hourglass silhouette was adopted by many other designers into the 1950s.

zippers and buckles typical of biker style

shawl collar

fringed sleeves

Leather jacket

Popularized by Hollywood, the leather jacket became universal wear from the 1950s. The look evoked rebellion and youth, and was adopted by all classes.

Winklepickers

With distinctively pointed toes, these shoes have been popular with rock-and-roll fans since the 1950s, although the sharpness of the point has changed over the decades.

outseam made of grosgrain (heavy, ribbed silk)

pull-on style with decorative laces

Tuxedo

Men were still required to wear formal attire for evening functions in the 1950s. The smart, iconic tuxedo never went out of fashion, but its tailoring was relaxed.

strapless bandeau top

Bikini

The bikini was fashionable in the 1950s, although it was regarded as controversial attire and took time to become popular.

full, pleated skirt emphasizes cinched waist and padded hips

That fresh-as-spring Courtelle feeling at Marks & Spencer

Synthetic fibers

Following the invention of nylon in the 1930s, a profusion of commercial man-made fibers was developed. This 1960s magazine ad promotes acrylic, a washable and durable alternative to wool.

Butterick 6243

Sewing pattern
In the 1960s, British designer Mary Quant created unique styles for teenagers, including miniskirts and hot pants. Her sewing patterns brought her designs to an even wider market.

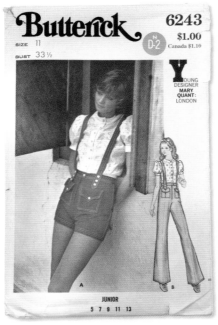

sloping raglan sleeves

padded shoulder emphasizes silhouette

Power dressing
In the 1980s, women wore clothes that were confident and tailored. This body-hugging dress gave a bold, hourglass shape.

bolero-style jacket

distinctive yellow stitching

Dr. Martens
The original Doc Marten boot was designed by a German soldier in 1945. They were later adopted in the UK by blue-collar workers and skinheads in the 1960s.

petal-shaped collar

short hemline

Shift dress
The classic 1960s dress had no waist or sleeves, and a stiff, printed collar. This example was made from linen dyed a vibrant pink.

corduroy fabric

Platform shoes
Platforms were impractical footwear, but that didn't stop thousands of women (and men) in the 1970s strapping them on.

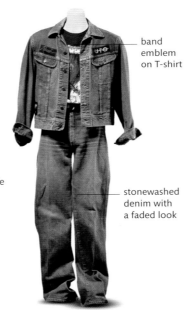

band emblem on T-shirt

stonewashed denim with a faded look

Denim outfit
In the 1980s, denim became part of the heavy metal "headbanger" subculture. Often the sleeves of the jacket would be cut off, to create a vest.

patch pockets

flared pants

Jumpsuit
Following the moon landing in the late 1960s, fashion looked to the future. This bright 1970s jumpsuit was fittingly modern and futuristic.

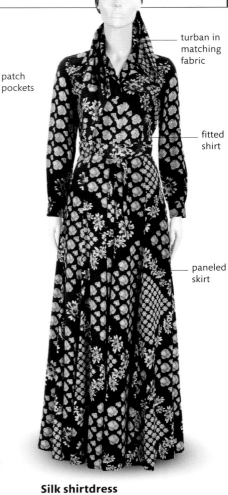

turban in matching fabric

fitted shirt

paneled skirt

Silk shirtdress
Long dresses in feminine prints became popular as hemlines dropped again in the 1970s. This silk ensemble includes a matching turban.

THE RISE OF JEANS

Originally designed for cowboys by Levi Strauss in the 19th century, and used as sturdy work wear by factory laborers, jeans have grown to be a truly universal garment. Rival companies, such as Wrangler and Lee, launched into the mainstream market in the 1940s, but James Dean popularized them in 1955 in *Rebel Without a Cause* (left). From this symbol of teen rebellion, jeans have been adopted across societies and subcultures and are now embraced the world over.

THE SPACE AGE

Until the second half of the 20th century, our knowledge of space came mainly from peering through telescopes. Space travel has greatly enhanced our understanding of both the Universe and life on Earth.

First man in space ▷
Russian Yuri Gagarin (1934-68) made history by becoming the first man in space. This poster celebrates his orbit of the earth on 12 April 1961. Gagarin's success shocked the Americans.

The dawn of the Space Age came on October 4, 1957, when the USSR launched Sputnik 1, the first artificial object to enter Earth orbit. What followed was an extraordinary era of innovation that captured the public imagination, although it was also linked to military developments and tensions between the US and the USSR. In 1961, President John F. Kennedy pledged that the United States would be the first nation to land a man on the moon. With the Soviet Union equally determined to achieve further success, a "space race" began. On July 20, 1969, Apollo 11 made the first Moon landing, and

American astronaut Neil Armstrong took the first steps on the lunar surface. The event was watched on television by one-fifth of the world's population. Since that historic moment, the latest technology has been harnessed to enable longer flights, larger crews, and spacecraft that can act as orbital laboratories.

In recent decades, unmanned missions have visited the outer reaches of the solar system, and thousands of satellites have been launched. Robotic spacecraft have explored inhospitable planets, and people spend months living and working in space.

SPACECRAFT

Space exploration only became possible when technology allowed astronauts to escape Earth's atmosphere and survive outside it. The American Apollo Space Program (1963–72) sent men to the Moon. Today most spacecraft are unmanned, from satellites to remote-controlled robots and space probes.

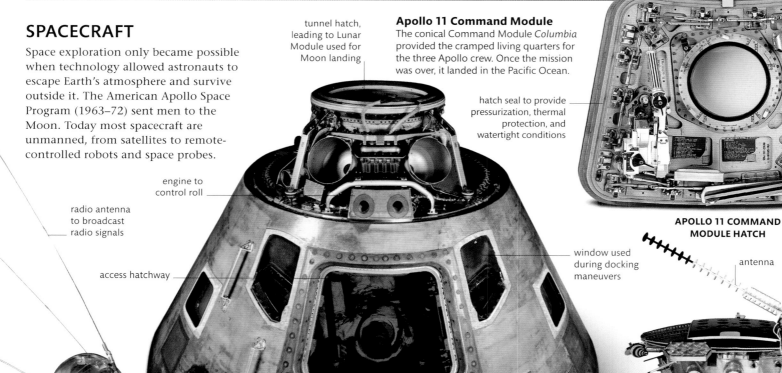

tunnel hatch, leading to Lunar Module used for Moon landing

Apollo 11 Command Module
The conical Command Module *Columbia* provided the cramped living quarters for the three Apollo crew. Once the mission was over, it landed in the Pacific Ocean.

hatch seal to provide pressurization, thermal protection, and watertight conditions

engine to control roll

radio antenna to broadcast radio signals

access hatchway

window used during docking maneuvers

APOLLO 11 COMMAND MODULE HATCH

antenna

Sputnik (model)
The size of a basketball, Russia's Sputnik 1 was the world's first artificial satellite. It orbited the Earth 1,440 times in October 1957.

Lunokhod 1 space probe
This unmanned Russian-built craft landed on the Moon in November 1970. Controlled from Earth, it spent 322 days analyzing the lunar soil.

SPACE EQUIPMENT

The history of space travel, from NASA's Apollo Program to modern space stations, is linked to the development of pioneering gadgets. It includes some of the most significant technical accomplishments in human history. Some tools and devices needed to be reinvented to deal with the unique challenges of working in space.

water container

Apollo 11 rucksack
Once back on Earth, the Apollo 11 crew was prepared to wait three days to be rescued. In the event, they splashed down just 15 miles (24 km) from a waiting US naval ship.

three pairs of sunglasses

instructions include alternative plans in case of emergency

razor-sharp stainless steel blade

machete sheath made from aluminum

aluminum body

wide-angle lens

HAMMER   CRIMPER-PLIERS

Apollo TV camera
Cameras like the one above were used on many Apollo missions to capture live images of the astronauts in space, enabling people on Earth to watch the space travelers.

Apollo 11 checklist
This checklist outlines the precise steps Neil Armstrong needed to take for the Lunar Module landing, his moonwalk, and the return to the Command Module.

Apollo 11 timer
Part of the cabin equipment, this timer is similar to a kitchen timer. It can be switched between a 60-minute interval and a 6-minute mode.

Mir space tools
This lightweight hammer was used onboard the Mir space station. The pliers could be gripped by a gloved hand and were used on spacewalks outside the space station.

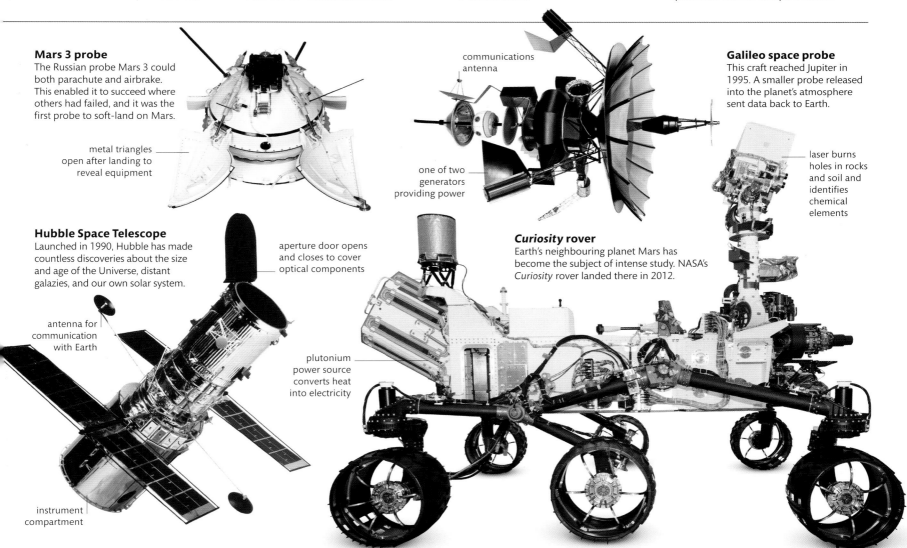

Mars 3 probe
The Russian probe Mars 3 could both parachute and airbrake. This enabled it to succeed where others had failed, and it was the first probe to soft-land on Mars.

metal triangles open after landing to reveal equipment

communications antenna

one of two generators providing power

Galileo space probe
This craft reached Jupiter in 1995. A smaller probe released into the planet's atmosphere sent data back to Earth.

laser burns holes in rocks and soil and identifies chemical elements

Hubble Space Telescope
Launched in 1990, Hubble has made countless discoveries about the size and age of the Universe, distant galazies, and our own solar system.

aperture door opens and closes to cover optical components

antenna for communication with Earth

Curiosity rover
Earth's neighbouring planet Mars has become the subject of intense study. NASA's *Curiosity* rover landed there in 2012.

plutonium power source converts heat into electricity

instrument compartment

WALKING IN SPACE

THE ISS SPACESUIT

The International Space Station (ISS) is one of the world's greatest feats of engineering. In orbit since 1998, the craft was built to enable a crew to live and work in space. The ISS is as large as an American football field, and it took 13 years to assemble. Sixteen countries now use it as a habitable working laboratory, not only to find out more about space but also how to improve life on Earth.

Life for the astronauts is unique. Orbiting the Earth at 17,500 mph (28,000 km/h) every 92 minutes, the crew sees 15 or 16 sunrises and sunsets a day. Many experiments take place both inside the ISS and out.

LAYERS OF PROTECTION

Working in space requires the very latest in space suits to enable the astronauts to leave the craft and explore outside. The ISS suit shown below was based on a design from the early 1980s that was used on NASA's Space Shuttle. The suit was upgraded in 1998 to meet the demands of building and working on the space station. Technically referred to as an Extravehicular Mobility Unit (EMU), the complex suit was engineered to protect the wearer from harsh temperatures, radiation, and space debris. With 14 layers between the wearer's skin and the vacuum of space, it weighs over 240 lb (108.9 kg) on Earth. It provides life support for up to nine hours, offering water, oxygen, and temperature control. The suits are kept on the ISS for up to two years to be used again by new astronauts coming aboard.

Mission patches
These patches celebrate different missions carried out by ISS space crews. Since the 1960s, astronauts have worn patches, usually ones they have designed themselves, to commemorate their missions.

> **"We opened the hatches...** and it was very pleasant to find ourselves in a place with... **good, clean air."**
>
> Sergei Krikalev, cosmonaut, on the first mission to the ISS, November 2, 2000

Primary Life Support Subsystem mounted on back of suit

mini workstation attached to chest

temperature control valve removes excess heat and prevents dehydration

cuff checklist summarizes tasks to be carried out on spacewalk

helmet light mounted to illuminate the working area

gold-tinted sun visor protects astronaut's vision

Backpack

The EMU contains a pack, worn on the back, called the Primary Life Support Subsystem. It holds equipment for oxygen supply, carbon dioxide removal, two-way communication, and water-cooling, as well as an electricity supply and a fan.

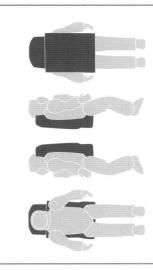

UNTETHERED SPACEWALKS

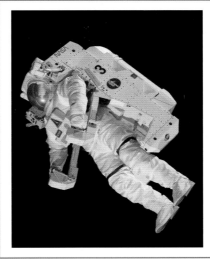

On March 18, 1965, Russian astronaut Alexei Leonov became the first man to walk in space, followed three months later by the American Edward White. In 1984, Bruce McCandless became the first astronaut to make an untethered spacewalk. He flew 320 feet (100 m) from the Space Shuttle *Challenger*. After just two further flights, the practice was considered unsafe and has not been repeated since.

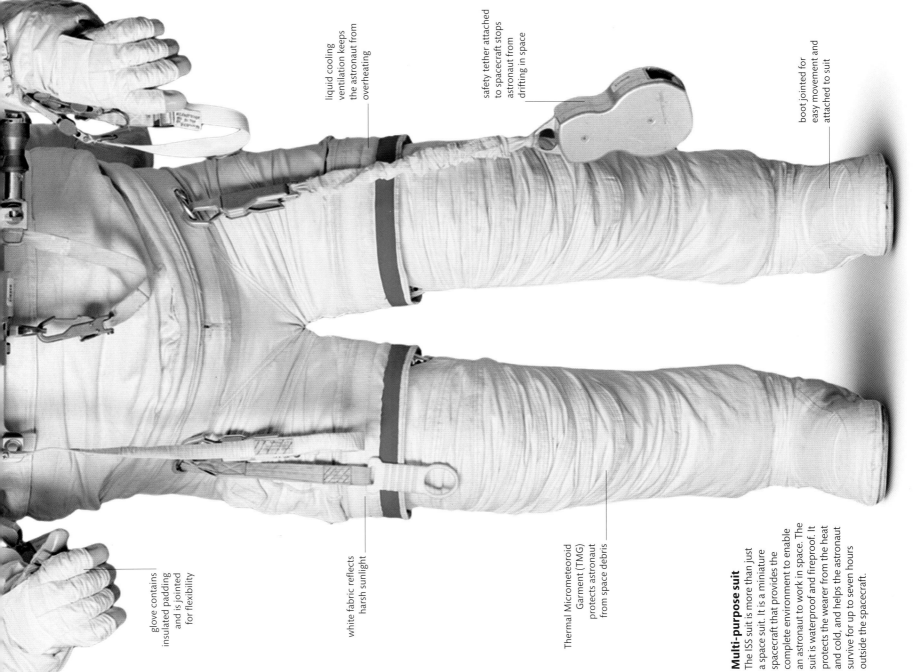

glove contains insulated padding and is jointed for flexibility

liquid cooling ventilation keeps the astronaut from overheating

safety tether attached to spacecraft stops astronaut from drifting in space

boot jointed for easy movement and attached to suit

white fabric reflects harsh sunlight

Thermal Micrometeoroid Garment (TMG) protects astronaut from space debris

Multi-purpose suit

The ISS suit is more than just a space suit. It is a miniature spacecraft that provides the complete environment to enable an astronaut to work in space. The suit is waterproof and fireproof. It protects the wearer from the heat and cold, and helps the astronaut survive for up to seven hours outside the spacecraft.

THE TECHNOLOGY OF MODERN WAR

The wars of the 20th century have led to many technological advances. Aircraft and weapons have become faster and deadlier, and enemy positions can be spotted by satellite or radar and eliminated with long-range missiles or drones.

Controlling the skies ▷
Fighter and bomber jets like this American F-4 Phantom play a dominant role in modern warfare. Air supremacy is derived from the aircraft's speed, maneuverability, and navigation and communications systems.

World War I saw men shot down in unprecedented numbers due to the advent of the machine gun. In 1945, the terrible force unleashed by the atomic bombs dropped on Japan brought a close to World War II but led to decades of global uncertainty and fear of nuclear war.

The ensuing Cold War resulted in further development of missiles and launchers. When new challenges were faced in the Gulf War in 1990, the US unleashed an arsenal of "smart"

technological weaponry, much of it never used before. Among the new weapons were devastating cruise missiles equipped with computerized guidance systems. Meanwhile, stealth fighter aircraft reflected radar signals and night-vision gadgets sought out enemies through the dark.

The United Nations, formed in 1945, utilized military technology to keep peace, while in guerilla warfare improvised weapons have come up against more advanced firepower.

WEAPONS

Since World War II, there have been attempts to make increasingly destructive weaponry as accurate as possible, using digital technology to avoid civilian casualties. Machine guns and assault rifles have become more lethal than ever, being used extensively during periods of political unrest in parts of Africa, the USSR, and the Middle East.

flight fins help steer missile

stabilizing wings

electric motor in tip

Sidewinder missile
Introduced in 1956 by the US Navy, this air-to-air "smart" missile finds its target using an infrared honing system. With a range of 18 miles (29 km) it carries a warhead that explodes on impact.

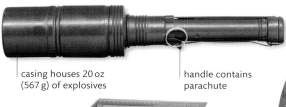

casing houses 20 oz (567 g) of explosives

handle contains parachute

RKG-3 anti-tank grenade
This Soviet grenade entered service after WWII. Used widely during the Vietnam and Cold Wars, it has a blast radius of 6.5 ft (2 m).

radar antenna

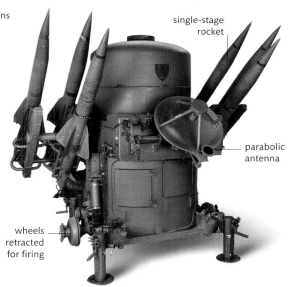

single-stage rocket

parabolic antenna

wheels retracted for firing

"Fat Man" bomb (replica)
Harnessing the explosive power of nuclear fission, this second US atomic bomb hit Nagasaki, Japan, on August 9, 1945, initially killing 50,000 people.

square tail box to keep bomb on stable flight path

Rapier missile launcher
Used by the British Army in the Falklands War (1982), the Rapier is a large rotating cylindrical unit that carries six missiles.

UNIFORMS

Military uniform has changed dramatically. Materials have improved, along with flexibility and maneuverability. In recent years, with the need for concealment in hostile and difficult terrain, camouflage has played a crucial role, making soldiers almost invisible.

digital camouflage

Night-vision goggles
These night-vision goggles attached to a helmet allow troops to operate at night. They played a crucial role during the Afghanistan and Iraq wars.

cleated sole

Tropical combat boots
These US Marine boots were made specifically for the hot, wet, and humid conditions of Vietnam. In the mid-1960s 5,000 pairs were produced a day.

Army desert camouflage
This type of camouflage was worn by British troops during conflicts in Iraq and Afghanistan from the 1990s. Its two-tone pattern blends in with the desert landscape.

Disruptive Pattern Material (DPM)

additional protection to collar

UN combat gear
The distinctive United Nations blue identifies UN soldiers as neutral wherever they are in the world. The tactical vest is lightweight and bulletproof.

sole made from old truck tires

Viet Cong sandals
Iconic for their use by the Viet Cong during the Vietnam War, these sandals, made of tire rubber, were simple but effective. The straps were made from strips of inner tube.

■ GUNS

solid wooden stock

AK-47 assault rifle
Developed in the Soviet Union in 1947, the Kalashnikov AK-47 is the most widespread assault weapon, with 100 million in use worldwide. It is cheap to manufacture and can fire 580 rounds per minute.

pistol grip

distinctive curved box magazine holds 30 rounds of ammunition

polymer frame flexes under impulse of firing and absorbs some recoil

accessory rail for lights or lasers

Glock 17 pistol
Designed in 1982 by Austrian Gaston Glock, this semiautomatic pistol is regarded as an exemplary firearm. It is widely used by military forces and law-enforcement agencies.

catch locks barrel in place

barrel can be changed in seconds

sight with low-light capacity and four-power magnification

MG 43 machinegun
This belt-fed light machinegun was developed in the late 1980s by German company Heckler and Koch. It is one of the most deadly guns ever invented.

safety catch can be set to fully automatic fire only

retaining bolt

Improvised pistol
Homemade guns, such as this 1980s South African model, have been used globally by insurgents and revolutionaries. Crudely made, they are often very dangerous to the user.

CONNECTING THE WORLD

The latter part of the 20th century saw an astounding evolution in computers and communications technology. Built on powerful devices, the "communications age" transformed the way we communicate with and connect the entire globe.

Fiberoptics ▷
Fiberoptics forms the backbone of the global telecommunications system. A single optical fiber slightly thicker than a human hair can carry huge amounts of information over long distances, as pulses of red light or infrared radiation.

The first technology that people used to communicate speedily over long distances was the telegraph. The first telephone networks opened in the 1880s, but uptake was slow until prices fell in the 1920s. It was not long after this that millions of people were also tuning in to radio broadcasts.

Electronic computers were first introduced in the 1950s, and from the late 1960s they gave businesses a new way to communicate, via computer networks. From the 1970s onwards, the miniaturisation of electronic components on small integrated circuits, or "chips," has enabled the development of electronic devices that were smaller and cheaper. The mobile phone and the personal computer became widespread in the 1990s, and access to the Internet — first via computers, then using smartphones and tablets — grew rapidly in the early years of the 21st century.

COMPUTERS AND THE INTERNET

The first computers were expensive and difficult to use. Smaller, cheaper, user-friendly personal computers became widespread in the 1980s. By the 1990s, companies called Internet service providers (ISPs) began providing the general public with access to the Internet, through which people can communicate via e-mail, the World Wide Web, and video conferencing.

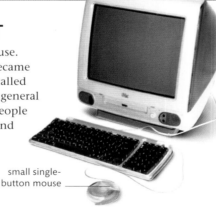

small single-button mouse

Apple computer
Apple introduced its first Macintosh computer in 1984. Later models, such as this iMac from 1998, were designed to make it easy for home users to connect to the Internet.

two floppy disk drives

IBM personal computer
In 1981, the US company IBM introduced the popular and influential IBM Personal Computer. It ran a text-based operating system supplied by the US company Microsoft.

Laptop
Small, portable computers with rechargeable batteries first became popular in the early 1990s, giving people the chance to continue with their work away from their desks.

Tablet
Apple's iPad, introduced in 2010, kick-started rapid development of tablet computers. Users interact via a touch screen interface rather than a mouse and physical keyboard.

touch screen interface

TELEPHONES

When a person makes a telephone call, a signal carrying his or her voice travels across a network that includes metal wires, optical fibers, and radio waves. That same network carries texts, images, and data, as well as voice calls. Today, Internet traffic shares much of the telephone network's infrastructure too.

1930s dial telephone
The automatic telephone exchange, introduced in the early 1900s, enabled callers to connect their own calls using a dial, instead of via switchboard operators.

1970s mobile phone
Mobile phones for use in moving vehicles date back to the 1950s, but handheld mobile phones and extensive cellular mobile networks were introduced in the 1970s.

battery takes ten hours to charge

base unit recharges phone battery

Cordless phone and handset
Cordless phones first became available in the 1980s. The handset communicates with a base station that is connected via cables to the telephone network.

touch screen

2000s smartphone
Smartphones have Wi-Fi access and serve as portable media players, cameras, Web browsers, and satellite navigation devices. They have revolutionized communication.

Telstar satellite
Launched in 1962, Telstar 1 was the first satellite to relay telephone calls and television pictures. Today, around 3,000 communications satellites orbit the planet.

solar panels with 3,600 solar cells in total on outer hull to generate power

aluminum body of satellite contains nickel-cadmium battery

typewriter linked to a telephone line

Teleprinter
Teleprinters were used to transmit and receive messages, at first over the telegraph network. From the 1920s to the 1980s, such messages were transmitted over a dedicated "telex" network.

number keys to dial recipient's fax machine

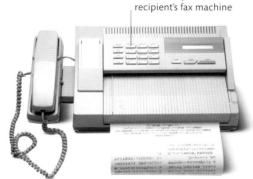

1990s fax machine
Fax machines scan documents and send a copy over the telephone. They were popular in the 1980s and 1990s, but Internet-based communication has largely superseded them.

TIMELINE OF WORLD HISTORY

EARLY SOCIETIES

In the millennia after 12,500 BCE, people in many parts of the world began cultivating plants, raising animals, and establishing settled communities. The era of the first farmers (known as the Neolithic era) saw many technological developments, including textiles and early metalworking, and monumental architecture such as Europe's megalithic tombs. Farming spread through trade and colonization. Agricultural productivity was increased by irrigation, by plows, and wheeled vehicles, and by using animals to draw them and to provide milk and wool. The first cities emerged and the first civilizations arose in the 3rd millennium BCE, in southern Mesopotamia, the Indus Valley, and Egypt, and later in China's Yangtze Valley, Mesoamerica, and Andean South America.

PAINTED HALAF JAR

c.18,000 BCE
Pottery-making begins
Hunter-gatherer communities in China begin to make pottery. Pottery-making develops in Japan in 14,000 BCE and then in other parts of the world at later dates, including c.6900 BCE in western Asia.

c.12,000 BCE
Permanent settlement begins
In the eastern Mediterranean and some parts of western Asia, many hunter-gatherers begin to live year-round in permanent settlements.

c.9000 BCE
Metalworking begins
Gold and native (naturally occurring, pure) copper are worked by cold-hammering in western Asia. By 7000 BCE, smelting copper ores to extract metal begins.

c.7000 BCE
First European farmers emerge
Agriculture spreads from Anatolia (modern Turkey) into southeastern Europe (Greece and the Balkans). Settling on fertile plains, farmers grow wheat and barley, and raise sheep and goats.

c.6000 BCE
Village cultures prosper
Prosperous agricultural village communities, such as the Halaf culture in Mesopotamia spread widely. Halafian pottery is decorated with multicolored geometric and animal-themed designs.

c.6000 BCE
Mummification begins
The Chinchorro culture of coastal Peru and Chile develop mummification techniques.

c.5900 BCE
Euphrates Valley farming communities established
The first farming communities are established in the Euphrates Valley in southern Mesopotamia, with cultivation dependent on irrigation.

20,000–7000 BCE

7000–5000 BCE

c.10,500 BCE
Farming begins
Sedentary communities in Syria begin cultivating rye. By 8000 BCE, farmers in the eastern Mediterranean are growing wheat, barley, pulses, and flax. Cultivation begins in the Americas and in New Guinea by 8000 BCE.

c.9000 BCE
Animals are domesticated
Farmers in western Asia begin to herd sheep and goats. Cattle and pigs are also domesticated. By 7000 BCE, zebu cattle are domesticated in Mehrgarh in modern Pakistan.

c.8000 BCE
First farmers in China
People near the Yellow River, China, cultivate broomcorn millet. Later, rice starts to be cultivated in the Yangtze River valley.

c.7000 BCE
Changes in the Green Sahara
Hunter-fisher communities of the Sahara, at this time grassland with lakes and rivers, start to herd cattle. After 6500 BCE, conditions become arid and people become more dependent on domestic animals and plants.

c.5500 BCE
European copper metallurgy develops
Copper metallurgy develops in the Balkans. Some of the earliest copper tools are made in this area.

c.5500–4500 BCE
Linear Pottery culture develops
The Linear Pottery culture, associated with the spread of European farming communities, emerges. Its distinctive pottery is found across central Europe and in some adjacent regions.

c.6000 BCE
Çatalhöyük prospers
Çatalhöyük, in modern Turkey, is a large early settlement, covering an area of 32 acres (13 ha). It is occupied by up to 8,000 people living in houses. Its inhabitants participated in obsidian exchange networks, grew crops, and raised sheep.

c.6000 BCE
Irrigation developed
Simple irrigation agriculture in central Mesopotamia begins. The development of water-control techniques enables farmers to colonize the Mesopotamian plains.

c.5100 BCE
Ai Bunar copper mining flourishes
A copper mining industry, based on a series of mine trenches, flourishes at Ai Bunar (modern Bulgaria).

SAHARAN ROCK PAINTING SHOWING CATTLE

MEGALITHIC TOMB, SOUTHERN FRANCE

c.3100 BCE
Egypt's First Dynasty established
King Menes (Narmer) unites the kingdoms of Upper (southern) and Lower (northern) Egypt, creating the First Dynasty of Egypt. He founds the first capital, at Memphis.

c.3200 BCE
South American mounds built
Complexes of large ritual structures on platform mounds with staircases begin to be built, and cotton is cultivated in coastal modern Peru.

c.4800 BCE
Megalithic tombs built
In north and west Europe, monumental tombs are often built for communal burials.

c.4500 BCE
Alloying discovered
In western Asia, a type of bronze, harder than soft copper is made by adding either copper ore containing arsenic or by adding arsenic to smelted copper.

c.4000 BCE
Earliest paddy fields created
In China, wet-rice cultivation using plowed, flooded paddy fields begins.

c.3200 BCE
Egyptian hieroglyphs developed
The Egyptian script is first used—it includes signs for words and for sounds. The hieroglyphic script is used in formal contexts, while a simpler version of the script, hieratic, is used for everyday writing. Hieroglyphs remain in use until the 4th century CE.

5000–4000 BCE

4000–3000 BCE

c.4500 BCE
Corn develops
Domestic corn is developed from wild teosinte in Mexico. Owing to the slow development of larger corncobs, corn only becomes a staple food supporting permanent settlements after 2000 BCE.

c.4500 BCE
Plowing invented
In western Asia, North Africa, and Europe, domestic animals are kept for milk, as well as for meat, and are used for pulling plows. Animal traction is one of the most labor-saving techniques invented.

c.3300 BCE
First written script developed
The first proper written script, including many pictographic signs, is developed by the Sumerians of Uruk, Mesopotamia, for administrative and accounting purposes.

c.3500 BCE
Stamp seals used
Stamp seals begin to be used in the new towns of western Asia for administrative and economic purposes.

c.3200 BCE
First bronze manufactured
In western Asia, tin is alloyed with copper to produce bronze, a hard metal that can be used to make effective tools.

c.5000–1000 BCE
The Old Copper Culture flourishes
The Old Copper Culture, a major industry and trade network based on cold-hammered native copper, locally mined in the Great Lakes region, flourishes in eastern North America.

c.4000 BCE
Grapes and olives farmed
Grape vines and olive trees are domesticated in the eastern Mediterranean. Olive oil and wine become important traded commodities in this region.

c.3500 BCE
Wheeled transportation invented
Wheeled transportation emerges and spreads rapidly through Eurasia. Carts are used for local transportation and as elite military vehicles.

c.5000 BCE
Andean agriculture develops
Farmers in the Andes start to keep llamas, for meat and transport, alpacas, for wool, and guinea pigs, for meat. A wide range of crops is grown in the Andes and in the Andean coastal areas.

c.3500 BCE
Indus plains farmed
Farmers move into the basin of the Indus River, establishing villages such as Harappa in Punjab, which grows eventually into a great city.

c.3200 BCE
Uruk emerges
Uruk, in Sumer (modern southern Iraq), grows into one of the world's first cities. By 2900 BCE, it has a population of around 60,000.

DEVELOPMENT OF WRITING

Writing evolved separately in different cultures, usually to keep economic and administrative records or for religious purposes. Writing meant people could communicate over distance and record information. As it developed, writing was used to reinforce royal authority, through propaganda such as monumental stone texts glorifying the deeds of kings and attributing their success to divine approval.

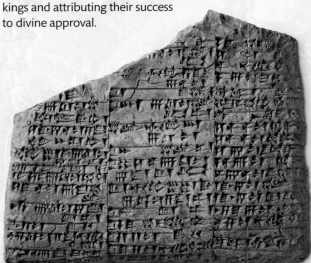

CUNEIFORM TABLET

800

The length, in years, of the Uruk period, which saw the dawn of urban life in Mesopotamia.

c.2600 BCE
King Gilgamesh rules
The semilegendary King Gilgamesh rules the Sumerian city of Uruk. He becomes the subject of a series of epic poems.

c.2900 BCE
Cuneiform script develops
In Sumer (modern southern Iraq), signs in the evolving script become less pictorial. They are formed of wedge-shaped (cuneiform) lines made by pressing sharpened reeds into soft clay.

c.2600–2500 BCE
Indus civilization emerges
More towns develop in the Indus basin, including the great city of Mohenjo-daro. Houses have bathrooms and often toilets, and an efficient drainage system.

c.2600 BCE
Bell Beaker culture spreads
The practice of burial with distinctive pottery vessels (Bell Beakers) spreads through much of Western Europe, along with copper metalworking. Graves also often contain archer's equipment, copper daggers, amber beads, and gold jewelry.

c.2600 BCE
Mummification practices develop
Natural preservation of the body in Egypt's desert ground is improved upon by artificial mummification during the Old Kingdom and mummification develops further in later times.

3000–2800 BCE | 2800–2600 BCE

---

c.2900 BCE
Early Dynastic period begins
The Early Dynastic period in Sumer (modern southern Iraq) begins. City-states including Uruk, Ur, and Shuruppak grow in power and extent.

c.3000 BCE
Aegean cultures flourish
Early Bronze Age societies cultivating vines, olives, and grains flourish in Crete, southern Greece, and the Cycladic islands. Sea trade is important to obtain copper and tin for making bronze.

c.3000 BCE
Longshan culture develops
In the Shandong Province and central plains of northern China, the Longshan culture develops. Following agricultural success, craftsmen make bronze tools and jade vessels, and weave silk.

c.2686 BCE
Old Kingdom established
King Sanakht accedes to the throne of Egypt, marking the beginning of the Third Dynasty and the Old Kingdom era—a time of strong, centralized rule.

c.2900–2400 BCE
First Stonehenge structures built
Wooden structures are built at the Stonehenge ceremonial complex in southern England.

c.2650 BCE
Step Pyramid of Saqqara built
Designed by the architect Imhotep, the first Egyptian pyramid, the Step Pyramid of Saqqara, is completed for King Djoser.

c.2600 BCE
South American cities emerge
The first known city in South America develops at Caral in the Supe valley (in modern Peru), supported by irrigation agriculture and rich coastal fisheries. Other settlements featuring temple complexes, such as Aspero, are also known in coastal Peru.

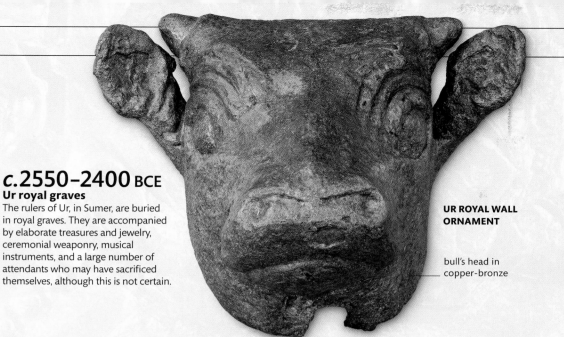

c.2550–2400 BCE
Ur royal graves
The rulers of Ur, in Sumer, are buried in royal graves. They are accompanied by elaborate treasures and jewelry, ceremonial weaponry, musical instruments, and a large number of attendants who may have sacrificed themselves, although this is not certain.

UR ROYAL WALL ORNAMENT

bull's head in copper-bronze

c.2334 BCE
Akkadian Empire formed
King Sargon of Akkad (in Mesopotamia) defeats the ruler of Sumer to control both Sumer and Akkad. Through subsequent campaigns to Elam in modern Iran, the eastern Mediterranean, Syria, and Anatolia (modern Turkey), Sargon and his ancestors carve out the world's first empire—the Akkadian Empire—with influence from the eastern Mediterranean to the Gulf.

c.2550–2370 BCE
Umma–Lagash conflict
The border conflict between Umma and Lagash, in Mesopotamia, is the earliest international conflict to be recorded.

c.2500 BCE
Indus civilization reaches peak
The Indus civilization reaches its peak, stretching 1,060 miles (1,700 km) from east to west and 800 miles (1,300 km) from north to south. The region's prosperity is based on farming, mining, crafts, and trade.

c.2500 BCE
Syrian city-states emerge
In Syria and the eastern Mediterranean, fortified cities such as Ebla and Mari develop.

c.2300 BCE
Stonehenge stones erected
Large stones are erected at Stonehenge in southern England. The entrances and stone arrangements mark astronomical events—the midsummer sunrise and midwinter sunset. The stones are rearranged several times over succeeding centuries.

2600–2400 BCE

2400–2200 BCE

c.2575–2500 BCE
Pyramids of Giza constructed
The three great pyramids at Giza are built for the Fourth Dynasty pharaohs Khufu, Khafra, and Menkaure. They are guarded by the statue of the Sphinx, which may bear the features of King Khafra.

c.2500 BCE
Trade routes developed
Long-distance trade routes develop in South America, linking the coast with the Andes.

c.2345–2181 BCE
Sixth Dynasty established
Egypt's Sixth Dynasty sees a weakening of the power of the Old Kingdom rulers in favor of regional governors called nomarchs. By the end of this period, the authority of the Egyptian rulers has steadily eroded.

c.2200 BCE
European Bronze Age begins
Copper ores and tin ore are used to make bronze, which replaces copper for metalworking across Europe.

6.5 million

The estimated mass, in tons, of the Great Pyramid of Giza.

THE SPHINX AND PYRAMIDS AT GIZA

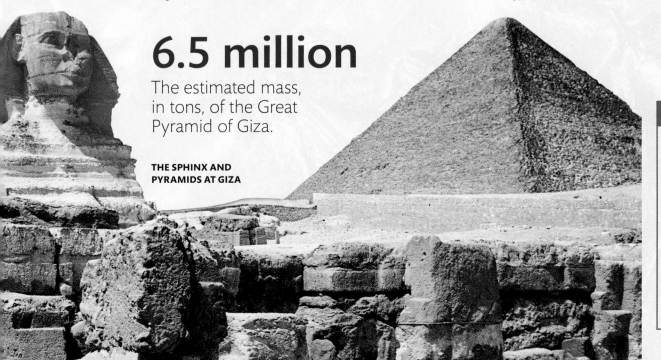

PYRAMID CONSTRUCTION

Incredible feats of engineering, the pyramids at Giza were constructed not by slaves as was once thought, but by a staff of full-time craftsmen and masons supplemented by farmers performing a type of national service during the Nile floods. Huge blocks of stone were cut from local quarries, hauled onsite using sleds, and then heaved up ramps, which grew ever higher as construction progressed.

c.2193 BCE
Akkadian Empire collapses
The Guti, mountain people from the east, defeat weak Akkadian kings. Sumerian city-states such as Kish, Ur, and Lagash reassert their independence. For the next 80 years, the city-states campaign against the Guti and Elam and vie with each other for dominance of Sumer.

c.2181 BCE
Old Kingdom ends
The Sixth Dynasty and the Old Kingdom period ends in Egypt after a series of natural disasters, including famine, weakens the authority of the king. The First Intermediate period begins.

c.2150 BCE
Nubian Kingdom flourishes
In southern Egypt, the Nubian Kingdom, with its capital at Kerma on the Nile, prospers after the collapse of the Egyptian Old Kingdom.

2004 BCE
Fall of Ur
The city of Ur falls to the Elamites, ending the dynasty of Ur.

c.2000 BCE
Chariots spread
Light, maneuverable chariots drawn by horses spread from the steppe regions west of the Caspian into West Asia, Europe, and China. Chariots are used particularly in warfare, as a fighting platform by high-status individuals.

c.2000 BCE
Philippines colonized
Farmers from Taiwan spread into the Philippines around 2000 BCE. From there people gradually spread into Indonesia, nearby islands in Southeast Asia, and Micronesia.

c.2000–1500 BCE
Minoans reach height
The Minoan civilization flourishes. Crete's prosperity is based on agriculture and trade including luxury craft products. The Minoans build great palaces near sanctuaries where they hold processions and feasts.

c.1894 BCE
Babylonian dynasty founded
The First Dynasty of Babylon is founded. The city-state grows in importance after the Euphrates River shifts westward in the 2nd millennium BCE, depriving more easterly states of its waters.

bird

snake

FIGURINE OF MINOAN MOTHER GODDESS

2200–2000 BCE

2000–1800 BCE

c.2055 BCE
Middle Kingdom begins
The Theban ruler Nebhepetre Mentuhotep II becomes king. In 2040 BCE, he defeats his rivals and unites Egypt once more. This begins the era known as the Middle Kingdom.

c.2112–2095 BCE
Reign of Ur-Nammu
Ur-Nammu founds the third dynasty of Ur, which witnesses a revival of Sumerian power, as well as an artistic and cultural renaissance. He commissions the first ziggurat in Ur—an imposing stepped platform topped with a temple—and others at Uruk, Eridu, and Nippur.

c.2000–1750 BCE
Arctic settlers spread
The Arctic Small Tool population, ancestors of the Inuit, spread from modern Alaska across Canada to settle in Greenland.

c.1900 BCE
City of Ashur flourishes
In northern Mesopotamia, the important city-state of Ashur develops a trading network across eastern Anatolia (modern Turkey).

c.1965 BCE
Egypt takes Nubia
Senwosret I conquers northern Nubia, extending Egypt's borders as far as the Second Cataract of the Nile. Nubia yields gold and copper and is a source of slaves.

1813 BCE
Kingdom of Upper Mesopotamia established
The Assyrian King Shamshi-Adad conquers northern Mesopotamia to establish the kingdom of Upper Mesopotamia—the forerunner of the Greater Assyrian Empire.

c.1900 BCE
Cretan script developed
A hieroglyphic script is developed by the Minoans, evolving by c.1750 BCE into the Linear A script.

THE ZIGGURAT OF UR

cuneiform text describes prayer for the well-being of the king

STELA OF HAMMURABI OF BABYLON

c.1800 BCE
Andean culture develops
Pottery-making and textile-weaving begins in modern Peru, canal-irrigation agriculture develops, and settlements such as El Paraíso, Sechin Alto, and La Florida are dominated by massive temple complexes.

c.1792–1750 BCE
Babylonian Empire established
Under King Hammurabi, Babylon becomes the foremost state in Mesopotamia. Hammurabi conquers the city-states of southern and central Mesopotamia and creates the Babylonian Empire. His law code presents his view of legal and ethical principles, and he exercises personal control over the affairs of his state.

c.1450 BCE
Lapita people migrate
People making distinctive stamp-decorated Lapita pottery begin to colonize the Pacific Islands, spreading eastward from Melanesia in their single outrigger canoes.

c.1750 BCE
Sechin Alto constructed
The large ceremonial complex of Sechin Alto is constructed in Peru, and by 1200 BCE, it is the largest temple complex in the Americas.

c.1600–1400 BCE
Mycenaean civilization emerges
On the Greek mainland, magnificent burials furnished with gold death masks and weaponry herald the emergence of the Mycenaean civilization.

c.1450 BCE
Alphabetic scripts develop
Various scripts using a sign to represent each consonant develop in the eastern Mediterranean. Around 1150 BCE, the precursor of the modern alphabet emerges.

c.1500–900 BCE
Aryans migrate
Speakers of the Aryan branch of the Indo-European language family from southern Russia settle in northern India.

c.1800 BCE
Indus declines
In south Asia, the Indus civilization goes into decline and its cities are gradually abandoned, but farming communities continue to flourish.

c.1725 BCE
Second Intermediate Period begins
The Middle Kingdom in Egypt is torn by unrest. In the subsequent Second Intermediate Period, an Egyptian dynasty rules Upper Egypt from Thebes, while Lower Egypt is controlled by Asiatic rulers (the Hyksos).

c.1595 BCE
Hittites sack Babylon
The Babylonian Empire, declining under Hammurabi's successors, is finally destroyed by the Hittites, who themselves soon decline as a result of succession disputes.

c.1500 BCE
Power struggles begin
The Egyptians, Mitanni, and New Kingdom Hittites compete for control of the eastern Mediterranean.

1800–1600 BCE   1600–1400 BCE

c.1700 BCE
Shang dynasty begins
The Shang dynasty develops along the Yellow River. Their first capital is established at Zhengzhou. The Shang develop a script ancestral to that of modern China.

c.1628 BCE
Eruption of Thera
A massive volcanic eruption destroys the center of the Aegean island of Thera (Santorini), burying three-story houses painted with frescoes in the Minoan-related town of Akrotiri.

c.1550 BCE
New Kingdom begins
The Theban King Ahmose I drives the Hyksos from Lower Egypt, ushering in the third period of settled rule in Egypt, known as the New Kingdom.

c.1500 BCE
Micronesian islands colonized
Palau and the Marianas in western Micronesia are colonized by 1500 BCE from the Philippines. Reaching the Marianas involves a remarkable open-sea crossing of 1,550 miles (2,500 km).

c.1650 BCE
Hittite Kingdom established
The Hittites establish the Old Kingdom in central Anatolia (modern Turkey), with Hattusa as its capital. They use cuneiform, but also develop their own script, Luwian hieroglyphic.

c.1500 BCE
Valley of the Kings used for burials
Egyptian rulers are buried in rock-cut tombs in the Valley of the Kings, near Thebes, for the first time.

c.1450 BCE
Mycenaeans take Crete
Most of the Minoan palaces in Crete are destroyed, leaving Knossos as the only functional palace. The Mycenaeans take control of the island. They use the Linear B script, an adaptation of Linear A to suit their own, early Greek language.

IRON-WORKING

By c.1500 BCE, the Hittites were employing iron working to make luxury objects. Later, as technology developed, the Hittites created weapons, such as the blade of this ceremonial ax. Although the Hittites traded iron goods, they kept this technology secret for about 300 years. Around 1200 BCE, iron-working spread through West Asia and to Greece, and then through Europe after 1000 BCE.

CEREMONIAL AX

134
The number of massive columns in the famous Hypostyle Hall at the Theban complex of Karnak.

c.1500–1150 BCE
Karnak Temple built
Most of the Karnak Temple complex is constructed at Thebes.

cup depicts an octopus pattern

MYCENAEAN KYLIX (DRINKING CUP)

c.1400–1200 BCE
Shang capital moves
In China, the capital of the flourishing Shang civilization moves from Zhengzhou to Xi'ang (Huanbei). Anyang eventually becomes the last of several Shang capitals.

c.1350 BCE
Assyria reasserts its independence
The small state of Assyria, centered on the city of Ashur, breaks free from domination by the Mitanni Empire and concludes a treaty with Babylonia.

c.1300 BCE
Mycenaeans at their peak
The Mycenaean civilization reaches its peak between 1400 and 1250 BCE. The Mycenaeans build massive defenses around their palace citadels, with underground cisterns, and drain Lake Kopais for agricultural land, a remarkable feat.

c.1279 BCE
Ramesses II comes to power
Pharaoh Ramesses' 67-year reign is a time of stability and prosperity for Egypt. Through a combination of war, diplomacy, and strategic marriage, Ramesses extends Egyptian influence to western Asia.

c.1259 BCE
Peace treaty signed
Pharaoh Ramesses II negotiates a pioneering peace treaty with the new Hittite king, Hattusilis III, partitioning the eastern Mediterranean between Egypt and the Hittites. He also takes two Hittite princesses in marriage.

c.1200–1050 BCE
Olmec culture flourishes
In Mexico, the Olmec culture rises to prominence with the development of the ceremonial center and city at San Lorenzo.

> **"King of Kings** am I... If anyone would know **how great I am** and **where I lie,** let him surpass one of my works.**"**
>
> Diodorus Siculus, from the inscription on the base of a statue of Ramesses II taken from *Bibliotheca historica*, 1st century BCE

c.1200 BCE
Nomadic pastoralism fully developed
After 2000 BCE, some agricultural communities, settled around the steppe margins of Central Asia, began a more mobile lifestyle herding animals in the region. By 1200 BCE, a fully nomadic pastoral way of life has developed.

c.1180 BCE
Hittite Empire collapses
Following the sacking of their capital, Hattusas, Hittite possessions in the eastern Mediterranean are lost and the empire fragments.

1400–1200 BCE | 1200–1050 BCE

---

c.1300 BCE
Urnfield culture emerges
New funerary practices sweep through most of Europe, suggesting a major change in religious beliefs. It becomes the norm to cremate the dead and bury their ashes in funerary urns within large cemeteries.

c.1336 BCE
Tutankhamun reigns
Akhenaten's son Tutankhamun ascends the throne at the age of nine in Egypt. During his reign the old gods are restored and the new capital is abandoned.

c.1352 BCE
New religion founded
Amenhotep IV becomes Egypt's pharaoh. In 1347 BCE, he breaks with the traditional religion and initiates the worship of a single deity, the Sun-disk Aten. He changes his name to Akhenaten, meaning "glory of the Aten," and founds a new capital called Akhetaten, "horizon of the Aten."

c.1200 BCE
Fiji colonized
Lapita colonists reach the Solomon Islands, Vanuatu, New Caledonia, and as far as Fiji and its archipelago by 1200 BCE.

c.1210 BCE
Assyria expands
Assyria defeats the Hittites, the kingdom of Urartu (modern Armenia), the Mitanni, and conquers Babylonia.

c.1200–1100 BCE
Sea Peoples rampage
Waves of migrants, known collectively as the Sea Peoples, move through the eastern Mediterranean, leading to attacks on Cyprus, Egypt, Anatolia (modern Turkey), and Canaan and Syria in the eastern Mediterranean.

1070 BCE
Third Intermediate Period begins
The Egyptian New Kingdom ends as the power of the pharaohs is eroded by a priestly elite who have gained control of many areas. Egypt enters a time of unrest called the Third Intermediate Period.

c.1050 BCE
Dark Age of Greece begins
Mycenaean palaces are abandoned by 1050 BCE. This triggers the so-called Dark Age of Greece, when writing falls out of use. It is not reintroduced until c.750 BCE.

RELIGION IN EGYPT
Egyptian religion was immensely complex, with a large number of gods, many of them localized and appearing with different aspects. Earlier pharaohs associated themselves with the sky god Horus or the Sun god Re, but gradually the cult of Osiris, king of the dead, became dominant. The need to ensure the immortality of the ruler's soul after death was the primary focus of Egyptian religious belief.

OSIRIS, KING OF THE DEAD

c.1027 BCE
Zhou dynasty begins
In China, a new dynasty replaces the Shang when King Wu of Zhou defeats the last Shang ruler, Di Xin. The Zhou dynasty rules China for 700 years.

c.1000 BCE
Ganges Valley communities settle
Farming communities begin to settle in the Ganges Valley, in India.

c.1000 BCE
Israelite capital founded
King David unites the Israelite tribes and makes Jerusalem his capital. David's son Solomon increases Israelite territory and builds a magnificent palace and temple in the capital, employing Phoenician craftsmen.

c.900 BCE
Chavín culture develops
Most Peruvian Andean ceremonial centers are abandoned after 900 BCE, but a new complex is founded at Chavín de Huantar, probably the center of a religious cult.

c.900 BCE
Olmecs influence neighbors
La Venta, in modern Mexico, becomes the main Olmec center. This large settlement is dominated by a tall pyramid—the forerunner of Mayan and other Mesoamerican temples. The Olmecs also devise a script of glyphs. Their influence spreads across Mesoamerica, impacting on the emerging Zapotecs and Maya.

c.900 BCE
Lapita spread continues
Colonists spread further into Polynesia, reaching Samoa and Tonga around 1000 BCE and outlying islands such as Tikopia and Anuta by 900 BCE.

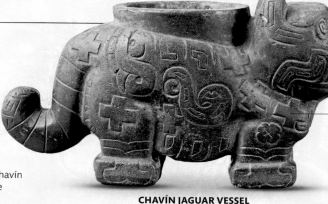

incised with geometric motifs

CHAVÍN JAGUAR VESSEL

c.800 BCE
Hallstatt region flourishes
The area around Hallstatt in modern Austria becomes a center for an early Iron Age culture. Hallstatt chieftains dominate local salt-mining and ironworking. They live in hilltop forts and are buried with rich grave goods.

776 BCE
Panhellenic Games held
The first Panhellenic Games are held in Olympia, Greece, and every four years thereafter.

753 BCE
Rome founded
According to legend, the Latin chief Romulus founds the city of Rome. In its early days, the city, built on seven hills, is ruled by various peoples, including the Etruscans, Latins, and Sabines.

c.750 BCE
Wet-rice cultivation spreads
Paddy fields to grow rice begin to be created in Korea in the early 1st millennium BCE and the practice spreads to Japan.

1050–800 BCE   800–700 BCE

---

c.1000 BCE
Phoenicians gain power
The Phoenicians become a major maritime power as individual Phoenician city-states establish colonies and ports around the Mediterranean.

RELIEF CARVING DEPICTING A PHOENICIAN COMMERCIAL SHIP

c.911 BCE
Assyria expanding
Strong Assyrian kings expand Assyria, conquering states in Syria and the eastern Mediterranean.

c.814 BCE
Carthage founded
Phoenicians from Tyre (in modern Lebanon) found a colony at Carthage, in modern Tunisia, to engage in trade.

c.850 BCE
First settlement at Rome built
The earliest settlement is built on the Palatine hill on the site of Rome, in Italy.

c.750 BCE
Kushites conquer Egypt
Piye, the Kushite ruler of Nubia, conquers both Upper and Lower Egypt, and unites them under Kushite rule.

c.726–721 BCE
Revolts against Assyria
Revolts in Israel were quickly suppressed, and the "ten lost tribes" of Israel are deported to northern Mesopotamia.

771 BCE
Eastern Zhou period begins
In China, fleeing northern invaders, the Zhou, move their capital east to Luoyang, marking the beginning of the Eastern Zhou period.

701 BCE
Assyrians invade Judaea
A revolt in Judaea is savagely put down by the Assyrian ruler Sennacherib; he sacks Lachish and other Judaean cities, but fails to take Jerusalem.

ANCIENT CIVILIZATIONS

The millennium that followed 700BCE saw much of the world's population incorporated into the great Classical civilizations of Eurasia—the Greek, Roman, Persian, Indian, and Chinese civilizations. These empires went on to reach unparalleled levels of sophistication and military superiority, and set models for administration and scholarship that would be followed for many centuries. In Central and South America, Africa, and Japan, new civilizations also emerged, in many ways equally advanced, but with much smaller reach than those of Eurasia. The Classical era also saw the birth of some influential religions—Buddhism, Judaism, and Christianity.

*c.*700 BCE
Etruscans expand
The Etruscans expand southward from modern Tuscany and Umbria, Italy. Their language remains undeciphered, but lavish tombs indicate a rich material culture.

terracotta jug

ETRUSCAN VASE

*c.*630 BCE
Assyria suffers losses
Assyria loses Egypt and Palestine, and in 626 BCE the Babylonians regain their independence.

663 BCE
Assyrian Empire peaks
The Assyrians sack Thebes in Egypt. The Assyrian Empire reaches its greatest extent.

*c.*630 BCE
Greek colonies formed
Greek settlers found Cyrene (in Libya) and, in about 600 BCE, Massilia (Marseilles). New cities are established as far west as Spain, and around the Black Sea coast.

621 BCE
Draconian law written
Shortly after a damaging popular uprising by the nobleman Cylon, Athens' first law code is drafted by Draco. The Draconian law is later known for the severity of the punishments it prescribed.

605 BCE
Nebuchadnezzar victorious
King Nebuchadnezzar II, ruler of the Neo-Babylonian Empire, defeats the Egyptians, repairs Babylon's main ziggurat, and orders the building of the famous Hanging Gardens of Babylon.

612 BCE
Assyrian state disappears
The Babylonians, Medes, and Scythians sack the Assyrian capital of Nineveh, and the Assyrian Empire crumbles. By 609 BCE the Assyrian state has disappeared.

700–650 BCE

650–600 BCE

689 BCE
Babylon sacked
Babylon is destroyed by Sennacherib, ruler of Assyria.

668 BCE
Ashurbanipal expels Taharka
The Assyrian King Ashurbanipal expels King Taharka from Memphis, reestablishing the Assyrian government in Egypt.

660 BCE
Emperor Jimmu begins reign
The traditional date for the start of the reign of Jimmu, the legendary first emperor of Japan and believed to be descendant of the sun goddess Amaterasu.

*c.*610 BCE
King Alyattes issues coins
King Alyattes of Lydia in Anatolia (modern Turkey) issues the world's first coins.

ASHURBANIPAL HUNTING LIONS

*c.*700 BCE
Greek city-states flourish
In Greece, the rise to preeminence of a number of city-states begins—notably Athens, Sparta, and Corinth. In Corinth, a new type of ruler, the "tyrant," emerges with the overthrow of the Bacchiadae kings in 658 BCE.

*c.*700 BCE
Scythian settlements formed
Nomadic Scythians from Central Asia begin to establish permanent settlements in Eastern Europe.

c.600 BCE
The Medes take control
Much of the Middle East falls under the control of the short-lived Median Empire.

c.600 BCE
Paracas culture emerges
The Paracas culture emerges in the Andes. They are famed for their intricate textiles.

c.600 BCE
Aryan kingdoms dominate
Aryan kingdoms dominate northern India.

597 BCE
Jerusalem captured
The Neo-Babylonian Empire under Nebuchadnezzar II captures Jerusalem and installs its own ruler. But he turns against the Babylonians, who retaliate by burning much of the city and destroying the Jewish Temple.

GLAZED BULL, ISHTAR GATE, BABYLON (BUILT BY NEBUCHADNEZZAR II)

539 BCE
Cyrus captures Babylon
Cyrus the Great captures Babylon, acquiring most of Mesopotamia and making the Persian Empire the greatest in the Middle East.

c.515 BCE
Darius I builds palace
Darius I of the Persian Achaemenid Empire, builds a royal residence at Susa, the former capital of Elam, in Mesopotamia.

19
The number of battles fought by Darius I over the period of a single year.

509 BCE
Roman Republic established
A group of Romans expel the Etruscan king, fearing the growing tyranny of his rule. They establish a Republic where supreme authority is held by two magistrates, called consuls, who are elected each year.

600–550 BCE

550–500 BCE

c.600 BCE
Sparta dominates
Sparta conquers almost all of the southern Peloponnese and establishes a stratified social system.

550 BCE
Persian Empire founded
The Persian King Cyrus the Great defeats Medes and founds the Persian (Achaemenid) Empire.

c.563 BCE
Buddha is born
The Buddha—Gautama Siddhartha, the primary figure in the Buddhist religion—is born.

c.530 BCE
Etruscan civilization reaches its peak
The Etruscan civilization reaches its peak in Italy.

525 BCE
Persian king becomes pharaoh
The Persian King Cambyses II annexes Egypt, capturing the royal capital at Memphis and installing himself as pharaoh.

507 BCE
Democracy established
The statesman Cleisthenes establishes a democratic government in the Greek city-state of Athens.

c.520–460 BCE
Sanskrit grammar developed
The Indian scholar Panini organizes Sanskrit grammar.

THE BUDDHA (c.563–483 BCE)

Around 530 BCE, Gautama Siddharta, a Hindu prince of Kapilvastu in modern Nepal, had a religious revelation and rejected his noble upbringing to embark on a quest for "enlightenment." Six years later he began to preach a way of moderate asceticism, known as the Middle Way, to gain release from the suffering of material life. He is known as the Buddha—the "awakened one" in Sanskrit—and his followers, who became known as Buddhists, spread his ideas throughout South Asia.

> "It is better to **conquer yourself** than to win a thousand battles. Then the **victory is yours.** It **cannot be taken from you...**"
>
> The Buddha, Gautama Siddharta

*c.*500 BCE
Zapotec hieroglyphs developed
The Zapotecs develop hieroglyphic writing in Central America. They begin to build the city of Monte Albán in the Oaxaca Valley, Mexico.

480–479 BCE
Battle of Salamis
The Persian King Xerxes I invades Greece and burns Athens, but is defeated by Athenian general Themistocles at the naval Battle of Salamis.

30 percent
The estimated proportion of the Athenian population that died during the Peloponnesian War.

GREEK HELMET

486 BCE
Xerxes becomes king
Xerxes becomes the Persian King on the death of his father, Darius, the architect of the Persian Empire.

490 BCE
Battle of Marathon
Led by Miltiades, the Athenian Greeks defeat a far larger Persian force at the Battle of Marathon.

475 BCE
Warring States period begins
In China, the political system of the Spring and Autumn period evolves into the Warring States period.

431 BCE
Peloponnesian War begins
The Peloponnesian War begins between the rival Greek states of Athens and Sparta.

413 BCE
Shishunaga dynasty founded
The Shishunaga dynasty is founded in Magadha, India.

500–450 BCE

450–400 BCE

*c.*490 BCE
Hanno makes epic voyage
The Carthaginian mariner Hanno sails far down the west coast of Africa.

*c.*500 BCE
Ironworking spreads
Ironworking spreads to Southeast Asia and East Africa.

478 BCE
Delian League founded
Athens founds the Delian League to counter Sparta's attempts to dominate Greece. The League soon evolves into the Athenian Empire.

*c.*450 BCE
La Tène culture emerges
The Celtic La Tène culture emerges in Central Europe.

447 BCE
Golden Age begins
Athens flourishes during its "Golden Age" under the statesman Pericles. In 447 BCE the construction of the second Parthenon begins.

413 BCE
Athenians defeated
The Athenians are defeated by the Syracusans in Sicily. Virtually their entire army is captured in this major encounter in the Peloponnesian War.

404 BCE
Fall of Athens
The Spartans capture Athens, ending the Peloponnesian War. The pro-Spartan Council of Thirty is set up to govern it.

THE PARTHENON ON THE ACROPOLIS, IN ATHENS, GREECE

"Know thee not that the end and **object of conquest is to avoid doing the same thing as the conquered.**"

Alexander the Great, from Lives by Plutarch

ALEXANDER THE GREAT LEADS HIS TROOPS INTO BATTLE

378 BCE
Thebans defeat Spartans
Exiled Theban democrats lead an uprising against the pro-Spartan ruling party. The Spartan garrison abandons the city of Thebes.

359 BCE
Philip II comes to power
The Macedonian King Philip II comes to power and begins to transform a minor kingdom into a major power.

338 BCE
Latin League dissolved
The Romans defeat the Latin League, a confederation of neighboring tribes. Many of the former Latin cities are absorbed into the Roman state.

323 BCE
Alexander dies
Alexander dies in Babylon. His empire begins to disintegrate among warring factions.

400–350 BCE

350–300 BCE

c.390 BCE
Celts sack Rome
An army of Celts attacks the Etruscan city of Clusium, defeats a Roman army at the Battle of the Allia, and then takes Rome itself.

343 BCE
Nectanebo II
Nectanebo II, the last native Egyptian pharaoh, is overthrown by the Persians.

338 BCE
Macedonians control Greece
King Philip II of Macedonia defeats a coalition of Greek states and gains control over most of Greece.

322 BCE
Empire divided
Wars break out between Alexander the Great's former generals, who carve up his empire to create rival kingdoms.

336 BCE
Alexander becomes commander
After Philip II's assassination, his son Alexander becomes commander of the major Greek city-states.

322 BCE
Mauryan Empire founded
In India, Chandragupta Maurya founds the Mauryan Empire.

371 BCE
Battle of Leuctra
The Theban general Epaminondas wins the Battle of Leuctra against Sparta. Thebes is now the dominant power in Greece.

ALEXANDER THE GREAT (356–323 BCE)

At the age of 20, Alexander inherited much of modern Greece from his father. By his death, just 13 years later, he had extended his empire to cover a vast area from the Indus River in the east to Illyria in the west. Alexander was a brilliant general but prone to acts of impetuous violence. He alienated many native Macedonians when he adopted Persian court rituals. Alexander did not name an heir and his empire fell apart after his death.

329–327 BCE
Bactria and Sogdiana conquered
Alexander conquers Bactria and Sogdiana, in the easternmost regions of the Persian Empire. In 326 BCE Alexander crosses the Indus River, in India, and wins the Battle of Hydaspes.

331 BCE
Battle of Gaugamela
At the Battle of Gaugamela, the Persian Empire falls to King Alexander.

*c.*300 BCE
Empire partitioned
King Alexander's empire is partitioned and ruled by the Seleucid, Antigonid, and Ptolemaic dynasties.

TERRACOTTA
MAURYAN
SCULPTURE

295 BCE
Battle of Sentinum
A huge Roman army overcomes the formidable combined forces of the Samnites and the Gauls at the Battle of Sentinum. This allows Rome to control central Italy.

241 BCE
First Punic War ends
The Romans win a naval victory against Carthage at the Aegades Islands. The First Punic War ends with Rome controlling Sicily.

225 BCE
Romans defeat Celts
At the Battle of Telamon, the Romans defeat Gallic tribes. The Romans go on to establish colonies in Celtic territories.

*c.*268 BCE
Ashoka ascends throne
Ashoka ascends the Mauryan throne and embarks on imperial conquests in modern India.

300–275 BCE   275–250 BCE   250–225 BCE

272 BCE
Fall of Tarentum
Tarentum, the leading Greek city in Italy, falls to the Romans after Pyrrhus, King of Epirus, withdraws his support.

*c.*250 BCE
Rome rules
Rome gains control of the entire Italian Peninsula.

230 BCE
The Satavahanas established
The Satavahana dynasty is established in India.

285 BCE
Ptolemaic dynasty reigns
King Ptolemy I of Egypt abdicates in favor of his son, Ptolemy II Philadelphos. The Ptolemaic dynasty will rule Egypt until 30 BCE.

wig with
lappets
on chest

253 BCE
Syrian War ends
War between the Seleucids and the Ptolemies over the possession of Syria is concluded by a marriage alliance.

238 BCE
Carthaginian conquests in Spain
The Carthaginian general Hamilcar Barca reestablishes North African power in Spain.

262 BCE
Ashoka revokes war
Having slain many thousands during his campaign against the Indian region of Kalinga, a remorseful Emperor Ashoka promotes the Buddhist concept of Dharma, meaning mercy or piety.

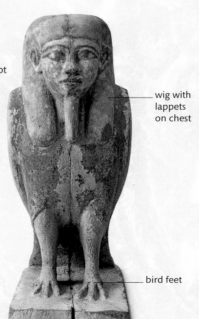

bird feet

PTOLEMAIC
MODEL OF
BA BIRD

264 BCE
First Punic War begins
The First Punic War between Rome and the North African power of Carthage begins.

100,000
The number of people said to have been killed during Ashoka's conquest of Kalinga.

"I will either **find a way or make one.**"

Hannibal, in response to the suggestion that it is impossible to cross the Alps with elephants

HANNIBAL (247–182 BCE)

Despite being a brilliant tactician, the Carthaginian general, Hannibal, lacked the strategic judgment to convert his triumphs against the Romans into final victory. Following the surrender of Carthage in 201 BCE to Rome, Hannibal was the city's chief magistrate until the Romans exiled him in 195 BCE. He then offered his services to a succession of Rome's enemies before poisoning himself in Bithynia.

218 BCE
Second Punic War
The Carthaginian general Hannibal besieges Saguntum in Spain, beginning the Second Punic War.

218 BCE
Hannibal crosses Alps
Hannibal invades Italy after crossing the Alps, and routs the Roman army. Two years later, at Cannae, Hannibal inflicts upon the Romans one of their worst-ever defeats.

215 BCE
First Macedonian War
King Philip V of Macedonia invades Illyria, starting the First Macedonian War.

206 BCE
Han dynasty begins
The Qin dynasty is succeeded by the Han dynasty under Liu Bang.

202 BCE
Battle of Zama
Scipio defeats Hannibal's army at the Battle of Zama. The Carthaginians' surrender to Rome ends the Second Punic War.

c.200 BCE
Maya build pyramids
The Maya begin to build pyramid temples in the rain forests of Mesoamerica.

c.200 BCE
Hopewell culture develops
The Adena peoples begin to adopt the Hopewell culture. These people live by hunting and gathering, but they also build large, elaborate burial mounds for their chieftains.

180 BCE
Chinese enjoy stability
Wen becomes the Chinese emperor. His 23-year reign provides a period of stability.

168 BCE
Roman territory expands
The end of the Third Macedonian War heralds a period of expansion for the Romans in the eastern Mediterranean.

225–200 BCE | 200–175 BCE | 175–150 BCE

221 BCE
Qin dynasty begins
Shi Huangdi, the first emperor of China, unites China under the Qin dynasty.

SHI HUANGDI'S TERRACOTTA ARMY, XIAN, CHINA

c.200 BCE
Nazca civilization emerges
The Nazca civilization emerges in modern South America. The Nazca create textiles and pottery.

c.185 BCE
Sunga dynasty takes power
The Sunga dynasty takes power in Magadha, India, when its founder Pusyamitra Sunga, a former Mauryan general, assassinates the last Mauryan ruler.

171 BCE
Mithridates I reigns
Mithridates I becomes king of the Persian League and the Parthian Empire.

164 BCE
Judah Maccabee revolts
Following the outlawing of Jewish religious practices in Judaea by the Seleucid ruler Antiochus IV, Judah Maccabee enters Jerusalem, reconsecrates the temple, and reestablishes Judaism.

149 BCE
Third Punic War begins
Rome crushes Carthage in the Third Punic War. It creates the province of Africa from former Carthaginian possessions.

62,000
The approximate number of Carthaginians killed by the Romans during the Third Punic War.

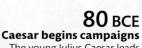

c.100 BCE
Celtic towns emerge
Celtic peoples of southern Britain start to expand their existing hill-forts into towns that are defended by extensive fortifications.

141 BCE
Parthian Empire founded
The Parthian King Mithridates the Great invades the Seleucid Empire and conquers Mesopotamia. He founds the Parthian Empire.

142 BCE
Hasmonean dynasty rules
Simon Maccabeus seizes control of Jerusalem from the Seleucids. He founds the Jewish Hasmonean dynasty that rules until Jerusalem is captured by the Romans in 63 BCE.

102–101 BCE
Marius defeats Germans
The Roman military commander Marius leads the Roman army in two victories over Germanic tribes—the Cimbri and the Teutones. He becomes Rome's dominant politician.

80 BCE
Caesar begins campaigns
The young Julius Caesar leads a series of successful Roman campaigns in Asia.

150–125 BCE   125–100 BCE   100–75 BCE

106 BCE
Caravan route established
First caravan trade route begins along the Silk Road, between Parthia, in modern Iran, and China.

c.100 BCE
Great Serpent Mound constructed
The Great Serpent Mound is constructed by the Fort Ancient peoples in modern Ohio.

GREAT SERPENT MOUND, OHIO, US

89 BCE
Roman citizenship extended
Roman citizenship is extended to all Italians.

146 BCE
Rome takes Greece
The Roman army takes and destroys the city of Corinth. Greece falls under Roman rule.

82 BCE
Sulla becomes dictator
Lucius Sulla is appointed dictator of Rome, following purges against supporters of Marius, and packs the Senate with his own supporters.

THE ASSASSINATION OF JULIUS CAESAR IN THE SENATE

31 BCE
Battle of Actium
Octavian defeats Mark Antony at the Battle of Actium. Antony and Cleopatra both commit suicide the following year.

200
The number of ships in Antony and Cleopatra's fleet that were sunk or captured at the Battle of Actium.

73 BCE
Spartacan revolt begins
In southern Italy, Spartacus leads a slave revolt—one of the most serious that the Roman Empire ever faces.

58 BCE
Gallic Wars begin
Julius Caesar begins his conquest of Gaul, which lasts until 50 BCE.

44 BCE
Caesar assassinated
Julius Caesar is assassinated just before a session of the Senate.

19 BCE
Herod rebuilds temple
The Judean King Herod I rebuilds the temple at Jerusalem.

c.4 BCE
Jesus is born
The Jewish preacher Jesus is born in Galilee, in modern northern Israel.

75–50 BCE | 50–25 BCE | 25 BCE–0 CE

63 BCE
Pompey takes Jerusalem
Having made Syria a Roman province the previous year, Pompey captures Jerusalem and annexes Judaea.

55 BCE
Caesar invades Britain
Julius Caesar invades Britain, but is forced to retreat. He returns the following year and takes hostages back to Rome, but does not make Britain part of the Roman Empire.

44 BCE
Cleopatra rules
A member of the Ptolemaic dynasty, Cleopatra becomes ruler of Egypt.

27 BCE
Octavian becomes first emperor
Octavian assumes the title of Augustus, and effectively begins rule as the first Roman emperor.

59 BCE
First Triumvirate formed
Julius Caesar forms the First Triumvirate with Pompey and Crassus.

46 BCE
Caesar made dictator
Having defeated Pompey at Pharsalus, in modern Greece, Julius Caesar is proclaimed dictator of Rome for life.

THE FORUM OF AUGUSTUS, ROME, ITALY

JULIUS CAESAR (100–44 BCE)

Julius Caesar was a rising military star when he became consul and the junior member of Rome's First Triumvirate in 59 BCE. His conquest of Gaul (58–50 BCE), in western Europe, brought Rome new provinces and furthered his political power. Having expelled the statesman Pompey from Italy, Julius Caesar won the supreme power he sought as dictator for life. This exalted position ultimately led to his murder in the Senate.

43 BCE
Second Triumvirate formed
Caesar's adopted son, Octavian, forms the Second Triumvirate with Mark Antony and Lepidus.

*c.*1 CE
Kushans invade India
The Kushans, an Indo-European nomadic people, invade northwest India.

COIN FROM THE KUSHAN PERIOD

200,000
One estimate of the number of people that died during the first Jewish revolt.

*c.*40 CE
The Arawaks migrate
The South American Arawak peoples migrate down the Orinoco River and settle in the Caribbean.

66 CE
Jewish revolt begins
The first Jewish revolt against Roman rule begins. Jewish strongholds are gradually reduced until, in 70 CE, Jerusalem falls and the Temple is destroyed.

47 CE
Paul begins missions
The Jewish missionary Paul begins a series of journeys to spread the word of Jesus to non-Jews. He travels through Anatolia (modern Turkey) and Greece to Rome, where he is martyred in around 62 CE.

*c.*60 CE
Kushan Empire established
The Kushan Empire is established in India and Central Asia.

0–25   **25–50**   **50–75**

---

*c.*1 CE
Buddhism spreads
Buddhism spreads through coastal Southeast Asia.

14 CE
Augustus dies
The Roman Emperor Augustus dies and his stepson, Tiberius, succeeds him.

43 CE
Romans invade Britain
Claudius, the new Roman Emperor, orders the invasion of Britain. By 47 CE most of the south and east of Britain is subjugated.

60 CE
Boudicca leads revolt
In Britain, Boudicca leads the Iceni revolt against the Romans.

9 CE
Xin dynasty established
Wang Mang seizes the Chinese throne and establishes the Xin dynasty. In 23 CE it collapses and the Han dynasty is restored.

12 CE
Artabanus becomes king
Artabanus II defeats the Scythians and Pahlavas, and becomes King of Parthia.

33 CE
Jesus crucified
Jesus Christ is crucified and his followers begin to spread his message. By around 50 CE communities of Christians will be established through Western Asia.

9 CE
Romans annihilated
Occupying Roman forces are driven back to the Rhine in Germany. The Roman frontier will remain here for the next 400 years.

JESUS CHRIST (*c.*4 BCE–33 CE)

Jesus, a preacher from Galilee, began his ministry in his early 30s. He taught in the Jewish tradition, calling for the reform of the Temple and for the love of one's neighbor to take precedence over the strict observance of religious law. Jesus gathered a group of twelve disciples around him, but was targeted by Jewish conservatives afraid of his growing influence. In 33 CE the Roman authorities in Judaea executed Jesus by crucifixion, but the disciples, convinced that Jesus had risen from the dead, continued his teaching.

PLASTER CASTS OF VICTIMS IN POMPEII, ITALY

123

The number of days of celebrations throughout the Roman Empire that Trajan announced following victory in the Second Dacian War.

*c.*101 CE
Dacian wars begin
Emperor Trajan begins the first of two wars with Dacia, in Central Europe. These generate a huge amount of treasure for the Romans.

79 CE
Vesuvius erupts
The eruption of the volcano of Vesuvius, near Naples in southern Italy, buries the Roman towns of Pompeii and Herculaneum.

112 CE
Trajan's forum completed
Trajan completes the building of a new forum in Rome.

132 CE
Second Jewish revolt begins
The second Jewish revolt against Rome begins. In 135 CE, the Romans recapture Jerusalem and expel the Jews from the city.

99 CE
Indians visit Rome
The Kushan Empire dispatches an embassy to Rome.

*c.*100 CE
Buddhism spreads
The Kushan Emperor Kanishka encourages the spread of Buddhism in Central Asia.

117 CE
Rome reaches greatest extent
The Roman Empire is at its greatest extent. Its frontiers may measure more than 6,213 miles (10,000 km).

75–100   100–125   125–150

80 CE
Colosseum completed
The Flavian Amphitheater, now known as the Colosseum, is completed in Rome.

*c.*100 CE
Teotihuacán expands
The city of Teotihuacán, in modern Mexico, expands and the building of the Temples of the Sun and the Moon begins.

*c.*105 CE
Paper invented
In China, the earliest form of paper is produced.

122 CE
Hadrian's Wall built
The building of Hadrian's Wall at the Roman frontier in northern Britain begins. It measures 73 miles (117.5 km).

147 CE
Romans celebrate anniversary
Celebrations are held for the 900th anniversary of the foundation of the city of Rome.

TEOTIHUACÁN, MEXICO

87 CE
Kushans visit China
An embassy from the Kushan Empire of India travels to the new eastern Han capital of Luoyang.

c.150
Ptolemy completes atlas
Ptolemy of Alexandria's *Geographia*, the first world atlas, is completed.

MAP BASED ON PTOLEMY'S *GEOGRAPHIA*

"Let no one escape **sheer destruction.**"

Septimus Severus, to his soldiers during his campaign of Caledonia, in modern Scotland, from Dio Cassius's *Roman History*, 76

193
Septimius Severus becomes emperor
The assassination of the insane Emperor Commodus leads to a civil war that results in African-born Septimius Severus being declared emperor.

c.200
Korea gains independence
The Chinese occupation of modern Korea ends and native states including Koguryo, Silla, and Paekche start to appear.

c.150
Christianity spreads in Africa
Christianity spreads west across Roman North Africa.

165
Plague hits Rome
Rome is devastated by an outbreak of the plague. By the end of the year it has spread widely across the Mediterranean region.

180
The Goths settle
The Goths—an East Germanic people—start to settle on the Black Sea coast.

150–175   175–200   200–225

---

c.150
Nok culture peaks
The Nok Iron Age culture in Nigeria reaches its peak.

166
Marcomannic Wars begin
The Marcomannic Wars begin with Germanic tribes invading northern Italy. The wars drag on for more than 10 years until the Romans establish strong provinces on the frontier.

180
Marcus Aurelius dies
The Roman emperor Marcus Aurelius dies. He is succeeded by his son, Commodus, who makes peace with the Marcomanni.

184
Yellow Turbans revolt
In China, a peasant revolt threatens the imperial government. Up to 400,000 rebels, known as the Yellow Turbans due to their distinctive headdress, march on the capital.

c.200
Moche culture emerges
The Moche civilization emerges in modern Peru.

c.220
Han collapses
The Chinese Han dynasty collapses and is replaced by three kingdoms—the Shu, Wu, and Wei.

c.150
Han dynasty flourishes
Han China regains dominance of Central Asia.

GERMANIC TRIBES

The Romans had faced Germanic tribes ever since they reached the Rhine at the time of Julius Caesar. Germanic groups across the Danube, such as the Quadi and Marcomanni, proved troublesome in the 2nd century, but by the late 3rd century new and more dangerous confederations of Germanic tribes arose, such as the Franks, Alamanns, and Goths, who overran much of the Roman Empire by the mid-5th century.

224
Sasanian dynasty founded
Parthian rule collapses after the revolt of Ardashir I, governor of the Pars, who founds the Sasanian dynasty.

SHAPUR I DEFEATS VALERIAN

carved figures
in Egyptian
porphyry marble

THE FOUR COEMPERORS

260
Persians defeat Romans
Shapur I, the Persian King, defeats Roman Emperor Valerian and takes him prisoner. This marks a period of Persian dominance in Syria and Mesopotamia.

277–79
Probus takes power
The Roman Emperor Probus defeats the Goths on the Danube, expels the Franks from Gaul, and puts down unrest in Egypt and Illyria.

c.250
Classical Mayan period begins
The Classical period of the Mayan civilization in Mesoamerica begins.

c.250
Yamato kingdom emerges
In Japan, the Yamato kingdom emerges, conquering most of central Japan.

267
Goths rampage
A massive army of Goths pillages Thrace, Macedonia, and Greece.

293
Tetrarchy formed
The Roman Emperor Diocletian sets up a system of four coemperors—the Tetrarchy—which enjoys early successes in Britain and Egypt.

235
Germanic raids begin
Germanic peoples start serious raids on the Roman Empire's Rhine and Danube frontiers.

225–250   250–275   275–300

235
Military anarchy begins
When the Roman army chooses the officer Maximinus Thrax as emperor, a period of military anarchy begins. There are more than 20 emperors in the next 50 years.

267–73
Queen Zenobia takes territories
Queen Zenobia of Palmyra takes Egypt and Syria from Rome, but is in turn defeated and taken prisoner by the Roman Emperor Aurelian.

ANCIENT RUINS OF PALMYRA, SYRIA

297
Persians take Armenia
The Persians, under ruler Narseh, invade Armenia and defeat Roman Emperor Galerius.

280
China united
The Western Jin conquer the south of China and unite the country under their leader, Sima Yan.

285
Empire divided
Emperor Diocletian reorganizes the Roman Empire, dividing power between two emperors. Diocletian rules the East and he appoints Maximian to rule the West.

ETCHMIADZIN CATHEDRAL, ARMENIA

CONSTANTINE THE GREAT (c.272–337)

Constantine is best known for his support of the Christians, following their persecution under Diocletian. As Roman emperor, he decreed freedom of worship by the Edict of Milan, sponsored the first large churches in Rome, and allowed bishops to take an important role in politics. Constantine was baptized on his deathbed and became the first Christian emperor.

c.300
Christianity becomes state religion
Armenia becomes the first country to accept Christianity as the state religion. Etchmiadzin Cathedral—the world's oldest cathedral—is built in the Armenian capital between 301 and 303.

330
Constantinople founded
Constantine founds a new capital for the Eastern Roman Empire at the ancient city of Byzantium, strategically sited between Europe and Asia. He demolishes pagan temples and builds new churches. The city is named Constantinople (modern Istanbul).

312
Battle of Milvian Bridge
The Roman Emperor Constantine defeats rival Maxentius at the Battle of Milvian Bridge and takes control of the Western Roman Empire.

362
Julian the Apostate restores paganism
The newly ascended Roman Emperor Julian—later known as Julian the Apostate—begins a campaign to restore pagan worship in the Roman Empire.

370
Huns invade
The Huns, a nomadic people from Central Asia, begin to invade Eastern Europe. They defeat the Ostrogoths in the Ukraine.

300–310

310–350

350–375

304
Xiongnu invade China
The Xiongnu invade China, leading to the breakdown of order in the north and the start of the Sixteen Kingdoms period.

c.350
Aksum kingdom embraces Christianity
One of the earliest states to embrace Christianity outside the Roman Empire, the kingdom of Aksum in Ethiopia becomes the most powerful independent state in Africa.

369
Sasanians gain security
The Sasanian King Shapur II occupies Armenia. He signs a peace treaty with the Romans that is beneficial to the Persians.

313
Edict of Milan issued
Constantine issues the Edict of Milan, which grants toleration to all forms of worship and, effectively, legalizes Christianity.

303
Christians persecuted
The Roman Emperor Diocletian issues an edict ordering the destruction of churches and the handing over and burning of Christian books. Subsequent edicts call for the arrest of Christian clergy, and order Christians to offer a sacrifice to the pagan gods. Many Christians are martyred.

320
Gupta Empire founded
The Emperor Chandragupta I, the founder of the Gupta Empire of India, ascends to the throne. The Guptas rule northern India for the next 150 years.

studded with precious gems

CROWN WORN BY AKSUM KINGS

"The man **who does not know scripture** does not know the **power and wisdom of God.**"

Jerome, in his commentary on *Isaiah*

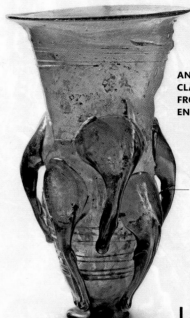

ANGLO-SAXON CLAWED BEAKER FROM SOUTHERN ENGLAND

clawlike projections

378
Battle of Adrianople
The Goths, under Fritigern, defeat the Romans at Adrianople, near the Danube frontier. The victory leaves the Eastern Roman army destroyed and the Balkans open to the Goths.

404
Bible translated
Jerome, the Christian priest, theologian, and historian, completes his Latin translation of the Bible.

420
Liu Song dynasty founded
In southern China, the Eastern Jins are overthrown and the Liu Song dynasty is founded under Song Wudi.

447
Huns invade Thrace
In the Balkans, the Huns, under Attila, invade Thrace and extract heavy tribute from the Eastern Roman Empire.

386
Northern Wei dynasty formed
The Toba Wei reunify northern China, ruling as the Northern Wei dynasty.

391
Official religion
Theodosius forbids all pagan sacrifices throughout the Roman Empire, and makes Christianity the official religion.

406
Barbarians invade
Hordes of invading groups including Vandals, Alans, and Sueves penetrate deep into the Roman Empire.

c.445
Saxons settle
The Saxons begin to settle in southern England. Within a few years, Saxon, Angle, and Jutish raiders occupy large parts of the former Roman province.

375–400   400–425   425–450

383
Roman–Goth truce agreed
The Roman Emperor Theodosius agrees a truce with the Goths, giving them land and political autonomy in exchange for military service.

395
Roman Empire splits
Following the death of Theodosius, the Roman Empire is split into eastern and western divisions. No one emperor will rule the whole empire again.

436
Huns defeat Burgundians
The Roman general Aëtius recruits the Huns to defeat the Burgundians, who had raided across the lower Rhine.

c.450
Temple of the Sun completed
The Moche culture in modern Peru completes the Temple of the Sun, using 50 million bricks.

379
Chinese adopt Buddhism
Buddhism becomes the state religion of China.

410
Goths sack Rome
Following their invasion of Italy in 408, the Goths, under Alaric, sack Rome. The event shakes the entire Roman world.

439
Vandals take Carthage
Under Gaiseric, the Vandals capture Carthage from the Romans and establish an independent Vandal kingdom in North Africa.

GOTH LEADER ALARIC ENTERS ROME

440
Chinese adopt Taoism
Taoism replaces Buddhism as the state religion.

250,000
The population of the city of Teotihuacán, in the Valley of Mexico, by 400.

c.450
Teotihuacán peaks
In the Valley of Mexico, the city of Teotihuacán reaches the peak of its power. Its main street—the Avenue of the Dead—is lined with the residences of the lords of the city.

890

The length, in feet, of the largest desert geoglyphs created by the Nazca people of Peru.

HUMMINGBIRD GEOGLYPH, SOUTHERN PERU

c.450
Nazca desert images created
The Nazca people of modern Peru create huge geoglyph pictures on the desert floor over hundreds of years.

478
Shinto shrine built
The first shrine of the Shinto religion is built in Japan.

518
Justin becomes emperor
Justin becomes Emperor of the former Eastern Roman Empire—the Byzantine Empire. He develops good relations with the Ostrogoths of Italy and the Vandals of North Africa.

c.496–506
Clovis converts
Clovis, the first Frankish king, converts to Catholic Christianity, setting him apart from other barbarian rulers.

455
Vandals sack Rome
The Vandal army, led by King Gaiseric, plunders Rome. This is the second time in fewer than 50 years that Rome has been sacked.

476
Last western emperor deposed
Romulus, the Western Roman emperor, is deposed and not replaced. This marks the end of the Roman Empire in the West after 500 years.

502
Persians invade
The Persians, under Kavadh, invade the Byzantine Empire, sacking Amida in Mesopotamia. In 506 CE the Persians and Byzantines agree a truce.

450–475   475–500   500–525

452
Huns invade Italy
Having been defeated by a Roman-Goth coalition in Gaul the year before, the Huns, led by King Attila, invade northern Italy, attacking Padua and Verona.

475
Visigoths rule Spain
The Romans acknowledge the rule of Euric, King of the Visigoths, in Spain and southwest Gaul in modern France.

507
Battle of Vouillé
The Franks defeat the Visigoths at the Battle of Vouillé and drive them out of Aquitaine in modern France.

453
Attila dies
Attila the Hun dies after his wedding feast. His sons begin a civil war that leads to the Hunnic Empire falling apart.

467
Gupta Empire declines
With the death of Skandagupta, the Gupta Empire in India starts to decline. Pressure comes from the Hephthalite Huns, who have conquered much of western India.

493
Ostrogoths conquer Italy
The Ostrogoths, under Theodoric, conquer Italy. In 497 CE the Byzantine Emperor Anastasius I recognizes Theodoric's right to govern Italy, and to extend his rule into Gaul.

ATTILA THE HUN (c.406–453)

King of the Huns from 434 to 453, Attila was the scourge of the Roman world. By the 400s, the Huns controlled a sizeable territory in Eastern Europe. Attila aimed to maintain a steppe empire placed strategically on the plains of modern Hungary, at the doorway to Western Europe. He subdued neighboring tribes and won victories over the eastern Romans, even extracting tribute money from them.

inlaid with precious gems

OSTROGOTHIC BROOCHES

MOSAIC IN THE HAGIA SOPHIA, CONSTANTINOPLE (ISTANBUL, TURKEY)

600
Printing invented
The Chinese invent printing, using carved wood blocks.

529–534
Justinian writes Codex
In his Codex *Justinianus*, Emperor Justinian codifies Roman law. A great builder, he orders the building of the huge church of Hagia Sophia in Constantinople.

536
Byzantines take Rome
The Byzantine army, led by Belisarius, occupies Rome. Belisarius goes on to capture Ravenna, the Ostrogothic capital, in 540.

563
Columba founds Iona
Columba sets up the abbey of Iona on an island off Scotland's western coast. Iona becomes a center of Irish-influenced monasticism, which extends into northern England, Scotland, and the Frankish Kingdom, in modern France.

*c.*570
Muhammad born
Muhammad, the prophet of Islam, is born in Mecca.

*c.*580
Avar state established
Under Khan Bayan, the Avars—nomadic horsemen from the northern Caucasus—exploit the vacuum left by the departure of the Lombards to carve out a vast territory centered around modern Austria.

525–550 | 550–575 | 575–600

533
Vandals conquered
Justinian sends an army, under General Belisarius, to Vandal-controlled North Africa. The Romans take Carthage and Vandal resistance collapses.

568
Lombards invade Italy
Byzantium concedes much of Italy to the Lombards, who had settled in the former Roman province of Pannonia (modern Hungary).

581
Sui dynasty founded
In northern China, Yang Jian, general of the Zhou rulers, takes the throne as the Emperor Wen. He goes on to invade southern China and becomes the first emperor of the Sui dynasty. China is united for the first time in three centuries.

538
Buddhism arrives in Japan
Buddhism is officially recognized in Japan. Emperor Kimmei accepts a gold and copper Buddhist image from the ruler of the Korean state of Paekche.

596
Augustine begins mission
Pope Gregory I sends Augustine on a mission to England to evangelize the Anglo-Saxon kingdoms. He converts Aethelbert, the pagan king of Kent.

540
Persians capture Antioch
Khosrau I, the Persian ruler of the Sasanian Empire, invades Syria and captures Antioch. He forces Justinian to pay 5,000 pounds of gold to regain it.

SUI DYNASTY BUDDHA CAVE CARVING, YUNGANG CAVES

TRADE AND EMPIRE

Following the fall of the Western Roman Empire in the 5th century, civilization in Europe entered a long period of comparative decline. In this period, China proved to be politically strong and technologically innovative under the Tang and Song dynasties, while much of the Middle East and North Africa was united under an Arab empire inspired by the new religion of Islam. The Americas, India, and Southeast Asia gave rise to distinctive cultures. However, from the late medieval period movements began to emerge in Europe that would lead to European domination of the globe until the mid-20th century.

surface covered with engraved decoration

SUTTON HOO HELMET (REPLICA)

c.602
Grand canal constructed
The Chinese Emperor Yangdi orders the construction of a grand canal linking Yangtze with Chang'an. The project is completed in 610.

636
Battle of Qadisiyya
At the Battle of Qadisiyya, Arab forces defeat the Persian army and hold Persian territory as far north as Mosul.

c.641
Sutton Hoo treasure buried
A great Anglo-Saxon ship burial at Sutton Hoo, Suffolk, England, is filled with marvelously worked artifacts, weapons, and treasures. A rare survival of elite pagan burials in England, the artifacts comprise a fusion of Christian and non-Christian elements, suggesting transition as Christianity gains in popularity and strength.

606
Last early Indian empire begins
Harsha accedes to the thrones of Thanesar and Kannauj, establishing the last native Indian empire of ancient times.

618
Tang dynasty established
In 616–17, rebellions against the despotic rule of Yangdi cause the collapse of the Sui dynasty. A year later military governor Li Yuan founds the Tang dynasty, which rules until 906.

600–619   620–639   640–669

613
Frankish kingdom established
King Clothar II reunites the Frankish kingdom, bringing an end to the civil war. His Edict of Paris, issued in 614, introduces reforms to the Merovingian church and state.

632
Death of Muhammad
Muhammad, the founder of Islam, dies aged 62. The young Muslim community—united by a religion that transcended traditional rivalries—selects Abu Bakr as the first caliph.

661
Sunni-Shi'ite split
Following fierce disagreement over how succession to the caliphate ought to be decided, Sunni and Shi'ite Muslims split into opposing branches of Islam.

622
Beginning of Islamic era
Hostility from the Meccan authorities forces Muhammad to flee to Medina with his family and followers. The start of the Islamic era is traditionally marked by the Hegira, or hijra, the flight to Medina.

668
Unification of Korea
With the help of Tang China, the Unified Silla kingdom in Korea brings to an end the long Three Kingdoms period.

614
Persian Empire restored
The Persian conquests of Syria, Mesopotamia, and Palestine are complete. In 619, the Persians go on to take Egypt.

MUHAMMAD (570–632)

Born in Mecca, Muhammad ibn Abdallah worked as a merchant and shepherd before growing discontented and retiring to a life of contemplation. Muslims believe that in 610, he received the first of a series of divine revelations—these became the Qu'ran. He preached a monotheistic faith, Islam, based on complete submission to God (Allah). Before his death he unified Arabian tribes within his new religion.

645
Japanese land reforms
In Japan, the Fujiwara clan enacts the Taika reforms, which follow the Chinese model by bringing all land into imperial ownership and centralizing power.

> # "I have not seen the equal; neither have I heard of anything... that could rival in grace this Dome of the rock..."
>
> Mukaddasi, Arab geographer, c.10th century

elaborate headdress

big ear spools

protruding fangs

STATUE OF CHAAK, MAYAN GOD

698
Loss of Carthage
The Arabs conquer and destroy Carthage, the last Byzantine stronghold in North Africa, and build Tunis.

692
Dome of the Rock built
Commissioned by Caliph Abd Al-Malik, the great shrine built on the Temple Mount in Jerusalem, known as the Dome of the Rock (or Qubbat as-Sakhrah), is completed.

c.700
Lindisfarne Gospels written
The Lindisfarne Gospels, an illuminated manuscript, are produced at the priory of Lindisfarne on Holy Island, off the northeast coast of England.

c.730
Mayan high point
The Mayan city-states of the Late Classical period reach the peak of their power and sophistication. The population of Tikal swells to at least 60,000 people, in a city spread out over 29 sq miles (76 sq km).

670–699 | 700–724 | 725–749

690
Reign of Empress Wu
In China, the Empress Wu takes the throne in her own name—the only woman in Chinese history to do so.

c.700
Teotihuacán collapses
In the Valley of Mexico, the great city-state of Teotihuacán collapses, bringing six centuries of growth and dominance to an end.

725
Dating system established
The Anglo–Saxon scholar, Bede, popularizes the Christian AD—Anno Domini—dating system, which spreads across Europe.

726
Iconoclasm starts
Emperor Leo III of Byzantium initiates the heretical movement of iconoclasm, which bans and destroys religious images, including icons.

672
Resurgence of Tikal
The Mayan city state of Tikal begins its resurgence after a century-long period of political and cultural domination by neighboring city-states. The city's rulers engage in a construction program to match their political ambitions, building many impressive structures including massive pyramids, ball courts, causeways, observatories, and palaces.

711
Conquest of Spain
A Muslim army crosses the Strait of Gibraltar and defeats the Visigothic king, Roderick, at the Battle of Guadalete. By the end of the year, most of the Iberian peninsula is under Islamic control.

732
Battle of Tours-Poitiers
Muslims are defeated by Frankish troops, marking the farthest extent of Muslim expansion in Western Europe.

c.725
Casa Grande established
The Hohokam settlement of Casa Grande, in modern Arizona, is founded. Its success lies in the watering system that allows a great range of crops to be grown, despite the arid environment.

TEMPLE II AT TIKAL, MODERN GUATEMALA

3,000
The number of major stone buildings constructed in Tikal's Late Classical period.

740
Battle of Acroinon
The Byzantine army defeats the Umayyad caliphate at Acroinon and expels the Umayyads from Anatolia (modern Turkey).

TIWANAKU SNUFF TABLET

inscribed Sun image in rectangular depression

c.750
Tiwanaku at its height
The city of Tiwanaku on the Altiplano, or high plain, of Bolivia reaches its zenith. Its advanced agricultural system supports the development of a sophisticated culture. The Tiwanaku people build pyramids, temples, and colossal statues.

755
An Lushan gains power
A Chinese general, An Lushan, rebels against the Tang dynasty and founds a rival dynasty in northern China.

c.760
Numerical system adopted
The Indian system of numerals is adopted by the Abbasid dynasty.

762
Founding of Baghdad
Baghdad becomes the first truly Islamic imperial city. It emerges as a trading hub that attracts merchants from Northern Europe, India, and China.

c.782
Cultural renaissance emerges
Scholars attracted to Charlemagne's court stimulate a Carolingian cultural renaissance. Charlemagne's first concern is to create an educated clergy with a good understanding of the Bible and the Christian faith.

794
Japanese capital moves
Emperor Kammu moves the Japanese capital to Kyoto, away from the Buddhist sects of Nara.

750–759   760–779   780–799

754
Franks invade Italy
Pepin III, the first Carolingian king of the Franks, invades Italy and forms a treaty with Pope Stephen II. This breaks the Frankish treaty with the Lombards, the ruling tribe in Italy.

750
Abbasid caliphate established
The foundation of the Abbasid caliphate is the culmination of growing tension in the Islamic world. The rival Umayyad clan is massacred.

756
Emirate of Cordoba begins
One of the last surviving Umayyads, Caliph Abd al-Rahman I, declares an independent Emirate of Cordoba, Spain. This marks the start of the breakup of the united Arab caliphate.

THE MOSQUE OF CORDOBA

774
Franks conquer Lombards
The Franks, led by Charlemagne, conquer the kingdom of the Lombards. This brings northern Italy into Charlemagne's Carolingian Empire and extends his reach down both sides of the Adriatic coast.

785
Offa's Dyke built
Offa of Mercia, effectively the overlord of Britain, starts to construct the monumental earthwork known as Offa's Dyke on the border between Wales and Mercia.

793
Viking raids begin
Viking raids against Western Europe gather pace. In 793 the rich monasteries of Lindisfarne and Iona, in the British Isles, are looted.

787
Council of Nicaea
The council restores icons to Byzantine churches, ending the period of iconoclasm.

> # "Right action is better than knowledge; but in order to do what is right, we must know what is right."
>
> Charlemagne, from *Epistola de litteris colendis*, c.780–800

831
Fall of Palermo
As the Islamic conquest of Sicily continues, Palermo falls after a yearlong siege. The city becomes the capital of Islamic Sicily, although total conquest of the island is not secured until 902.

830
Moimir established
Moimir, the first known ruler of the Moravian Slavs, founds the Kingdom of Moravia—a powerful Slavic state in Central Europe.

CHOLA SCULPTURE

c.800
Temple of Borobudur built
The Temple of Borobudur, a Buddhist monument in central Java, Southeast Asia, is completed in the early 9th century. The colossal structure—the largest Buddhist monument in the world—is a testament to the power of the Srivijayan Empire.

811
Bulgar victory
The Bulgar Khan Krum defeats the Byzantine Emperor Nicephorus I. Two years later, Krum attempts to besiege the Byzantine capital Constantinople, but is unable to breach the walls.

814
Death of Charlemagne
Charlemagne dies and his last surviving son, Louis the Pious, accedes to the throne, having been crowned co-emperor by his father the year before.

846
Rise of the Cholas
The Chola King Vijayalaya captures the city of Tanjore from the Pandya kingdom, signaling the rise of the Tamil Chola dynasty in southern India.

800–809 | 810–829 | 830–849

802
Khmer Empire founded
Proclaiming himself Chakravartin, meaning "god-king," Jayavarman II establishes the independent Khmer Empire in modern Cambodia. The authority of the Khmer kings rests on their direct link to the gods, which is reflected in the monuments they construct at the temple city of Angkor over centuries to come.

c.822
House of Wisdom founded
Caliph Al-Ma'mun consolidates the House of Wisdom in Abbasid Baghdad, continuing the tradition of intellectual patronage. Arabic translations of ancient Greek texts secure knowledge for the future.

841
Vikings found Dublin
Having raided inland Ireland four years earlier, the Vikings found the kingdom of Dublin. The following year the Vikings sack London, England.

843
Treaty of Verdun
The treaty of Verdun divides Charlemagne's empire into regions broadly equating to France in the West, Germany in the East, and a middle kingdom that becomes known as Burgundy.

800
Caliphs lose Africa
The Abbasid caliphs in Baghdad lose authority in Africa west of Egypt. They recognize the emir's hereditary right to rule over the province of Ifriqiya. The emir, Ibrahim ibn Aghlab, thus founds the Aghlabid dynasty.

ISLAMIC SCHOLARSHIP

Thanks to the House of Wisdom and other similar centers of scholarship across the caliphate, Islamic scholars developed ideas beyond what the ancient Greeks and Romans had done. Islamic scientists made great advances in fields such as alchemy (proto-chemistry), medicine, toxicology, metallurgy, mathematics, and astronomy.

825
Battle of Ellandun
Wessex, the Anglo-Saxon kingdom in south and west England, ruled over by King Egbert, wins victory over King Beornwulf of Mercia at the Battle of Ellandun, Wiltshire. Wessex becomes the dominant power in England.

848
Pagan established
The Burmese Kingdom of Pagan is founded in the Irrawaddy Valley. Cultural, religious, and mercantile ties with India influence the architecture of this part of Southeast Asia.

ARABIC ASTROLABE

874
Vikings settle in Iceland
Having already visited the island and even over-wintered there, the Vikings build their first permanent settlement on Iceland.

896
Bulgarian Empire founded
The Bulgar Khan Symeon defeats the Byzantine army at Bulgarophygon in modern Turkey, signaling the height of the Bulgarian Empire.

886
Danelaw begins
The Treaty of Alfred and Guthrum establishes Danish rule in part of England; this area becomes known as Danelaw.

c.890
Anglo-Saxon Chronicle produced
The first Anglo-Saxon Chronicle is written. This record of events, from wars and politics to the weather, is written by chroniclers until the mid-12th century.

c.850
Astrolabe perfected
Arab astronomers perfect the astrolabe, a complex instrument invented by the ancient Greeks and used by astronomers, astrologers, and navigators.

868
***Diamond Sutra* written**
An illustrated Buddhist text, the *Diamond Sutra*, is produced in China. It is the world's oldest complete surviving printed book.

866
Vikings take York
Vikings take the city of York and establish a kingdom in northern England.

c.889
Building at Tikal ends
The catastrophic decline of the Classic Mayan city-states of the southern lowlands continues after the last monument is built at Tikal.

850–859   860–879   880–899

858
Fujiwara regency begins
Yoshifusa, a member of the wealthy Fujiwara clan, becomes the regent of the child-emperor Seiwa, his grandson. This marks the beginning of the Fujiwara clan's domination of Japan.

867
Basil I gains power
Basil I, the founder of the Macedonian dynasty, comes to power in the Byzantine Empire.

871
Alfred the Great becomes king
Alfred the Great of England, an educated man who spent time in Rome with the pope, accedes to the throne of the Anglo-Saxon kingdom of Wessex. In 878 he defeats the Danes at the Battle of Edington and halts the Danish advance in England.

c.863
Cyrillic script introduced
The Cyrillic script is invented by the Byzantine missionary later known as St. Cyril. Sent to convert the Slavs in Moravia by the Byzantine Emperor Michael III, Cyril devises a new "Glagolitic" script to translate the Bible into Slavic; this later becomes Cyrillic script.

c.850
Mayan decline
The decline of the Mayan civilization continues. People abandon cities, starting with Palenque, at the end of the 9th century.

> " **I desired to live worthily** as long as I lived, and to leave after my life... **the memory of me in good works.**"

Alfred the Great, from *Boethius' Consolation of Philosophy*

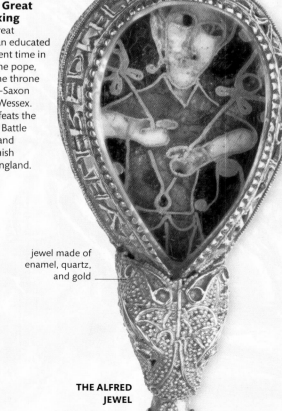

jewel made of enamel, quartz, and gold

THE ALFRED JEWEL

THE ABBEY OF CLUNY

William the Pious, Duke of Aquitaine, donated the land to found the Benedictine Abbey of Cluny. It became one of Europe's most important and powerful monastic institutions. Cluny governed more than 10,000 monks and its abbots were international statesmen of great influence. Pope Urban II, a former Abbot of Cluny, declared it "the light of the world."

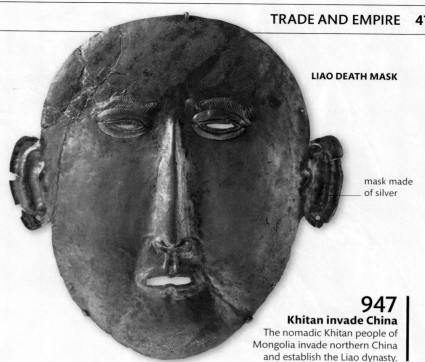

LIAO DEATH MASK

mask made of silver

907
Tang dynasty collapses
The Tang dynasty in China collapses following a period of military decline. A period of anarchy, known as the Five Dynasties and Ten Kingdoms, follows until the establishment of the Northern Song Dynasty in 960.

909
Fatimid dynasty begins
The Fatimids establish power in North Africa and create a capital in Mahdia, in modern Tunisia.

910
Monastic center founded
The Abbey of Cluny in Burgundy is founded. It becomes the center of a monastic "empire" in Europe.

919
Saxon dynasty begins
Henry the Fowler, Duke of Saxony, is elected King Henry I of East Francia (modern Germany), the first king of the Saxon dynasty.

947
Khitan invade China
The nomadic Khitan people of Mongolia invade northern China and establish the Liao dynasty.

937
Reunification of Korea
The Silla kingdom is conquered by the Koryo kingdom, completing the reunification of Korea.

900–909   910–929   930–949

c.900
Toltecs found Tula
The Toltecs settle in the Valley of Mexico and found a capital at Tula.

906–907
Magyars raid Europe
The Magyars destroy Moravia (modern eastern Czech Republic) and begin to raid Western Europe.

911
Vikings establish duchy
The Frankish King Charles III grants a large area of land, which becomes Normandy, to the Norse chieftain Rollo.

930
Vikings establish parliament
The Vikings of Althing in Iceland establish one of the earliest parliamentary assemblies in the world.

938
Independent Vietnam declared
The kingdom of Dai-co-viet in Vietnam gains independence after 1,000 years of Chinese rule.

937
Battle of Brunanburgh
The Anglo–Saxon King Athelstan's victory at the Battle of Brunanburgh cements his control of Britain and his kingship of the now unified Anglo–Saxon realm of England.

929
Abd al-Rahman III rules
The waning authority of the Abbasids in Baghdad prompts Abd al-Rahman III, ruler of Muslim Spain, to declare himself the true caliph. During the 10th century, his capital, Cordoba, Spain, becomes the largest and most developed city in Western Europe.

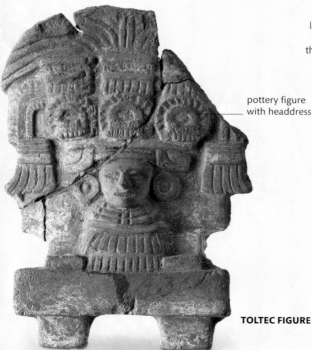

pottery figure with headdress

TOLTEC FIGURE

100,000
The population of the city of Cordoba by the end of the 10th century.

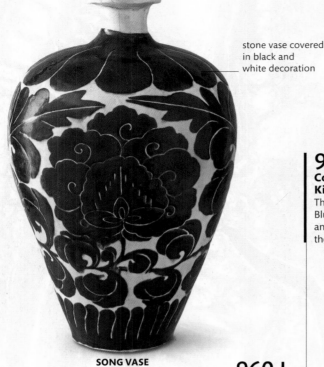

stone vase covered
in black and
white decoration

SONG VASE

986
Vikings reach Greenland
The Viking explorer Eric the
Red leads a party of Icelandic
colonists to the shores of
Greenland. They quickly
establish a thriving colony
that eventually numbers
around 5,000 people.

7,300
The weight of silver
in pounds paid by
the English to the
Vikings following
the Battle of Maldon.

965
**Conversion of the
King of Denmark**
The King of Denmark, Harald
Bluetooth, converts to Christianity,
and the religion spreads through
the Nordic region.

991
Battle of Maldon
Following the Battle of
Maldon, English monarchs are
forced to pay Danegeld tax to
Vikings for the first time.

981
Arab victories in Spain
The Islamic forces of Cordoba defeat the
Christian kingdom of Leon in Spain under
the leadership of Al-Mansur. He also
campaigns against Navarre and Catalonia,
making their kings subordinate to the caliphate.

987
Capetian dynasty established
In France, Hugh Capet founds the
Capetian dynasty. It becomes one
of the most powerful European
royal families.

960
Song dynasty founded
The establishment of the Song dynasty in
China brings an end to the anarchy and warfare
of the Five Dynasties and Ten Kingdoms era.

950–959   960–979   980–999

962
**Coronation of
Holy Roman Emperor**
The pope's imperial coronation
of Otto I as emperor revives the
Carolingian Roman Empire in
the West. He becomes the
first Holy Roman Emperor.

983
Great Wend Rebellion
The Great Wend Rebellion against the
East Franks results in the Wends—forcibly
converted Slavic tribes—restoring their
pagan religion and resisting colonization
for nearly two centuries.

987
**Toltec–Mayan
state established**
Toltec forces conquer the
Yucatán Maya and make
Chichen Itza the capital
of a Toltec–Mayan state.

969
Cairo founded
The Fatimids of Tunisia assume
control of North Africa, from
Tunisia to Egypt, and relocate
to a new capital, Cairo.

955
Battle of Lechfeld
Emperor Otto I, known as Otto the Great,
defeats the Magyars at the Battle of Lechfeld.
The son of Henry I, Otto had vigorously asserted
royal authority since his coronation in 936,
gaining control of all the East Frankish duchies.

THE TOLTECS

The Toltecs, who ruled a state centered
on Tula in modern Mexico, were notable
for their militarism, which changed society
in Central America and paved the way for
militaristic states such as the Aztec. The
term "Toltec" came to mean "city-dweller"
or "civilized person," but its literal meaning
is "reed person"—signifying an inhabitant
of Tollan ("Place of the Reeds," the city now
known as Tula). Toltec art and architecture,
characterized by monumental masonry
and giant statues, was influential
in the region.

**POTTERY
TEMPLE
MODEL**

THE ANCESTRAL PUEBLO PEOPLES

The Ancestral Pueblo peoples used sophisticated dryland agriculture and hydrology to thrive in a difficult environment. They controlled trade routes that extended as far as the Pacific coast of modern California and the Valley of Mexico. Noted for their impressive architecture, the Ancestral Pueblo constructed Great Houses such as Pueblo Bonito, one of 13 buildings in Chaco Canyon. Pueblo Bonito was six stories high and comprised more than 600 rooms. Well-maintained roads connected Chaco Canyon to thousands of Ancestral Pueblo settlements across the region.

1028
King Canute gains power
England, Denmark, and Norway are united under King Canute, the son of Svein Forkbeard.

CANUTE COIN

c.1000
Chaco Canyon developed
The Ancestral Pueblo civilization, centered on Chaco Canyon in southwest North America, reaches its climax.

1014
Battle of Clontarf
The Battle of Clontarf breaks Viking dominion in Ireland.

c.1002
Europeans reach America
The Norseman Leif Eriksson, son of Eric the Red, is thought to be the first European to set foot in North America.

1046
Deposition of the Three Popes
Benedict IX sells the papacy by resigning in exchange for payment. For a time, three popes claim authority until Henry III, King of Germany, oversees the Deposition of the Three Popes.

1001
Muslims raid India
Muslims, led by Sultan Muhammad of Ghazni (modern Afghanistan), launch their first raids into northern India.

1009
Ly dynasty established
The Ly dynasty is founded in the Vietnamese kingdom of Dai-co-viet.

1040
Battle of Dandanqan
The Seljuks defeat the Ghaznavids to establish the Seljuk Empire in modern Turkey.

1000–1009 1010–1029 1030–1049

1013
England conquered
Svein Forkbeard of Denmark conquers England.

1025
Cholas launch attacks
The Chola King Rajendra Choladevra launches an audacious naval expedition against the maritime empire of Srivijaya in Sumatra, also sacking the Pegu kingdom in Burma. His triumphs secure control of the lucrative Indian–Chinese trade routes.

1000
Chimú victory
The Chimú people establish an empire in northern Peru.

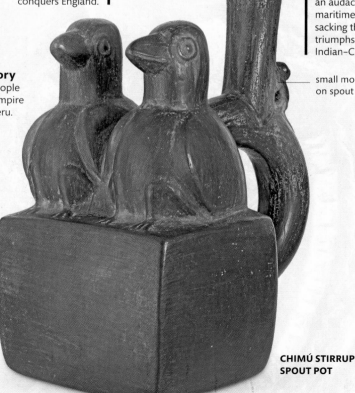

small monkey on spout

c.1000
Hungarians become Christians
Stephen becomes Grand Prince of the Hungarians and converts to Christianity.

1044
Burmese power shift
Anawrata seizes power in the Pagan kingdom in Burma. He develops Burmese as a written language, institutes a program of construction, and forges trade and cultural links with India and China.

c.1000
Italian city-states emerge
The Italian trading city-states Genoa and Venice begin to flourish. Venice, in particular, enjoys lucrative trade links with the Byzantine Empire.

CHIMÚ STIRRUP SPOUT POT

1055
Bagdhad captured
The Seljuk Turks capture Baghdad, ending the Buyid dynasty and restoring the Sunni branch of Islam.

1054
Almoravid dynasty founded
In Morocco, the founding of the Almoravid dynasty signals the start of the Islamic conquest of West Africa, where a number of powerful states have arisen, including Ghana.

1071
Battle of Manzikert
The Seljuks crush the Byzantine army at Manzikert; they capture and ransom Emperor Romanus IV and go on to conquer Anatolia (modern Turkey). This victory marks the beginning of Muslim-Turkish supremacy in the region.

UNIVERSITY OF BOLOGNA

1088
First university founded
University of Bologna is the first to be founded in the Western world.

1054
Church schism decreed
The excommunication of the patriarch of Constantinople marks the final schism between the Catholic Church of Rome and the Orthodox Christian Church of Byzantium.

1075
Investiture Controversy begins
The Investiture Controversy between the emperor and the pope concerns the right to appoint bishops. In 1076, Pope Gregory VII excommunicates the German Emperor Henry IV.

1050–1059   1060–1079   1080–1089

1066
Battle of Hastings
At the battle of Hastings, William, Duke of Normandy, defeats Harold Godwinson, the last Anglo-Saxon king of England.

1076
Empire of Ghana collapses
The Empire of Ghana, in West Africa, falls to the Almoravids.

WILLIAM THE CONQUEROR (1028–1087)

When William, Duke of Normandy, defeated his English rival, Harold, at the battle at Hastings, he became King William I. He introduced feudal government to England and appointed many French noblemen as his vassals. William built many castles and commissioned a famous survey, the Domesday Book, detailing the lands and wealth of his kingdom.

1071
Norman rampage
The Normans complete their conquest of Byzantine southern Italy.

776
A contemporary estimate of the number of ships in the Norman fleet during the conquest of England.

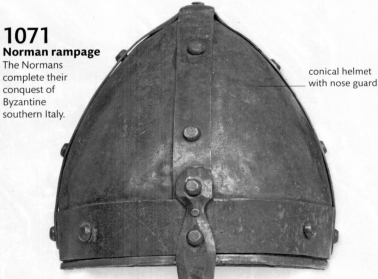

conical helmet with nose guard

NORMAN HELMET REPLICA

CRUSADERS STORM ANTIOCH

1100
King of Jerusalem crowned
Baldwin I becomes the first king of Jerusalem.

1095
Council of Clermont
At the Council of Clermont, Pope Urban II preaches to an assembly of mainly Frankish clerics and nobles about Muslim "defilement" of the Holy Land. The pope urges his audience to take up arms in a holy war, or crusade.

1119
Knights Templar formed
The Knights Templar, an order of Crusaders, is founded.

1122
Concordat of Worms
A synod at the German town of Worms, presided by a papal legate, draws up a concordat (agreement) ending the Investiture Controversy.

1125
Guelph–Ghibelline conflict begins
The death of Henry V triggers the start of what becomes known as the Guelph–Ghibelline conflict. Rival factions support either the pope or the Holy Roman Emperor.

1148
Siege of Damascus
The unsuccessful Second Crusade climaxes with the failed Siege of Damascus. After this the Frankish Crusader kingdoms decline.

1090–1119   1120–1129   1130–1149

1098
Siege of Antioch
Antioch falls to the Crusaders after a year-long siege in 1098.

1111
Imperial coronation
The German King Henry V launches a powerful expedition to Italy to force Pope Paschal II to crown him Holy Roman Emperor. Under duress, the pope offers major concessions on the Investiture Controversy, but he repudiates them the following year.

1122
Almohad movement established
The preacher Ibn Tumart founds the Islamic revivalist Almohad movement, which conquers Morocco by 1147 and Muslim Spain by 1172.

1127
Southern Song dynasty established
Kaifeng, the Song capital, falls to the Jurchen from Manchuria. The Song moved its capital to Hangzhou, forming the southern Song dynasty. The Jurchen rule northern China as the Jin dynasty.

1099
Crusaders take Jerusalem
The capturing of Jerusalem marks the end of the First Crusade.

c.1125
Angkor Wat built
The Khmer King Suryavarman II orders the construction of the great temple of Angkor Wat, in modern Cambodia.

1138
King of the Romans declared
Conrad III is elected the king of the Romans in Germany.

1144
Fall of Edessa
The Crusader state of Edessa falls to the Muslims. The loss of Edessa causes alarm and outrage in Europe, and provides the trigger for the Second Crusade.

1147
Almohad campaigns start
The Almohads seize the city of Marrakesh from the Almoravids and take control of North Africa. They also establish themselves in southern Spain.

" Undertake this journey for the **remission of your sins,** with the assurance of the **imperishable glory of the Kingdom of Heaven.**"
From Robert the Monk's account of Urban II's speech at the Council of Clermont

c.1150
Cahokia settlement at its height
The Cahokia mound settlement in the Mississippi River Valley reaches its peak. It sees the construction of more than 100 mounds, including one with a base larger than that of the Great Pyramid at Giza.

1152
Barbarossa crowned
Frederick I, known as Barbarossa, succeeds Conrad III as king of the Romans. Aware of historical precedent, Barbarossa aims to restore the imperial crown to Roman-era glory, and begins to style his realm the Holy Roman Empire.

1170
English invade Ireland
The Anglo–Normans under Robert "Strongbow" FitzStephen are active in Ireland.

1174
Ayyubid dynasty founded
With the death of the Zengid emir Nur al-Din, his nephew Saladin, who had already assumed control of Egypt, quickly marches north to secure Syria. Saladin is duly recognized as sultan of Egypt and Syria by the caliph in Baghdad, founding the Ayyubid dynasty.

1175
Ghurids invade India
Muhammad of Ghur, the leader of the Persian Ghurids, launches the Islamic invasion of northern India.

1180
Gempei War
The Gempei Wars begin in Japan as two clans battle for power.

c.1190
Angkor Empire ascendent
The Angkor Empire of Cambodia reaches its greatest extent under Emperor Jayavarman VII.

1192
Shogun rule established
In Japan, Minamoto Yoritomo becomes shogun. As an undisputed military dictator, his bakufu, or administration, at Kamakura now supplants the imperial court. Japan is ruled by shoguns for centuries to come.

KAMAKURA BUDDHA

1150–1169   1170–1189   1190–1199

1170
Becket slain
Thomas Becket, Archbishop of Canterbury, is murdered in Canterbury Cathedral, England, by four knights from the court of Henry II. Becket is canonized in 1173 and becomes one of the most popular English saints.

1187
Battle of Hattin
Crusader armies are destroyed by Sultan Saladin of Ayyubid dynasty at the Battle of Hattin. Following this victory, Saladin goes on to take the Crusader strongholds of Acre and Jerusalem.

1189
Third Crusade launched
King Richard I of England, known as the Lionheart, leads the Third Crusade. Although he wins most of his battles, he is unable to achieve his aim of "liberating" Jerusalem.

1192
Battle of Taraori
The Ghurids defeat a Hindu rebellion at the Battle of Taraori near Thanesar in India. The following year, Muhammad of Ghur founds the Sultanate of Delhi.

1192
Treaty of Ramla
Richard I and Saladin sign the Treaty of Ramla. Jerusalem remains under Muslim control, but the city is open to Christian pilgrimages.

enamel decoration on gilt-copper reliquary

THOMAS BECKET RELIQUARY

"Will no one **rid me** of this **turbulent priest?**"
Attributed to Henry II, referring to Thomas Becket

c.1200
Incas settle
The Incas, under Manco Capac, settle in the Andes near Cuzco.

c.1200
Aztecs migrate
Migrating from the north, the Aztecs enter the Valley of Mexico.

1212
Battle of Las Navas de Tolosa
At the Battle of Las Navas de Tolosa, a huge Christian army defeats the Almohads. This is a decisive point in the reconquest of Moorish Spain.

1204
Constantinople falls
Crusaders sack Constantinople during the Fourth Crusade.

1209
The Albigensian Crusade begins
The pope declares a crusade against heretics in southern France—the Albigensians and Waldenses—whose teachings challenge the worldliness of the established church.

GENGHIS KHAN (c.1162–1227)
Originally named Temüjin by his family of minor chieftains, Genghis Khan spent much of his childhood as a precarious semi-outlaw. He earned a military reputation in minor skirmishes against the Chinese, eventually securing a leading position among the Mongol tribes. In 1206 he was proclaimed Genghis Khan, or "universal ruler," going on to command a feared army of more than 200,000 men. He is thought to have died following a riding accident, and was buried according to custom in an unmarked grave in Mongolia.

1215
Magna Carta signed
In England, the Magna Carta is signed following civil war. It states that the king is not above the law.

1215
Mongols capture Beijing
The Mongol Emperor Genghis Khan continues his campaigns through China, capturing Beijing.

1227
Death of Genghis Khan
Genghis Khan dies; he is about 65 years old.

1237
Mongols invade Russia
Under Batu Khan, the Mongols invade Russia. These armies conquer the Russian principalities and go on to blaze a trail of destruction deep into Central Europe.

1244
Jerusalem sacked
Jerusalem, which has been under partial Christian control since the Holy Roman Emperor Frederick II's treaty with the sultan of Egypt, is taken by the Muslim forces of King Ayyub with the help of the Turks.

1200–1214   1215–1229   1230–1249

c.1200
Easter Island statues created
The inhabitants of Easter Island, or Rapa Nui, in the Pacific Ocean begin to carve monumental statues known as *moai*.

MOAI ON EASTER ISLAND

c.1209
Franciscan order established
The Franciscans form a new order of friars. They are mainly recruited from the middle classes—living off charity rather than farming—and are devoted to preaching in towns and cities.

1218
Mongols invade Persian Empire
Having conquered most of Central Asia and northern China, Genghis Khan invades the Persian Khwarazm Empire.

1235
Mali Empire ascendent
Sundiata, King of the Keita, a Mande people from sub-Saharan Mali, defeats the Susu King Sumanguru at the Battle of Kirina. This signals the rise of the Mali Empire.

1248
Conquest of al-Andalus
The Spanish King Ferdinand III completes the conquest of al-Andalus (apart from Granada) with the successful Siege of Seville.

pukao—huge stones for hats—made from red volcanic rock

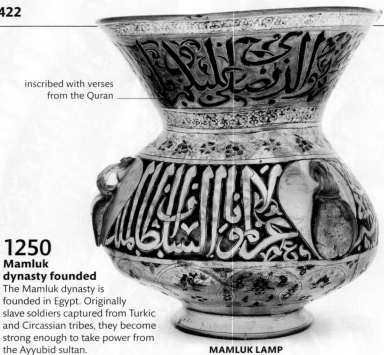

inscribed with verses from the Quran —

MAMLUK LAMP

7,000
The estimated number of Venetians killed at the Battle of Curzola.

1298
Battle of Curzola begins
At the Battle of Curzola, the Genoese fleet inflict a disastrous defeat on the Venetians, destroying all but a few of their ships. A peace treaty between the two powers is negotiated.

1298
Battle of Falkirk breaks out
Scottish forces led by William Wallace are defeated by the English at the Battle of Falkirk.

1250
Mamluk dynasty founded
The Mamluk dynasty is founded in Egypt. Originally slave soldiers captured from Turkic and Circassian tribes, they become strong enough to take power from the Ayyubid sultan.

1271
Yuan dynasty established
The Mongols led by Kublai Khan found the Yuan dynasty in China.

1287
Pagan Empire falls
The Mongols destroy the Pagan Empire in Burma.

1266
Mongol capital created
The Mongol leader Kublai Khan founds a new Mongol capital at Khanbaliq (modern Beijing).

1274
Mongols face failure
Kublai Khan's first attempt to invade Japan fails. He makes a second unsuccessful attempt in 1281.

1291
The fall of Acre
The Crusader port of Acre falls to the Mamluk Turks. After nearly 200 years, Christian presence in the Holy Land is extinguished.

1260
Mamluks conquer Mongols
The Mamluks, under Baybars, defeat the Mongols at Ain Jalut, Palestine.

1250–1259 | 1260–1279 | 1280–1299

1258
Mongols sack Baghdad
Having crushed the Order of the Assassins two years earlier, the Mongols sack the city of Baghdad and execute the Abbasid caliph—the figurehead of Islam.

1261
Byzantine sees victory
The Byzantines retake the city of Constantinople from the Crusaders.

1279
Pandya kingdom triumphant
In southern India, Kulasekhara of Pandya defeats the last Chola king, expanding the kingdom of the Pandyas to its greatest extent.

c.1280
Maori settlers arrive in New Zealand
The Maori settle in New Zealand, the last major land mass to be colonized by humans, with the exception of Antarctica.

1270
Solomonid dynasty established
The Solomonid dynasty is founded in Ethiopia.

1271
Marco Polo sets sail
The Italian explorer Marco Polo leaves Venice for China. In 1275, he visits the court of Kublai Khan.

MARCO POLO'S DEPARTURE FROM VENICE

> "I did not write **half of what I saw** for I knew **I would not be believed.**"
>
> Explorer Marco Polo, on his deathbed

ASHIKAGA GOLDEN PAVILION, JAPAN

THE BLACK DEATH

The effects of the Black Death are best recorded in Europe, where it had profound consequences. The disease depopulated the land, depressed the economy, checked intellectual and artistic progress, changed the social order, and contributed to the end of feudalism. It also triggered a wave of anti-Semitic pogroms (violent raids) on Jews, who were blamed for the pestilence, forcing many to migrate to Eastern Europe.

1337
Hundred Years War begins
The Hundred Years War between the nations of England and France begins.

30 percent
The proportion of the total population of Europe killed by waves of the Black Death.

1336
Ashikaga shogunate seizes power
Following the civil war in Japan, the Ashikaga shogunate takes power. It rules Japan for the next 240 years.

c.1300
Ottoman state founded
The Ottoman Turkish leader Osman I founds the Ottoman state, based in northwestern Anatolia (modern Turkey). During the first phase of the Ottoman expansion, they rapidly conquer Byzantine territory.

1340
Battle of Rio Salado
A Christian army defeats the Marinids at the Battle of Rio Salado, ending the threat of Islamic incursion into the Iberian peninsula from Africa.

1347
Deadly disease spreads
The Black Death reaches Europe after ravaging western Asia.

1316
Famine strikes Europe
Famine in Western Europe follows crop failure of the previous year.

1300–1319　　1320–1339　　1340–1349

1314
Knights Templar suppressed
The Grand Master of the Knights Templar is burned at the stake, as the order is suppressed.

c.1325
Tenochtitlán built
The Aztecs found a capital at Tenochtitlán, Mexico.

1336
Vijayanagar Empire founded
A Hindu rebellion establishes the Vijayanagar Empire in southern India—the last great Hindu empire in India.

1346
Battle of Crécy
The English, under King Edward III, inflict a crushing defeat on the French at the Battle of Crécy. They go on to besiege Calais, which falls in 1347 after a protracted siege.

1324
Pilgrimage of Gold begins
Mansa Musa, emperor of Mali, performs the Pilgrimage of Gold to Egypt and Mecca. He dispenses so much gold on his passage through Cairo that he destabilizes the economy.

1314
Battle of Bannockburn
At the Battle of Bannockburn, Robert the Bruce, king of Scotland, finally expels the English from Scotland.

1333
Hojo regency falls
In Japan, Emperor Go-Daigo defeats the Hojo regency in Kamakura.

1309
Papacy moves to France
Facing tumultuous conditions in Italy, Pope Clement V relocates the papacy to Avignon in southern France.

THE BURGHERS OF CALAIS BY AUGUSTE RODIN, LONDON

276 years
the duration of the Ming dynasty.

porcelain painted with underglaze decoration

MING VASE

1354
Ottomans sieze Gallipoli
John Kantakouzenos—claimant to the Byzantine throne—asks the Ottomans to help him gain power. However, the Ottomans soon seize Gallipoli, securing a foothold in Europe.

1362
Tamerlane becomes leader
Tamerlane—also known as Timur Leng—rises from modest beginnings to become the leader of the Turkic-Mongol Chagatai tribe in Transoxiana, Central Asia. Tamerlane is destined to become one of the greatest conquerors in history.

1368
Ming dynasty established
Zhu Yuanzhang expels the Yuan dynasty and founds the Ming dynasty. He sets up a strong, centralized government in which the position of the emperor is strengthened.

1389
Battle of Kosovo begins
At the Battle of Kosovo, the Ottomans defeat the Serbs and Bosnians, smashing the Serbian Empire and absorbing most of its territories. After the battle, the Ottomans control most of Anatolia (modern Turkey) and the Balkans south of the Danube.

1392
Yi dynasty established
In Korea, King Taejo founds the Yi (Joseon) dynasty. Taejo restructures his government on the Chinese model, and institutes wide-ranging land reforms.

c.1360
Vijayanagar Empire reaches its peak
The Vijayanagar Empire of southern India reaches its greatest extent.

1378
Western Schism starts
The Western or Great Schism sees rival popes installed in Rome as well as Avignon until 1417.

1398
Delhi destroyed
Tamerlane invades India and destroys Delhi.

1350-1359 1360-1379 1380-1399

1354
The Alhambra extended
Mohammed V murders his father and becomes King of Granada. Under Mohammed, the Alhambra—the fortress-palace of Granada—is further developed, becoming a treasure of Islamic architecture.

1360
Treaty of Calais signed
King Edward III of England campaigns in France and agrees to terms at the Treaty of Calais. This marks the end of the first phase of the Hundred Years War.

1381
War of Chioggia breaks out
The Venetians' victory at the War of Chioggia ends the Genoese maritime supremacy.

1396
Battle of Nicopolis
At the Battle of Nicopolis, the Ottomans repel a Crusader army.

THE ALHAMBRA, GRANADA, SPAIN

MAP OF
TENOCHTITLÁN

1415
Battle of Agincourt begins
At the Battle of Agincourt, Henry V of England inflicts a terrible defeat on a far larger French force, taking the Duke of Orléans prisoner, and going on to conquer Normandy.

THE HUNDRED YEARS WAR

The series of conflicts from 1337 to 1453, later known as the Hundred Years War, was triggered by a combination of factors: tensions over the status of the duchy of Guienne, which belonged to the kings of England but owed sovereignty to the French crown; English claims to France, based on descent from the Capetians; and the need of English kings to use foreign adventures to shore up support at home. There should have been little contest between France, the most powerful nation in Europe, and smaller, poorer England, but the English used new tactics and weapons, especially the longbow, to devastating effect. The war drained resources on both sides, but also forged a new degree of national identity for both countries.

c.1400
Tenochtitlán at its peak
Founded by the Aztecs in 1325, the city of Tenochtitlán in the valley of Mexico reaches its peak at the beginning of the 15th century. A huge population of up to 200,000 is supported by intensive agriculture and extensive networks of trade and tribute.

1415
Ceuta captured
The Portuguese capture Ceuta—the first permanent European possession in North Africa.

1428
Le dynasty established
The Le dynasty in Vietnam wins its independence from China.

1438
Inca expansion begins
The expansion of the Inca Empire begins under Sapa Inca Pachacuti. The empire triples in size by the 16th century.

1445
Portuguese discovers trade route
The Portuguese explorer Dinis Dias sights the mouth of the Senegal River. This offers a trade route deep into the African interior, and rounds Cape Verde, the westernmost point of Africa.

1400–1409 1410–1429 1430–1449

1402
Battle of Ankara
Tamerlane defeats the Ottomans and temporarily shatters their power in Anatolia (modern Turkey).

c.1400
Songhay kingdom expands
The African Songhay kingdom, centered on the trading metropolis of Gao, in West Africa, begins to expand. The kingdom eclipses the other two large empires of the late Iron Age in West Africa—Ghana and Mali.

1410
Battle of Grunwald starts
Polish–Lithuanian forces defeat the Teutonic knights at the Battle of Grunwald, one of the greatest cavalry confrontations of the age.

1429
Joan of Arc relieves the Siege of Orléans
Joan of Arc, a 16-year-old farmer's daughter, relieves the Siege of Orléans as the head of the French army. Joan goes on to defeat the English armies twice more before being captured.

1449
Council of Basel dissolved
The dissolution of the Council of Basel signals the triumph of the papacy over the Conciliar Movement. This movement claimed that the Church Council, rather than the pope, held power in spiritual matters.

1434
Rise of the Medici
The rise of Cosimo de Medici marks the start of the Medici domination of Florence. Cosimo combines business acumen with political shrewdness, winning popular support for his policies.

STATUE OF JOAN OF ARC, PARIS, FRANCE

covered in gold leaf

> "I was 13 when I had a **voice from God** for my **help and guidance.**"

Joan of Arc, during her second public examination, February 22, 1431

c.1430
Rise of the Mutapa Empire
As the Great Zimbabwe civilization declines, the Mutapa Empire, in modern Zimbabwe and Mozambique, is established. The Mutapa Empire remains the dominant regional power for more than a century.

ENLIGHTENMENT AND IMPERIALISM

Europe underwent a cultural revolution—the Renaissance—in the 15th and 16th centuries, when the knowledge of the continent's ancient scholars was rediscovered, fostering a spirit of scientific enquiry and inspiring technological advances and voyages of exploration. By the late 1500s, however, Catholicism in Western Europe was torn apart by the Reformation, and many of the fledgling colonies of European powers were soon settled by Protestants fleeing religious persecution. But European expansion was not straightforward—Ming and Qing China, Mughal India, and Edo Japan, and the Safavid Persians and Ottomans resisted Europe's incursions.

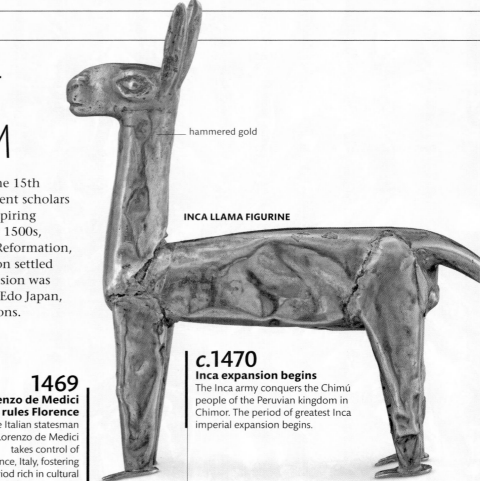

— hammered gold

INCA LLAMA FIGURINE

1455
Gutenberg Bible printed
German printer Johannes Gutenberg prints the first major book—the Gutenberg Bible—with a movable-type printing press. Thousands of copies of books can be made relatively easily using his printing method.

1467
Onin War begins
Beginning as a succession dispute between Hosokawa Katsumoto and Yamana Sozen, the Onin War leaves Japan devastated and leads to a century of turbulence—the Warring States Period—in which a series of regional magnates attempt to eradicate their rivals.

1469
Lorenzo de Medici rules Florence
The Italian statesman Lorenzo de Medici takes control of Florence, Italy, fostering a period rich in cultural and intellectual output.

c.1470
Inca expansion begins
The Inca army conquers the Chimú people of the Peruvian kingdom in Chimor. The period of greatest Inca imperial expansion begins.

1450–1459   1460–1469   1470–1474

1455
Wars of the Roses begin
In England, armies belonging to the rival Plantagenet houses of York and Lancaster clash at the Battle of St. Albans, the opening conflict of the Wars of the Roses.

1468
Songhay take Timbuktu
The Songhay recapture Timbuktu from the Tuaregs and become the leading power in West Africa.

1469
Portuguese begin trading on Gold Coast
The Lisbon merchant Fernão Gomes is granted a monopoly on lucrative commerce with the West African coast—Portuguese sailors had been trading on this coast since the 1440s—provided he continued to explore the Gulf of Guinea.

1472
Ivan III marries
King Ivan III of Russia, later known as Ivan the Great, takes as his second wife Zoë (later Sophia) Palaeologus, the niece of the last Byzantine emperor.

1471
Khmer civilization ends
The final decline of the Khmer civilization in Southeast Asia begins.

1453
Constantinople captured
Constantinople is captured by Muslim Ottomans; the Christian Eastern Orthodox Byzantine Empire falls.

THE SPANISH INQUISITION

The Inquisition was a medieval Catholic institution designed to root out heresy, but it became infamous in Spain and its territories. Isabella I of Castille and Ferdinand II of Aragon petitioned Pope Sixtus IV in 1478 to allow the establishment of these tribunals to expose heretics among converted Jews and, after the fall of Granada in 1492, Muslims as well. It was finally disbanded in 1834.

1471
Champa destroyed
The Hindu state of Champa, in modern South Vietnam, is effectively destroyed by Viet troops who lay waste the Champa capital, Vijaya.

"I should be judged as a captain who went from **Spain to the Indies** to conquer a people **numerous and warlike.**"

Christopher Columbus, in a letter to Doña Juana de Torres, October 1500

1492
Columbus crosses Atlantic
With the backing of the Spanish crown, the Genoese voyager Christopher Columbus makes the first Atlantic crossing, landing in the Bahamas, in the Caribbean.

MODEL OF COLUMBUS'S SHIP, THE *SANTA MARIA*

hull length 62 ft (19 m)

1479
Spain united
The Spanish succession crisis that began in 1474, and was triggered by the marriage of Queen Isabella I and King Ferdinand II in 1469, comes to an end and the two crowns rule over what becomes modern Spain.

1491
Kongo ruler converts
The ruler of Kongo, Nzinga a Nkuwu, and his son, Mvemba a Nzinga, convert to Christianity after meeting Portuguese missionaries, and become João I and Afonso I, respectively.

1494
Treaty of Tordesillas
Pope Alexander VI draws up the Treaty of Tordesillas, which effectively divides up existing and future New World discoveries between Spain and Portugal.

1497
Newfoundland "discovered"
With the backing of the English crown, the Italian navigator John Cabot reaches Newfoundland. He returns to England certain that he has reached China.

1475–1484   1485–1494   1495–1499

1480
Ivan the Great defies Mongols
Ivan the Great of Russia stops paying tribute money to the Tatar Mongols. He declares independence for his Muscovy state.

1485
Battle of Bosworth Field
At the Battle of Bosworth Field, in central England, Henry Tudor defeats the English King Richard III. He becomes King Henry VII and establishes the Tudor dynasty.

1494
Italian Wars begin
The Italian Wars, nominally sparked by the desire of Charles VIII of France to assert a claim to the kingdom of Naples, see an intermittent 65-year struggle between France and Spain for the control of Italy.

1499
Vespucci lands in South America
The Florentine navigator Amerigo Vespucci lands on the northern coast of South America at the mouth of the Amazon River.

1497
Bonfire of the Vanities
Florence comes under the religious dictatorship of the Dominican monk, Girolamo Savonarola. He imposes a puritanical campaign on the city in which he denounces tyrants and corruption, and institutes the Bonfire of the Vanities: the mass destruction of idolatrous goods, including books and artworks.

1498
Vasco da Gama reaches India
After a year's voyage, the Portuguese explorer Vasco da Gama arrives in Calicut, southwest India, having discovered a sea route from Europe around the Cape of Good Hope. The longest ocean crossing yet made, it initiates the route used throughout the "Age of Sail."

SEAL OF HENRY TUDOR

1477
Battle of Nancy
At the Battle of Nancy, the Burgundian forces, led by Charles the Bold, are comprehensively routed by the Swiss. King Louis XI of France seizes the Burgundians' French territories; those in the Low Countries pass to the Habsburgs.

1492
Fall of Granada
Spanish monarchs Ferdinand and Isabella preside over the fall of the Kingdom of Granada, marking the end of a decades-long campaign to reclaim the last Islamic territory in Iberia.

1499
France seizes Milan
French troops under King Louis XII invade Lombardy, Italy, and seize Milan. Louis allies with Ferdinand of Aragon, and they agree to divide Naples between them.

THE REFORMATION

The Reformation—the religious challenge to the Catholic Church instigated by German Martin Luther—tore the Western Church apart. Soon politics became linked to the religious ideas that spread across Europe. The consequence was a legacy of violent religious division between Catholics and Protestants that led to a permanent schism in European Christendom.

MARTIN LUTHER POSTS HIS *95 THESES*

c.1500
Sikhism founded
Sikhism is founded by Guru Nanak in the Punjab region of India.

1513
Florida settled
The Spanish explorer Juan Ponce de León, explores the coastline of Florida and claims the North American territory for Spain.

1517
Martin Luther publishes *95 Theses*
The priest and professor of theology Martin Luther nails his *95 Theses* to the door of All Saints' Church in Wittenberg, Saxony, in modern Germany, as part of what is a growing protest movement against religious practices and corruption in the Catholic Church.

1502
Slave trade between Africa and Americas begins
Juan de Córdoba sends his African slaves from Spain to Hispaniola in the Caribbean to work in Spanish settlements. By 1518 European slave traders were sending Africans directly to the Americas, after King Charles V of Spain granted the first licenses for the trade.

1519
Magellan seeks western passage
The Portuguese nobleman Ferdinand Magellan leaves Spain seeking the western passage to the Spice Islands.

1521
Edict of Worms issued
Having already been excommunicated by the pope at the Edict of Worms, Martin Luther is declared a heretic and his works are banned.

1500–1509 | 1510–1519 | 1520–1524

1504
Michelangelo sculpts *David*
In Florence, Italy, the sculptor and painter Michelangelo Buonarroti completes the monumental sculpture *David*. In 1508 he begins work on painting a fresco on the Vatican's Sistine Chapel ceiling.

1511
Portuguese take Malacca
The Portuguese take control of the trading post at Malacca (Melaka) on the Malay Peninsula.

1519
Spanish conquer Aztecs
The Spanish explorer Hernán Cortés marches on Tenochtitlán, capital of the Mesoamerican Aztec Empire. Within two years, the Spanish subjugate the entire nation.

1524
German Peasants War begins
In Germany and Austria, large numbers of people gather in hastily assembled armies in an attempt to end what they see as abuses against them—chiefly taxes and labor services—by the Church and the nobility. The uprising is savagely repressed, with thousands killed.

1514
Battle of Chaldiran breaks out
The Ottomans, under Sultan Salim I, defeat the Safavid Persians at the Battle of Chaldiran. Salim dramatically increases Ottoman territories and Muslim holy places in the Near East.

1506
***Mona Lisa* completed**
The Italian polymath Leonardo da Vinci completes his painting, the *Mona Lisa*.

1500
Portuguese claim Brazil
The Portuguese explorer Pedro Álvares Cabral, bound for India, sights Brazil. The Portuguese crown is quick to claim it once it is clear that this territory lies inside Portugal's zone as outlined by the Treaty of Tordesillas.

THE RENAISSANCE

The Renaissance—literally "rebirth"— grew out of the Italian Middle Ages and marked a reevaluation of European thought. At its heart was a reinterpretation of Europe's Classical past. It gave rise, first in Florence (left), to an artistic and architectural revolution, and later, to a scientific one. The early impact of the Renaissance was fitful but spread to most of Europe in the following 200 years.

quillon ends in a petalled dome

curved steel blade

MUGHAL SWORD

1526
Mughal Empire founded
The Mughal Empire is founded in northern India. It is the creation of Babur, a descendant of the Mongol leader Genghis Khan.

1529
Ottomans besiege Vienna
Following their conquest of Hungary, the Ottomans, fearing that the Habsburgs will try to recapture the lost territories, lay siege to Vienna. The task proves too ambitious even for the formidable Ottoman army that fails to take the city.

1534
St. Lawrence River discovered
The French explorer Jacques Cartier leads an expedition to the Americas to find a northwest passage to Asia. Instead, he encounters the St. Lawrence River, which links the Atlantic Ocean to the North American Great Lakes.

1534
Jesuit order established
The Jesuits, a Catholic order, is established by the Basque nobleman Ignatius of Loyola. His goal is to produce a new generation of highly educated priests to spread a new militantly Catholic faith. Given papal sanction in 1540, the Jesuits spearhead the Catholic revival.

1536
Dissolution of the monasteries
King Henry VIII's secretary, Thomas Cromwell, begins the dissolution of the monasteries in England. More than 800 monasteries in England are suppressed and their lands transferred to the Crown. This is the greatest transfer of land in England since the Norman conquest of 1066. In this process, many religious buildings are destroyed or vandalized.

1536
England and Wales united
England and Wales are formally united under one legal and administrative system through an Act of Union.

1545
Council of Trent founded
At Trent in the Italian Alps, the Catholic Church sets out to challenge the Protestant Reformation by reforming and remodeling itself. The Council of Trent aims to eradicate corruption, make the Church's teachings more coherent, and to project itself as a dynamic and competitive religious force.

1545
Silver deposits discovered
At Potosí, in modern Bolivia, Spanish colonists discover the biggest single concentration of silver ever found—almost an entire mountain of silver. Together with the silver found in northern Mexico, this discovery funds the further expansion of the Spanish Empire, as well as replenishing the coffers to fight conflicts back in Europe.

1547
Battle of Mühlberg
The Habsburgs, under Holy Roman Emperor Charles V, defeat the protestant Schmalkaldic League at the Battle of Mühlberg.

1525–1534   1535–1544   1545–1549

1529
Peace of Cambrai signed
A temporary truce is created between France and Holy Roman Emperor Charles V, with the Peace of Cambrai. France relinquishes its rights in Italy, Flanders, and Artois. Charles V renounces his claims to Burgundy.

1533
Spanish conquer Peru
The Spanish conquistador Francisco Pizarro launches the conquest of Inca Peru. Pizarro encounters, captures, and kills the Inca Emperor Atahuallpa, and conquers the Inca capital, Cuzco.

1534
Church of England founded
Having been denied a divorce by the pope, King Henry VIII of England breaks with Rome. He forms the Church of England under the Act of Supremacy.

PRINCE EDWARD, KING HENRY VIII, AND QUEEN JANE SEYMOUR

1543
Ethiopian Christian Empire triumphs
Islamic *jihadi* fighters are finally driven out of Ethiopia, leaving the empire Christian Orthodox.

> "**The King,** our sovereign... shall be taken, accepted, and reputed as the **only supreme head** on earth of the **Church of England.**"

The Act of Supremacy, 1534, which made King Henry VIII head of the English church

> "I know I have the body of a **weak and feeble woman;** but I have the **heart and stomach of a king.**"

Elizabeth I, speaking to her troops at Tilbury, 1588

QUEEN ELIZABETH I'S "ARMADA" PORTRAIT

1558
Elizabeth becomes queen
Following the death of Queen Mary I, Elizabeth I, the daughter of King Henry VIII and Anne Boleyn, becomes Queen of England.

1572
St. Bartholomew's Day Massacre
On St. Bartholemew's Day, thousands of French Protestants, known as Huguenots, are slaughtered. This event is triggered by an assassination attempt on a Huguenot guest after the wedding of Catherine de Medici's daughter, Marguerite of Valois, to the Bourbon Huguenot, Henry of Navarre.

1557
Süleymaniye mosque opens
The Süleymaniye mosque is completed, making it the largest mosque in Istanbul.

1555
Peace of Augsburg
Holy Roman Emperor Charles V concedes the Peace of Augsburg, giving German princes the freedom to select either Lutheran Protestantism or Catholicism and impose that religion on their territories.

1565
Manila Galleon Trade
Spanish navigator Andés de Urdaneta discovers a west-to-east route across the Pacific. His voyage helps the Spanish to colonize the Philippines and provides them with markets for products from Peru and Mexico.

1565
Reign of Terror begins
Tsar Ivan IV begins his Reign of Terror. He dispossesses and slaughters the boyars—the Russian aristocracy. Their former estates become Ivan's "private domain," the oprichnina—a vast area of central Russia parceled out among a new nobility loyal to the Tsar.

1550–1554 1555–1564 1565–1574

1550
Vasari's *Lives* published
The Italian painter and historian Giorgio Vasari publishes his *Lives of the Most Eminent Italian Painters, Sculptors, and Architects.*

1556
Akbar becomes Mughal emperor
The accession of the 14-year-old Akbar to the Mughal throne marks a decisive moment in the dynasty's fortunes. Mughal India enjoys expansion of territory, prosperity, religious tolerance, and cultural richness.

1558
England loses Calais
Queen Mary I of England is persuaded by her husband, King Philip II of Spain, to join him in a renewed war with France. This proves disastrous, leading to the loss of Calais, England's last foothold in continental Europe.

1565
Spain claims Philippines
The Spanish colonization of the Philippines begins with settlement on Cebu.

1571
Battle of Lepanto
The Battle of Lepanto, fought off the coast of western Greece, is the last major engagement between galleys—with the Christians and Ottomans having fleets of about 200 ships each. The Christian fleet triumphs, ending the threat of Ottoman expansion in the western Mediterranean.

IVAN THE TERRIBLE (1530–1584)

Tsar Ivan IV applied a ruthless brutality to his rule over the Russians. Although he was capable of bouts of remorse— he regretted killing his son and heir—Ivan's rule led to vast numbers of Russians fleeing the country during his reign from 1547 to 1584. This depopulated the country to the point that serfdom (bonded peasantry) was the only means of retaining an agricultural workforce.

1558
Ivan the Terrible begins conquest
Tsar Ivan IV, also known as Ivan the Terrible, continues his policy of Russian expansion by trying to gain access to the Baltic Sea, triggering a 24-year struggle against Livonia (modern Estonia and Latvia) known as the Livonian War.

ST. BASIL'S CATHEDRAL, MOSCOW, BUILT BY IVAN IV

one of nine onion-shaped domes

THE SPANISH ARMADA

130

The number of galleons and armed merchant vessels in Spanish King Philip II's Armada.

1598
Treaty of Vervins
After three years of war with Spain, King Henry IV of France signs the Treaty of Vervins with Spain and, along with the Edict of Nantes in the same year, ends the Wars of Religion.

1588
English defeat Spanish Armada
The victim of English seamanship, lengthening lines of supply, and the weather, the gale-wracked Spanish Armada is forced home in disarray. Spanish hopes of conquering and converting the Protestant country are decisively checked.

1579
Union of Arras
The Catholic provinces of the Low Countries assert loyalty to King Philip II of Spain with the Union of Arras.

1592
Seven Years War begins
The Seven Years War, or Imjin Waeran, begins when Japanese forces mount a sustained invasion of Korea.

1575–1579   1580–1589   1590–1599

1579
Union of Utrecht
The Protestant provinces of the Low Countries form a defensive alliance with the Union of Utrecht.

1576
Pacification of Ghent
Having been unable to suppress the Dutch Revolt in 1568, the authority of Spain's King Philip II disintegrates. The Low Countries (modern Netherlands) unite to call for the withdrawal of Spanish troops and an end to religious persecution.

1582
Japan begins reunification
The Japanese feudal lord Toyotomi Hideyoshi seizes power in Japan after the death of Oda Nobunaga. Within a decade, he has succeeded in reunifying almost the whole of Japan under his rule.

1590
Ottoman–Safavid peace treaty
Ottoman frontiers are extended to the Caucasus and the Caspian following the Ottoman–Safavid peace treaty.

1593
Long War begins
The Long War on the Ottoman–Habsburg frontier begins. The net result of the eventual peace settlement—the Treaty of Zsitvatorok, of 1606—leaves the frontier in a state of simmering uncertainty.

1582
Gregorian Calendar introduced
Pope Gregory XIII decrees a revision to the Julian Calendar, which overestimates the length of every year by 11 minutes. Gregory removes 10 days from the calendar to ensure that the spring equinox, from which the date of Easter was calculated, falls on the correct date.

1587
Sir Francis Drake raids Cadiz
Despatched by Queen Elizabeth I of England, the British privateer Sir Francis Drake raids Cadiz, in southern Spain, destroying about 30 Spanish vessels. The raid delays the Spanish Armada by more than a year.

1576
Mughals capture Bengal
The Mughal forces of Emperor Akbar capture Bengal, the richest province in northern India.

iron shaft reeded with raised ribs

chiseled knop

MUGHAL MACE

MAORI TIKI CARVING

intricately carved wooden surface

c.1600
Classic Maori phase
The Polynesian people of New Zealand, the Maori, have become established in their new lands since first arriving in the 13th century. Known as the Classic Maori phase, their culture is distinguished by elaborate wood carving, precisely patterned bone tools and weapons, and substantial earthwork settlements.

1602
Dutch East India Company founded
Like its English rival, the Dutch East India Company is founded and granted a trade monopoly. Over the following two centuries, it becomes one of the most successful commercial ventures in the world.

1622
Virginia colony massacre
Powhatan American Indians in the English colony of Virginia kill 347 settlers—men, women, and children—approximately 25 per cent of the total number of colonists.

1618
Thirty Years War begins
The Holy Roman Emperor Ferdinand II's quest to erase Protestantism from all his dominions becomes a Europe-wide fight for supremacy involving, at different points, every major European power.

1611
King James Bible published
The new King James Bible is the work of 47 scholars under the direction of the English Archbishop of Canterbury, Richard Bancroft. The text gains support gradually until it becomes the definitive English-language Bible used by all English-speaking Protestant churches.

1623
Persians recapture Baghdad
The Persians, under Shah Abbas, retake Baghdad after nearly 90 years of Ottoman rule, and extend the Safavid Empire deep into Anatolia, in modern Turkey.

1600–1604   1605–1614   1615–1624

1600
English East India Company established
The establishment of the English East India Company, with royal approval, is a clear statement to Spain and Portugal that they cannot expect exclusive domination of trade with East Asia.

1605
Plot to blow up the Parliament
Guy Fawkes is one of the English Catholic conspirators who attempt to blow up the Houses of Parliament. The plotters may have been encouraged by Robert Cecil, the chief minister to James I, in order to stoke anti-Catholic opinion.

1624
Cardinal Richelieu comes to power
Cardinal Richelieu becomes the chief minister to the King of France, Louis XIII. Richelieu's goals are "to destroy the military power of the Habsburgs, to humble the great nobles [of France], and to raise the prestige of the House of Bourbon in Europe."

1603
Japan's capital shifts to Edo
Japan's Tokugawa Ieyasu unifies the country under a successful shogunate, and moves the island's capital from Kyoto to Edo (modern Tokyo); this period of stability lasts for more than 200 years.

1616
Shakespeare dies
The English playwright William Shakespeare dies, at the age of 52. Widely regarded as the greatest writer in the English language, he produced at least 37 plays and 154 sonnets.

1600
Battle of Sekigahara
At the Battle of Sekigahara, the Japanese statesman Tokugawa Ieyasu defeats his enemies and affirms his position as Japan's most powerful warlord.

TITLE PAGE OF SHAKESPEARE'S FIRST FOLIO

1620
Arrival of the *Mayflower*
The English ship, the *Mayflower*, carrying the Puritan pilgrims—Protestant exiles looking for religious freedom in the New World—arrives in Plymouth, North America. A year later, the pilgrims celebrate the first Thanksgiving with American Indians.

GALILEO GALILEI (1564–1642)

Born in Pisa, Italy, Galileo Galilei was an Italian scientist whose work in astronomy, physics, and engineering, and the development of complex instruments, brought a revolutionary approach to understanding the world. The Church regarded his revelations as heresy but, reluctant to condemn the scientific pioneer outright, did its best to accommodate him. Heretic or not, Galileo died with his reputation assured.

1638
Ottomans take Baghdad
The intermittent conflict between the Ottoman Empire and the Safavid Persian Empire, which had begun in 1623, climaxes with Baghdad falling to the Ottomans, led by Sultan Murad IV.

1644
Qing dynasty established
In China, the Manchus, allying with a remnant Ming force, crush forces assembled by rebel leader Li Zicheng at the Battle of Shanghai Pass. The first Manchu Qing Emperor of China, the six-year-old Shunzhi, is installed in Beijing. The Qing rule until 1911.

1645
Battle of Naseby
At the Battle of Naseby, the main army of English King Charles I is annihilated by the Parliament's newly formed New Model Army. The Parliament's victory in the English Civil War is virtually guaranteed.

1633
Galileo put under house arrest
The Italian scientist Galileo Galilei is called before the Roman Inquisition of the Catholic Church. His crime is to support the theory that the Sun, not the Earth, is at the centre of the solar system. He is found guilty of heresy, and is forced to recant and spend the rest of his life under house arrest.

1626
Dutch buy Manhattan Island
Peter Minuit, director-general of the Dutch West India Company's New Netherlands settlement, buys Manhattan Island from its American Indian inhabitants. It had been the site of Fort Amsterdam since 1625.

1635
French declare war on Habsburgs
French intervention in the Thirty Years War prevents a pro-Habsburg settlement, provoking the final and most brutal phase of the war.

1642
English Civil War begins
King Charles I of England's declaration of war on Parliament starts the English Civil War between the royalist Cavaliers and the puritan Roundheads.

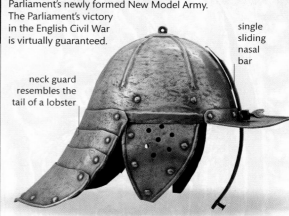

single sliding nasal bar

neck guard resembles the tail of a lobster

ENGLISH CIVIL WAR TROOPER'S HELMET

1625–1634   1635–1644   1645–1649

1631
Battle of Breitenfeld
At the Battle of Breitenfeld, Sweden's Lutheran king, Gustavus Adolphus, consolidates the position of the Swedes in Germany and restores Protestant fortunes after a decade of defeats.

1632
Gonder becomes a cultural center
Ethiopian Emperor Fasilides moves the capital to Gonder and the city becomes a cultural hub, especially in the copying of manuscripts and panel painting.

1642
Abel Tasman discovers remote lands
The Dutch explorer Abel Tasman is the first European to explore Tasmania and New Zealand.

1648
Treaty of Westphalia signed
After four years of negotiations, the Thirty Years War in Germany and the Spanish–Dutch Eighty Years War is brought to a close with a series of agreements, collectively known as the Treaty of Westphalia.

1645
Seat of Dalai Lama begins to be built
The 5th Dalai Lama—leader of Tibetan Buddhism—Lozang Gyatso, begins the construction of the modern Potala Palace, in Lhasa, Tibet. The construction ends in 1694, and it remains the seat of the Dalai Lama until 1959.

POTALA PALACE, LHASA, TIBET

1649
Charles I executed
King Charles I of England is beheaded. He is the only king of England to have been legally executed. The High Court of Justice convicts Charles as "tyrant, traitor, and murderer" by a vote of 68 to 67. Throughout his trial, Charles consistently rejects the idea that any court could legally try a king, because he rules by divine right.

6

The number of verified deaths caused by the Great Fire of London.

THE GREAT FIRE OF LONDON

1652
First Anglo–Dutch War begins
The first of three wars between England and the Netherlands begins. These naval wars are fought for the command of the sea and shipborne commerce. England's eventual victory signals the decline of Dutch commercial preeminence.

1654
Protectorate established
In England, a republic is established after Oliver Cromwell, a leading parliamentarian commander, is appointed Lord Protector of England.

1662
The Royal Society receives charter
The Royal Society in London, England, aims to pursue pure and applied science. King Charles II of England grants the society his royal charter, acknowledging the importance of science to the state.

1666
Great Fire of London breaks out
As the city's Great Plague ends, a new disaster overtakes London—the Great Fire. The whole of the city is destroyed, including the medieval St. Paul's Cathedral, 87 other churches, and more than 13,000 houses.

1668
Portugal gains independence
Spain recognizes Portuguese independence—the Iberian Union lasted from 1580 to 1640—with the Treaty of Lisbon. Portugal is ruled by the House of Braganza.

1668
Treaty of Aix-la-Chapelle signed
The Treaty of Aix-la-Chapelle concedes French gains in the Spanish Netherlands and brings an end to the War of Devolution between the Triple Alliance—England, Holland, and Sweden—and France.

1650–1659 | 1660–1669 | 1670–1674

1660
Monarchy is restored
Following the death of the English leader Oliver Cromwell, in 1658, King Charles II of England is swept to his throne on a wave of popular sentiment.

1653
Taj Mahal completed
The Taj Mahal in Agra, India, is built by the Mughal Emperor Shah Jahan as a mausoleum for his third wife, Mumtaz Mahal. This iconic structure combines Indian, Persian, and Islamic architectural styles.

1664
English seize New Amsterdam
A small English fleet arrives at New Amsterdam, modern Manhattan, the capital of the Dutch North American colony of New Netherlands, and demands its surrender. Director-general Peter Stuyvesant eventually complies.

1661
Rule of Louis XIV begins
King Louis XIV, crowned in 1643 when five years old, assumes his personal rule of France. He remains on the French throne for a further 54 years.

1670
Cossack uprising
In South Russia, an attempt to protect Cossack independence against the centralized Russian state becomes a revolt by a disaffected peasantry that sees several cities sacked and looted. The Cossack uprising is brutally suppressed by the tsar.

THE TAJ MAHAL, AGRA

LOUIS XIV (1638–1715)

King Louis XIV, known as *Le Roi Soleil*, the Sun King, had a greater impact on France than any other monarch. He was determined to be the absolute ruler of his nobles and his country—he centralized the state and fought numerous wars, but he also supported the arts. By the end of Louis' reign, France had expanded its territory and was the leading nation in Europe, much admired and imitated.

1677
Niagara Falls discovered
In northeastern North America, the discovery of the Niagara Falls, a waterfall larger than any in Europe, evokes wonder in the Old World. More than 6,000,000 cu ft (170,000 cu m) of water thunders over the edge every minute.

1682
Peter I becomes Tsar of Russia
Later known as Peter the Great, the Russian tsar introduces a program of modernization, including military and political reforms, that bears great fruit. Winning numerous wars, he expands his empire into a major European power.

precious stone inlay

fur trim

CROWN OF PETER THE GREAT

1690
Fort William established
Seeking greater security for its trade, the British East India Company establishes a new base in what became Kolkata (Calcutta), India. Fort William, named after King William III, continually enlarges and improves, and will be critical to the later British dominance in India.

1680
Pueblo revolt
The Pueblo people of the colony of New Mexico rise against the Spanish occupiers and drive them from the area, the revolt lasting 12 years. The Pueblo revolt is provoked partly by drought, but more particularly by Spain's determination to crush local religious practices—Pueblo shamans are consistently accused of witchcraft and executed.

1689
Treaty of Nerchinsk signed
The Treaty of Nerchinsk settles the territorial dispute between Russia and China in Siberia.

1689
Joint monarchs declared
King William III and Queen Mary II are declared joint Protestant monarchs of England, Scotland, and Ireland by the Parliament.

1694
Bank of England established
Closely modeled on the Bank of Amsterdam, founded in 1609, the Bank of England is formed. It allows England to finance its part in the War of the Grand Alliance, and becomes a significant factor in Britain's subsequent emergence on the world stage.

1675–1679   1680–1689   1690–1699

1682
French Court moves to Versailles
King Louis XIV establishes Versailles as the base for his court and government.

1689
Grand Alliance formed
A Grand Alliance of England, the Netherlands, and the Austrian Habsburgs is formed to counter the war of aggression launched by King Louis XIV of France against the Palatinate states in Germany. The atrocities carried out by the French rouse hatred towards Louis across Europe.

1682
La Salle explores the Mississippi
The French explorer René-Robert Cavelier, sieur de La Salle, a veteran of North American exploration, leads a party down the Mississippi River to its mouth. He proclaims the river and its hinterlands a French possession, naming it Louisiana, after the French king.

sun positioned at center

1687
Newton publishes the Law of Gravitation
The English physicist Isaac Newton publishes the Universal Law of Gravitation, one of the most remarkable of all scientific discoveries. It explains what holds the Universe together: all heavenly bodies exert a force called gravity, or weight.

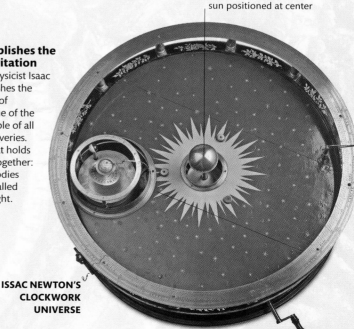

ISSAC NEWTON'S CLOCKWORK UNIVERSE

1683
Ottomans besiege Vienna
The Ottomans besiege Vienna—as they had in 1529—and again, they fail. The collapse of the Ottoman rule in Hungary follows, and an alliance that includes the Holy Roman Empire, Poland, and Venice, formed under papal authority, drives the Ottomans south across the Balkans.

1700
Great Northern War begins
Denmark, Saxony, Poland, and Russia declare war on Sweden in an attempt to end Sweden's preeminence in the Baltics. However, the army of King Charles XII, the "Swedish Meteor," beats the Danes, then annihilates a Russian army four times its size. It goes on to inflict a similarly crushing defeat on a combined Polish–Saxon force at Klissow in Poland. Sweden eventually loses the war in 1721.

1701
Asante rise to prominence
The Asante kingdom in West Africa begins its rise to prominence under the leadership of King Osei Tutu.

standing man

cobra

DECORATIVE WEIGHT MADE BY ASANTE

1713
Treaty of Utrecht
The War of the Spanish Succession is brought to an end by the Treaty of Utrecht. It confirms the separation of the French and Spanish crowns, and cements English control of Newfoundland and Nova Scotia, in modern Canada.

1720
Qing drive Mongols from Tibet
A force of Qing and Tibetan warriors drives the Zunghar Mongols from Tibet. The Qing force brings with it a replacement for the Dalai Lama, who was murdered by the Mongols. Tibet becomes a tribute-paying protectorate of Qing China.

1722
Persians annexed
The declining Persian Safavid dynasty is deposed by independent Afghans to the east. Mahmud Hotaki proclaims himself the Persian Shah.

1724
Dahomey becomes a West African power
King Agadja, the third ruler of the Kingdom of Dahomey, in the modern Republic of Benin, leads attacks on its neighbors and enlarges the state. Dahomey also profits from its involvement in the Trans-Atlantic slave trade.

1700–1704   1705–1714   1715–1724

1701
War of Spanish Succession
The War of the Spanish Succession sees a Grand Alliance, including England, the Netherlands, and Austria, oppose the unification of the French and Spanish thrones. The war lasts until 1714, when the Spanish King Philip V is forced to give up any claim to the French throne.

1707
Mughal Empire declines
The decline of the Mughal Empire begins with the death of the sixth emperor, Aurangzeb. His successors squander the dynasty's fortunes while losing control of regional governors, who go on to build their own empires.

1711
St. Paul's Cathedral completed
St. Paul's Cathedral, a London landmark, is officially completed. Designed by the British architect Christopher Wren, it is the fourth church to occupy its site; its predecessor was badly damaged in the Great Fire of London in 1666.

c.1717
Blackbeard strikes terror in the Atlantic
The notorious English pirate Edward Teach, known as Blackbeard, begins plundering ships in the West Indies, and along the coast of the North American colonies, including Virginia and the Carolinas.

BLACKBEARD THE PIRATE

"Imagination cannot form an idea of a **fury from hell** to look **more frightful.**"

Charles Johnson, describing the notorious pirate Blackbeard, in *A General History of the Robberies and Murders of the Most Notorious Pirates*, 1724

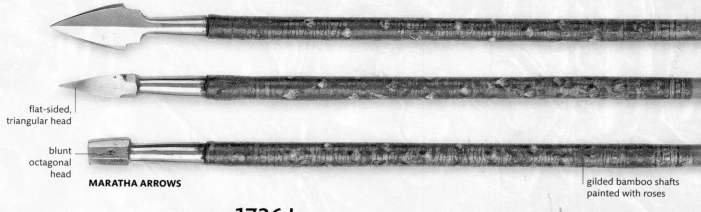

flat-sided,
triangular head

blunt
octagonal
head

MARATHA ARROWS

gilded bamboo shafts
painted with roses

c.1736
Maratha Empire expands
The Maratha Empire in India enjoys its
greatest expansion to the north, at the
expense of the Mughal Empire.

c.1740
**Mysore Kingdom
rises to prominence**
In southern India, the Mysore
Kingdom rises to prominence,
seizing territory from the Marathas,
Hyderabad, and neighboring kingdoms.

1746
French occupy Madras
A French force takes the British-held port of Madras
(modern Chennai), in southern India. The French
remain in occupation of Madras until the Treaty
of Aix-la-Chapelle returns the port to the British
in exchange for Louisbourg in Nova Scotia.

1748
Treaty of Aix-la-Chapelle
The War of the Austrian Succession is concluded
by the Treaty of Aix-la-Chapelle. Prussia's conquest
of Silesia is recognized; France regains some
colonies, but withdraws from the Netherlands;
and Britain's Asiento contract with Spain is
renewed. The Asiento contract permits Britain
to supply slaves to Spanish colonies.

1728
Battle of Palkhed
On the Indian subcontinent,
at the Battle of Palkhed, the
Hindu Marathas defeat Asaf
Jah I, the Nizam of Hyderabad.

1739
Treaty of Belgrade
The Treaty of Belgrade ends the
Austro–Russian–Turkish War. It
confirms Austria's loss of northern
Serbia and Belgrade to the Ottomans.

1725–1734   1735–1744   1745–1749

1736
Nader becomes Iranian Shah
Military leader Nader Shah, founder of the
Afsharid dynasty, is crowned Shah of Iran.

1739
Battle of Karnal
The Persians defeat the Mughals
at the Battle of Karnal, to occupy
Delhi, India. Persian forces now
control all territory to the north
and west of the Indus River.

1747
Afghanistan unified
Ahmad Khan Abdali, known as Durrani,
becomes head and founder of the modern
state of Afghanistan. Abdali unifies the
country under his rule and develops a
large empire, including parts of modern
Iran, Pakistan, and India.

1728
Bering Strait explored
The Danish seaman, Vitus Bering, is
commissioned to follow the Siberian
coast northward from the Kamchatka
Peninsula. He sails into the narrow
strait, now named after him, that
separates Siberia and Alaska.

1745
Jacobites rebel against Hanoverians
Charles Edward Stuart, "Bonnie Prince Charlie," Scottish
pretender to the English throne, rallies his Jacobite
forces and defeats the ruling Hanoverian army at
the Battle of Prestonpans. The Scottish force is
later overcome at the Battle of Culloden.

1748
Dahomey in conflict
The African Dahomey kingdom
under King Tegbesu grows richer
and stronger, but it continues to pay
tribute to the Oyo Empire in the
Yoruba states (modern Nigeria),
as it has done for decades.

30,000
The reward, in pounds, offered
for the capture of Bonnie
Prince Charlie following the
Jacobite uprising of 1745.

snake carving

**YORUBA
IVORY BRACELET**

INDUSTRY AND INDEPENDENCE

This was an era of unprecedented European global supremacy and imperial expansion on every continent, supported by rapid industrialization, expanding trade, and huge population growth. Revolutions in America and France in the late 18th century transformed Western political expectations and demands for liberation echoed through the 19th century. Democracy gradually gained ground in Europe, European colonies in Latin America won their independence, and slavery was eventually abolished everywhere in the Americas. However, those peoples who stood in the way of European expansion were harshly treated. Japan became the first Asian state to match the European powers in military and economic modernization.

1758
British victories in North America
The British score key victories over the French by taking Fort Duquesne on the Ohio River and Fort Louisbourg, on Cap Breton island, Nova Scotia, Canada.

1756
Seven Years War begins
Hanover, Britain, and Prussia (led by Frederick the Great) clash with the other major European powers: France, Austria, and Russia. The Seven Years War is fought in areas from India to North America to Europe, making it a truly global conflict.

c.1750
Agricultural revolution begins
New farming practices in Britain begin an increase in agricultural output that will feed a growing population in towns and cities.

1754
French and American Indian War
French and British colonial forces clash in the Ohio Valley, beginning a struggle for supremacy in North America. The conflict is concluded with the signing of the Treaty of Paris in 1763.

1755
Earthquake strikes Lisbon
The Lisbon earthquake, one of the deadliest in history, kills between 60,000 and 100,000 people in Portugal.

1757
Battle of Leuthen
Having defeated Austro-French forces in Rossbach (in modern Germany), Prussia defeats Austria at the Battle of Leuthen ensuring the control of Silesia.

1750–1754   1755–1759

1751
***Encyclopédie* published**
In France, the writer and philosopher Denis Diderot publishes the *Encyclopédie, ou dictionnaire raisonné des sciences, des arts et des métiers*. Known as the *Encyclopédie*, it becomes one of the defining works of the Enlightenment.

1758
Afghan–Maratha War begins
The Afghans, led by their chief Durrani, sack the Mughal city of Delhi. This provokes the neighbouring Marathas, who feel they should rule over the territory, to go to war against the Afghans.

1750
Treaty of Madrid
The Treaty of Madrid settles border disputes between Spain and Portugal in South America. Spain cedes most of modern Brazil to the Portuguese.

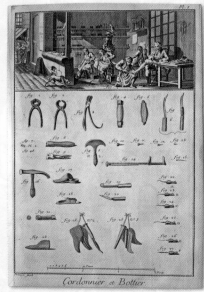

THE SHOEMAKER AND BOOTMAKER PAGE FROM DIDEROT'S *ENCYCLOPÉDIE*

1757
Battle of Plassey
The British officer Robert Clive recovers Calcutta for the East India Company and Britain by defeating the Nawab of Bengal at the Battle of Plassey.

1759
Britain takes Quebec
The French surrender Quebec, in modern Canada, to the British after a battle that sees the deaths of both rival commanders.

c.1750
Wahhabi movement begins
The Wahhabi movement to purify Islam begins in Arabia.

62,000
The number of Bengali troops defeated by Robert Clive's 3,000 men at the Battle of Plassey.

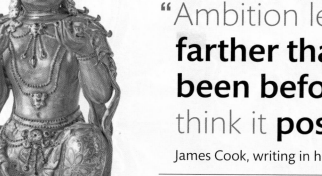

QING PORCELAIN FIGURE OF A KNEELING BUDDHA

1760
Qing dynasty suppresses Mongols
The ongoing revolts by Zunghar Mongol tribes in the northwest frontier of China, which started around 1755, are finally suppressed.

"Ambition leads me not only **farther than any other man has been before me,** but as far as I think it **possible for man to go...**"
James Cook, writing in his journal, 1774

1768
James Cook explores Pacific
English explorer James Cook begins his first Pacific voyage aboard the *Endeavour*. He travels to New Zealand and the unknown eastern coast of Australia.

1767
Jesuits expelled by Spanish
King Charles III of Spain expels the Jesuits from all Spanish territories. He had become worried about the order's growing wealth and influence in Spanish America.

1763
Treaty of Paris
Britain, France, and Spain sign the Treaty of Paris, ending the Seven Years War. The French cede most of their North American territories, including Canada, to the English.

1772
First partition of Poland
Russia, Prussia, and Austria sign a treaty—ratified by the Polish legislature—depriving Poland of one-third of its land, of which all three powers take a share.

1760-1764
1765-1774

1762
Rousseau publishes *The Social Contract*
French philosopher and writer Jean-Jacques Rousseau publishes his influential treatise, *Du Contrat Social (The Social Contract)*. It examines the relationship between governments and the governed, and the question of freedom in the face of political authority. The book is immediately banned.

1764
Spinning jenny invented
In Lancashire, England, a weaver and carpenter named James Hargreaves invents the spinning jenny, which enables cloth production to increase eightfold.

1762
Catherine the Great ascends throne
Following a conspiracy against her husband, Peter III, Catherine II, known as Catherine the Great, becomes the Empress of Russia.

1768
Russian–Ottoman War begins
The Russian–Ottoman War begins after Russian advances into Poland pose a threat in the Crimea.

1768
Nepal founded
Prithvi Narayan Shah, the Rajput King of Nepal, brings together kingdoms in the Kathmandu Valley to create the kingdom of Nepal.

1773
Boston Tea Party
In protest against British taxes on American colonies, angry protestors take 342 chests of tea from the *Dartmouth*, anchored in Boston, and tip them into the city's harbour. This is heralded as a key moment of resistance to British governance.

THE BOSTON TEA PARTY

CATHERINE THE GREAT (1729–1796)

The reign of the German-born Empress of Russia was marked by Russian aggression and territorial expansion. Catherine introduced wide-ranging reforms in agriculture, industry, and education. She also relaxed Russia's censorship laws and was known for her love of literature and particular fondness for French philosophers and writers—including Voltaire, with whom she corresponded for 15 years.

> "We must all **hang together** now, or assuredly we shall **hang separately.**"
>
> Benjamin Franklin, on the need for the Americans to fight together for independence, 1774

DECLARATION OF INDEPENDENCE

1776
Declaration of Independence
On July 4, the First Continental Congress issues a Declaration of Independence, formally announcing the separation of the North American colonies from the British rule and collectively calling this the United States of America.

1781
Articles of Confederation ratified
The Articles of Confederation are ratified to set up a "firm league of friendship" binding the states to assist each other against all forces made upon them on account of religion, sovereignty, trade, or any other pretense. The document will eventually be replaced by the US Constitution.

1775
War of Independence begins in America
Battle breaks out between American colonists and British troops in Lexington, Massachussets, as well as nearby Concord. This action signals the start of the American War of Independence.

1776
Cook begins third Pacific voyage
Captain James Cook sets out to search for the Northwest Passage, a fabled Arctic shortcut that is supposed to connect the Atlantic and Pacific Oceans.

1778
France joins war
France formally enters the American War of Independence against the British.

1784
The India Act
British Prime Minister, William Pitt the Younger's India Act puts the East India Company under government control.

1775–1779

1780–1784

1777
Treaty of San Ildefonso is signed
Spain and Portugal finally settle ongoing disputes in the Río de la Plata region of South America with the First Treaty of San Ildefonso. Spain cedes territory in the Amazon basin in return for control over the Banda Oriental (in modern Uruguay).

1781
Battle of Yorktown
General George Washington and his French allies defeat the British at the Battle of Yorktown, Virginia. This is the last major battle of the War of Independence.

1783
Treaty of Paris
The Treaty of Paris, which formally ends the War of Independence, is signed by Britain and its former American colony, calling for them to "forget all past misunderstanding and differences".

1775
Watt patents steam engine
In Britain, the Scottish inventor and engineer James Watt patents his steam engine. His work on steam engines spurs the development of steam-powered trains.

1783
First manned balloon flight
On 21 November 1783, the first manned balloon launches near the Bois de Boulogne, Paris, France. Invented by the Montgolfier brothers, the balloon is beautifully decorated in blue, gold, and red.

MONTGOLFIER BALLOON ASCENT

1785
Burmese–Siamese War begins

Having captured the kingdom of Arakan the year before, Burma's King Bodawpaya invades Siam, triggering the Burmese–Siamese War.

THE STORMING OF THE BASTILLE

1788
Australian colonists arrive

Six transports and two escorts, part of Britain's First Fleet shipping convicts to Australia, arrives at Botany Bay. The First Fleet sails inland to Port Jackson, which becomes Sydney.

1789
Storming of the Bastille

Some 600 people armed with weapons attack the Bastille, in Paris, a medieval fortress and prison that symbolizes the despotism of the monarchy. The Storming of the Bastille becomes a defining moment of the French Revolution.

1792
France declared a republic

King Louis XVI is overthrown. France abolishes the constitutional monarchy in favor of establishing a republic.

1793
Louis XVI is executed

The French king is executed on the guillotine, followed later by his wife Marie Antoinette.

1799
Napoleon becomes First Consul

Napoleon Bonaparte dissolves the Directory, the body that had been governing France since 1795. He replaces the Directory with the Consulate and takes charge of France as the First Consul.

1785-1789   1790-1799

1789
Declaration is published

In France, the _Declaration of the Rights of Man and of the Citizen_ is published. The document proclaims that "men are born free and remain free and equal in rights" and that "the source of all sovereignty lies essentially in the Nation."

1791
Saint-Domingue slaves revolt

A large-scale slave uprising begins in Saint-Domingue (modern Haiti), on the island of Hispaniola, in the Caribbean. The slaves attack estates, kill plantation owners, and torch cane fields.

1794
Robespierre is executed

A revolt in the National Convention, the governing assembly elected during the French Revolution, ends the ascendancy of Robespierre, who is executed. The Reign of Terror ends and a five-man Directory takes power.

1798
Napoleon invades Egypt

The French general Napoleon Bonaparte invades Egypt, defeating Mameluke troops at the Battle of the Pyramids. The French Mediterranean fleet is completely destroyed by the British navy, under the command of Horatio Nelson, at the Battle of the Nile.

1789
First US president elected

George Washington is elected first president of the US.

1793
Reign of Terror begins

In France, many suspected enemies of the Revolution are executed in the Reign of Terror instituted by Maximilien Robespierre, as war rages between France and a coalition of other European powers.

UNITED STATES CONSTITUTION

The US Constitution is the world's oldest written constitution still in use. It was adopted on September 17, 1787 and has been amended 27 times to deal with issues such as freedom of speech. George Washington led the Constitutional Convention and became the first US president in 1789. During his presidency, the first ten amendments, known as the Bill of Rights, were ratified.

17,000
The number of people executed during Robespierre's Reign of Terror.

1795
Poland destroyed

In the Third Partition of Poland, Prussia, Austria, and Russia complete their carve-up of Polish territory. Poland ceases to exist as an independent country.

15,000,000

The price, in dollars, paid by the United States to France through the Louisiana Purchase.

NAPOLEON BONAPARTE (1769–1821)

Napoleon Bonaparte was born in Corsica and educated in France, where he became an army officer in 1785. His successful campaign in Italy (1796–97) was followed by further military and political victories. In 1804, Napoleon was declared emperor and led France in more battles, although with diminishing success. This drained the nation's resources, ultimately leading to his downfall. Napoleon died in exile on the remote island of St. Helena, in the South Atlantic.

1803
Louisiana Purchase signed
Napoleon realizes that he can raise revenue by selling the large and mostly undeveloped area controlled by France in North America. Having become interested in the Louisiana territory, especially the port of New Orleans, the United States buys the territory stretching from the Gulf of Mexico to the Rocky Mountains.

1804
America explored
Explorers Meriwether Lewis and William Clark explore the territories of the Louisiana Purchase and chart a route to the Pacific coast. They make detailed maps and record the region's flora and fauna.

1806
Battle of Jena
Prussia suffers a devastating defeat against France at the Battle of Jena. As a result, King Frederick William III decides that internal reform in Prussia is necessary to bolster the country's flagging fortunes.

1814
Napoleon exiled
Anti-French allies pursue Napoleon and occupy Paris. Napoleon abdicates and is exiled to the island of Elba off the coast of Italy. The Congress of Vienna convenes to agree the future of Europe.

1803
Napoleonic Wars begin
Britain declares war on France, beginning the Napoleonic Wars.

1804
First steam train
The British engineer Richard Trevithick makes the first steam locomotive running on rails.

1805
Battle of Austerlitz
The French, led by Napoleon, defeat Russia and Austria at the Battle of Austerlitz, and occupy Vienna.

1812
Napoleon invades Russia
Having forced the Russians to retreat after the Battle of Borodino, Napoleon occupies Moscow. He is forced to retreat.

1800–1804 1805–1809 1810–1814

1803
Cape Colony restored to Dutch
Under the terms of the Treaty of Amiens, the Cape Colony, in South Africa, is restored to the Dutch.

1804
Napoleon becomes Emperor
Napoleon makes France an empire with hereditary rulers. Napoleon assumes the title Emperor of France and makes sweeping reforms to the legal system in France and the French territories. These reforms were known as the Napoleonic Code.

1807
Slave trade banned
The British parliament votes to outlaw the slave trade, and the United States bans the importation of slaves.

1810
Spanish American revolutions begin
In Mexico, a parish priest named Miguel Hidalgo y Costilla launches an appeal for Mexican independence. This signals the start of the Spanish American revolutions. By 1826 all Spanish mainland colonies in South America have gained independence.

1805
Battle of Trafalgar
France suffers a humiliating naval defeat at the hands of the British at the Battle of Trafalgar. The British navy is led by Napoleon's old enemy, Horatio Nelson, who is fatally wounded before the end of the battle.

NAPOLEONIC CODE

One of Napoleon Bonaparte's most far-reaching reforms was to codify French law. Enacted in 1804, the Napoleonic Code (*Code Napoléon*) declared all men equal, ending any hereditary nobility, but women were put under male control. The laws also dealt with issues such as property rights, marriage, and civil rights. The Napoleonic Code was disseminated throughout French-controlled territory in Europe and beyond, making it highly influential.

1811
Egypt revived
Muhammad Ali, Ottoman viceroy of Egypt, massacres his Mamluk rivals in Cairo. He embarks upon a programme of military and economic modernization that makes Egypt a major regional power.

inlaid decoration

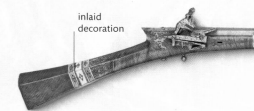

OTTOMAN RIFLE

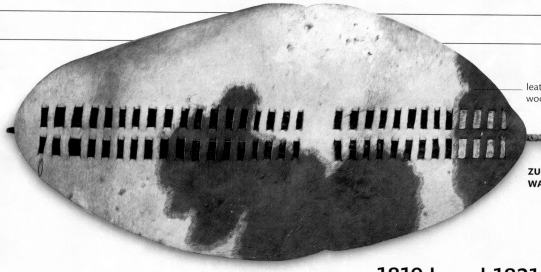

leather stretched over
wooden frame

**ZULU
WAR SHIELD**

1818
Chilean independence confirmed
In South America, General José de San Martín secures independence for Chile at the Battle of Maipú. The Spanish loyalist troops suffer a crushing defeat.

1815
Britain takes Ceylon
Britain's troops in Ceylon (modern Sri Lanka) take control of the kingdom of Kandy, meaning the entire island is under British rule.

1819
Zulus become dominant
In South Africa, the Zulus, under Shaka, defeat the Ndwandwe at the Battle of Mhiatuze River and emerge as the dominant military power in the Natal region.

1819
Singapore is founded
The British statesman Stamford Raffles negotiates a deal for the British East India Company to create a new base at the port of Singapore, in the Malay peninsula. This challenges Dutch dominance of trade routes between China and India.

1821
Mexico gains independence
Mexico secures its independence from Spain. Former royalist Augustín de Iturbide crowns himself Emperor Augustín I.

1821
Fight for Greek independence begins
In Greece, a fight for independence from the Turks begins. Resentful at years of living under oppression, people from across Greek society—including the Orthodox Church—begin to plot their liberation.

1823
Byron fights for Greece
Inspired by the Greek struggle for independence, the English Romantic poet Lord Byron goes to Greece to fight. He dies in 1824, having contracted an illness.

1815–1819

1820–1824

1815
Battle of Waterloo
Napoleon escapes from Elba and leads the French at the Battle of Waterloo, in modern Belgium, where he is defeated by British troops led by the Duke of Wellington and by Prussian forces. Napoleon is exiled to St. Helena in the South Atlantic Ocean. The French monarchy is later restored.

1819
Congress of Angostura begins
The Congress of Angostura begins, establishing the Republic of Colombia, comprising New Granada, Venezuela, and Quito (Ecuador).

1819
Adams-Onís Treaty
Spain cedes the Pacific Northwest and Florida to the United States and the boundaries of New Spain—modern Mexico—are agreed under the Adams-Onís Treaty.

1824
Peru gains independence
In Peru, a decisive victory at the Battle of Ayacucho means the end of Spanish rule. However, to the north, in the territory known as Upper Peru, Spanish loyalist forces still hold out against rebel troops.

**THE DUKE OF WELLINGTON COMMANDS HIS
TROOPS AT THE BATTLE OF WATERLOO**

1825
World's first railroad
The Stockton and Darlington Railway, masterminded by British engineer George Stephenson, opens in northeast England. It is the world's first public railroad, and uses steam locomotives to haul coal trucks.

1826
Russo-Persian War begins
The second Russo-Persian War begins after the Persians attempt to take back the territory of Georgia. The Russians defeat the Persians and the Caucasus territory returns to Russia.

1829
Independence won
The Ottomans agree to the independence of Greece and Serbia.

1828
Early photograph taken
French doctor Nicéphore Niépce produces a durable image by exposing a plate coated in bitumen in a camera obscura.

1830
French invade Algeria
A French expeditionary force invades Algeria, capturing Algiers and deposing the Ottoman ruler. This marks the start of French control over this North African territory.

1830
July Revolution
France is convulsed by the July Revolution. This insurrection forces the abdication of the King of France Charles X, who is replaced by Louis-Philippe, Duke of Orléans. The rebellion is triggered by Charles's attempt to enforce repressive ordinances, such as suspending the freedom of the press and modifying electoral law, so many people lose their right to vote.

BRONZE MEDAL CELEBRATING THE SLAVE EMANCIPATION ACT

1833
Slavery abolished in England
The Slave Emancipation Act abolishes slavery in the British Empire. The Act immediately sets free young children. All slaves are freed by 1840. Compensation is paid to slave owners.

c.1830
Immigration to US increases
Immigration to the US from Europe reaches 60,000 and keeps increasing.

1831
Belgium attains independence
A new state of Belgium is officially recognized by Britain and France, but not the Netherlands, following a revolution the previous year.

1832
Reform of Parliament
In Britain, a Reform Act rationalizes elections to the House of Commons, extending the franchise to one in six adult males.

1825-1829

1830-1834

1827
Treaty of London signed
Britain, France, and Russia sign the Treaty of London. This supports Greece's battle against the Ottoman Empire and demands the establishment of an independent Greek state.

1830
Trail of Tears
The US Congress passes the Indian Removal Act, under which American Indians in the southeastern US are forcibly relocated westward. Thousands of Cherokee, Creek, Seminole, Choctaw, and Chickasaw die on the trail to the west.

1831
Polish rebellion crushed
An armed uprising by Polish nationalists against Russian rule is suppressed. Poland loses its semi-autonomous status within the Russian Empire.

1830
Scheduled rail services begin
In the US, the Baltimore and Ohio Railroad Company begins the first scheduled passenger railroad service.

THE *ATLANTIC* LOCOMOTIVE PULLING BALTIMORE AND OHIO RAILROAD COMPANY CARRIAGES

QUEEN VICTORIA (1819–1901)

Queen Victoria ruled during one of the most prosperous periods of British history. She became queen at the age of 18 years and reigned for 63 years and 216 days. In 1840, she married her cousin, Albert of Saxe-Coburg and Gotha. She adored him and they had nine children together. The Victorian era contrasted sharply with the excesses of previous Hanoverian rulers, and Victoria's domestic life was held up as the model for families in this period.

80,000

The number of prospectors that arrived in California in 1849, following the discovery of gold.

1848
Gold discovered in California
American carpenter and sawmill operator James Wilson Marshall discovers gold in California. This prompts prospectors to seek their fortune in the California Gold Rush.

1842
US–Canadian border issue settled
The US and Britain sign the Webster–Ashburton Treaty, which settles several outstanding issues concerning the US–Canadian border.

1837
Victoria's reign begins
Victoria becomes the Queen of England. Her long reign is a time of growing prosperity, technological innovation, and colonial expansion.

1838
Battle of Blood River
In South Africa, at the Battle of Blood River, the Boers, under Andries Pretorius, massacre the Zulu army.

1839
Opium War begins
The first Opium War between Britain and China begins over trade and access to Chinese ports. The Chinese are forced to negotiate.

1845
Irish famine triggered
Successive failures of the potato crop in Ireland trigger a famine that lasts five years and leaves more than one million people dead.

1846
Mexican War starts
The US declares war on Mexico after a border dispute involving Texas, the 28th state. Mexico surrenders in 1847, also ceding California and New Mexico to the Americans.

1835–1839   1840–1844   1845–1849 ≫

1839
Darwin publishes journal
British naturalist Charles Darwin publishes the journal of his five-year voyage on the *HMS Beagle*. Darwin's account helps make his name in science.

1840
Treaty of Waitangi signed
Britain takes over New Zealand under the Treaty of Waitangi, signed by Maori chiefs and representatives of the British Crown. In exchange for ceding sovereignty, the British offer the Maori protection and stability.

1846
US approaches Japan
A US delegation is sent to Japan to try to persuade the isolationist nation to open its ports to trade. The delegation is sent away empty-handed, but the US would soon try again.

1848
Year of revolutions
Europe is swept by popular uprisings after a republic is proclaimed in France. Radicals and nationalists achieve temporary successes in Germany, Austria, Hungary, and Italy. In Britain, Chartist reformers stage mass demonstrations. By the year's end, the revolutionary tide ebbs.

1838
Great Western **crosses Atlantic**
British civil engineer Isambard Kingdom Brunel's *Great Western* steamship crosses the Atlantic in record time. Completing the journey in 15 days, the paddle-wheeled ship cuts the voyage time by half and arrives with fuel to spare.

1842
Treaty of Nanking agreed
The Opium War between Britain and China comes to an end when British troops reach Nanjing (Nanking). Chinese officials sue for peace, resulting in the Treaty of Nanking. China is forced to pay an indemnity to the British and officially cede Hong Kong.

1848
Communist Manifesto **published**
German philosophers Karl Marx and Friedrich Engels publish the *Communist Manifesto*. This calls for the overthrow of the bourgeoisie, with the cry of "working men of all countries, unite."

1836
Texas declares independence
Texans revolt against Mexican rule and become an independent state. Ten years later, Texas becomes a state in the US.

THE SIGNING OF THE TREATY OF WAITANGI

1849
Order reasserted in Europe
The armies of the Austrian and Russian Empires crush nationalist forces in Hungary. Austria regains control of northern Italy. The General National Assembly is dissolved.

FORCES CLASH DURING
THE SEPOY REBELLION

1851
Taiping rebels march
Christian-inspired Taiping rebels
march north through China,
causing immense devastation.

1852
Transvaal independence acknowledged
In South Africa, the British acknowledge the
independence of the Transvaal. Two years later,
this is followed by a similar acceptance of the
Boer settlers' new Orange Free State.

1853
US threatens Japan
Four US warships under
Commodore Matthew Perry are
sent to Edo (modern Tokyo), Japan,
and threaten military action if the
Japanese refuse to open their
country to foreign contact.

1852
Second Empire founded
In France, Louis Napoleon
is proclaimed Emperor
Napoleon III, replacing
the Second Republic
with the Second Empire.

1854
Crimean War begins
Making an alliance with
the Ottoman Empire, which
is at war with Russia, Britain
and France send troops
to invade Crimea and lay
siege to the Russian base at
Sevastopol (Sebestopol). The
war continues until 1856.

1857
Sepoy Rebellion begins
Sepoys—local Indian soldiers in the
British forces—rise against their British
officers in northern India. This revolt
is also known as the Indian Mutiny.

1859
***On the Origin of Species* published**
British naturalist Charles Darwin cements his
reputation with the publication of *On the Origin
of Species by Means of Natural Selection*. The
work explains the process of evolution and sets
out Darwin's ideas about species adaptation
and the survival of the fittest.

1850–1854

1855–1859

1851
Great Exhibition opens
The "Great Exhibition of the Works
of Industry of all Nations" opens in
London, England. The Great
Exhibition, as it becomes known,
is housed in the Crystal Palace, an
exhibition hall made of glass and
iron built for the occasion.

1857
Second Opium War starts
The British and French send an expedition to
attack China's ports, culminating in the Second
Opium War. In 1860, British and French forces
occupy Beijing (Peking) and force China to open
more ports and legalize opium importation.

1858
Start of the Raj
The Government of India Act passes
control of India from the British East India
Company to the British Crown. This starts
the period known as the Raj.

INSIDE THE CRYSTAL PALACE

1859
Suez Canal begins to be built
Construction of the Suez Canal in
Egypt begins and is completed
in 1869. It will link the Mediterranean
Sea and the Red Sea, cutting voyages
between Europe and Asia by
thousands of miles, and allowing
ships to avoid sailing around the
Cape of Good Hope, Africa.

6 million
The number of visitors to the
Great Exhibition between
May 1 and October 31, 1851.

1860
Lincoln wins presidency
Abraham Lincoln, leader of the newly formed Republican party, becomes President of the US. The Republican party is established to curtail the power of existing slave states, in which slavery continues to be allowed, and to stop the creation of new ones.

1861
Italy unifies
Victor Emmanuel II of Piedmont-Sardinia is declared King of Italy. This follows a series of wars that drive out Austrian rule in Italy.

1862
Otto von Bismarck takes office
The Prussian statesman Otto von Bismarck becomes the Prime Minister of Prussia. He builds up the army and masterminds the unification of Germany.

1863
Slavery outlawed
Abraham Lincoln signs the Emancipation Proclamation, freeing slaves in Confederate areas. In 1865, slavery is abolished across the US.

1865
American Civil War ends
The American Civil War ends with victory for the Union— the Confederacy is devastated. The bloodiest conflict the US has seen claims more than 600,000 lives.

brass eagle emblem

rounds of ammunition

UNION INFANTRYMAN'S AMMUNITION POUCH

1874
British defeat Asante Empire
In West Africa, a British expedition led by Sir Garnet Wolseley defeats the Asante Empire (modern Ghana). This asserts Britain's control over the southern part of the territory, known as the Gold Coast.

1871
South African diamond rush starts
In South Africa, a diamond rush in the Northern Cape is followed by the discovery of gold in the Transvaal region. This sparks the arrival of thousands of prospectors to the region.

1871
Germany unifies
Following victory against France, King Wilhelm I of Prussia declares himself emperor, unifying Germany. He names Otto von Bismarck chancellor.

1860–1864   1865–1869   1870–1874

1864
War of the Triple Alliance
War erupts between Paraguay and an alliance of its neighbors—Uruguay, Brazil, and Argentina. The war devastates Paraguay, reducing the population of 525,000 to 221,000.

1867
US purchases Alaska
The US purchases the vast Alaska territory from Russia. For the price of $7.2 million, the US increases in size by 663,268 sq miles (1,717,856 sq km).

3 million
The number of soldiers that fought in the American Civil War. Union soldiers outnumbered those of the Confederacy by 2 to 1.

1861
American Civil War begins
In US, the southern slave states leave the Union and form the Confederacy. As the situation grows increasingly tense, the American Civil War begins.

1867
Austro-Hungarian dual monarchy established
Weakened by defeat in a war with Prussia, the Austrian Empire compromises with Hungarian nationalists. Hungary becomes a separate state with its own government, but with the Austrian emperor as its king.

1868
Japanese Meiji period starts
In Japan, after the fall of the Tokugawa shogunate, Emperor Meiji Tenno rises to power. He reverses Japan's policy of isolationism and begins a program of westernization.

1870
Franco-Prussian War begins
War breaks out between France and Prussia. The French eventually surrender to the German forces and the regions of Alsace and Lorraine are ceded to Germany.

1871
Paris Commune declared
Parisians establish a radical committe, the Commune, in protest at the French government's surrender after the Franco-Prussian War. A council of citizens governs Paris for over two months. The retaliation of the ruling National Assembly is swift—troops are sent to Paris, and 20,000 people are killed.

POSTER DEPICTING THE PARIS COMMUNE ARRESTED BY IGNORANCE AND REACTION

BOX TELEPHONE DESIGNED BY ALEXANDER GRAHAM BELL

> " Mr. Watson, **come here. I** want to see you..."
>
> Alexander Graham Bell, speaking the first words transmitted over the telephone, 1876

1876
Telephone patented
In the US, Scottish-born inventor Alexander Graham Bell patents the telephone. This development will forever change the way the world communicates.

1877
Britain annexes Transvaal
The discovery of gold in South Africa exacerbates tensions between the Boer settlers and the British, who annex Transvaal.

1879
Anglo–Zulu War ends
The British defeat the Zulu in a war in southern Africa. Britain annexes the Zulu kingdom.

1882
British occupy Egypt
The British place Egypt under military occupation, making it a British protectorate. Britain is fearful of what a nationalist uprising might mean for its access to the Suez Canal.

1882
Triple Alliance formed
Germany, Austria–Hungary, and Italy form an anti-French alliance.

1875–1879

1880–1884

1875
Balkan rebellion starts
The rift between the Ottoman Empire and its subjects in Bosnia and Herzegovina grows wider as the Christian inhabitants of the two territories rebel against Ottoman rule.

1877
Russian Balkan victory
Russia goes to war with Ottoman Turkey in support of Balkan nationalists. Defeated in 1878, the Ottomans lose almost all influence in the Balkans. Austria takes control of Bosnia and Herzegovina.

1881
Tsar assassinated
Russian Tsar Alexander II, who abolished serfdom in 1861, is assassinated by left-wing terrorists of the People's Will movement.

1881
First Boer War ends
The Boers resist a British invasion, maintaining the Transvaal's independence.

1884
Africa partitioned
The Berlin Conference agrees to the European partition of Africa.

THE BOERS

The Boers ("farmers" in Dutch) were settlers of Dutch, French Huguenot, and German descent who left the Cape Province in South Africa to search for autonomy farther to the north. They spoke Afrikaans, a language that evolved from Dutch. The earliest settlers arrived in the Cape of Good Hope after the Dutch East India Company established a port in 1652. The Boers had a strong ethnic identity and clashed with the Zulus and the British.

postage stamps

BOER WAR DISCHARGE PAPERS

1885
Belgium acquires Congo
King Leopold of Belgium formally proclaims the Congo Free State. This follows concessions made to him by other European powers at the Berlin Conference in Africa.

1889
Brazil declared a republic
The ruler of Brazil, Dom Pedro II, is overthrown by a military coup, and a republic is declared. Pedro remained popular with Brazilians even after his forced exile.

1889
Rhodesia colonized
Rhodesia (modern Zimbabwe) is colonized after a charter to the British South Africa company, under the British-born South African politician Cecil Rhodes, permits the colonization of parts of southern Africa.

1892
British defeat Ijebu
The British take advantage of divisions among Yoruba rulers—in the region of modern Nigeria—and overthrow the Ijebu government.

43
The number of events competed in by the 241 athletes who took part in the 1896 Athens Olympics.

1892
Franco–Russian alliance
The French Republic and the Russian Empire form a defensive alliance against Germany and Austria, causing an upheaval in European international relations.

1893
Women's suffrage
New Zealand becomes the first country in the world to give women the right to vote. This follows formidable efforts by suffragists and tireless campaigners.

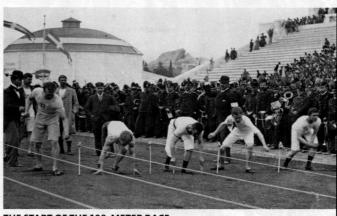

THE START OF THE 100-METER RACE, ATHENS OLYMPICS, 1896

1896
Olympics reborn
Greece sees the modern rebirth of the ancient Olympic games. It is organized by the enthusiastic Frenchman, Baron Pierre de Coubertin.

1894
First Sino–Japanese War begins
War is declared between China and Japan following the intervention of both countries in Korea. A year later the war ends in a victory for Japan.

1885-1889   1890-1894   1895-1899

1889
Eiffel Tower completed
In Paris, France, Gustave Eiffel dazzles all of Europe with his tower. Eiffel had won a design contest to build the tower as part of the International Exposition of 1889, in honor of the centenary of the French Revolution.

1885
First automobiles developed
German engineers Gottlieb Daimler and Karl Benz develop the first automobiles. Independently, they have both developed internal-combustion engines.

1890
American Indians massacred
At the Lakota reservation near Wounded Knee Creek, South Dakota, the army kills 150 Sioux including women and children.

1894
Ottomans suppress Armenians
Under Ottoman rule, the Christian-Armenians suffer a particularly brutal suppression that sees systematic massacres of Armenian people throughout the empire.

250,000
The estimated number of Armenians killed out of a population of 2 million between 1894 and 1897.

THE EIFFEL TOWER, CENTERPIECE OF THE PARIS INTERNATIONAL EXPOSITION OF 1889

1897
Cuba granted autonomy
Following the Cuban War of Independence, Cuba becomes autonomous but not fully independent from Spain.

1898
US declares war on Spain
The Spanish–American War ends Spain's colonial empire in West, and Cuba gains independence from Spain after a 30-year struggle.

1899
South African War begins
The Transvaal and the Orange Free State declare war on Britain. The Boers have demanded that the British troops protecting mining interests withdraw from Transvaal, but Britain has ignored these demands.

A SHRINKING WORLD

In command of much of the world's territory, the powers of Europe began the new century confidently, but World War I's human and economic cost brought a period of turmoil that engulfed the continent. It also sparked the Russian Revolution, ushering in the world's first communist state, the USSR. Following World War II, Europe was forced to abandon most of its colonies in Africa, the Middle East, India, and Southeast Asia and embark on a process of unification, while the Cold War—an ideological confrontation between the democratic capitalist US and communist USSR—took center stage. The end of this power struggle, in the 1990s, briefly promised a new era of peace, but soon gave way to a period of political uncertainty and regional conflict.

HENRY FORD'S MODEL T

1900
Boxer Rebellion erupts
In China, the growing presence of westerners leads to the Boxer Rebellion, a peasant uprising that aims to eject all foreigners from China. International forces invade Beijing to free European hostages.

1901
Commonwealth of Australia proclaimed
The many colonies that have been founded in Australia begin a new era by drafting a constitution and establishing the Commonwealth of Australia.

1904
Russo–Japanese War begins
War begins between Russia and Japan when Japan sinks two Russian warships. Japan's victory against Russia marks its emergence as a major world power.

1905
Einstein publishes Relativity theory
German-born physicist Albert Einstein explains the relationship between mass and energy in the *Special Theory of Relativity*.

1908
First Model T car produced
American car manufacturer Henry Ford produces the Model T— the first affordable, mass-market car.

1908
Young Turks Revolution begins
The Young Turks Revolution demands reform in the Ottoman Empire. These Turkish nationalists force Sultan Abdul Hamid II to restore the constitution.

1900–1903 1904–1906 1907–1909

1903
First controlled flight completed
American bicycle shop owners Wilbur and Orville Wright make the first successful heavier-than-air controlled flight. With Wilbur at the controls, the fourth test flies 852 ft (259 m) in 59 seconds.

1905
Russians mount uprising
Russian revolutionary forces, organized into soviets (councils), mount a series of uprisings. What becomes known as the Russian Revolution of 1905 is caused by discontent with the Tsar Nicholas II. Leon Trotsky, one of the key revolutionary leaders, is later jailed.

1906
Earthquake devastates San Francisco
In US, San Francisco bears the brunt of a 7.8 magnitude earthquake. The quake lasts less than a minute, but it wreaks damage that will take years to repair. Buildings collapse and many catch fire throughout the city.

1908
Austria–Hungary annexes Bosnia–Herzegovina
Austria–Hungary annexes Bosnia–Herzegovina, shocking other European powers. It is concerned that the Ottoman "Young Turks" may undermine Austro–Hungarian power in the Balkans.

THE 1903 WRIGHT FLYER PILOTED BY ORVILLE WRIGHT

37 million

The number of military and civilian casualties of World War I.

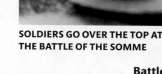

SOLDIERS GO OVER THE TOP AT THE BATTLE OF THE SOMME

1910
Mexican Revolution begins
Mexico heads toward revolution, following 30 years of stable government under President Porfirio Diaz. Political fighting spills over into violence, and warfare continues for decades.

1913
Harriet Tubman dies
African American abolitionist (anti-slavery activist) and reformer Harriet Tubman (born 1821) dies.

1913
Suffragette trampled to death
In England, the suffragette Emily Davison throws herself in front of King George V's horse during the Epsom Derby. She later dies of her injuries.

1914
Battle of Tannenberg starts
At the Eastern Front, the Germans crush the Russian First and Second Armies at the Battle of Tannenberg and at the Masurian Lakes.

1915
Lusitania sinks
The ocean liner, the *Lusitania*, is torpedoed off the coast of Ireland by a German U-boat. More than 1,200 people are drowned, including 128 US citizens. The attack provokes anti-German riots in British cities and a hostile response in the US.

1916
Battles of Verdun and the Somme begin
In France, battles of unprecedented scale are fought at Verdun and the Somme. At Verdun, each side suffers around 400,000 casualties. At the Somme, four months of fighting costs 300,000 lives.

1918
World War I ends
As Germany's momentum stalls, the Allies mount a series of offensives that break through Germany's last fortified defense lines. The Germans sign an armistice on November 11, bringing World War I to an end.

1918
"Spanish Flu" kills millions
A global pandemic of "Spanish Flu" reaches its peak. One of the worst natural disasters in human history, the disease kills more than 50 million people.

1918
UK women gain the vote
The right to vote is given to women over the age of 30 in Britain. Women in the US have to wait until 1920.

1917
The US enters war
The US declares war on Germany after German submarines torpedoe three American ships.

1910-1912　　1913-1915　　1916-1918

1914
Panama Canal opens
The first ship completes its passage through the Panama Canal. This amazing feat of American engineering connects the Atlantic and Pacific Oceans.

1911
Chinese Republic established
In China, the Wuchang Uprising leads to the collapse of the Qing dynasty, which has been in power for 260 years. Sun Yat-sen becomes the first president of the Chinese Republic.

1914
Germany invades Belgium
Having declared war on France, the Germans invade Belgium. As Britain guarantees Belgium's neutrality, it declares war on Germany.

1914
Battle of the Marne begins
As German forces threaten Paris, the French launch a counteroffensive at the Marne. The German army is forced to retreat, and their hopes of a swift victory in the war are left in ruins.

1910
Portuguese monarchy overthrown
A republican-led coup ends the short reign of King Manuel II. The Portuguese Republic is recognized by Europe's leading nations.

1914
World War I begins
The assassination of the Austrian Archduke, Franz Ferdinand, and his wife, by a Serbian nationalist, resulting in Austria–Hungary declaring war on Serbia, with the backing of Germany, sets World War I in motion. Within a week, all the major European powers are at war.

1916
Irish nationalists stage uprising
In Ireland, Irish nationalists stage an uprising against British rule. On Easter Monday, they occupy key buildings in Dublin and proclaim a Provisional Government of the Irish Republic. The British send troops to Dublin, and after five days of fighting the rebels surrender.

1915
Allies make advances
Allied French and English advances at Neuve Chapelle, Ypres, and Loos result in enormous Allied casualties. In an attempt to break the deadlock, the Germans use poison gas at Ypres.

1917
Russian Revolution begins
In Russia, the Provisional Government of Prime Minister Alexander Kerensky is ousted in a Bolshevik coup. Bolshevik leader Vladimir Lenin sets up a revolutionary government of People's Commissars and proclaims a unilateral armistice.

> " **Factories** to the **Workers!** **Land** to the **Peasants!** "
>
> A slogan of the Russian Revolution

REVOLUTIONARY POSTER—LENIN POINTS THE WAY FORWARD

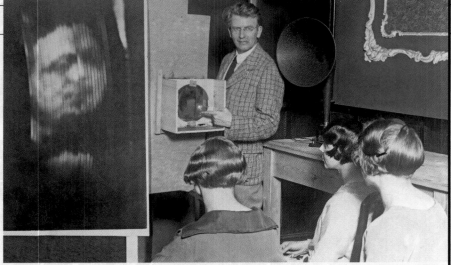

JOHN LOGIE BAIRD DEMONSTRATES HIS "TELEVISOR"

1927
Lindbergh flies solo across the Atlantic
Aviator Charles Lindbergh completes the first non-stop solo transatlantic flight from New York to Paris in the monoplane he built, which was named the *Spirit of St. Louis*. His achievement stimulates the rapid growth of commercial aviation in the US.

1926
First television picture created
The Scottish engineer John Logie Baird makes the first public demonstration of a television transmission in London, England. Fifty members of the Royal Institution see the indistinct, but recognizable, moving image of a face.

1919
Treaty of Versailles signed
With the Treaty of Versailles, World War I's victorious Allies impose peace terms on Germany without negotiation. Germany loses all of its colonies and substantial territory in Europe.

1921
Russians suffer famine
Russia experiences one of the most destructive famines of the 20th century. Hundreds of thousands die of starvation and disease.

1924
Lenin dies
Vladimir Lenin, founder of the Soviet Union, dies of a stroke. Statues of Lenin are erected across the Soviet Union, and the city of Petrograd is renamed Leningrad in his honor. A power struggle between Joseph Stalin and Leon Trotsky follows.

1929
Stock Exchange crashes
The Wall Street Crash sees share prices on the New York Stock Exchange fall dramatically. The crash is the start of a long-lasting collapse in share prices, and the start of a worldwide depression.

1919–1924   1925–1929

1920
League of Nations established
The League of Nations, dedicated to the peaceful resolution of disputes and the collective deterrence of aggression, is formed. It is created by the American president Woodrow Wilson, but the US Congress refuses to ratify it.

15,000
The number of exhibitors at the International Exhibition of Modern Industrial and Decorative Arts, in Paris.

1925
Paris Exhibition opens
Paris, France, reasserts its status as the world leader in style with the International Exhibition of Modern Industrial and Decorative Arts. The exhibition gives a name—Art Deco—to the design of angular shapes and patterns. Art Deco soon sets the style for items from scent bottles to skyscrapers.

1922
USSR established
The Union of Soviet Socialist Republic (USSR), or the Soviet Union, united Russian and other neighboring states under the government of the Communist Party.

1923
Turkish Republic founded
The Turkish army officer Mustafa Kemal, later known as Ataturk, formally founds the Turkish Republic. He embarks upon a series of radical reforms designed to turn Turkey into a modern secular state.

1928
Stalin begins reforms
The Soviet leader Joseph Stalin begins radical economic and social reforms. Stalin launches a Five-Year Plan to transform the Soviet Union into a major industrial country.

1919
First nonstop transatlantic flight completed
British aviators John Alcock and Arthur Whitten Brown complete the first nonstop flight across the Atlantic. It takes 16 hours 27 minutes in a Vickers Vimy biplane.

1922
Irish Free State proclaimed
Southern Ireland becomes the Irish Free State. However, many Irish Republicans are outraged by the compromises in the Anglo-Irish Treaty, which leads to civil war.

JOSEPH STALIN (1879–1953)

Born Iosif Dzhugashvili, in Georgia, Stalin joined Lenin's Bolsheviks in 1903. After Lenin's death, he cleverly outmaneuvered other leading Bolsheviks to achieve dictatorial power by 1929. Stalin ran a ruthless police state that murdered millions of its citizens, yet he presided over the country's transformation into a major industrial power and led it to victory over Nazi Germany in 1945.

MOHANDAS GANDHI (1869–1948)

Known as Mahatma ("Great Soul"), Gandhi was born into a privileged Indian family and studied law in London. His first campaigns of nonviolent civil disobedience were in South Africa. Returning to India in 1915, he led the opposition to British rule. In 1948, Gandhi was assassinated by Hindu extremists, outraged by his conciliatory attitude toward Muslims.

HITLER'S ELECTION POSTER

1930
Gandhi makes Salt March
In India, Mohandas Gandhi mounts a campaign of civil disobedience against British rule. Gandhi dramatizes his opposition to the government's salt monopoly by staging a 24-day march from Ahmedabad, in Gujarat, to the Indian Ocean. On reaching the sea, he scoops up a handful of salt water in public defiance of the government's ban on unlicensed salt gathering.

1932
Great Depression peaks
The peak year of the Great Depression leads to mass unemployment in the world's leading industrial nations.

1933
Hitler becomes German Chancellor
In Germany, the Nazi (National Socialist) leader Adolf Hitler is invited to become Chancellor (head of government). The conservatives believe they have Hitler under their control. Hitler, however, celebrates his appointment as if it is a seizure of power.

1934
Hitler cements his power
Hitler cements his hold on German power through a massacre, known as the Night of the Long Knives. The main targets are Stormtrooper paramilitaries who had aided his rise to power. After President Hindenberg dies, Hitler becomes Führer (leader) of the Third Reich.

1938
Munich Conference held
The leaders of Britain, France, Germany, and Italy strike a deal to keep peace in Europe. This is at the expense of Czechoslovakia, which hands over Sudetenland. The British and French are relieved to have avoided war.

1937
Second Sino–Japanese War begins
Gradual Japanese encroachment on Chinese territory erupts into a full-scale war. Having forced the Chinese to abandon Shanghai, the Japanese take the Nationalist capital Nanjing (Nanking), and massacre the population.

1936
Great Purge commences
In the Soviet Union, Joseph Stalin begins the Great Purge. This campaign of political repression kills at least 680,000 people.

1930–1934   1935–1938

1930
Vargas comes to power
In Brazil, an army revolt brings nationalist Getúlio Vargas to power. Vargas installs a populist dictatorship that pushes for the industrialization of Brazil and suppresses political dissent. He also introduces social welfare measures for the poor.

1931
Empire State Building constructed
In New York, the Empire State Building is officially opened. Standing 1,454 ft (443 m) tall to the top of its spire, it becomes the world's tallest building.

EMPIRE STATE BUILDING CONSTRUCTION WORKERS TAKE A BREAK

1933
US President Roosevelt launches "New Deal"
The US President Roosevelt pushes through legislation to fulfil his promise of a "New Deal." Roosevelt's personal leadership has a dramatic effect on American morale. His radio broadcasts, known as "fireside chats," convince many Americans that they have a friend in the White House.

1936
Spanish Civil War is declared
Nationalist Spanish army officers led by General Francisco Franco in Spanish Morocco launch a military uprising against Spain's Popular Front government. Although the revolt fails across much of Spain, it turns into civil war when Franco's Army of Africa arrives in southern Spain.

THE HOLOCAUST

Hitler's German Nazi (National Socialist) government murdered people from many minority groups, including Slavs, homosexuals, and gypsies, but their treatment of the Jews was without parallel. By 1942, they had begun to implement the "final solution," with the aim of exterminating all the Jews in Europe. The Nazis transported Jews to specially built camps equipped with gas chambers. About 6 million Jews—two-thirds of Europe's Jewish population—were murdered.

SUPERMARINE SPITFIRE RAF FIGHTER—A KEY AIRCRAFT IN THE BATTLE OF BRITAIN

all-metal monocoque fuselage structure

1939
World War II begins
Germany invades Poland, triggering World War II. Britain and France declare war on Germany. Australia, New Zealand, Canada, and South Africa follow.

1940
Germans advance through Europe
German forces invade Denmark, Norway, the Netherlands, Luxembourg, Belgium, and France. The Germans occupy Paris, and France is forced to sign an armistice with Germany.

1941
Japanese bomb Pearl Harbor
Japanese carrier aircraft deliver a surprise attack on the US naval base at Pearl Harbor, in Hawaii. The attack provokes the US to enter the war.

1944
Battle of the Bulge
Hitler's final campaign is a massive offensive in the Ardennes, France. The battle ends with the Germans retreating.

1939–1940

1941–1944

1939
Spanish Civil War ends
General Francisco Franco's Nationalists triumph in the Spanish Civil War. Franco executes thousands of his enemies and imposes a dictatorship.

1940
The Battle of Britain begins
An aerial conflict between Germany's Luftwaffe and the British Royal Air Force rages over southeastern England. By failing to destroy Britain's air defenses, Germany suffers its first defeat of the war.

1940
Britain subjected to the Blitz
British cities are subjected to a bombing campaign—the Blitz. Night raids by Luftwaffe bombers cause heavy casualties and widespread destruction.

1941
Germany invades USSR
Hitler assembles more than 4 million troops to invade the USSR (the Soviet Union). At first, the invasion is a success, but in the face of Soviet resistance and freezing winter conditions, the offensive grinds to a halt.

1942
Battle of El Alamein starts
In North Africa, the British Eighth Army, commanded by General Bernard Montgomery, wins a great victory at Alamein, Egypt.

1942
Battle of Stalingrad starts
German forces attack Stalingrad, in the USSR. The Soviets launch a counterattack that traps German troops inside the city and eventually the Germans surrender.

1942
US wins Pacific victories
The US defeats Japan at naval battles in the Coral Sea and at Midway, in the Pacific.

1944
Paris is liberated
French armored units and Resistance fighters liberate Paris from German occupation. Parisians welcome the return of General Charles de Gaulle as leader of the Free French.

1944
Allies invade Normandy
The Normandy invasion begins with the D-Day landings along the French coast. A fleet of 5,000 ships takes part in the largest amphibious operation in history.

1944
Allies reoccupy Burma
British Indian troops withstand an attempt by the Japanese to invade northeast India from Myanmar (Burma). Allied forces go on to retake much of Myanmar from the Japanese later that year.

WINSTON CHURCHILL (1874–1965)

British wartime leader Churchill led an adventurous life as a soldier and war correspondent before entering politics. As First Lord of the Admiralty in World War I, he was blamed for the Gallipoli disaster. A backbench MP during the 1930s, he opposed the appeasement of Hitler. In 1939, he returned to the Admiralty before becoming prime minister in May 1940. He led Britain through the war but lost the 1945 general election.

laminated wood
propeller blade

**TENZING NORGAY AND EDMUND HILLARY,
CONQUERORS OF MOUNT EVEREST**

1947
Palestine partitioned
The UN General Assembly agrees to the partition of Palestine into separate Jewish and Arab states. The proclamation of the state of Israel leads to the first Arab-Israeli War, in 1948.

1953
Everest conquered
The New Zealander Edmund Hillary and Nepalese sherpa Tenzing Norgay become the first people to reach the summit of Mount Everest.

1945
Battle of Iwo Jima breaks out
US forces take the Pacific island of Iwo Jima from the Japanese. The US plans to use the island as a base for fighters supporting bombing raids on mainland Japan.

1945
War ends in Europe
Soviet forces retake Berlin. Hitler commits suicide and Germany surrenders.

1947
India and Pakistan gain independence
Both India and Pakistan gain their independence from Britain, ending 200 years of British rule.

1953
DNA structure discovered
The American scientist James Watson and the British Francis Crick discover the double helix structure of DNA. The new model helps explain how genes replicate and carry information.

1945–1949

1950–1954

1945
Atomic bombs dropped on Japan
The US planes drop atomic bombs on the Japanese cities of Hiroshima and Nagasaki, killing thousands and causing devastation. Emperor Hirohito announces the Japanese surrender. World War II comes to an end.

ATOMIC BOMB EXPLODES IN HIROSHIMA

1946
United Nations formed
Representatives of 51 countries form the United Nations (UN) General Assembly. It aims to provide a forum for nations and to uphold peace and security.

1949
People's Republic of China formed
The Chinese Communist leader Mao Zedong proclaims the founding of the People's Republic of China.

1948
Apartheid introduced
The Afrikaner D. F. Malan comes to power in South Africa. Believing that Africans threaten the prosperity of the Afrikaner (Dutch settlers') culture, Malan introduces a system—apartheid—that enforces a racial hierarchy in favour of white South Africans.

1948
Berlin blockade
In 1945, Berlin was split into four zones. In the first crisis of the Cold War, Stalin cuts off road and rail links to West Berlin. The West responds by supplying rations by air to prevent starvation. The Berlin Blockade lasts 318 days.

80,000
The number of people killed instantly by the atomic bomb that fell on Hiroshima.

1954
France defeated in Southeast Asia
French rule in Indo-China comes to an end. Laos and Cambodia become independent, while Vietnam is divided into North Vietnam, with a communist government, and South Vietnam.

1952
Mau Mau Rebellion begins
In Kenya, opposition to British rule leads to the Mau Mau Rebellion. The Mau Mau, an anticolonial insurgent army, raids white-settler farms, and the British declare a state of emergency.

1950
Korean War begins
The communist leader of North Korea Kim Il-Sung orders an invasion of South Korea. The South Koreans are backed by the UN Command forces, while North Korea has the support of China. The war continues until 1953, when an armistice is signed.

FIDEL CASTRO (1926–2008)

Fidel Castro was jailed for his revolutionary activities in Cuba in 1953. After his release he went into exile, but returned in 1956. He was Cuban prime minister in 1959–76 before becoming president, and the first communist head of state in the Americas. His relations with the US were originally good, but speedily deteriorated. Castro remained a prominent figure, after he retired as president in 2006.

1959
Fidel Castro comes to power
Cuban revolutionary leader Fidel Castro overthrows the corrupt regime of Fulgencio Batista and becomes the Cuban prime minister. Eventually, Cuba becomes a Soviet-style, socialist state.

1961
Berlin Wall erected
Troops in East Germany close the border between East and West Berlin with barbed wire fences. Within days, these are replaced by concrete blocks.

MEDAL GIVEN TO WORKERS INVOLVED IN BUILDING THE BERLIN WALL

1955
Juan Perón ousted
President of Argentina Juan Perón is overthrown in a coup and exiled to Paraguay. His position had been weakened by the death of his popular wife, Eva Perón, and a quarrel with the Roman Catholic Church.

1957
Treaty of Rome signed
The Treaty of Rome sets up the European Economic Community (EEC) and provides for the European countries' social and economic programs.

1960
Sharpeville massacre
In South Africa, an antiapartheid protest in Sharpeville results in the deaths of 69 demonstrators. The African National Congress, (ANC) which fights for the rights of black South Africans, is banned.

1955–1959

1960–1963

1956
Suez Crisis mounts
British and French forces invade the Suez Canal Zone in Egypt, after President Nasser nationalizes the Suez Canal. International criticism forces a cease fire and withdrawal.

1957
Space Age begins
The Space Age begins when Russia launches its *Sputnik I* satellite into orbit.

1960
Kennedy elected president
The Democrat candidate John Fitzgerald Kennedy is elected 35th president of the US.

1961
Gagarin launched into space
The USSR scores a victory in the space race when Yuri Gagarin becomes the first person to go into space and orbit the Earth.

45 million
The number of people who are worked, starved, or beaten to death during Mao's "Great Leap Forward" program.

KENNEDY'S ELECTION POSTER

1962
Cuban Missile Crisis erupts
The Cuban Missile Crisis brings the world to the brink of nuclear war. President John F. Kennedy delivers an ultimatum to the Russian leader, Nikita Khrushchev, to remove Soviet missiles from Cuba. Khrushchev eventually backs down.

1963
Kennedy assassinated
President John F. Kennedy is assassinated as he travels through Dallas, Texas, in an open top car. Lee Harvey Oswald, a former marine, is arrested and charged with Kennedy's murder.

1958
China starts "Great Leap Forward"
Chinese leader Mao Zedong initiates a program of reform known as the "Great Leap Forward." It is intended to rapidly industrialize China's rural economy. However, Mao's scheme plunges the country into one of the worst famines in history.

> "There are some things **so dear**... some things **so eternally true**, that they are **worth dying for.**"

Martin Luther King Jr., in a speech in Detroit, June 23, 1963

1969
US makes first moon landing
American astronauts Neil Armstrong and Edwin "Buzz" Aldrin walk on the moon from their spacecraft Apollo 11. Millions watch this televised event, which represents a symbolic victory for the US over the USSR in the Cold War.

THE APPLE II

keyboard integrated with body of computer

1968
Martin Luther King Jr assassinated
The African American civil rights leader is assassinated in Memphis, Tennessee. King is shot on the balcony of his hotel as he prepares to lead a march of workers protesting against low wages.

1965
US enters Vietnam War
The US President Lyndon Johnson orders US Operation Rolling Thunder, a massive bombing campaign against North Vietnam. The following month, the first American ground troops arrive to fight alongside South Vietnamese forces against the communist Viet Cong.

1967
Israel wages Six-Day War
As tensions run high in the Middle East, Israel wages war on its Arab enemies. The Six-Day War leaves Israel in control of Sinai, Gaza, the West Bank, the Golan Heights, and Jerusalem.

1972
Northern Irish protesters killed
British troops open fire on demonstrators in Londonderry, Northern Ireland, killing 13 people and injuring 14. The marchers are protesting against the policy of internment without trial. This day comes to be known as "Bloody Sunday."

1973
First personal computers introduced
The first personal computer to use a microprocessor, the Micral, is introduced in France. It is followed by the Commodore, PET, Apple II, and TRS-80, among others.

1964–1969

1970–1974

1964
Civil Rights Bill passed
The US passes the Civil Rights Bill which creates equal rights for all, regardless of race, religion, sex, or color. The signing is witnessed by civil rights campaigner Martin Luther King Jr. At 35, he becomes the youngest man to receive the Nobel Peace Prize.

1966
Cultural Revolution launched
Chinese communist leader Mao Zedong launches the Cultural Revolution, aiming to purge the country of "impure" elements. One-and-a-half million people die and much of the country's cultural heritage is destroyed.

1973
Pinochet leads Chilean coup
Chilean president Salvador Allende is killed in a coup led by his trusted ally General Augusto Pinochet and backed by the US. Pinochet kills 3,000 supporters of the Allende regime, shuts the Chilean Parliament, and bans all political activity. In 1974, he makes himself president.

1973
Global fuel crisis begins
Following the Yom Kippur War between Arab and Israeli forces, the Arab oil-producing countries impose an oil embargo on all nations that had supported Israel. Oil prices soar from under $3 a barrel before the war to over $11 by early 1974.

1971
Bangladesh gains independence
The state of Bangladesh is created when the Indian army crushes Pakistani forces in what was East Pakistan.

CHINESE CULTURAL REVOLUTION POSTER SHOWING CHAIRMAN MAO AS THE RED SUN OF THE WORLD'S PEOPLE

1968
US troops massacre at My Lai
In the village of My Lai in Vietnam, US troops, who have been on a "search and destroy" mission to root out communist fighters, kill more than 500 Vietnamese civilians, many of them women and children. The massacre helps turn public opinion against the Vietnam War.

1974
Turkey invades Cyprus
Turkish troops invade northern Cyprus following a coup in which President Archbishop Makarios is deposed. The island is split in two, with Greek-Cypriots fleeing to the south and the Turkish community remaining in the north.

1975
Khmer Rouge takes Cambodia
The Cambodian capital, Phnom Penh, falls to the radical communist movement, the Khmer Rouge, led by Pol Pot. They transform Cambodia into a communist, rural society.

1,074,000
The distance, in miles, traveled by *Columbia* during the first shuttle mission.

1978
Camp David peace accord signed
Egyptian President Anwar Sadat and Israeli Prime Minister Menachem Begin sign the Camp David peace accord for peace in the Middle East. US President Jimmy Carter hosts the meetings at Camp David, Maryland.

1980
Solidarity formed
The first noncommunist trade union, Solidarity, is formed in Poland. Led by Lech Walesa, it becomes a social movement and a symbol of struggle against Soviet domination.

1977
Pakistan sees military coup
In Pakistan, Army Chief General Mohammad Zia ul-Haq deposes Prime Minister Zulfikar Ali Bhutto in a military coup. Bhutto's Pakistan People's Party (PPP) is accused of vote-rigging at the recent general elections.

1980
Iran–Iraq War
Iraq invades Iran, triggering an eight-year war, in which Iraq uses chemical weapons.

1981
Space shuttle launched
The US space shuttle *Columbia* completes its first orbital flight. As the world's first reusable spacecraft, it heralds a new era in space exploration.

1975–1977   1978–1979   1980–1982

1975
Vietnam War ends
After almost two decades of fighting, the Vietnam War ends as the government in Saigon surrenders to the North Vietnam forces. Saigon is renamed Ho Chi Minh City and, the following year, North and South Vietnam are reunified.

1979
Khomeini gains power in Iran
In Iran, support for Ayatollah Ruhollah Khomeini, a Shi'ite Muslim cleric, leads to revolution. The Shah of Iran leaves and the Islamic Republic of Iran is proclaimed.

1981
AIDS comes to prominence
A new infectious condition is noted in Los Angeles, California. The condition becomes known as AIDS (Acquired Immune Deficiency Syndrome).

1980
Zimbabwe gains independence
Former Marxist guerrilla leader, Robert Mugabe, becomes Prime Minister of the new independent state of Zimbabwe, formerly Rhodesia.

FIRST TEST TUBE USED TO FERTILIZE EGGS

1978
First test-tube baby born
The world's first test-tube baby is born in Oldham, England. Dr. Robert Edwards and Dr. Patrick Steptoe fertilize Lesley Brown's egg in a laboratory dish before implanting the embryo in her uterus. Her baby, Louise Brown, develops normally.

1979
USSR invades Afghanistan
Fearing an Iranian-style Islamist revolution, the USSR invades Afghanistan to restore order. The Soviet forces face fierce resistance from antigovernment forces, the Mujahideen, who have been trained covertly by the US.

1982
Falklands War begins
Argentina invades the British territory of the Falkland Islands in the South Atlantic. The sovereignty of the islands has long been disputed. Britain sends a naval task force to regain the islands. The conflict lasts 74 days when the Argentine surrender

COLUMBIA LIFTS OFF FROM THE FLORIDA COAST

1985
Gorbachev launches reform of USSR
Mikhail Gorbachev becomes the leader of the USSR and sets about reforming the nation. He is the architect of *glasnost* (openness) and *perestroika* (restructuring). He builds bridges with the West and renounces many Stalinist ideas.

1986
Space shuttle *Challenger* explodes
The US space shuttle *Challenger* explodes 72 seconds after takeoff, killing all seven crew members. The accident is witnessed by millions of television viewers.

1986
Collapse of Marcos regime
The Philippine President Ferdinand Marcos is deposed and exiled, after the military and world opinion turn against him. Corazon Aquino, the first female leader of the country, is his successor.

1986
Chernobyl reactor explodes
An accident at a nuclear power station in Chernobyl, Ukraine, USSR, is the worst disaster in the history of nuclear power.

1987
Intifada begins
Palestinian Arabs of the Gaza Strip and West Bank rise up in an "intifada" against Israeli occupation of Palestinian territories. In 1988, the Palestine Liberation Organization (PLO) accepts the "two-state solution", officially recognizing Israel's right to exist.

1987
World population reaches landmark
The world population reaches five billion. This is double the population in 1950. The population of the world is growing at a rate of 220,000 people a day.

1989
Demonstrations held in Tiananmen Square
In China, a demonstration held in Tiananmen Square, Beijing, ends in bloodshed after civilians are killed by the People's Liberation Army.

1988
Pan Am flight 103 crashes
US Pan Am flight 103 crashes at Lockerbie, Scotland, killing all passengers and crew. Two Libyan intelligence agents are linked to the bombing, although it will take more than 11 years to bring them to trial.

1983
Civil war begins in Sri Lanka
In Sri Lanka, civil war begins between government forces and the militant group the Liberation Tigers of Tamil Eelam—the Tamil Tigers—who want an independent Tamil state.

1983–1985

1986–1987

1988–1989

1984
Bhopal gas tragedy
A gas leak at a Union Carbide chemical plant in Bhopal releases more than 40 tons of poisonous gas over the Indian city of Bhopal, killing thousands and injuring tens of thousands. A bitter dispute follows over who should take the blame.

1984
Indira Gandhi assassinated
Indira Gandhi, the Prime Minister of India, is assassinated by Sikh extremists. This is in response to an attack on the Sikh shrine, the Golden Temple of Amritsar, ordered by Gandhi to remove Sikh separatists, who were thought to be amassing weapons at the temple.

1985
Live Aid rocks the world
Two huge concerts are held simultaneously in London, Britain, and Philadelphia, Pennsylvania, to raise money for famine relief in Ethiopia. The Live Aid concerts are watched by two billion television viewers in 150 countries.

1989
Cold War ends
The US and the USSR declare the end of the Cold War. At a joint news conference, US President George H. W. Bush and USSR President Mikhail Gorbachev announce plans for reductions in weapons in Europe. This follows the collapse of the communist states in Europe and the fall of the Berlin Wall.

LIVE AID CONCERT, WEMBLEY STADIUM, UK

190 million
The amount of money, in US dollars, raised by the Live Aid concerts.

HUBBLE TELESCOPE

solar arrays power the telescope

1990
Hubble Space Telescope launched
NASA launches the Hubble Space Telescope, which is taken into orbit by the space shuttle *Discovery*. Still in operation in 2014, Hubble has produced stunning images of deep space, and its observations have led to a greater understanding of the Universe.

1994
Assassination triggers Rwandan genocide
The president of Rwanda, Juvénal Habyarimana, a Hutu, is killed when his plane is shot down above Kigali airport. The incident catalyzes a mass genocide of ethnic groups.

1996
First mammal cloned
Dolly, a sheep born in Edinburgh, Scotland, becomes the first mammal to be cloned from an adult cell.

1994
The Channel Tunnel opens
Queen Elizabeth II of Britain and President François Mitterrand of France formally open the Channel Tunnel that links the two countries.

1997
Hong Kong returns to China
Hong Kong is handed back to the Chinese authorities after 150 years of British rule. The new chief executive, Tung Chee Hwa, formulates a policy based on "one country, two systems", to preserve Hong Kong's role as a capitalist centre in Asia.

1990–1991   1992–1994   1995–1997

1990
Ban on ANC lifted
In South Africa, the 30-year ban on the African National Congress (ANC) is lifted by President de Klerk. This starts the long process of dismantling the apartheid system. Nine days later, Nelson Mandela, the South African leader of the ANC, walks free after spending 27 years in prison.

1991
USSR disbands
Heads of three of the USSR's 15 republics— Russia, Ukraine, and Belarus—meet to disband the USSR and form a new union, the Commonwealth of Independent States (CIS). Boris Yeltsin becomes the first president of the Russian Federation.

1991
Yugoslavia disintegrates
Slovenia and Croatia are the first republics within Yugoslavia to declare independence. Serbian President Slobodan Milošević sends troops to both regions to prevent their secession.

1990
Germany is reunited
Nearly a year after the fall of the Berlin Wall, Germany is reunited. Helmut Kohl is elected as the first chancellor of the reunified nation.

1993
Czechoslovakia splits
Czechoslovakia splits into Slovakia and the Czech Republic, dissolving the 74-year-old federation. The creation of the new countries becomes known as the "Velvet Divorce" following the Velvet Revolution, which freed Czechoslovakia from communism in 1989.

1992
Bosnian War begins
Bosnia and Herzegovina declare independence, but Serbs living in Bosnia resist the move. War breaks out, and the Yugoslav army under president Slobodan Milošević attacks the Muslim population of Bosnia. The vicious conflict ends in 1995, when the leaders of Bosnia, Croatia, and Serbia sign the Dayton Peace Accord.

1991
Iraq expelled from Kuwait
US and coalition forces launch the First Gulf War, code named "Operation Desert Storm," to expel Iraqi forces from Kuwait. Kuwait is liberated after five weeks.

1994
Mandela becomes president
Nelson Mandela becomes South Africa's first black president after more than three centuries of white rule. His party, the African National Congress (ANC), wins 252 of the 400 seats in the first democratic elections in South Africa's history.

PRESIDENT MANDELA WITH HIS DEPUTIES F. W. DE KLERK AND THABO MBEKI

UN PEACEKEEPING

United Nations Peacekeeping emerged out of World War II to help warring countries or communities to create the conditions for world peace. UN forces include military and police personnel. They were first used to monitor the armistice between Israel and the Arab states in 1948. Their role has grown substantially since then: supervising elections, ensuring human rights are respected, clearing land mines, and intervening in failed states. By 1992, UN Peacekeeping forces had made 26 interventions worldwide.

SYDNEY, AUSTRALIA, WELCOMES THE NEW MILLENNIUM

2003
Civil war begins in Sudan
Civil war erupts in Darfur, in the west of Sudan, as rebels rise up against the government. They claim that the region's non-Arab population is being oppressed by the authorities in the capital Khartoum. It is estimated that more than 200,000 people have died, and several million have fled to refugee camps.

2003
Invasion of Iraq begins
Iraq's regime crumbles when US-led troops invade and topple Saddam Hussain's government. This triggers years of civil conflict in Iraq between rival religious factions.

2000
New millennium celebrated
Huge celebrations across the world usher in the new millennium. Sunrise in New Zealand's Chatham Islands is watched worldwide to start the celebrations.

2001
Afghan War begins
The US and Britain launch attacks on targets in Afghanistan, where Osama Bin Laden, head of the militant Islamic organization al-Qaeda, is believed to be hiding. Operation "Enduring Freedom" aims to establish a democratic government.

1999
Euro launched
The single European currency, the Euro, is launched. 11 European Union member states decide to adopt the Euro, which becomes a full economic currency in 2002.

1998-2000   2001-2002   2003-2004

1998
Good Friday Agreement signed
The Good Friday Agreement marks a major breakthrough in the Northern Ireland peace process. A referendum held in Northern Ireland and the Republic of Ireland is overwhelmingly in favor of the accord.

2001
iPod launched
US technology company, Apple, launches its new digital music player, the iPod. The device can store hundreds of music tracks, yet is around the same size as a deck of cards.

2002
Bali nightclub bombed
A bomb in a nightclub on the Indonesian Island of Bali kills more than 200 people. Members of a violent Islamist group, Jemaah Islamiyah, are convicted of the attack.

2004
Tsunami kills thousands
An earthquake under the Indian Ocean near the Indonesian island of Sumatra unleashes a series of killer waves (tsunami). In 11 countries, more than 270,000 people are killed and millions are made homeless, making this the most destructive tsunami in history.

2001
America suffers terrorist attacks
The US experiences an unprecedented day of terror on September 11, when 19 al-Qaeda terrorists hijack four passenger airlines. Two are flown into the twin towers of the World Trade Center, while another targets the Pentagon. The fourth crashes into a field near Pittsburgh. Nearly 3,000 people are killed. These events leave the US, and the rest of the world, in a profound state of shock.

2001
Human Genome published
The Human Genome Project, which aims to identify all the genes in the human body, publishes its first draft.

2003
Concorde retired
Concorde, the supersonic passenger aircraft, makes its last flight. It has flown for 27 years, but spiraling costs and dwindling ticket sales lead to its demise.

British airways
G-BBDG

CONCORDE

108 billion

The estimated cost, in US dollars, of the property damage inflicted by Hurricane Katrina.

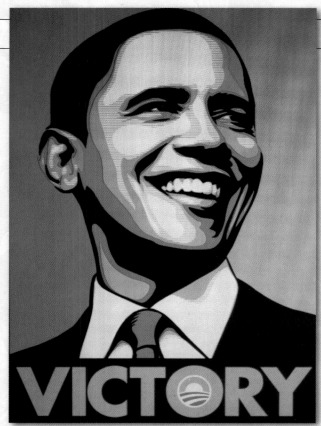

OBAMA'S VICTORY POSTER

2007
Dark matter discovered
The mysterious dark matter that makes up a quarter of the Universe is revealed via a 3-D map created by the Hubble telescope. It helps explain how the Universe was formed.

2005
Hurricane Katrina strikes
Hurricane Katrina hits New Orléans in the US, causing unprecedented destruction in the area. The hurricane also batters large swathes of the Louisiana and Mississippi coastlines, leaving two oil rigs adrift in the Gulf of Mexico.

2006
Dolphin becomes extinct
The baiji, also known as the Yangtze river dolphin, is declared functionally extinct. It is the first aquatic mammal to become extinct since the 1950s.

2008
Barack Obama elected president
Democrat Barack Obama wins the US presidential election, becoming the first African American president. He wins 52.5 percent of the popular vote.

2005–2006

2007–2009

2005
Kyoto Protocol comes into force
Seven years after it was first agreed, the Kyoto Protocol comes into force. It aims to curb the air pollution blamed for global warming.

2006
ETA cease fire
The armed Basque separatist group ETA declares a permanent cease fire, making a definitive end to almost four decades of domestic terrorism in Spain.

2008
Large Hadron Collider started
The world's largest "atom smasher," the Large Hadron Collider, built near Geneva, Switzerland, is started. It is designed to investigate the "Big Bang" and other mysteries of the Universe.

2009
World's tallest building completed
In Dubai, the Burj Khalifa skyscraper becomes the world's tallest building. Standing at 2,722 ft (829.8 m) high, it has 163 floors. It cost $1.5 billion to build.

2005
Terrorists target London
Explosions rip across London, England. Coordinated terrorist attacks strike underground trains and a bus, killing 52 people and injuring several hundred more. The British suicide bombers are backed by militant organization al-Qaeda.

2006
Three Gorges Dam completed
The Three Gorges Dam in China is completed. At 1.4 miles (2.3 km) long, it is one of the world's largest dams, and one of the most controversial public works in modern times. The dam is engineered to prevent flooding along the Yangtze River, but has huge social and ecological implications.

2008
Apology made to Aboriginals
The Australian Prime Minister Kevin Rudd makes an official apology for years of mistreatment inflicted on the country's Aboriginal people.

y-shaped structure

2005
YouTube launched
YouTube, the video-sharing website, is launched and soon grows into one of the most popular websites on the Internet. After only a year, 100 million videos are being viewed every day.

2008
World economy suffers crisis
Crisis in world finance leads to the collapse of large financial institutions, governments bailing out banks, and stock markets plummeting. This is a major cause of what will become the worst global recession since World War II.

THE BURJ KHALIFA

2010
Volcano erupts
An Icelandic volcano, dormant for 200 years, erupts near the Eyjafjallajökull glacier. It sends clouds of ash soaring as high as 36,000 ft (11,000 m), delaying millions of air passengers across the world.

2011
Last World War I veteran dies
The last known combat veteran of World War I, British Claude Choules, dies in Australia aged 110. He had served in both World Wars. Conflict shaped his life, and he became a staunch pacifist.

> "If I had **my time** over again I **wouldn't change a bit** of it."
>
> Claude Choules, the last surviving veteran of World War I, talking in an interview with the BBC

2010
Oil rig explodes
The US experiences an environmental disaster when the Deepwater Horizon oil rig explodes and sinks. About four million barrels of oil are pumped into the Gulf of Mexico and eleven men are killed.

2013
Global surveillance operations revealed
American former National Security Agency (NSA) contractor Edward Snowden releases classified documents revealing details of global surveillance operations carried out by the NSA and its international partners. The US charges Snowden with espionage; he is granted asylum by the Russian government.

2011
Arab Spring begins
Protests, riots, and civil wars erupt across the Arab countries of the Middle East and North Africa. What becomes known as the "Arab Spring" sees rulers forced from power and governments overthrown.

2012
Skydiver breaks sound barrier
Austrian skydiver Felix Baumgartner becomes the first person to break the sound barrier without traveling in a vehicle. He travels an estimated 24 miles (39 km), reaching a speed of 844 mph (1,358 kph), or Mach 1.25.

2014
Ukraine Revolution
In Ukraine, a revolution ousts the president, Viktor Yanukovych; an interim government is put in place, and an old version of the constitution is restored. Russia refuses to recognize the new government and seizes Ukraine's Crimean Peninsula, beginning the Crimean crisis.

2010–2011

2012–2014

2010
Chilean miners trapped underground
Following a cave-in, 33 Chilean miners are trapped underground. They spend 69 days in the mine and the world becomes transfixed by their ordeal, which ends in a successful rescue.

2011
Japanese earthquake causes huge tsunami
Japan experiences its most powerful earthquake since records began. Measuring 9.0 on the Richter scale, the earthquake strikes the northeast coast, causing a massive tsunami. A wall of water sweeps away cars, ships, and buildings, and many thousands are killed. A state of emergency is declared at several nuclear power plants.

2013
New Pope elected
Pope Benedict XVI becomes the first pope to resign since 1294. He is succeeded by the Argentine Jorge Mario Bergoglio, who becomes Pope Francis. He is recognized for his humility and a less formal approach to the papacy.

2011
Osama Bin Laden killed
Osama Bin Laden, the leader of al-Qaeda and the most hunted man in the world, is killed in a firefight with US forces in Pakistan. The news leads to immediate fears of retaliation.

2010
Earthquake devastates Haiti
An earthquake measuring 7.0 on the Richter scale devastates the Haitian capital Port au Prince. About 230,000 people are killed, many housed in badly constructed buildings.

3 million
The estimated number of people affected by the earthquake in Haiti in 2010.

AFTERMATH OF THE JAPANESE TSUNAMI

INDEX

Page numbers in **bold** type refer to main treatments of a topic; *italic* page numbers refer to the illustrations

ACKNOWLEDGMENTS

Dorling Kindersley would like to thank the following people for their help in making this book: Shaila Brown, Lizzie Munsey, Alyssa Hingre, Frankie Piscitelli, Anita Kakar, Dharini Ganesh, and Sonia Yooshing for editorial help; Steve Crozier, Philip Fitzgerald, Tom Morse, Jonny Burrows, Dave Ball, Ethan Carlin, Mahua Mandal Sharma, Devika Dwarkadas, Ankita Mukherjee, Namita, Surpriya Mahajan, Neha Sharma, Parul Gambhir, Konica Juneja, Vanya Mittal, and Tanvi Sahu for design assitance; and Sachin Singh, Nand Kishor Acharya, Vijay Kandwal, and Anita Yadav for DTP design assistance.

The quotation on p.18 has been reproduced from Black, J.A., Cunningham, G., Ebeling, J., Flückiger-Hawker, E., Robson, E., Taylor, J., and Zólyomi, G., The Electronic Text Corpus of Sumerian Literature (http://etcsl.orinst.ox.ac.uk/), Oxford 1998–2006. "A Praise poem of Šulgi (Šulgi B)" t.2.4.2.02, lines 258-261.

NEW PHOTOGRAPHY

For allowing us to photograph their collections and help with photography, Dorling Kindersley would like to thank: Neil Curtis, Louise Wilkie, Shona Elliott, Nicole Stahl, and Hannah Clarke at **University of Aberdeen Museums**; Craig Bowen and Philip Hadland at **Canterbury Museums and Galleries**; Jackie Westlake and Hilary Riva at **Faversham Town Council**; Lauren Ryall-Stockton, Brigid Bradley, and Alan Humphries at the **Thackray Medical Museum**, Leeds; Rachel Barclay, Ashleigh Sheppard, Helen Armstrong, Lauren Barnes, and Craig Barclay at **Durham University Oriental Museum**; Samantha Harris and Giles Guthrie at **Maidstone Museum and Bentlif Art Gallery**; Inbal Livne, Mike Cobb, and Christopher Date at the **Powell-Cotton Museum**, Quex Park, Kent; Andrew Parkin and Audrey Glasgow at the **Great North Museum: Hancock**, Newcastle; and Jim Matthieu, Bob Thurlow, Jen Houser, Katy Blanchard, Bill Wierzbowski, Steve Lang, Dwaune Latimer, Adria Katz, and Lynn Makowsky at the **University of Pennsylvania Museum of Archaeology and Anthropology** (Penn Museum).

(Key: a-above; b-below/bottom; c-center; f-far; l-left; r-right; t-top)

2 Penn Museum: (c). **4 Durham Oriental Museum**: (fbl). **Maidstone Museum**: (fcla). **Penn Museum**: (ftl). **6 Canterbury Museum**: (tl). **Durham Oriental Museum**: (tc). **7 Powell Cotton Museum**: (tc). **8 Penn Museum**: (c). **12 Aberdeen Museum**: (tr). **13 Great North Museum**: (br). **Penn Museum**: (fcl). **14 Aberdeen Museum**: (bc). **Great North Museum**: (cl). **20 Aberdeen Museum**: (ca). **Durham Oriental Museum**: (fcla). **21 Penn Museum**: (bc, bl, c, cb, cbl, cr, cra, fclb). **22–23 Penn Museum**: (all). **24-25 Penn Museum**: (all). **28 Aberdeen Museum**: (cr). **Durham Oriental Museum**: (bl, tl). **Penn Museum**: (bc, bl, c, fcla). **29 Aberdeen Museum**: (cla). **Canterbury Museum**: (br). **Durham Oriental Museum**: (c, cbl). **Great North Museum**: (ftl). **30 Aberdeen Museum**: (bl, ftr, tc). **Canterbury Museum**: (c). **Durham Oriental Museum**: (bc, cl). **Great North Museum**: (cr, fcr). **Penn Museum**: (fcra). **31 Aberdeen Museum**: (tc, fcra). **Great North Museum**: (cb). **32 Aberdeen Museum**: (tc). **33 Penn Museum**: (c). **34 Aberdeen Museum**: (ca, cb, cla, clb, fcla, fclb). **Great North Museum**: (fcra). **35 Canterbury Museum**: (cl, cla, cr, fcr). **Durham Oriental Museum**: (c, cr). **Penn Museum**: (bc, fcl). **36 Penn Museum**: (ca). **37 Aberdeen Museum**: (cra). **Durham Oriental Museum**: (fcla, ftr). **Penn Museum**: (ca, cla). **38 Penn Museum**: (br, c). **41 Aberdeen Museum**: (fcla, cl). **Great North Museum**: (ca). **Penn Museum**: (bc). **42 Maidstone Museum**: (br). **Great North Museum**: (bc, fcra, ftr). **46 Penn Museum**: (tr). **47 Durham Oriental Museum**: (br). **Penn Museum**: (c, cla, crb, fbr, fcla, fcrb). **50 Durham Oriental Museum**: (bl, c, cr). **Penn Museum**: (fcl). **51 Durham Oriental Museum**: (b, ca, cla, clb, tc, tr). **53 Durham Oriental Museum**: (bl). **Penn Museum**: (bc, br). **54 Penn Museum**: (br). **55 Aberdeen Museum**: (br). **Penn Museum**: (bc, bl, fbl). **56-57 Penn Museum**. **60 Aberdeen Museum**: (bl, clb, fbl, fclb). **Great North Museum**: (cla, tr). **61 Aberdeen Museum**: (bl, br, c, cl, fbr). **Great North Museum**: (fbl, tc, tr). **64 Canterbury Museum**: (bl). **Great North Museum**: (cra, fcla). **Penn Museum**: (cla). **65 Great North Museum**: (bc, bl, c, ca, cla, cr, cra,fcr, fcrb, tc). **Penn Museum**: (br, fcra). **66 Canterbury Museum**: (tr). **69 Maidstone Museum**: (cb). **70 Aberdeen Museum**: (bc, bl). **Maidstone Museum**: (fbr, fcrb). **71 Penn Museum**: (c). **74 Great North Museum**: (tl). **75 Great North Museum**: (bc, bl, br). **Penn Museum**: (c, cra, fbr, fcl, fcr). **76 Penn Museum**: (cla, tl). **78 Great North Museum**: (cr). **Penn Museum**: (br, ca, cla). **78 Penn Museum**: (cra, tb, tc). **79 Penn Museum**: (bl, cbl, cr). **82 Canterbury Museum**: (ca, cr, cra). **Maidstone Museum**: (tr). **Thackray Museum**: (br, crb, fcrb). **83 Aberdeen Museum**: (tc). **Canterbury Museum**: (c, cla, br, cb, cr, cra). **Penn Museum**: (bl). **86 Canterbury Museum**: (c, cb, cla, fcra, tc, tr). **Great North Museum**: (ca). **Penn Museum**: (bc, bl, br, fbr, fcla). **87 Canterbury Museum**: (ca, clb, crb, tc). **Great North Museum**: (bc, c, cla). **Penn Museum**: (cb, fcrb, tr). **90 Aberdeen Museum**: (tr, cb). **91 Durham Oriental Museum**: (c, cla, clb, clb, ftr, tc, tr). **Maidstone Museum**: (fcla). **Great North Museum**: (br). **Penn Museum**: (cr, tl). **94 Aberdeen Museum**: (bc, crb, fcla). **Penn Museum**: (tc, tl, tr). **95 Penn Museum**: (c, cr). **96 Aberdeen Museum**: (c). **Durham Oriental Museum**: (bl). **Penn Museum**: (tl). **97 Durham Oriental Museum**: (bc, br, ftl, ftr, tr, tc, tr). **Great North Museum**: (bl). **Penn Museum**: (tl). **98 Aberdeen Museum**: (cl, clb). **100 Durham Oriental Museum**: (clb, crb). **101 Aberdeen Museum**: (cra, fcra). **Durham Oriental Museum**: (bl, cl, cla, cr, fcl, fcla, tl). **104 Durham Oriental Museum**: (bl, br, cl, cr, fcr). **Penn Museum**: (cr, fbr, fcl). **105 Maidstone Museum**: (cb). **Penn Museum**: (br, crb). **106 Penn Museum**: (tr). **107 Aberdeen Museum**: (br, fcla, cla, cr, cra, fcra, ftr). **108 Penn Museum**: (c, cla, clb). **109 Aberdeen Museum**: (ca, tr). **Penn Museum**: (bl, br, cb, cla, crb, fcrb, tl). **110 Penn Museum**: (bc, bl, cla, clb, cr, ftr, tc, tl, tr). **112-113 Canterbury Museum**. **114 Canterbury Museum**: (tr). **115 Canterbury Museum**: (cl). **Great North Museum**: (bl). **116 Canterbury Museum**: (cr, tr). **Maidstone Museum**: (c, cb). **117 Great North Museum**: (bc, bl, br, c, crb, fbr). **118 Canterbury Museum**: (br, c, cr, crb, fbr, fcr, tr). **Maidstone Museum**: (cla, cra). **119 Canterbury Museum**: (cb, fcl, tc, tr). **Maidstone Museum**: (c, cl, clb, fbl). **Powell Cotton Museum**: (cr). **131 Penn Museum**: (c, cb, cl, clb, tc). **134 Penn Museum**: (bc, cr). **140 Aberdeen Museum**: (tr). **Canterbury Museum**: (c, cr, cra). **Faversham Town Council**: (tl). **Great North Museum**: (cl). **142 Maidstone Museum**: (bc). **143 Aberdeen Museum**: (cb). **Canterbury Museum**: (bc, br, c, ca, clb, cr, cra, fcra, tr). **Great North Museum**: (tr). **144 Faversham Town Council**: (br, c). **147 Aberdeen Museum**: (cla, fcla). **160 Penn Museum**: (tr). **162 Aberdeen Museum**: (cr, fcr). **Durham Oriental Museum**: (bc, br, cl, cra, tc). **Penn Museum**: (c, ca). **163 Penn Museum**: (c, cr, fcr, tl, tr). **165 Durham Oriental Museum**: (bc, bl, br, c). **166 Durham Oriental Museum**: (br, cb, cl, cr, fcl, tc). **Penn Museum**: (bl, c). **171 Durham Oriental Museum**: (bc, bl, br, c, ca, cl, crb, fbr, tr). **177 Penn Museum**: (bl, br). **180 Aberdeen Museum**: (bl, cr). **Penn Museum**: (br, cra, crb). **181 Aberdeen Museum**: (tc). **Penn Museum**: (bc, cl, tl, tr). **182 Aberdeen Museum**: (fcla, fclb, ftr tr). **Penn Museum**: (bl, c, ca, cb, cl, cr, crb, tc). **183 Penn Museum**: (bc, bl, ca, tc, tr). **184 Penn Museum**: (tl). **190 Penn Museum**: (bl, c, cl, cla, cr, fcl, fcr). **191 Penn Museum**: (br, c, cb, cr, tc, tr). **194-195 Maidstone Museum**. **198 Aberdeen Museum**: (cfr, cr). **208 Canterbury Museum**: (tc). **Maidstone Museum**: (cbl). **Powell Cotton Museum**: (cla). **209 Thackray Museum**: (c, ca, cb, cbr, cr, tl). **212 Aberdeen Museum**: (fclb). **Maidstone Museum**: (tc). **216 Maidstone Museum**: (c, tc). **217 Canterbury Museum**: (c). **Maidstone Museum**: (tc). **217 Powell Cotton Museum**: (cb, clb). **218 Canterbury Museum**: (cl, fcl, ftl, tl). **Faversham Town Council**: (c). **Maidstone Museum**: (fbl). **Powell Cotton Museum**: (bc). **222 Aberdeen Museum**: (cl). **Durham Oriental Museum**: (br). **Penn Museum**: (bl). **223 Durham Oriental Museum**: (bc, tc). **Penn Museum**: (bl). **225 Durham Oriental Museum**: (c). **229 Durham Oriental Museum**: (fcr, tc). **Penn Museum**: (c). **230 Penn Museum**: (bc, bl, br). **231 Penn Museum**: (c). **232 Durham Oriental Museum**: (bc, bl, br, c, cr, fcr, fbr). **Penn Museum**: (tr). **233 Durham Oriental Museum**: (bl, tc, tr). **Penn Museum**: (c, ftl, ftr, tl). **238 Durham Oriental Museum**: (c). **Durham Oriental Museum**: (fbr, fcr, fcra, fcrb). **Maidstone Museum**: (bl). **Powell Cotton Museum**: (tr). **239 Penn Museum**: (bl, c, cl, cr). **240 Durham Oriental Museum**: (cl, cla, tl). **240-241 Durham Oriental Museum**: (c). **241 Durham Oriental Museum**: (bc, tr). **242 Durham Oriental Museum**: (br, cb). **Penn Museum**: (cr, fcr). **Powell Cotton Museum**: (bc). **243 Durham Oriental Museum**: (cla, cr). **Maidstone Museum**: (bl). **Powell Cotton Museum**: (ca). **245 Durham Oriental Museum**: (c). **246 Durham Oriental Museum**: (bl, br, c, ca, cb, cl, cla, clb, tc). **247 Durham Oriental Museum**: (br, cr, fbr). **Maidstone Museum**: (fcr, ftl, ftr, tr). **Powell Cotton Museum**: (bl). **248 Maidstone Museum**: (bc, bl, cb, clb). **248-249 Maidstone Museum**: (c). **249 Maidstone Museum**: (bl, clb). **250 Durham Oriental Museum**: (bl, ca, tl). **Maidstone Museum**: (bc, br, c, cla, cr, cra, tc, tr). **251 Aberdeen Museum**: (tr). **Durham Oriental Museum**: (cla, cr, tl). **Maidstone Museum**: (bl, br, cra). **252 Durham Oriental Museum**: (tc, tl, tr). **Maidstone Museum**: (c, crb). **253 Durham Oriental Museum**: (bl). **256 Canterbury Museum**: (ca). **257 Durham Oriental Museum**: (c). **258 Durham Oriental Museum**: (bl, cb, cbl). **259 Durham Oriental Museum**: (br, cr, tr). **262 Aberdeen Museum**: (tr). **263 Penn Museum**: (bc, bl, cl, cr, fcla). **264 Penn Museum**: (c). **265 Penn Museum**: (cr, fcr). **Powell Cotton Museum**: (bc, br, fbr). **266 Powell Cotton Museum**: (c). **267 Powell Cotton Museum**: (bc). **272 Maidstone Museum**: (tr). **274 Maidstone Museum**: (c). **278 Aberdeen Museum**: (ca). **281 Maidstone Museum**: (bc). **Thackray Museum**: (br, c, cb, clb, cr, tr). **282 Powell Cotton Museum**: (tr). **285 Aberdeen Museum**: (cr, fcr). **291 Aberdeen Museum**: (ca, cra, fcr, fcra, ftr, cla). **293 Penn Museum**: (bl). **296 Maidstone Museum**: (c, tl, tr). **297 Maidstone Museum**: (bl, br, cb, crb). **298 Aberdeen Museum**: (ftr, tr). **299 Durham Oriental Museum**: (cla, tc). **304 Durham Oriental Museum**: (c, tc, tl). **Maidstone Museum**: (cr, tr). **305 Durham Oriental Museum**: (bl, cla, clb, tl). **Maidstone Museum**: (br, c). **306 Durham Oriental Museum**: (bc, bl, br, cr). **307 Durham Oriental Museum**: (cl, cr). **308 Penn Museum**: (tl, tr). **309 Durham Oriental Museum**: (br). **310 Canterbury Museum**: (tc). **Durham Oriental Museum**: (c, ca, tr). **Maidstone Museum**: (br). **Penn Museum**: (cl, cra). **311 Durham Oriental Museum**: (bc, br, c, ca, cl, cr, cra, fcl). **Powell Cotton Museum**: (ftl, tl, tr). **313 Durham Oriental Museum**: (c). **314 Aberdeen Museum**: (fcr). **316 Aberdeen Museum**: (tr). **317 Aberdeen Museum**: (bc, cla, clb, cr, fclb). **Maidstone Museum**: (bc, crb). **Penn Museum**: (c). **319 Aberdeen Museum**: (cb). **325 Penn Museum**: (br, c, tr). **326 Penn Museum**: (c, tc, tl). **327 Penn Museum**: (clb). **360 Thackray Museum**: (bc). **361 Thackray Museum**: (bl, clb, cr, cra fcla, ftr, tc). **362 Thackray Museum**: (bc). **362 Thackray Museum**: (bl). **363 Thackray Museum**: (c). **363 Thackray Museum**: (tc). **363 Thackray Museum**: (tl). **373 Thackray Museum**: (fcra). **384–385 Aberdeen Museum**: (c). **388 Durham Oriental Museum**: (tl). **389 Penn Museum**: (tc). **391 Penn Museum**: (br). **392** The University of **Aberdeen Museum**: (bc). **393 Penn Museum**: (tc). **394 Great North Museum**: (tc). **398 Durham Oriental Museum**: (bl). **407 Maidstone Museum**: (tr). **412 Penn Museum**: (tl). **415 Penn Museum**: (tr). **Aberdeen Museum**: (bl). **416 Durham Oriental Museum**: (tl). **Penn Museum**: (br). **417 Canterbury Museum**: (tr). **420 Durham Oriental Museum**: (tr). **426 Penn Museum**: (tr). **433 Maidstone Museum**: (tr). **436 Aberdeen Museum**: (tl). **437 Penn Museum**: (br).

Dorling Kindersley would like to thank the following for their kind permission to reproduce their photographs:

(Key: a-above; b-below/bottom; c-center; f-far; l-left; r-right; t-top)

1 Dorling Kindersley: Whipple Museum of History of Science, Cambridge. **4 Dorling Kindersley:** Birmingham Museum And Art Gallery (clb). **5 Dorling Kindersley:** Courtesy of Durham University Oriental Museum (cra); Courtesy of the Powell-Cotton Museum, Kent (crb). **Statens Historiska Museum:** (tr). **6 Dorling Kindersley:** Danish National Museum (tr). **7 Dorling Kindersley:** The Wallace Collection - DK Images (tl). **10-11 Corbis:** EPA. **12 Alamy Images:** Interfoto (b). **13 Dorling Kindersley:** The Natural History Museum, London (tr); Science Museum, London (bl). **14 Corbis:** Nathan Benn (c); Sakamoto Photo Research Laboratory (bl). **Dorling Kindersley:** Courtesy of the University Museum of Archaeology and Anthropology, Cambridge (tl); Courtesy of the Museum of London (cl, cla, cr); Amgueddfa Cymru - National Museum Wales (tr). **Getty Images:** De Agostini (t). **15 Alamy Images:** The Art Gallery Collection (bl); The Art Archive (tl). **Dorling Kindersley:** Courtesy of the University Museum of Archaeology and Anthropology, Cambridge (cr, fbr, fcl); The Natural History Museum, London (br). **Getty Images:** AFP (bc). **Statens Historiska Museum:** photo by Christer Åhlin (tr). **16 Alamy Images:** Globuss Images (b). **Dorling Kindersley:** Courtesy of the University Museum of Archaeology and Anthropology, Cambridge (t). **17 Corbis:** (br); Alfredo Dagli Orti (bl). **Dorling Kindersley:** Courtesy of the Booth Museum of Natural History, Brighton (ca); National Museum, New Delhi (tl, tr); National Museum, New Delhi (cr). **18 Dorling Kindersley:** Courtesy of the University Museum of Archaeology and Anthropology, Cambridge. **19 Alamy Images:** Martin Bache. **20 Dorling Kindersley:** The Trustees of the British Museum (tr); The Trustees of the British Museum (br); The Trustees of the British Museum (c). **21 Alamy Images:** Peter Horree (fbr). **Dorling Kindersley:** The Trustees of the British Museum (cl); Imperial War Museum North (clb). **26 Dorling Kindersley:** Courtesy of Durham University Oriental Museum . **27 Corbis:** Charles & Josette Lenars. **29 Dorling Kindersley:** The Trustees of the British Museum (cla). **30 Dorling Kindersley:** Ashmolean Museum - DK Images (cla). **34 Dorling Kindersley:** Courtesy of Ure Museum of Greek Archaeology, University of Reading (crb). **35 Alamy Images:** MCLA Collection (tr). **36-37 Dorling Kindersley:** The Trustees of the British Museum. **40 Alamy Images:** Peter Adams Photography Ltd (b). **Corbis:** Arne Hodalic (t). **41 Dorling Kindersley:** Courtesy of the University Museum of Archaeology and Anthropology, Cambridge (bl, tr); © The Board of Trustees of the Armouries (ftr); Courtesy of the Museum of London (ca, c). **42 Corbis:** EPA (bl). **Dorling Kindersley:** Courtesy of the University Museum of Archaeology and Anthropology, Cambridge (tc, tl, fbr); Courtesy of Ure Museum of Greek Archaeology, University of Reading (tr). **The Art Archive:** Prehistoric Museum Moesgard Højbjerg Denmark / Gianni Dagli Orti (cla). **43 Alamy Images:** Odyssey-Images (tr); Zev Radovan (bc). **Getty Images:** De Agostini (bl, cb). **Glowimages:** Werner Forman (br). **44 Alamy Images:** The Art Archive (b). **45 Corbis:** Michele Falzone (tr); Roger Wood (bl). **46-47 The Trustees of the British Museum**. **48 Corbis:** Royal Ontario Museum. **49 Getty Images:** China Tourism Press. **50 Alamy Images:** The Art Archive (cla). **Corbis:** Asian Art & Archaeology Inc. (bc). **Dorling Kindersley:** Courtesy of the University Museum of Archaeology and Anthropology, Cambridge (cra, ca). **Encyclopedia of China Publishing House:** (cb). **51 Dorling Kindersley:** Courtesy of the University Museum of Archaeology and Anthropology, Cambridge (cb). **52 The Bridgeman Art Library:** Arthur M. Sackler Museum, Harvard University Art Museums,USA / Bequest of Grenville L. Winthrop. **54 Alamy Images:** The Art Gallery Collection (tr); The Art Archive (bl). **Corbis:** Werner Forman (bc). **55 Alamy Images:** Kenneth Garrett / Danita Delimont (tr). **Glowimages:**

SuperStock (fbr). **58 Dorling Kindersley:** Board of Trustees of the Royal Armouries (t). **59 Alamy Images:** Ball Miwako. **60 Dorling Kindersley:** The Trustees of the British Museum (br); © The Board of Trustees of the Armouries (tl). **61 Dorling Kindersley:** Courtesy of the Trustees of Sir John Soane's Museum (tl). **62-63 Courtesy of the Trustees of Sir John Soane's Museum. 63 Courtesy of the Trustees of Sir John Soane's Museum:** (t). **64 Getty Images:** De Agostini (r). **66 Corbis:** National Geographic Society (b). **67 The Trustees of the British Museum:** (t). **Dorling Kindersley:** Courtesy of the Museum of London (bc, crb, cr, br, cra); Courtesy of the University Museum of Archaeology and Anthropology, Cambridge (fbl, bl). **Getty Images:** De Agostini (cl). **68 Corbis:** Werner Forman (t). **Getty Images:** Print Collector (b). **69 Amgueddfa Cymru - National Museum Wales:** (bl). **The Bridgeman Art Library:** Ashmolean Museum (cl). **Corbis:** Heritage Images (cla). **Dorling Kindersley:** The Trustees of the British Museum (r). **Getty Images:** De Agostini (ca). **70 Alamy Images:** Heritage Image Partnership Ltd (ca). **The Trustees of the British Museum:** (tl). **Dorling Kindersley:** Courtesy of the University Museum of Archaeology and Anthropology, Cambridge (tr); The Trustees of the British Museum (cb). **Getty Images:** De Agostini (cl). **71 The Trustees of the British Museum:** (bc). **Dorling Kindersley:** Alan Hills and Barbara Winter / The Trustees of the British Museum (clb). **Getty Images:** (br); De Agostini (tr). **72 Getty Images:** De Agostini (bl). **72-73 The Trustees of the British Museum. 74 Getty Images:** Bridgeman Art Library (b). **75 Dorling Kindersley:** Courtesy of Ure Museum of Greek Archaeology, University of Reading (ca); Ashmolean Museum - DK Images (cl). **76 Getty Images:** De Agostini (br). **80 Dorling Kindersley:** The Trustees of the British Museum. **81 Alamy Images:** Ken Kaminesky. **82 Corbis:** Araldo de Luca (bl); Sylvain Sonnet (c). **83 The Trustees of the British Museum:** (cl). **Dorling Kindersley:** The Trustees of the British Museum (tr). **84-85 Dorling Kindersley:** National Museums of Scotland. **88 Alamy Images:** Frank Bach. **89 Alamy Images:** A.A.M. Van der Heyden (bl). **Getty Images:** Independent Picture Service (cl). **The Art Archive:** National Museum Bucharest / Dagli Orti (cb). **90 Getty Images:** Universal Images Group (b). **91 Alamy Images:** Collection Dagli Orti (tl). **92-93 The Trustees of the British Museum. 98 Dorling Kindersley:** The Trustees of the British Museum (bc); National Museum, New Delhi (c). **99 The Trustees of the British Museum:** (t). **Dorling Kindersley:** The Trustees of the British Museum (b). **100 Corbis:** Viewstock / Yi Lu (t). **100-101 Corbis:** (b). **102-103 The Trustees of the British Museum:** With kind permission of the Shaanxi Cultural Heritage Promotion Centre, photo by John Williams and Saul Peckham. **102 Corbis:** Design Pics (tc); Robert Harding World Imagery (tl); Mike McQueen (ca). **103 The Trustees of the British Museum:** With kind permission of the Shaanxi Cultural Heritage Promotion Centre, photo by John Williams and Saul Peckham. **104 Dorling Kindersley:** The Trustees of the British Museum (tl). **Encyclopedia of China Publishing House:** (tr). **105 Alamy Images:** Interfoto (bl). **Glowimages:** Tohan Aerial Photographic Service / AFLO (tr). **107 Dorling Kindersley:** Birmingham Museum And Art Gallery (bl). **110 Alamy Images:** Nathan Benn (cr); The Art Archive (br). **Corbis:** Keren Su (tr). **114 Getty Images:** British Library / Robana (b). **115 Dorling Kindersley:** The Trustees of the British Museum (tr); Courtesy of the Museum of London (br); © The Board of Trustees of the Armouries (crb). **116 The Bridgeman Art Library:** Kremsmunster Abbey, Upper Austria (l). **Dorling Kindersley:** Ashmolean Museum, Oxford (tc). **Getty Images:** De Agostini (bc). **RMN:** Grand Palais (Musée du Louvre) / Martine Beck-Coppola (br). **118 Getty Images:** De Agostini (tc). **120 Statens Historiska Museum. 121 Photo SCALA, Florence:** Pierpont Morgan Library / Art Resource. **122 Dorling Kindersley:** Peter Anderson / Danish National Museum (cl); Universitets Oldsaksamling, Oslo (br); © The Board of Trustees of the Armouries (tl, cla, clb); Vikings of Middle England (tc); Danish National Museum (tr, cra). **123 Dorling Kindersley:** Danish National Museum (tl, clb); Statens Historiska Museum, Stockholm (cla, br, cl, bl); Universitets Oldsaksamling, Oslo (t). **124 Dorling Kindersley:** The Trustees of the British Museum (tr); Statens Historiska Museum, Stockholm (cra, br); York Museums Trust (Yorkshire Museum). Reproduced by courtesy of the Yorkshire Museum (ca). **Statens Historiska Museum, Stockholm:** Gabriel Hildebrand (bl). **125 Dorling Kindersley:** Peter Anderson / Danish National Museum (bl, br); Statens Historiska Museum, Stockholm (tc, fbl); Universitets Oldsaksamling, Oslo (cra); Statens Historiska Museum, Stockholm (cla); Danish National Museum (fbr, cl). **Statens Historiska Museum, Stockholm:** Gabriel Hildebrand (cb). **126-127 The Trustees of the British Museum. 127 Getty Images:** British Library / Robana (b). **128 Dorling Kindersley:** The Trustees of the British Museum (tc); Danish National Museum (b, cl). **Statens Historiska Museum, Stockholm:** Ulf Bruxe (tr, cra). **129 Dorling Kindersley:** Danish National Museum (clb); Statens Historiska Museum, Stockholm (cra, crb). **Statens Historiska Museum, Stockholm:** Christer Åhlin (cla, c, cr); Gabriel Hildebrand (tl). **130 Getty Images:** Universal Images Group (b). **Glowimages:** Heritage Images (t). **131 Dorling Kindersley:** The Trustees of the British Museum (tr); Statens Historiska Museum, Stockholm (bl). **Getty Images:** Universal Images Group (cr). **Werner Forman Archive:** British Museum, London (br). **132-133 The Trustees of the British Museum. 134 Glowimages:** Werner Forman (bl, cb, bc); ImageBroker (t). **135 Glowimages:** Werner Forman (cb, cr, bl). **Photo SCALA, Florence:** The Metropolitan Museum of Art / Art Resource (br). **136 Getty Images:** (b). **Photo SCALA, Florence:** The Metropolitan Museum of Art / Art Resource (t). **137 Deutsches Historisches Museum, Berlin:** A. Psille (fcr). **Dorling Kindersley:** © The Board of Trustees of the Armouries (c, fcl, cl, tc, ca, br). **Getty Images:** British Library / Robana (tr). **138 Getty Images:** De Agostini (cl); Bridgeman Art Library (t). **Robert Harding Picture Library:** Walter Rawlings (c). **138-139 Getty Images:** Bridgeman Art Library. **140 Dorling Kindersley:** Courtesy of the Museum of the Order of St. John, London (cb, bc, bl); Courtesy of the Museum of London (br). **141 The Mappa Mundi Trust and Dean and Chapter of Hereford Cathedral. 142 Alamy Images:** The Art Archive (t). **146 Alamy Images:** The Art Gallery Collection (t). **The Bridgeman Art Library:** Musée Condé, Chantilly / Giraudon (b). **147 Alamy Images:** Interfoto (cl). **Corbis:** Austrian Archives (br). **Getty Images:** Bridgeman Art Library (bl). **Wikipedia:** (t). **148-149 Statens Historiska Museum:** (all). **150 Dorling Kindersley:** The Trustees of the British Museum (bc); The Wallace Collection - DK Images (tr, c, cr, bl); The Wallace Collection - DK Images / By kind permission of the Trustees of the Wallace Collection (cl). **Getty Images:** De Agostini (tc). **151 Alamy Images:** The Art Archive (c). **Corbis:** (cr). **Dreamstime.com:** Seregal (tr). **Getty Images:** De Agostini (tc). **Glowimages:** SuperStock (br). **152 Dorling Kindersley:** Courtesy of the Churchill College Archives, Cambridge University (cb); © The Board of Trustees of the Armouries (bl, br). **Smithsonian Institution, Washington, DC:** Arthur M. Sackler Gallery. Purchase, Smithsonian Unrestricted Trust Funds, Smithsonian Collections Acquisition Program and Dr. Arthur M. Sackler (tr). **153 Photo SCALA, Florence:** The Metropolitan Museum of Art / Art Resource (b, tc, tr). **154 Dorling Kindersley:** National Museum, New Delhi (tr). **Thinkstock:** Skouatroulio (b). **155 Corbis:** Angelo Hornak (bl). **Dorling Kindersley:** Ancient Coins Canada (tr, tc). **Glowimages:** SuperStock (c). **Photo SCALA, Florence:** The Metropolitan Museum of Art / Art Resource (cr, br). **SuperStock:** Tomas Abad (bc). **156-157 Dorling Kindersley:** The Trustees of the British Museum. **156 Dorling Kindersley:** The Trustees of the British Museum (t). **158-159 Corbis:** Brooklyn Museum of Art. **159 Alamy Images:** Photosindia.com (b). **161 Photo SCALA, Florence:** The Metropolitan Museum of Art / Art Resource. **162 The Bridgeman Art Library:** Crown, Northern Song dynasty or Liao dynasty, 10th-11th century (bronze with gilding & repoussé decor), Chinese School / Saint Louis Art Museum, Missouri, USA / Funds given by Edith Spink in memory of her husband, C. C. Johnson Spink (tl). **The Trustees of the British Museum:** (bl). **166 Dorling Kindersley:** Ashley Leiman (bc). **Encyclopedia of China Publishing House:** (tr). **167 The Trustees of the British Museum. 168 Photo SCALA, Florence:** The Metropolitan Museum of Art / Art Resource (t). **168-169 Photo SCALA, Florence:** The Metropolitan Museum of Art / Art Resource. **169 Corbis:** Radius Images (tl). **170 Getty Images:** De Agostini (t). **Photo SCALA, Florence:** The Metropolitan Museum of Art / Art Resource (b). **171 Getty Images:** De Agostini (cra). **172-173 Alamy Images:** Gary Dublanko (b). **173 Alamy Images:** Paul Carstairs (c). **Corbis:** Hemis / Jacques Sierpinski (tl). **Getty Images:** Steve Allen (cla); Luis Castaneda Inc (cr). **174-175 Photo SCALA, Florence:** The Metropolitan Museum of Art / Art Resource. **176 Dorling Kindersley:** American Museum of Natural History Library (t). **Getty Images:** National Geographic (b). **177 Dorling Kindersley:** National Museum of the American Indian / Smithsonian Institution, Washington, DC (cra). **Smithsonian Institution, Washington, DC:** National Museum of the American Indian (tl, tc, cla, cl, clb, ca, tr, cb, bc). **178 Dorling Kindersley:** Courtesy of the University Museum of Archaeology and Anthropology, Cambridge. **179 Corbis:** Hans Georg Roth. **180 Dorling Kindersley:** CONACULTA-INAH-MEX. Authorized reproduction by the Instituto Nacional de Antropología e Historia (tc, cl, bc). **181 Dorling Kindersley:** Birmingham Museum And Art Gallery (c); CONACULTA-INAH-MEX. Authorized reproduction by the Instituto Nacional de Antropología e Historia (cr). **182 Glowimages:** Werner Forman Archive / Dallas Museum of Art (crb). **183 Dorling Kindersley:** CONACULTA-INAH-MEX. Authorized reproduction by the Instituto Nacional de Antropología e Historia (br). **Glowimages:** Werner Forman Archive (cla); Werner Forman Archive (cl). **184-185 The Trustees of the British Museum. 186-187 Sächsische Landesbibliothek - Staats- und Universitätsbibliothek Dresden (SLUB). Dresdner Digitalisierungszentrum (DDZ):** http://digital.slub-dresden.de/id280742827 (all). **188 Alamy Images:** The Art Archive (tr). **Getty Images:** Ennio Vanzan (b). **189 Alamy Images:** Peter Horree (bc); The Art Archive (br). **Dorling Kindersley:** University Museum of Archaeology and Anthropology, Cambridge (tr); Pitt Rivers Museum, University of Oxford (tl). **Getty Images:** De Agostini (bl); DEA / M. Carrieri (tc). **Glowimages:** Werner Forman Archive (cl, c). **190 Dorling Kindersley:** Bolton Metro Museum (tr, ftr). **191 Getty Images:** De Agostini (l). **192-193 Corbis:** Hemis / Richard Soberka. **193 Corbis:** Martin Finkbeiner (bl, br). **196 Dorling Kindersley:** National Maritime Museum, London (tr). **197 Glowimages:** ImageBroker. **198 Dorling Kindersley:** The Trustees of the British Museum (cla); National Maritime Museum, London (br); Whipple Museum of History of Science, Cambridge (bl). **199 Getty Images:** Universal Images Group. **200-201 Dorling Kindersley:** Whipple Museum of History of Science, Cambridge (all). **202 Photo SCALA, Florence:** White Images (cla). **204 Dorling Kindersley:** The National Music Museum (tr, fcl, cl, c, cr, fcr); The National Music Museum (clb, b). **205 Alamy Images:** Bildarchiv Monheim GmbH / Paul M. R. Maeyaert (cl). **Corbis:** Derek Bayes (bl); Nathan Benn (br). **Getty Images:** Stuart Gregory (cr). **Glowimages:** SuperStock (c). **206-207 Corbis:** Laurie Chamberlain. **206 Corbis:** Araldo de Luca (cr); Arte & Immagini slr (b). **207 The Bridgeman Art Library:** St. Peter's Vatican, Rome, Italy (tr). **210 Dorling Kindersley:** National Maritime Museum, London. **211 akg-images:** André Held. **212 Dorling Kindersley:** Courtesy of the English CIvil War Society (tc); © The Board of Trustees of the Armouries (ca, cl, clb, cb, bl). **212-213 Dorling Kindersley:** © The Board of Trustees of the Armouries (c). **213 Dorling Kindersley:** © The Board of Trustees of the Armouries (tc, cr, tr, b, cb, cra, tl). **214-215 Photo SCALA, Florence:** The Metropolitan Museum of Art / Art Resource. **215 Corbis:** Leonard de Selva (br). **Photo SCALA, Florence:** The Metropolitan Museum of Art / Art Resource (bl). **216 Dorling Kindersley:** © The Board of Trustees of the Armouries (tl); The Wallace Collection - DK Images (tr, b). **217 Dorling Kindersley:** Courtesy of the Museum of the Order of St. John, London (tl, cl); The Wallace Collection - DK Images (r, bl). **218 Dorling Kindersley:** Courtesy of The Shoe Museum (cr). **219 Dorling Kindersley:** Courtesy of the Museum of London (all). **220 Dorling Kindersley:** Science Museum, London (clb); Science Museum, London (bl); Calcografia Nacional, Madrid (bc); Science Museum, London (br). **Getty Images:** British Library / Robana (c); Hulton Archive (tc); Time & Life Pictures (cla). **221 Dorling Kindersley:** Science Museum, London (cla); Whipple Museum of History of Science, Cambridge (tc, r); Science Museum, London (cl); Science Museum, London - DK Images (c); The Natural History Museum, London (bl). **222 Getty Images:** De Agostini / G. Dagli Orti (tr, bc). **SuperStock:** Christie's Images Ltd. (br). **223 Alamy Images:** Gianni Dagli Orti / The Art Archive (cra). **The Bridgeman Art Library:** Christie's Images (br). **Getty Images:** De Agostini / G. Dagli Orti (cl, cla, ca). **Nour Foundation / Nasser D. Khalili Collection of Islamic Art / Courtesy of the Khalili Family Trust:** (cb). **224 Dorling Kindersley:** © The Board of Trustees of the Armouries (t, cla, cl, ca, scabbard, c, clb, crb). **224-225 Dorling Kindersley:** © The Board of Trustees of the Armouries (cb, b). **225 Dorling Kindersley:** © The Board of Trustees of the Armouries (tl, tc, tr, cl, cr, fcr). **226-227 Alamy Images:** Images and Stories (all). **228 Alamy Images:** B. O'Kane (b). **Photo SCALA, Florence:** The Metropolitan Museum of Art / Art Resource (tr). **229 Alamy Images:** The Art Archive (bl). **Dorling Kindersley:** The Trustees of the British Museum (tr); Courtesy of Durham University Oriental Museum (br, c). **233 The Bridgeman Art Library:** Christie's Images (cr). **234-235 Wikipedia. 236 Alamy Images:** Interfoto (tr). **237 Getty Images:** Peter Gridley. **238 Dorling Kindersley:** Courtesy of Durham University Oriental Museum (cl, tr); The Wallace Collection - DK Images (ca). **242 Dorling Kindersley:** The Trustees of the British Museum (cla); Courtesy of Durham University Oriental Museum (clb, bl, bc). **Encyclopedia of China Publishing House:** (tc). **243 Dorling Kindersley:** Courtesy of Durham University Oriental Museum (tc, cb, bc). **244 Dorling Kindersley:** Courtesy of Durham University Oriental Museum (t). **246 Dorling Kindersley:** © The Board of Trustees of the Armouries (clb, bc). **247 Dorling Kindersley:** © The Board of Trustees of the Armouries (cb). **251 Dorling Kindersley:** Courtesy of Durham University Oriental Museum (c). **252 Dorling Kindersley:** Courtesy of Durham University Oriental Museum (cr, br, bl, bc). **253 Dorling Kindersley:** Courtesy of Durham University Oriental Museum (r). **255 Getty Images:** Grant Faint. **256 Dorling Kindersley:** Courtesy of Durham University Oriental Museum (bc, br); © The Board of Trustees of the Armouries (cl, tr, cra, ftr); The Wallace Collection - DK Images (clb). **257 Dorling Kindersley:** Courtesy of the City Palace Museum, Jaipur (bl); © The Board of Trustees of the Armouries (cla, cl); Courtesy of Durham University Oriental Museum (cb). **Getty Images:** AFP (tr). **Photo SCALA, Florence:** The Metropolitan Museum of Art / Art Resource (br). **Smithsonian Institution, Washington, DC:** Freer Gallery of Art / Gift of Dr. Stephen R. Turner F1984.3a-b (tl). **260 Alamy Images:** Dinodia Photos (tr). **Getty Images:** De Agostini (bl, bc). **Glowimages:** Werner Forman (br). **Nour Foundation / Nasser D. Khalili Collection of Islamic Art / Courtesy of the Khalili Family Trust:** Acc. No joy2151.3 (cr). **261 Dorling Kindersley:** Pitt Rivers Museum, University of Oxford (r); © The Board of Trustees of the Armouries (tl, cla, bc, bl, cl); The Wallace Collection - DK Images (c). **262 Corbis:** Stapleton Collection (b). **263 Alamy Images:** Image Asset Management Ltd (c). **Corbis:** Werner Forman (tc). **265 Corbis:** Heritage Images (c). **Glowimages:** Werner Forman (l, t). **268 Dorling Kindersley:** Wilberforce House, Hull City Museums (t). **Glowimages:** SuperStock (b). **269 The Bridgeman Art Library:** Private Collection / Christie's Images (r). **Dorling Kindersley:** Pitt Rivers Museum, University of Oxford (t). **Beto Durán:** (br). **Jamestown-Yorktown Foundation, Williamsburg, Virginia:** (ca). **Photo SCALA, Florence:** The Metropolitan Museum of Art / Art Resource (cla, bc). **The Art Archive:** The British Library, London (c). **The Library of Congress, Washington DC:** Image No 004r (bl). **272-383 Dorling Kindersley:** Southbank Enterprises (sidebar). **273 Getty Images:** Heritage Images. **274 Dorling Kindersley:** Museum of English Rural Life, The University of Reading (tl); The Science Museum, London (cl, tc). **Abudulla Saheem:** (cr). **Science & Society Picture Library:** Science Museum (bl, tr). **274-275 Dorling Kindersley:** Courtesy of the Royal Artillery Historical Trust (b). **275 Dorling Kindersley:** National Motor Museum, Beaulieu (tl); Courtesy of The National Railway Museum, York / Science Museum, London (tr). **276 Science & Society Picture Library:** Science Museum (bl). **276-277 Dorling Kindersley:** The Science Museum, London. **278 Corbis:** Bettmann (bl). **Dorling Kindersley:** The Science Museum, London (tr, cla, clb, cb, bc, br); Whipple Museum of History of Science, Cambridge (tc). **Science & Society Picture Library:** National Media Museum (crb). **279 Dorling Kindersley:** The Science Museum, London (t, b). **280 Dorling Kindersley:** Blandford Fashion Museum (cra); Washington Dolls' House and Toy Museum (bl); The Science Museum, London (tr); National Cycle Collection (crb). **Science & Society Picture Library:** Science Museum (tc). **281 Dorling Kindersley:** HPS Museum of Leeds University (ca, tc); The Science Museum, London (crb). **Getty Images:** Hulton Archive (ftl). **Science & Society Picture Library:**

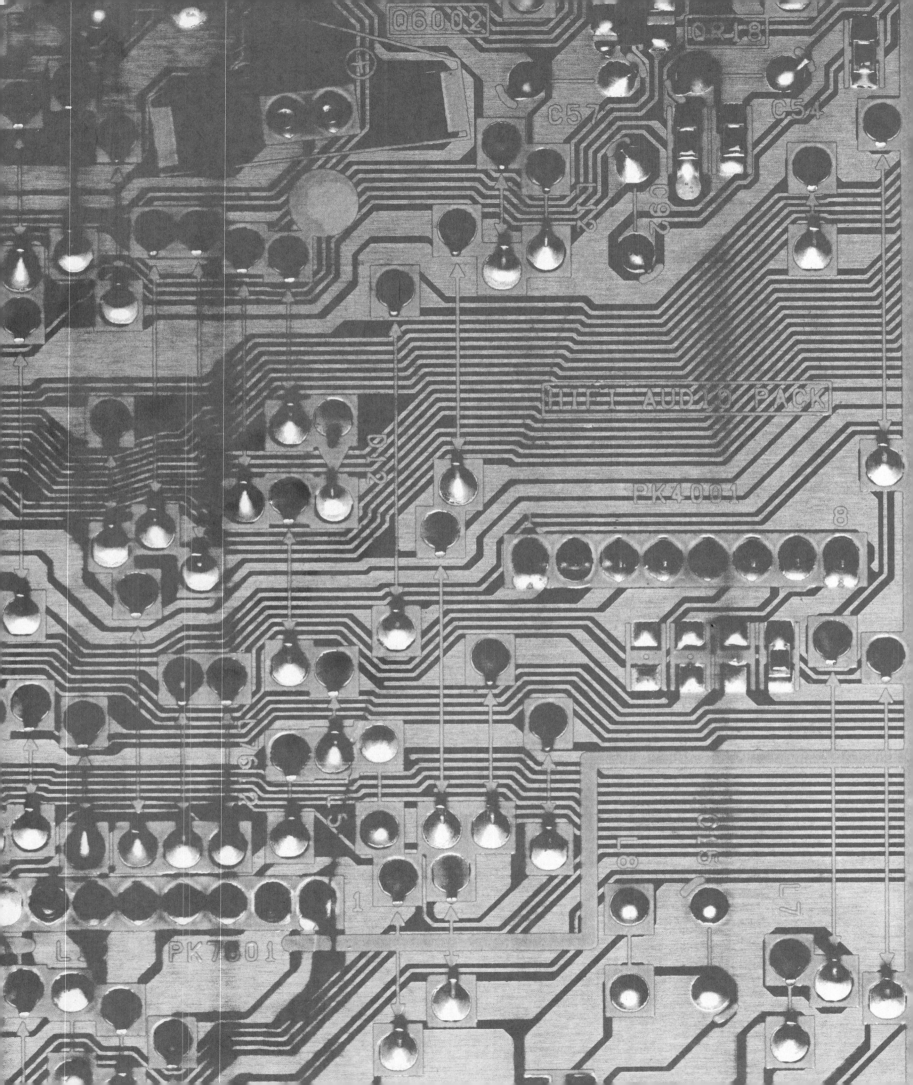